JOHN HOWE'S
ULTIMATE
FANTASY ART
ACADEMY

DAVID & CHARLES

www.davidandcharles.com

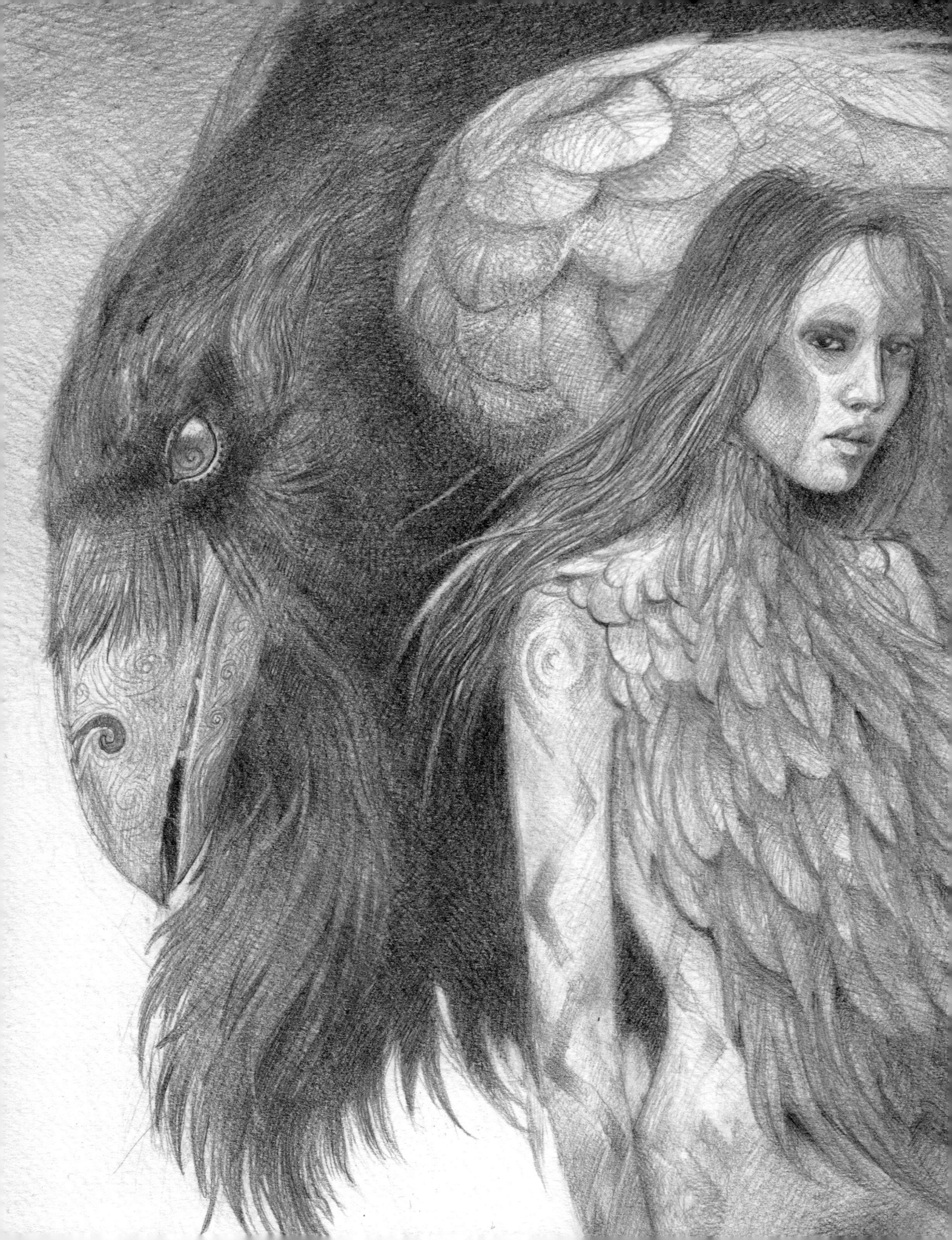

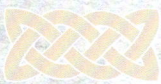

CONTENTS

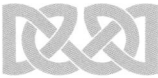

FOREWORD
BY TERRY GILLIAM

OK … let's be totally honest.

This book has depressed me … really depressed me.

Let me explain.

T thought I could draw, I thought I could paint, and I believed I had a vivid imagination but, having studied this book, I realize I have been fooling myself. I've been living in a fantasy world. Here is the real thing … a man who draws beautifully, paints like a Leonardo, and is able to imagine worlds that I gave up dreaming about long ago. Not that I wanted to give up dreaming about them but, unable to render them as I saw them in my mind's eye, I shut them out. So you can understand my depression at being reminded of my failings.

Nevertheless, John Howe is the kind of artist the world needs. An ancient pagan returned to live among us. A wizard from the North West. He looks deep into flowers. He knows their inner lives. He understands moss. He knows that stones harbour spirits. He can taste the flavour of a wind. He has felt how deep water can cut. He has seen the sky fall. Yet, with a wave of his brush, he defies gravity and tames the elements. He makes all of this so real that I want to dive in and never return. I'm a child again, willing to adventure into these worlds. He makes me believe once again, that there are still heroes and great deeds to perform.

With this book he inducts us into the secrets of how he breathes life into his imaginings. He encourages us to develop the skills that will allow us to render our dreams on paper. He's articulate and open about how he develops his ideas, inviting us into his studio to share his techniques. Nothing is withheld. Or so he wishes us to believe. But these are clever diversions. The secret never revealed.

Unfortunately for him, he has unwittingly left a clue to the truth of his magic. Look closely at him drawing. Do you see the giveaway clue. No? Look again. Note the way he holds his pencil. Is it between the thumb and forefinger? Like a normal person? No! Do you know why? I'll tell you. It's clear as day that John Howe has made a pact with the devil! Shocking? Yes … but true! How else could a human being create such sublime art?

Don't let him blind you with moist pages for watery skies or toothbrushes for spattering sea foam. The secret is in the way he holds the brush. I have been trying for some hours now and am slowly getting the hang of it. I've also turned off the lights, burned sulphur and chanted incantations to the demonic forces. I think it's beginning to work.

So, look out John Howe. I'm on your tail. I'm giving up directing movies and am going to show the world that I too can paint wondrous worlds of imagination and dreams. And I'm going to beat you, John Howe! You should have cropped those photos more carefully.

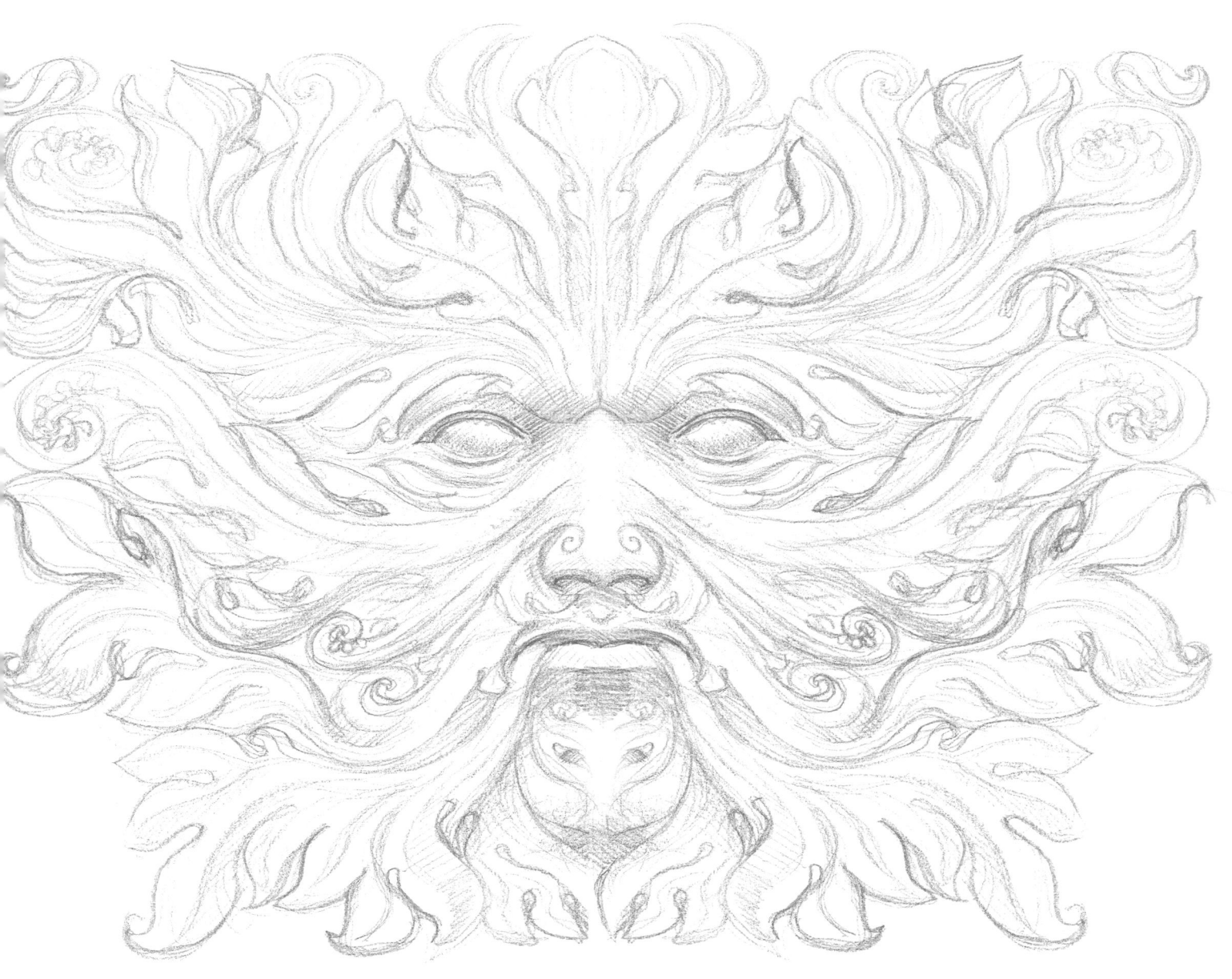

⬆ *Green Face*

'Green Faces' or 'Green Men' are one of the most fascinating, inscrutable and enduring motifs in medieval art, from Celtic forest spirit to high Gothic flamboyance.

"HE ENCOURAGES US TO DEVELOP THE SKILLS THAT WILL ALLOW US TO RENDER OUR DREAMS ON PAPER"

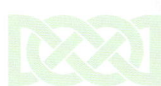

INTRODUCTION

When a book long out of print is republished, the most
compelling urge is to rewrite it all, to amend and correct,
to bring to it new experiences and thoughts that fill the
interim since that initial publication. On the other hand,
one should not invalidate the existing work, nor create
a sort of hybrid volume which is neither old or new.

This book, which combines *Fantasy Art
Workshop* and *Fantasy Drawing Workshop*, is
both old and new. The original books compose
the major part of it, with new amendments,
and a new portfolio section with more recent work and
thoughts. The result is a book about drawing and painting,
and how to take the right steps to achieve whatever goals
you might have set for yourself. There are exercises and
examples, vehicles for your imagination and your capacity
to visualize, but the most important role is played by you.

If you know how to draw already and you are quite satisfied
with the results, then this book is not really for you. If you
feel that figurative and narrative imagery is not your cup
of tea, this book is not for you. If you feel that mythology
and fantasy have little to say to our modern world, then
this book is most definitely not for you. If you are searching
for off-the-shelf methods and sure-fire technical tricks of
the trade, then this book is most definitely not for you.
However …

… if your mind is full of images that keep escaping from
your fingertips, this book may be of help. If you are unsure
of the direction your art wishes to take, but know you
should be heading somewhere, this book may be a signpost
of a kind for your journey. If you find pleasure in telling
stories in pictures, then this book may help you clarify your
thoughts. If life has obliged you to leave pages of yourself
unturned, and you'd feel better with a little company for a
chapter or two, then this book is definitely for you.

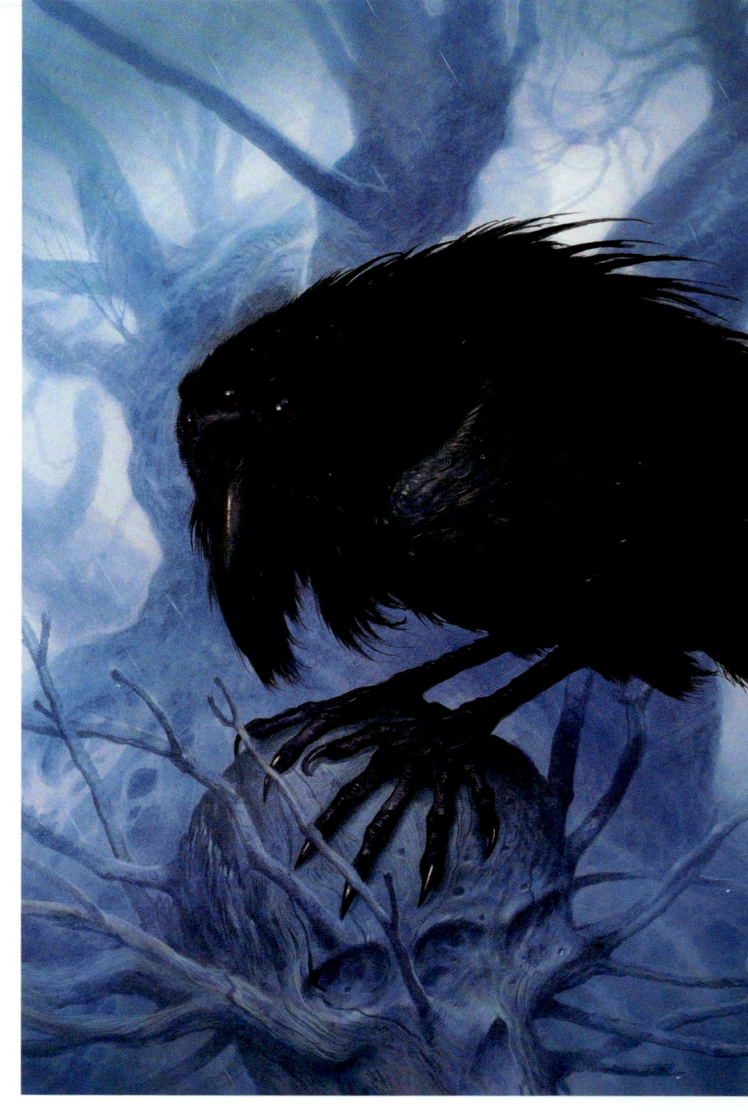

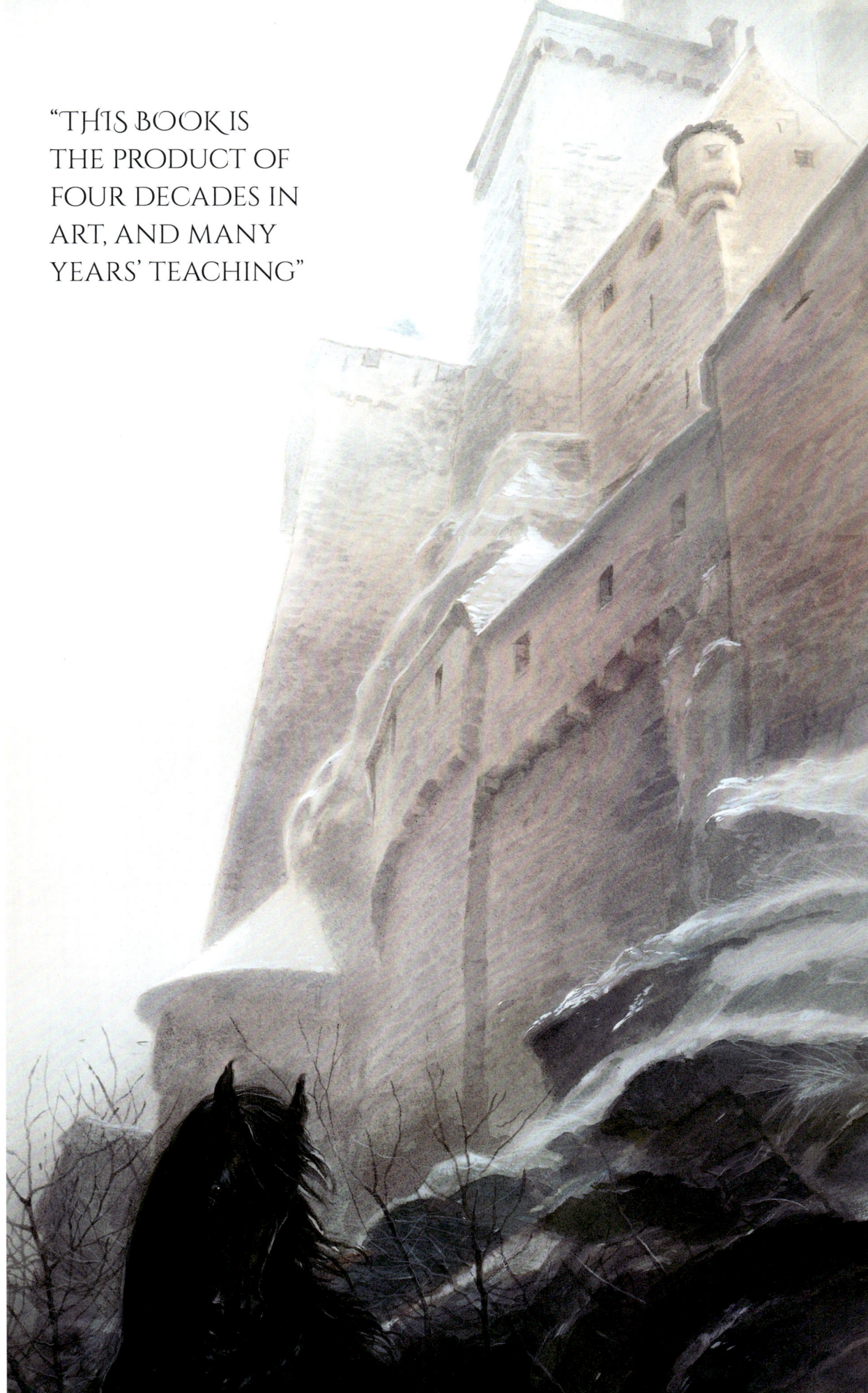

"THIS BOOK IS
THE PRODUCT OF
FOUR DECADES IN
ART, AND MANY
YEARS' TEACHING"

←

*Nightmare
Crow*

This illustration
for *A Clash of
Kings* by George
R.R. Martin
is the stuff of
bad dreams: a
three-eyed raven
that pecks at a
dreamer's face.

➙ *The
Forged Horse*

Back cover
illustration for
The Golden Fool,
Book II of *The
Tawny Man* by
Robin Hobb. This
castle is one I
know very well
and have visited
frequently. The
ability to go and
walk around
places like this is
perhaps the main
thing that keeps
me in Europe.

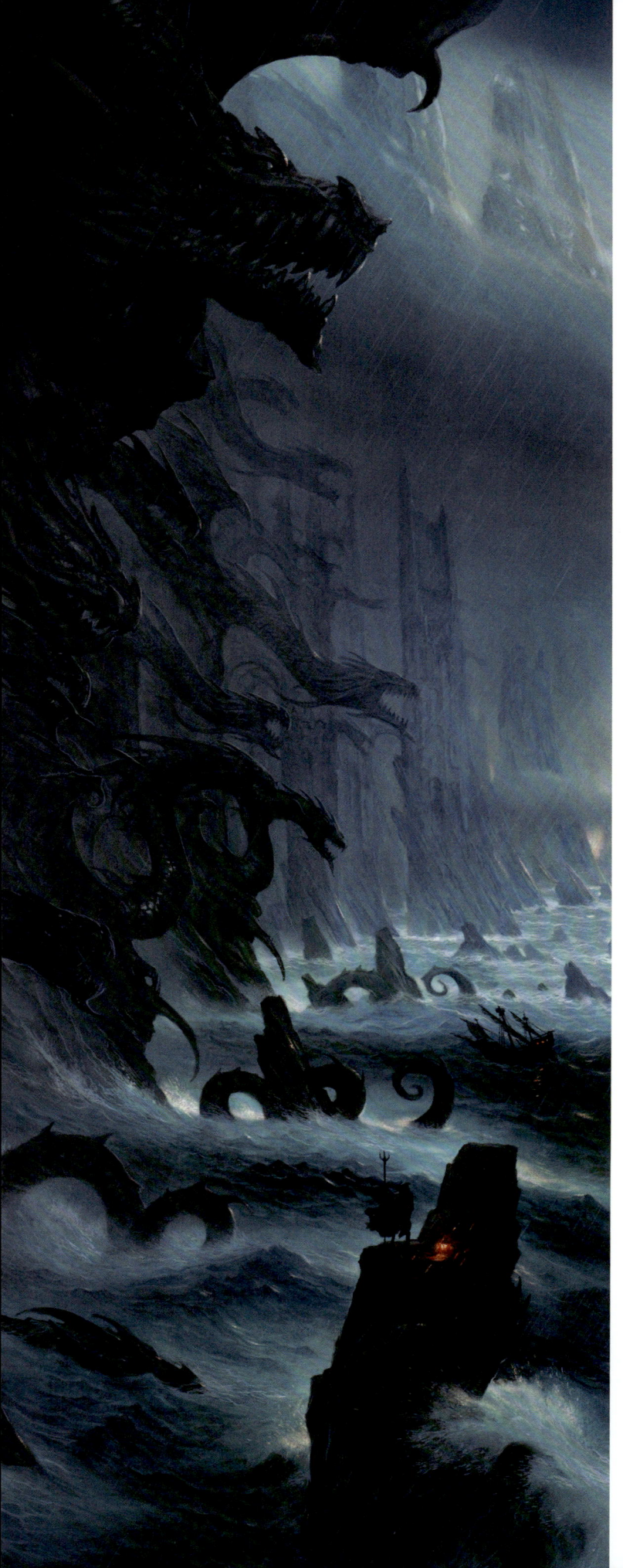

I will say from the start that I dislike 'How To ...' books, unless purely technical and about carpentry, hot-water pipes or pruning. I dislike the temptation to reduce an intuitive, personal process to a 'system' applied to any circumstances. I am dubious of rectangles and circles that magically turn into animals. I dislike seeing archetypes transformed into stereotypes. I sigh in dismay when I see famous paintings divided into arbitrary shapes and golden means. These leave little place for serendipity, imagination and instinct, your most precious allies and tools.

Pencil drawing is giving yourself up to an exercise in the incidental. It is a form of communion with your subject, whether the subject is in front of you or inside your head. Expertise and skill, intuition and imagination, information and experience go hand in hand with your desire to express feelings, to tell stories, to create and share worlds. This mix of the universal and the personal is unique to you. I have tried to say in words how I feel about all of that. (With each picture being worth a thousand of them, that makes quite a few.) I'm grateful to the editors for allowing my thoughts such unruly growth, pruning only when necessary.

This book is personal, too. I speak for myself, not for the art of drawing and painting. It is the product of four decades in art, and many years' teaching. While much of this time has been spent locked up in the studio, these studios have been in many countries, on varying projects. Events have allowed me to meet people the world over. This has all enriched and enchanted me, part of the experience I wish to share.

Finally, to my comrades-in-art and fellow illustrators, I beg your indulgence for this foray into the dreaded land of Explanation and the perilous realm of Reason, momentarily forsaking the foggy shores of Inspiration. I am speaking only for myself, not for my profession. All of you have your own voices. (But buy the book anyway.)

← *Dragonstone*

One of the most compelling fortresses in George R.R. Martin's *A Song of Ice and Fire* – a towering and jagged keep on a ragged coast of precipitous and dizzying cliffs … and it's covered in stone dragons. What more could an artist ask for?

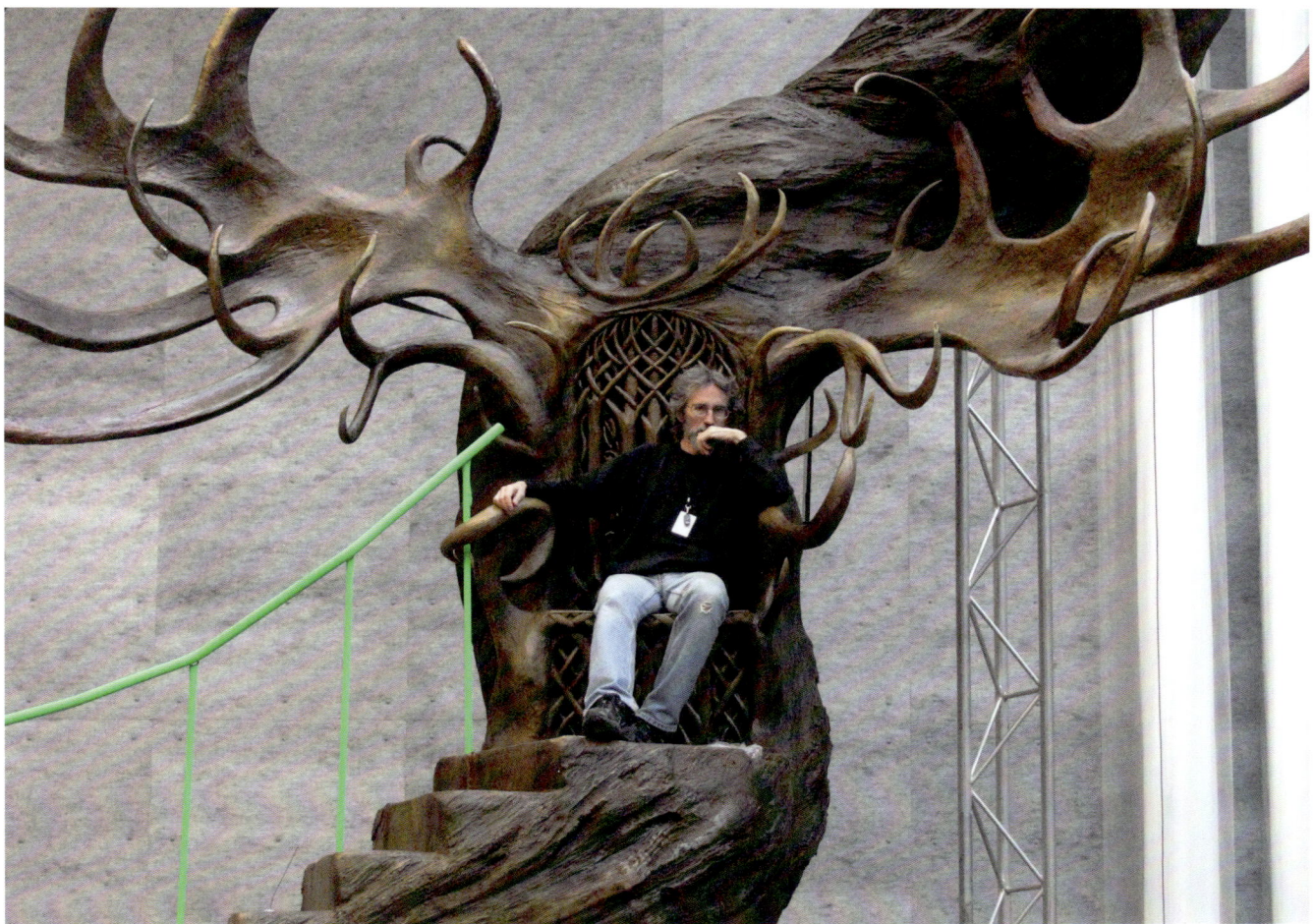

Step into this book …

To begin, I discuss how I get along with the muse and find my inspiration; the second section is about the materials and techniques I use, and how I use them.

The third part looks at a selection of my work, with case studies breaking down the process (these are a real-world slice of life, complete with deadlines and last-minute deliveries). The initial colour washes define the atmosphere of most pieces; the second stage is usually a re-defining of the initial sketch and a blocking-in of volumes and forms. Then choices become more arbitrary. Many pictures go through unattractive, laborious phases, so I have singled these out. They may not be pretty, but they are instructive. The final stage, adding light and highlights, is the final injection of life before you move on to the next picture.

You will then find some of my most recent images, with words on creativity in the fantasy realm. From artist's block to world-building, I describe the journeys taken to capture

King for a day …

Thranduil's throne, from Peter Jackson's *Hobbit* trilogy. I set the self-timer and rushed up the steps – thank goodness for that green railing – and managed to look suitably possessed of the ennui of kingship.

ideas and transform them into pictures. There is even a neatly numbered list bearing advice that may not only help in the short term, but will leave you exploring your own approach to concept art and creativity in general.

A course of step-by-step exercises is dedicated to modest tools: pencil and paper. Designed to advance your skills as you work through them, they are written to be as helpful as possible. Follow each step, and you will end up with a drawing and, if we have done our job properly, you will have gleaned something more. Finally, I look at working in various aspects of the profession, including books and film, and presenting your own portfolio to potential employers.

THE CREATIVE PROCESS

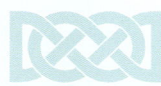

Where does inspiration come from? Or, more importantly, where does it go when you can't find it? It is wise not to confuse information and inspiration. The former is the result of studious application, the latter is what happens when you don't think about it. Each has a role to play, but must not look to play the role of the other. Inspiration may be the bright tower in the clouds; information is the solid rock of the foundations.

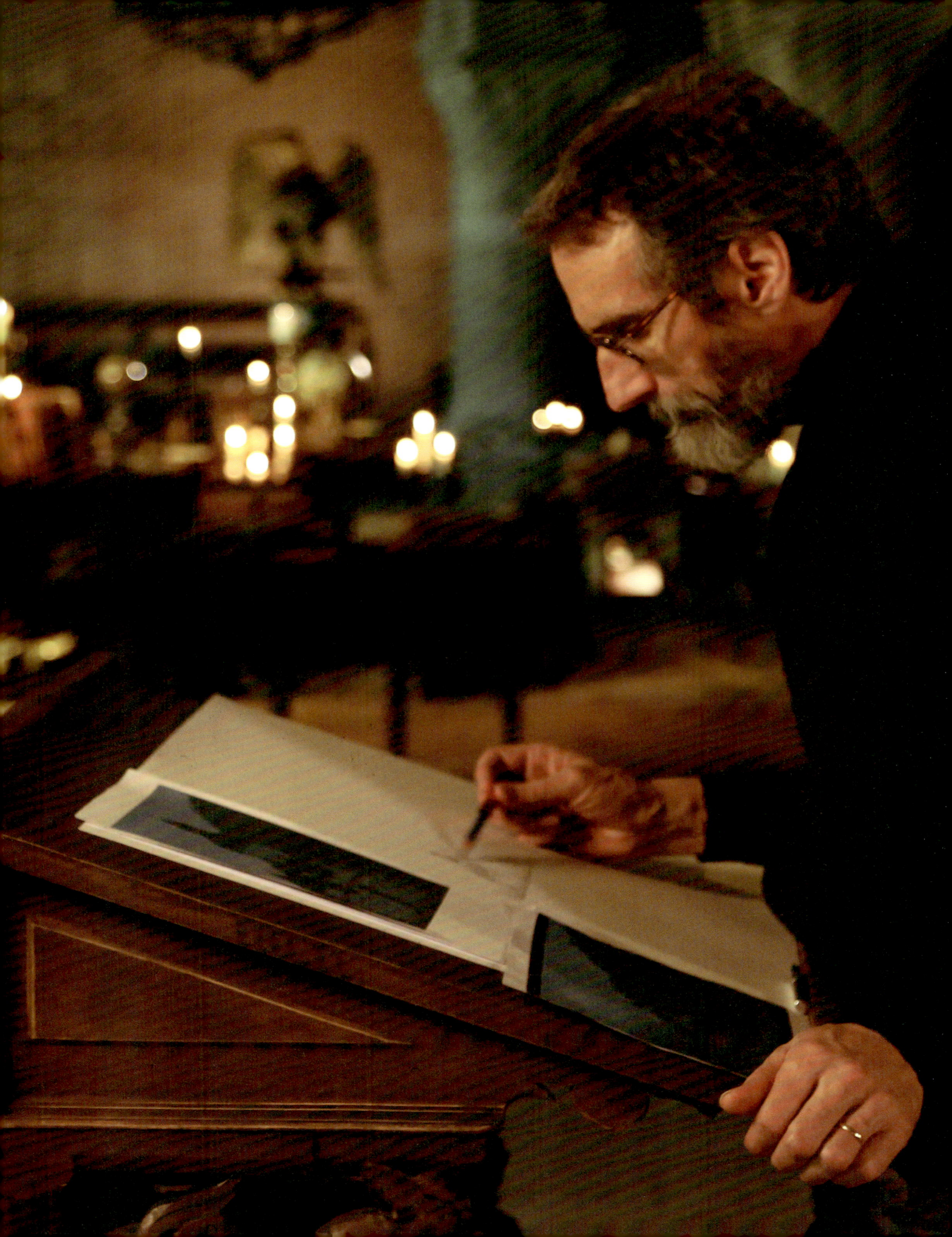

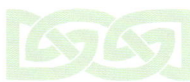

MY ARTISTIC JOURNEY

I'm sure it comes as no surprise if I say I never remember not drawing ... My first memory is of drawing something – or rather *not* being able to draw something.

When I was four or so, my attempts to draw a cow were not satisfying (I grew up on a farm, they were familiar creatures) so my mother did her best to sketch one for me. Alas, her skills did not extend to draughtsmanship, and it wasn't much better than my scribble. I've had few opportunities to draw cattle, but did wish to do something with pencils and paints. In school, I ended up in power mechanics or some other class I loathed – art classes were full of kids too unacademic for any other discipline. I got into art class for my last two years, and owe a great deal to the art teacher, who put up with the rowdy crew and provided the first critical appreciation of my work outside friends and family.

At 19, I enrolled in an English-language school in France to spend a year abroad, and never went back. The next year, I was happily sitting in first year illustration at the École des Arts Décoratifs in Strasbourg, not understanding a thing. I kept almost nothing from my three years there, but did enjoy that time. I only truly appreciated what I had learnt two decades later. It did me good, despite launching a roundabout route through children's books and the French publishing industry, and imposed a clarity of thought on the ambiguous business of putting enough of oneself into what one does to be of interest, but not clouding the looking glass.

Most of my early jobs were just that, paid jobs in which I took pleasure, but do not recognize myself. Comics, adverts, maps, charts and graphics, half-sections of automobiles, logos, billboards and more. I'm not proud of any. I accepted offers not meant for me, hoping to find an advantage in them. I re-did sketches three times for a children's publication, each batch a greater torture than the last. I started one of my first book covers seven times, drew caricatures of 1980s politicians, and slaved over acres of scratchboard to design lettering for ungrateful clients.

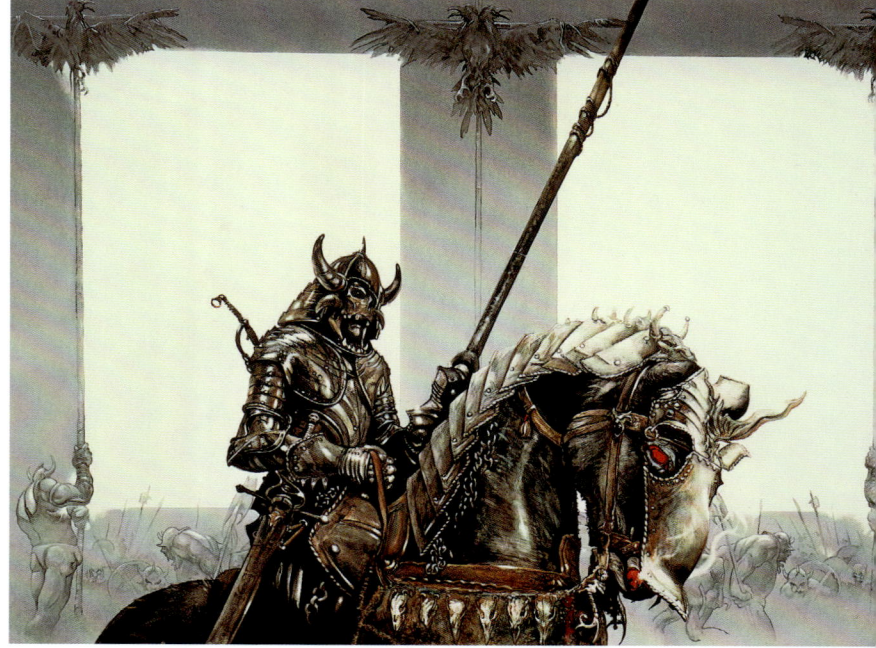

⬆ *Witch King*
1979

Done at art school, the king and steed are cut from one sheet of card pasted on to another – I had ruined the background. The frames were intended to hold text. It is one of my first published Tolkien pieces, appearing in the 1987 Tolkien calendar.

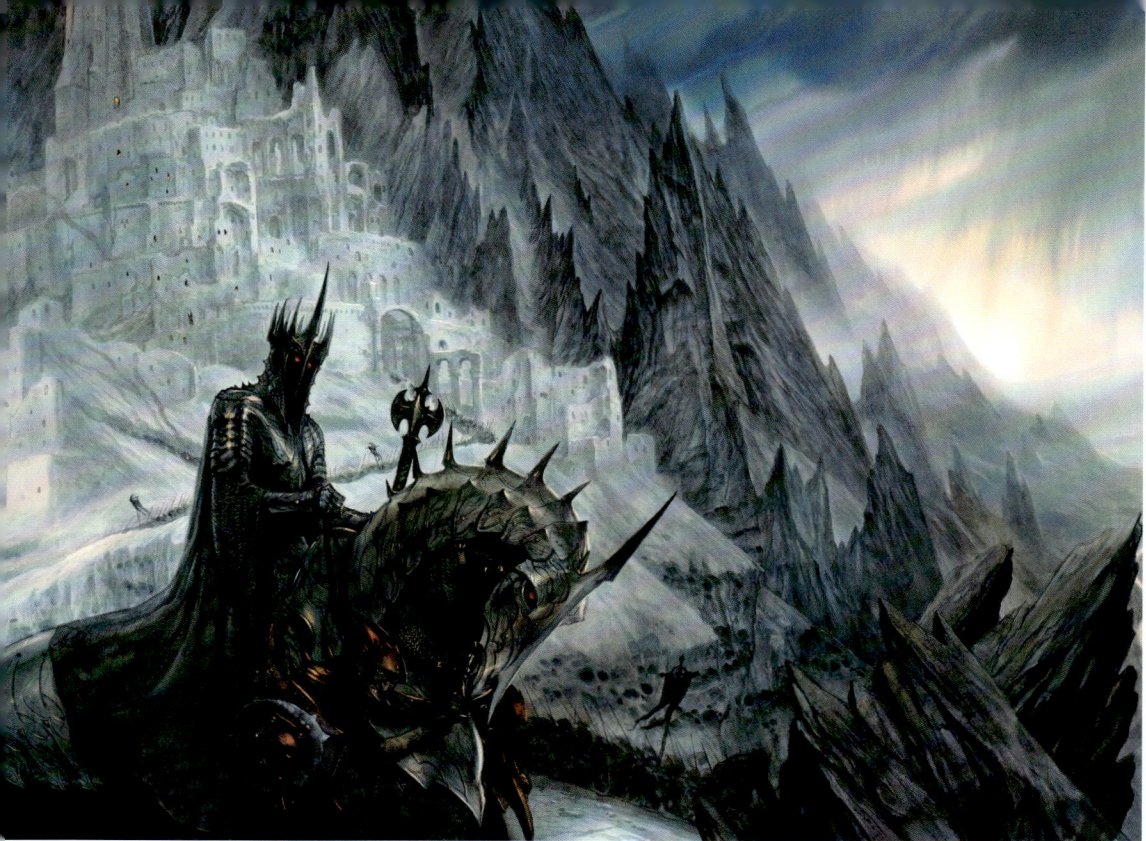

← *Witch King*
2006

The return of the *Witch King*, 27 years later, for a board game box. I enjoy revisiting themes and could happily paint versions of the same theme for months. So, what's changed? Certainly a firmer grasp of armour and a few technical tricks. I should do another in 2033, to see if there is a pattern.

On the other hand, I've met extraordinary people through illustration, and had the privilege to work, and exhibit my work, the world over. I've gained membership of a confraternity of artists, many of whom I admired as demigods in my teens, and are now friends. I've been privileged to make images for writers whose words have marked generations of readers. I've been allowed to make images the way I wished them to be, and the desire, or rather the need, to make them has opened my eyes to many things I would otherwise never have noticed. I have been privileged to work at home, to allow family life to intrude so fully in my work that there is no way I can separate the two.

It's hard work, filled with frustrations, dead ends and occasional sleepless nights, but I have never considered an alternative. It is probably the feeling that I had something to say with images that drove me on. That conviction, more than anything else, is an inner voice to which it is worthwhile listening. That voice has always urged me down whatever path my pencils lead me. I'm eager to get on with it. There is so much left to draw.

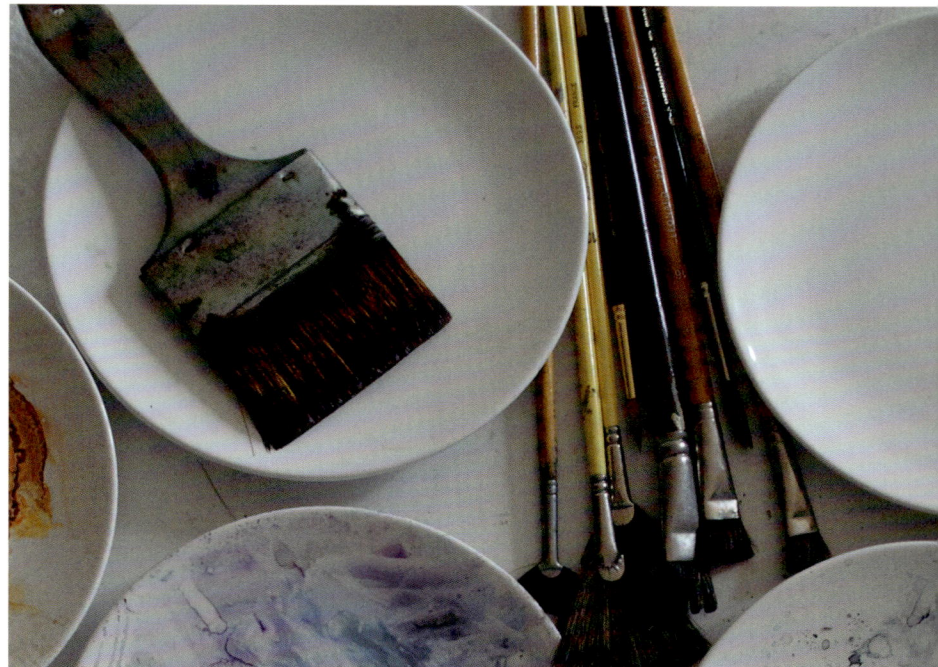

↑ ... and, camera!

Being filmed drawing a landscape for a documentary. The only way is to not worry about messing up and forget there is a crew watching. The most traumatic drawing I have done on camera was a hobbit, then deciding (it was in the script) I didn't like it and erasing it, hoping we would not have to reshoot. I can't recall the last time I erased a drawing.

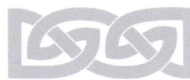

NARRATIVES, THEMES
& INSPIRATION

I spend all my time being shocked and delighted at how beautiful
things can be – light, waves, rocks, faces, architecture, stories,
music, whatever. All this beauty makes me feel vulnerable,
because it's perfection far beyond what I can ever hope
to render, but it also makes me burn to try.

I see compositions, translucencies, light, shadow, things sharp and things hazy, always things that can make pictures. Inspiration is like breathing, and it's no surprise these two words share an etymology. People ask where inspiration comes from. I think it comes down to three worlds: the one in which we all live, the world of words we are enticed to enter, and the world somewhere between the first two, where images are. This third sphere is a secret, the walled garden where the carefully tended flowers blossom, or the blasted heath where the cauldron steams and bubbles. Pellucid or adumbrative, cluttered or spotless, it's the place where even your closest friends can't go. But you can wander about there and return with the travel pics.

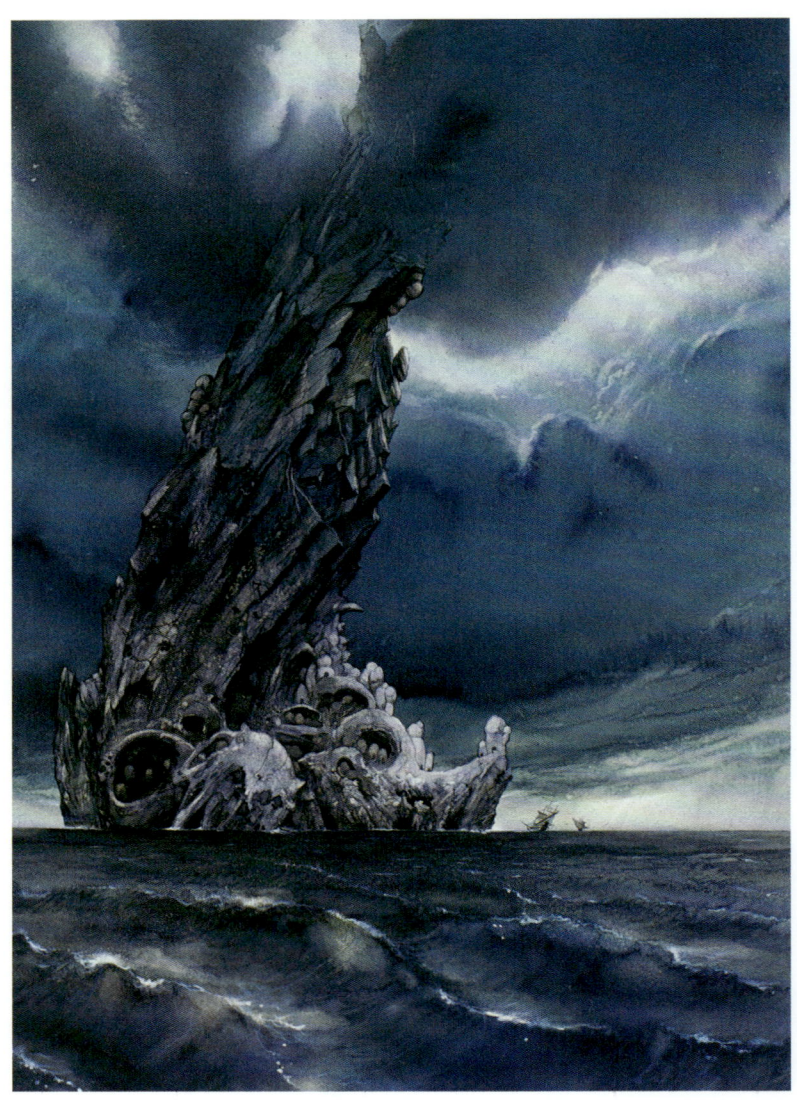

➥ *The Nameless Isle*

Painted in art school, this image is based on an episode from H.P. Lovecraft's novel *The Dream-Quest of Unknown Kadath*. A classmate had a collection of small animal skulls that we piled up and photographed. Those photos led to this image, which led to 'The Dark Tower' in the 1991 Tolkien calendar, and finally to New Zealand, to a rather larger version of the same. Teenage obsessions can go a long way.

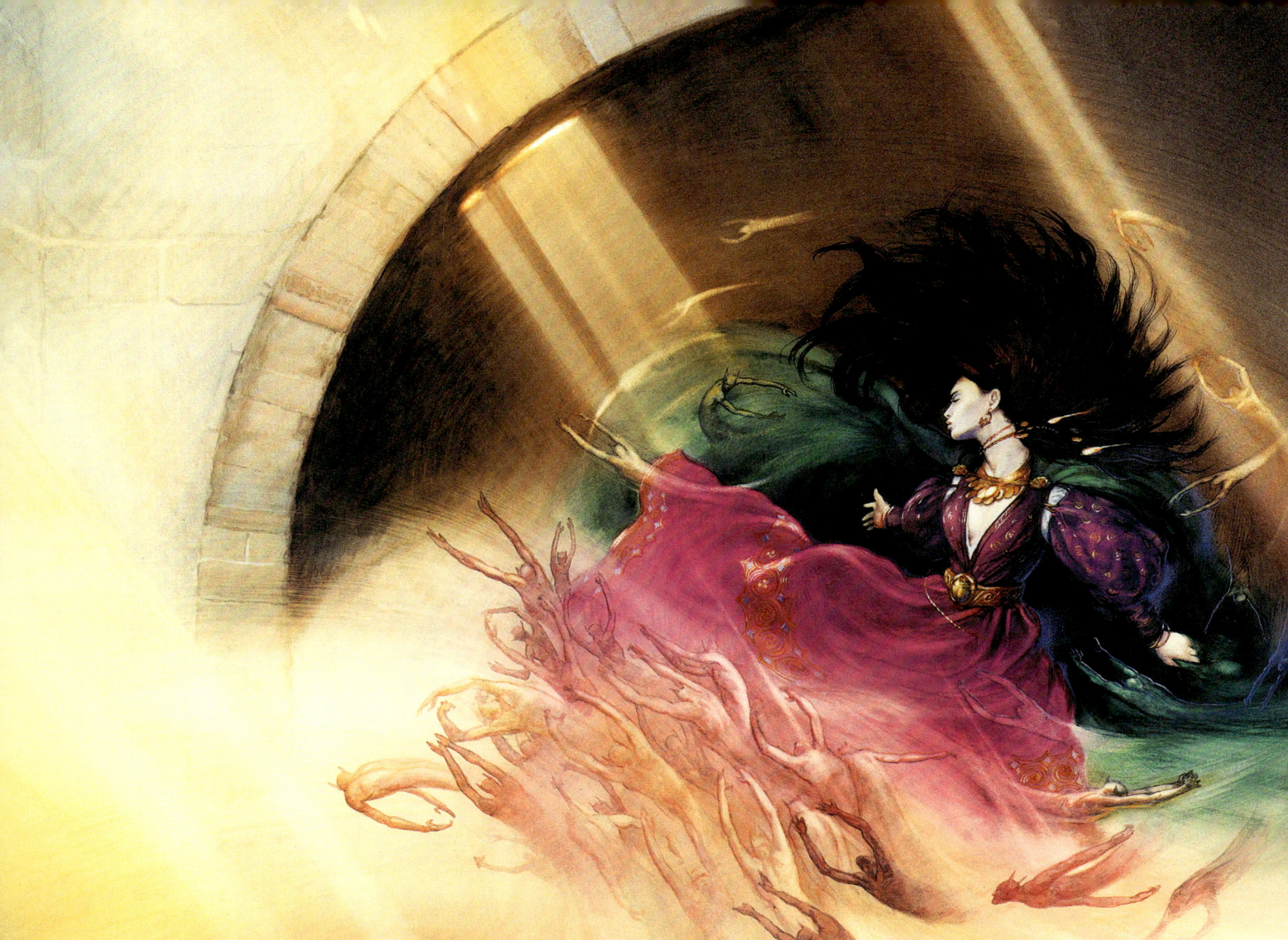

There has been fantasy illustration for centuries, but the notion of literary fiction heralded a shift of perspective. Consciously conceived fantasy literature is not that old. So what makes fantasy 'fantasy'? I think it has something to do with our distance from the subject. When fantastical creatures were part of the common culture – devils dancing in a hellmouth, for example – the artist was giving visible form to a shared reality. When illustrating a cycle of legends, however meaningful, the viewer's perception is not the same. It's a subtle and ultimately savoury paradox that the ousting of fantasy from the everyday has led to the erection of its modest pedestal.

Myth and legend is the arena where humanity carries on its most enduring struggles; I like to think that modern fantasy illustration can be a part of that. Of course there is an element of pleasure in it, but it can also be a way of proposing a path of thought or stirring an emotion that may lead to resolving personal issues. There are dragons within and dragons without. Fantasy illustration should be a lantern that tries to shed a little light on things, not just posters for teenagers' bedrooms.

⬆ *Chimeras*

This was one of my first non-Tolkien covers for HarperCollins. I recall reading the manuscript carefully to find a theme to illustrate. The background is inspired by an orientalist painting. *Chimeras* reproduced courtesy of HarperCollins Publishers.

"SO WHAT MAKES FANTASY 'FANTASY'? I THINK IT HAS SOMETHING TO DO WITH OUR DISTANCE FROM THE SUBJECT"

The difference between iconography and narrative imagery is like the difference between a photographic portrait in which the complicity of the subject and photographer is evident and one where the subject seems unconscious of the camera. With photography, it's a given that both artist and subject belong to the same world, but with fantasy art, we are looking through to another world. It becomes really intriguing just where the regard of the subject stops short of actively engaging the spectator. Characters can look directly at the viewer without the gaze actually leaving their universe, allowing the looking glass to remain intact. Unlike 'poster art', fantasy illustration should open a window on another world, rather than clothing our own in fantasy trappings.

Before the era of mass media, any encounter with art would have been rarer and more significant than it is today. Modern life has pruned away many of the uses of enchantment (to quote Bruno Bettelheim) and science has explained many others. So in a way, fantasy has left the wider world to find a home inside our heads. We project our fantasy outwards rather than encountering it in inexplicable phenomena. Today, fantasy is a largely solitary game, though with the complicity of many in the case of a popular theme such as *The Lord of the Rings*. This makes the 'validity' of the artist's vision an issue: it must convince the viewer, since what things look like is now a personal rather than a cultural choice.

I think the 'personalizing' of fantasy goes hand in hand with our freedom of choice in modern society: with our 'smorgasbord' approach to spirituality and philosophy, it is often relegated to the world of distraction and entertainment – literature, film, games. But dragons may not yet have breathed their last.

↓ *The Mad Ship*

Illustration for the cover of *The Mad Ship* by Robin Hobb. The story features a seafaring merchant people who have unusual ships: the figureheads are more than wooden effigies – they are alive. The ship rots on the shore, eyes blinded by axe blows. He is befriended by a ragged beggar girl. Mismatched and crippled friendships are always moving.

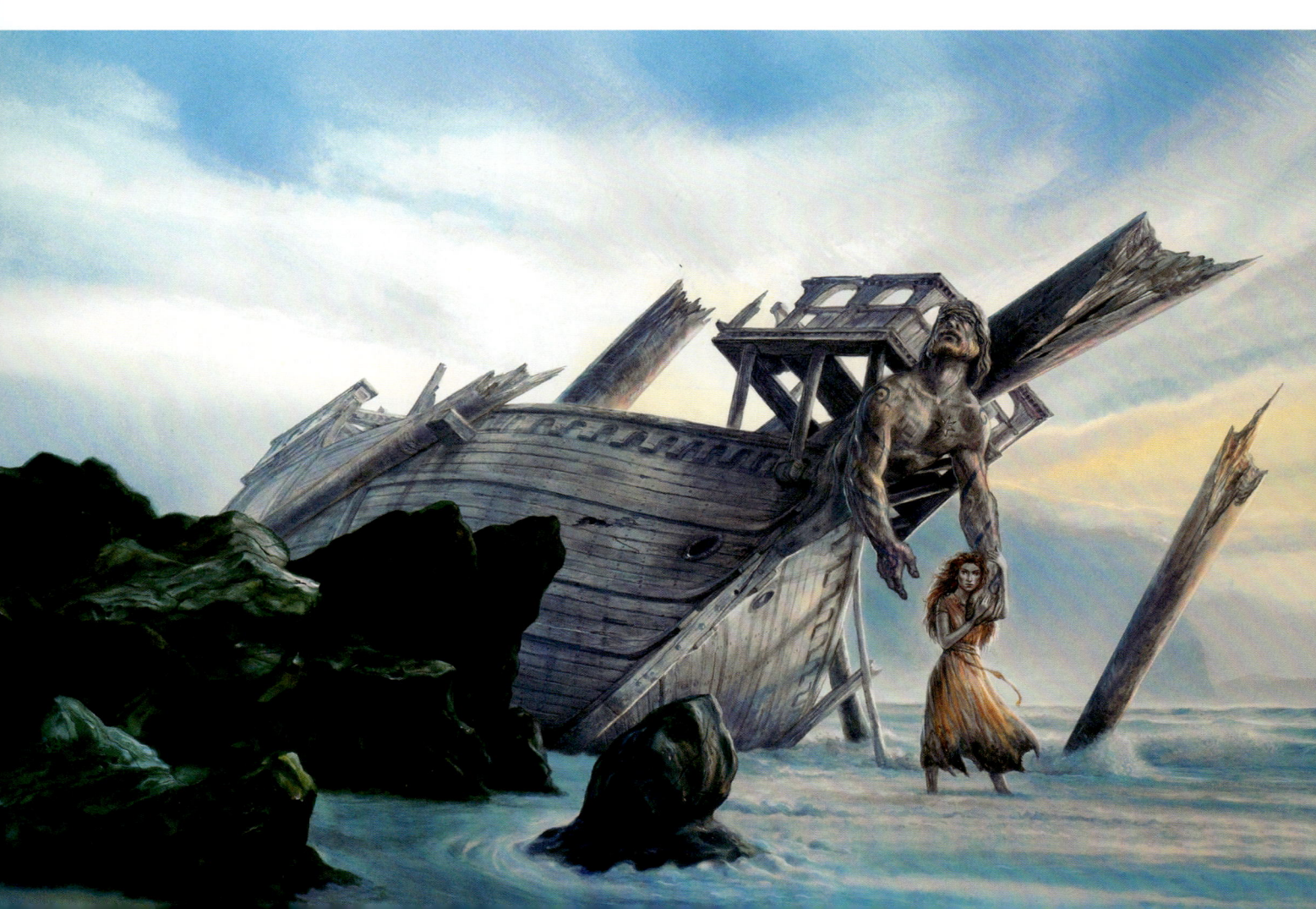

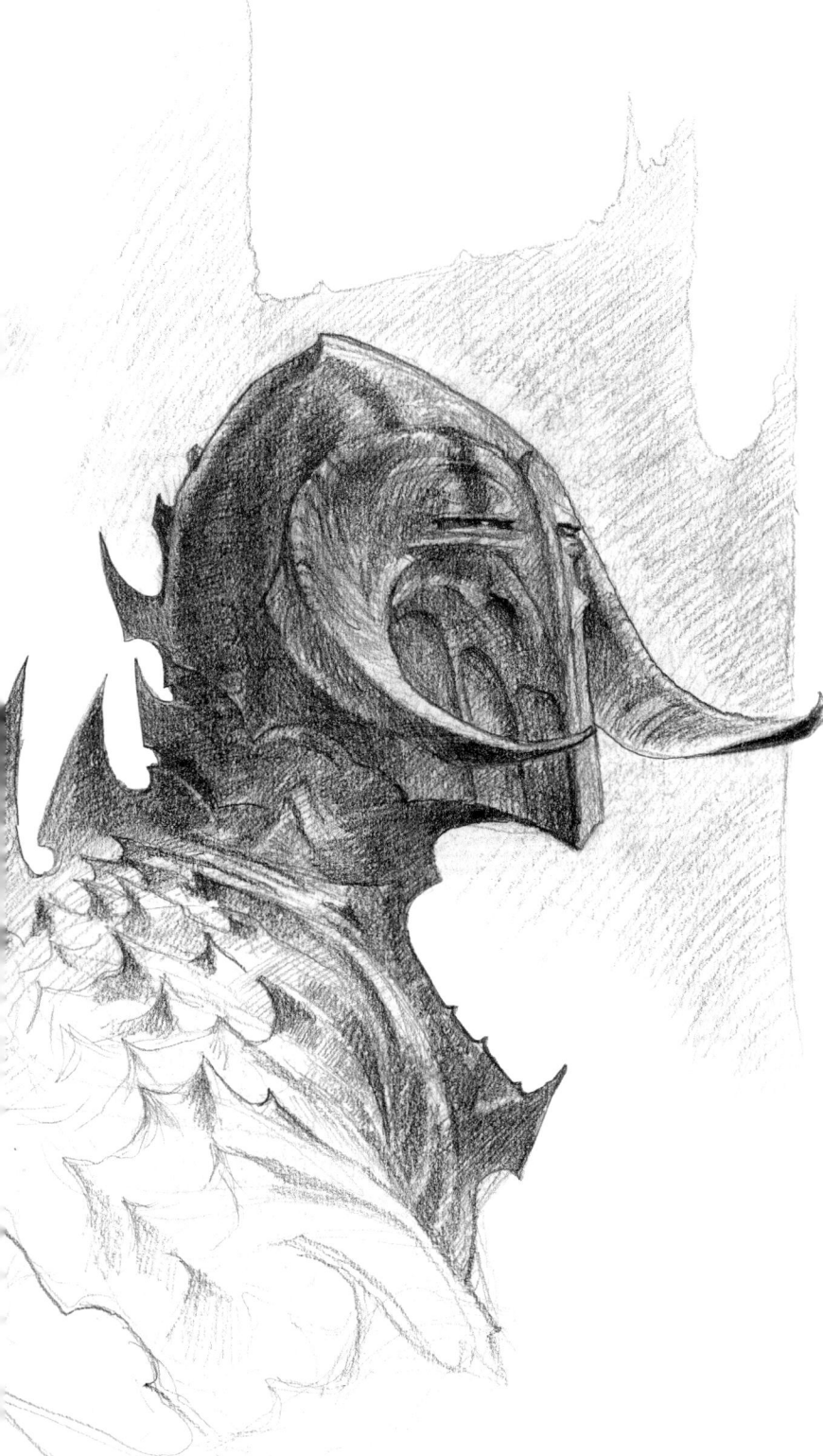

"MODERN LIFE HAS PRUNED AWAY MANY OF THE USES OF ENCHANTMENT (TO QUOTE BRUNO BETTELHEIM) AND SCIENCE HAS EXPLAINED MANY OTHERS"

In many ways, we are not so different from the people who invented the myths, and, as myths are invented for solid reasons, fantasy has a contribution to make. Ancient beliefs have been the richest source, drawing on the mythology of the ancient Greeks, Celts and other cultures. The line between religion and fantasy is not cut and dried: religious symbols such as the Grail are rampant in what we now call fantasy. On the edges of belief roam fantastical creatures such as gargoyles and dragons, which are part of the history of religion.

For me, fantasy imagery involves 'glamour' (in its archaic sense of enchantment), and implies a suspension of rationality. It refers to worlds and creatures derived from myth or invented by creative minds in the same vein. Its fully realized worlds have elements that we cannot physically experience. They are generally pre-industrial, slowly blending into science fiction as they move forward in time, trading suspension of disbelief for belief in the promise of science. Teleportation, for example, is magical in a medieval setting if done by a mage, but it's sci-fi on the Starship Enterprise.

Awe is not enough, there must be something in fantasy that is beyond our grasp. It is about empowerment: the shedding of the mundane, the pruning of the everyday and the transposing of human preoccupations into an environment where the 'possible' reigns, coupled with a richness of imagination and a common cultural inheritance. It is something we should never grow out of.

↜ *Sauron*

Tolkien never really describes Sauron's physical appearance, preferring to describe the horror and fear he inspires in all who come near him. Not only is this more effective, but it offers liberty to illustrators. Rather than matching a description, it means capturing an atmosphere.

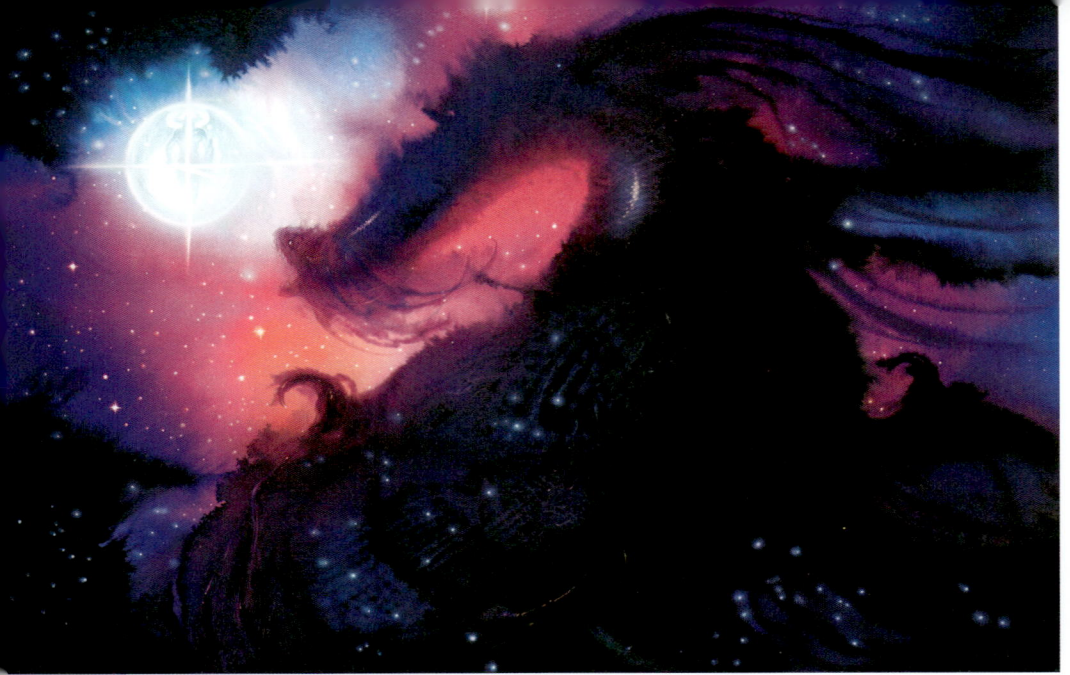

← Dragon of Chaos

Babylonian god Marduk slays the dragon Tiamat and builds the world from the smoking ruin of her body. A protean, dissolving form seemed to best express time before time. I worked up the lighter parts on very damp paper, then dropped a *lot* of black with an eye-dropper, coaxing shapes with a feathered brush as colours ran. The white acrylic stars are airbrushed to make them shine.

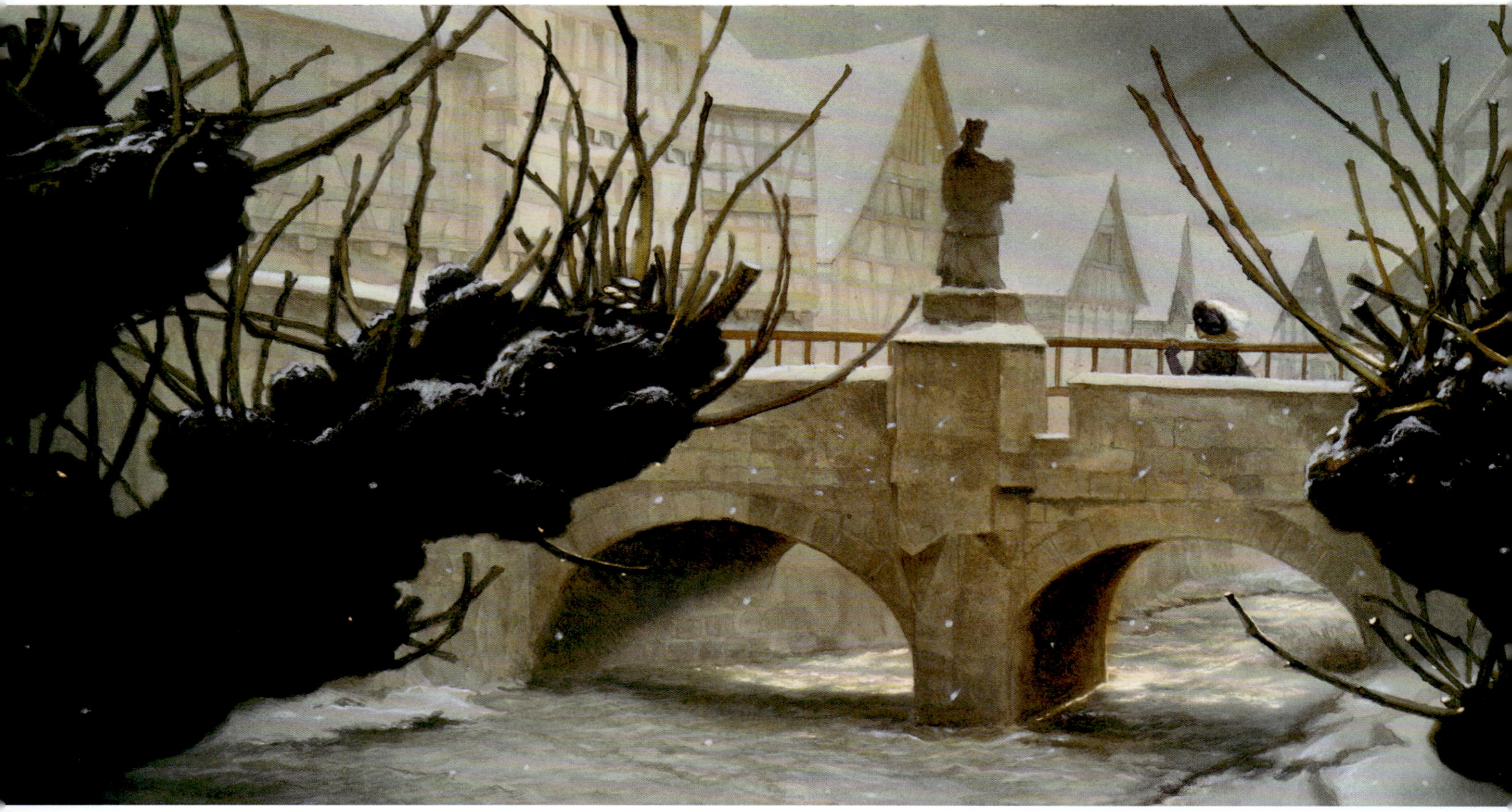

⬆ The Man Who Lit the Stars

The bridge in this illustration for a children's book by Claude Clément is taken from a town in the Jura, the buildings from another town in the Alsace, and the pollarded willows from across the lake where we live. My only addition to the scene is the man with his ladder, which allows him to climb up high enough to clean stars, so you never see either end of it until he reaches the top. *The Man Who Lit the Stars,* from *La Ville Abandonnée,* John Howe © CASTERMAN S.A.

➡ Yggdrasil

Isn't this grim? What *was* I thinking? This picture grew from the sword hilt. A word or phrase can trigger sketches that go far astray from the original idea, leading to new ideas. Following your pencil as it wanders is often more rewarding than pushing forcefully before you.

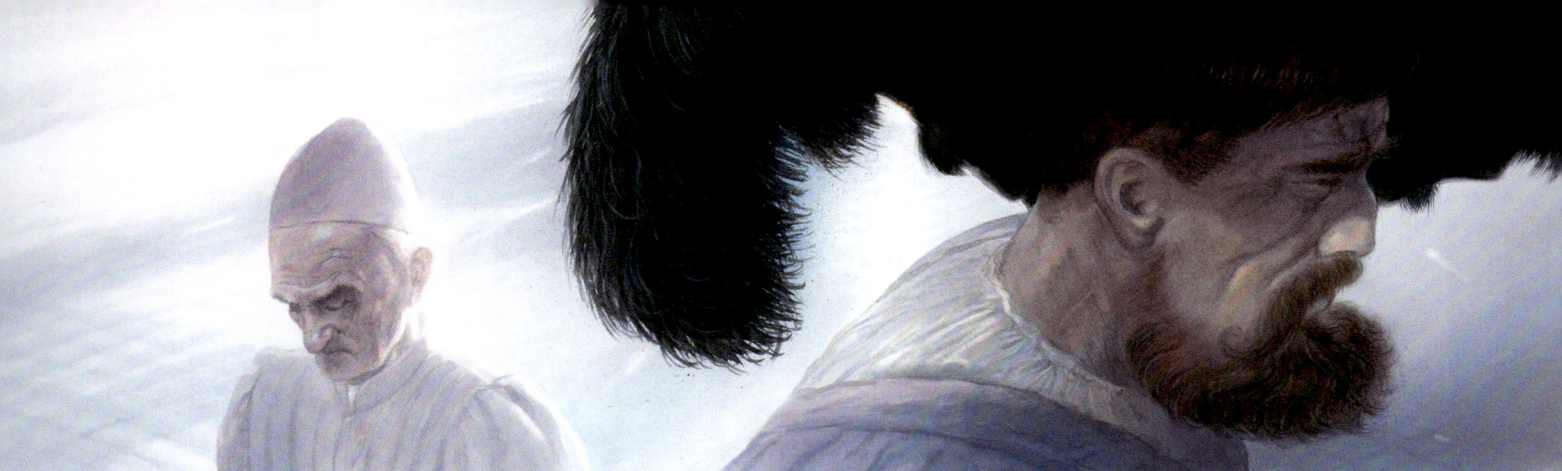

↑ The King and the Glassblower

Illustration *from The Abandoned City* by Claude Clément. The king's profile is from a stock images book with a beard and hat added. The glassblower is my wife's father, who obligingly posed for the portraits of this character. *The King and the Glassblower*, from *La Ville Abandonnée*, John Howe © CASTERMAN S.A.

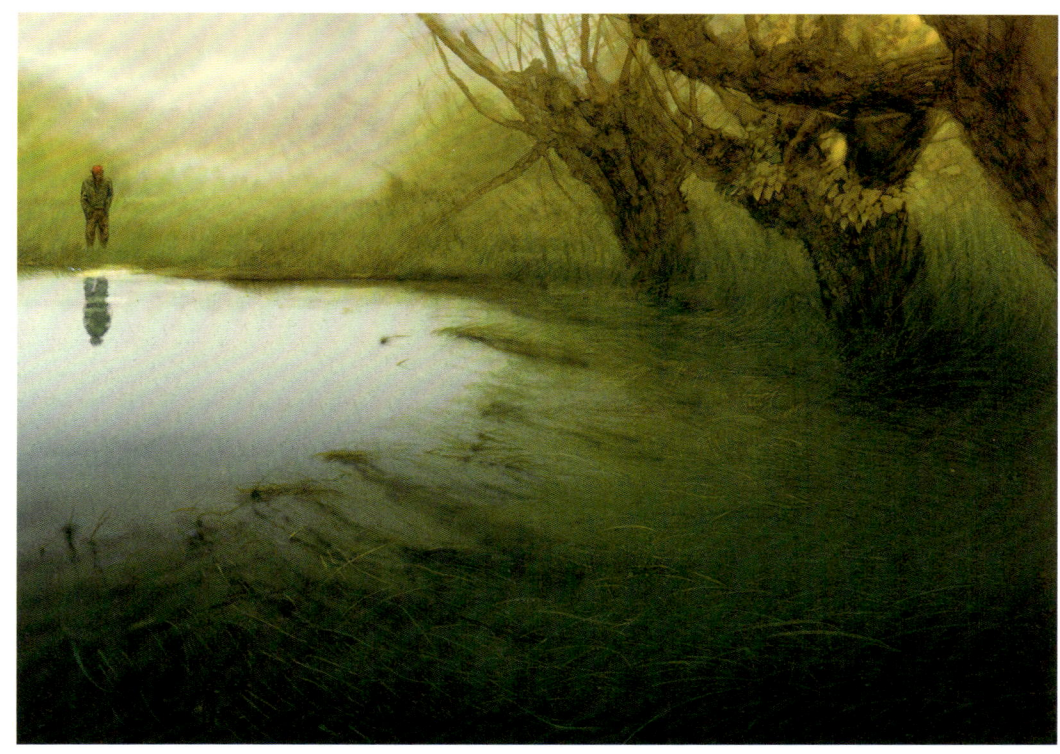

↑ The Pond

This was for *Rana-la-Menthe*, by J.L. Trassard, a tale of a poacher haunted by galloping hooves. One moonless night he manages to stop the horse, ridden by a beautiful, silent woman. She is not human and eventually returns to the marshes – he is disconsolate. I wanted to show how the world that was once a refuge is now a barrier between him and his lost love. The unfathomable pool, dragging weeds and brooding willows are the result of this line of thought.

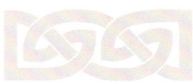

GATHERING & USING REFERENCE MATERIAL

Being something of a magpie is a useful quality for any illustrator. Gathering material – whether you store it in your head, in your sketchbook, on your computer or in a folder – is essential. Organizing it so that you can find it when you need it also helps.

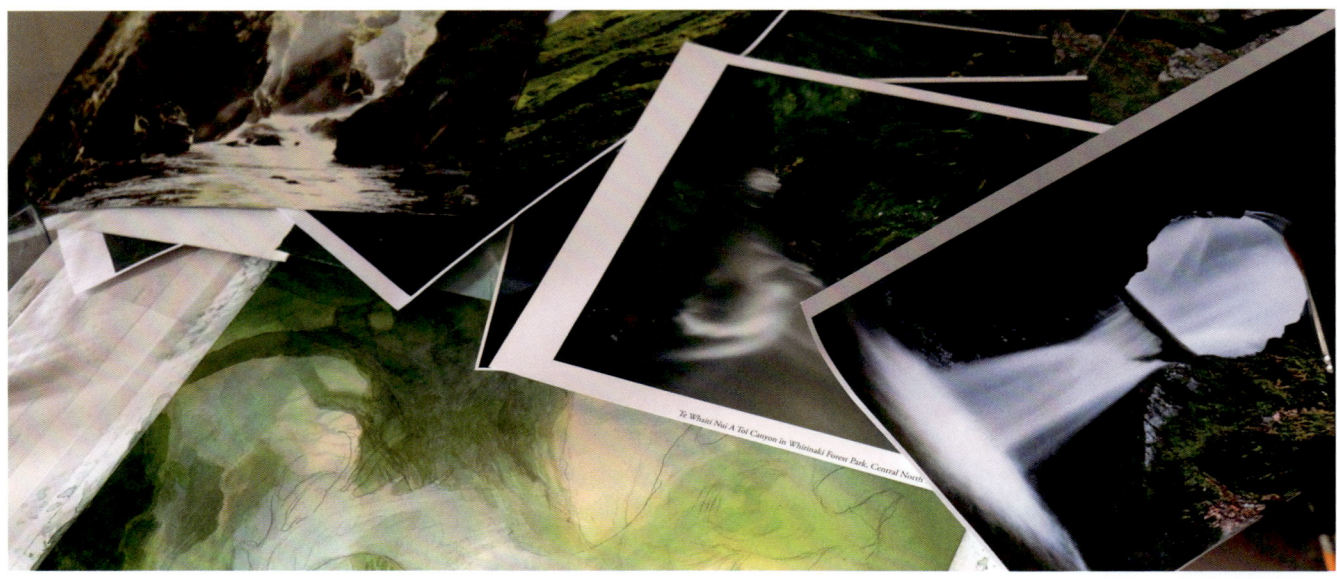

Te Whaiti Nui A Toi Canyon in Whirinaki Forest Park, Central North

To anyone who is keen to convey a certain sense of reality in fantasy, reference materials are crucial. Our house is full of books in languages I can't read, purchased for their images alone. The wall behind my computer supports a daunting set of shelves containing over a hundred drawers, filled with photos, printouts and pictures cut out of books and magazines. There are drawers labelled 'ravens', 'rhinos', 'ruins' and 'rust', others 'King Arthur', 'Beowulf' or 'Mythago Wood'; these themes end up defining themselves. They change, merge or separate. My filing system would make a dedicated documentalist faint in dismay, but I'm the only one who uses it and your documentation should fit your needs and not any pre-defined system. (It is entirely visual, and I must say that only an intensely creative mind would call three successive drawers 'rocks', 'more rocks' and 'yet more rocks'.) I also have a large reference library (yes, of books, remember those?), principally on subjects I am attracted to: architecture,

⬆ Creative disorder
Allow clutter freedom. Documentation accumulates in drifts as I work through a painting. When I am done, books, drawers of images and photos are piled all around. They will be tidied up and put away when the painting is done.

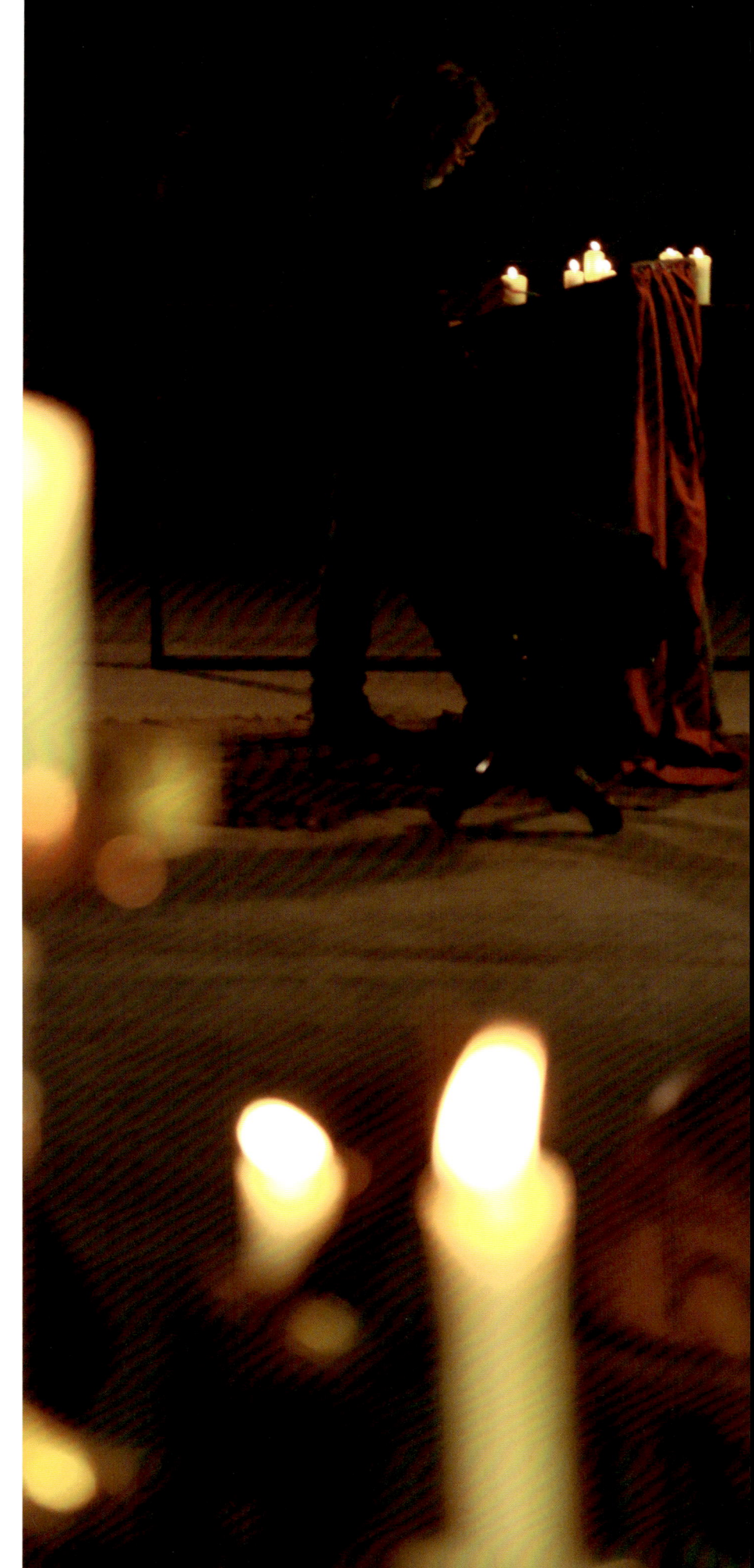

➜ Unusual circumstances

Drawing by candlelight for a documentary. I wish this was my studio (the real one is a lot smaller and fortunately easier to heat). Drawing is the perfect way to settle in to a new space; you can – and should happily – draw everywhere.

history, costume, armour, etc., and a diligently collected selection of books on ancient culture, myth and legend. I also take an inordinate amount of photos, principally of landscapes.

Imagination cannot function in a vacuum. Faced with the hopeless ideal of memorizing everything I see, and blessed with a squirrel-like tendency to store things away just in case, I stack my reminders away, rather like the forgetful actor who knows he can count on the prompter to jog his memory. However, this kind of reference is to be used with some care. Unless a photo coincides so closely with an idea that the two are intertwined, the sketch must come first. To invert the order is to make an error that will, if it does not compromise the spirit of an illustration, indenture it to the document and misdirect the focus.

While we are all happy picture-snappers of the instant camera age, where our perception of the world is often (over-)defined by the speed of a shutter. The superiority of sketching over the camera resides in the pace of a sketch, which paradoxically stops time, permitting a look that can stretch over many minutes, even hours. An out-of-time communion, subject to passing clouds, the movement of the sun, failing light, it is the antithesis of the snapshot. Photos have a role, but a subordinate one.

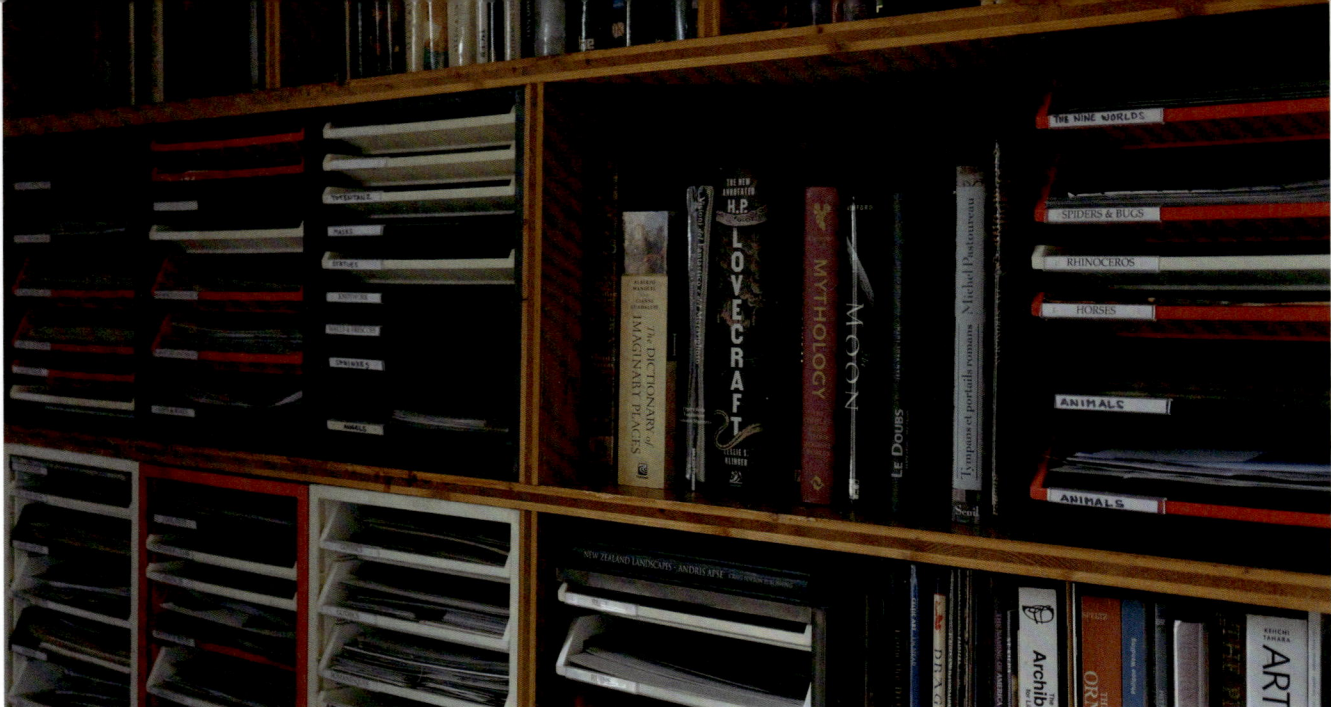

The wealth of detail and colour masks the fact that they are incomplete, and can easily end up being 'hollow' – all surface, no substance.

Obviously, the constant accumulation of imagery is not enough. Good illustrations are not done with the copy/paste function, nor do they have anything to do with a lavish laying-on of detail. The value of information and knowledge, visual or other, is the time it spends kicking around inside one's head. The mind is not an idle place where things are stored away collecting dust. They talk to each other, exchange information, get together, make groups and friends, and eventually are there when you are doing the one thing you cannot do consciously – being inspired.

It's easy to confuse information and inspiration – and fatal to the latter. The bulwark of documentation can wall you in and kill any spark of creativity. However, one word can unlock the door to a vastness of options: when I think 'window', I want the history

of it through the ages and the world over to flash before my inner eye – pueblos, step gables and arrow slits, from Mycenae to my neighbourhood, from caverns to cathedrals; the whole lot to borrow and invent. What one draws so often relies on recognition, not observation. An aggregation of recognizable elements, not real invention. But somewhere in the many drawers on mountains are images that will take me to Asgard or Shambhala, and Yggdrasil or Avalon are tucked away. If I pay attention to the pictures, I'll get there. Somewhere in this accumulation of anecdote are the signposts pointing out the path to the universal. That's what myth is all about.

Fantasy requires a heightened sense of believability, exactly the opposite of what one might expect of this world. The willing suspension of disbelief on the part of the viewer needs a supplementary layer of credibility, which can only be reached by judicious mix of what we know is real and what we would love to dream could be.

⬩ Evolving labels

Documentation is a crucial resource. Drawers seem to be the most efficient way of storing loose reference images, the subjects and labels composing themselves as images accumulate.

⮕ Head to toe

A bit of everything, from medieval armour to movie props. Fantasy illustration can benefit from the authenticity of reconstructed accessories, not necessarily for copying outright, but to gain a sense of proportion, weight and feel. I use the raven's foot often. Narsil (bottom right) is, to my knowledge, the only movie sword ever designed with a hollow pommel.

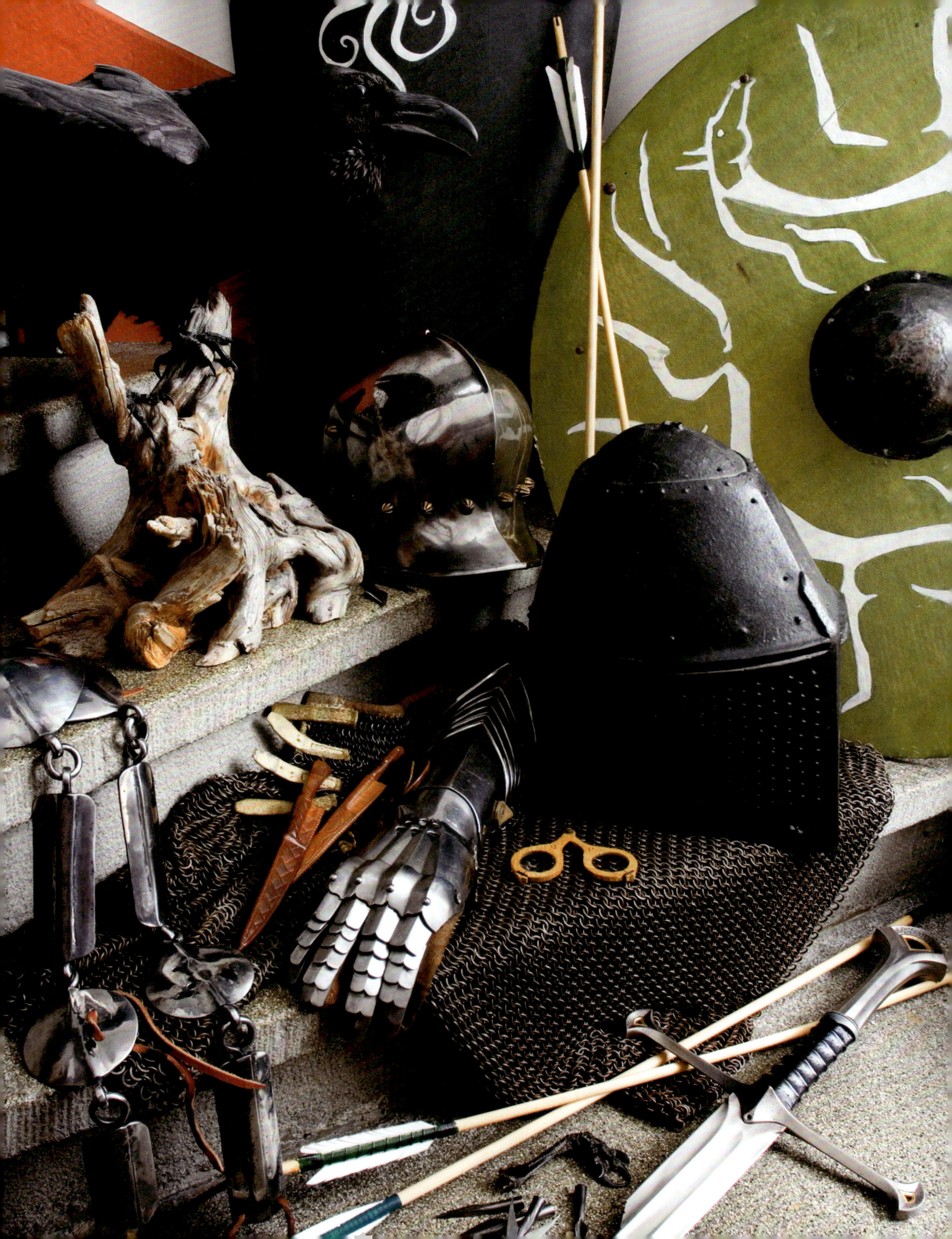

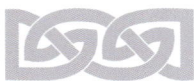

ORGANIZING YOUR WORK ENVIRONMENT

A comfortable working environment may be every illustrator's dream, but is not always possible. The most important element is that it is your space for your pursuit of imagery, whether it be the size of a broom cupboard or a loft – you must be able to leave your things and not have to clear them away every night.

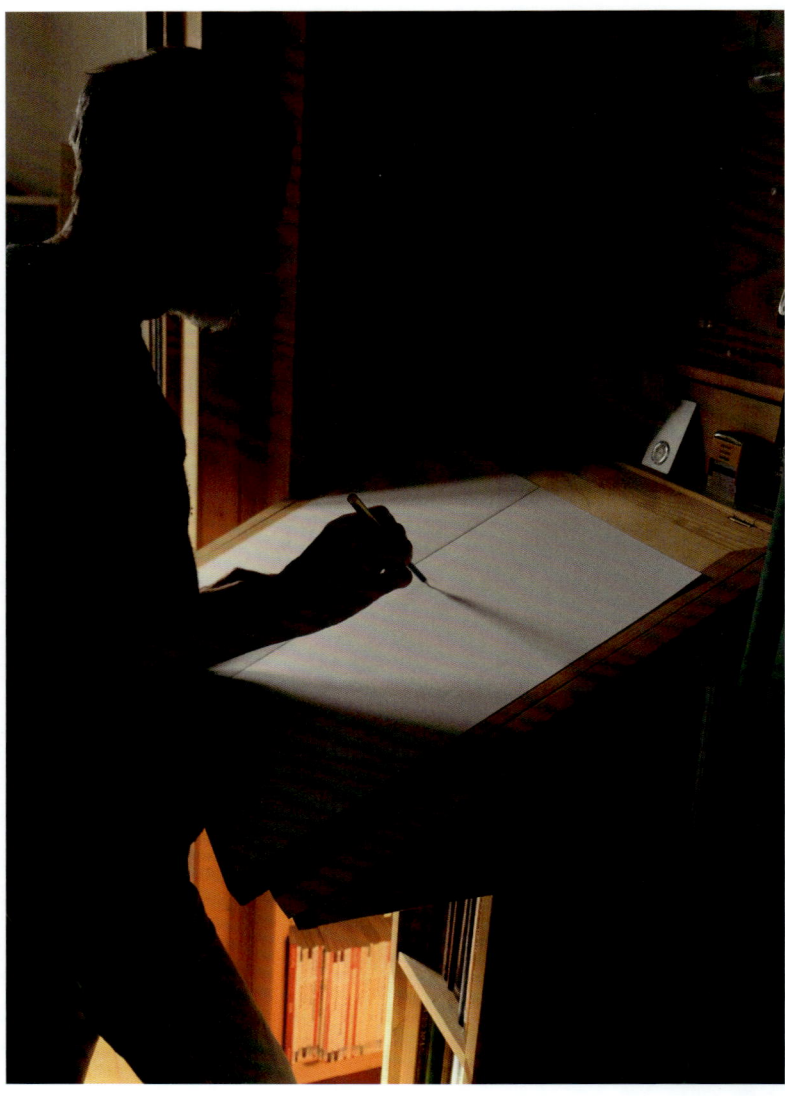

Whether you work in your home or out is a personal choice: I am so accustomed to the intermingling of professional and family life that I no longer feel qualified to judge what works for others. But while illustrating is of course a job, it is also a waltz with the muse. A sudden inspiration should not have to wait for you to drag your art materials from a cupboard and set them up.

Choosing a place to draw or paint
Drawing is rather like fencing – you need to master the correct skills when using pointed instruments – and you must control the distance between you and your sparring partner. If you are not yet sure of your proficiency, placing the paper on a table can plunge you back into a 'scholastic' situation more adapted to writing than drawing.

➔ At the pulpit
I have a sort of drawing pulpit, which allows me to draw standing up; distancing yourself from the reflexes of writing will allow you to approach your drawing with fresh perspective. You can create similar conditions yourself by propping a board upon a table, or by fixing your board to a sketching easel.

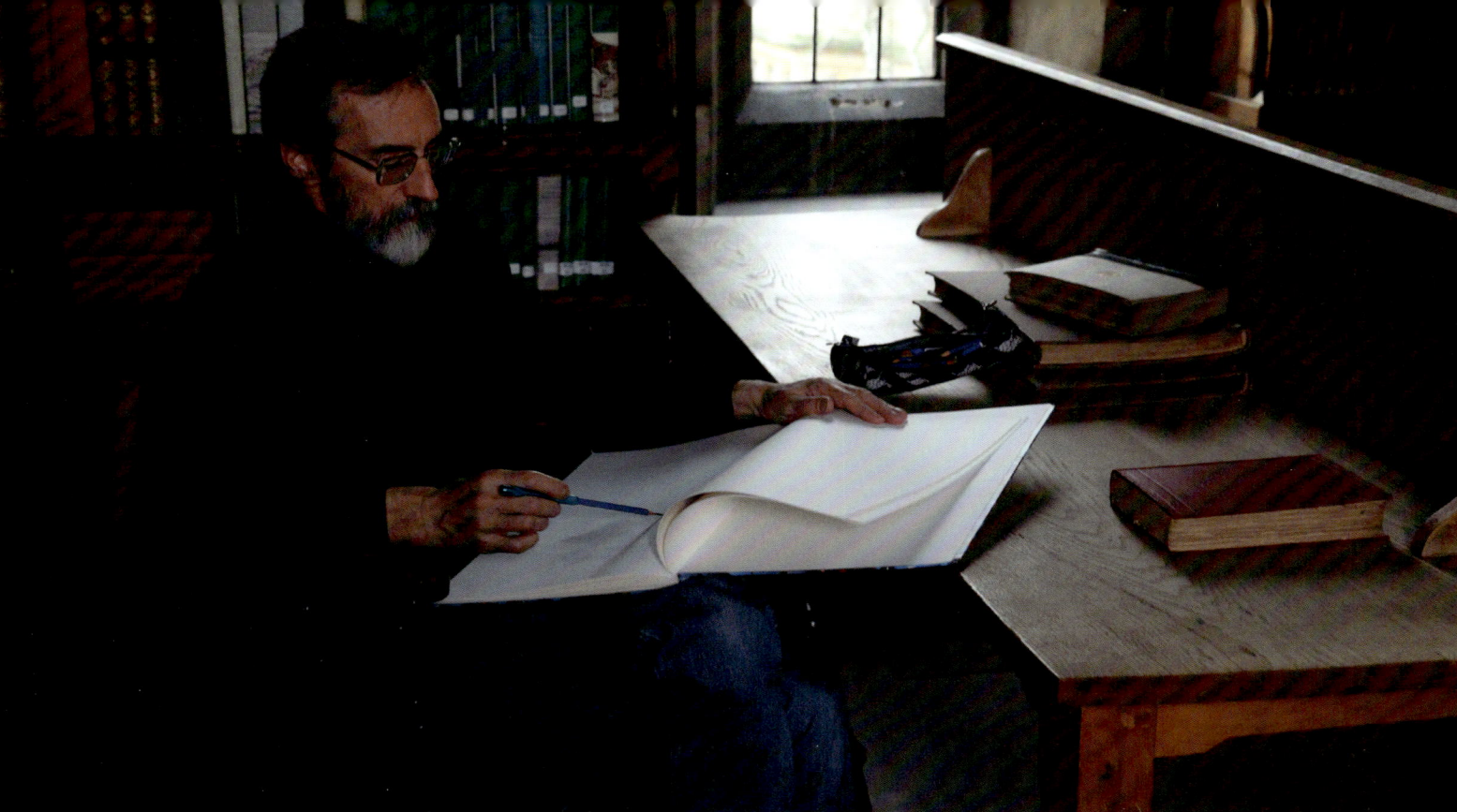

At Tolkien's desk

Drawing in the Bodleian Library. The most comfortable way to draw is with the sketchbook perched on your knee. You can more or less draw anywhere you can find a seat.

For sketching you need to loosen up, sit back, get your arm free from the shoulder down and let your pencil wander. I see people studiously sketching with an HB pencil, heel of hand firmly planted on page, working in a square centimetre of space, and want to yell at them.

There is a spot in my studio dedicated to sketching, dubbed my sketching pulpit. Built rather as an afterthought between shelving and a window, it has an angled surface just big enough to take the large sheets of drawing paper. I can pile a dozen sketchbooks inside it and there is a handy shelf for drawing materials. Nowhere near as cumbersome as a full-fledged draughtsman's table, it takes up surprisingly little room. It is high enough to comfortably use standing without resting elbows on it. An effective way to work, it encourages using the whole arm, sketching freely from the shoulder, with the hand free to allow the pencil to wander. The drawing itself is also easier to see in its entirety.

Workspace

Smaller paintings can happily rest propped up on a table, while the larger ones need to be set on an easel. The compressed air cylinder on the right is for the airbrush.

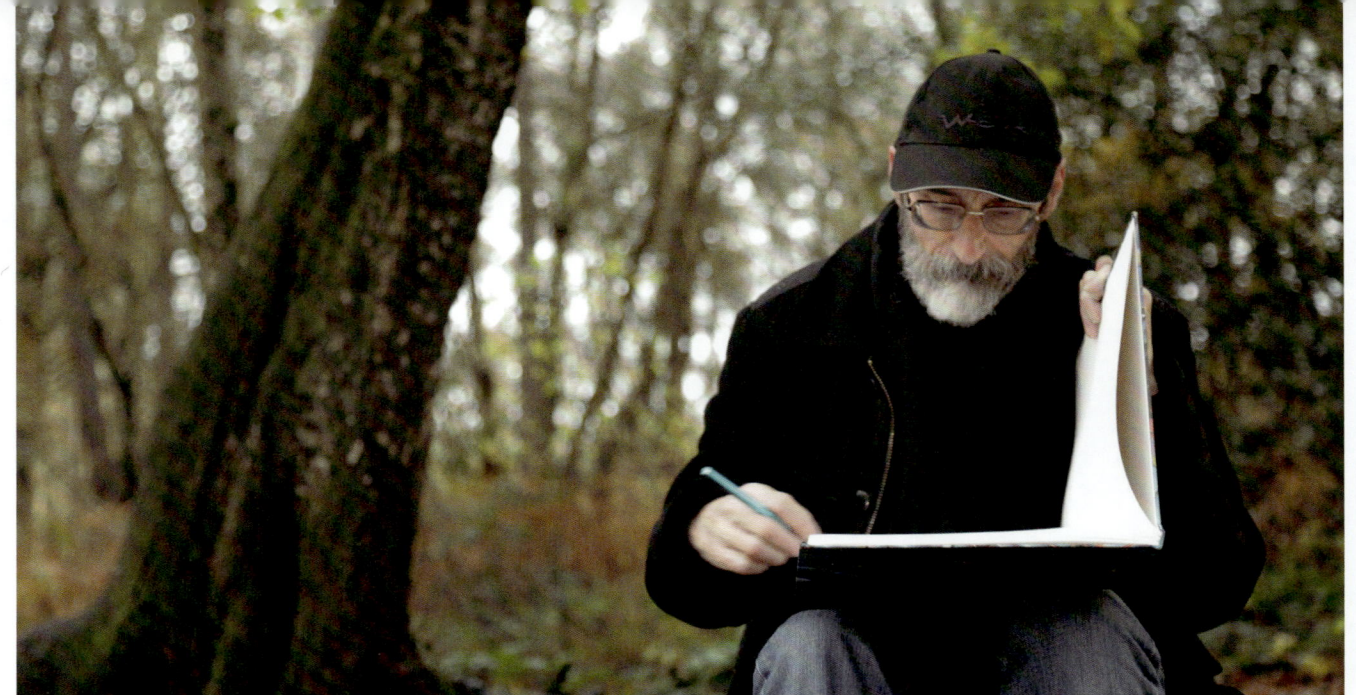

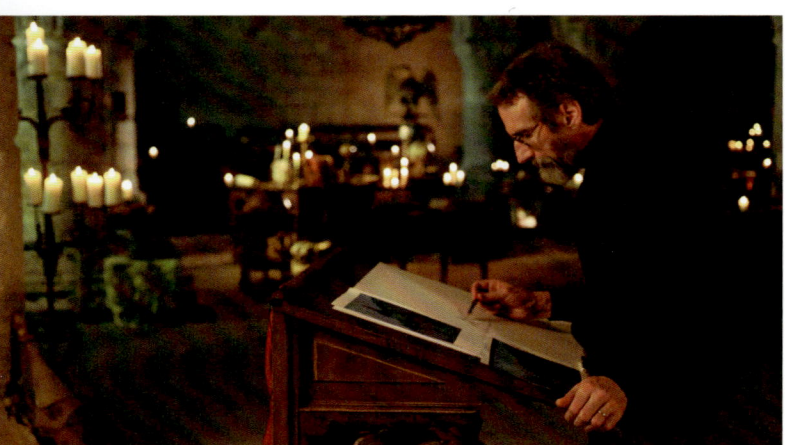

From idea to paper

Painting usually takes place in the studio, but at that stage, hesitations and 'blank-paper block' should be swept away by sketched ideas. You do require personal space for this, but itinerant colour work can be done easily if you have to.

Starting on a big painting may require a ritual, exploiting opportunities to procrastinate – I tidy the studio, vacuum the floor and do something else totally pointless that could wait. When I've run out of options for wasting time, I'm just about ready to start. Beginning requires a heightened level of attention and awareness to get the first washes right, and this initial hurdle needs to be taken at a certain speed. If you confuse the two – the blank-page musing and the actual starting – you may run into insurmountable obstacles. If you have drawn something once, you can redraw it for your finished piece. If you have the feeling that you'll never be able to draw it again as well as you just did, you are only on the very edge of your achievement, having not really drawn your idea but only approached it.

Redrawing is the only way to maintain the spontaneity of line necessary for the germination and elaboration of ideas and the integrity necessary for colour. You are freer to make errors in a sketch and correct them later than if you endlessly erase and re-erase details on a piece that is neither a sketch nor a finished drawing. Separating the two, and their inherent contingencies, lets you work anywhere.

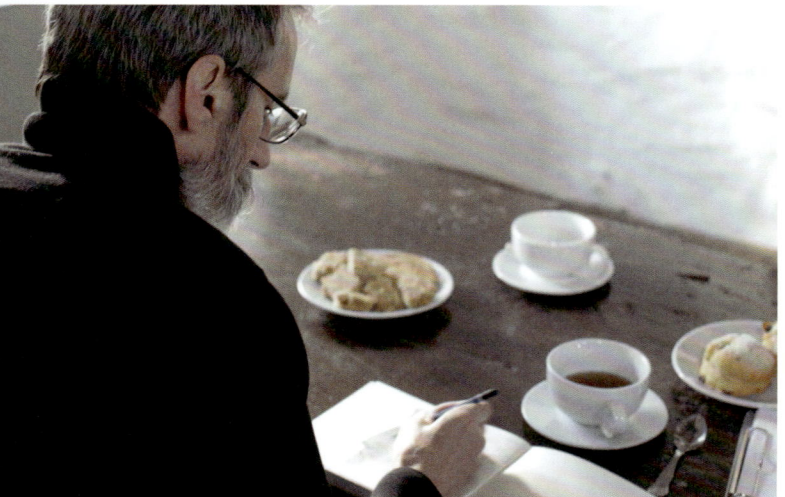

⬩ Here and there

Keeping a small sketchbook to hand lets you draw during meetings, perhaps the most efficient way to concentrate and take visual notes. (I was always drawing in class at school.)

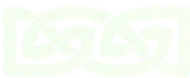

OUT & ABOUT

There is no substitute for drawing from life – getting out of the studio and acquiring the confidence to quickly sketch 'in situ' can be a real asset. It's easy enough to sketch in pretty much any condition except rain or strong winds. Even if your sketch isn't that exciting or satisfying, you have gained from the observational exercise.

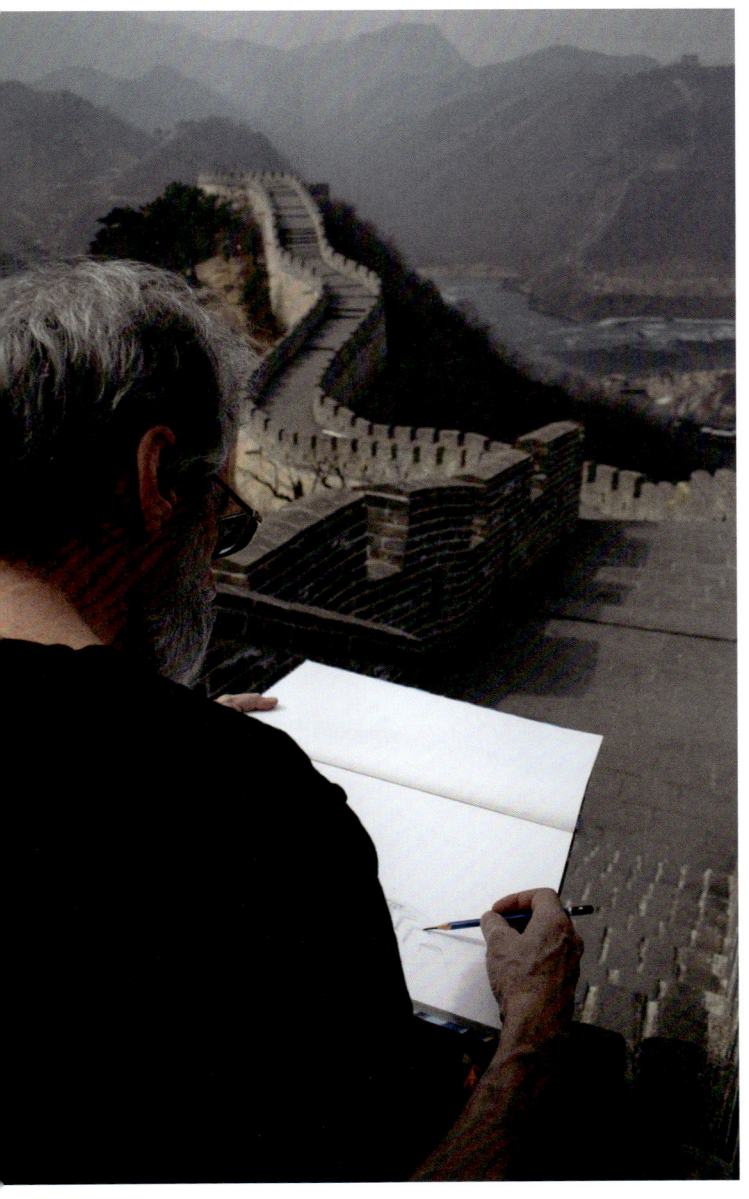

For an artist, sketching on location is the equivalent of a musician playing scales on a piano. Time spent drawing a vista may not give you as attractive a result as a camera can, but you have spent time understanding what it is that you are drawing. When drawing outside, travel light. Review your materials: they should be trim and transportable, while not leaving you with a cramped drawing surface. You should be able to take them anywhere. My small knapsack contains a pouch with pencils, erasers and a couple of craft knives, and I use a sketchbook that opens to A3 size, which just fits in the bag and leaves me hands free. I can happily cart my current sketchbook everywhere I go – perhaps half of my sketches are done while waiting for appointments or travelling.

Carrying a sketchbook means that your doodles are going to be with you for a while, so you can build on themes and subjects. I often get quite a lot of thinking done on long trips, and like to fill up a sketchbook in the summer if I can, since the weather is so conducive to idly sitting out of doors. Generally, unless I am being rained upon or the wind is tearing pages from my sketchbook, I can draw anywhere and at any time, if there is enough light.

← On the Great Wall

Perhaps the most exotic place I have had the pleasure of drawing in. My sketchbook and camera provide two complementary things: the deep impression gained from looking at a landscape for the time needed to draw it, and the back-up details captured in the photos.

PROTECTING & STORING YOUR ARTWORK

While most of my work is done in traditional media, it is all ultimately digitized. The physical artwork can happily live in plan chests, and the work that is framed is stored in a dedicated area when it is not on the road.

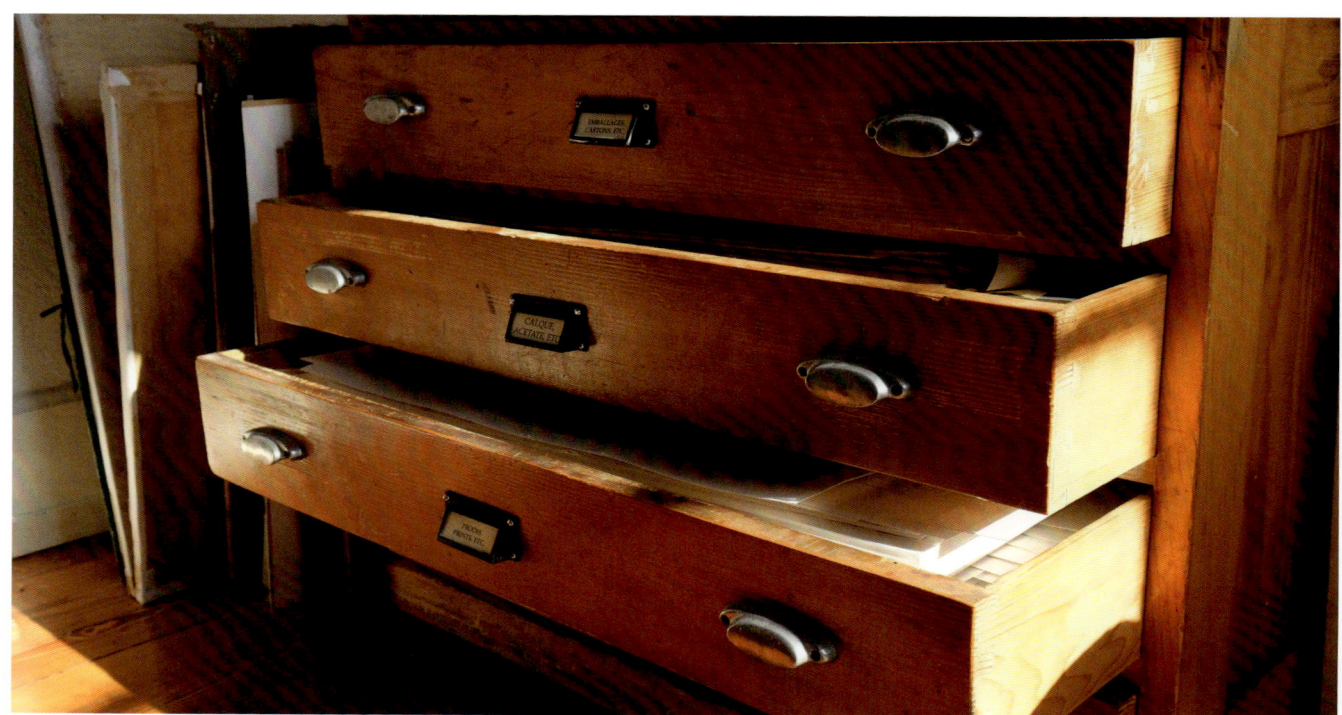

The main enemy of finished artwork is light, particularly ultra-violet (UV) light. There are plenty of ways to protect against this, the easiest being to store your work in folders, boxes or drawers (a plan chest is best). UV light will eventually yellow and decay paper, and alters pigments. The most durable medium is the practically indestructible egg tempera. Oil paint comes next, pastels and watercolour after that. If you display your work, frame it with UV filter glass, or give it a light coat of fixative containing a UV filter. The other enemy is humidity, and this is a matter of storing your work somewhere that isn't damp and hopefully won't flood.

⬆ Stay out of the sun

The plan chests in my studio have drawers that are a little deep, so I've installed an extra tray in each. My original artworks live in the plan chests. (I prefer not to have them on the walls – I've already seen them.)

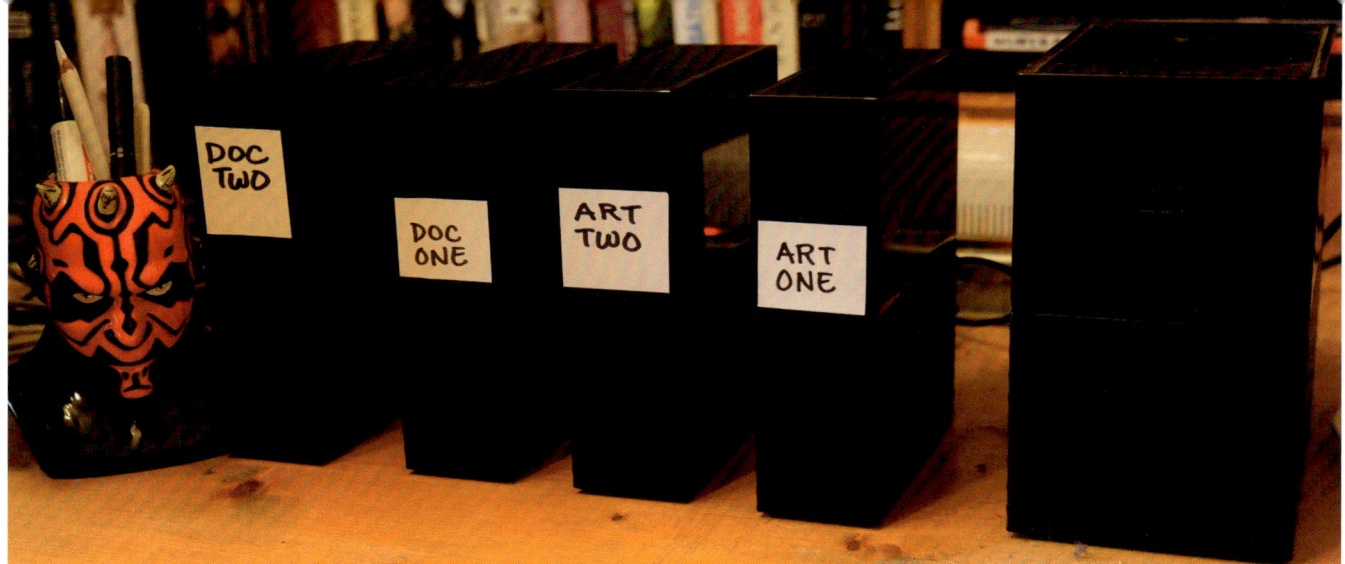

Using fixative

Pictures do not need a thick coat of fixative, but it is a practical expedient against damage caused by greasy fingers, stray water droplets and general handling. If stored and handled competently, work shouldn't need large amounts of fixative; but if you do use it, apply as little as you can – two light coats rather than one thick one. It cannot be used on pastels, which demand special care; watercolours don't really require fixative, but other drawing media can often do with a light coat. I put a spray of fixative over the pages in my sketchbook, as travel results in wear and tear, and I put a sheet of tracing paper over every original drawing.

Digitizing images

I scan all my work at 600dpi on an A3 scanner. A large format can end up being a jigsaw puzzle of overlapping scans before being pieced together. While the photomerge option is helpful I prefer to do most of it myself. Once the patchwork has been assembled seamlessly and corrections made, I send a flat RGB TIFF file at 300dpi to the commissioning editor. The folder for any given painting usually contains folders with the original scans, a 600dpi layered file, and a 300dpi flat file, as well as various screen captures and low res jpegs. (I scan in RGB format, and let publisher or printer convert files to CMYK as required.)

Files can be quite large, but I would not reduce them in size. I use external hard drives that I update and organize myself. The oldest digital files have migrated through several drives, so it is worthwhile checking them to make sure they are still accessible. Everything is immediately backed up at least twice.

You can photograph your work, but need studio quality equipment to do this, otherwise even a 20MB shot may not give you the results you are looking for. One option is to go to a professional photographer who has the required lights, studio space and so on, but this can be expensive as you will be charged for the time spent setting up. So, if you go down this route, wait until you have a group of pictures to be photographed, then the same set-up can be used for all of them.

↑ Double drives

Digital files are backed up at least twice on external hard drives.

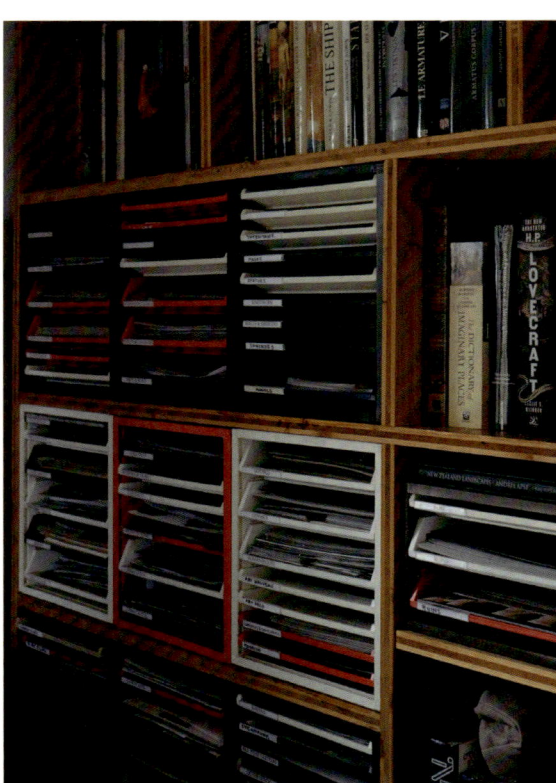

↑ Intuitive filing

For years I tried to classify papers in binders, but if searching for a reference was laborious, returning it to its proper place was torture. So I abandoned binders for drawers, which largely compose themselves. Documents rarely used sink to the bottom like sediment and may eventually be discarded.

TOOLS & TECHNIQUES

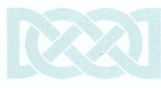

Methods must be mastered before you can decide if they are right for you. Digital tools are ever more exciting – you need time to bend those to your will, but it is worth the investment. Traditional tools are simpler – or appear so – as many are similar to those we used in childhood. Finding the right paper, brushes and pencils can mean trying many, but when you find ones that correspond well to your sensibilities, you will wonder how you ever did without.

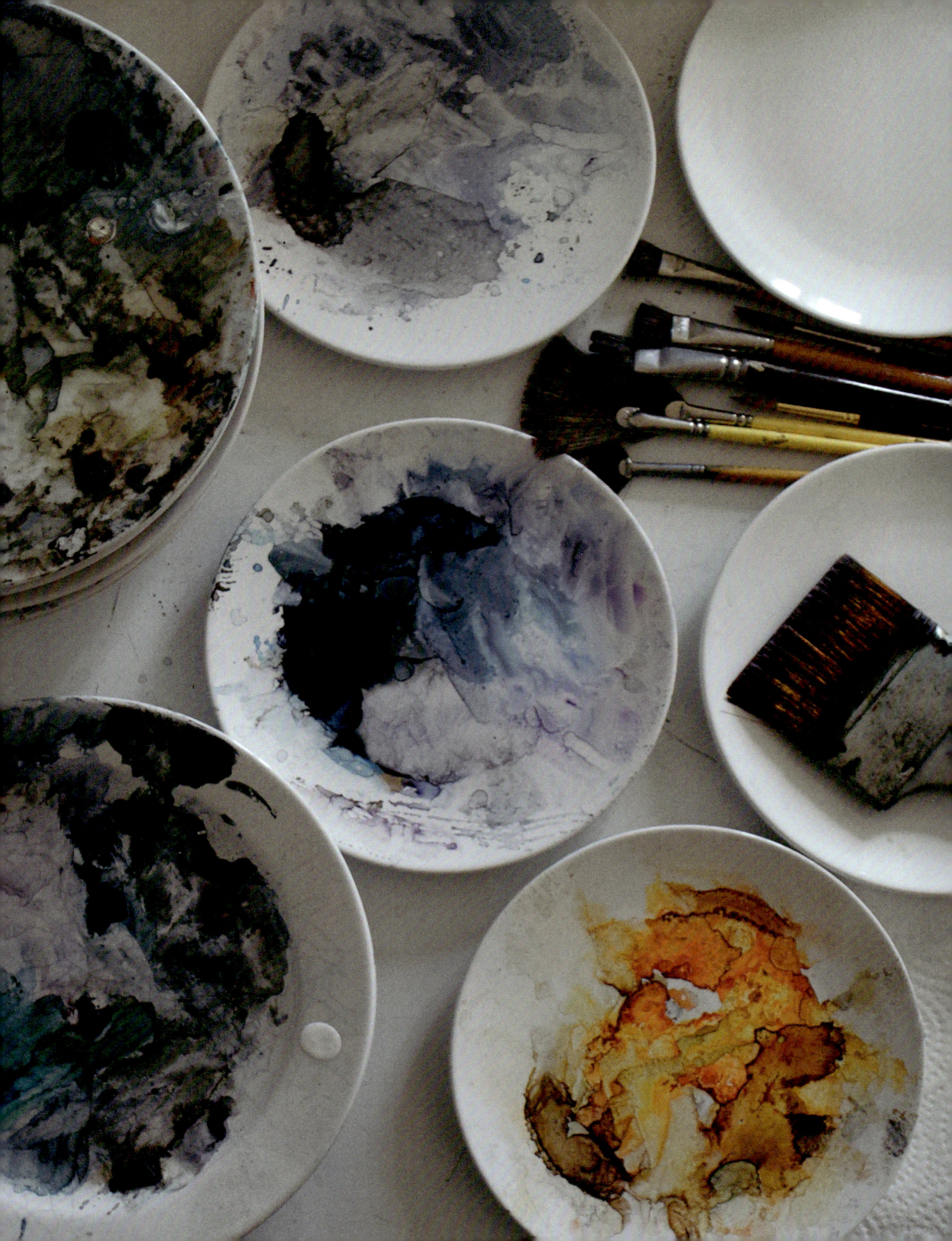

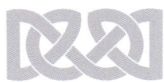

DRAWING TOOLS & MATERIALS

The pencil – a truly marvellous invention! First mass-produced in the late 1600s, modern pencils date from around 1795. They are the perfect low-maintenance method for putting thoughts and ideas on paper. Their companion, the eraser, was invented in 1770 (an improvement on the fresh kneaded bread previously used). I go nowhere without pencils, a craft knife and an eraser.

For work in black and white, and for sketches, use a 2B or 4B pencil and nothing harder. It is a personal choice, but for sketching, a hard pencil will slow you down. Do not automatically associate a light line with a hard lead – a light line is done with a light touch. Softer-grade pencils allow freedom and looseness when drawing, but many people are accustomed to pressing hard on a pencil (the fault of writing) and think a soft pencil will break. You hardly need more than the actual weight of the pencil to make a decent line. Putting weight on the pencil means that it and the paper are not giving you feedback; your line will lack that serendipitous quality that leads to further ideas and new sketches.

To do more photorealistic, detailed work, get a good set of pencils from 9H to 8B and painstakingly work through them in that order. For a pencil rendering of this kind, you're best off with satin-smooth paper. For sketching, if your pencil literally engraves the paper, then something is definitely not right. I use mostly 3B and 4B, and have no trouble erasing – but I don't lean on the pencil until I know the line is there to stay. You can get a very fine point on a 4B pencil if you use a sharp craft knife, and you can dive in with your nose to the paper to do very fine details.

Pastel pencils

The pastel pencil is a wide, hard pastel lead contained within a shaft. Pastel pencils have all the advantages of pastel sticks without the drawbacks: they won't break easily and the colour will not come off in your hand. They can painlessly introduce colour to your drawings and possess a rough texture that creates an attractive finish. Beginners and improvers will find pastel pencils easier to work with than traditional coloured pencils: the colour, which can be applied vividly and thickly for fast results, is reasonably easy to remove with a putty eraser.

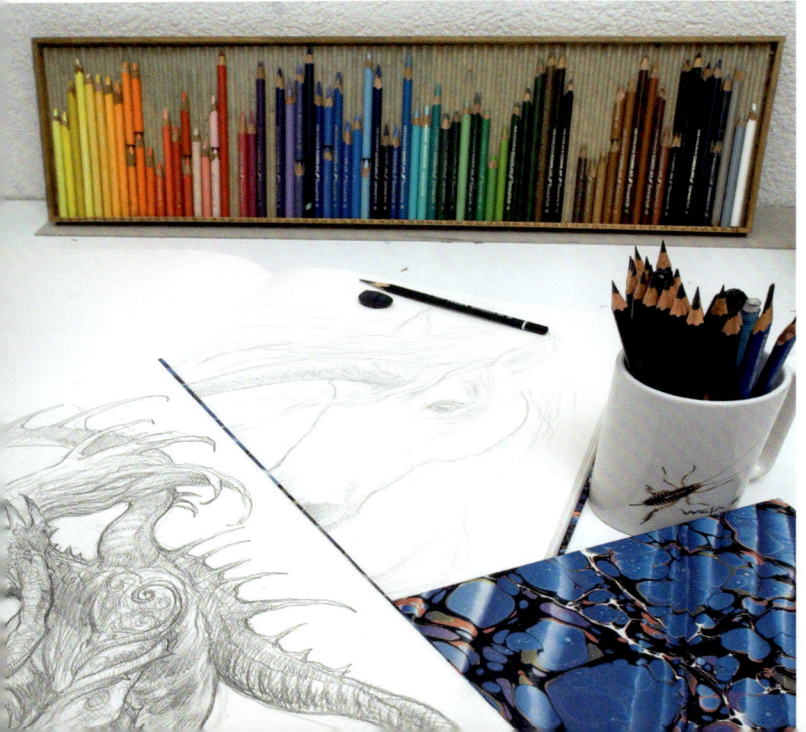

← Colourful characters

In addition to graphite, I have used pastel pencils for two of the projects in this book – Lancelot and the mermaid. Details of the colours required can be found within the instructions.

Sharpening pencils

I dislike traditional sharpeners, which create a mechanical and perfect point. I prefer a craft knife as it enables you to carve a long point, which will correspond better to the way you sketch. The fixed length of a mechanical point dictates the angle at which you hold the pencil; a long, hand-sharpened point lets you hold it nearly flat to the page if necessary. If a pencil lead breaks constantly, it has weakened within the pencil itself. Usually, pencils are sturdy and you should have no trouble getting a very long point even with a soft lead. Keep your knife sharp by replacing the blade regularly, or better still buy one with snap-off blades.

The following steps for sharpening with a craft knife are for a right-handed person, so left-handers should reverse them:

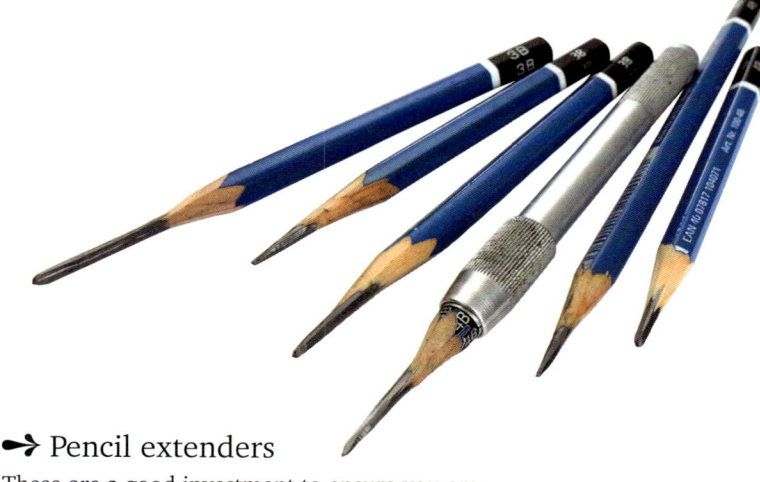

➔ Pencil extenders

These are a good investment to ensure you are able to use the pencil down to its very end. Place the pencil into the extender 'backwards', to protect your lead from breaking while travelling.

Erasers

These are some of my best friends. I have erasers of varying hardness, and white ones that won't colour paper. Most useful are kneadable erasers, which leave no scraps, perfect for sketching in any situation. Although not as effective at eradicating marks as a hard white eraser is, they are good for removing parts of sketches and defining highlights, and can also draw in negative (*see* Drawing & Sketching).

Other types of eraser I own offer enough precision to erase very small areas. These include an electric eraser, which makes a buzzing sound but is very accurate. A soft eraser by Tombow 'lives' in a plastic tube, rather like the lead in a mechanical pencil, is equally handy for erasing small areas.

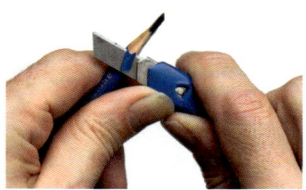

1 Hold the craft knife in your right hand and the pencil in your left, grasping each firmly between thumb and forefinger, using your other fingers to hold them in place. Rest the knife above the left thumb.

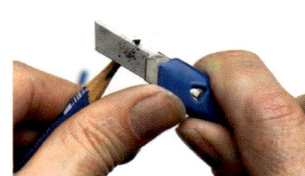

2 To sharpen, draw the pencil back against the blade, keeping the knife steady throughout. Do *not* push the blade forwards through the wood. It's important to retain contact between the thumbs and a firm but controlled grasp on the knife.

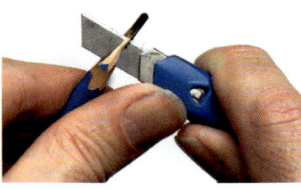

3 As the long graphite point develops, shave the top of the nib as you turn it to achieve a fine point. A 'personalized' point will be better suited to your drawing style.

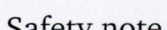

Safety note

Craft knives are very sharp, so be careful when using to sharpen pencils. Always keep the blade away from your fingers and never sharpen towards yourself.

➔ Ruler

While a craft knife and putty eraser are essential, a ruler is not, but is useful for defining and erasing straight edges (that said, any straight-edge will do in a pinch).

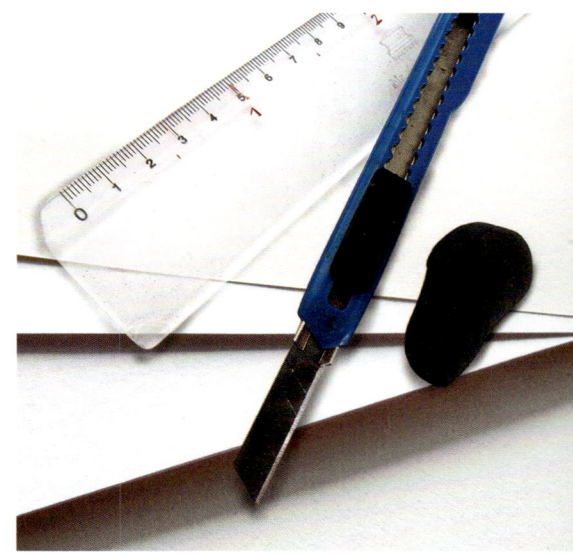

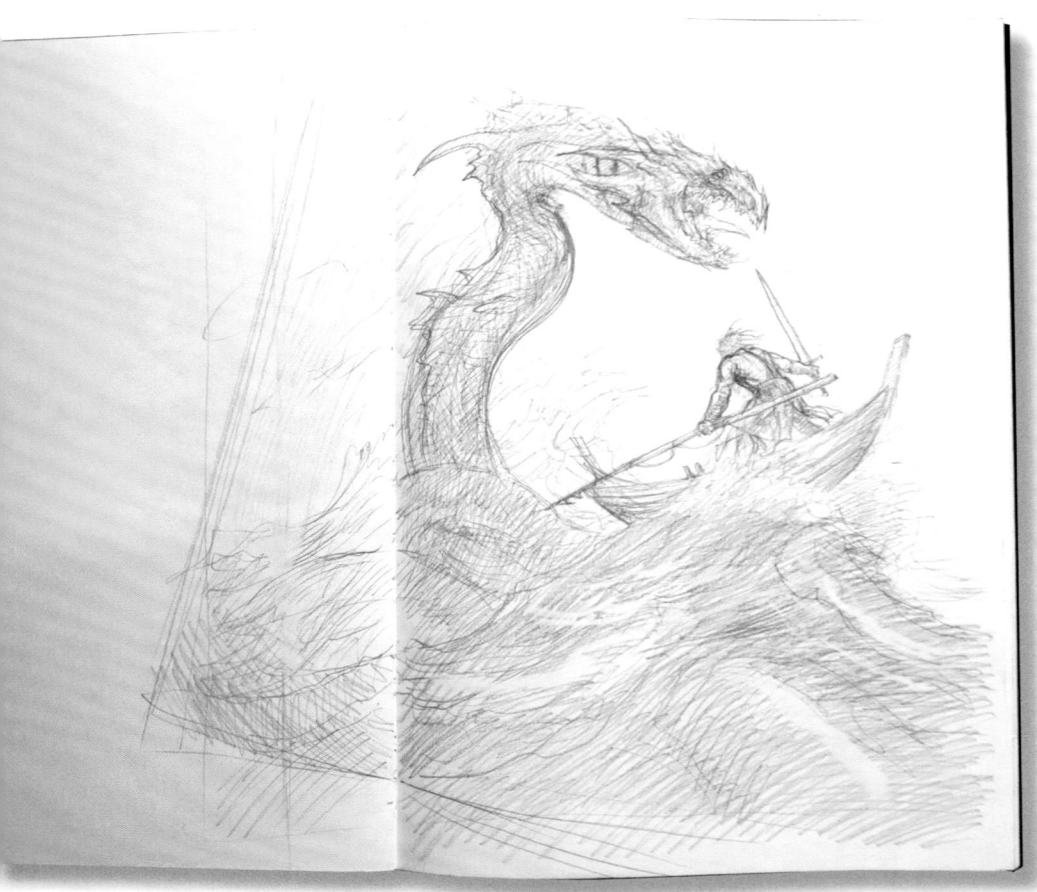

Papers

When selecting paper for drawing, avoid anything too thin or smooth. Your pencil won't apply well, it will tear easily and store poorly. I used regular cartridge paper for the projects in this book. With a thickness of 150gsm (40# bond), it is good-quality, decent-sized, acid-free and available at art stores. Remember, even doodles deserve a decent paper.

← *The Grey King*

Sketch for George R.R. Martin's *A Song of Ice and Fire*. Quite often a sketch will end up crossing the gutter of your sketchbook to the left-hand page.

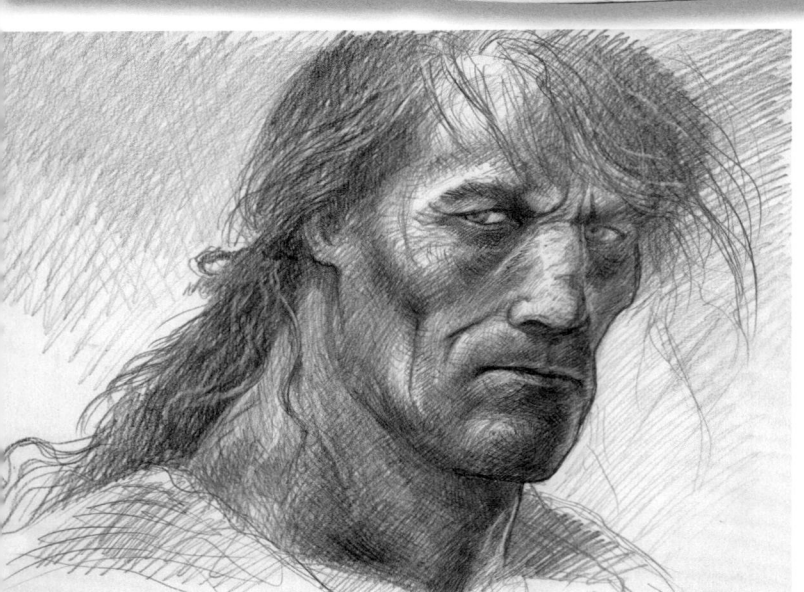

↑ *Frankenstein's Monster*

I have never been able to reconcile the monstrous creature depicted on film with the lofty ambitions of Victor Frankenstein. I imagine him rather more … presentable.

↪ *Schmendrick*

Schmendrick, the earnest but bumbling magician who befriends Lady Amalthea in Peter S. Beagle's wonderfully written *The Last Unicorn*. I would jump at the chance to illustrate this book one day.

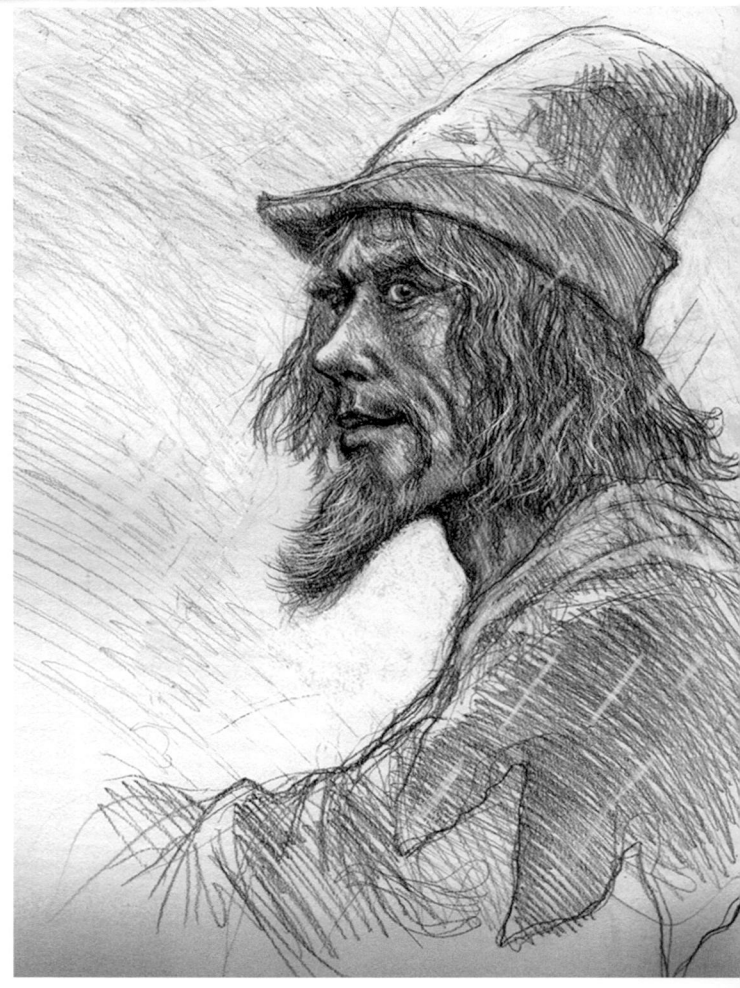

Sketchbooks

A landscape or portrait sketchbook close to A3 size allows you to draw wherever you wish, and quickly pack up and move on (*see* Out & About). It should have good paper, acid-free if possible. I prefer hard-bound; the temptation with spiral-bound is to tear out the drawing you are unhappy with – an imperfect sketch can be a stepping-stone to a better drawing. If you have trouble starting, open the book in the middle and start there.

Included here is a selection of pages from my own sketchbooks, some that were preliminary ideas subsequently developed into colour paintings. A stack of full sketchbooks is a treasure-trove of forgotten ideas to be later rediscovered.

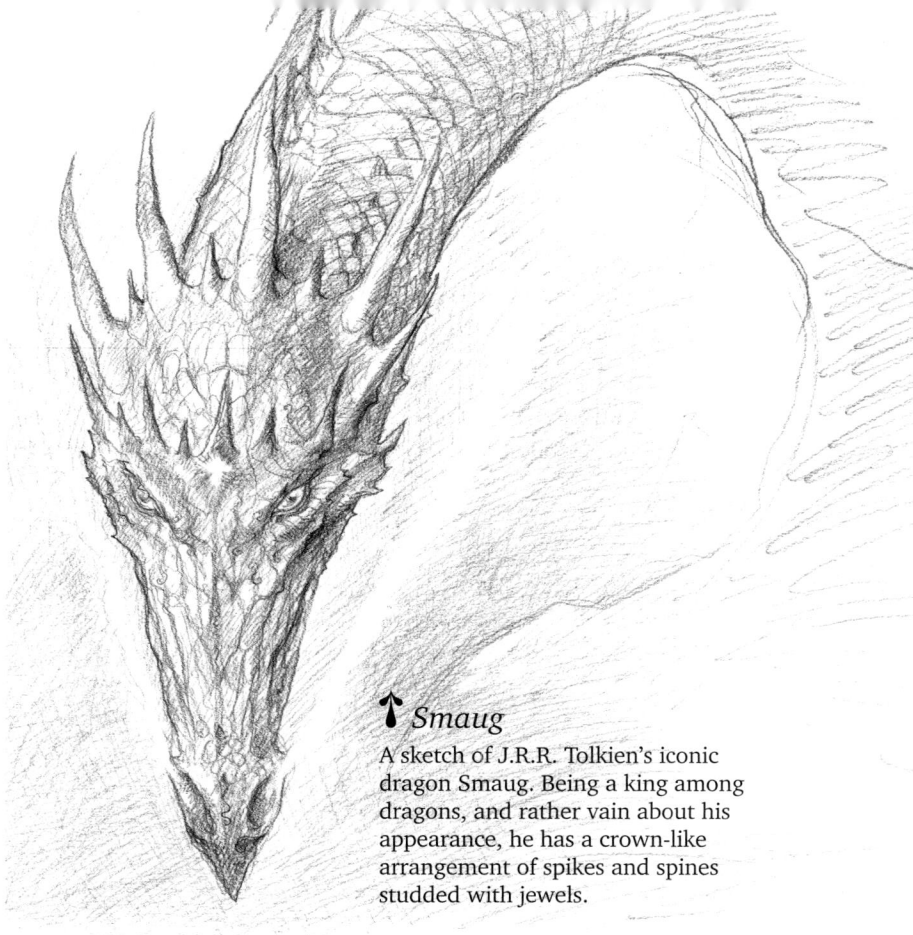

↑ *Smaug*

A sketch of J.R.R. Tolkien's iconic dragon Smaug. Being a king among dragons, and rather vain about his appearance, he has a crown-like arrangement of spikes and spines studded with jewels.

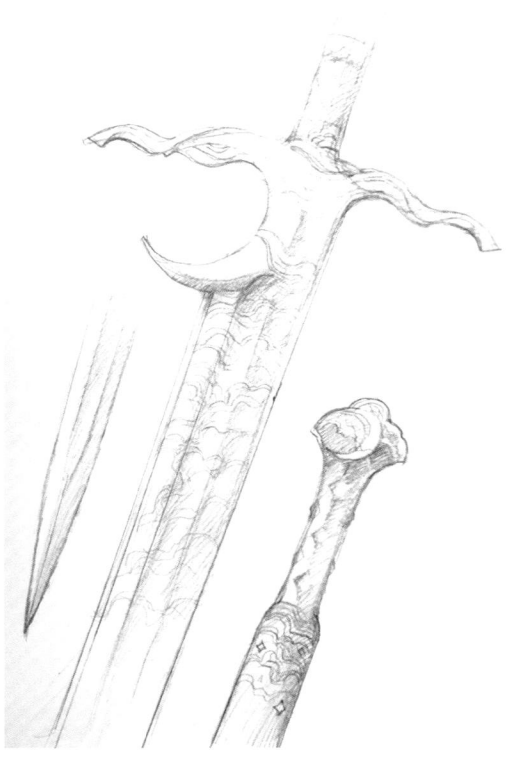

↑ *Sword of Moon and Shadows*

Sketch for a Chinese story. Swords never seem to fit on a page in one piece, but the pieces are easily assembled in Photoshop.

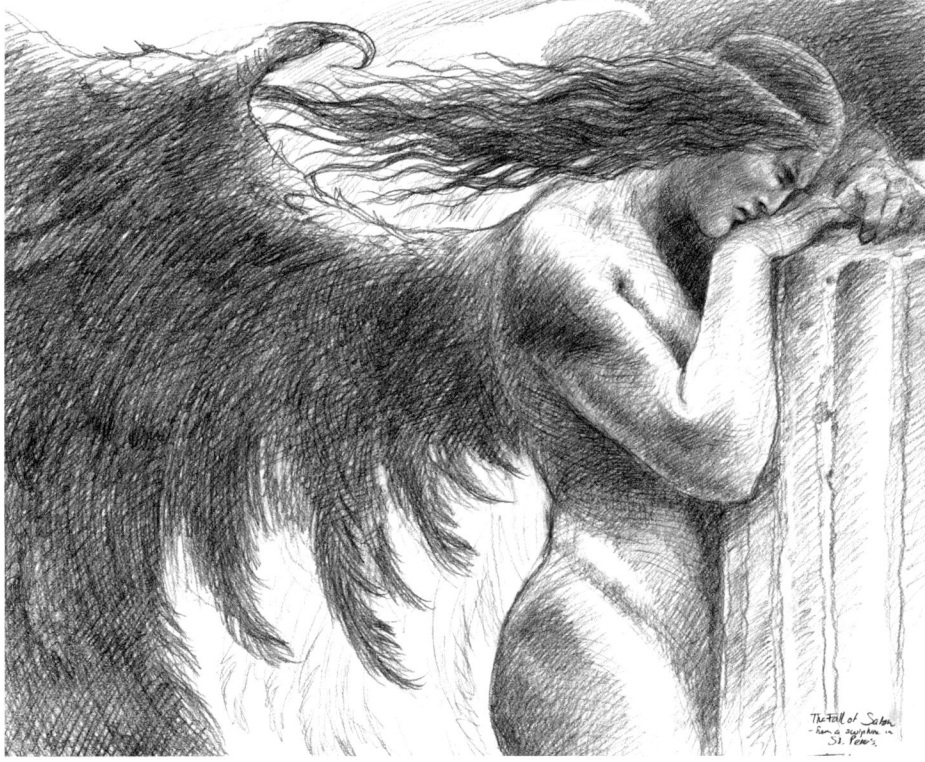

↑ *The Fall of Satan*

Lucifer after the fall, plotting revenge. The sketch is based on a figure in a Roman cemetery, and is one of those done on a whim, to give tangible form to an idea for future reference.

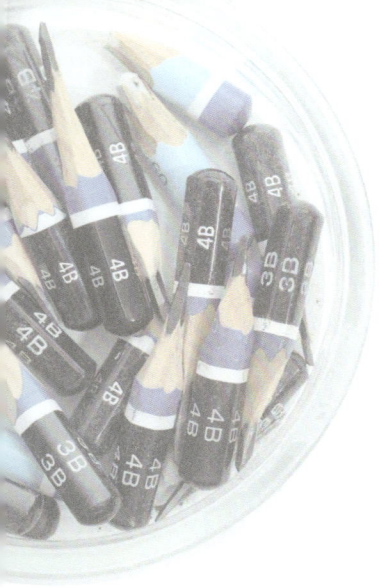

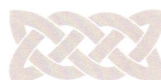

HOLDING THE PENCIL

Give an adult a pencil and ask him to hold it the way he would to draw, and nine times out of ten he will hold it in exactly the same manner as he would to write with. While the tools are identical, the two activities couldn't be more different.

Writing is an intellectual, linear process, managed by the left-hand side of the brain. The mind concentrates on the letter at hand, staying on the lines, being neat and legible. Drawing, however, relies heavily on the right-hand side of the brain – instinctive, intuitive, non-linear. To work freely, see the bigger picture, explore proportions and the overall composition is the purpose of this exercise. By picking up a pencil as if we are about to write, we immediately send the wrong message to the wrong parts of our brains.

To rediscover the ease with which children draw, it may well be necessary to unlearn our writing reflexes and replace them with those better adapted to drawing. For those who have acquired a certain number of bad drawing habits, this may not be easy, but it can be done.

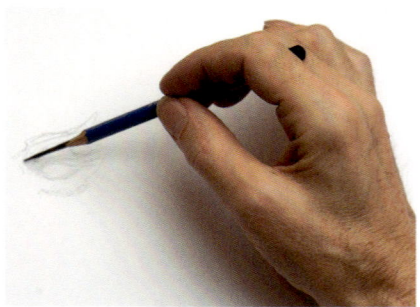

Sketching and establishing lines
I would be tempted to forbid holding a pencil as if to write. Never hold it close to the writing end unless working on tiny details. Holding it halfway down like a conductor's baton raises the hand and wrist off the page and allows for large, open drawing movements. You can apply very light pressure with looser control over the pencil and greater suppleness of line.

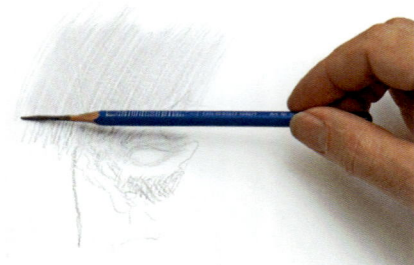

Shading
Holding the pencil right at the end of the shaft, I am using the weight of the pencil alone to create marks. In a way, this position allows you to have even more freedom than the previous hold. Cross-hatching holding the pencil like this, you can build up an even, grey background. (Don't worry about running over the outlines; you can always tidy up with a putty eraser.)

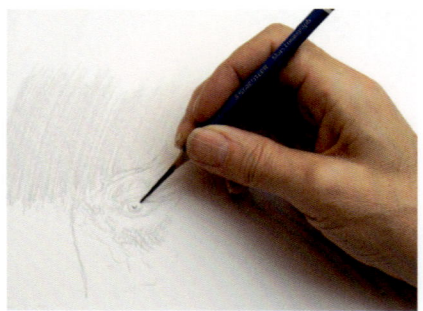

Working on details
This is the exception to the rule. When you wish to do very fine detail over a very small area, hold the pencil as you would to write, and take advantage of the vertical angle and concentrated field of vision to work on those tiny bits.

Free your drawing hand

Ask someone to write a few words in large letters in a given space. Habitually, the letters start out amply sized, but end with the last few crammed in. *Drawing* the same letters will be more likely to produce a harmonious arrangement – the eye sees the whole space, not just the letter being made. If I had five top tips to help you release your drawing hand from your writing one, they would go like this:

✦ Stay sharp

Sharpen your pencils into long points with a craft knife (*see* Drawing Tools & Materials) so that you can hold your pencil as flat to the paper as possible when necessary.

✦ Get a grip, lightly

Hold your pencil as far away from the tip as you can. Just the weight of the pencil will leave a light line that can easily be erased, allowing you to sketch and block in ideas freely.

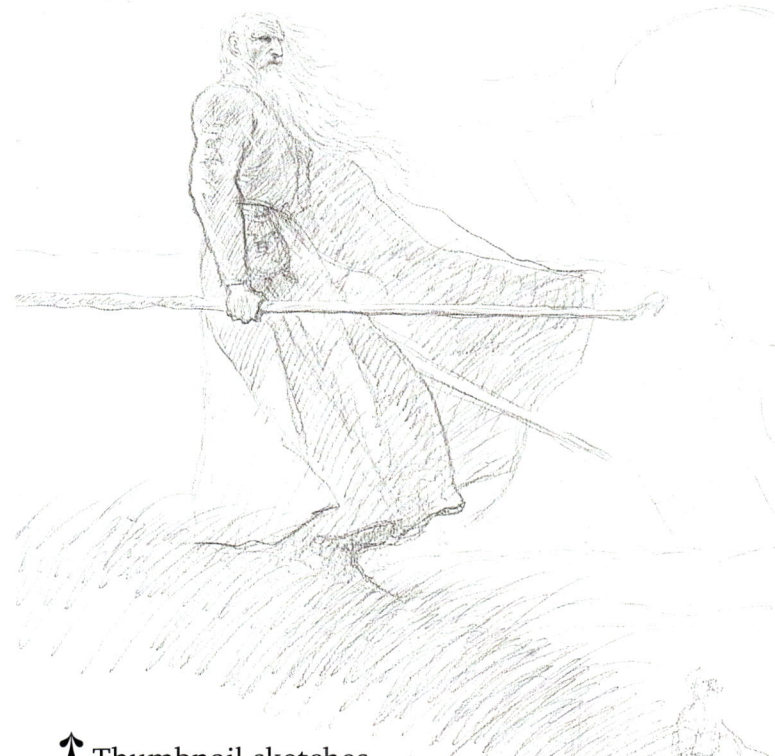

⬧ Thumbnail sketches

A thumbnail helps to make decisions about the composition and to work within the available space. Tucked away in the corner it remains useful throughout, until it gets covered and eventually erased by the drawing itself.

✦ Back off

Get your hand and wrist off the page. Allow your arm to be free from the shoulder or, at least, from the elbow. You have an area half a metre (half a yard) square to work with, so don't be afraid to use it. Lean in close and pose your hand to work details, but don't forget to keep stepping back to …

✦ … see the bigger picture

Don't confuse stationery with art material – A3 is quite small; twice the size is better. Sketching is like fencing: you want to see your entire opponent, not just the sword point. Work with the whole surface and don't be afraid to adjust, develop and even change your ideas. Keep your eye on the whole picture, not just the line you're drawing. Choose your distance from the drawing surface; do not let bad habits choose for you.

✦ Switch off

Let your pencil wander; let your instinct and intuition take over. Have you ever wondered what happens in an illustrator's head when he draws? Well, in mine, not a lot, at least not on the thinking side.

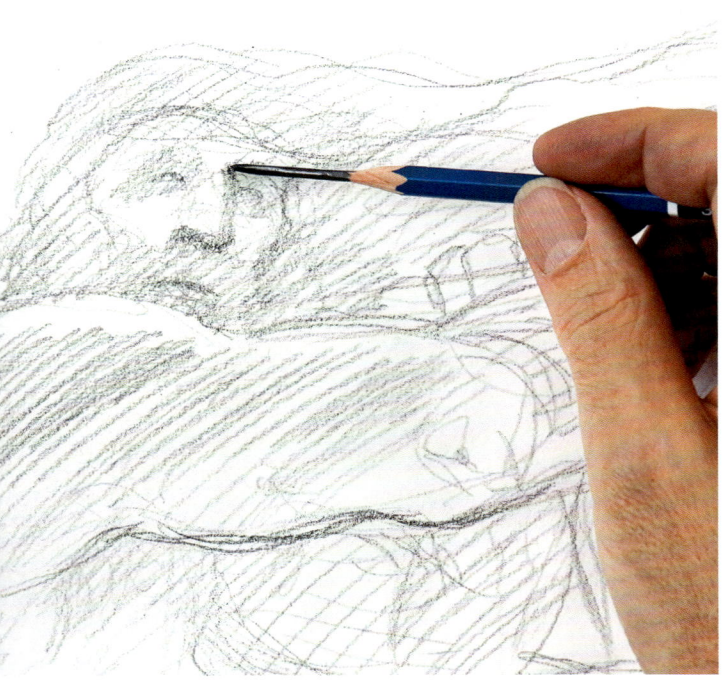

⬧ Keep your drawing loose

In *Thor and the Giant* I was undecided how to position the giant's left arm. Initially, one was around the stern, the other on the rudder. Rather than compromise a whole picture for an ill-placed detail, it's better to erase or start anew.

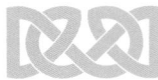

DRAWING & SKETCHING

Together with a few words about techniques, I hope you will
forgive me for giving in to my love of the origins of words,
for 'drawing' and 'sketching' have very different ancestries,
and distinguishing between them today is worthwhile.

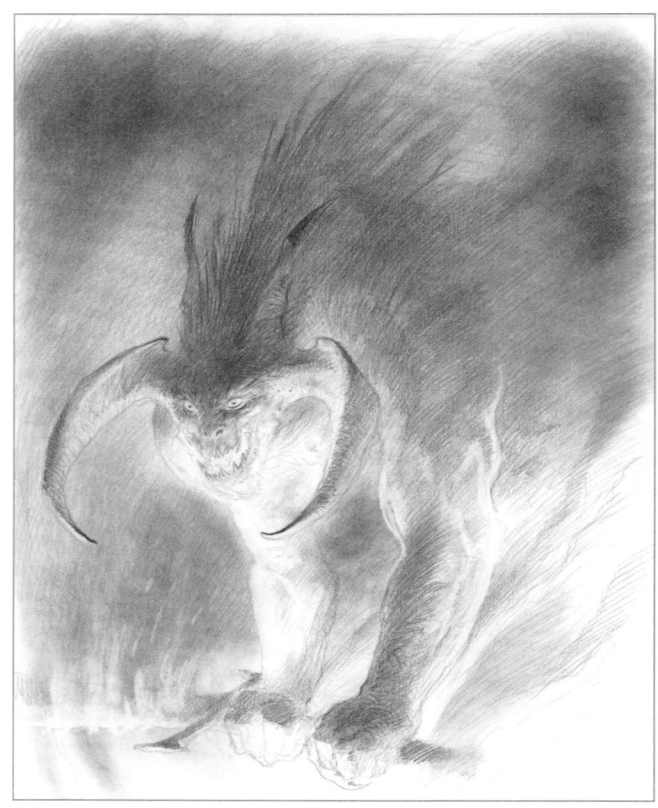

Drawing and sketching have become quite
interchangeable, but have very different
etymological roots. 'Draw', in the sense of
'making a line or figure' is attested from *c.*
AD1200, from the old English *dragan*, meaning to draw,
drag or pull. We also draw swords, ploughs and cards.
'Sketch', a rough drawing that is preparation for a finished
picture, is attested from the 1660s, from the Italian *schizzo*.
'Sketchbooks' are first mentioned in 1820. Drawing implies
a careful, measured gesture; sketching evokes something
more spontaneous. (A 'study' falls between the two, but
implies focusing on only a portion of an image.)

Put another way …
A drawing is a thorough exploration, implying a more
finished quality that considers complex aspects. A sketch
is unfinished, a question or exclamation mark quickly put
on paper to capture a fleeting or urgent idea. Incidental and
often abridged, once a few lines have captured the spirit
of the sketch, it can be abandoned (working too long on a
sketch is not necessarily sound practice). It is impossible
to catalogue every drawing and sketch as one or the other.
More important is keeping your aim in sight.

In general, softer pencils are better for sketching. Pen and
ink, coloured pencils, charcoal, fusain and watercolours
or oils can be wonderful too, but these examples focus on
simple pencils.

✦ Smudging
I am not a fan of smudging techniques, but there are times
when you want to push a landscape back as if there was
mist or cloud. Here, it is the smoke and flames of the fiery
demon *Balrog* (above). The simplest tools are the best, in
this case a folded paper towel.

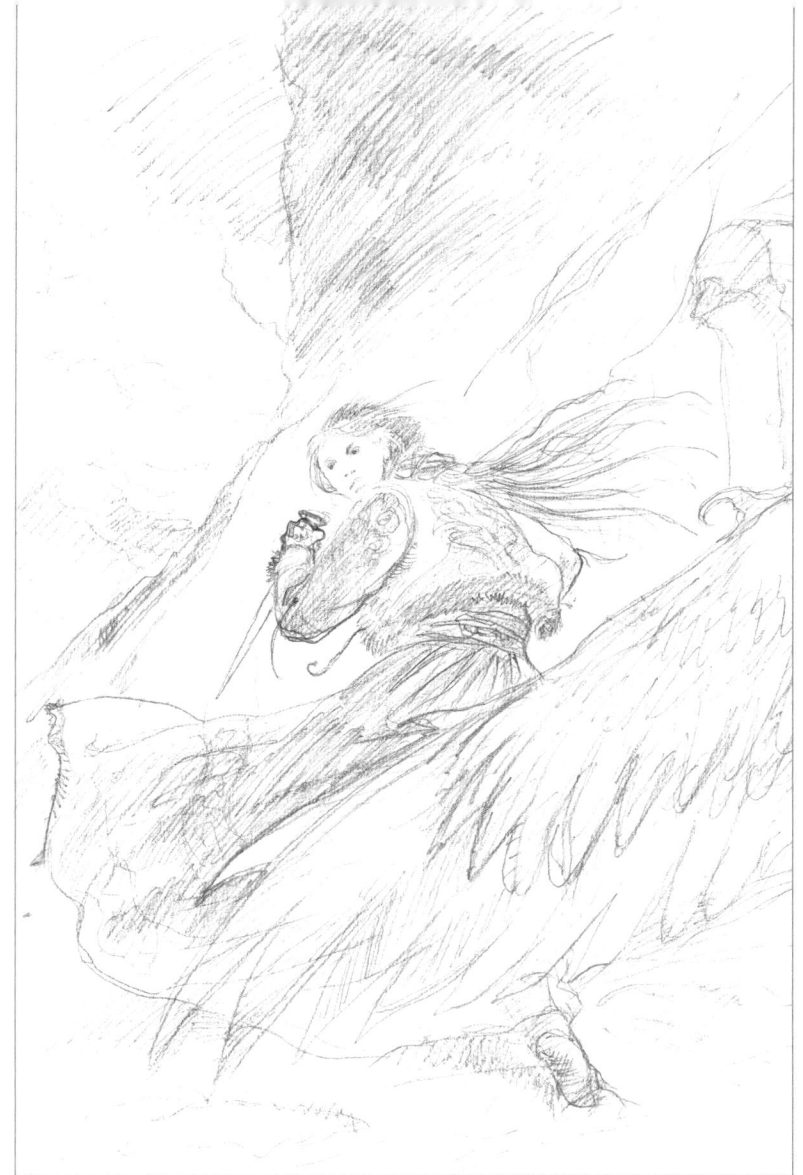

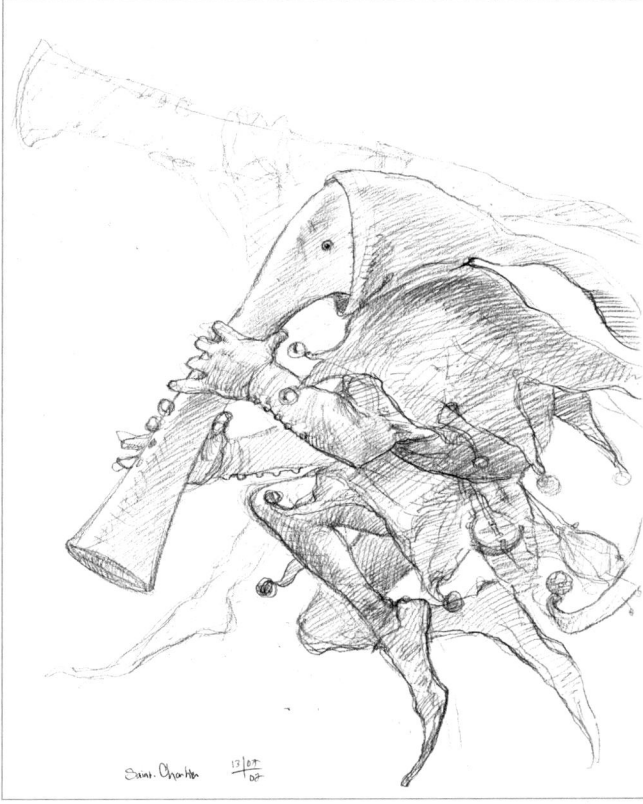

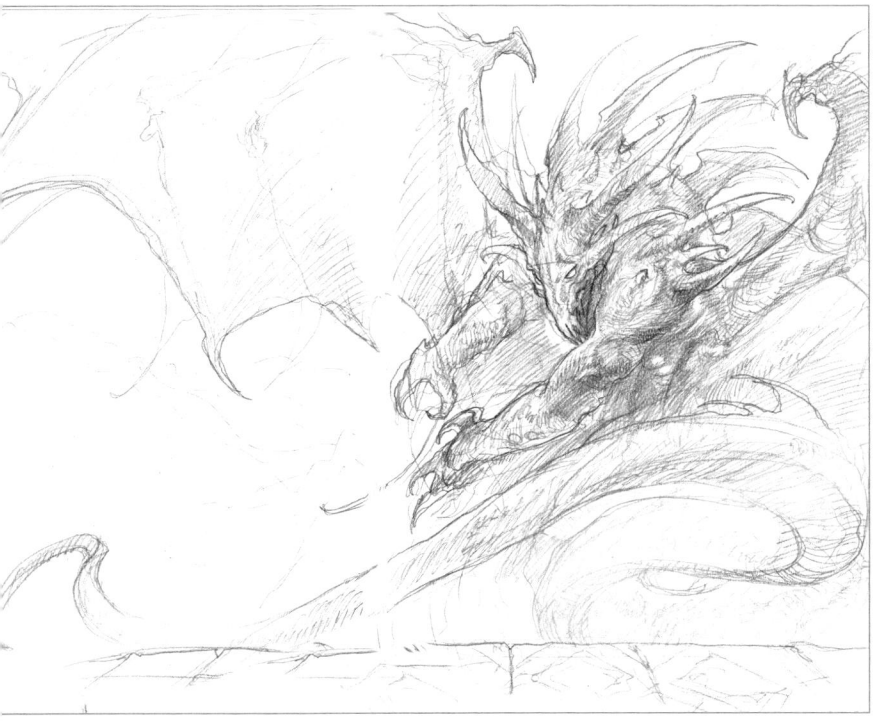

✦ Bold lines

The perfect line may take a while to find. Keep your sketching gestures light but bold, let spontaneity work for you and don't go back over lines unless you are certain they are in the right spot. Keep everything moving. You can block in a figure with just a line or two as needed. When you find the confidence to sketch quickly and lightly, your pencil has no trouble keeping up with your imagination.

Sketches such as *Harpy's Flight* and *Serpent Gate* (left and above left) and *Fantastical Musician* (above) are all quickly done. (I am fond of this character playing his nose, inspired by a medieval choir stall.) They are akin to thinking out loud, looking for volumes, blocking out shapes. Very little is erased. They are done when they have set out the idea clearly enough that the essential elements have been explored.

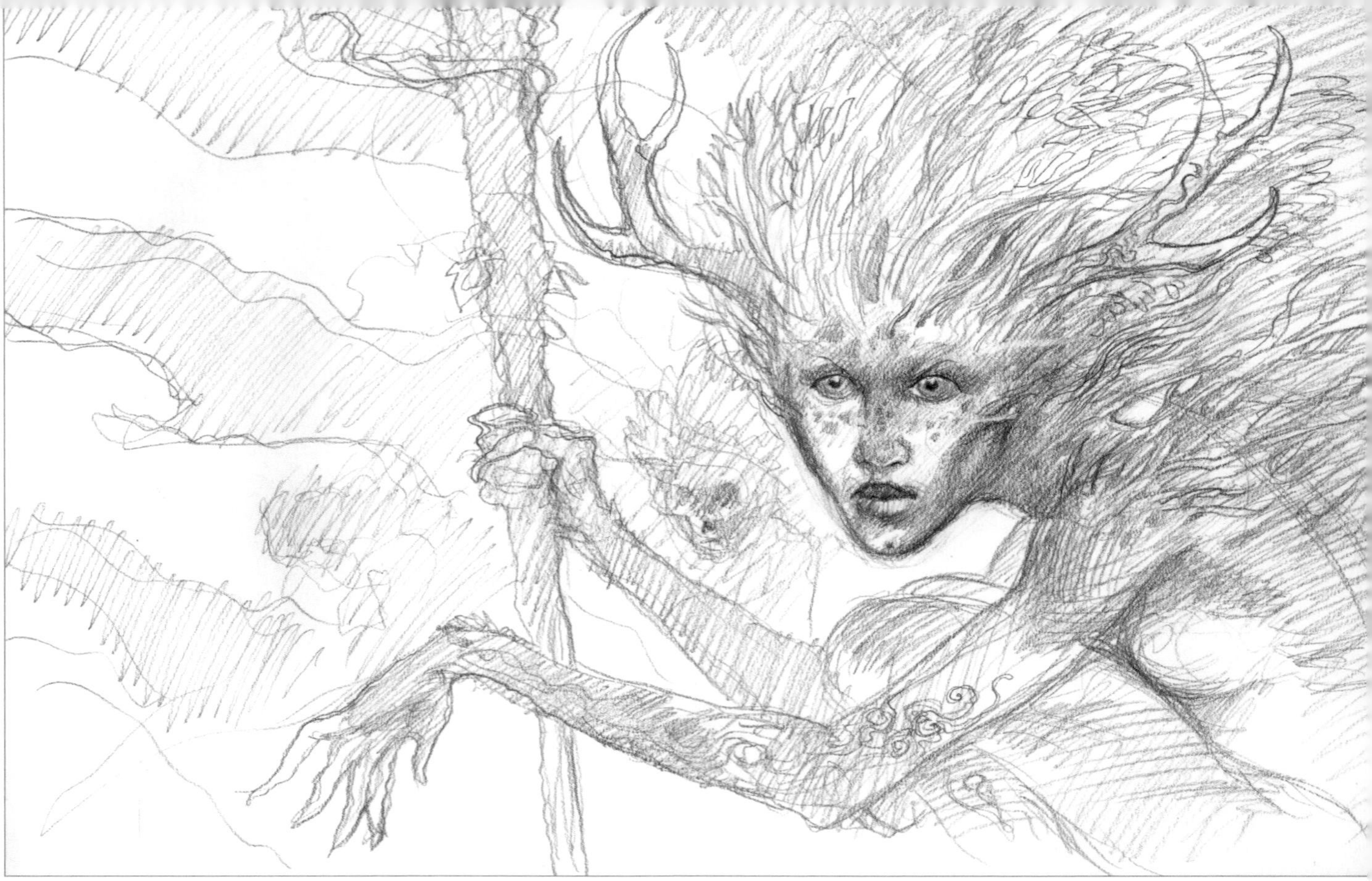

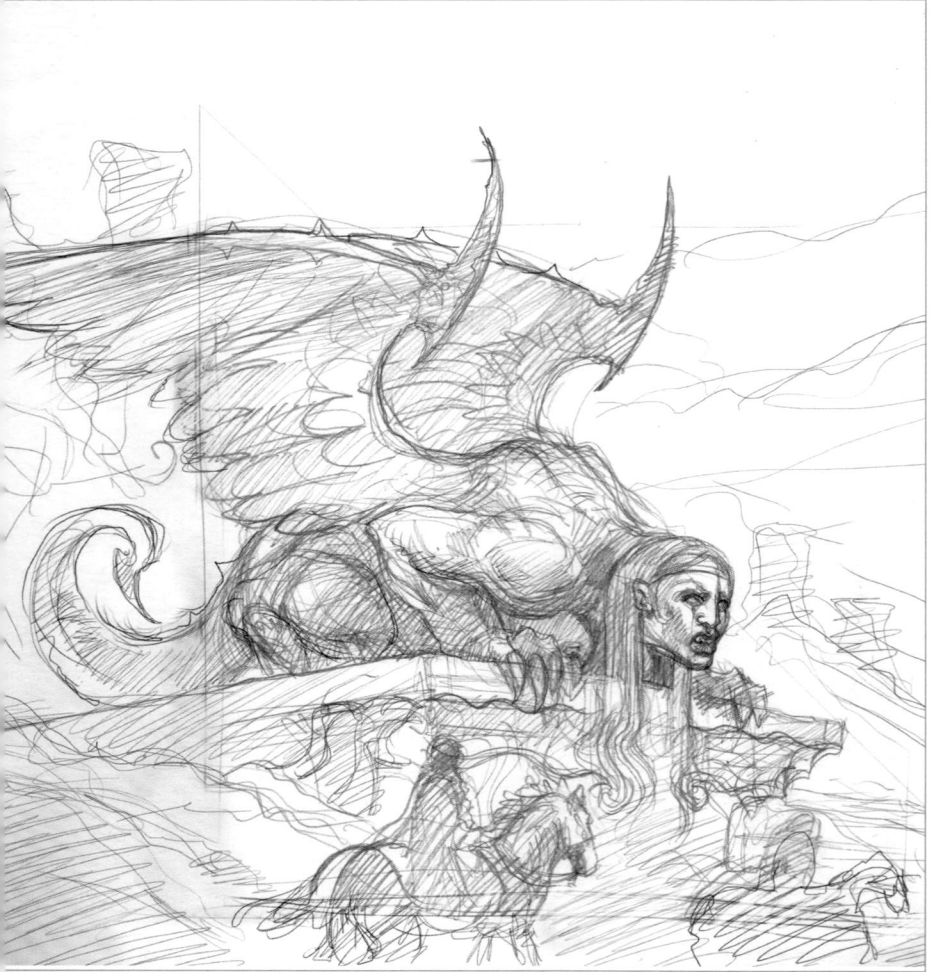

✦ Building up tones

Line and tone are the same: line is simply the limit of the surface. Do not split them into different actions. A common error is to draw an outline, then try to fill it with a tone. Even in a quick sketch, keep shifting between the defining form with a line, enhancing with tone.

Children of the Forest (above), and *Valyrian Sphinx* (left) take sketches a step further, with volumes blocked out and halftones more fully rendered. They remain sketches, and are a crucial step (but still a step) towards preparing a painting. When drawing, keep lines light – they are a form of shorthand; rendering the volume convincingly should be the end result.

Transferring a sketch

To transfer to stretched paper, I scan the sketch, enlarge/reduce it to the right size, flip it horizontally, print it out and trace important lines onto tracing paper. When placed on the paper, the sketch is transferred with a burnisher.

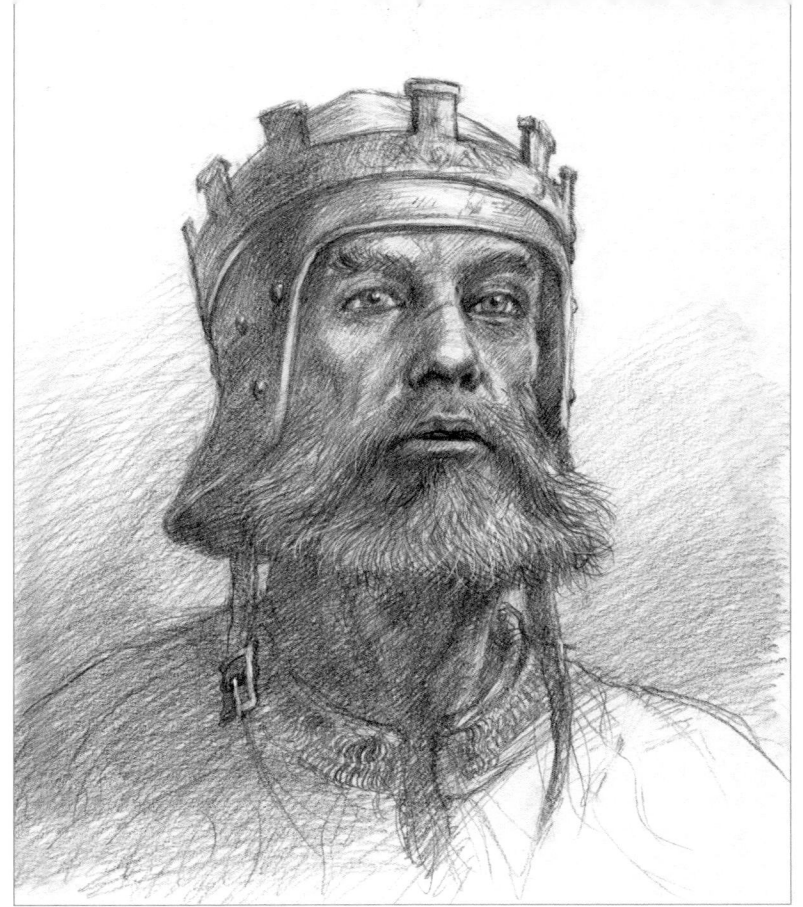

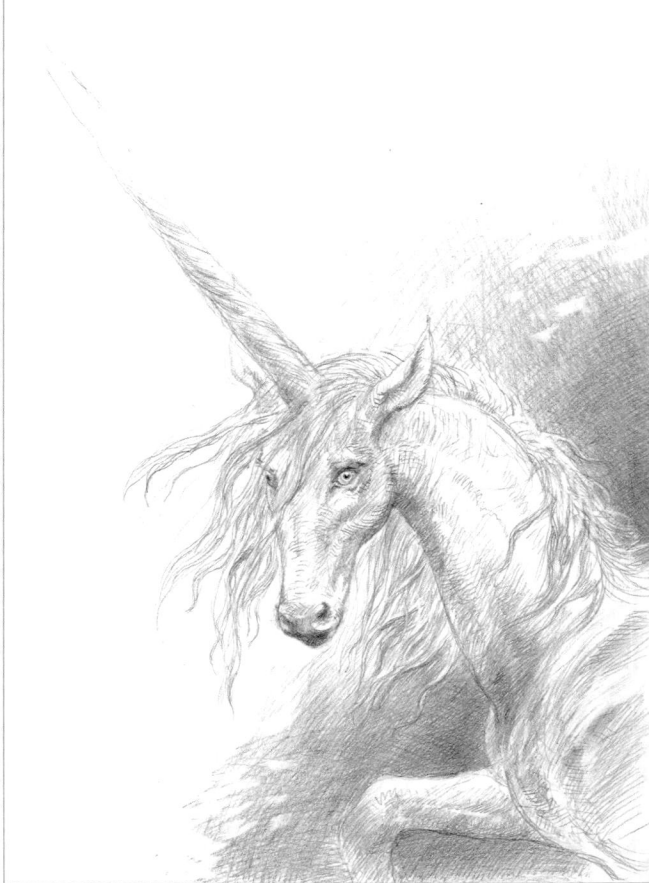

✦ Drawing with the eraser

A putty eraser can be pinched to an edge for thin lines, a lumpy piece dragged across a halftone to form the basis of smoke. Be creative – an eraser can be as vital as a pencil. *King Lir* (above) shows highlights done with an eraser, as are the leaves in the background of *Unicorn* (above right). More painstaking are the lighter hairs in the King's beard, formed one by one with the sharp edge of a putty eraser.

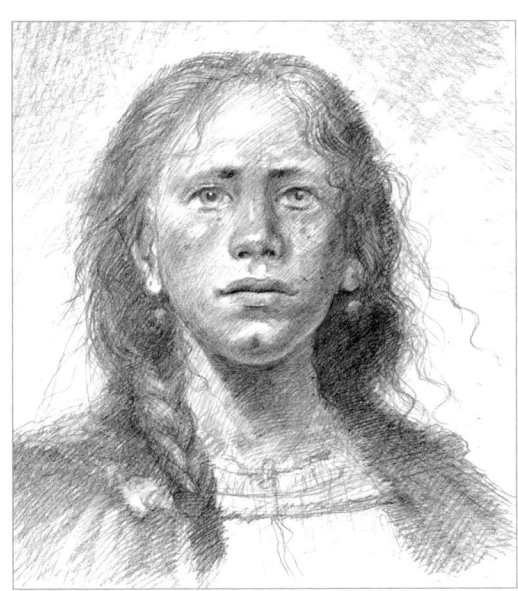

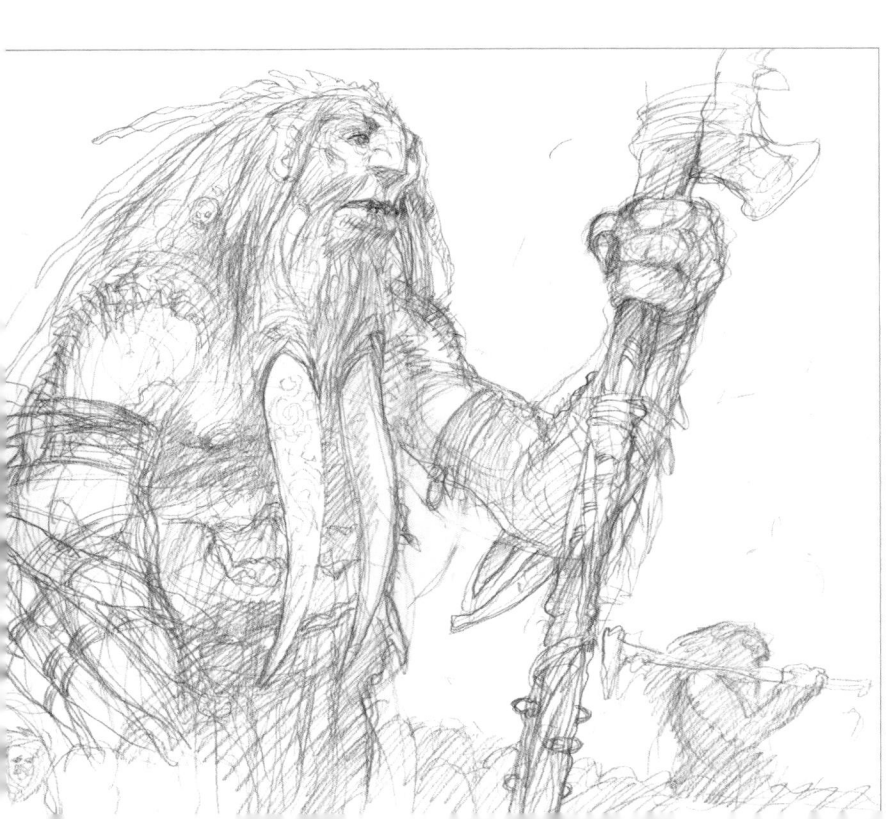

✦ Directional modelling

Follow form when shading. Foreshortening is better served by curving lines than straight, which do not necessarily translate the form accurately. In quick sketches such as *Giant* (left) shading is only lightly and partially applied. In more finished drawings such as *Sooz* (above) volumes are more fully rendered.

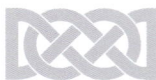

PAINT & INK

Among the myriad types of media, brushes, papers and other equipment available are the particular tools and materials you need if you want to add paint and ink to your process.

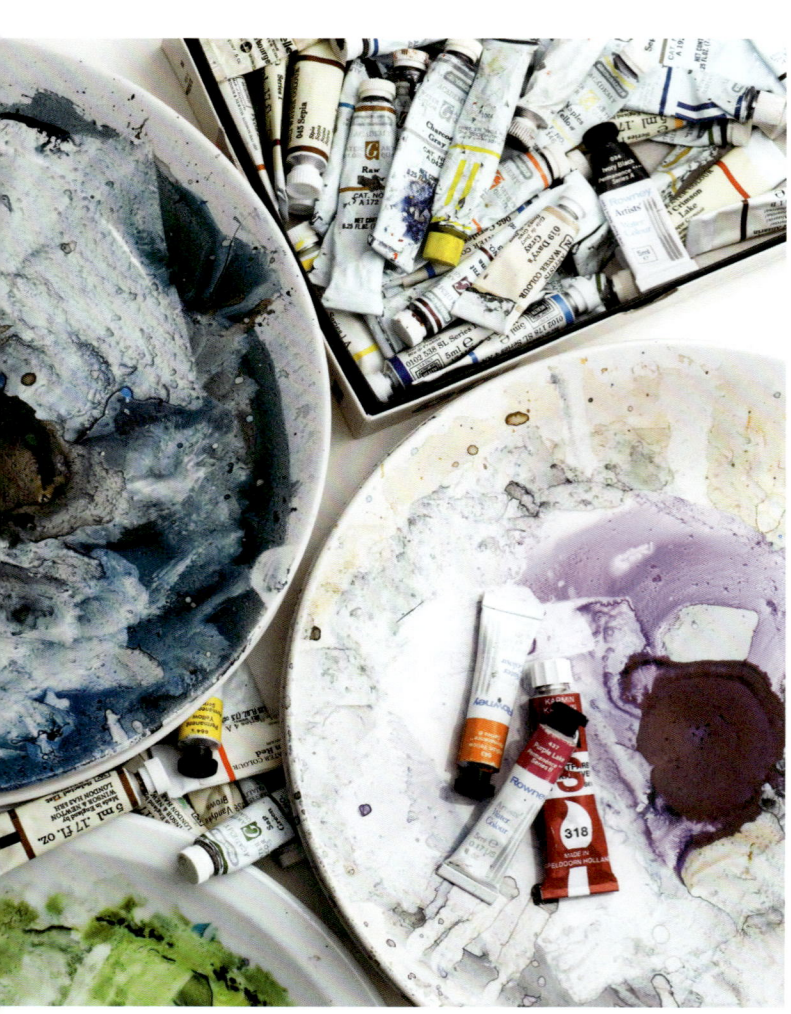

No two artists have the same requirements from their tools and materials; buying the trademark watercolours or ink of some name in the art world will not help you paint. This section outlines the tools and materials I use in my work, and how I use them. I hope that it will help you build a kit that works for you and your methods.

Brushes

Money spent on brushes is money well spent, but you are better off with one or two expensive brushes than a fistful of cheap ones. The brushes I use range from the house-painting variety (10cm (4in) wide) to fine watercolour brushes (generally No. 6). The widest are used to wet the full page evenly, and do large areas of colour. Stiff oil-painting brushes are good for drybrush work, and I have a few fan-shaped ones, which are wonderful for work on a damp ground. Watercolour brushes are an all-round tool, and for the finest work.

Airbrushes

I own a few airbrushes, which are reserved mostly for those uses where a regular brush will not do the job – adding a tone here and there, darkening a sky or painting armour.

Watercolours

My preferred painting colours are watercolours, available in tubes or pans or cakes. They end up on cheap white porcelain plates, which make inexpensive and durable palettes. While light-fast and durable, watercolours are not indelible, so can be left on the palette to dry and revived with water next time you start work.

↑ Palettes

White plates really are the best palettes, far superior to anything designed especially for watercolours and inks. They are cheap, so you can have lots, and happily let colours dry and sit until the next time you need them.

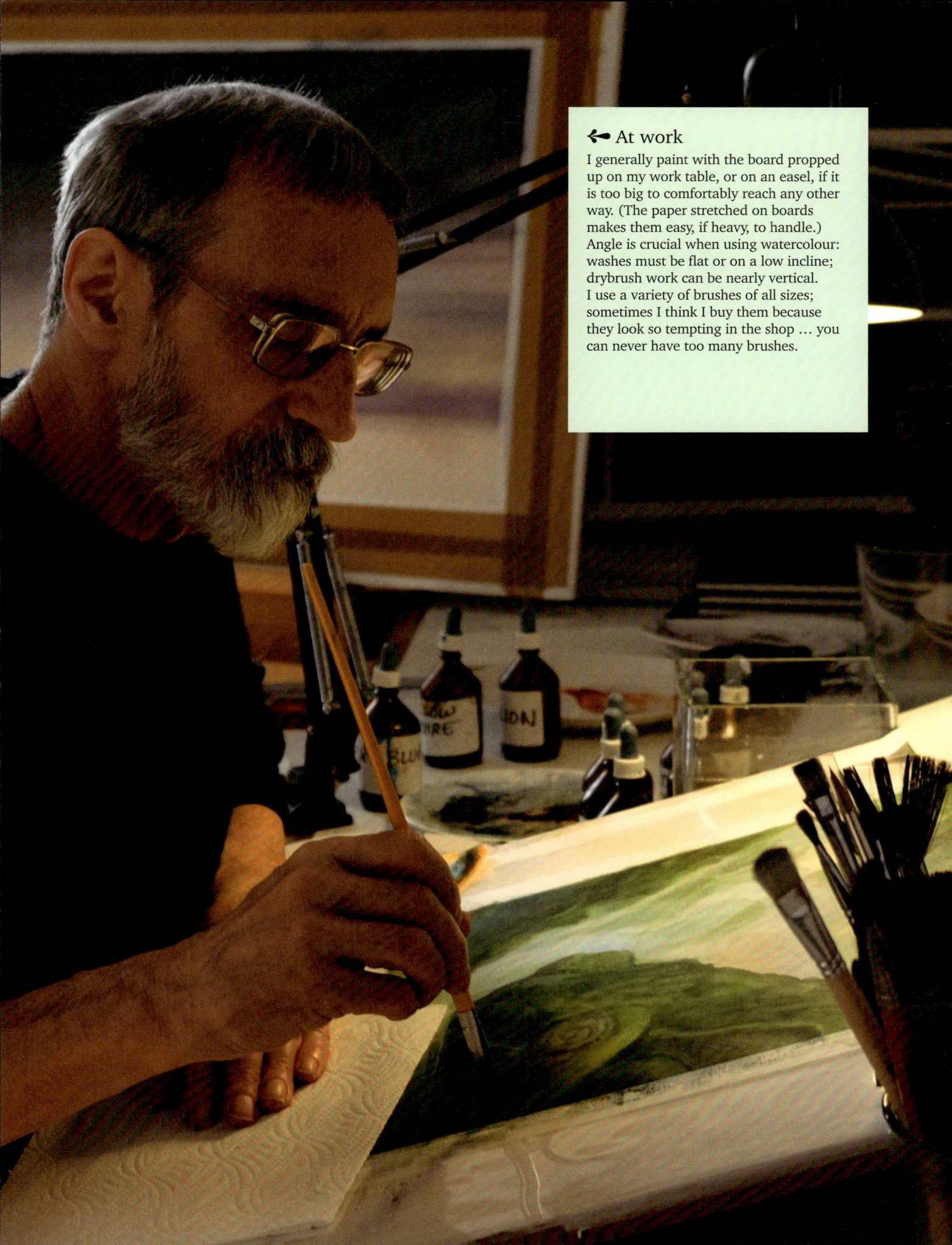

✒ At work

I generally paint with the board propped up on my work table, or on an easel, if it is too big to comfortably reach any other way. (The paper stretched on boards makes them easy, if heavy, to handle.) Angle is crucial when using watercolour: washes must be flat or on a low incline; drybrush work can be nearly vertical. I use a variety of brushes of all sizes; sometimes I think I buy them because they look so tempting in the shop … you can never have too many brushes.

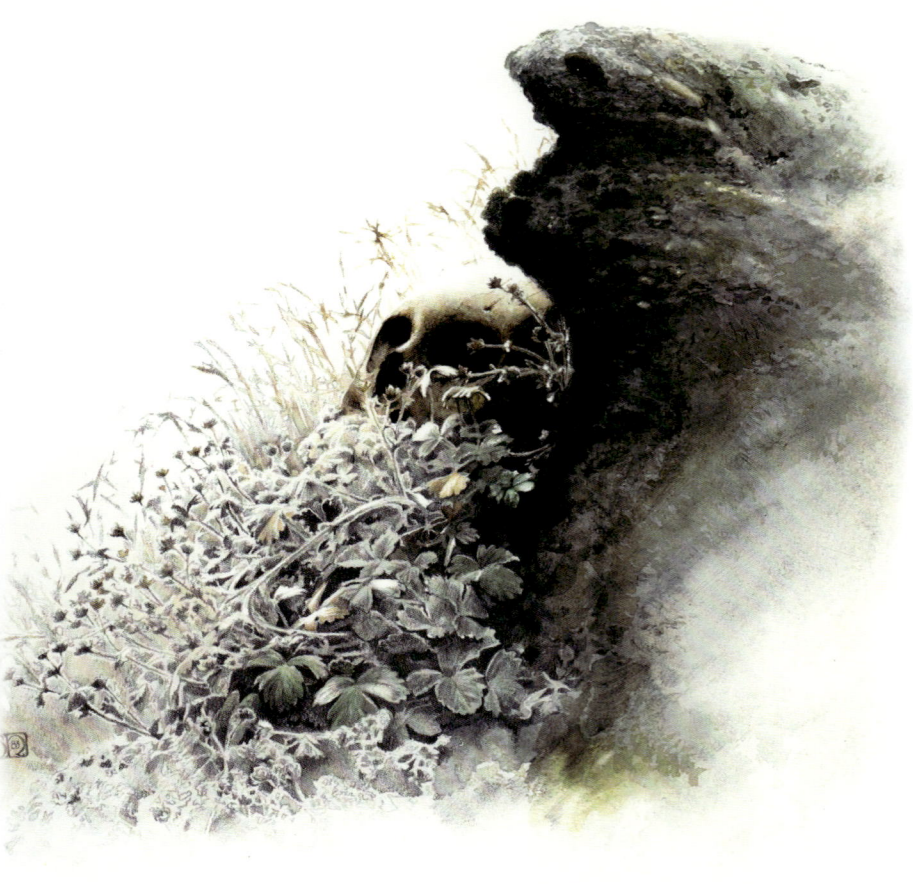

Pastels

Dry pastels are useful for rendering fog and smoke. I leave a light wash for mist, or a darker wash for smoke. It's not always possible to control the values, but a layer of pastel (scraped from the stick into a pile of dust, then carefully spread with a soft paper towel) creates the effect I want. If using several layers, fix the work lightly between each one.

Paper

I mostly work on an all-purpose, sturdy 250gsm (120lb) paper. This comes in large sheets, and holds up to the abuse I sometimes give it. The paper must first be stretched on boards so that it will dry flat. The bathtub in our house is often occupied by paper soaking in preparation for stretching. (Stretching paper can be tedious, so soak only one sheet at a time.) Water-soaked paper will 'grow' substantially; when taped down, it will dry and stretch like the skin of a drum. When humidified once more (often repeatedly) while painting, it will always dry flat, even if valleys and ridges form when you wet it thoroughly.

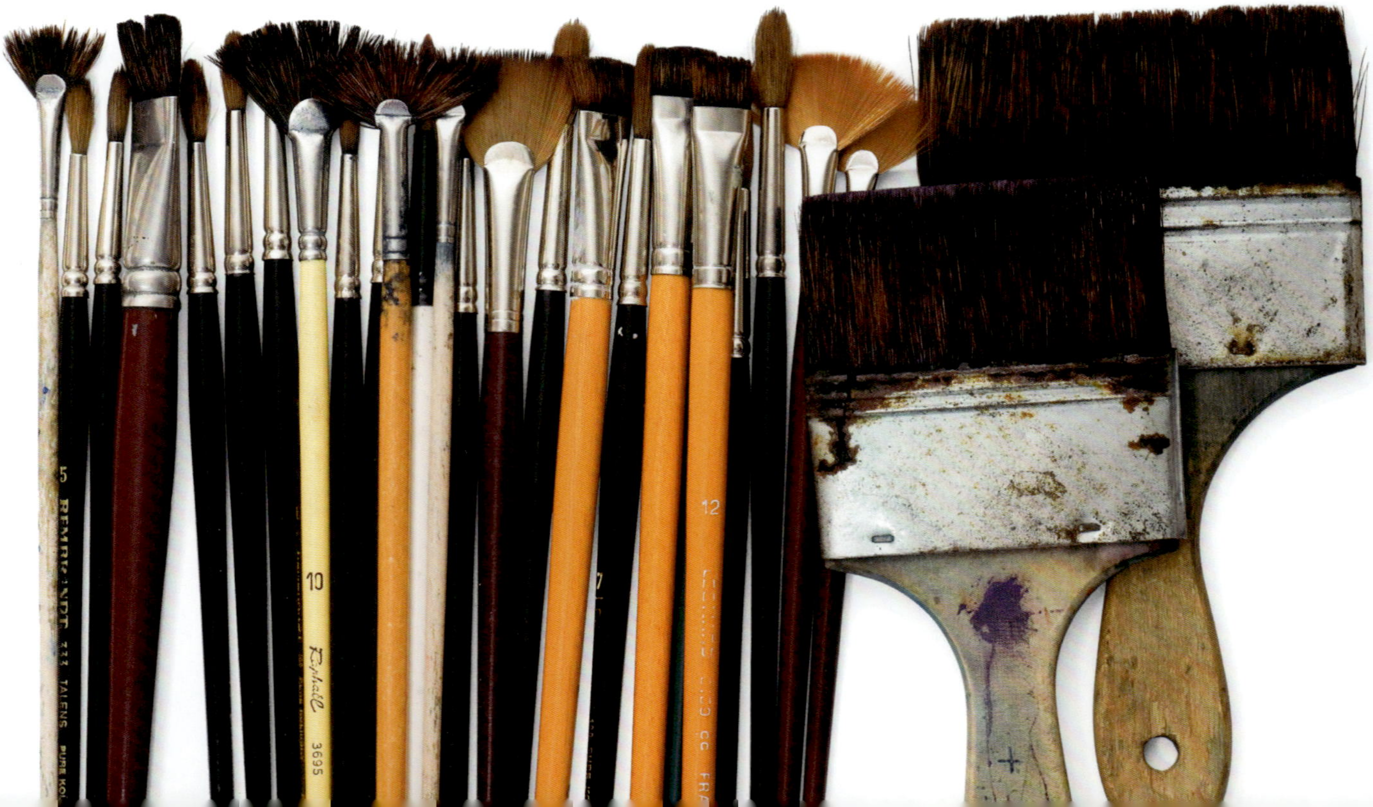

⬆ *Still Life with Skull*

This watercolour was done from a photo. I thought of lying, saying I drew it from life, perched on a cliff facing the Pacific, to make it sound more romantic, but that wouldn't be right. (I did take the photo, though.)

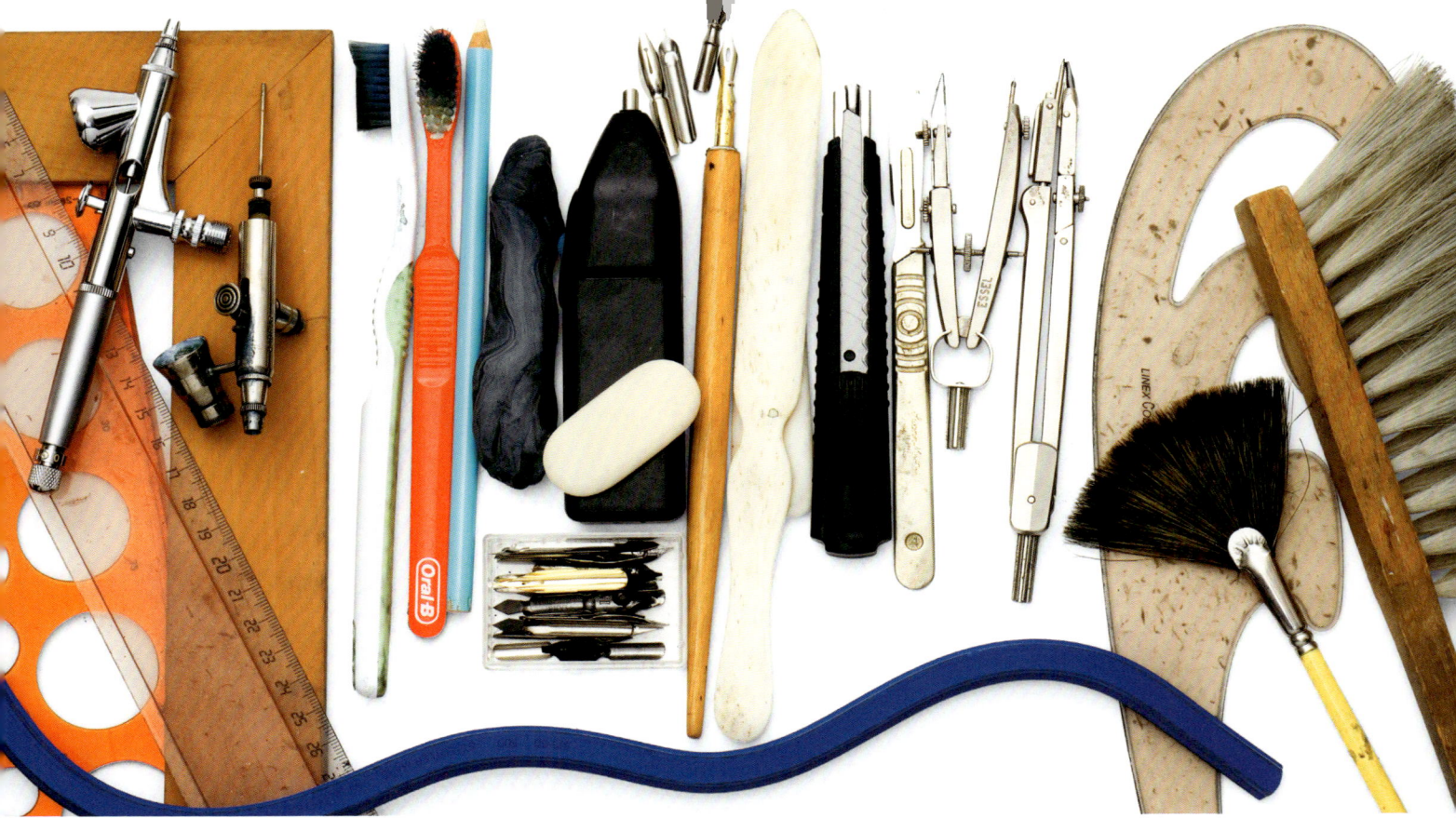

❦ Other tools

A selection of my tools including airbrushes, erasers, toothbrushes, knives, dip pens, compasses, rulers and various curves. I use the bone folder to the left of the craft knife for transferring drawings from tracing paper to stretched paper.

← Brushes

The full range of my brushes, from a 10cm (4in) house painter's to a No. 6 sable.

Masking tape and sheets

I tend not to mask surfaces prior to painting objects in the background if I can possibly do otherwise. I've often found my judgment is not sound enough when initially laying a picture out, and I decide to move or change things halfway through. Reserving an area in white means one is stuck with it, for better or worse.

Use clear matt tape labelled 'invisible', not the shiny kind. Do not use repositionable tape, as this does not stick down well enough. To avoid putting down masses of tape, acetate is a useful way of covering large surfaces. Any plastic sheet will do – if you can't get acetate (it can be expensive), in a pinch you can use the clear plastic sleeves sold to hold A4 documents. Frisket is a sticky thin plastic sheet, but this is designed for airbrush work, and anything too liquid may get underneath.

✦ Mask application

Place the acetate on your picture, use an indelible pen to outline the shape you need to mask, cut it out with scissors and place it on the drawing. Go no closer than 10mm (³⁄₈in)

to the edge of the form you wish to mask. Tape all around, creating minimal overlaps – every overlap is a potential disaster area.

When cutting a masking sheet, I can feel when the blade is far enough through the tape to cut it before it touches the paper. It's not that hard, and you need never score the paper. It is more delicate with overlapped tape, so cut the upper layer first, then the other. Cut out your shape and press down the tape. Pay special attention to overlaps, running your nail along these: the tape must adhere fully and firmly where it rides over the edge of the piece beneath it. Take a deep breath and go for the colour.

✦ Mask removal

A hair dryer is the crucial tool to soften the glue on the tape, allowing you to lift it off easily without tearing the paper. (Test your paper if you have never tried tape on it. Some will not take it.) Make sure your paper is dry: even dry to the touch may not be truly dry. To test it, place a small sheet of thin tracing paper on the stretched paper; if the tracing paper curls up, your paper is still damp.

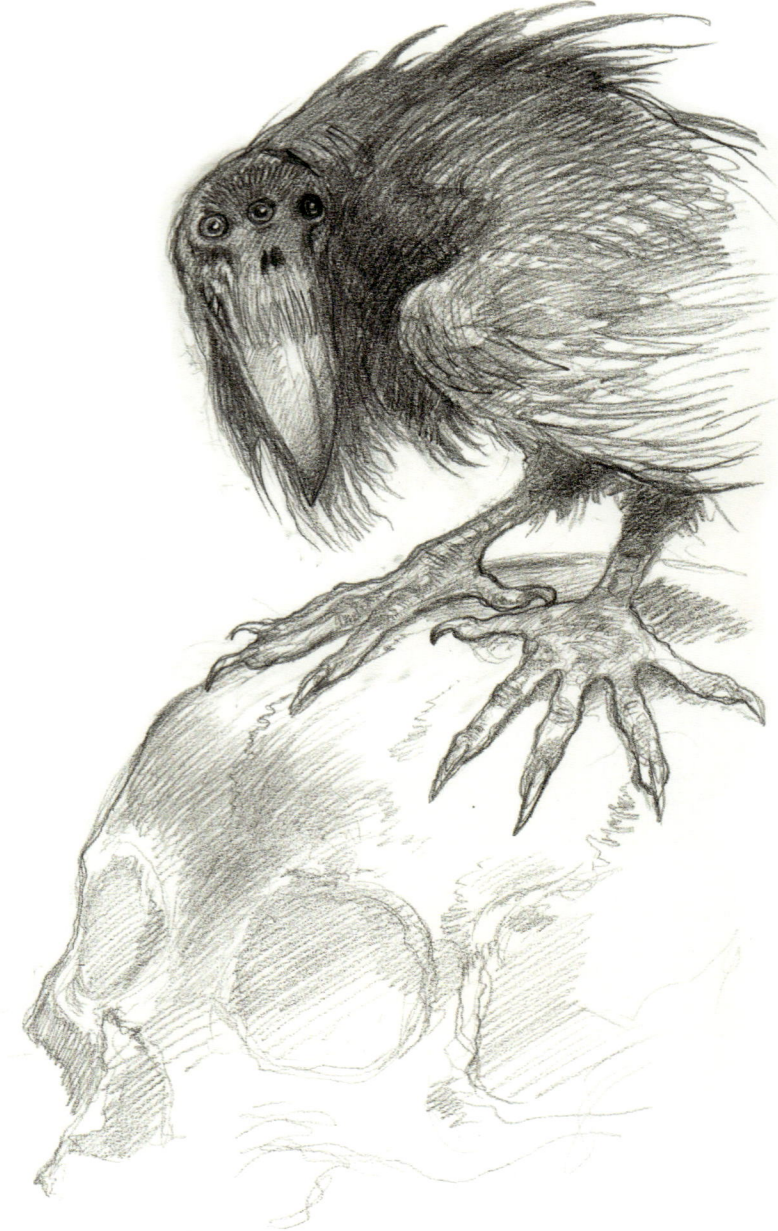

➜ *Nightmare Crow*

An initial pencil sketch for the image featured in my introduction; creatures with an odd number of eyes are ... well, odd.

Fixatives

Any will do: preferably one suitable for your medium. Don't use hairspray – it may contain oils, which are not recommended for artwork, even if split ends appreciate them.

Backing boards

Board thinner than 1.5cm (½in) will warp; the bigger the board, the thicker it should be. Buy plywood, the denser the better: marine ply is the best, but any decent ply will do. The wood should not be too tender, and must be smooth. Don't try to save money with thinner or cheaper options – the best is not expensive and lasts forever. Order boards from a DIY store that are the size of the paper you habitually use, plus 5cm (2in) or so around the edge. I have formats for full, half and quarter sheets.

Illustration board

Illustration board avoids the problems of paper, but needs more storage space, and may be stripped by eager photolithographers in order to go through a scanner.

Pens and inks

Some cheap ballpoints are superb for drawing and easy to replace. Dip pens are useful for fine line work, especially grass and hair. If you find nibs you like, buy lots – they are cheap and you may not find more. For colour I use drawing inks – like watercolours, they can be left to dry on a palette then revived.

Scratchboard

Excellent for ink work, and you can achieve just about any effect on this. If you are cautious when you scrape and scratch you can rework the same area several times. Check that your ink is compatible with the board.

➜ *Old Man Willow* final artwork

Old Man Willow is actually several willows. Where we live, there is an extraordinary row of pollarded willow trees that I use regularly in my illustrations. I've been photographing them for years, and they continually crop up in my work.

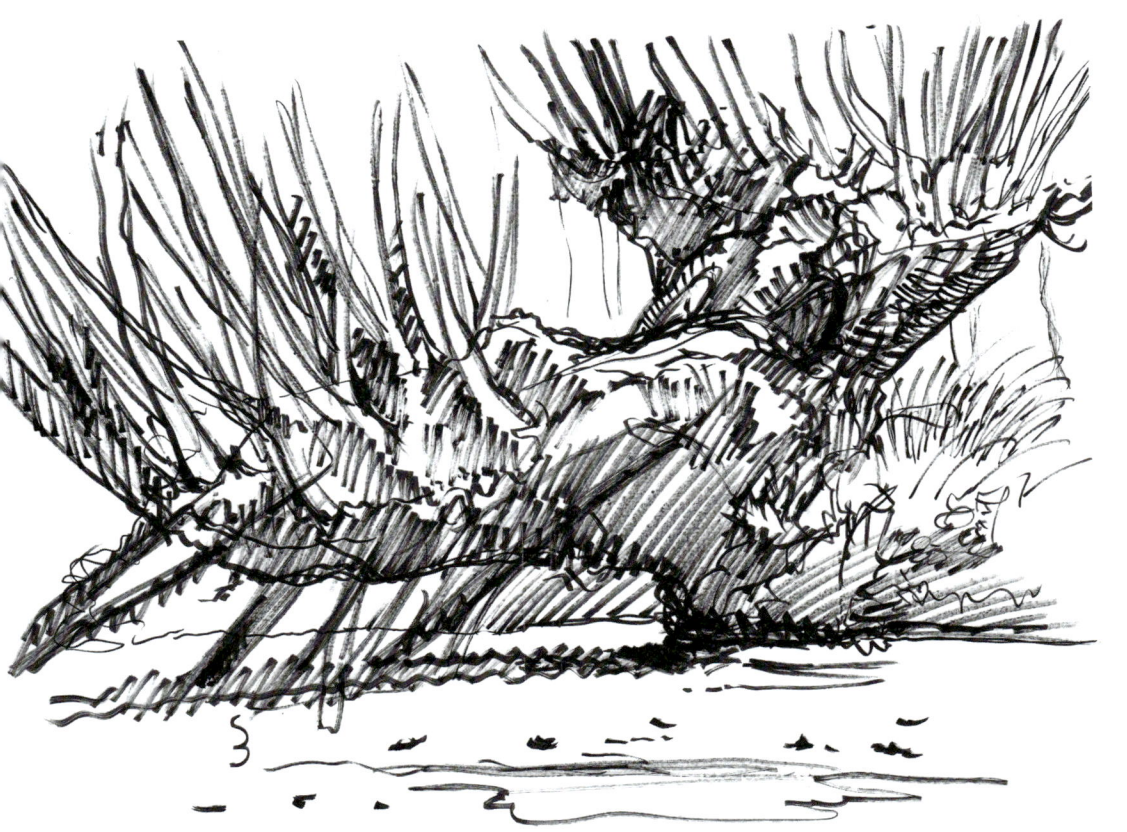

← *Old Man Willow* sketch

It's unusual for me to sketch in felt tip, but this piece must have been the result of a moment of unusual clarity, as I dashed it off in a few minutes. 'Sketches' like this are a visual shorthand, done more to remember ideas than as preparatory drawings. They are done on anything from shop receipts to book margins to restaurant tablecloths (only if paper).

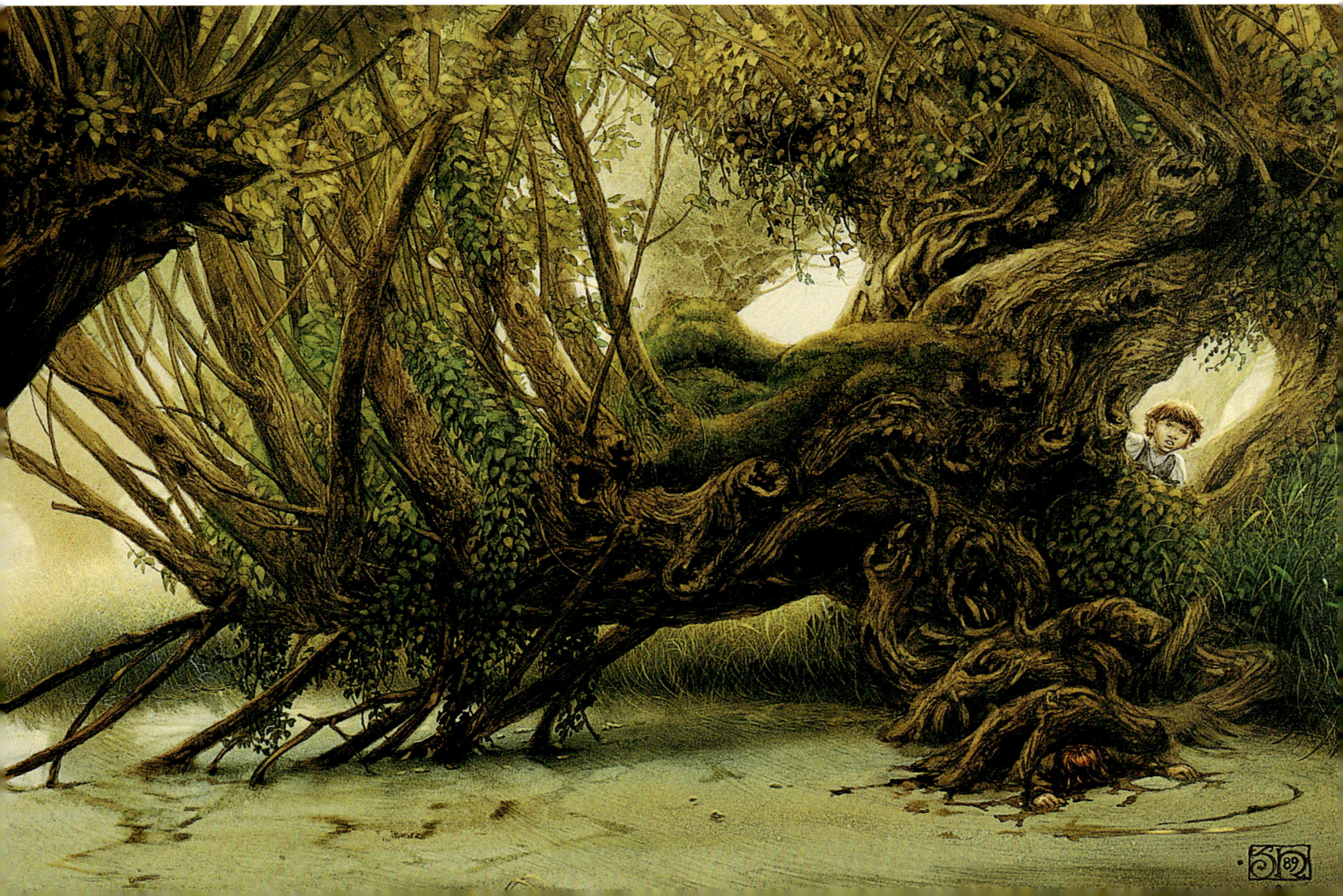

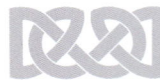

DIGITAL WORKFLOW

Concept work for video games and films of course means
digital. I confess I don't – yet – master 3D programs but working
digitally is the only way to remain agile, reactive and of course
fast enough to happily thrive in an art department.

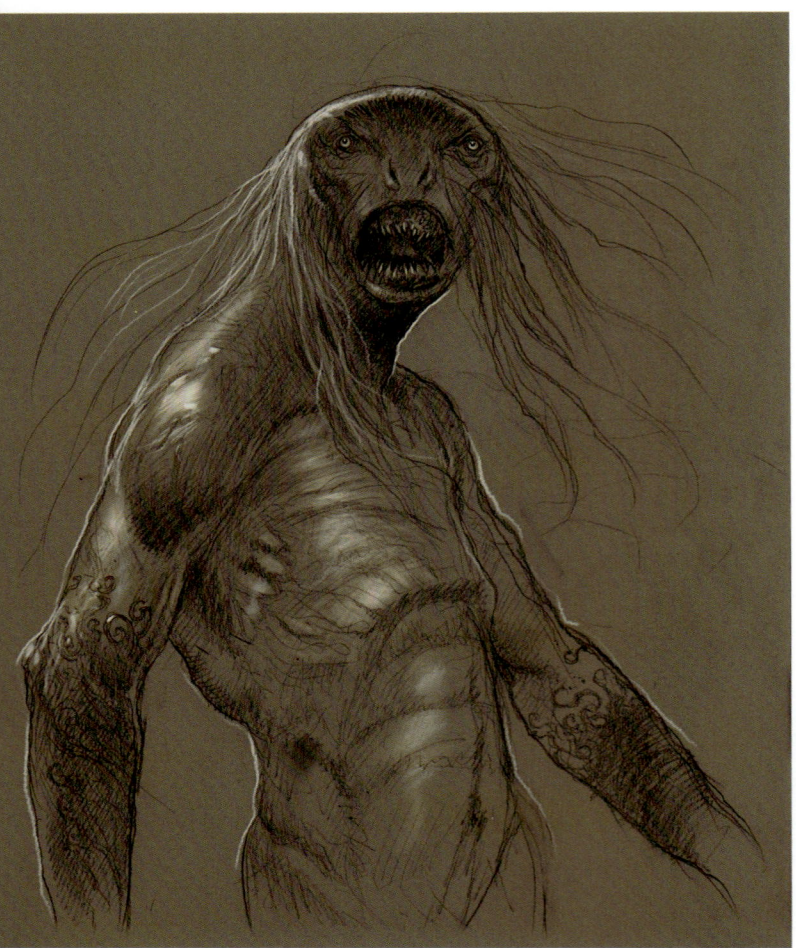

↑ Pencil, digital sepia and highlights
Quick study for the monster Grendel from the tale of
Beowulf. The original pencil sketch is in the Beasts &
Beings section.

Coming to digital art mid-career, I confess I
have been slow to acquire new skills beyond
the basics, and am only slowly tackling 3D. I
think better with a sketchbook, so will often
start with a pencil sketch to outline my thoughts. The
sketch is scanned and reworked, or taken into full colour.

Agility and creativity
Today's artists must master tenfold the number of tools of
only a few years ago, and, given the sophistication of these
digital tools, it takes time to bend them to your will – I envy
those who grew up with Photoshop. Conversely, what does
not change is the need for creative, energetic, inquisitive
and bold artists in every field. With that in mind, while it
is crucial to keep abreast of new programs and updates, to
pick and choose wisely the ones that correspond not only
to what you do but what you would happily explore, it is
equally crucial to maintain creativity and inventiveness.

Protect your work
It is an understatement to say that there are many amazing
artists out there (they were there before, just not as readily
visible). Now, you have the same choice of platforms as
everyone to display your work. While no one is immune
to having their work 'borrowed', that too is also a longtime
(mal)practice, so upload only low-resolution versions of
your work (72dpi screen resolution).

While visibility is crucial, originality and creativity are the
keys to your art being noticed.

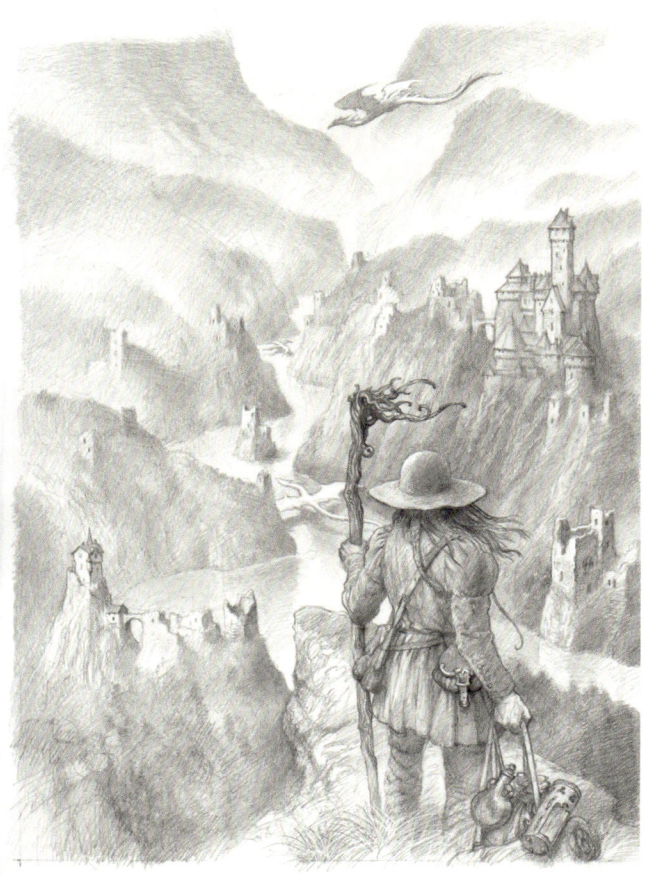

Poster illustrations for the cultural program "Les Portes du Temps". Produced with permission of the Collectivité européenne d'Alsace.

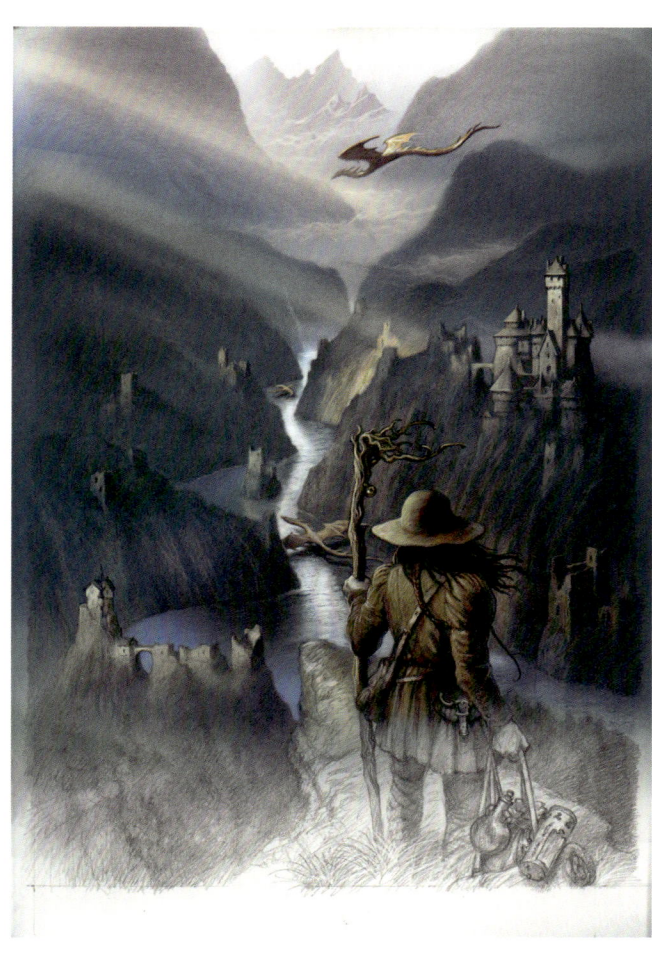

↓ Combining digital and traditional

The portrait of Hester Shaw, the plucky heroine of Philip Reeve's dystopian novel *Mortal Engines* is traditional but the background is digital.

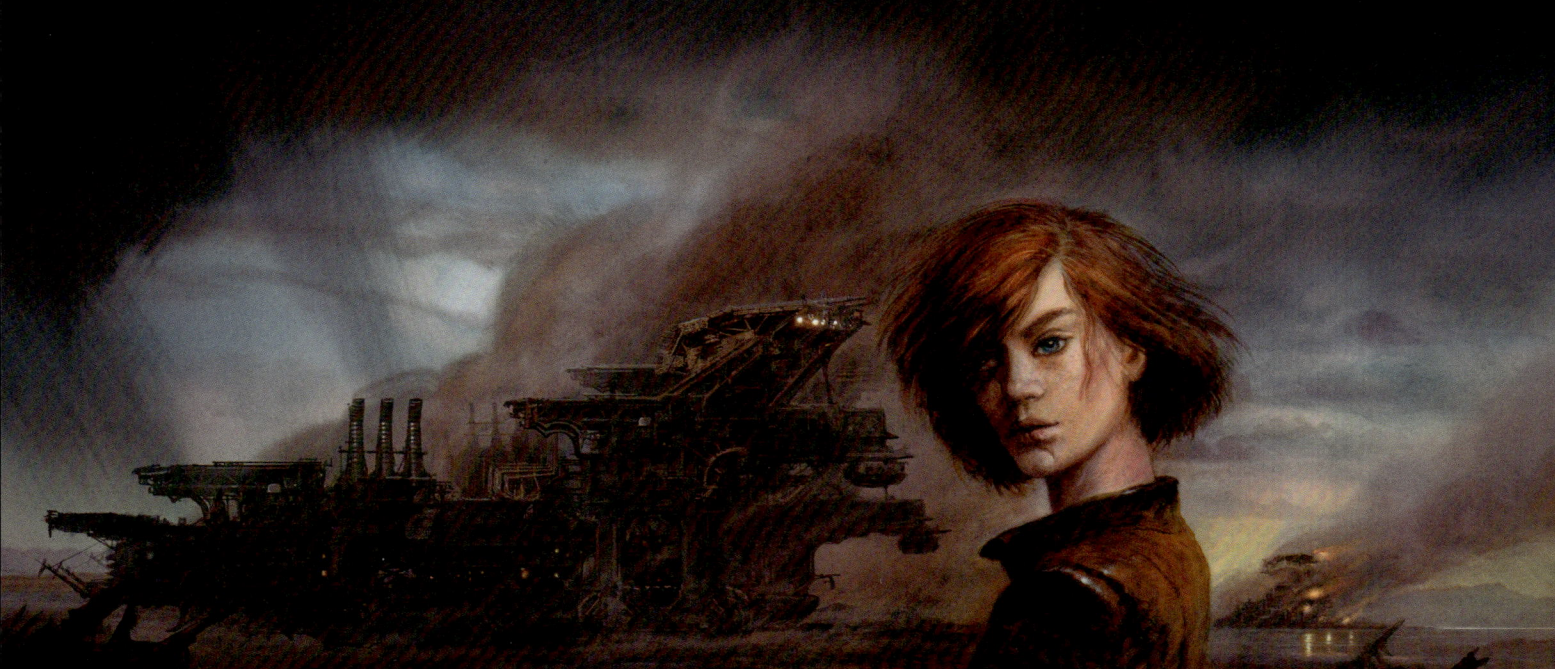

DIGITAL WORKFLOW IN ACTION

Like the rest, digital art should be fun. This colour piece is done just to try something I would not do traditionally. I imagined a futuristic fallen angel, his armour burnt, bent and battered.

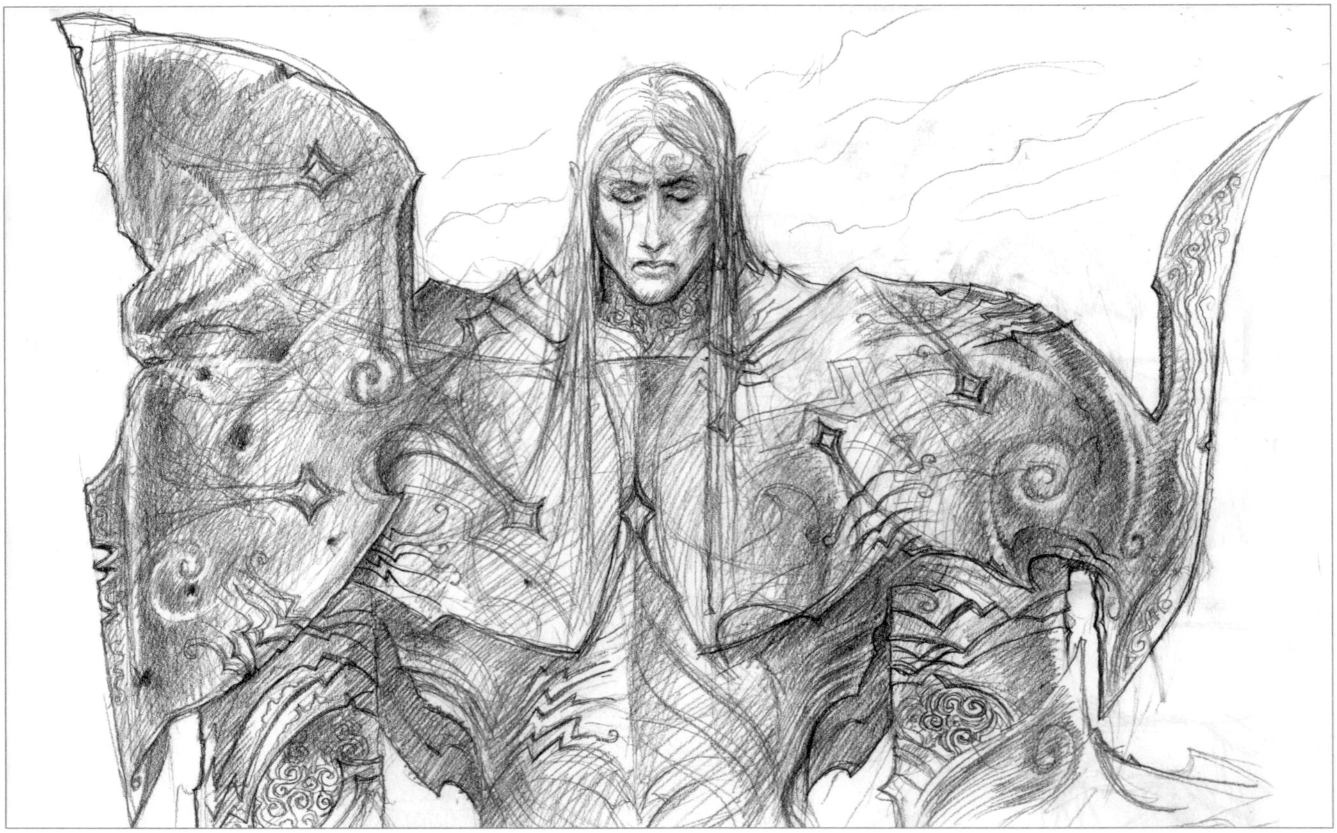

↑ *Fallen Angel*

An idle sketch made while travelling. It will be done when I no longer feel like playing around with textures and effects. I will come back to it though, and paint his wings one day.

Preparation

Importing the scan

The original sketch scanned and taken into Photoshop. Always keep the original scan as the master copy, and make an additional copy to work with.

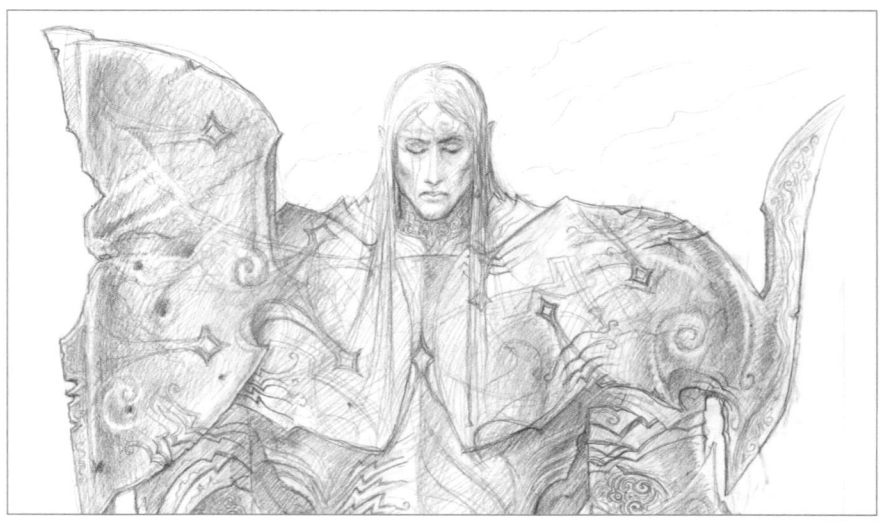

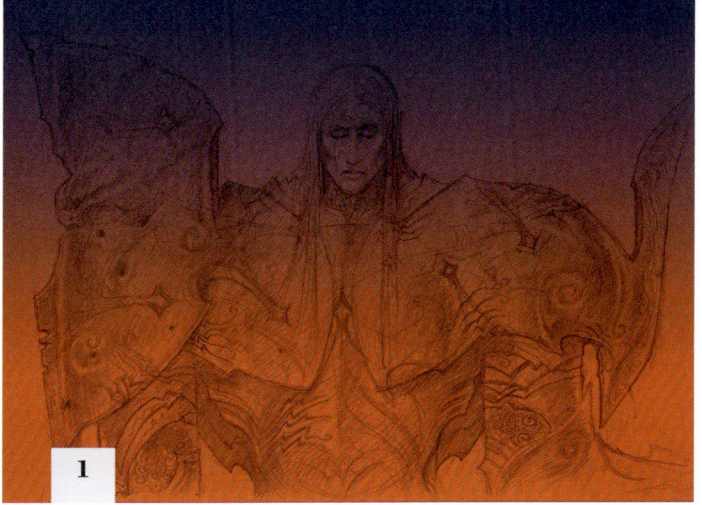

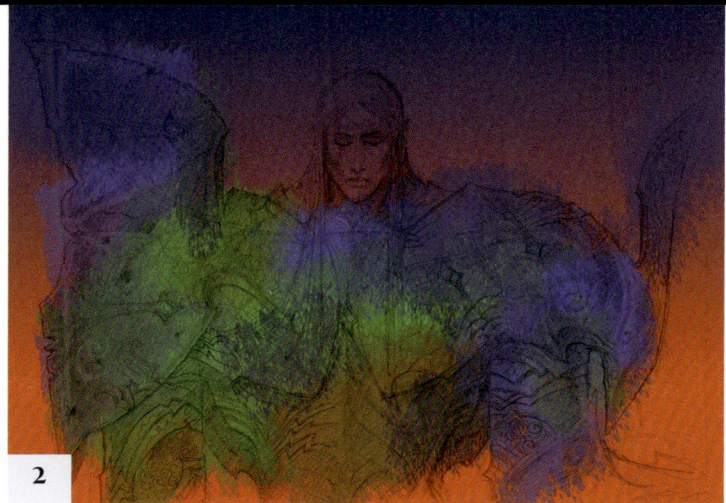

Stage 1
Setting up the canvas
Dropping in some colour on a flat background with a gradient layer; the sketch is on a multiply layer.

Stage 2
Blocking in tones and textures
I start with very big brushes, painting loosely – this is really the equivalent of a first watercolour wash. It is fine to remain very loose at this point.

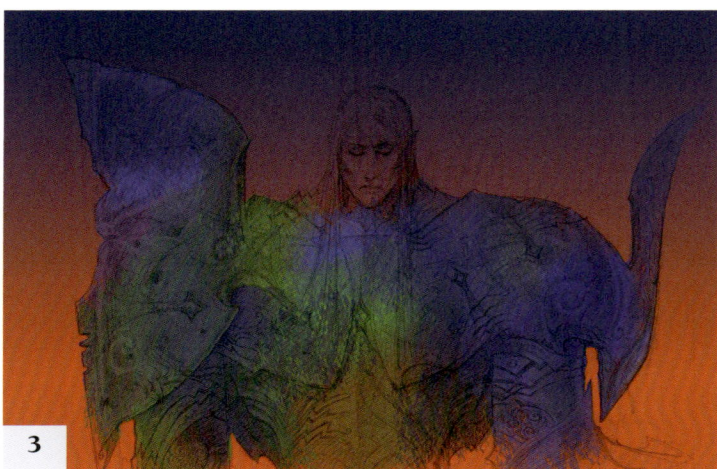

Stage 3
Finding the forms
The outline of the figure has simply been determined with a hard eraser.

Stage 4
Putting in a face
The main features of the face are blocked in; I will adjust the shadows and light on a new layer. Given that this painting is of a figure, with no real background, it is possible to work more or less wherever you like, and build up the volumes as you go.

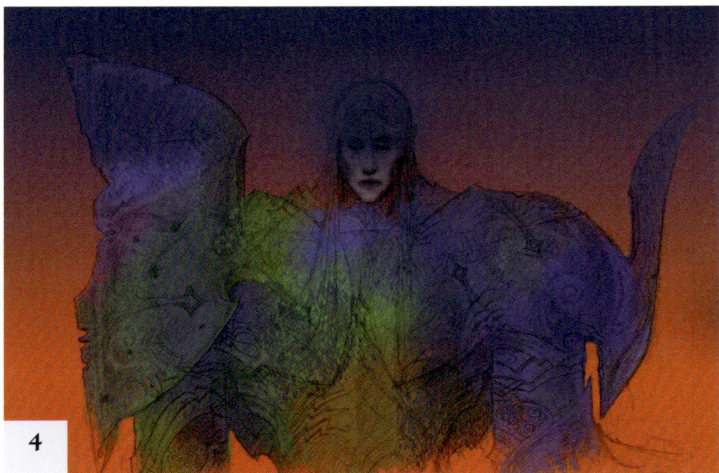

Stage 5
Textures and volumes
Now that things are starting to take shape (adding the head helps) I have started adding textures and more volume.

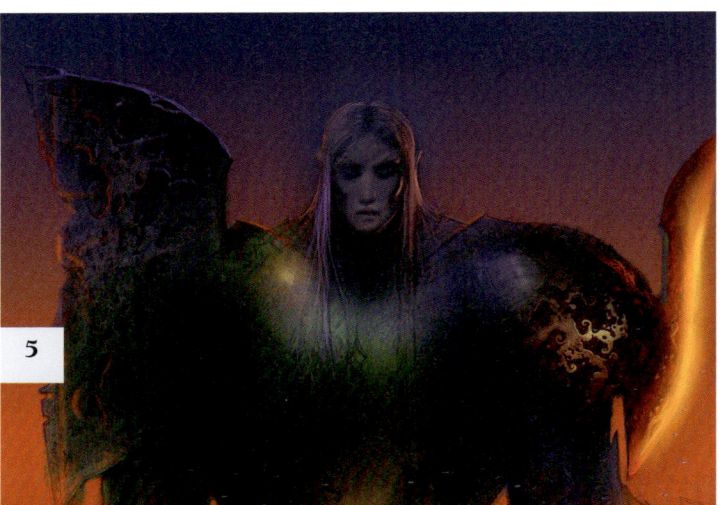

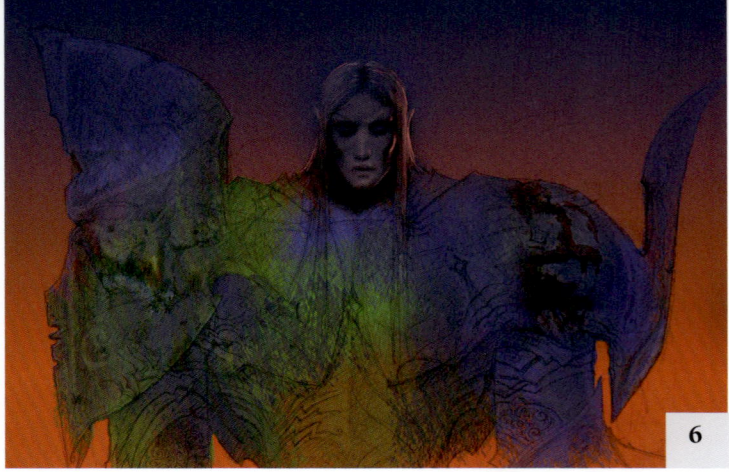

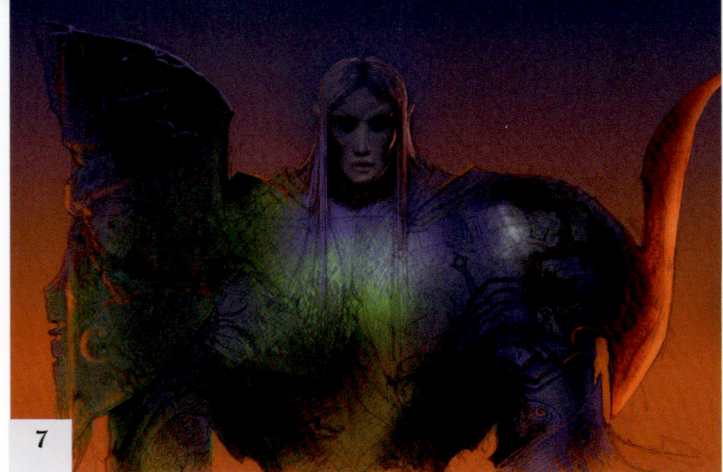

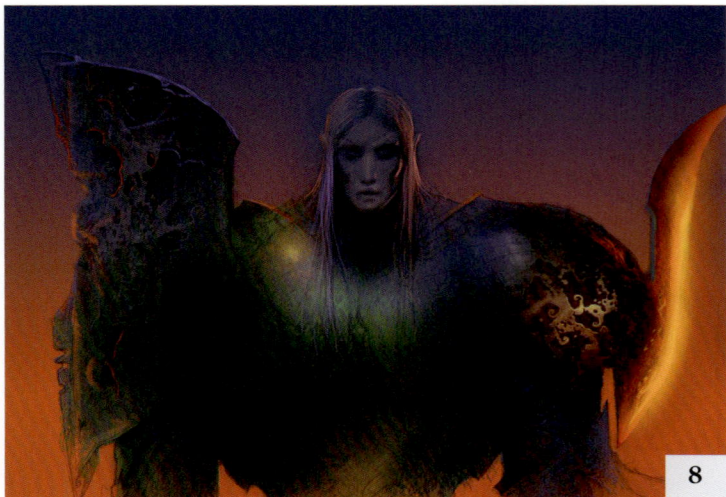

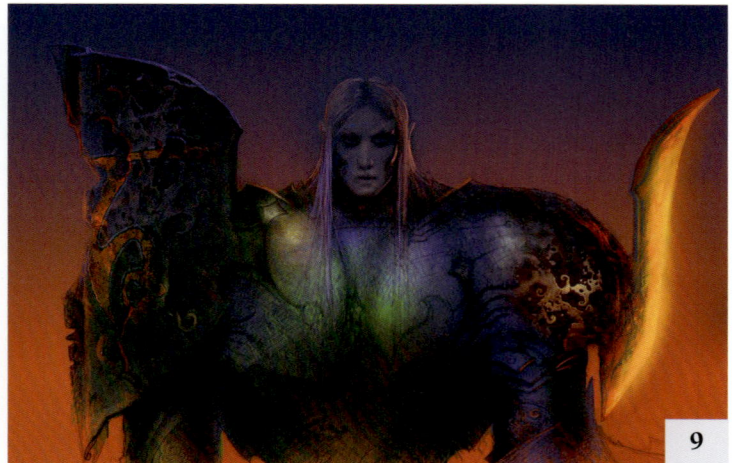

Stage 6
Armour details
Adding textures to make the armour look weathered, worn and damaged.

Stage 7
Trying a new idea
I have suddenly decided that the blade on his pauldron should be red-hot and glowing. Whether this will really work remains to be seen so I do it on a separate layer, but it is worth a try.

Stage 8
Adding further details
I add more light, details and volume, assessing the overall effect as well as the details themselves.

Stage 9
Adding further details
I have stencilled a number onto the shield, and the same number is now imprinted on the figure's face. I have also played with the hair a little.

Stage 10
Last details
Working in the final details, trying not to lose sight of the overall volumes and atmosphere.

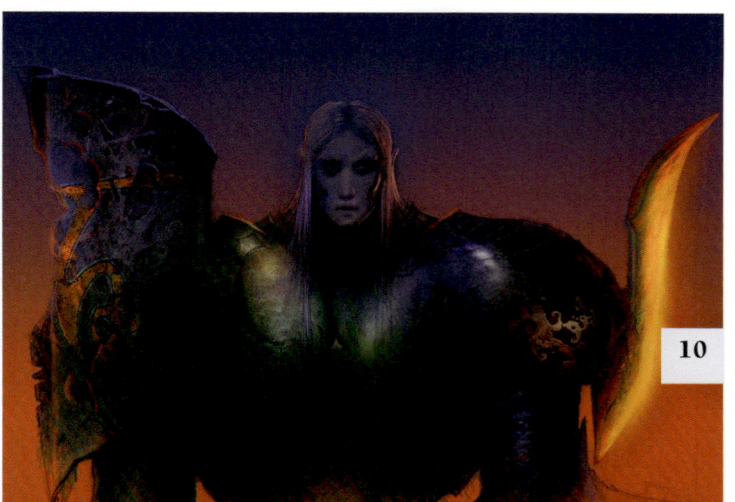

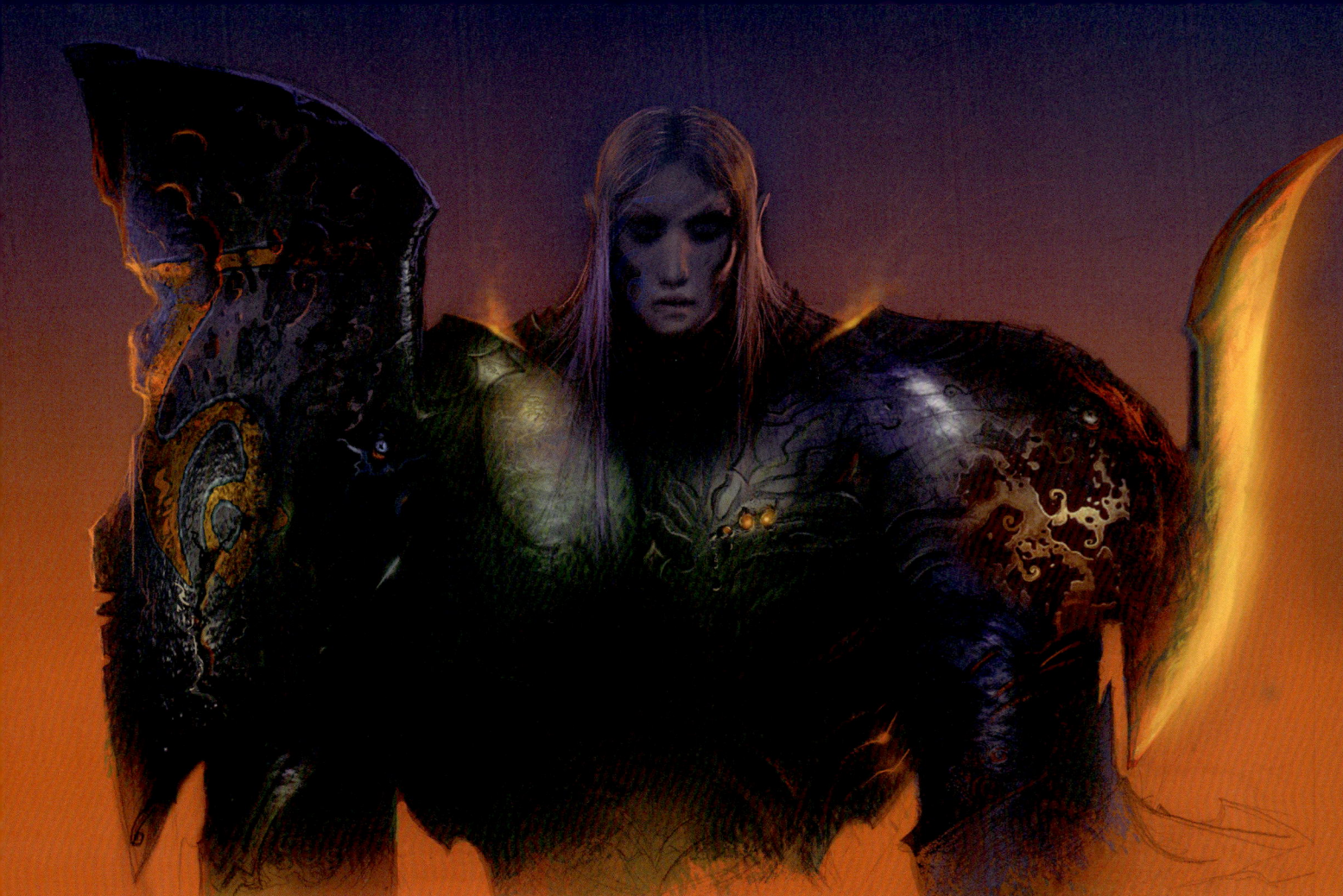

↑ Final artwork
The finished painting – for now. If I have time, I will return to it later and perhaps add a background (something suitably apocalyptic, of course), but I do not mind the sketchy quality it still retains.

MANAGING PIXELS & PAINT

Most of my work is done using non-digital techniques, but is all scanned and digitized. Film concept work is a mix of both, from quick sketches scanned and watermarked to detailed digital paintings. If traditional techniques are important to you, there are several things to get right in the digital realm:

Scan your work in
Number one – scan your work. I go into more detail about this in Protecting & Storing Your Artwork, but in general, I scan mine as RGB TIFF files at 600dpi.

Back it up
Once the digital file has been cleaned up, contrasts and colours balanced to your satisfaction, and a final version created (I also keep the raw scans as a back-up), we arrive at number two: back up your work. Check your drives regularly, files can become unexpectedly corrupted for mysterious reasons. Don't compress work or reduce the resolution of files unless it is a copy. Keep full-size copies of your files in two safe places.

Fix the original
Personally, I resist the temptation to leave something unresolved in an original painting, even when retouching it digitally would be less laborious and time-consuming. Navigating between the two worlds is a balancing act, and I wish to preserve the integrity of the actual paintings, so resist the siren song of digital convenience as best I can. This said, and depending on the nature of a commission, it is often advantageous to mix the two.

BEASTS & BEINGS

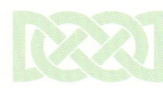

Fantasy is both a magnification and an enhancement of reality, a stripping away of the commonplace and an exploration of the potential of imagination. Fantasy beings are the generous hosts who allow the imagination to travel freely in these parallel worlds. It's surprising how much we can have in common with things that don't exist.

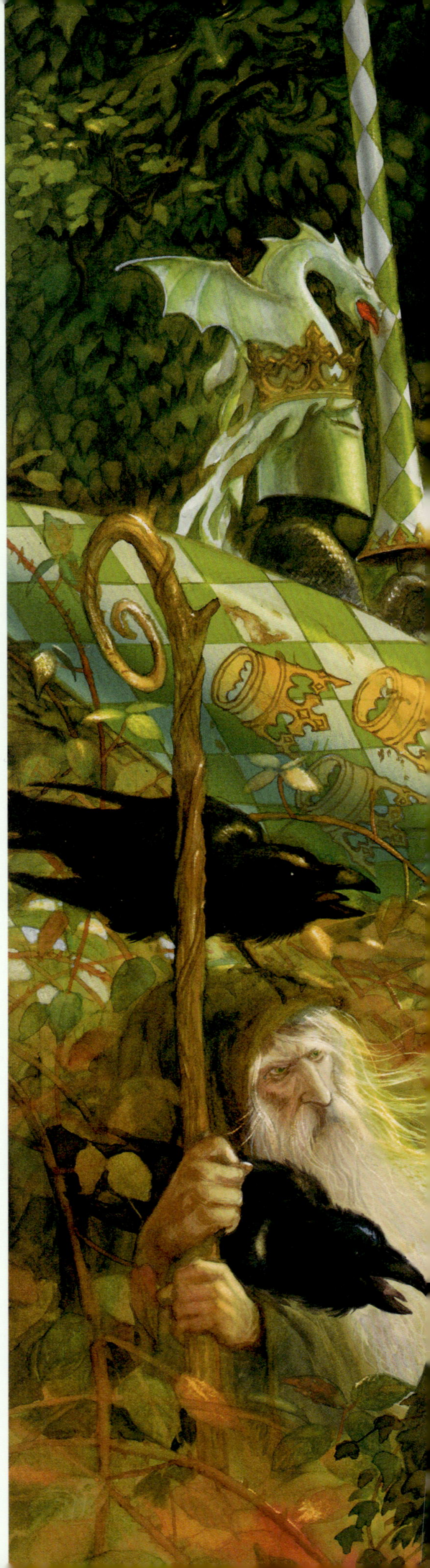

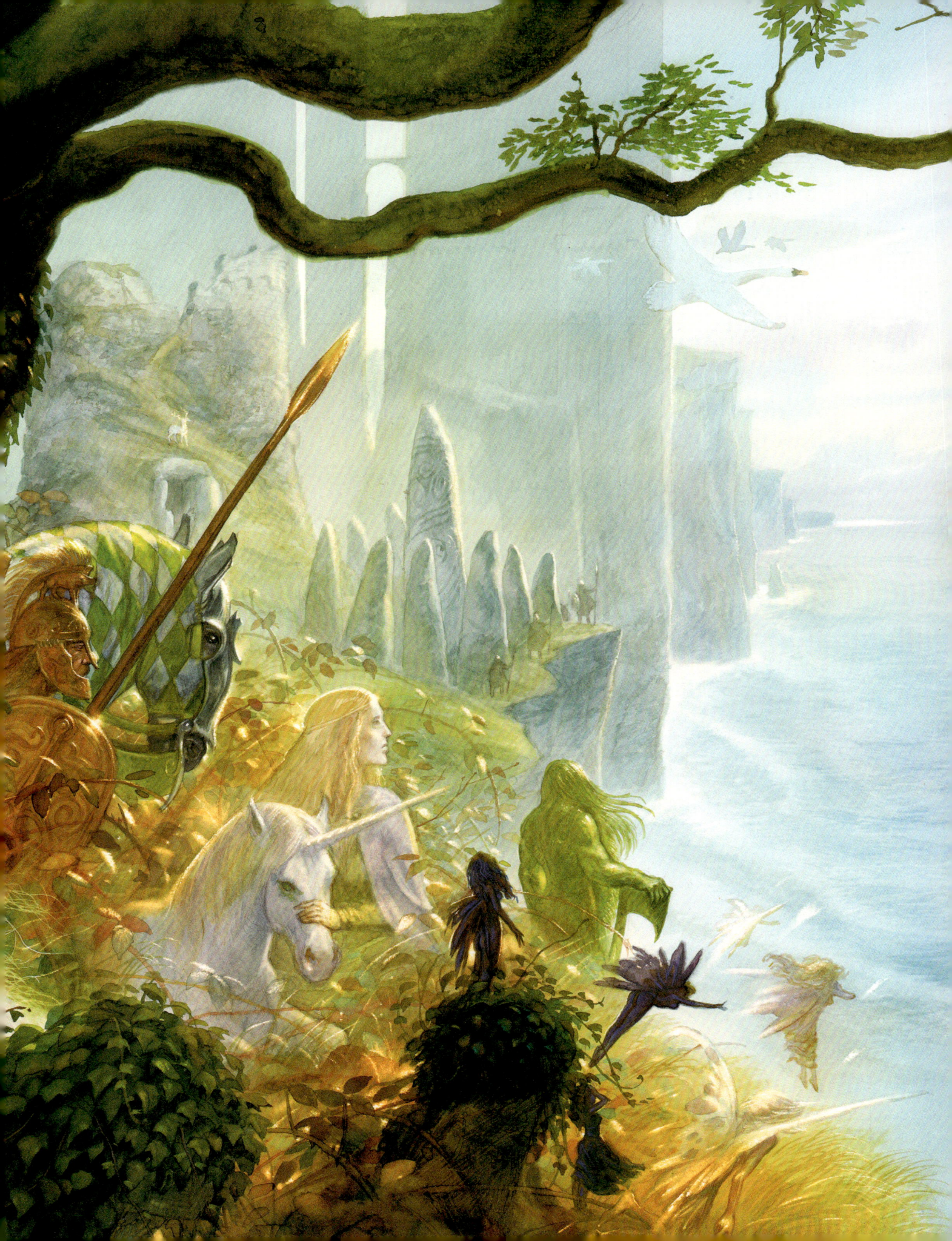

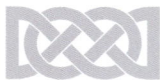

FANTASY BEINGS
APPROACHES & INSPIRATION

The notion of fantasy beings is of creatures that are composed of elements from thousands of years of human fears and aspirations, that are extensions of our qualities and faults, that are allegories.

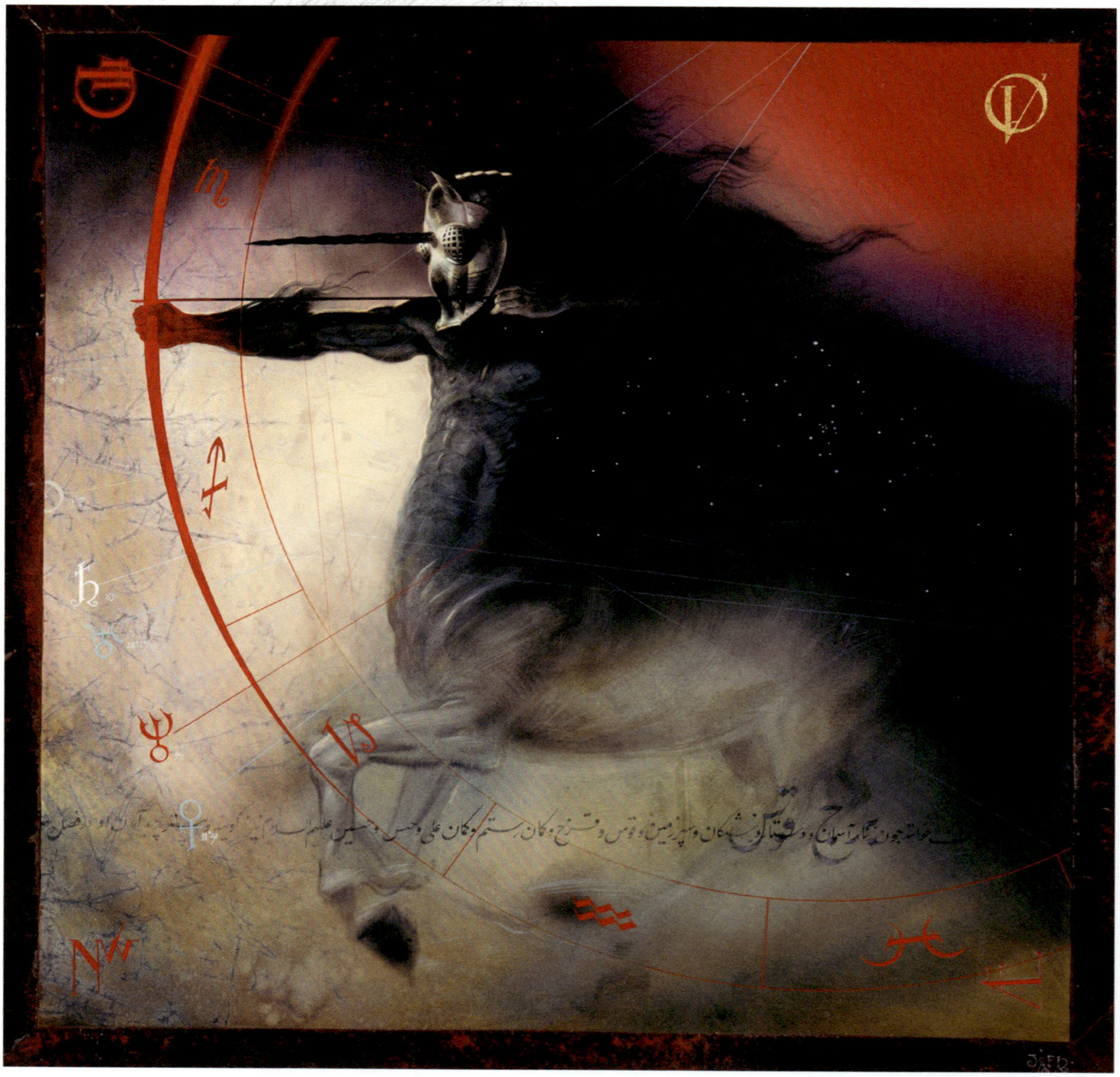

"THIS IS THE KIND OF IMAGE I MOST ENJOY DOING: HUGE DRAGONS AND ELVES IN IMPOSSIBLE ARMOUR"

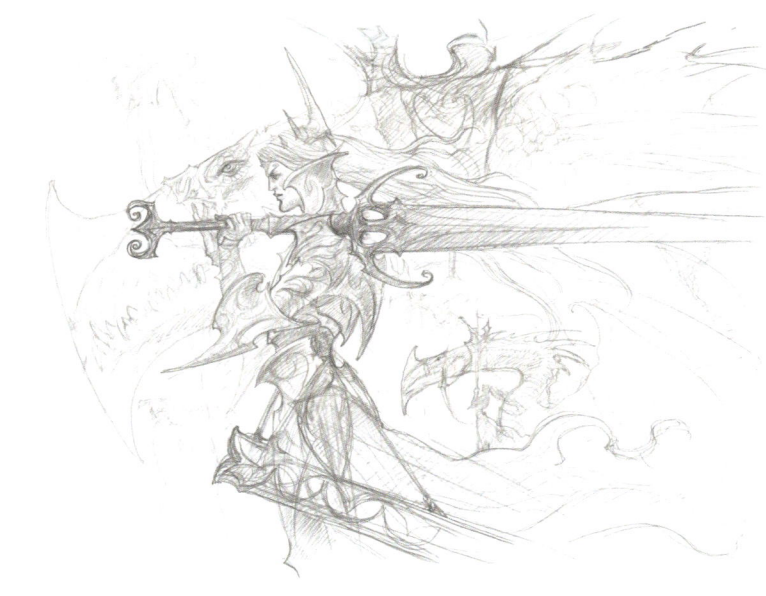

T here is a fine distinction between fantasy and science fiction, which mythology occasionally strays across. A centaur, mythologically, is a horse's body with a human torso. Period. As soon as one questions its bone structure, digestion (omnivore? herbivore? how do they eat enough to keep that huge horse's body going?) or intellect, then it turns into a speculative proposition for an alien race. The distinction is subtle, and the frontier not clearly defined, but it will establish the tone of an image and eventually influence its evolution.

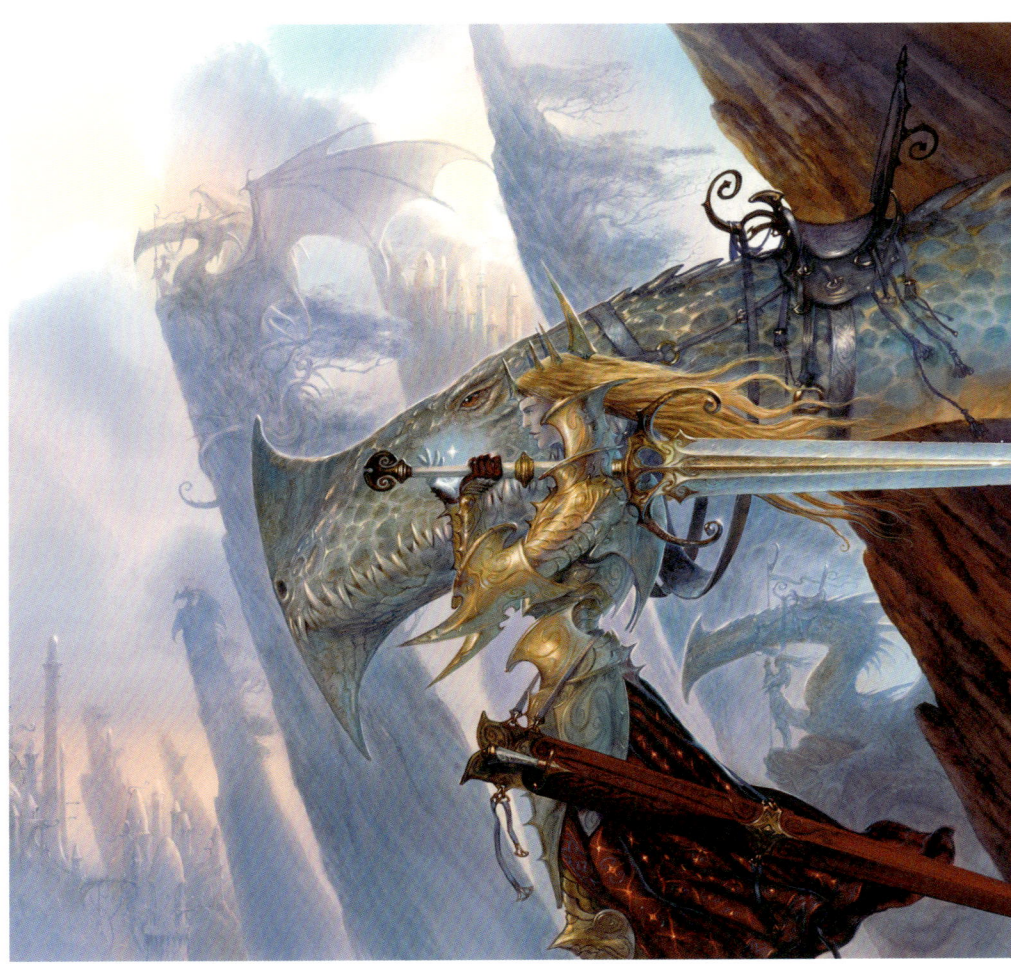

← *Sagittarius*

A painting done for an exhibition on the signs of the zodiac. I posed myself for the torso and the position of the arms. The horse is from a magazine, and the astrological symbols are the sky chart at the time of my son's birth (easy to order from any astrologer).

↑ *Elves and Dragons*

This is the kind of image I most enjoy doing: huge dragons and elves in impossible armour – the full fantasy menu. I spent ages trying to discover a novel shape for the dragons, until I finally stumbled on this silhouette. The passage from the sketch to the colour artwork was quite straightforward. The details are only defined as the colour moves ahead.

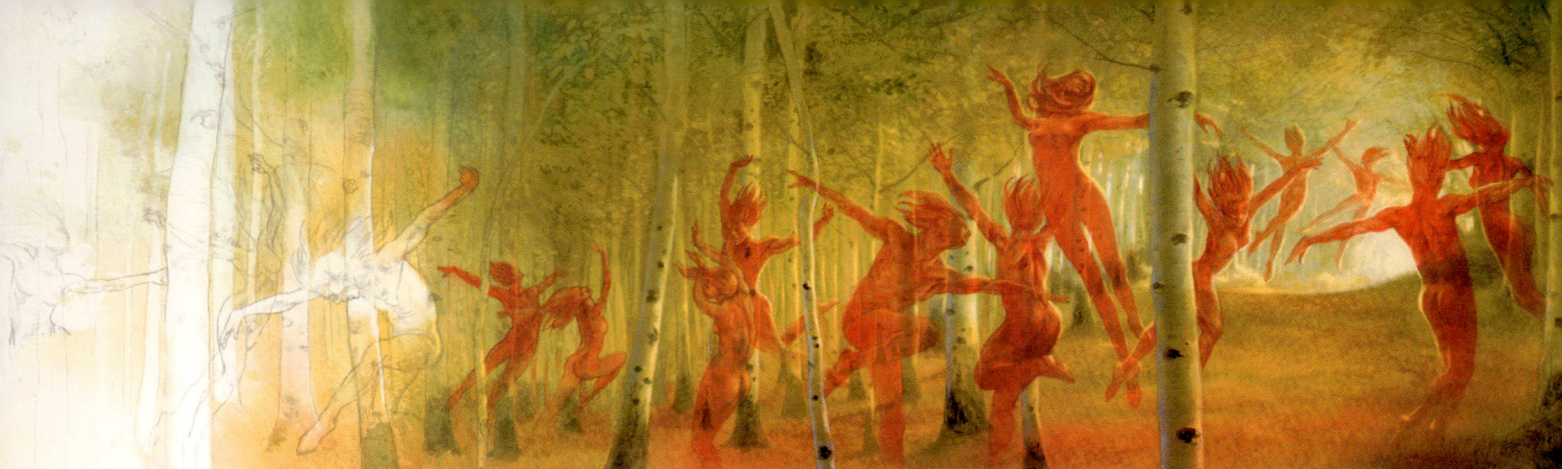

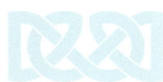

FANTASY BEINGS

CHARACTERS, SYMBOLISM & ACCOUTREMENTS

History provides a stable terrain on which to build fantasy. It is also the stone from which one may quarry the blocks to build one's own universe; a deep well from which to draw information.

Possessing a solid grounding in visual history results in overflowing ideas and creativity, especially for fantasy. The ingenuity, creativity and skill of the societies that bequeathed our legacy of myth and legend, evidenced by their surviving artefacts, is astonishing and rich. It is largely illusory to imagine that with a pencil and paintbrush, today's illustrator can capture the beauty of a La Tène spearhead, a Viking sword hilt or a Minoan helm. But a declared and dedicated interest and a certain intimacy with these things naturally leads to the desire to find that same beauty in one's own 'subcreations'. (Much of what we 'know' about history is largely fantasy, anyway.)

Tolkien, who coined that neologism, created Middle-earth from an overflowing of enthusiasm for the words of lost languages. In the same way that his delight in the sound and etymology of those vestiges led to the devising of new tongues for the peoples of Middle-earth, a modern maker of fantasy imagery can largely ignore the constraints and dictates of archaeology and mine the surviving riches freely. This isn't in any way a superficial copy-and-paste approach: attentiveness to the essence of visual history comes equipped with the notions of what 'feels right' for any fantasy design. And a little knowledge of the 'real thing' rules out the patently ridiculous, or the terrible tendency to look to Hollywood for authenticity.

But does all this really tell us what ogres look like? Does this supply a foolproof method for depicting fairies? Does it tell us for sure that elves have pointed ears? Of course not. The 'idea' of elves is something we share collectively, but those shared clues do not an elf make. Rather, they are a guide to what is outside the genre, of what does not 'feel right', as much as they are a list of ingredients. Inside this loose framework, the artist has the leeway needed to make a personal contribution to the eternal renewing of the themes.

← *Memory and Dream*

The cover brief stated: 'Crowd of naked red semi-transparent figures dancing in forest setting. Male and female.' In the end, it was not too complicated, although I absolutely emptied the modern dance shelf at the local library. They are pure fantasy, in that they do not rely on any particular reference other than their clearly fantastical nature.

→ *Elf Fantastic*

The commission sheet basically said: 'Mass-market paperback format on elf/fantasy theme.' Commissions that leave a lot to the imagination are often hard to do, as there is no narrative, only the evocation of a subject.

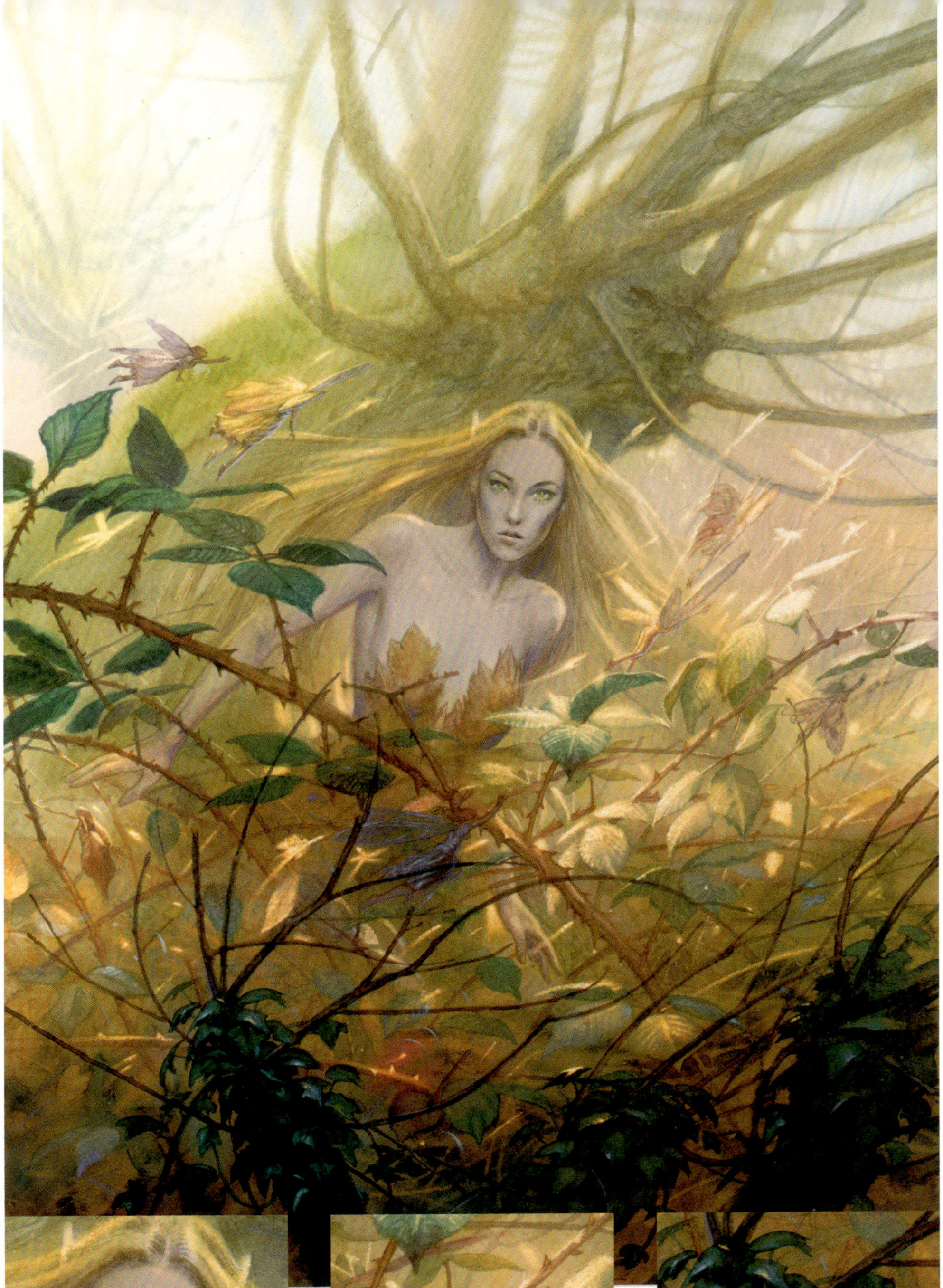

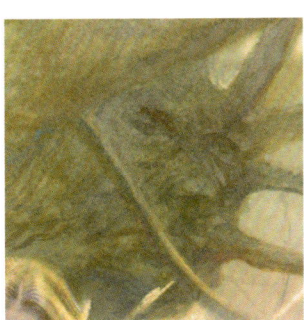

✦ I have always thought that faërie should be an anthropomorphization of the forest for the purpose of making us heavy-footed and careless humans take more notice of nature.

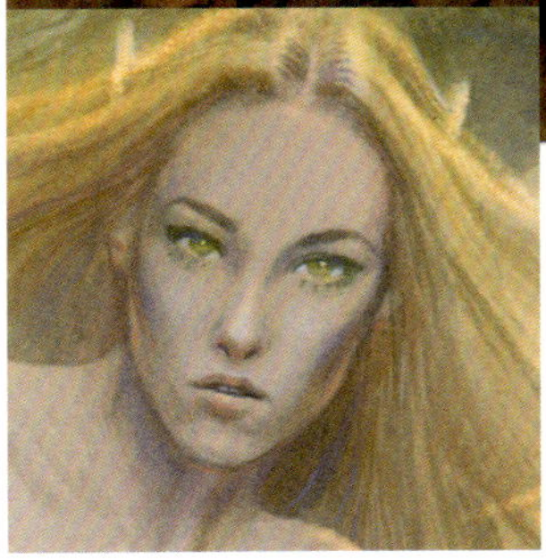

✦ The most enticing of elves can stand on the threshold we cross at our peril. The winged sprites of this vision are the fare of nursery rhymes, but faërie is a dangerous place.

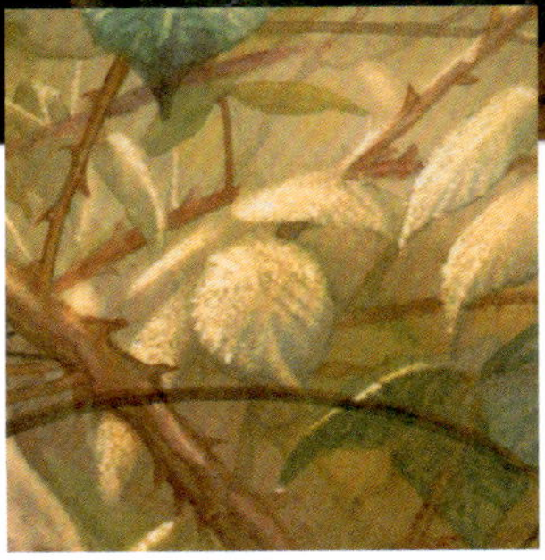

✦ The highlights on the blackberry leaves were obtained by scraping the surface of the paper with a scalpel. The broader highlights were done with a hard eraser.

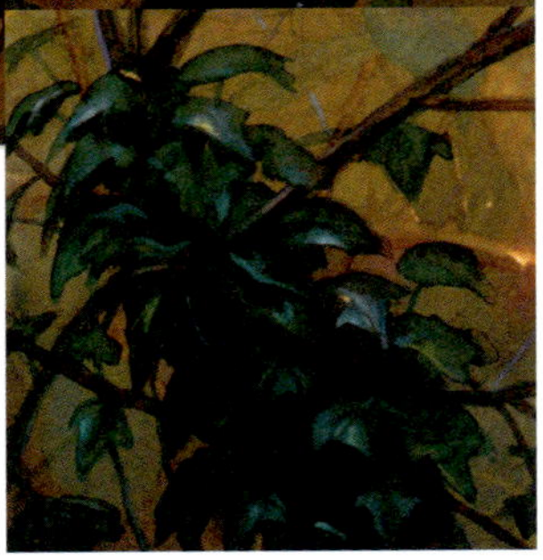

✦ Ivy is a wonderful element to explore – the brilliance of the leaves, the patterns of growth, and its propensity to thrive in the most unlikely places.

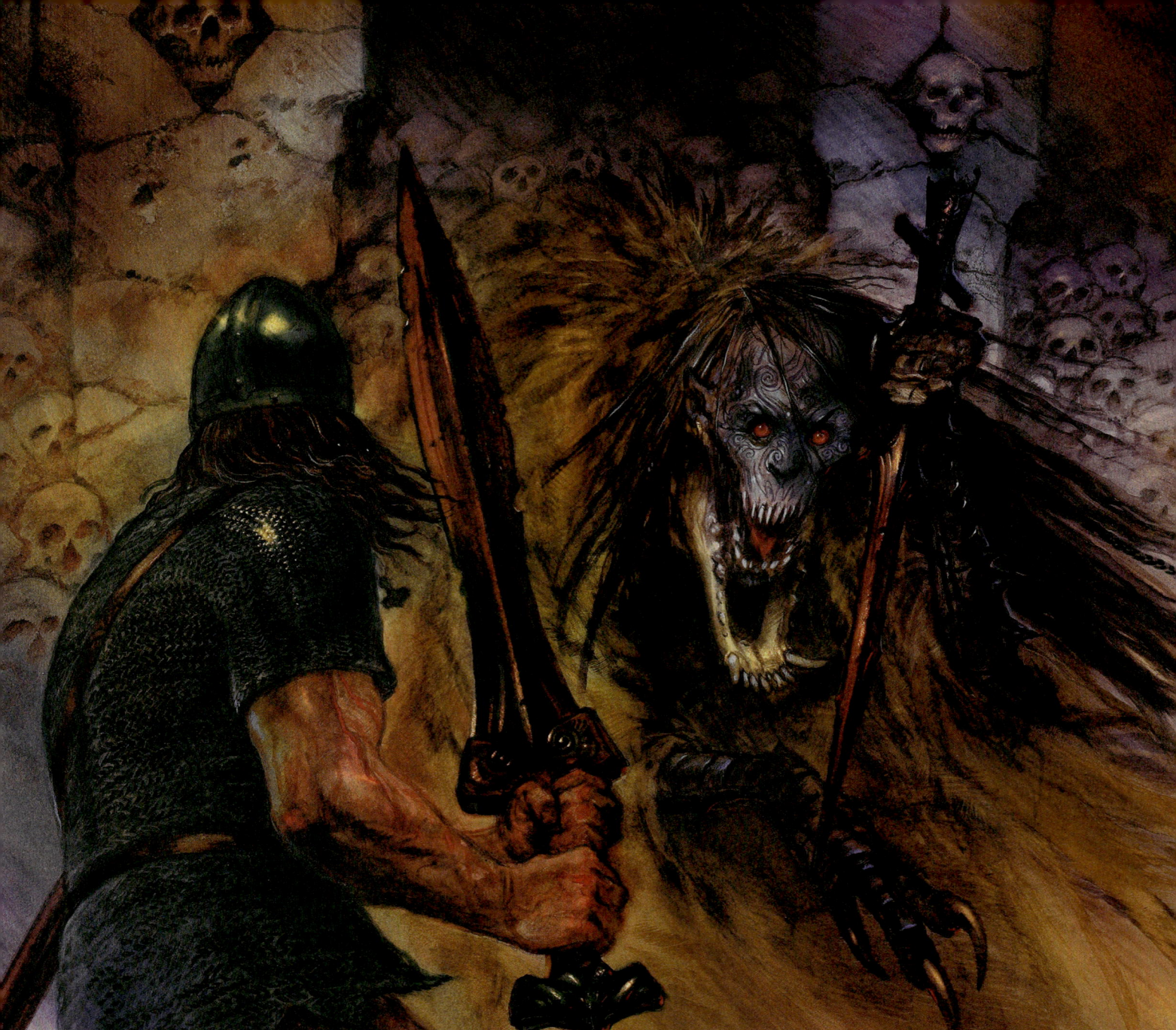

Nothing is permanent – the rules aren't set in stone in the realm of fantasy. Tolkien's elves are perhaps the best example. From the otherworldly Tuatha de Danaan and the powerful figures of Norse legend to the nursery rhymes and flower fairies of the Victorian era, theirs was an inexorable decline, both in stature and glamour, until an Oxford professor forever changed the way we see them. Elves have never been the same since. For one author to have achieved such a feat single-handedly is unprecedented in modern fantasy literature.

↑ *Beowulf and Grendel's Mother*

The monster's heavy tattoos are a vivid memory of the ancient Maori manner of tattooing, which left furrows in the skin, and her scaly, taloned hands are based on ravens' feet. I really think very little about how to depict fantasy beings: generally there is some element of them that tells me which way the image needs to go.

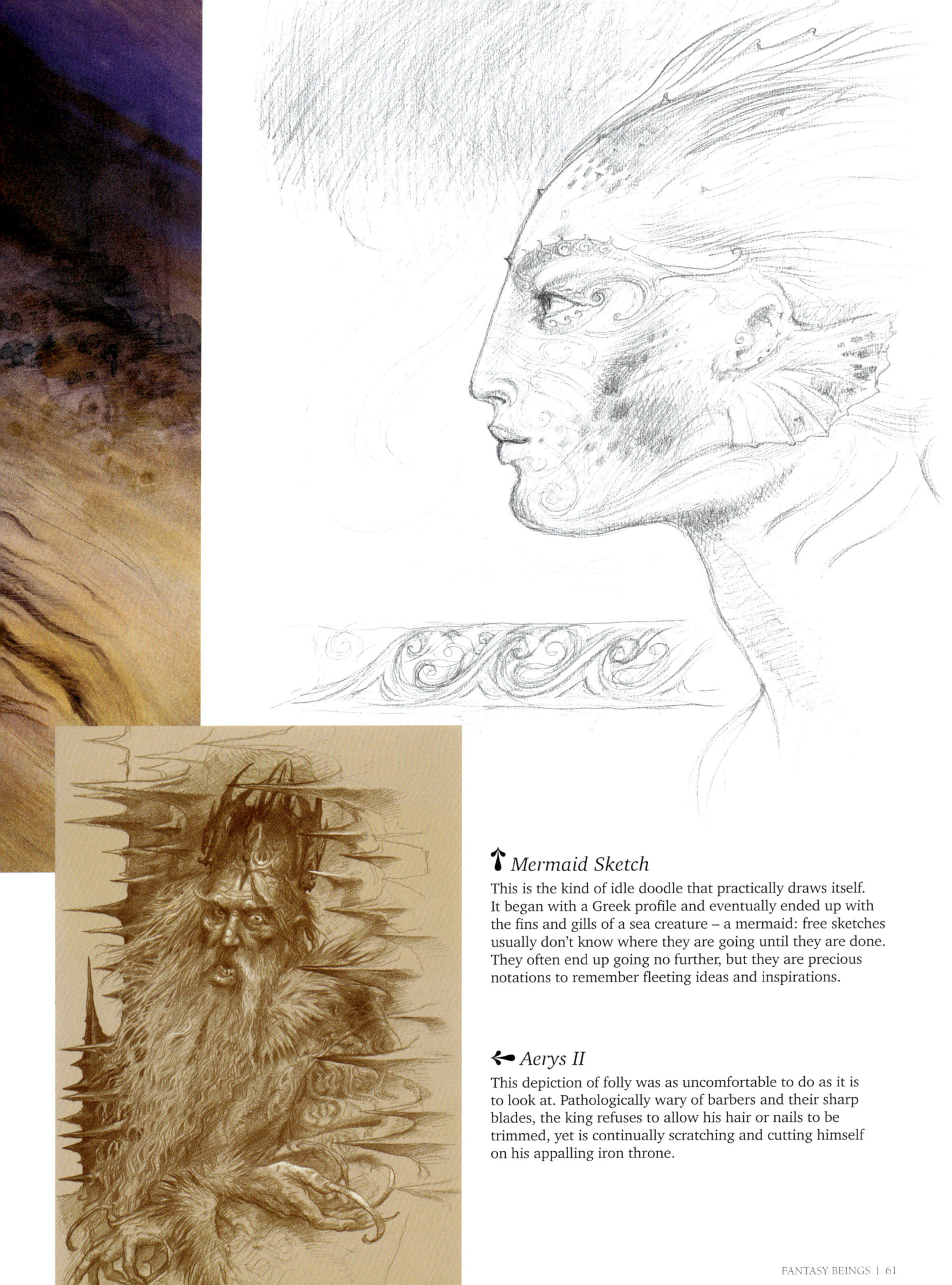

⬆ Mermaid Sketch

This is the kind of idle doodle that practically draws itself. It began with a Greek profile and eventually ended up with the fins and gills of a sea creature – a mermaid: free sketches usually don't know where they are going until they are done. They often end up going no further, but they are precious notations to remember fleeting ideas and inspirations.

⬅ Aerys II

This depiction of folly was as uncomfortable to do as it is to look at. Pathologically wary of barbers and their sharp blades, the king refuses to allow his hair or nails to be trimmed, yet is continually scratching and cutting himself on his appalling iron throne.

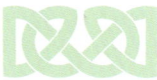

FANTASY BEINGS
CERNUNNOS

Like any admirer of Celtic myth, I was eager to depict Cernunnos, the antlered god. I have many books on the subject and look in awe at reproductions of the Gundestrup Cauldron, on which he appears. I also admit to considerable influence from fantasy author Robert Holdstock's revisitings of traditional Celtic mythos.

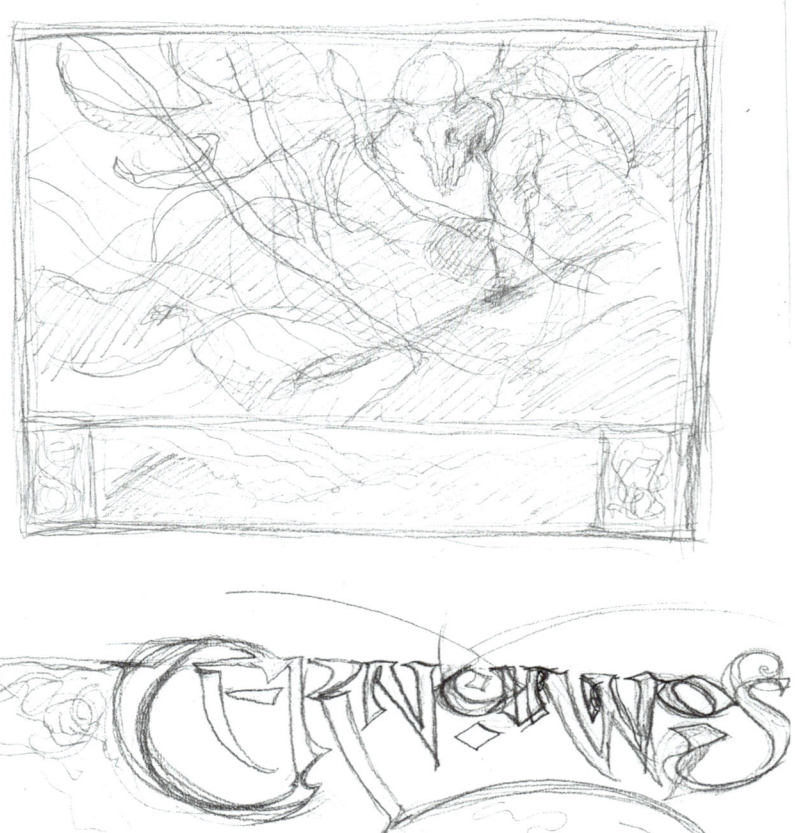

⬆ Sketch

My sketch is really a scribble, a visual note-to-self – I spent far more time on the lettering. Reconstructions of prehistoric Irish elk give an idea of their massive antlers, and I dug out information on elk skulls. I want Cernunnos to be a hulking figure, dangerous and swift with his huge lance.

Stage 1
Initial washes

This stage is just a matter of breaking the ice. I often find it hard to know where to start, so starting all over seems best. Most of this will disappear later, but serves as a base.

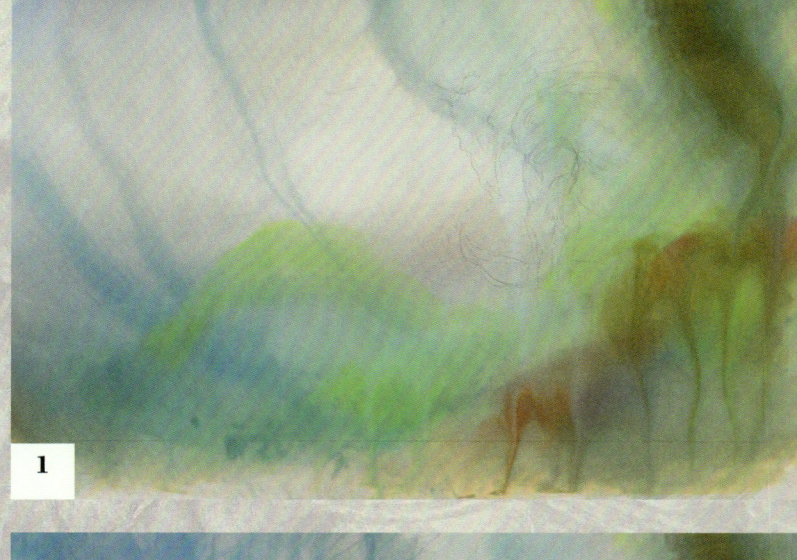

Stage 2
Resolving the background

I decide to put a huge oak in the background, so the whole page is dampened again to keep the tree from being too present. It can be worked up later (if enough of it remains visible behind what I've not yet decided to put in front).

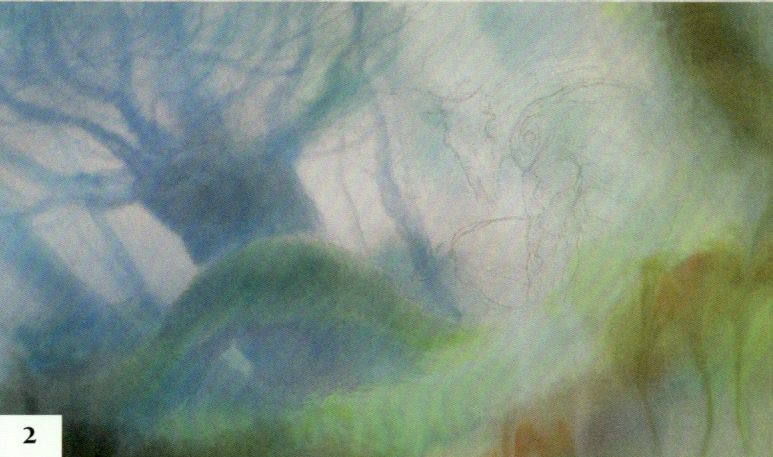

Stage 3
Blocking in the foreground

Starting on Cernunnos himself, and blocking in the roots and trunks in the foreground. I've decided to add a snake coiling around the lance, as serpents are apparently the god's familiars. His body is painted with a wide brush, building muscle mass. I used my own arm as a model (it's much thinner, of course). It's hard to find photos of muscular bodies that are not body-built out of all semblance to reality.

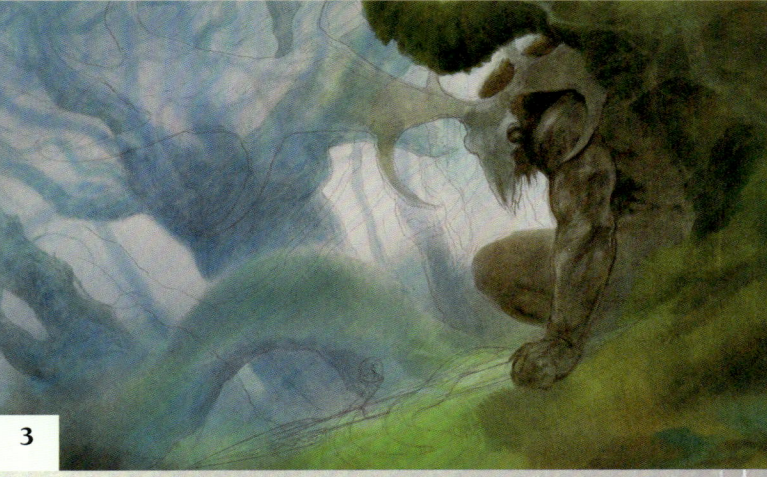

Stage 4
Working up detail

While working up roots and branches, I've suddenly decided to add a standing stone, painted with a wide brush and a quick (and indelible) stroke of colour. The right antler is blocked out, waiting until I decide what will go in front of it. At this stage, nothing looks good: his skin is dull, the area behind his head is confused, the branches aren't working. His skull mask has been reworked but is still not quite right. This often happens in the middle of a picture, but there's no choice but to carry on and hope for the best.

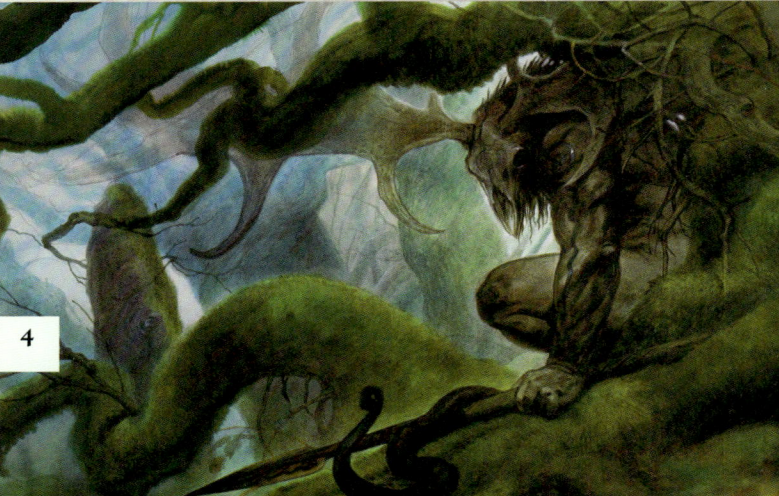

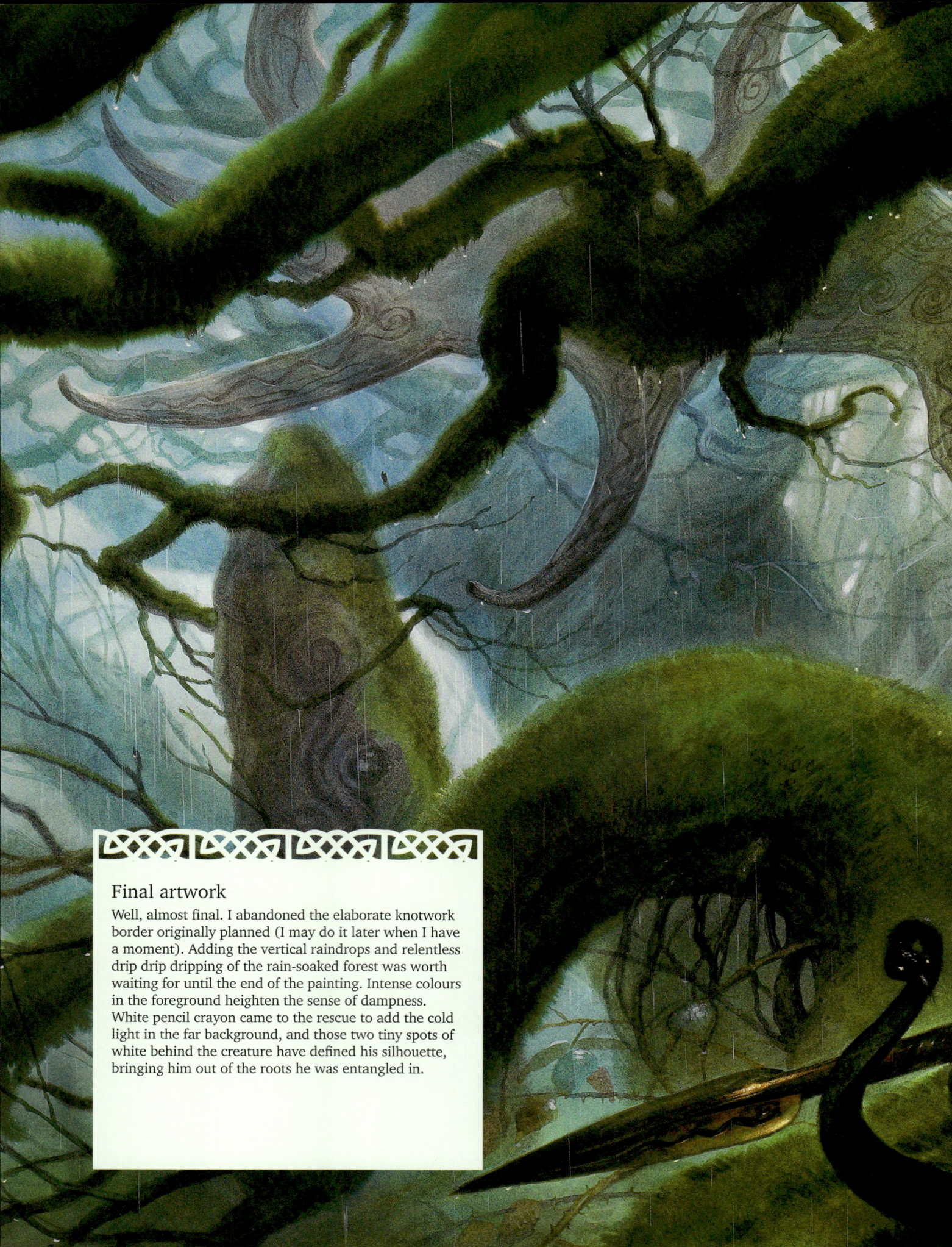

Final artwork

Well, almost final. I abandoned the elaborate knotwork border originally planned (I may do it later when I have a moment). Adding the vertical raindrops and relentless drip drip dripping of the rain-soaked forest was worth waiting for until the end of the painting. Intense colours in the foreground heighten the sense of dampness. White pencil crayon came to the rescue to add the cold light in the far background, and those two tiny spots of white behind the creature have defined his silhouette, bringing him out of the roots he was entangled in.

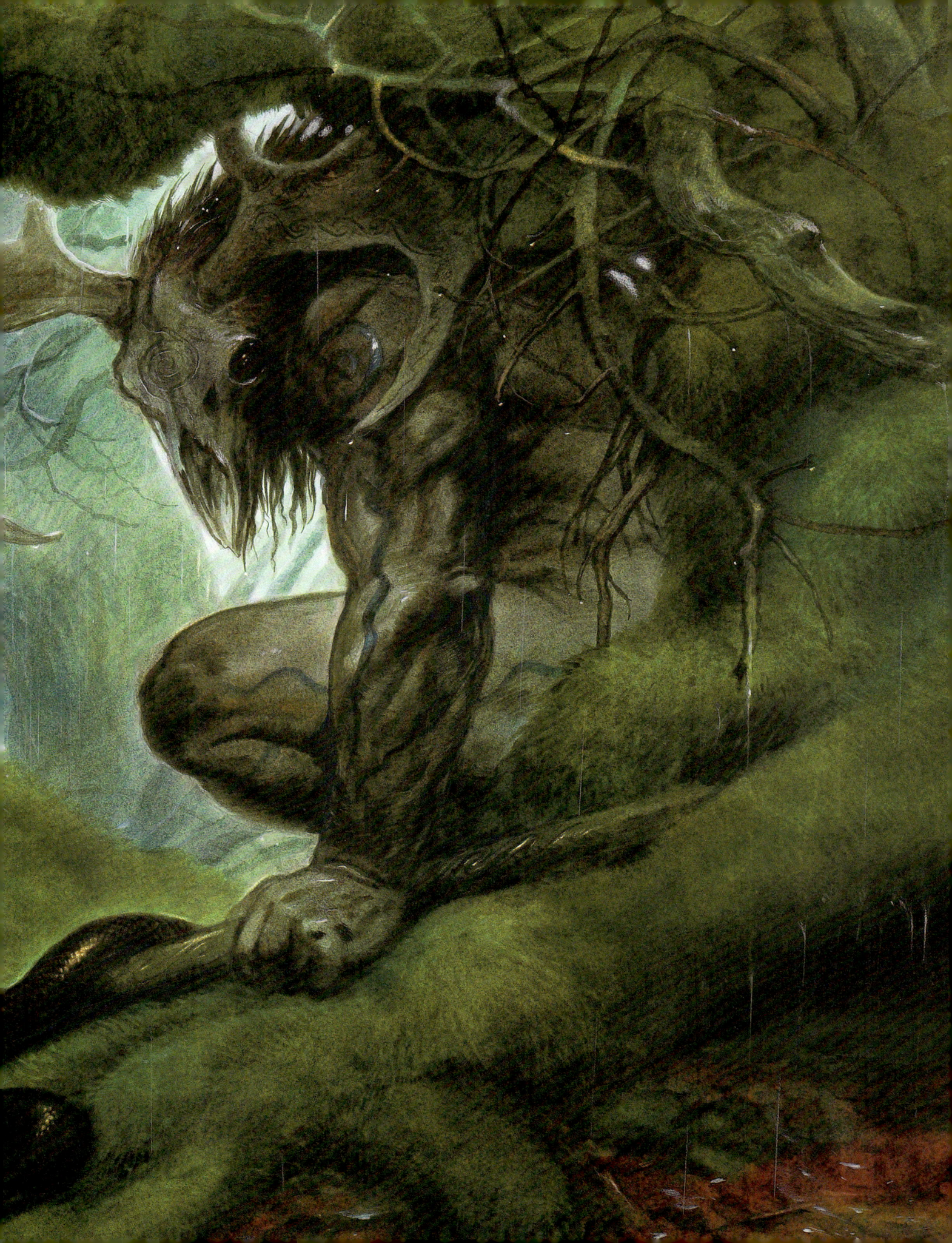

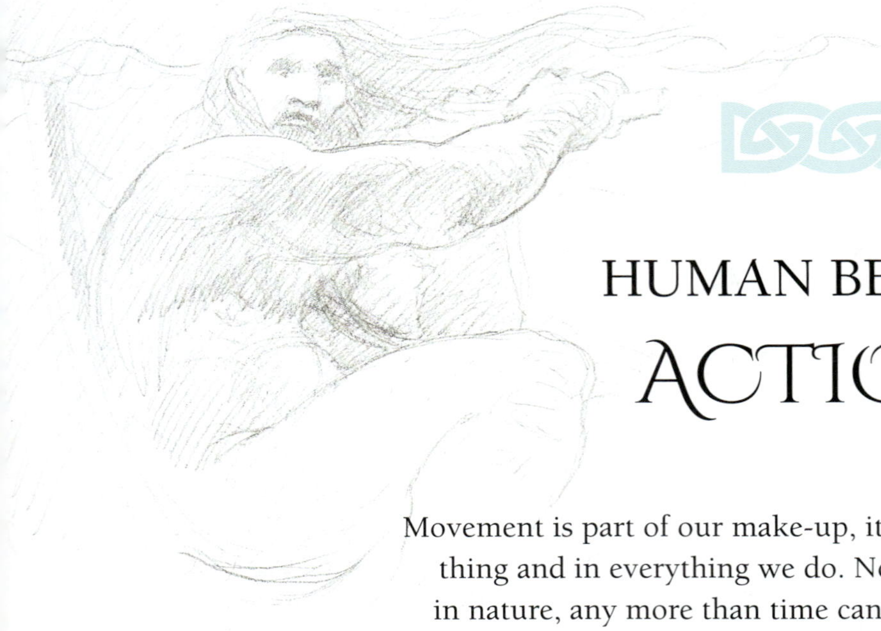

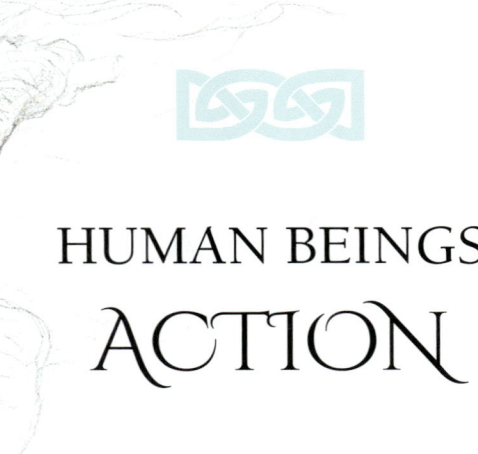

HUMAN BEINGS
ACTION

Movement is part of our make-up, it is inherent in every living
thing and in everything we do. Nothing is ever really still
in nature, any more than time can stand still, and we have
to reflect that in the drawings and paintings we make.

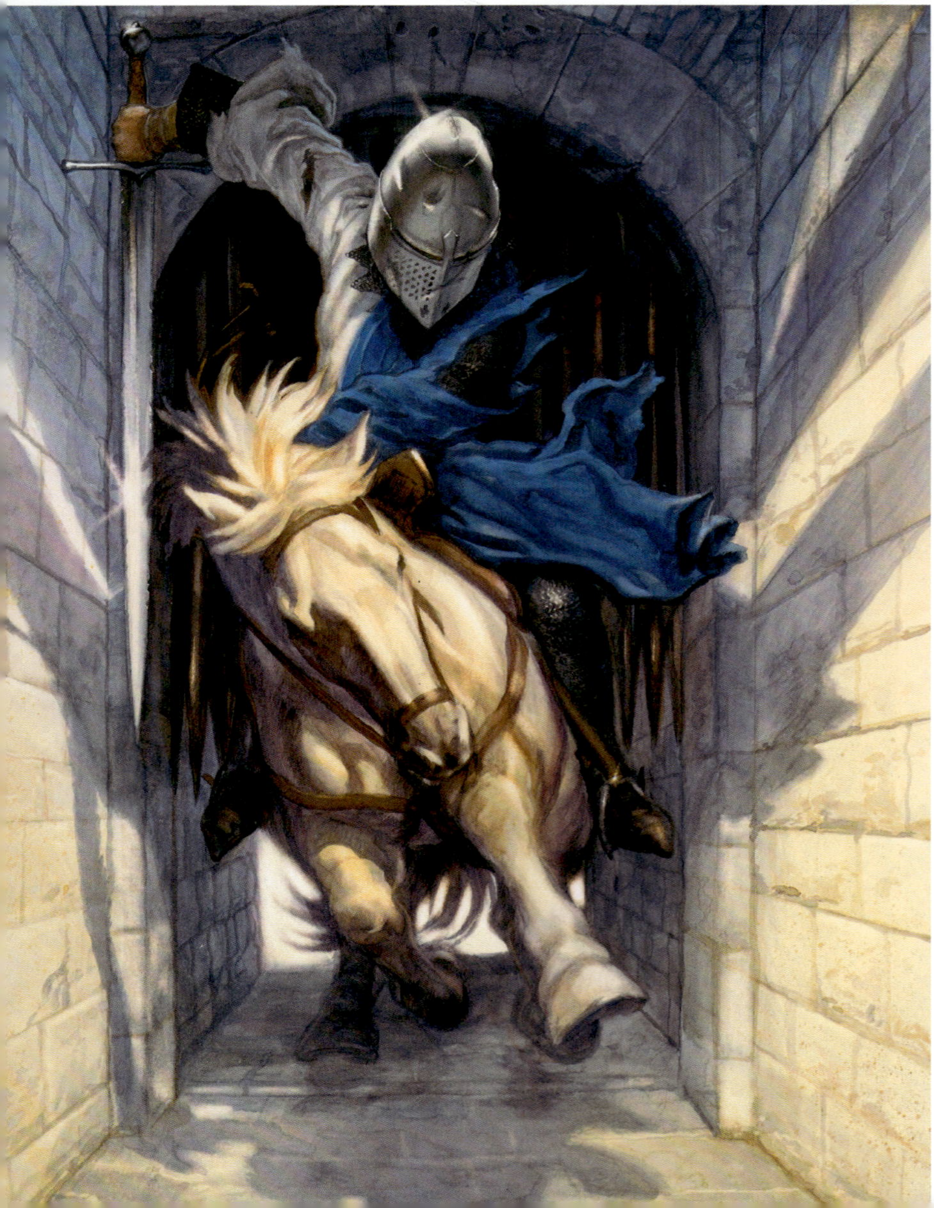

There are many ways to treat action. Photography has given us the ability to seize movements invisible to the eye, slowing and freezing them as we wish. More powerful than the action itself, however, is the split second that precedes it – the indrawing of breath or tensing of muscle that can contain the potential of the action. Rather than attempt to achieve split-second freeze frames in fantasy illustration, it is often more eloquent to convey the spirit of the movement more naturalistically, by leaving some things blurred by speed. I often find myself blurring hard edges, or blocking in forms with a wide brush and stopping short of providing more detail than the subject requires.

← Yvain's Escape

In the original story by Chrétien de Troyes, Yvain's horse is cut in two. That was judged a little grisly for children, so here the falling spikes just clip the heels. Everything is exaggerated, from the horse's pose to the impossibly long sword Yvain manages to wield while galloping madly down a narrow passage.

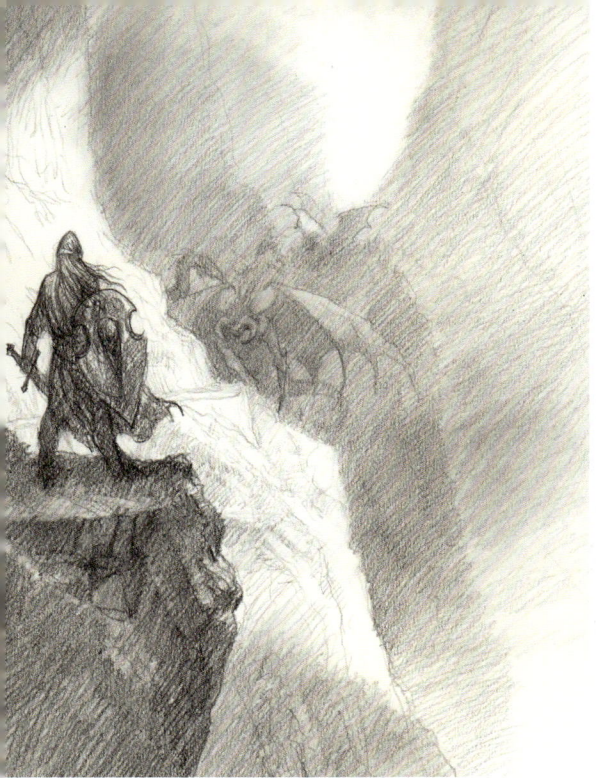

🌢 *The Flight from Gondolin*

An image like this is really about what is
about to happen. The action is contained
and suspended in the narrative: while the
protagonists are immobile, the confrontation
draws inexorably nearer.

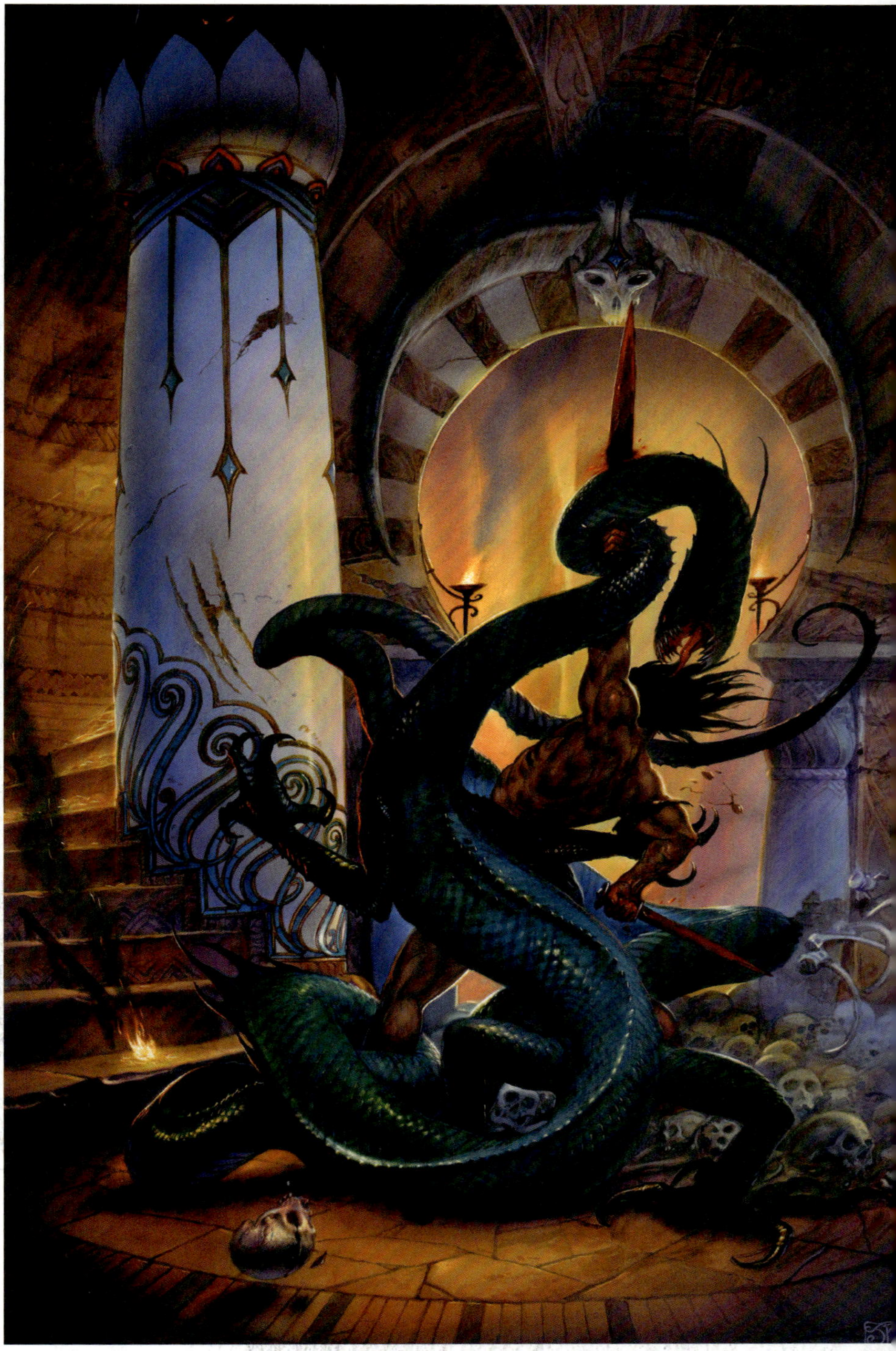

"MORE POWERFUL
THAN THE ACTION
ITSELF, HOWEVER, IS
THE SPLIT SECOND
THAT PRECEDES IT"

🌢 *The Slithering Shadow*

Fantasy stripped back to the bare bones – and muscles: barbarian versus
monster in an exotic setting. This is a stop-action image, everything
poised in mid-air, in mid-gesture. 'Freezing' movement is not a natural
process: movement can be arrested through an understanding of motion
and anatomy, though not with the clarity provided by photography or
slow-motion film sequences. Every detail added will 'slow' movement.

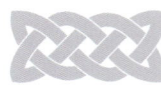

HUMAN BEINGS
WEAPONS & ARMOUR

Weapons are nasty sharp pointed things destined for one purpose only, but they contain a slim elegance and power that is forged in the metal itself. The lumpy, clumsy heave-aloft-and-bash swords of yore never really existed.

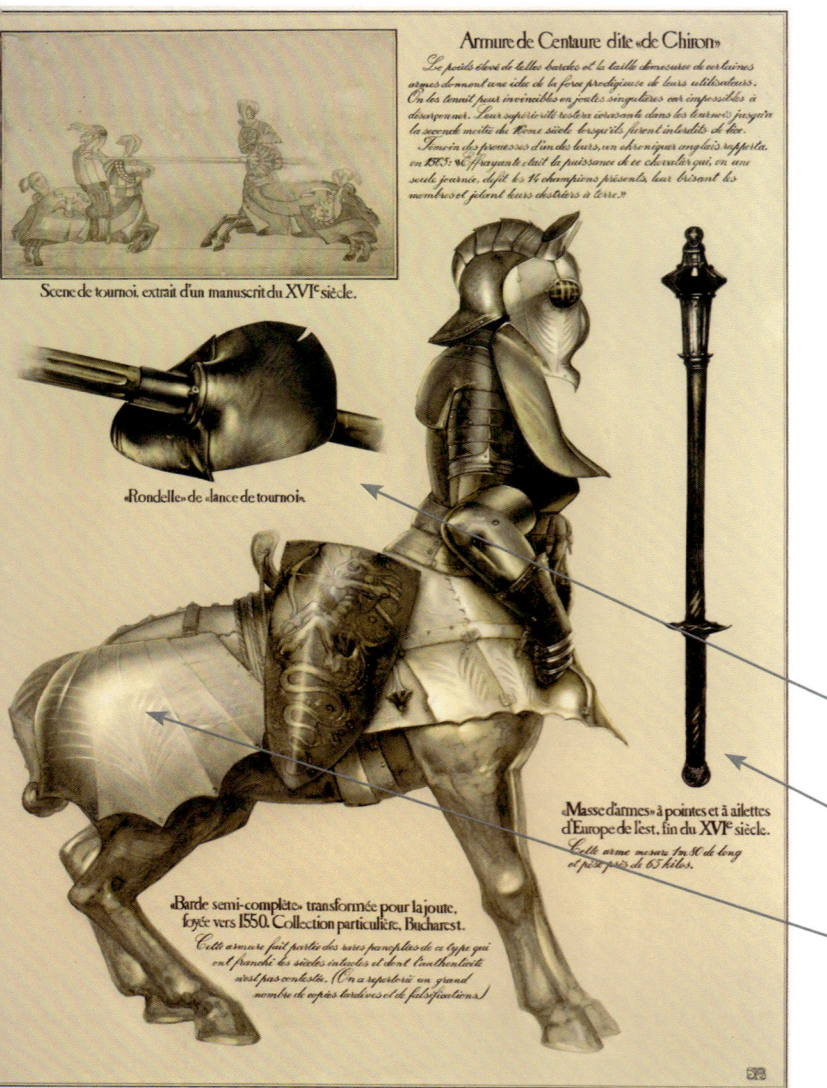

Armure de Centaure dite «de Chiron»

Le poids élevé de telles bardes et la taille démesurée de certaines armes donnent une idée de la force prodigieuse de leurs utilisateurs. On les tenait pour invincibles en joutes singulières car impossibles à désarçonner. Leur supériorité restera croissante dans les tournois jusqu'à la seconde moitié du XVème siècle lorsqu'ils furent interdits d'être. Témoin des prouesses d'un de leurs, un chroniqueur anglais rapporta en 1385: «Effrayante était la puissance de ce chevalier qui, en une seule journée, défit 14 champions pissants, leur brisant les membres et jetant leurs destriers à terre.»

Scène de tournoi, extrait d'un manuscrit du XVIᵉ siècle.

«Rondelle» de «lance de tournoi».

«Masse d'armes» à pointes et à ailettes d'Europe de l'est, fin du XVIᵉ siècle. *Cette arme mesure 1m 30 de long et pèse près de 65 kilos.*

«Barde semi-complète» transformée pour la joute, forgée vers 1550. Collection particulière, Bucharest.
Cette armure fait partie des rares panoplies de ce type qui ont franchi les siècles intactes et dont l'authenticité n'est pas contestée. (On a répertorié un grand nombre de copies tardives et de falsifications.)

The late medieval jousting helms encased a system of padding and straps as sophisticated as today's American football helmet. Weight and balance are key, but fantasy allows liberties, and a familiarity with real medieval weaponry adds believability. As metal plate doesn't stretch, armour will work or it won't. It doesn't stay on by magic. Straps, buckles and leather thongs secure it, so add them when you are blacksmithing. A sturdy garment was worn beneath armour as a foundation and to protect the body, from concussion and the armour itself. A working knowledge of styles and periods will help.

← *Centaur Armour*

An early 1980s painting in the style of 19th-century treatises on the art of war, which in turn was produced in imitation of Renaissance works. Horse armour reached extravagant proportions, sometimes encasing the whole animal.

✦ The rondel on the lance is taken from a book on jousting. The huge funnel-shaped guards are typical.

✦ Real war-hammers, axes and maces are surprisingly small – unlike film props. This one is exaggerated to fit the equine strength of the centaur.

✦ The hard edges of the metal and 'segmented' nature of armour mean that it lends itself well to repeated masking.

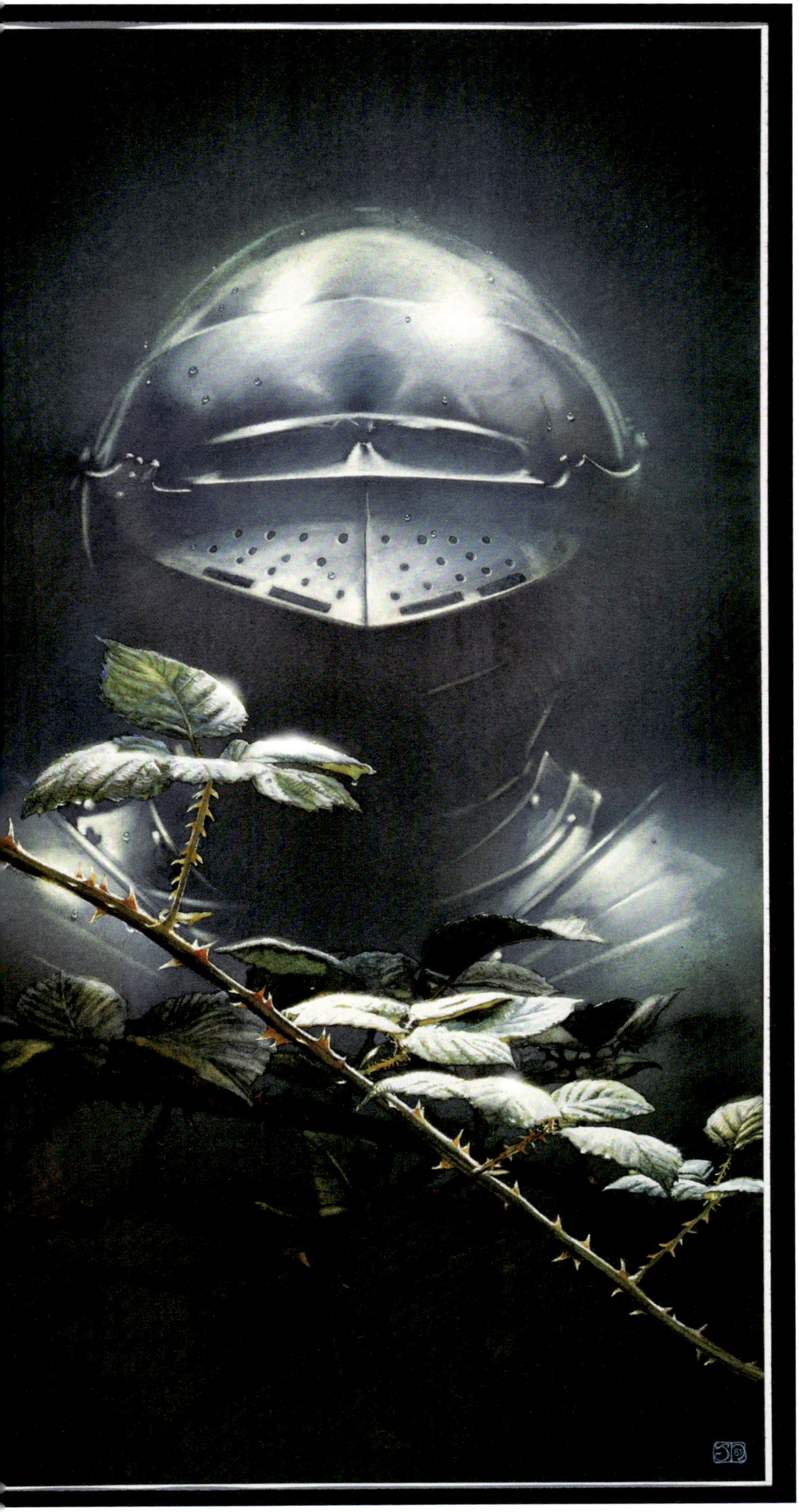

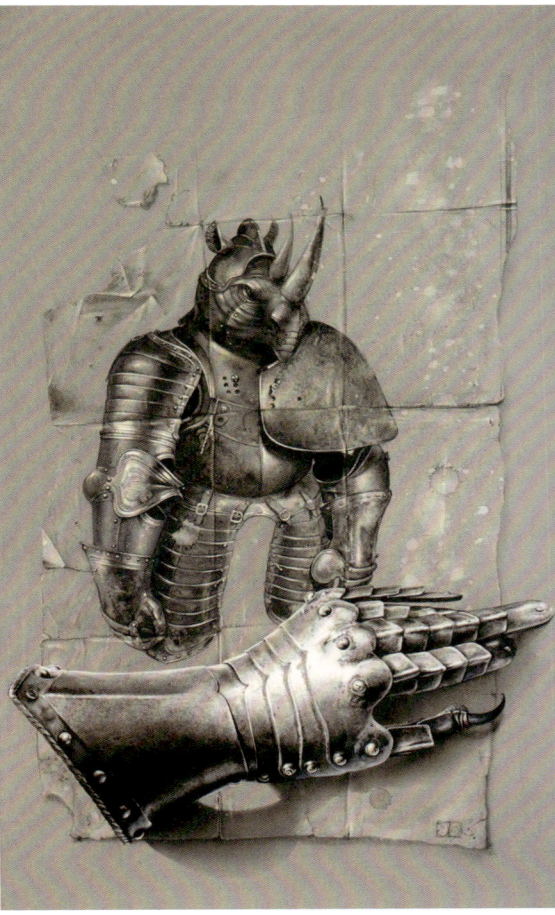

↑ Rhino Armour

I imagined these creatures in a fantastical sort of Thirty-Years-War Europe, carrying huge bronze muzzle-loading cannon, seconded by an artillery crew with powder and shot. Paintings often open up unexpectedly on worlds of their own. The gauntlet's clawed thumb was inspired by a raven's foot.

↩ Lancelot

Polished steel has a mirror-like surface, so an airbrush is often indispensable to obtain smooth curves, though in fact there is no airbrush work in this painting. Contrasts can be strikingly sharp, and mastering the highlights is as crucial as getting the shapes right. Like a mirror, armour will reflect a good deal of the atmosphere surrounding it. The armour itself is in the Paris Army Museum.

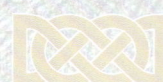

HUMAN BEINGS
FACES, EXPRESSIONS & HANDS

Faces and hands are understandably among
the hardest things to draw well, as they are
the features we know the most intimately.

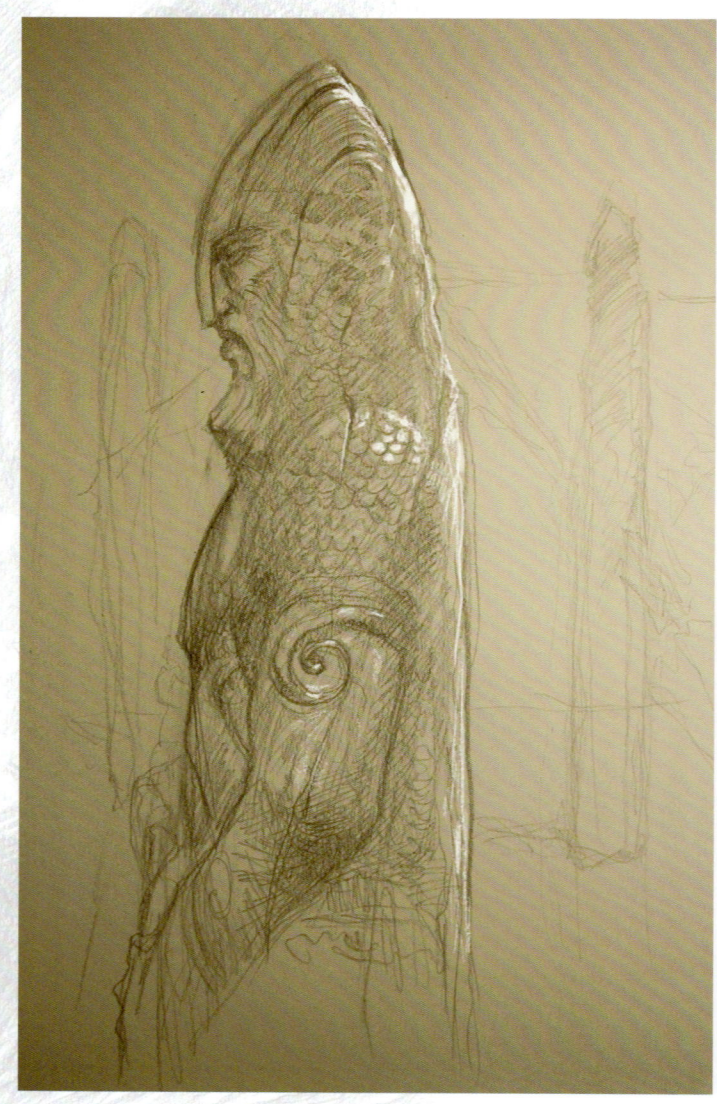

Mervyn Peake, author of the
Gormenghast trilogy and a renowned
illustrator, wrote in *The Craft of the
Lead Pencil*: 'The beginner doesn't
think in terms of "heads". He thinks of "faces".' It's easy
to forget that the features are anchored to the head, and
to think in terms of detail rather than volume. One of the
better ways to capture a face is to begin from the inside,
finding the foundations on which the features rest before
losing yourself in an accumulation of detail.

Heads and hands abound. Your friends may initially be
reluctant to pose; you may be reluctant to show them your
efforts, but persist. It can help if you are not consciously
drawing the person, but using them as a model for another
character, liberating you from the task of producing a
'faithful' likeness.

➤ *Pillars of Heorot*

This is a sketch for a film project based on the tale of
Beowulf. Attempting to emulate sculpture from another
period and culture is a revealing exercise. It is very hard
to keep modern realism from intruding, and to keep
sophistication at bay. The face and figure on the Viking
post have been reduced to simple forms.

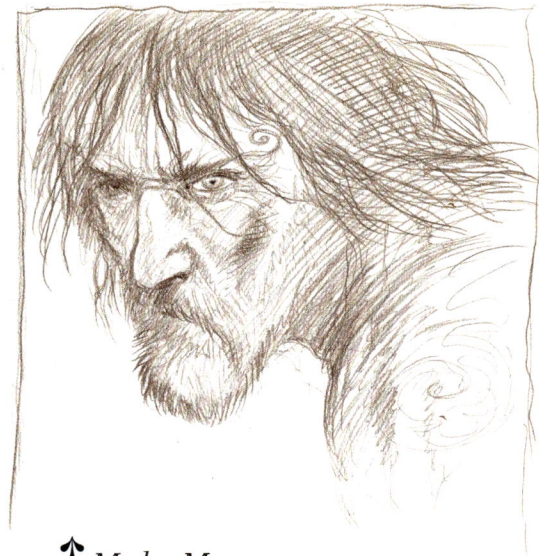

Me by Me

Most illustrators insert themselves into imagery here and there. I have a soft spot for Boromir – failed heroes are always more interesting. Occasionally the inner dilemmas of a character make you take on all manner of expressions, and from there it is a short step to ending up in the drawing yourself. This Wild Man is very much me, except for the tattooed brow.

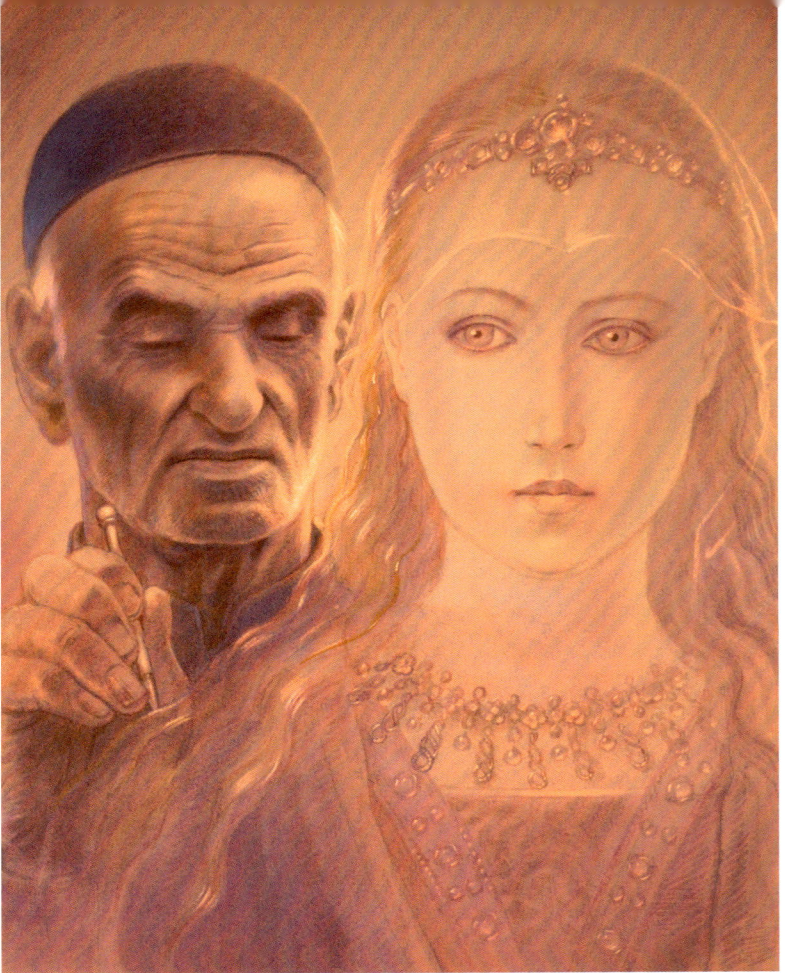

The Glass Princess

Characters from *The Abandoned City* by Claude Clément, drawn from very different models. The glassblower is my wife's father; the princess is based on the 15th-century painter Hans Memling's *Reliquary of Saint Ursula* in Bruges. *The Statue*, from *La Ville Abandonnée*, John Howe © CASTERMAN S.A.

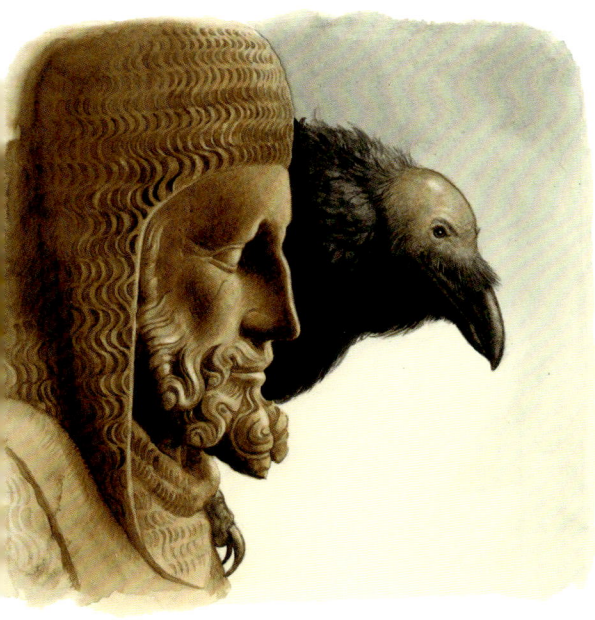

King and Crow

The profile of the King is taken straight from a statue once on Strasbourg Cathedral (now replaced by a reproduction). Medieval faces are often disconcerting to modern eyes, but contain an inherent elegance that it is worthwhile trying to understand and capture.

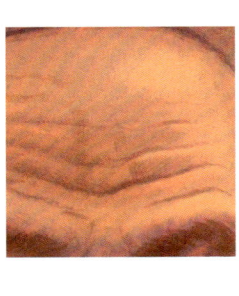

✦ Concentration that widens the eyes and wrinkles the forehead, rather than narrowing them and knitting the brows, indicates application to the subject without attempting to dominate it.

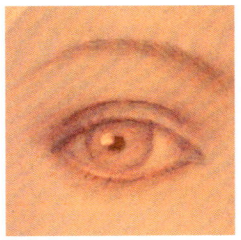

✦ The eyes in the original painting are downcast, but it was important to have them looking out of the picture with the ambiguous, unfocused gaze of a statue coming to life.

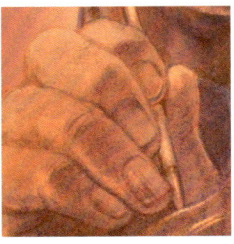

✦ This is my hand, drawn by looking in a mirror. Hands are better achieved by thinking first in terms of volume before tracing careful contours.

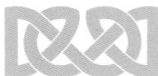

HUMAN BEINGS
HAIR & COSTUME

Clothes may not make the man, but for fantasy beings, they certainly help. Convincing costume is fundamental to well-dressed mythological individuals, or they will not be perceived as 'real'.

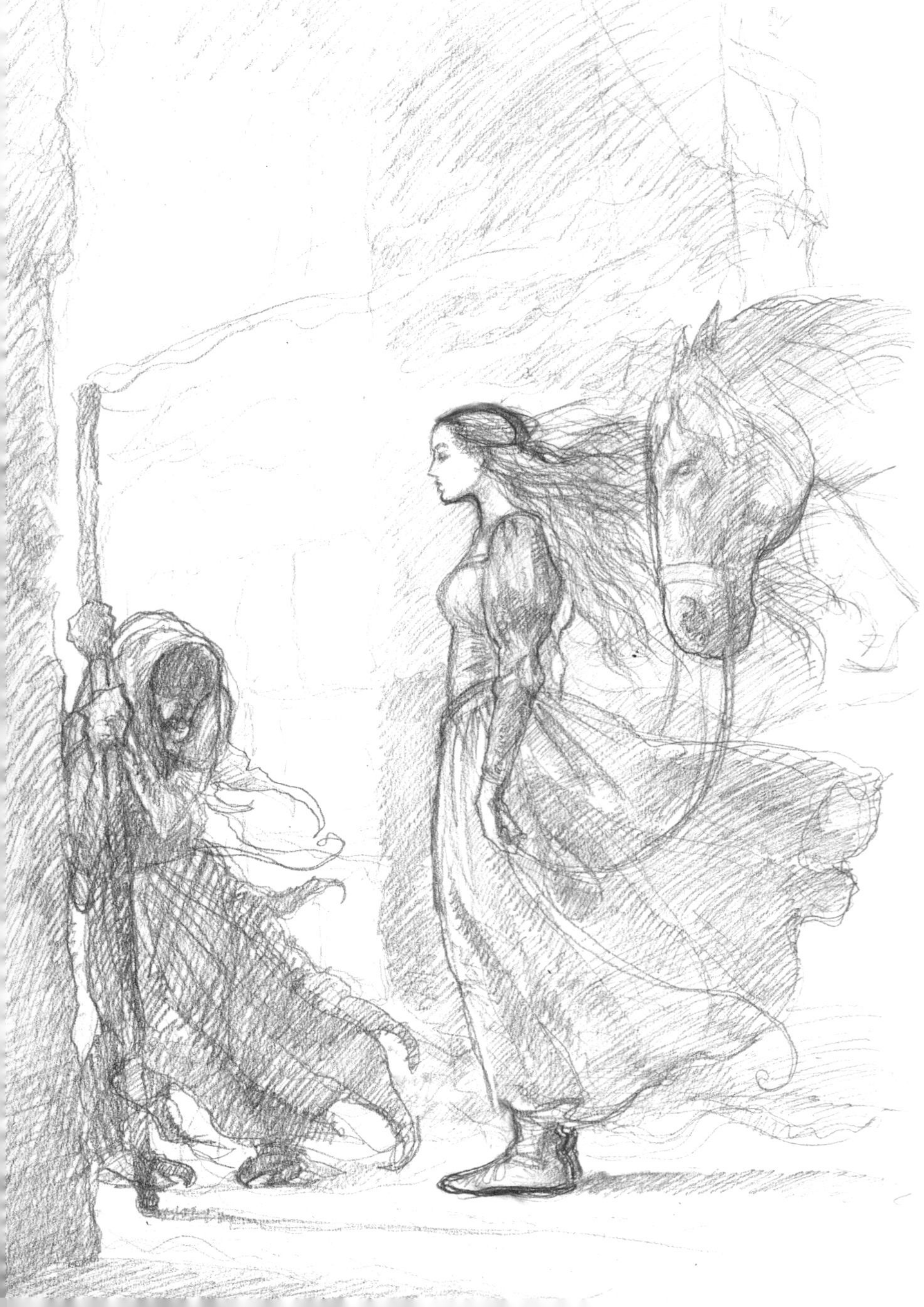

Once again, there is no substitute for the real thing. Spend time in museums, take home catalogues, learn to appreciate period images and take photos if allowed. But try to sketch on the spot. Photos, although a useful additional reference, may not show clearly enough how costume actually works. Even a quick sketch will help you remember when it comes to using it in a picture.

Hair is obviously impossible to paint, all one can do is suggest it, getting the brightness in the right place and making sure that the volumes and state of the hair (wind-blown, in motion, wet, dry) are captured. The viewers' imagination will do the rest.

⬅ The Limbreth Gate

Sketch for a book cover. It was important to convey the heroine's tight-lipped determination and readiness to step into the unknown through the Limbreth Gate. The billowing dress and hair add to the tension, as if there was a difference of pressure between her world and the one beyond the wall, making the passage more than just taking a few simple steps.

◆ Only orcs and down-at-heel bandits wear rusty metal. Soldiers spend time cleaning their armour. Polished steel can be like a mirror, so rendering it means mastering sometimes startling reflections.

◆ Methods for painting metal vary with the light and location. The volumes of armour are done with an airbrush, and highlights with a scalpel and hard eraser.

◆ Rendering chain mail can be irksome: alternating lines of closely packed 'c' strokes is one method. Adding highlights at the end helps. It is not cloth – it hangs heavily so the weight should be apparent.

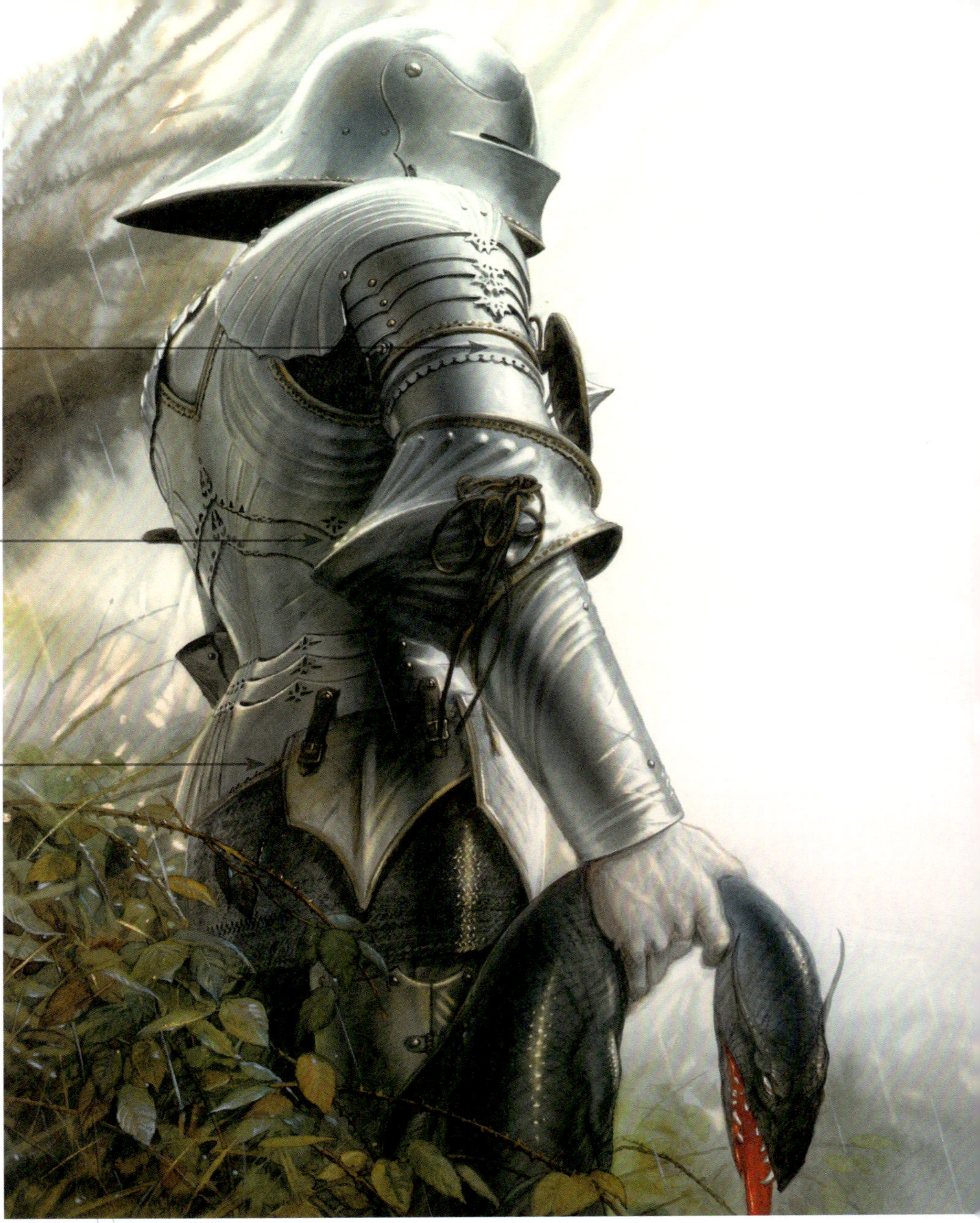

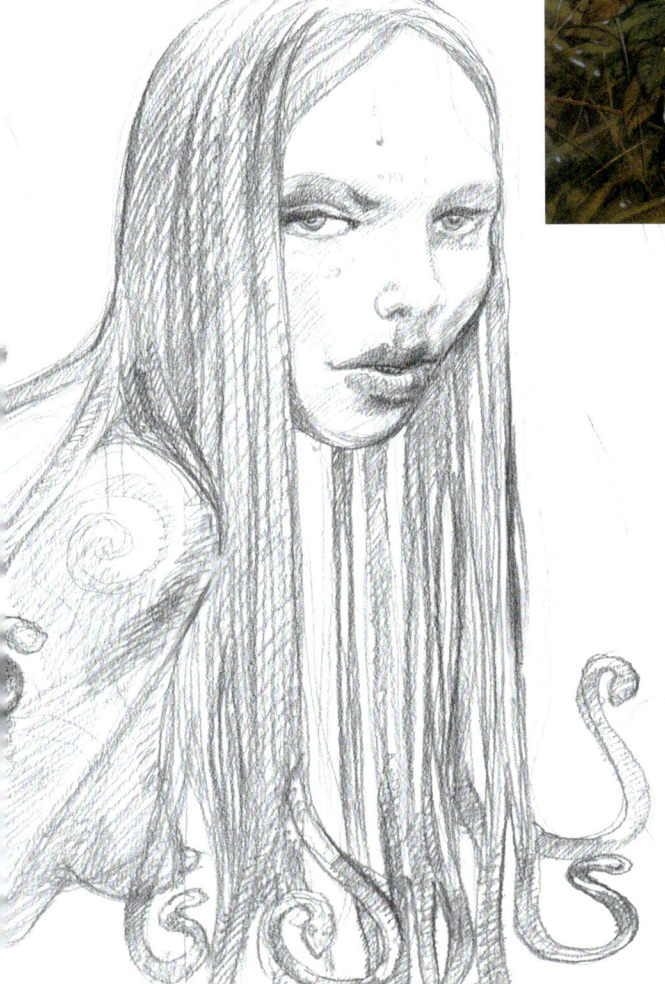

⬩ Lancelot

The armour is done from a photo. (That's me inside – I am skinny enough to fit into most armour, which is handy.) Beware of armour displayed in museums: unless strapped to a life-size, properly proportioned figure, they may be sitting wrong and be misleading. Modern reproductions rarely get the proportions right, so also beware of photos of re-enactors unless their costume is impeccable. This armour, a 19th-century copy of a 15th-century harness, belongs to a friend.

← Medusa

There is something disquieting about a snake held by the tip of the tail; even when hanging limply, the head is always level, and the snake ready to tense. That seemed more hair-like and more apt for this seductive Medusa than a halo of writhing serpents.

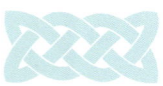

HUMAN BEINGS
TOM BADGERLOCK

Occasionally I'm lucky enough to have a real person and book character coincide, the real person here a circus strongman in the South of France. When he had finished breathing fire, breaking chains and rolling on broken glass, I asked if I could take photos. Years later, when illustrating covers for Robin Hobb, everything fell into place: I had my Tom Badgerlock.

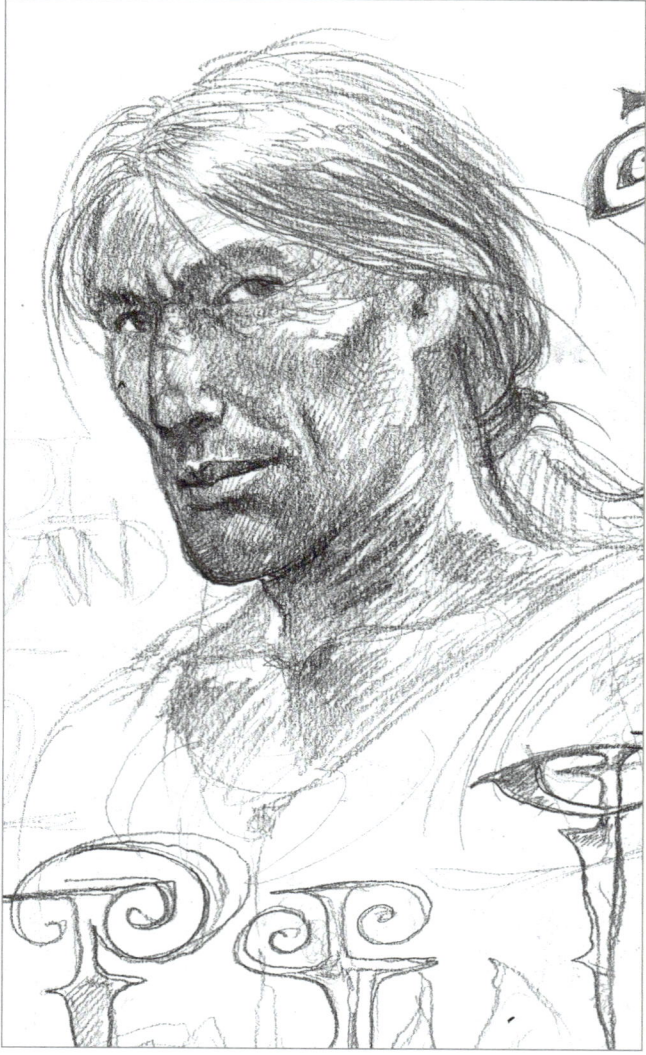

⬅ Sketch

The first sketch is from several years ago, when I did the cover of Robin Hobb's *The Golden Fool* (*see* Book Cover Illustration). A page full of doodles ended up featuring a sketch of FitzChivalry, or Tom Badgerlock as he is called later in the novels. For the rest of the figure, a friend posed: I did thumbnail sketches and took photos. The arming doublet is his, the rest of the gear is mine.

Age-old question

Consider stage of life inhabited by your character. Here, he is in his late thirties or early forties, still unafraid to fight and confident in his skills, but possibly pondering on the wisdom of it all. I would happily do a series of portraits from youth to old age. It is unusual to find such complexity and depth in a fictional character. (And next time I'll get the colour of his eyes right – Robin Hobb tells me they are dark, not blue.)

Stage 1
Groundwork

A picture that consists of such independent elements has really no logical step-by-step methodology. When working with detailed figures, I prefer to reverse the order and work from front to back, rather than masking off an element before I'm really sure where it will go. In this case, many of the elements shifted place several times.

Stage 2
Foreground first

This step may not actually be a logical one – it could have come a little earlier or a while later. I did want the picture to be contrasted, hence the early blocking in of the shadows. At this point, much is still undecided, especially in the background. A painting at this point is very unsatisfying, and it can be hard to maintain a view of the whole and not to let the paint-by-number reflexes take over. This means doing quite a lot of work on reflected light, filling cold shadows with warm sidelights and generally trying to sculpt and situate the volumes within the space of the image.

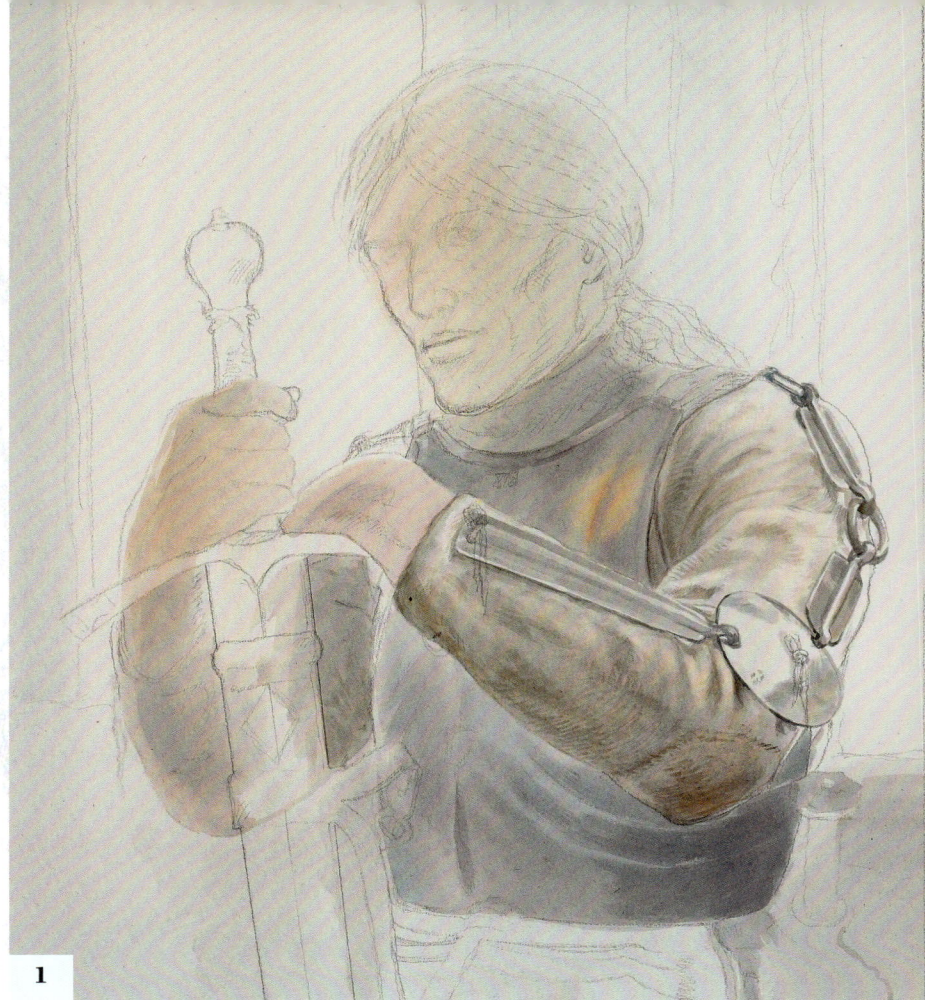

1

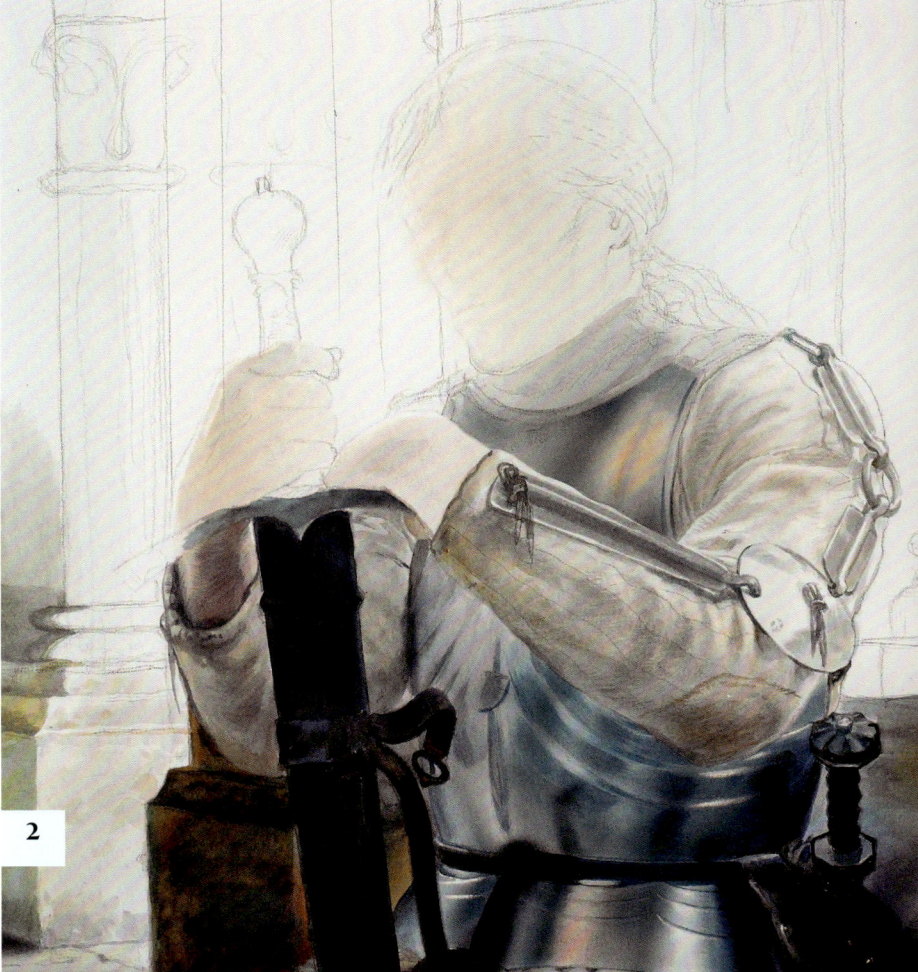

2

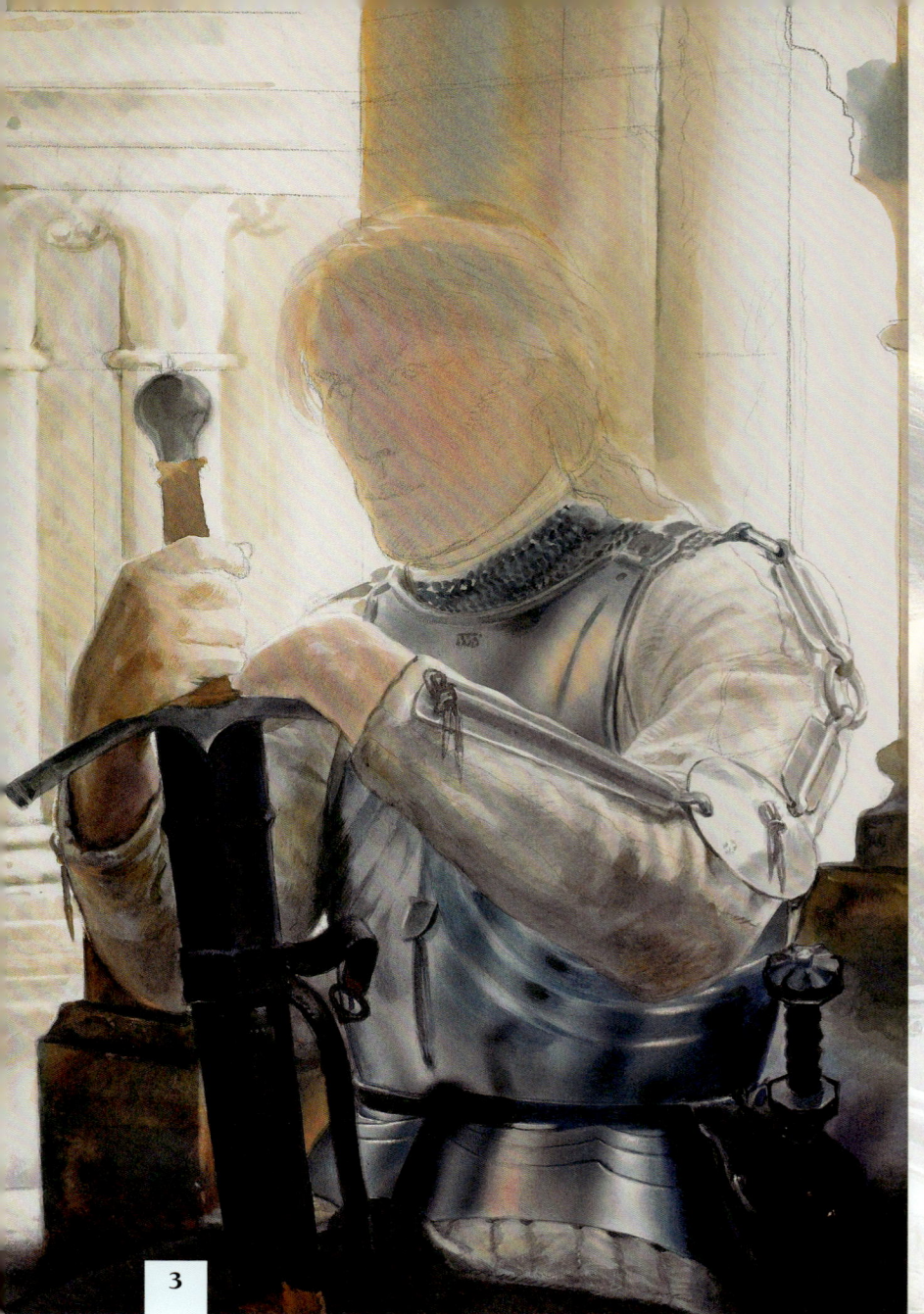

3

Stage 3
Working backwards

The background has almost resolved itself, but the face is awful. Sketching in faces with pencil is something I rarely manage convincingly, and the picture is even more unsatisfying at this point, as the mix of near-finished elements throws attention on the blank spots. Actually, the slightly haphazard approach is simply to defer making decisions. The haphazard defining of detail after detail slowly builds the atmosphere and the place (the castle of Buckkeep, in this case, the site of much of the novels' action), which in turn makes the 'encounter' with Fitz possible.

This sounds precious and esoteric, but it really is like stalking wildlife. Saving the face until last means that by the time I arrive at that point, I know what expression and features are required to convey my thoughts on the character. (This is, admittedly, what happens in an ideal world – not only is it not possible with every commission, but one can also easily miss the mark.)

↪ Final artwork

Tom Badgerlock is an ambiguous and reluctant hero, a puppet of causes and powers both beyond and within him. His gear is well worn – missing point ends, scabbard broken and repaired with the knife and file gone, breastplate marked, sword with worn grip and matt pommel, with the crossguard broken and re-forged – signs of trustworthy but well-used equipment. His face has scars, and his expression, well, I tried to catch my own mixed feelings about his place in the novels: something of resignation without submission, of loss without defeat, of strength and doubt.

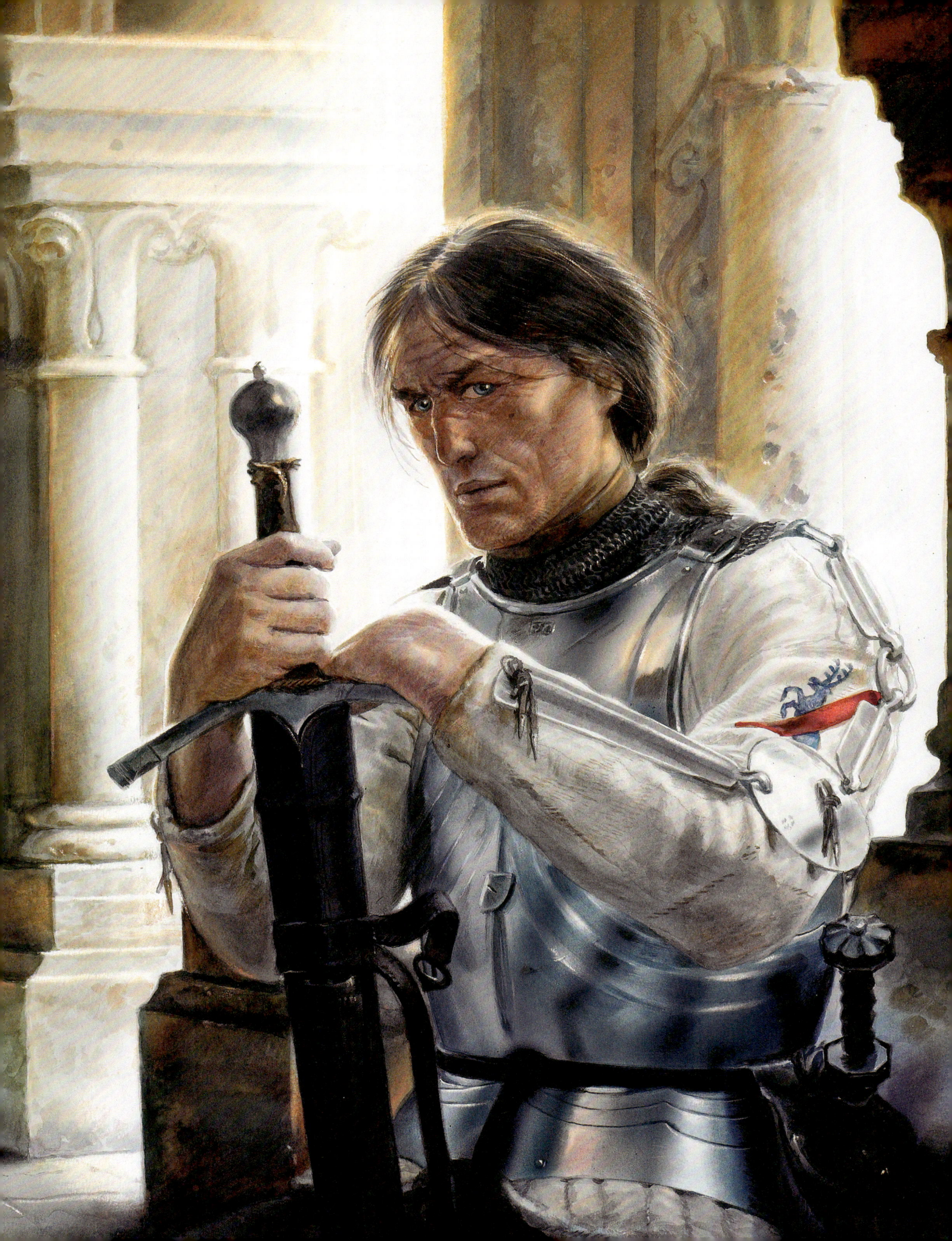

FANTASY BEASTS
APPROACHES & INSPIRATION

I often wonder about what we call 'collective consciousness' in relationship to beings that do not exist outside the realms of imagination.

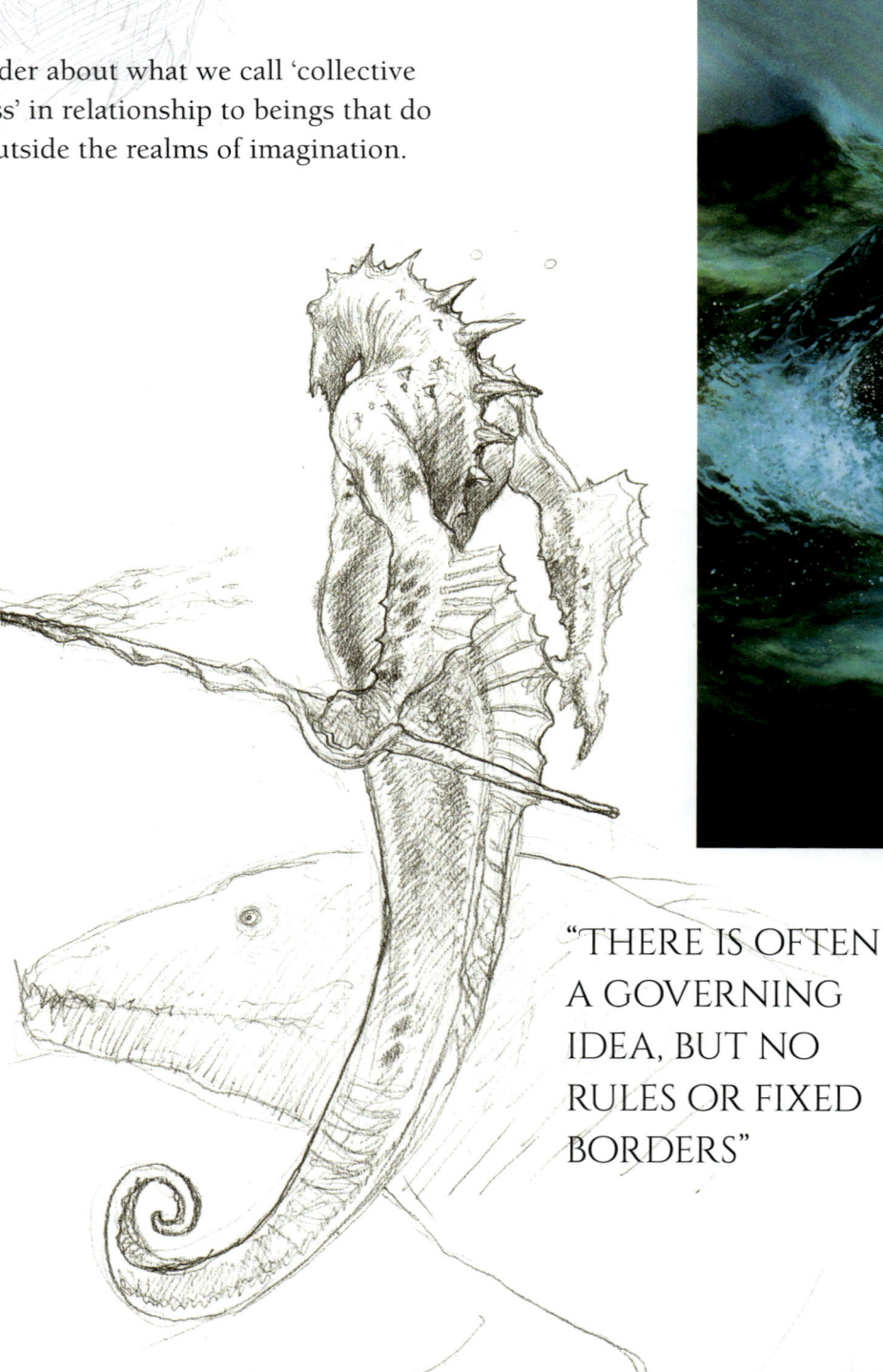

Throughout time, it seems, humans have filled the spaces they cannot explore with creatures drawn from fears and hopes. But myth-history is just a point of departure; the only limits are those of the imagination. I could say, 'Unicorns are often described as slim horses, with cloven hooves and a horn on their foreheads', but never 'To draw a unicorn, start with …'. Formulae should be banished from fantasy. There is often a governing idea, but no rules or fixed borders. A regrettable tendency towards inherited stereotypes that capture none of the incredible diversity of fantasy creatures can transform them into a resumé of typology rather than individuals. I often find my pencil stopping mid-stroke, and wonder why I am drawing the way I am. The pencil is often obeying convention and habit rather than innovation and originality – a good time to get out the fantasy eraser and begin anew.

"THERE IS OFTEN A GOVERNING IDEA, BUT NO RULES OR FIXED BORDERS"

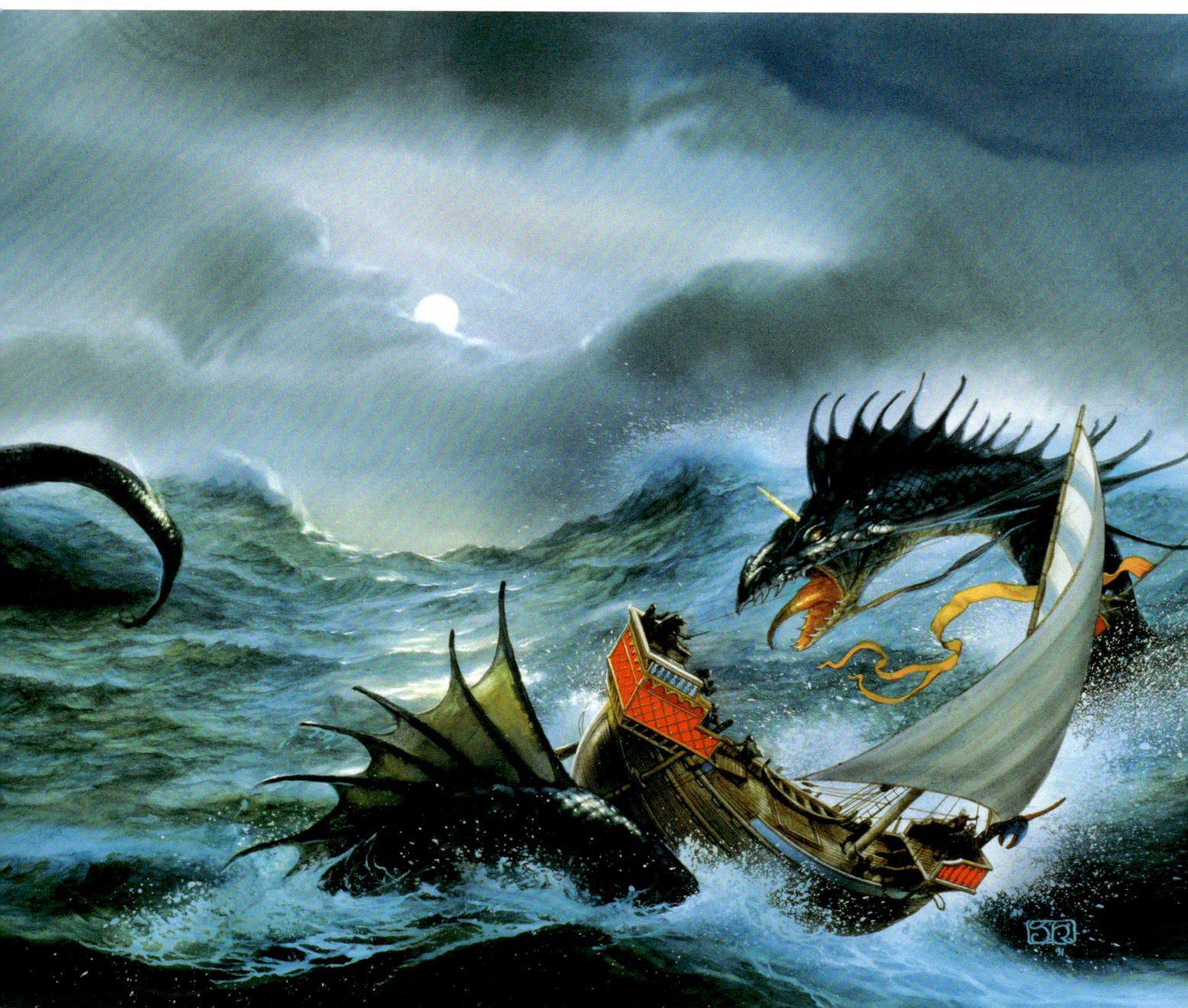

⬅ *Seahorse Sketch*

A summer sketchbook doodle. I do
my best to do one sketch per day
whenever we are away. Usually there
is a moment of idleness that can be
turned into a few lines. If centaurs
exist, then why not sea-centaurs?

⬆ *The Wandering Fire*

This is by far my favourite cover of Guy Gavriel Kay's
Fionavar trilogy. I keep a collection of photos of large marine
mammals for the manner in which they break the surface of
the water, and another drawer full of photos of snakes for
scales. A snake's body is never simply round, like a sausage,
it is a sinuous continuum of intersecting lines of force. A few
highlights on scales help make the creature come alive.

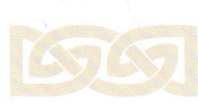

FANTASY BEASTS
TALONS, WINGS, FANGS & FIRE

Fantasy creatures often have family trees stretching back beyond history. The concepts may be universal, but their applications are myriad. Many live exclusively in folklore, under one particular bridge, or in a certain tree; others go by a hundred names in as many places and times.

Today's illustrators can be worthy successors of medieval illuminators, who filled manuscript margins with vouivres, sciapods, blemmyae and cynocephali. The genesis of fantasy beasts has often followed a complex path. Bestiaries were one of the grand inventions of the Middle Ages. Many archetypal beasts that haunt the edges of the world appeared there – unicorns, manticores, amphisbaenae, ant-lions and others – continue to be depicted by artists over the centuries.

Modern fantasy has conscientiously revisited archetypes, transforming, extrapolating, rationalizing (applying 'scientific' reasoning) and grandly expanding the genre. Their fantastical nature, which need not obey the laws of biology, allows for some cut-and-paste freedom, a welcome respite from bestowing 'convincibility' on fantasy. Hairy, scaly, clawed and feathered, the palette of textures required is enough to make you want to spend time in the nearest natural history museum. They are the perfect excuse to study real animals and build your reference portfolio. For example, the apparent weightlessness of flying creatures means a lot of pushing heartily and repeatedly downwards. Wings are exquisite creations of nature – careful attention to their real-world form will lend credibility to an illustration.

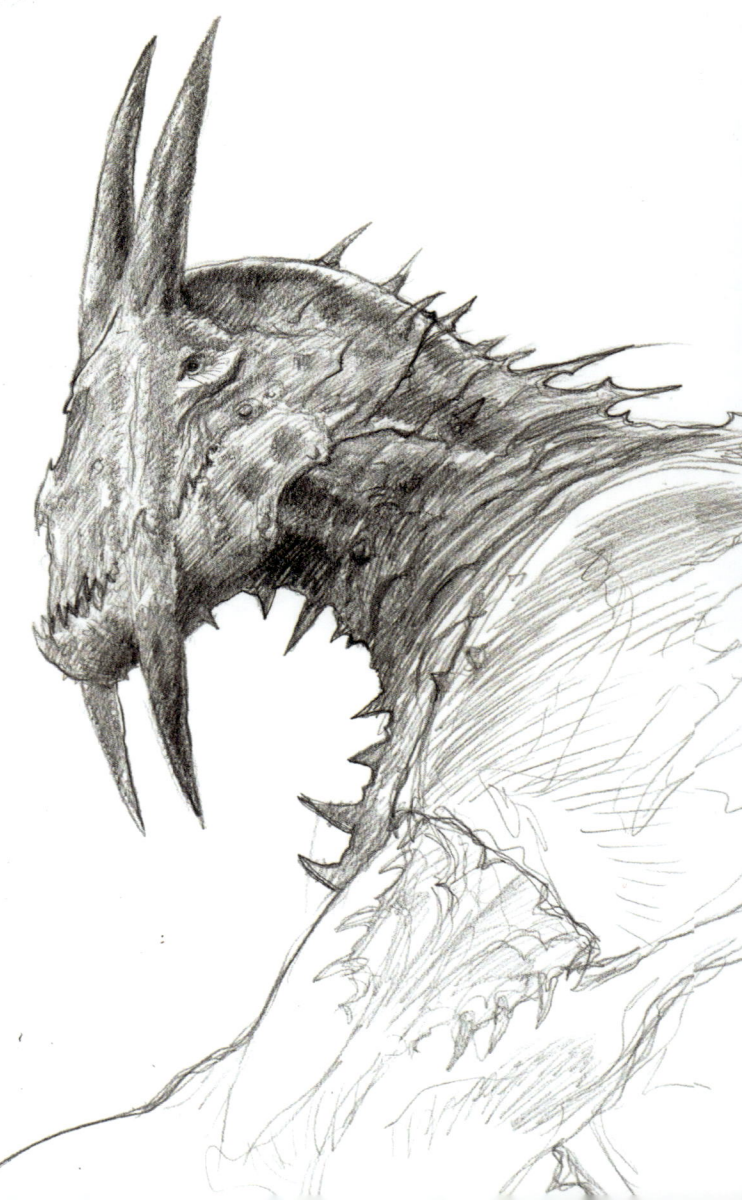

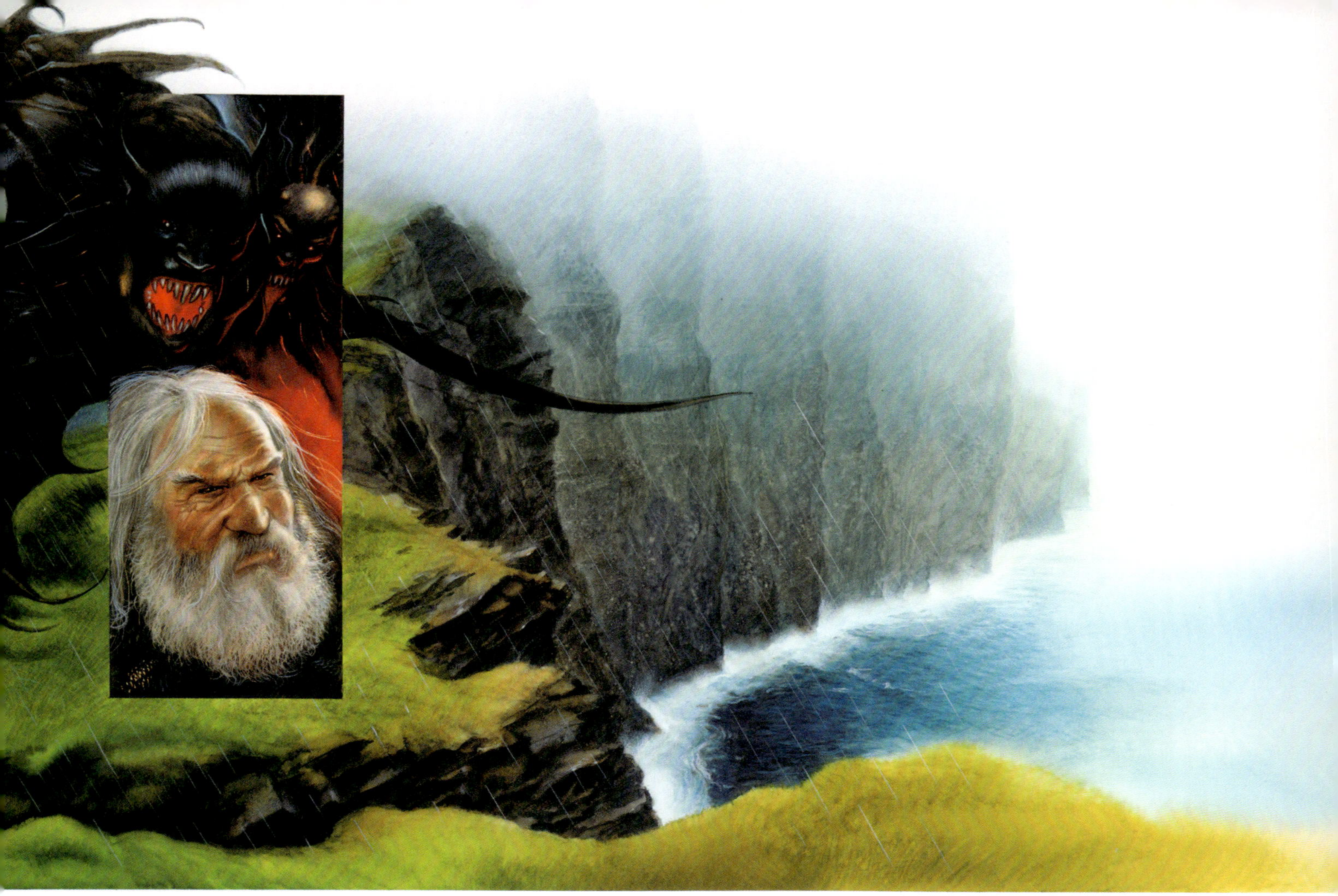

☝ The Dragon Comes

Beowulf is now old, his strength gone. He must now confront the dragon, knowing it may be his last battle. I wanted to sum up his life in the vignette – the legacy of the creatures he vanquished, and his reluctant resolution when faced with a new threat. I imagine the dragon sweeping in low over the sea before rising and skimming the cliff tops to alight and spread destruction.

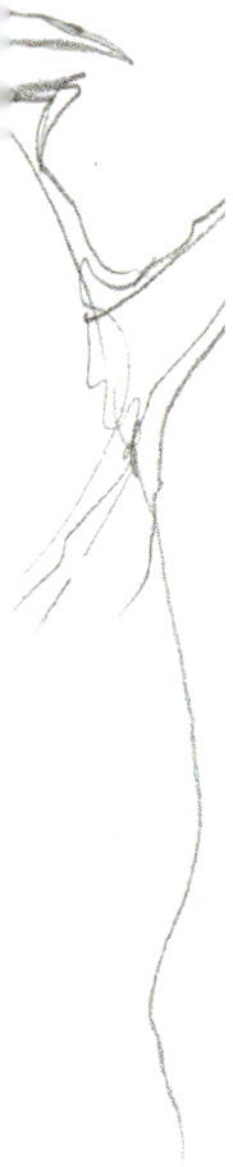

⬅ Quay Sketch

The Quay are an alien race designed for a card game. When small, my son would wear two Batman masks at once, with one upside down, transforming ears into fangs. An interesting idea, I thought at the time. Much later, the idea sparked the Quay design process. *Quay* © Decipher Inc.

➡ Grendel Sketch

Taking time over a theme lets your mind wander; ideas occur 'en route', here the tattoo-like scars from wrestling with fire-snakes. The face is a cross between a sea otter and a lamprey. *See* Digital Workflow for a digitally rendered version.

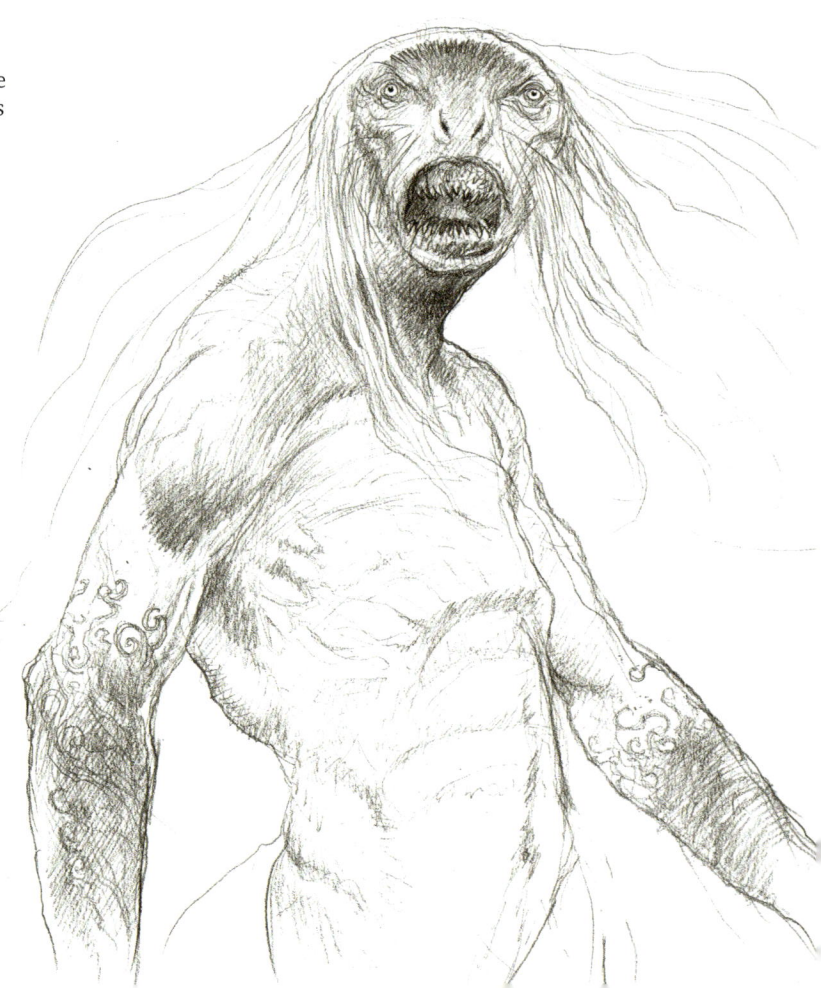

The bone structure of a bat's wing is not dissimilar to a human arm, with a few notable modifications, especially in the 'hand' and length of the fingers, so you can use your own arm as a basis. I have tried to borrow stuffed creatures and animal skulls from the local museum, but they didn't seem to trust me (I should never have mentioned the word 'dragon'). But your luck may be better. Birds are harder due to all the feathers in the way, but there are more books on birds than on bats, and if you have a falconer among your acquaintances, you have a ready-made supply of subjects.

➜ Earthsea

The hero of Ursula Le Guin's *Earthsea* novels visits a land ruled by dragons. Marine iguanas and the Galapagos Archipelago were my inspiration. The clouds were blocked out with a brush, then masked off to equalize the sky behind with the airbrush. To mask them, I took a single layer from a sheet of paper towel, sprayed it with repositionable glue, then tore it into small pieces to lay over the existing clouds. The ragged, fibrous edges make natural-looking cloud edges.

⬇ Quay Sketch

The full body of the Quay alien in 'battle mode'. The game developer wanted a transformed version of the creature for gladiatorial combat. This rough sketch establishes the anatomy and proportions. *Quay* © Decipher Inc.

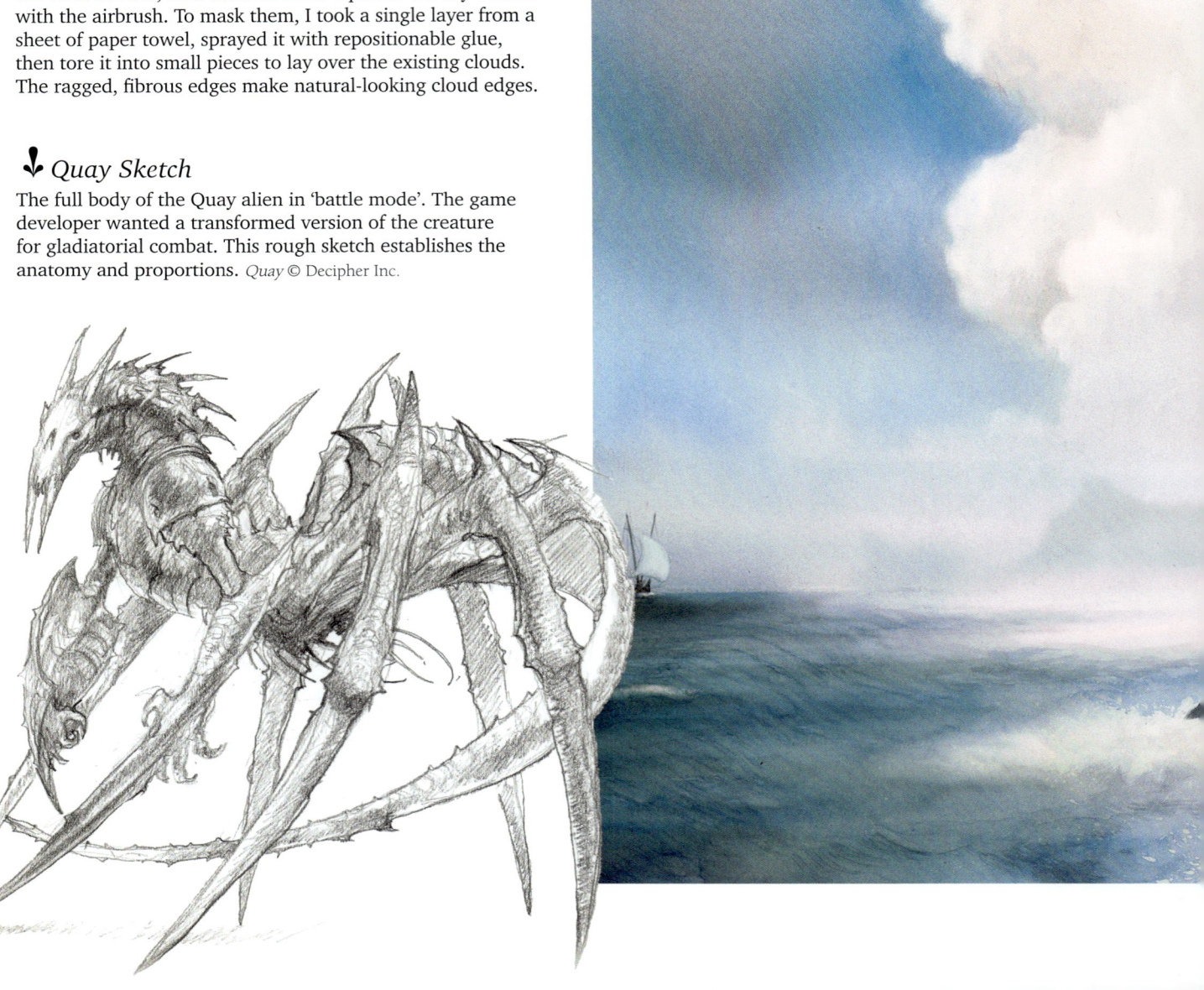

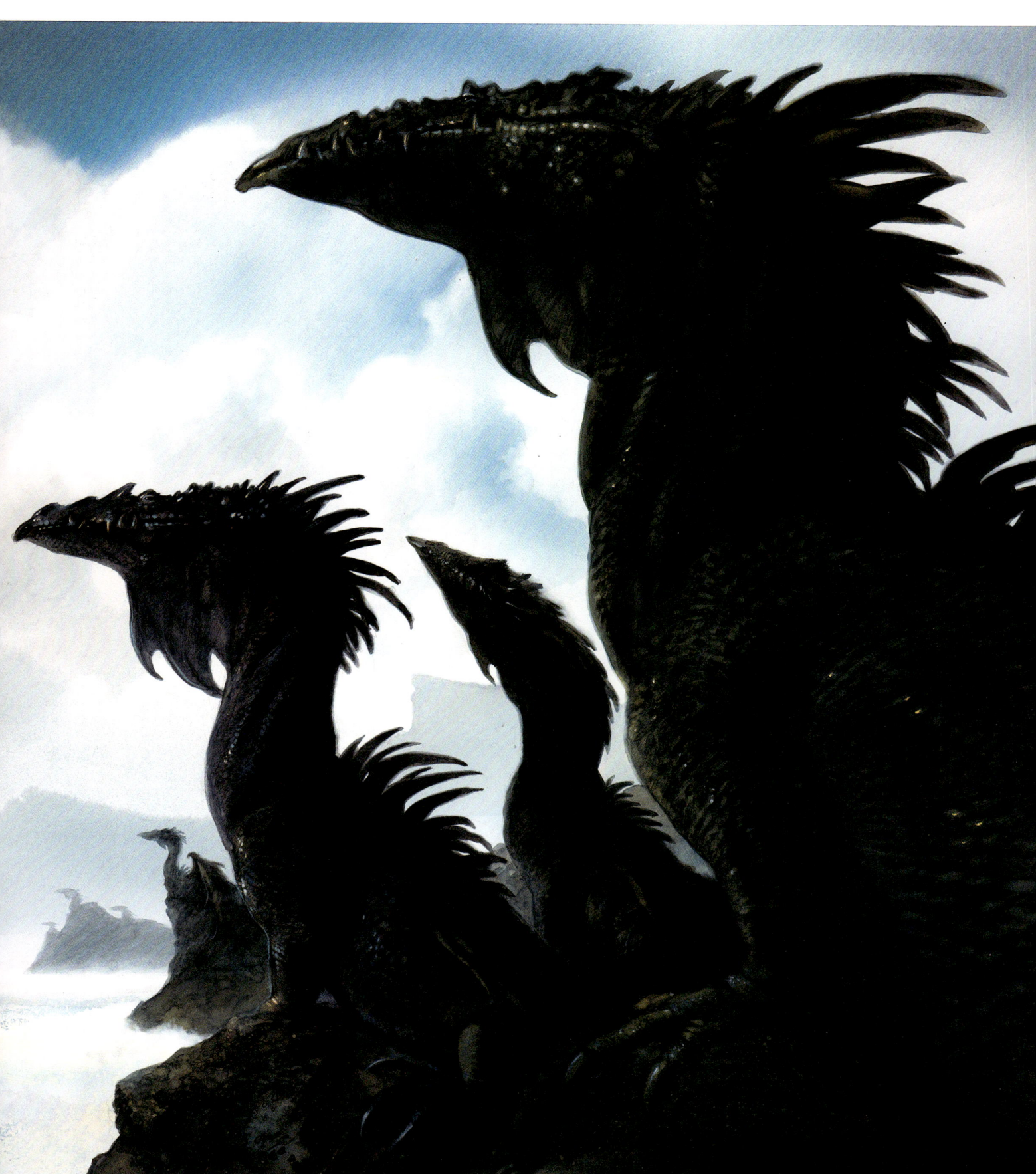

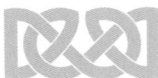

FANTASY BEASTS
NOBLE ANIMALS

Some creatures hold a particular fascination. They may be familiars
of the gods, like Hugin and Munin soaring above Odin in his guise as
a hooded traveller, or objects of desire such as unicorns, hunted as if
such beauty must be possessed even at the cost of its destruction.

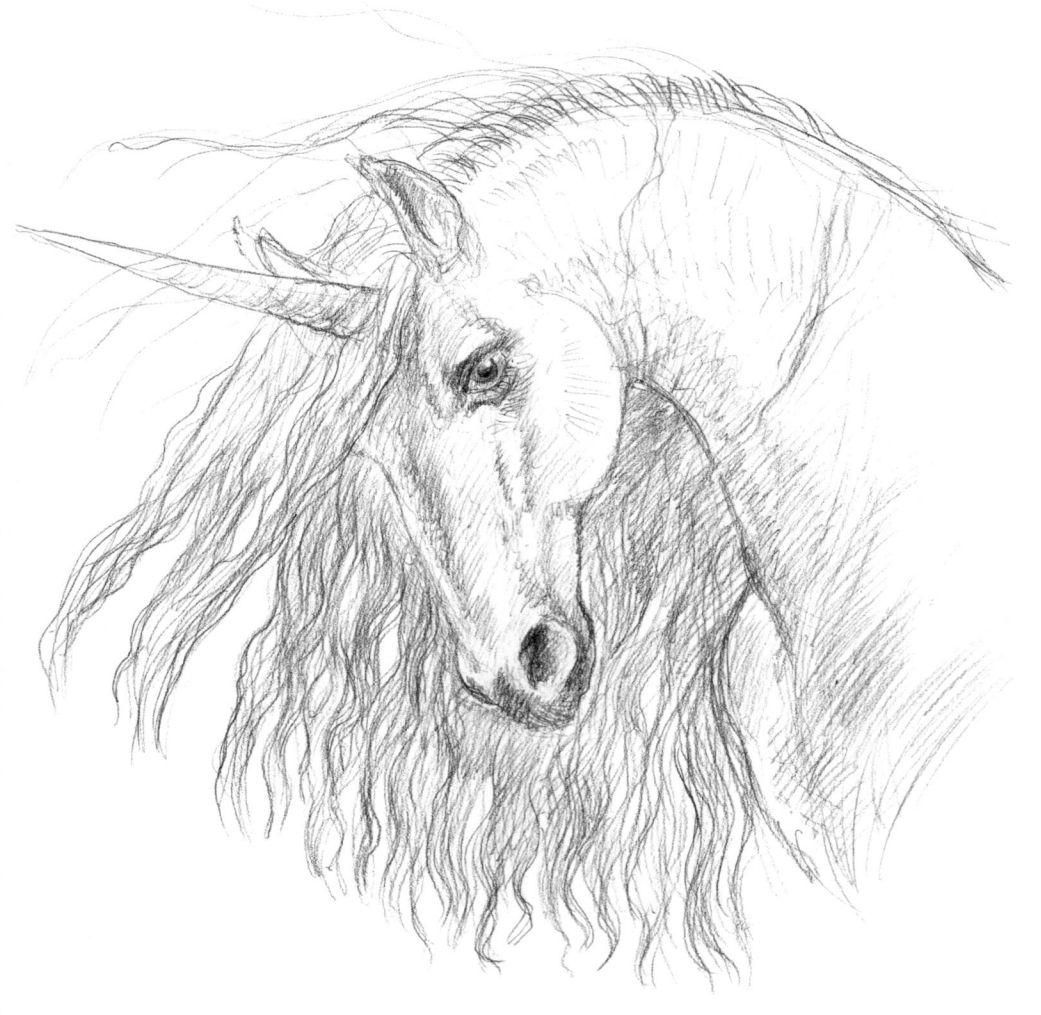

Some are embodiments of nature, or guardians of the otherworld, there to warn us away or lure us to our fates. Sacred places have watchful creatures too; it seems there is a mythical animal waiting at every twist in the path. How to depict them is another matter. Unless physically fantastical, they require a careful dose of the subliminally anthropomorphic to show their supernatural nature. It is a fine balance: too much and they look 'Disneyfied', too little and they are simply animals in nature paintings. It is often a question of scale and proportion, and conferring a certain sentience in their bearing and regard, establishing a parity between such animals and ourselves.

← *Unicorn Sketch*
There is a good deal of unicorn lore about, from Pliny to Peter Beagle, so we all know what unicorns look like.

➜ *Celtic Myth*

Originally intended for a compendium of Celtic myth, this image includes a Green Face, an oak, the Green Knight, a maid with a unicorn, a sacred stag and a stone circle, not to mention Cuchullain, a Merlin-like figure, and more.

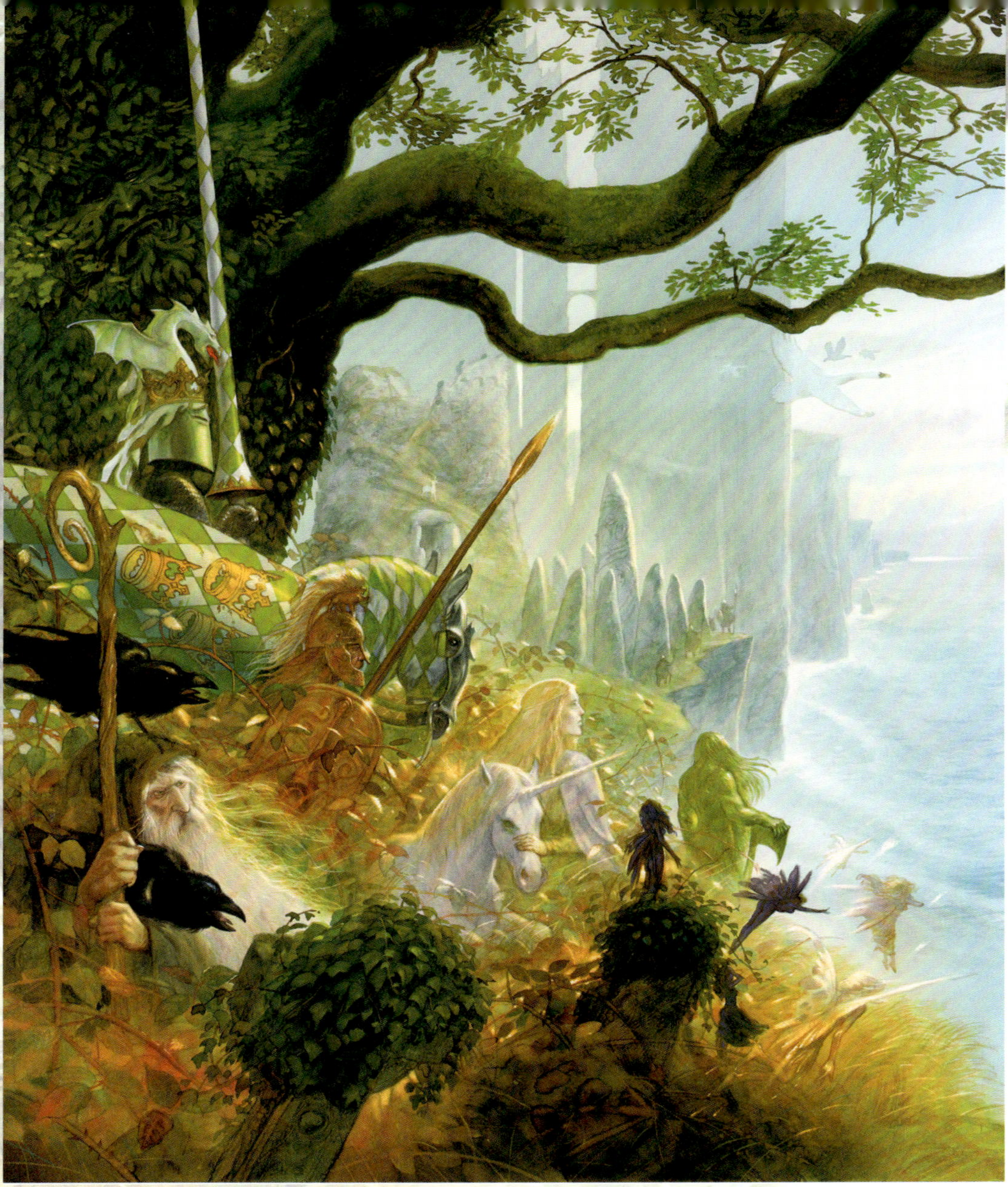

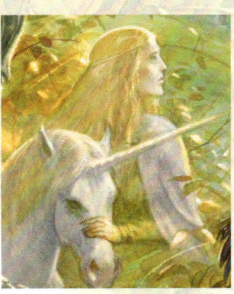

✦ The characters gaze out at something we cannot see, rather than 'posing for the camera'. Only the wise and knowing unicorn turns towards us.

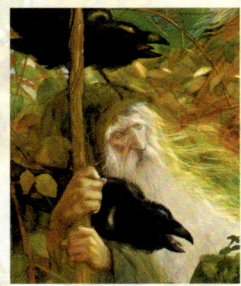

✦ Ravens, bearers of ill news, are the ubiquitous familiars of wise old men. These may be Hugin and Munin, but is the figure Odin, Merlin or Gandalf? I'm not sure.

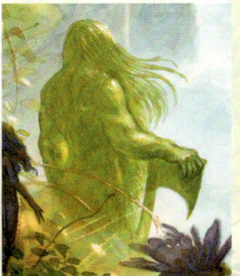

✦ The ambiguous figure of the Green Man originated in the Middle East in early Roman times, but flourished in medieval Europe, where he merged with his wilder Celtic counterpart. As a spirit of vegetation he is portrayed as a strange face made of leaves, as he appears on the tree above.

FANTASY BEASTS

BEOWULF & THE DRAGON

This painting was originally planned for an illustrated retelling of Beowulf, but I ran out of time, and an existing illustration was used instead. I was so eager to do the picture I proposed it as this case study. (It actually did make it into the Beowulf book, just under the wire. That doesn't mean there's a moral to the story – meeting deadlines properly is by far the best policy.)

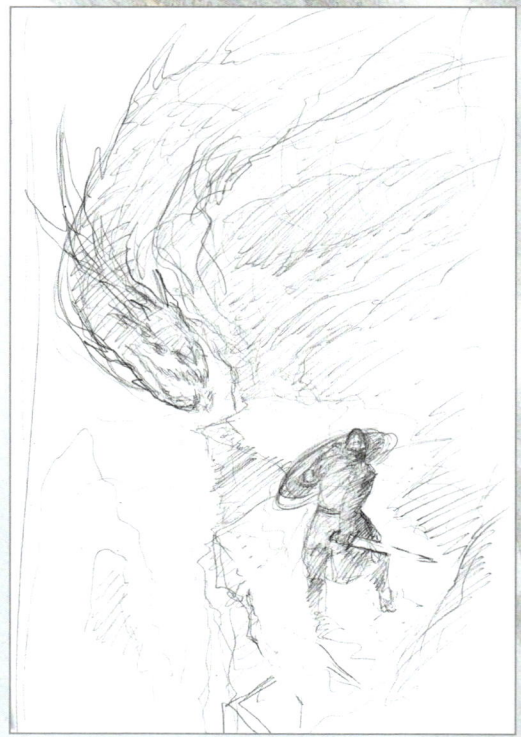

Sketches

Two scribbles for this one. A detail of the positions of Beowulf and his foe (left), and a quicker sketch to establish the general layout (below). Neither need be transposed to the colour work – a few guidelines are enough to start working with.

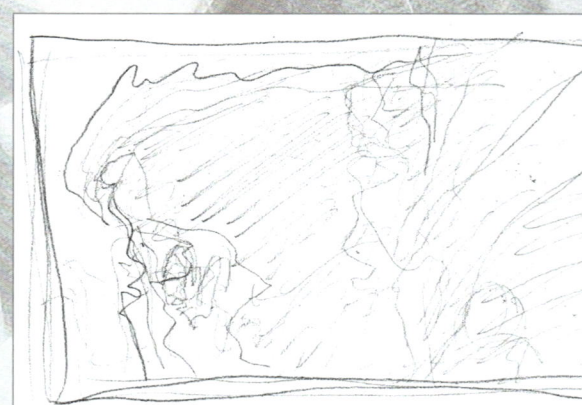

Stage 1
Initial colour wash

Blocking out the general colours and, above all, getting colour on to the whole page, which I usually dampen even if I'm not planning on putting colour on it all. This prevents the paper being treated unevenly. In misty scenes, the light takes on a most curious tint, so it is worthwhile 'warming up' the lightest tones so that the cooler tones will stand out properly. If it is to be raining, this is also a good stage to hint at the falling drops by running a large brush diagonally over the whole image.

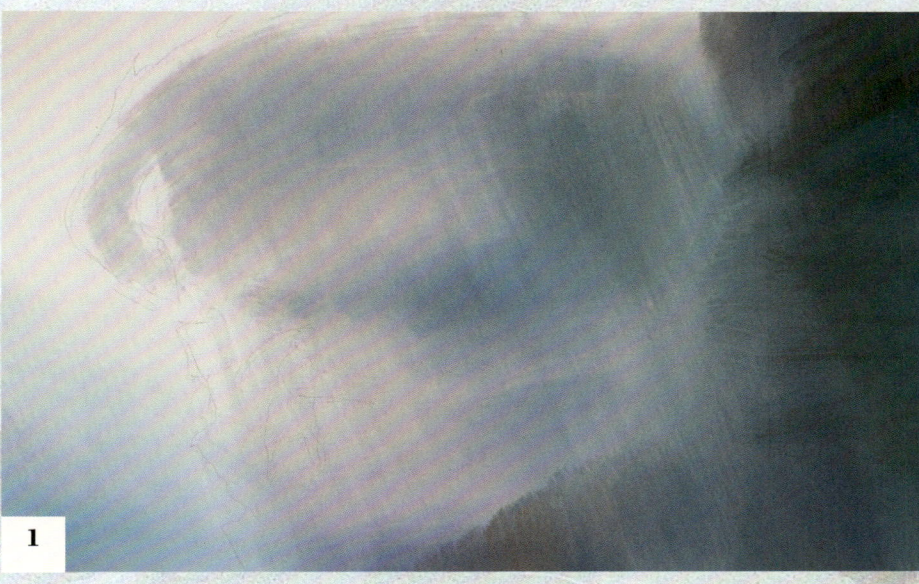

Stage 2
Establishing scale

Figuring out where to start placing details and working on the different planes and perspectives. Most of this is done wet-on-wet with a wide brush, adding a few details with a finer watercolour brush – the surface of the sea, the cliff edge, the rocks below. Painting barely visible waves often means working slowly forward from the horizon, stroke by tiny stroke. It can be painstaking, but establishing scale and distances now is important. It's best to have pecked away at these throughout, rather than counting on the human figure to do the job for you at the end.

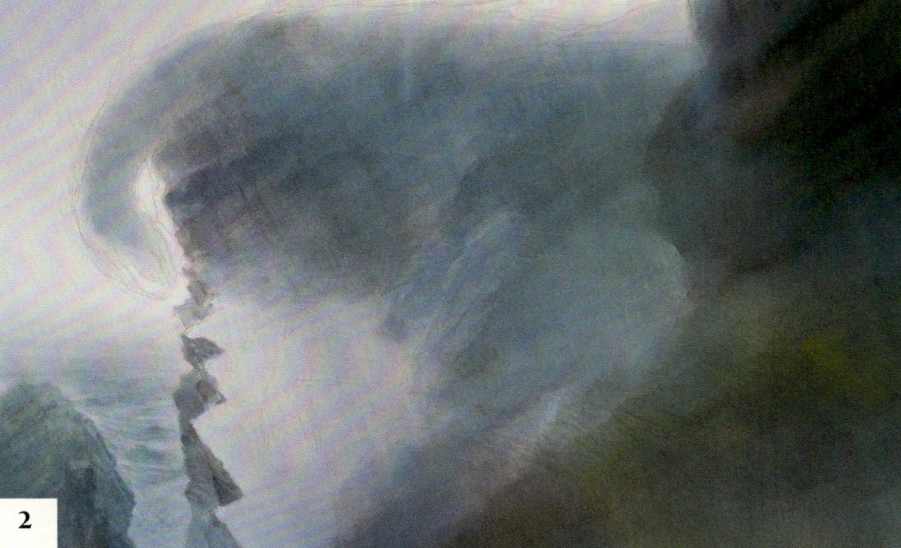

Stage 3
Building depth

Working up the volumes of the rocks and beginning to define the foreground. The sea and rocks lower left have a wash over them to push them back into the mist. The blades of grass lower right are premature, but sometimes it's helpful to go too far forward in a safe area for reassurance that things will work.

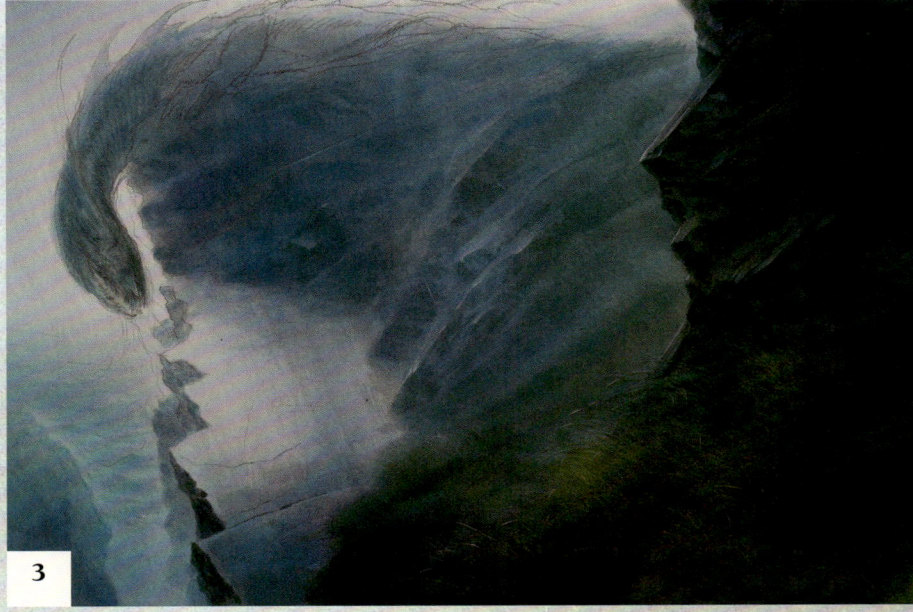

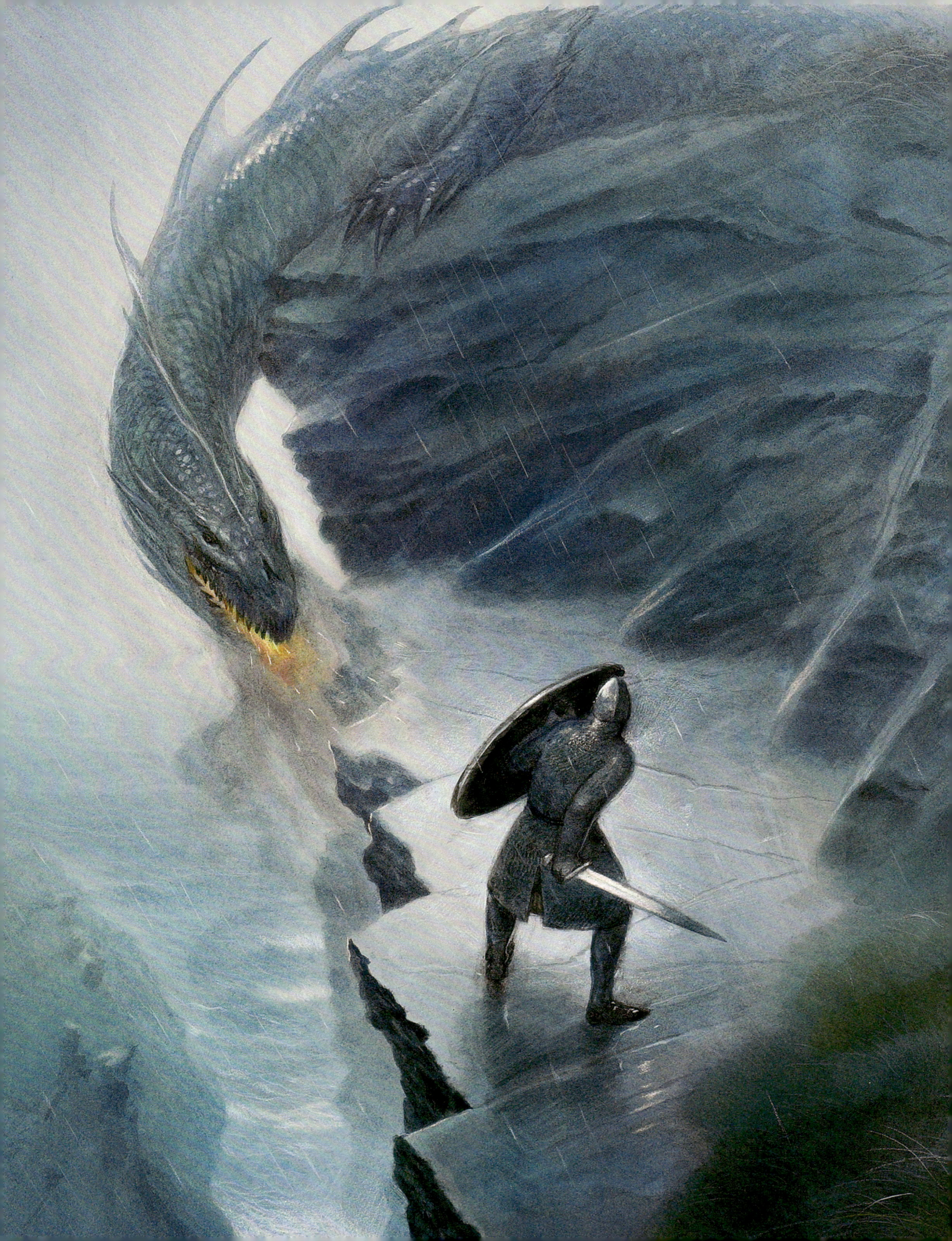

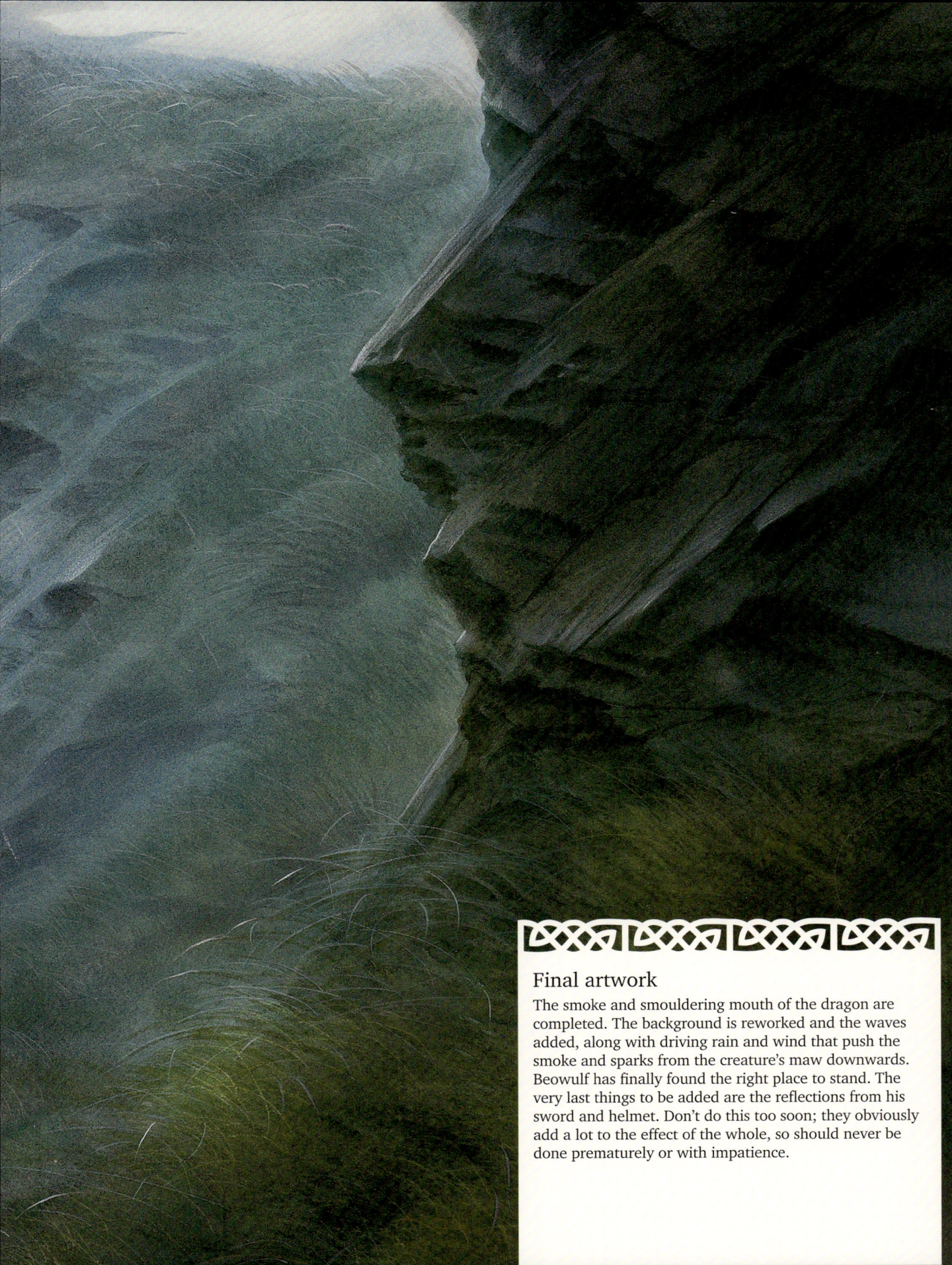

Final artwork

The smoke and smouldering mouth of the dragon are completed. The background is reworked and the waves added, along with driving rain and wind that push the smoke and sparks from the creature's maw downwards. Beowulf has finally found the right place to stand. The very last things to be added are the reflections from his sword and helmet. Don't do this too soon; they obviously add a lot to the effect of the whole, so should never be done prematurely or with impatience.

BACKDROPS

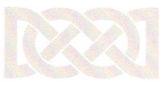

The four 'elements' of the ancient
world – Earth, Air, Fire and Water –
are truly the illustrator's elements.
The practice of illustration
has as much in common with
Empedoclean theory as it does
with the colour wheel or the rules
of perspective. Juggling all four of
these elements is akin to alchemy.

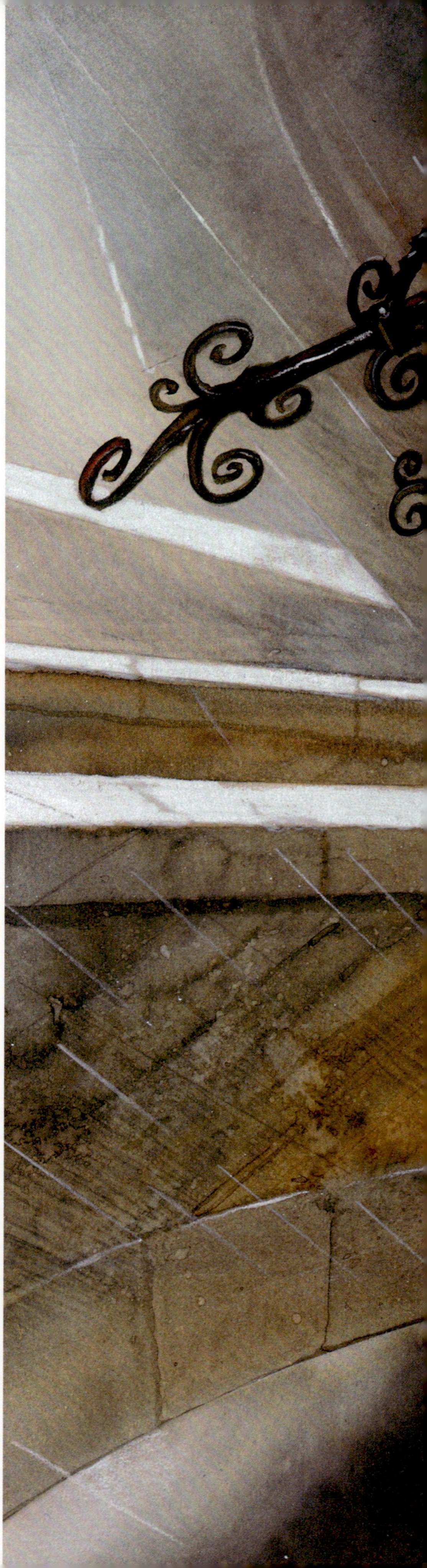

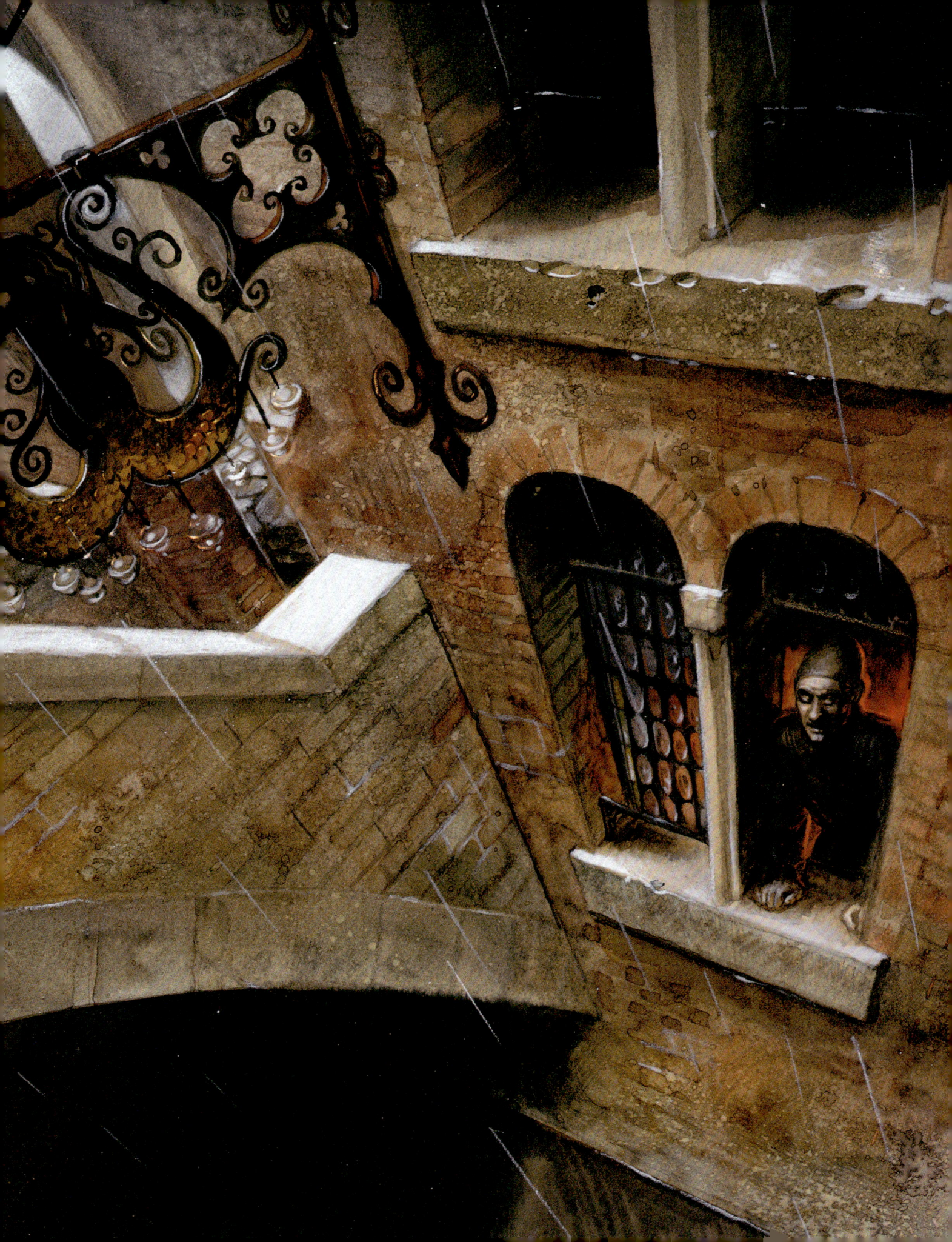

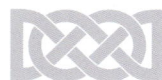

LANDSCAPES
APPROACHES & INSPIRATION

In fantasy landscape, mountains are higher, oceans deeper, rivers broader, clouds more menacing. Vistas are grander, groves are sacred, stars shine on vast cities of marble and porphyry. How fortunate we are to have such countries of the mind to wander in.

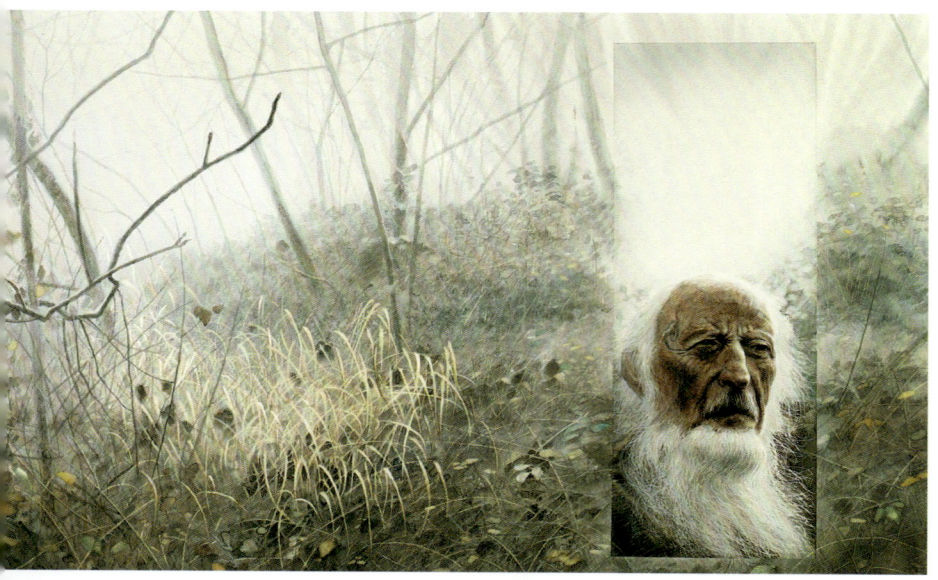

⬅ *Merlin*

This cover for a book on Merlin (later shelved) uses a landscape on the shores of Lake Neuchâtel. On an incredible afternoon with fog on the lake and sun above, I took photos. Occasionally a certain landscape will seem to sum up a particular myth or character. It's very personal, but according a little thought and attention to just what draws you to such a choice can help you approach the character themself. I believe in associating real locations with those places where the mind goes when inventing or enhancing an approach to fantasy.

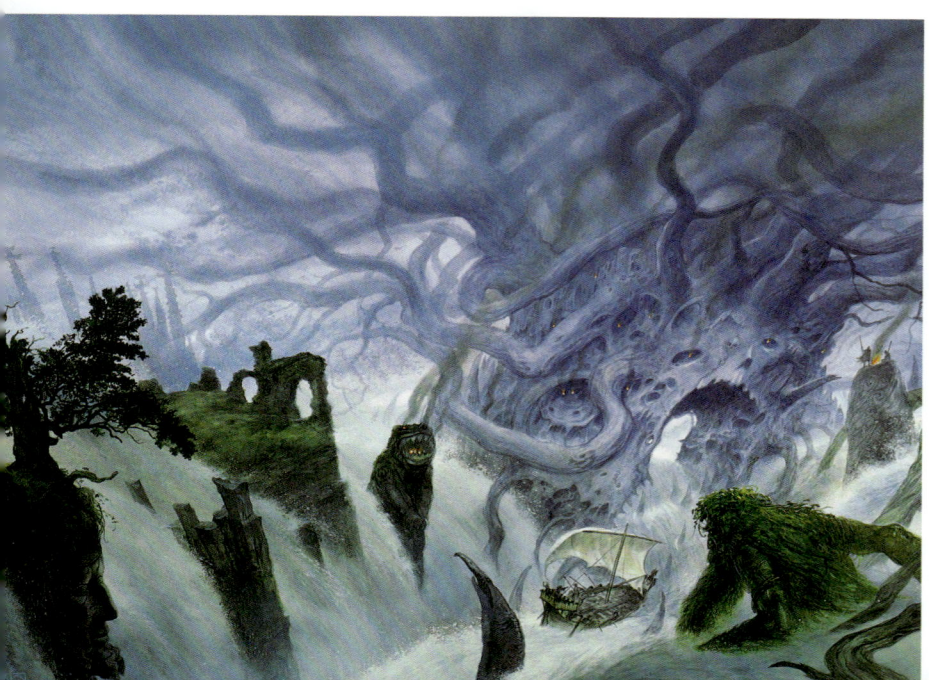

⬅ *Gate of Ivory*

I tried to echo the slip-sliding landscapes and juxtaposition of worlds and time that Robert Holdstock's books carry off so well, by incorporating elements from disparate sources and playing with their scale. The giant head on the left is from Strasbourg Cathedral, the tree from England. Behind is a ruin from Scotland. The statue with fire is a Scandinavian sculpture, the roots on the far left are from the Gulf Islands, the leafy giant is from inside my head, and the huge tree from our back yard. That's not true – it was just to see if you were paying attention. We have a more mundane magnolia.

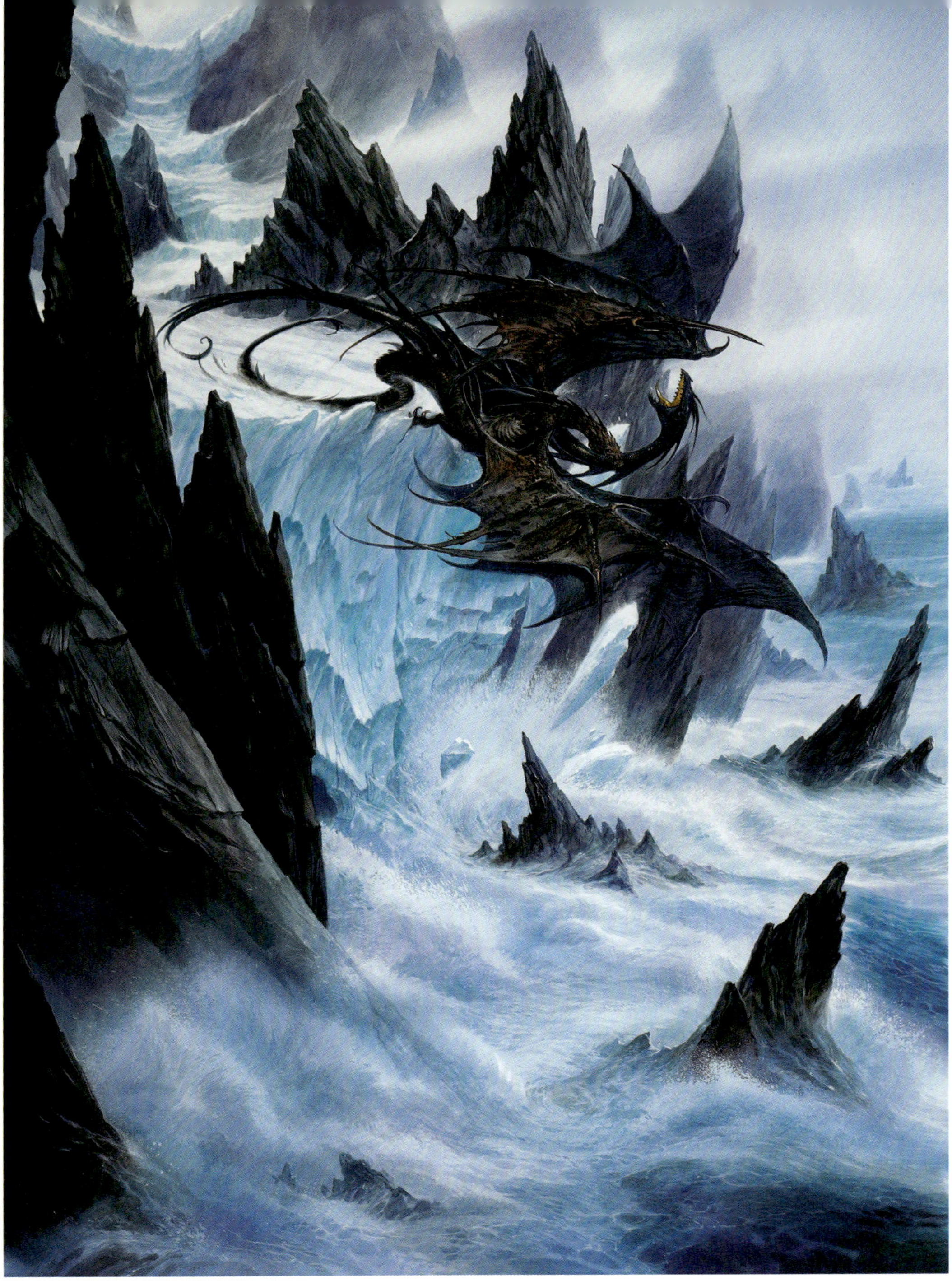

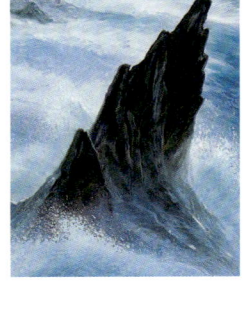

← *Fool's Fate*

Cover illustration for *Fool's Fate* by Robin Hobb. The end of Robin's trilogy features a cataclysmic struggle between two dragons in an equally cataclysmic setting – the islands of Askjeval, two ragged rocks jutting up from an ever-stormy sea and joined by a glacier. It felt natural that every element of the image would reflect the dragons' struggle. They are the centre of the action, but appear altogether as an extension of the turbulent landscape.

✦ The foremost rocks serve to enhance the inhospitable nature of the environment.

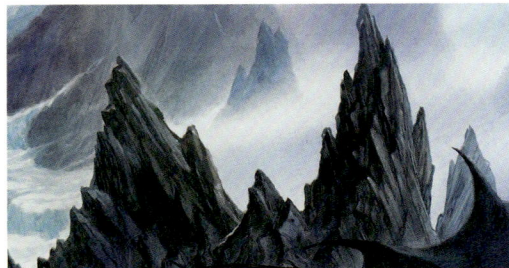

✦ The jagged rocks echo the shape of the dragon's wings, almost like a stop-motion photo of the movement.

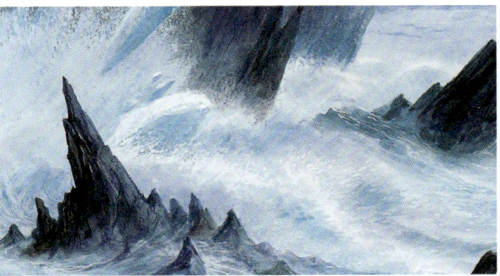

✦ The dragons' struggle has dislodged blocks of ice from the glacier's edge.

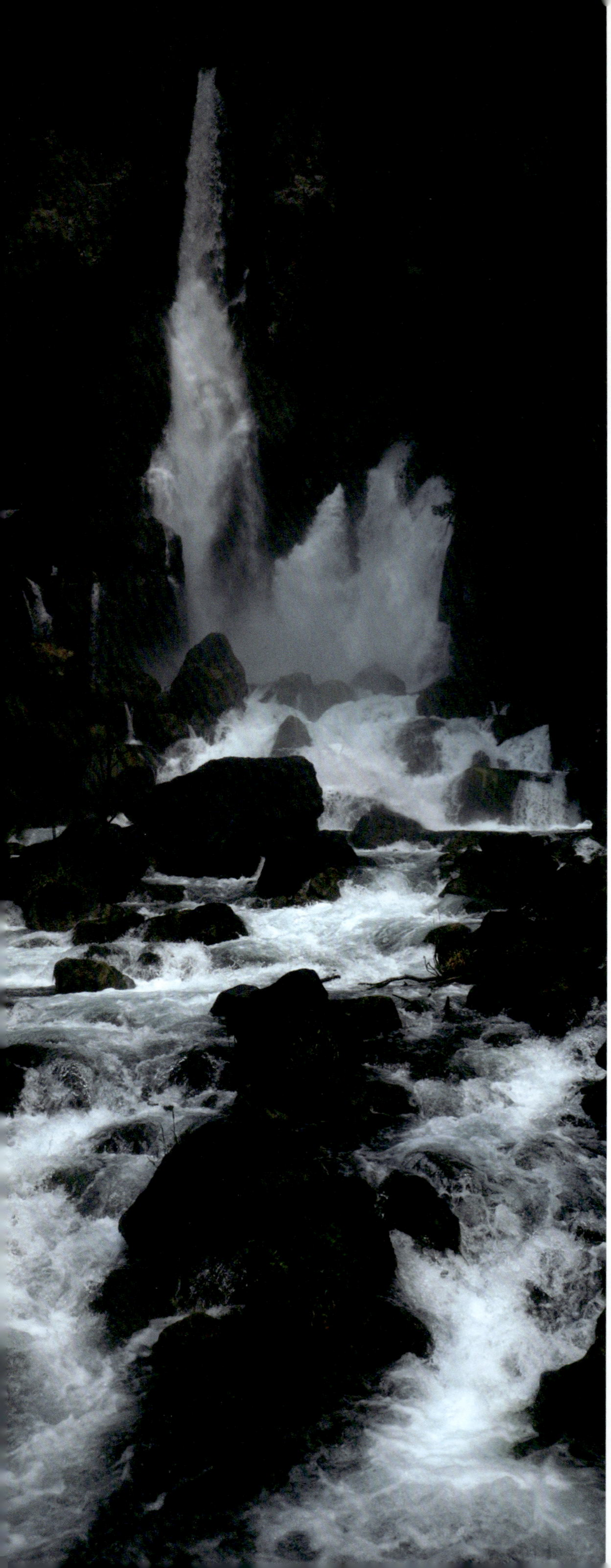

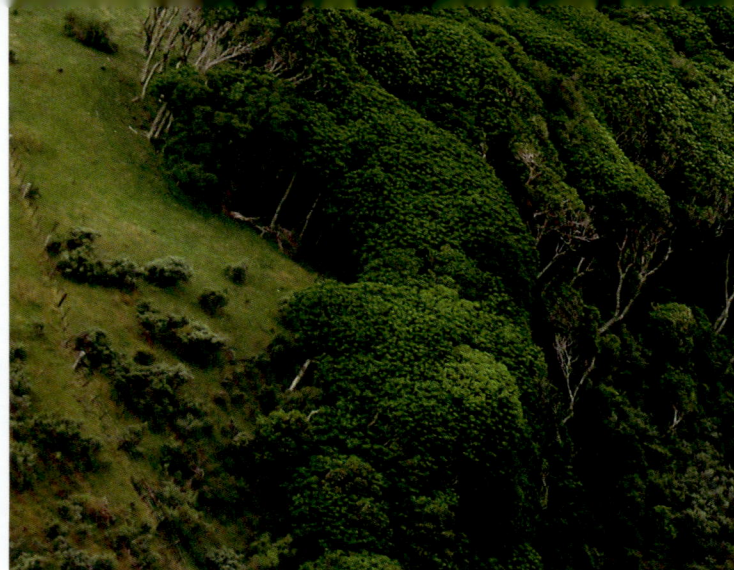

There are few sensations closer to the sublime than gazing at inaccessible landscapes, the places where we may not go, or only go in spirit. The edge of the sea or a precipice, high mountain or fleeting light we cannot retain but must rapidly savour; the impossibility of doing aught else but gaze places us squarely in the paradox of our presence: the view is beautiful because it is all we are not.

Nature is beautiful because it does not need us.

Landscape is an integral participant in fantasy art worth our particular attention, not only for the wealth of detail we glean from it, but perhaps more importantly for the archetypal qualities we can try to capture. I do my best to capture those things with a camera, and the more lasting memories of truly looking at the landscape. (This also applies to urban landscapes, focusing on period and style.)

↓ Travel photography

I rarely travel without a camera, snapping everything of interest that strikes a chord or may be useful one day. Your choices of landscape and light will run parallel to those you make when you paint. This landscape and the others on these pages are all in New Zealand.

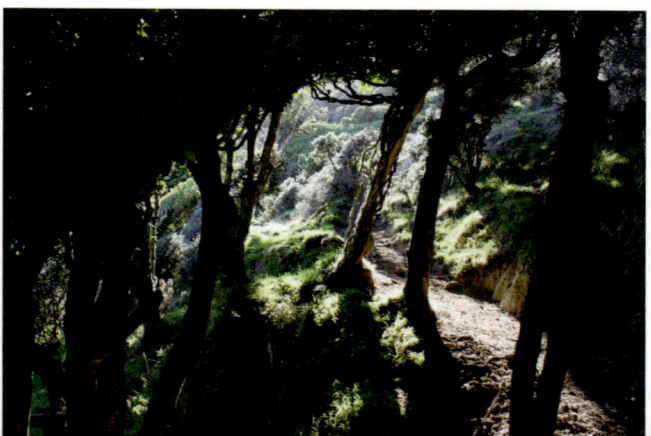

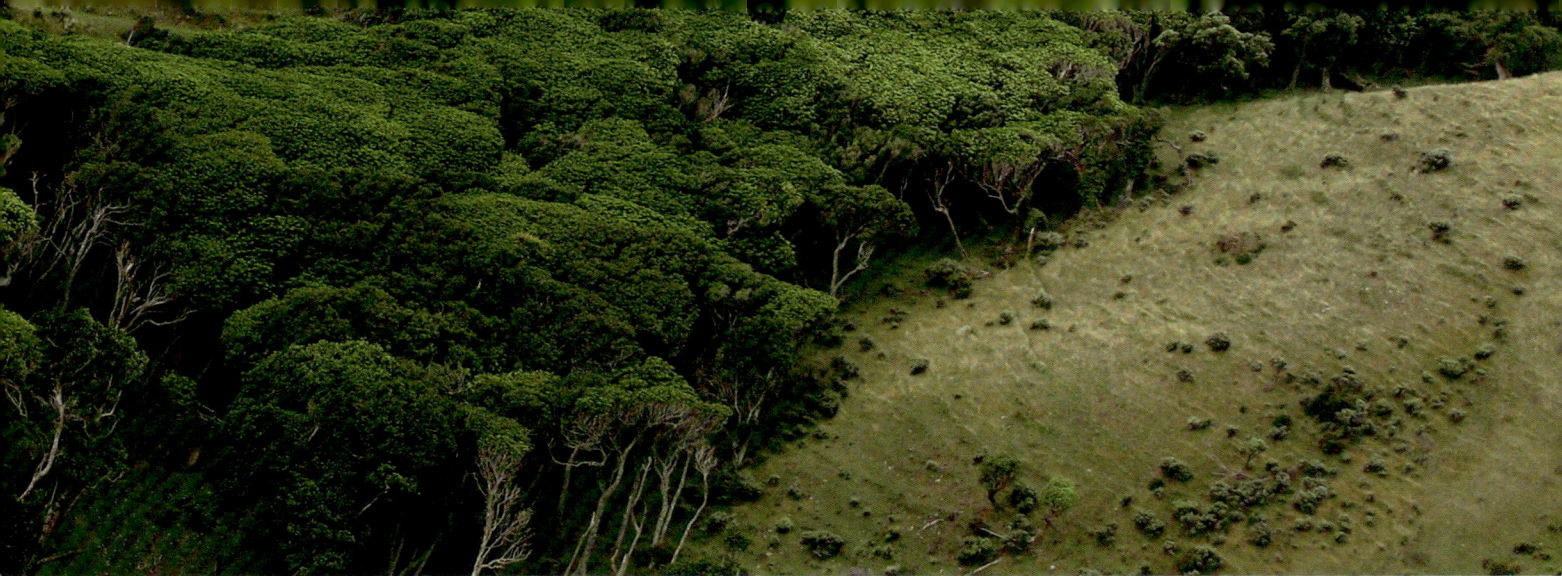

Standing on the edge of a landscape, especially one I cannot walk further into, I am deafened by voices and music. A landscape is not unlike a choir. These are the voices of everything that is not us. Everything is speaking, singing, chanting. I wish to understand and be part of the exchange, but cannot. I don't understand those languages anymore. They have been speaking to us for a long time, we have just not been listening. It is time we do.

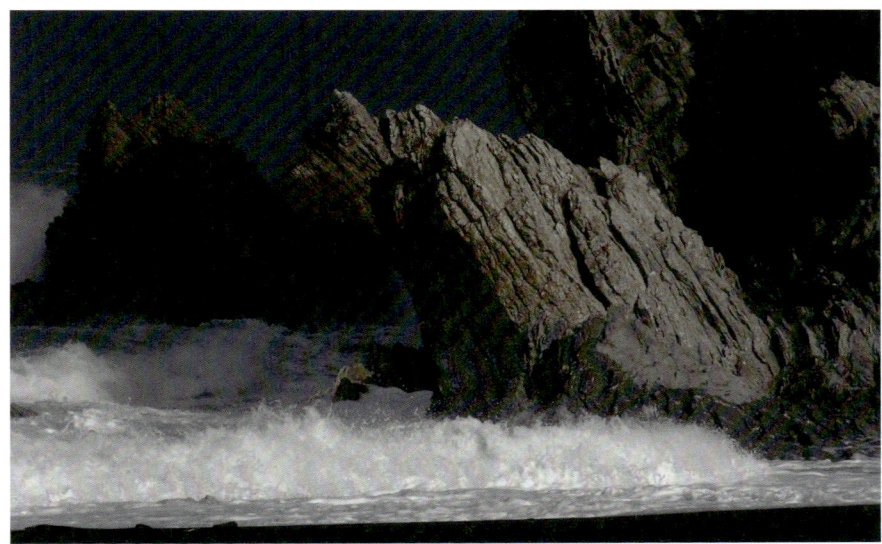

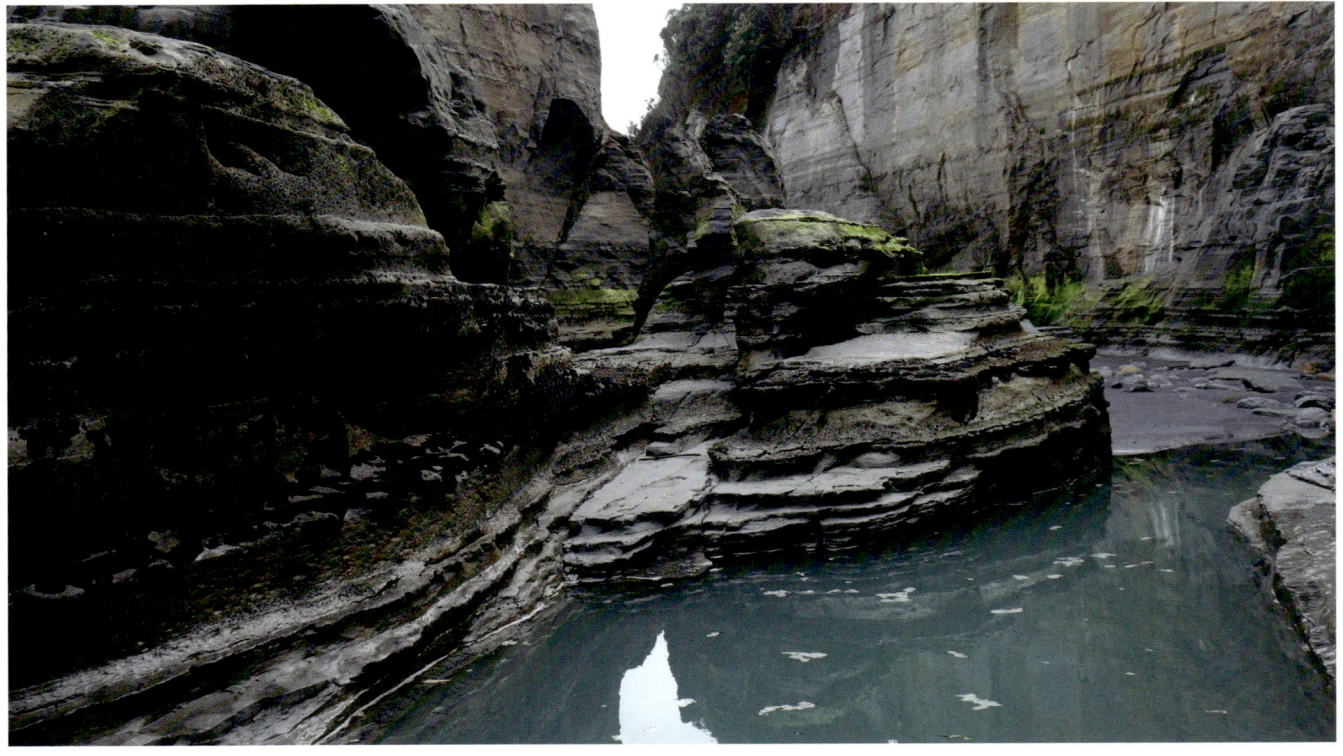

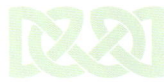

LANDSCAPES
EARTH

There is a well-defined symbolic role to be played
by landscape, and rock is its backbone, defined
by the forces that went into shaping it.

Whichever world one has at hand is underpinned by
this, and the nature of rocks should be harmonious
with the world they crop out of. Keeping track of the
many surface textures and volumes that compose a
landscape can be hard; it is tempting to revert to a 'system' to render
large areas of stone, water, grass or trees. Fight this – it reduces your
palette to a graphic language that relies on recognition rather than
depiction. The results will be far removed from the real thing. If you
have, say, a huge tree to paint, start with the area to which the eye
will be drawn by your composition, and work on that important
section, supported by photographic reference if needed, until you've
captured something of the true likeness of bark. This 'system' of
sorts will let you faithfully render less important areas without
relying too heavily on visual shorthand.

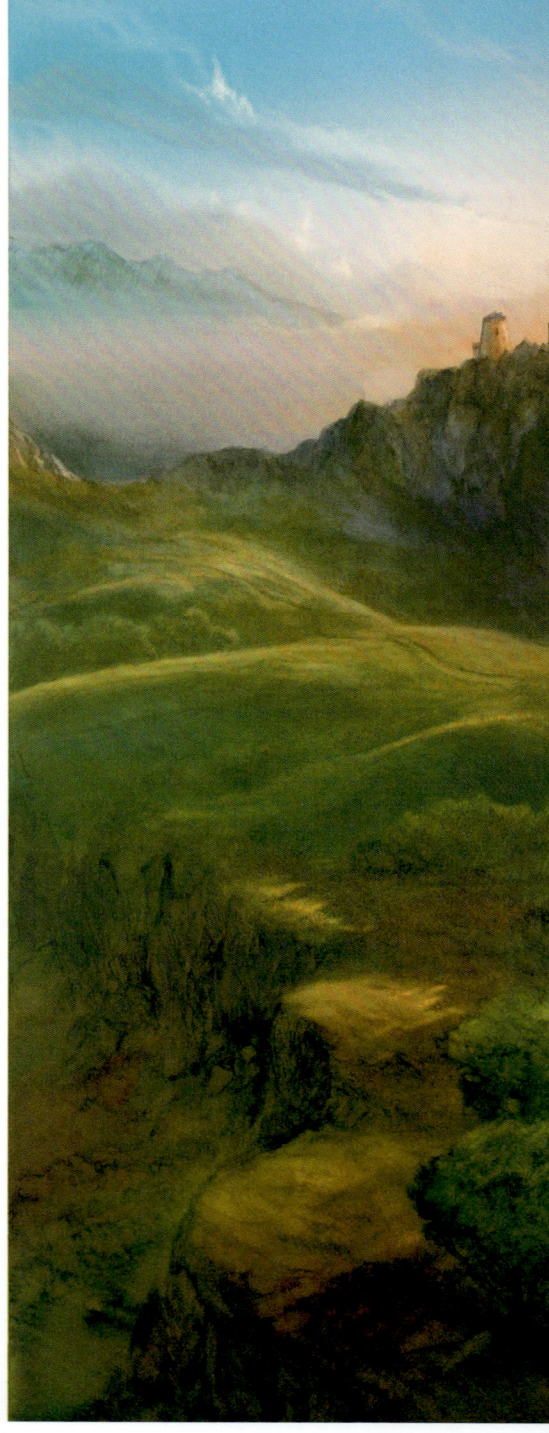

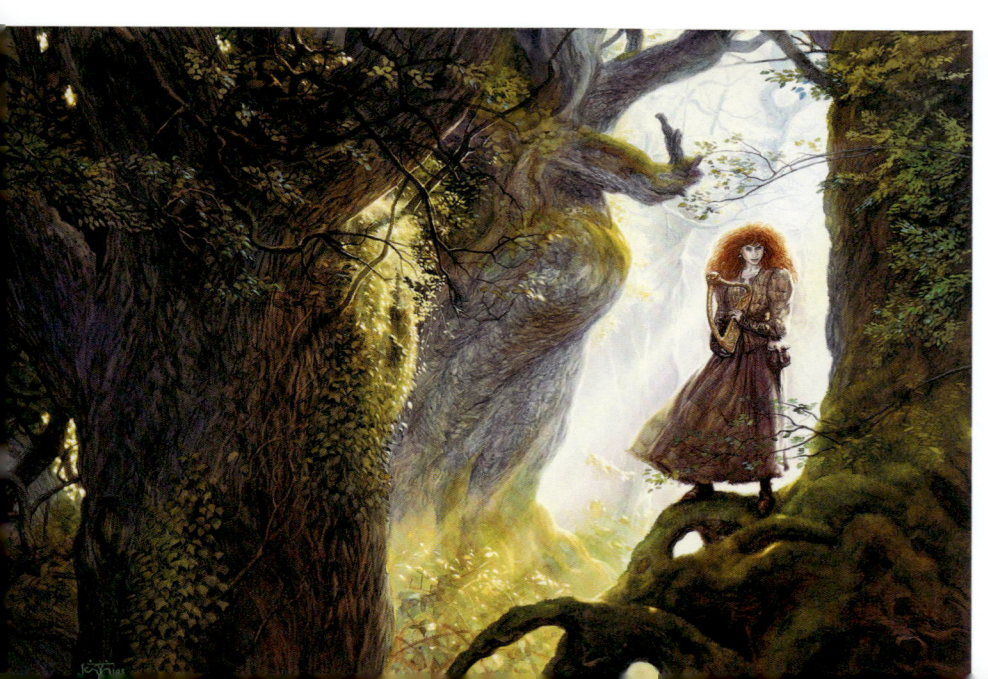

← *Into the Green*

The main character of Charles de Lint's
novel personifies the forest – alluring and
a little dangerous. The rocks of Betws-y-
Coed in Wales inspired the trees (recipe for
tree: just add bark). The arbitrary eddies of
forest light and shade mean you can apply
any degree of atmospheric perspective.

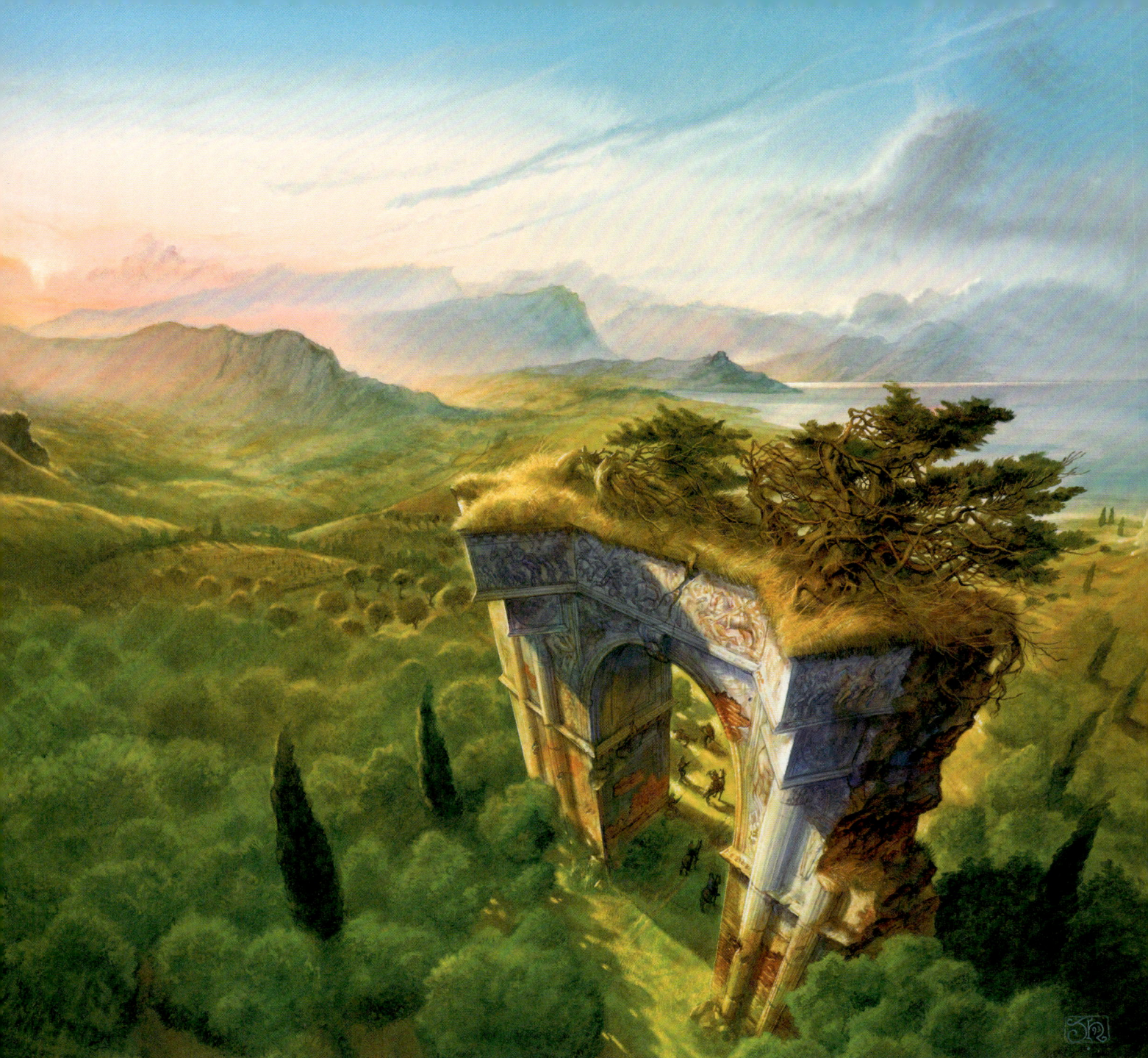

"KEEPING TRACK OF THE
MANY SURFACE TEXTURES
AND VOLUMES THAT
COMPOSE A LANDSCAPE
CAN BE HARD"

☝ *A Song for Arbonne*

The landscape depicts a fictional medieval Mediterranean world.
I even made the effort to briefly research the planting patterns
of olive groves and vineyards in 15th-century Italian paintings.
This was admittedly an aside, but it does illustrate the occasional
detour one can make while elaborating an image.

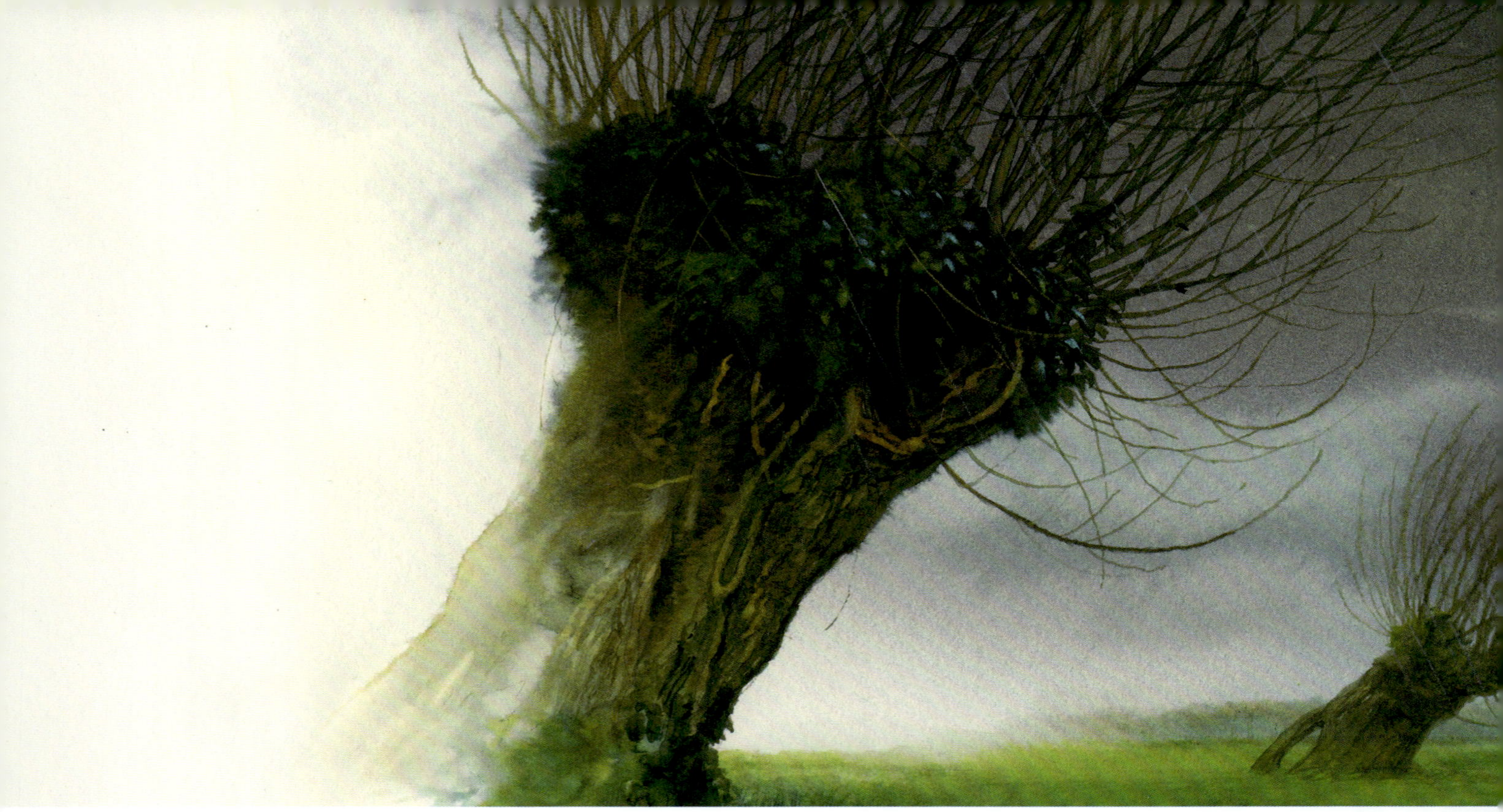

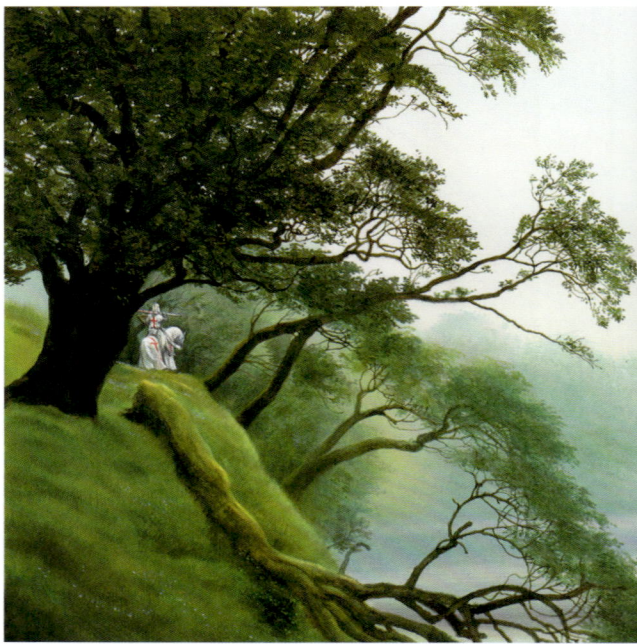

LANDSCAPES
AIR

You may not be able to see air, but you can
certainly see what it's up to. Such sumptuous
emptiness is a gift to be used generously.

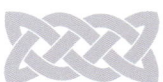

The air is full of dust, light, clouds, rain. Distant, hazy views, of mountains, say, in watercolour are generally best done when the paper is quite wet, so it's best to visualize what you have in mind before you begin. You can work back over with drybrush, but it can be hard. Distant features can be blocked out wet and details added later, being careful not to compromise the blurred edges. Atmospheric effects are often volatile, best achieved with freedom, rather than being laboured over.

⬆ *The Red Cross Knight*

The story of the Red Cross Knight is something of an afterthought in fantasy. Knights have ridden far from Arthur's legendary kingdom into the realms of folklore, on their way to children's literature. The benign-looking dragon and idyllic pastel setting reflect this fairy-tale landscape for characters who have lost much of their own substance in successive retellings. There is more depth to the landscape itself than to the inhabitants.

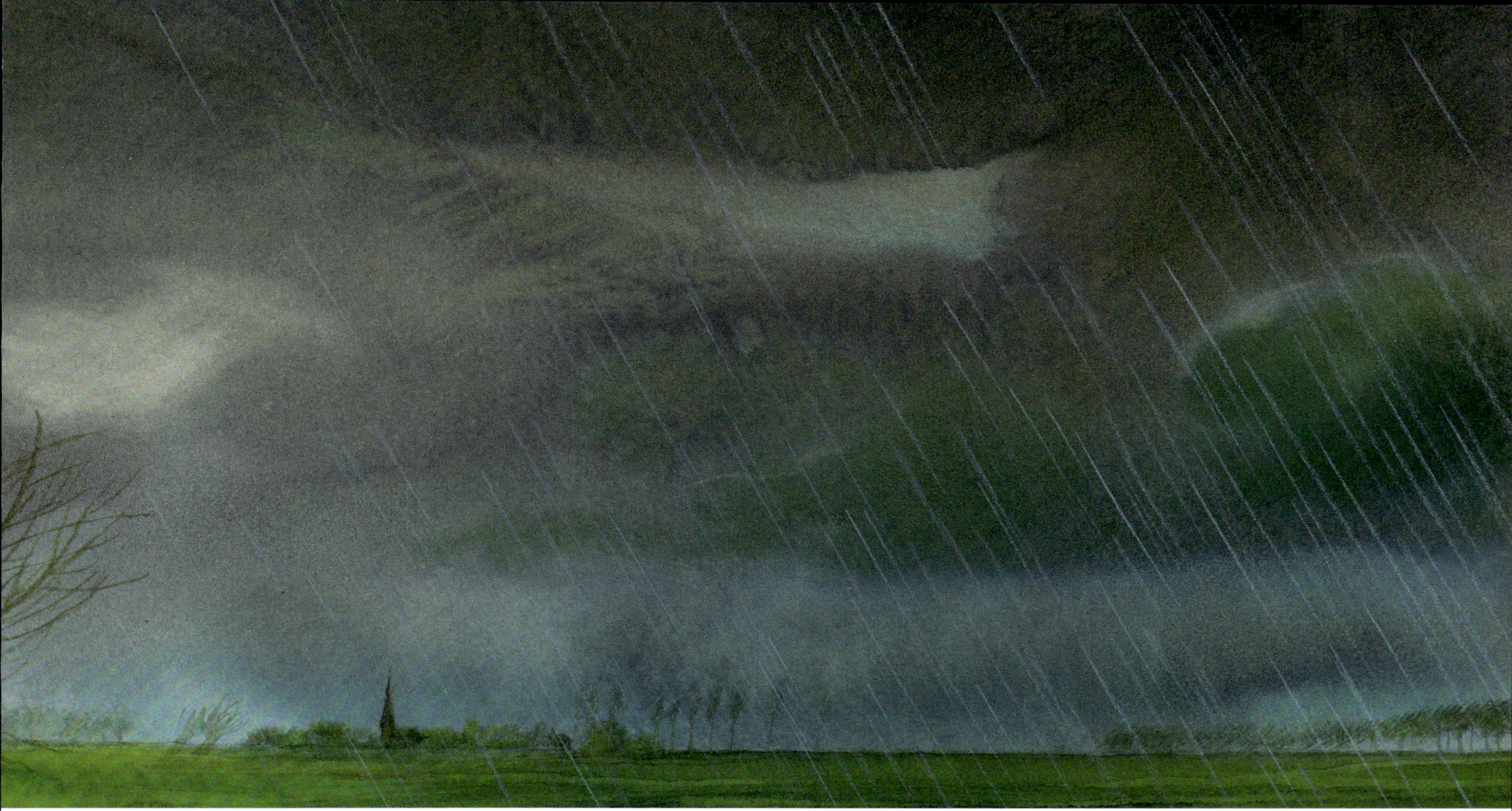

⬆ *Willows*

This is the opening and closing illustration for a children's book by Claude Clément, *The Man Who Lit the Stars* – the rising and falling curtains on the narrative. Spring and fall often bring the best light, when the sun is low, and wet grass can be the most intense green. Sun and rain in the landscape together can cause the most extravagant effects of light and contrast. These landscapes are similar to watercolours when still damp, or the wet pebbles children pick up on the beach. Capturing that saturation of tint can be a challenge. *Willows, from La Ville Abandonnée*, John Howe © CASTERMAN S.A.

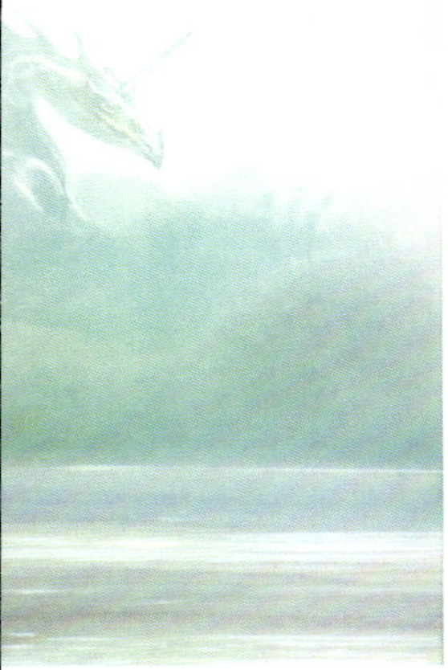

⬇ *Nighteyes and Buckkeep*

So much of the incredible range of contrasts of cloud is comprised of minute variations between warm and cool colours of similar density.

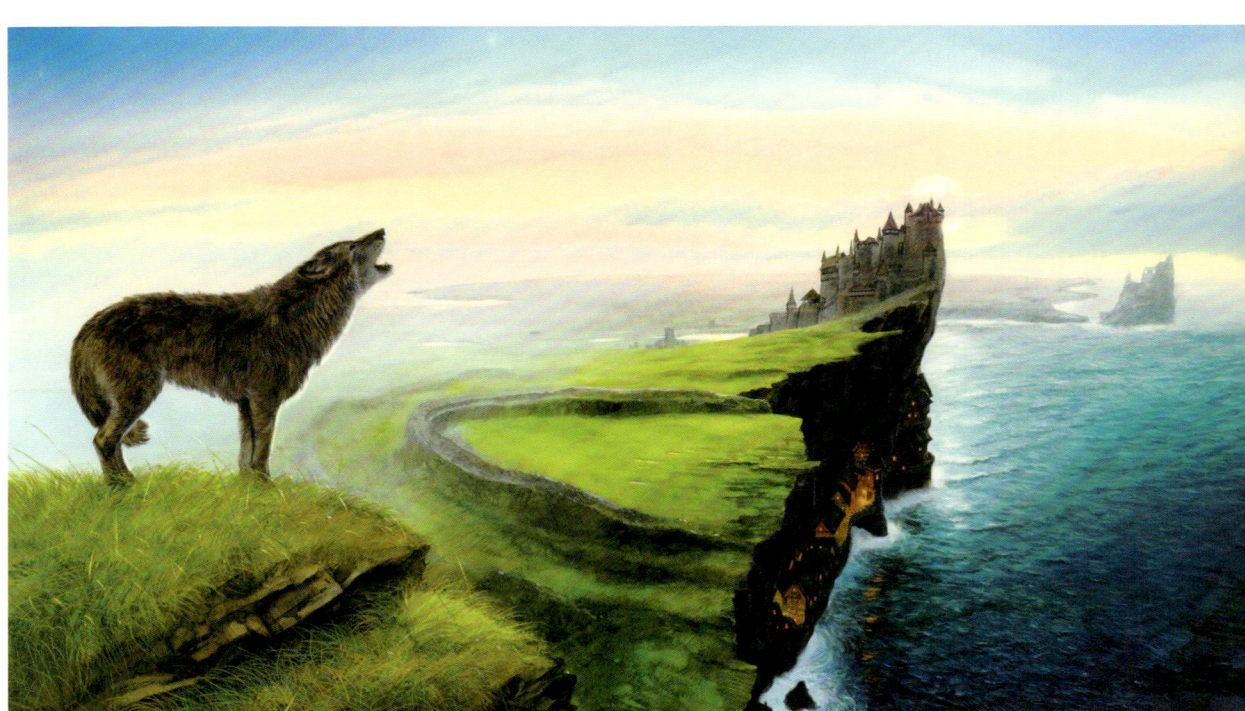

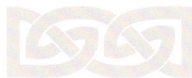

LANDSCAPES
FIRE

I have always loved drawing fire and smoke, and my library is full of books on vulcanism. Any flame can become a principal light source in an image.

The rendering of such a volatile effect demands taking a deep breath and diving into a very well-dampened area on your paper. As with clouds, the work needs to be done quickly or the spontaneous nature of flame can be lost. Inks and watercolours are transparent, so it's crucial to start with lots of fresh, clean water and paper towels – you will need to clean your brushes as you work from the bright yellow heart of the flames to the darkness of the clouds of smoke.

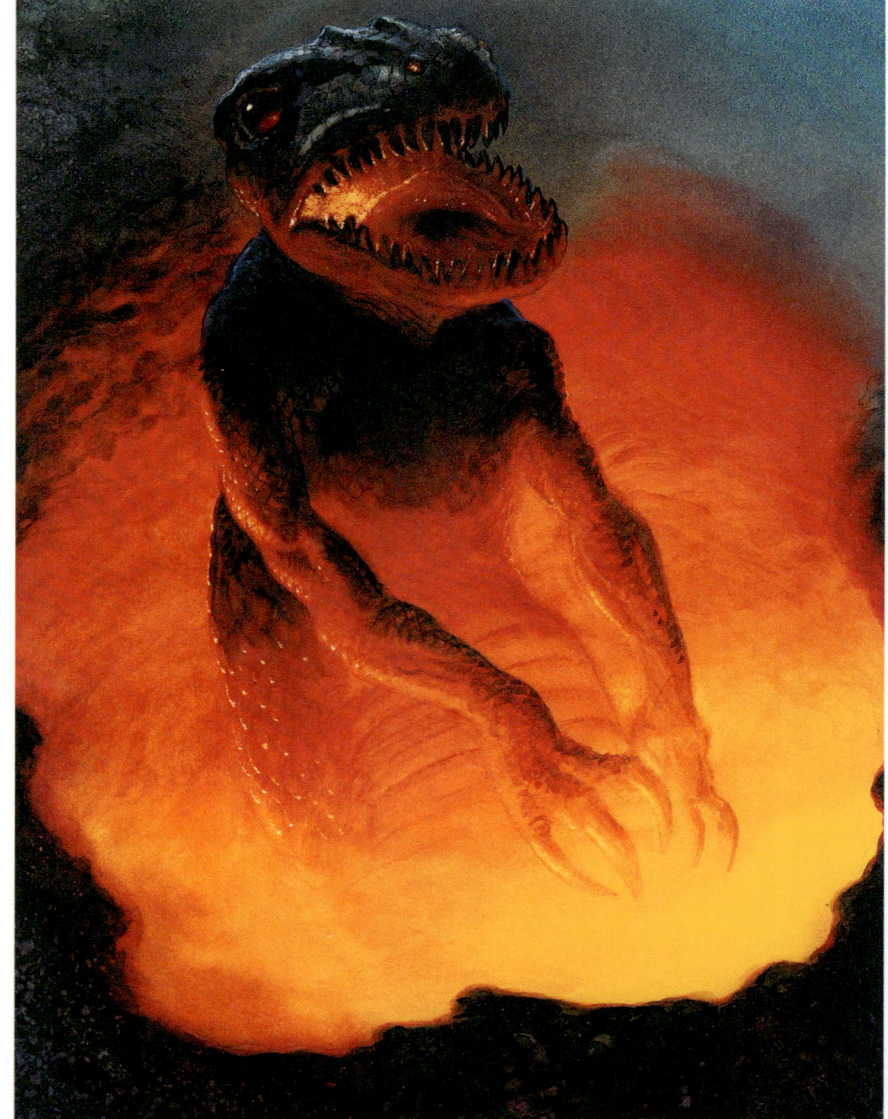

➼ *Fire Dragon*

I wanted to explore the theme of vulcanism, with dragons spawned in molten rock. Images of this kind are not technically difficult. You need only a few decent photos of lava. The two distinct light sources – warm (incandescent here) and cold – do not mix, so work from their lightest parts to where they meet but do not mingle.

Slow Dragon

Everything – approaching storm, waves, walls, inexorable belly-dragging progress of the dragon – moves to the right. Only the dragon's head turned left pulls the eye back into the picture. The narrative, however, continues out to the right, to the next chapter in the story.

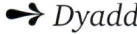 *Dyadd*

The fire is painted on a well-dampened ground to capture its movement and volume. Vermillion repels black ink, so flames can reach up into the smoke without being dirtied.

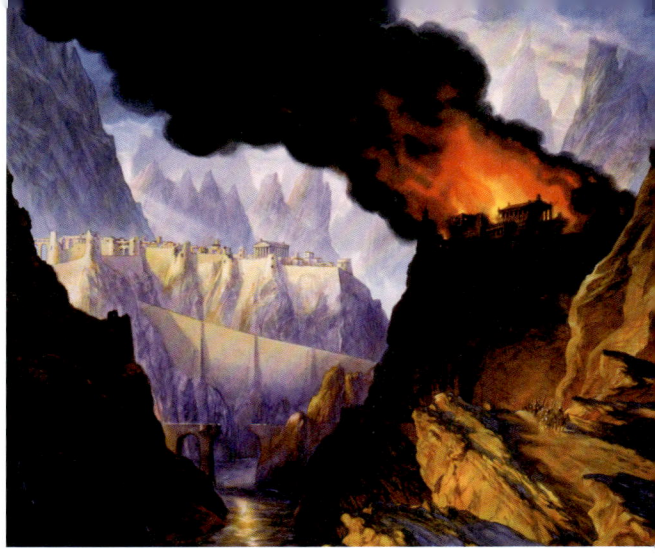

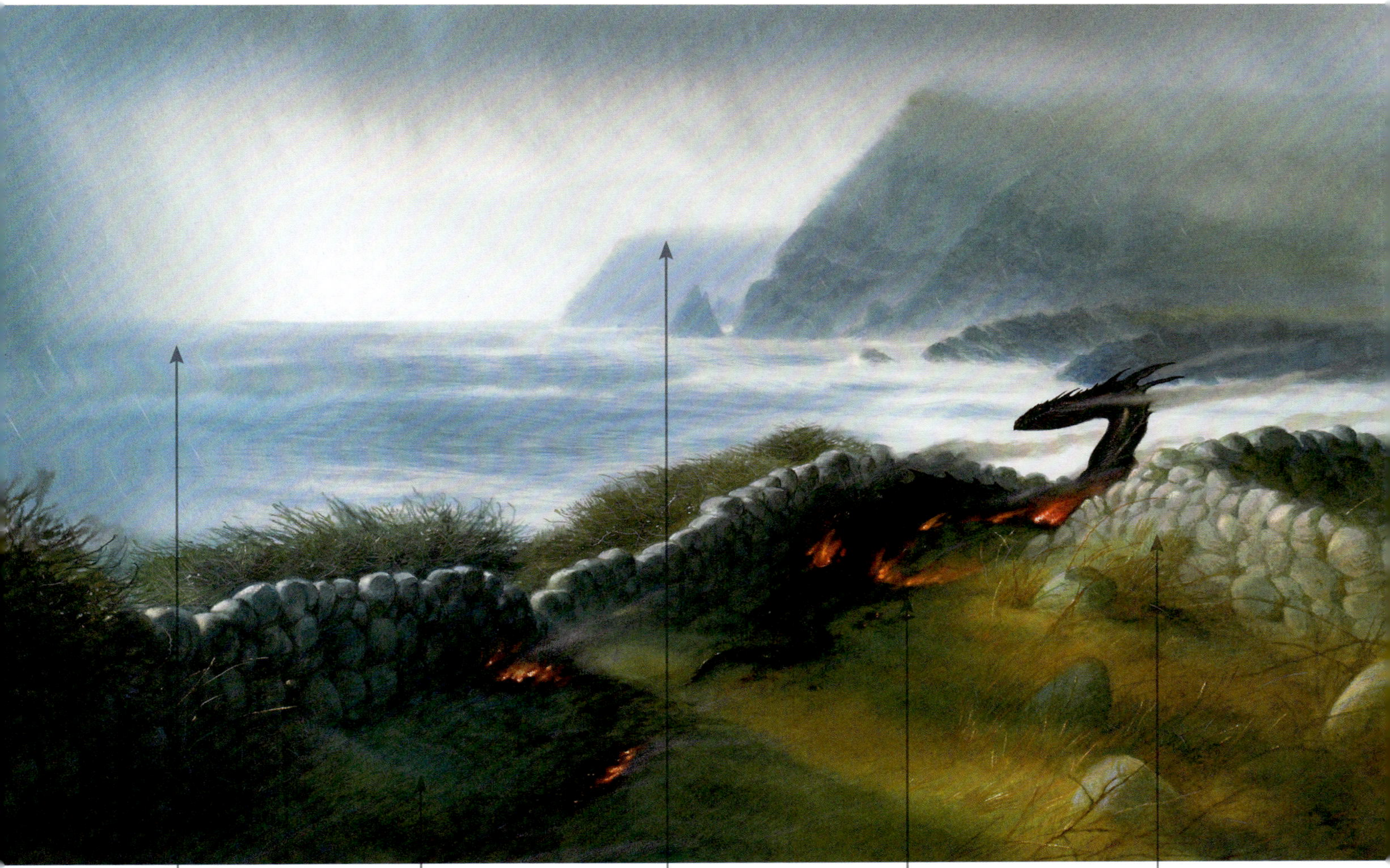

✦ Detail fades quickly to the horizon; texture is used only to intimate the depth of the breakers.

✦ A shadow echoes the line of the coast towards the dragon's head, forming a narrow band of focus.

✦ The cliffs provide focus by blocking off the horizon to the right; the blue of the hills brings the attention on to the dragon.

✦ Sometimes less is more: a few patches of fire are enough to give an indication of the power of the dragon.

✦ Almost white in the weak light, the wall curves out of the picture to leave the plight of the settlement to the imagination.

LANDSCAPES
WATER

Water comes in all kinds – mirror-smooth, clear as glass, murky,
turbulent or tempestuous. And in all forms – rain, waterfalls, waves,
rivers and more. Depicting this diverse element is always exciting.

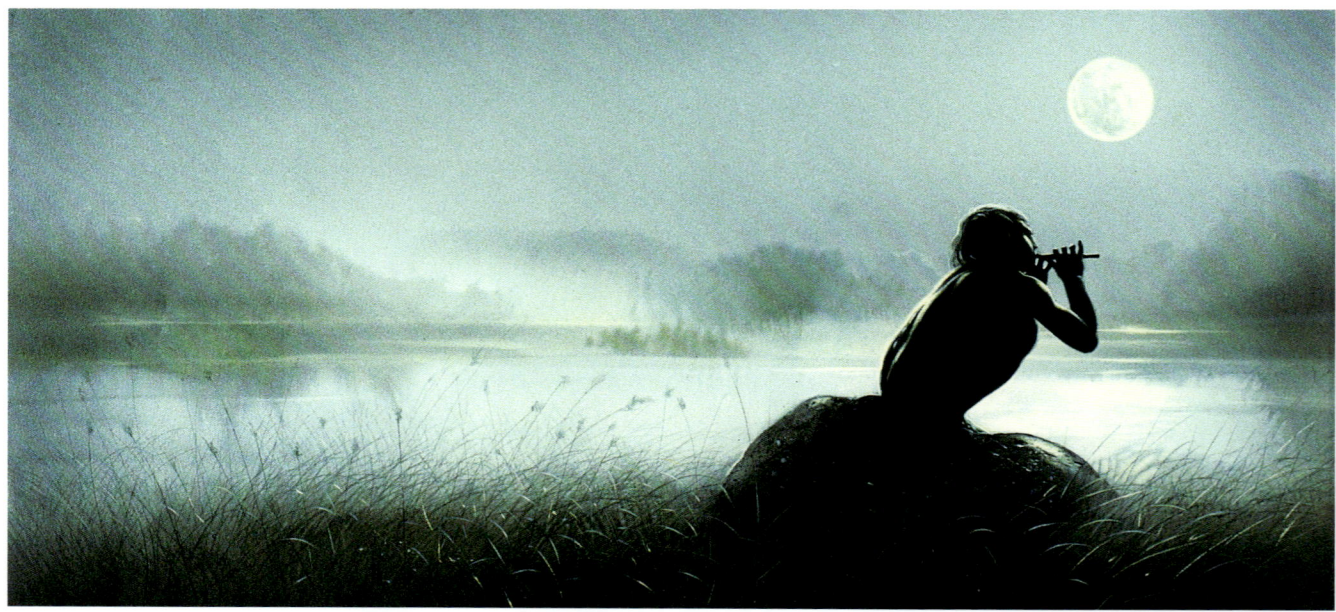

Usually, an expanse of still water is composed of only a handful of tones.
A wide brush is useful for blocking in a smooth surface, even more so
a reflective one like water. Toothbrushes are useful when painting wild
water, as you can spatter masking fluid all over and get very realistic
splash patterns – on clothes, in coffee, on important things left too close. Old
toothbrushes in our house end up on my work table, lasting for two or three
waves, a river or a flash flood before becoming clogged then discarded. You can
do the spattering in layers rather than all at once; put down a very light initial
wash to soften the glare of white paper. For rain I generally use a white pencil
crayon, unless of course the rain is backlit, in which case scraping with a scalpel
can be better; of course, this depends on the nature of the background.

⬆ *Musician from the Darkness*

Still water hinges on convincing
reflections. I made the paper quite wet
and angled the board to let the ink
bleed and run. Horizontal drybrushing
adds perspective to the water, and the
highlights and moon were done with an
eraser. A hair dryer is essential to avoid
water pooling and drying unequally,
and to halt the run of ink when
necessary. The musician is me, posing
with a ruler in my mouth. *Musician from
the Darkness*, from *La Ville Abandonnée*, John
Howe © CASTERMAN S.A.

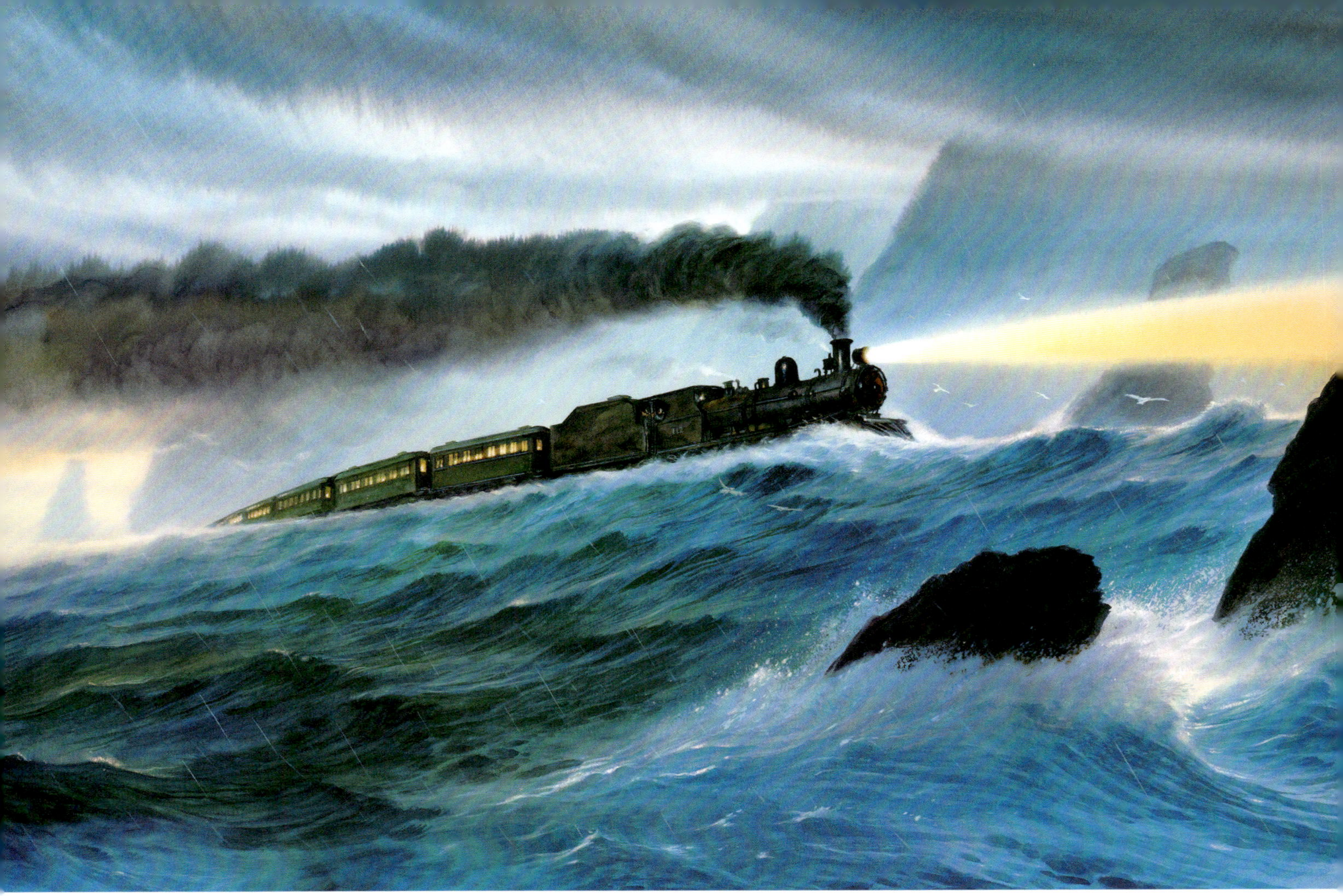

⬆ Rolling Harbour

Cover art for a CD by the band Elandir. This illustration was enormous fun to do. I needed to keep the waves 'solid' enough to visually support the train while still looking like water. The foreground waves and spray were first done in a warm tone, masked (to paint the water behind), then cooled and darkened with the airbrush. The highlights were added with a hard eraser and a scalpel, scraping back to the warm undercoat.

➜ The Rising Sea

The cover illustration for *The Abandoned City* by Claude Clément, in which the king of the city breaks his word to a humble glassblower. As a result, the sea invades the streets. While the rising sea is an inexorable consequence of the king's arrogance, the stirring-up of the cosmos, reminiscent of the Flood, is not hinted at. However, Claude's awareness of what binds us to nature is clear in the restless sea; it seemed crucial to visualize a purposeful conjunction of the elements as retribution for the oathbreaking. I used waterfalls as reference for cascading water, splattering masking agent with a old toothbrush and reworking in coloured pencil. *The Rising Sea*, from *La Ville Abandonnée*, John Howe © CASTERMAN S.A.

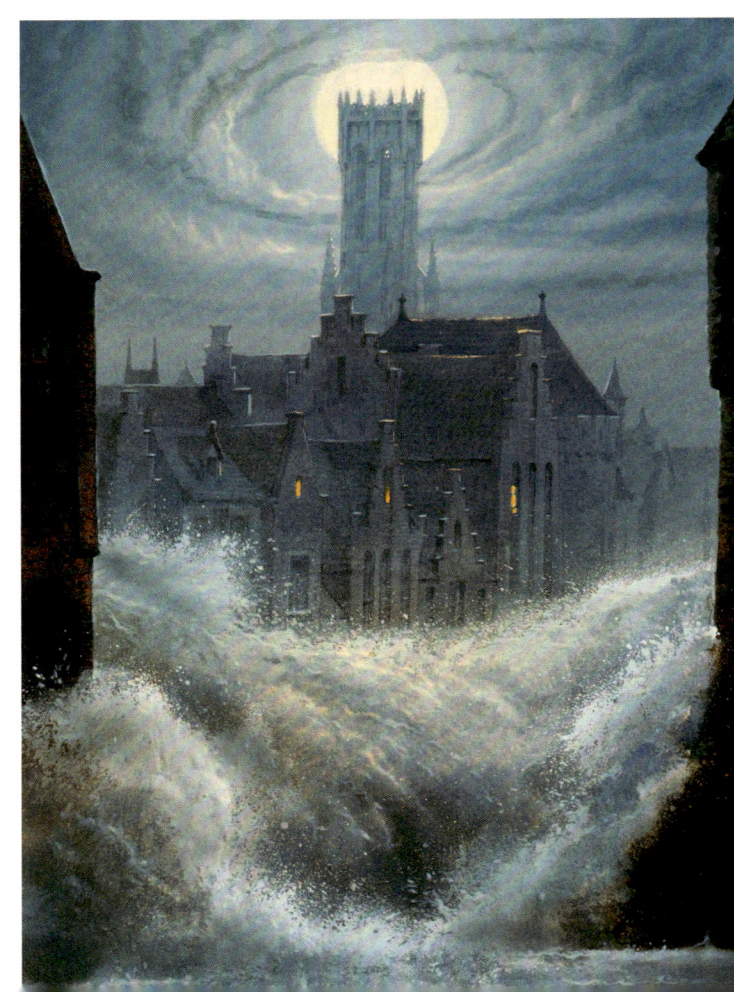

LANDSCAPES
ATLANTIS

This illustration is a double-page, full-bleed, full-colour opener for a picture essay on the drowned civilization. It seemed that there was no avoiding the catastrophic fate of Atlantis, but I did want to emphasize the fact that it was destroyed by Poseidon. Hence the huge and stern-visaged statue of the sea god presiding over the sinking.

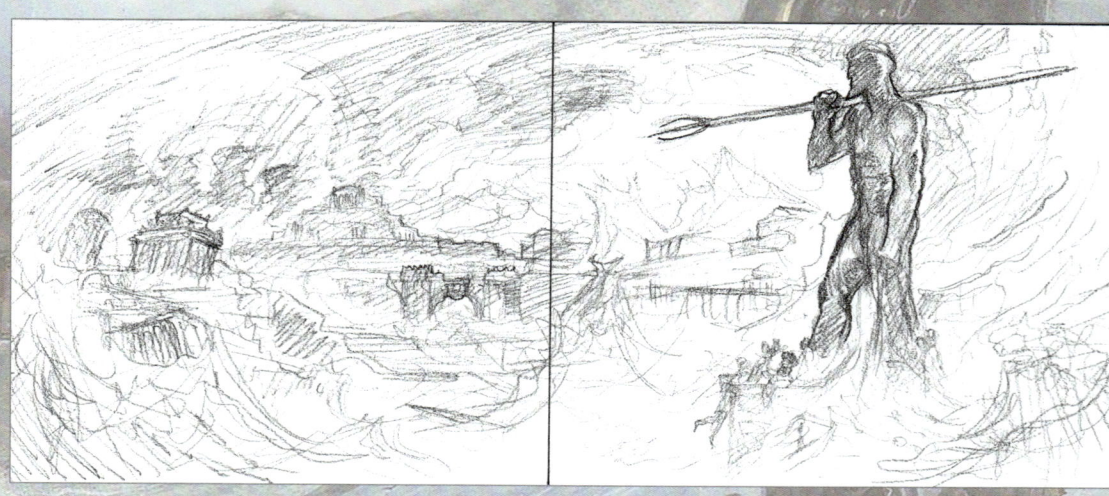

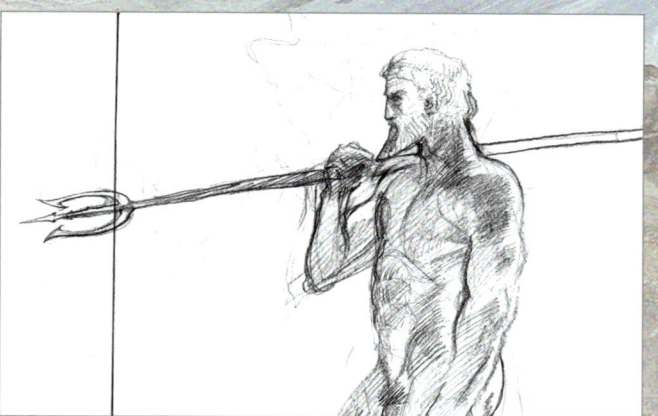

Sketches

A few constraints are imposed by the book's layout. A title and text will be placed on the left-hand page of the spread, and of course it's wise to keep important elements out of the gutter. For more rigorous layouts like this, it is worthwhile sketching in the correct format. I did a first sketch with Poseidon too large (left), then placed him in context in a second (above).

1

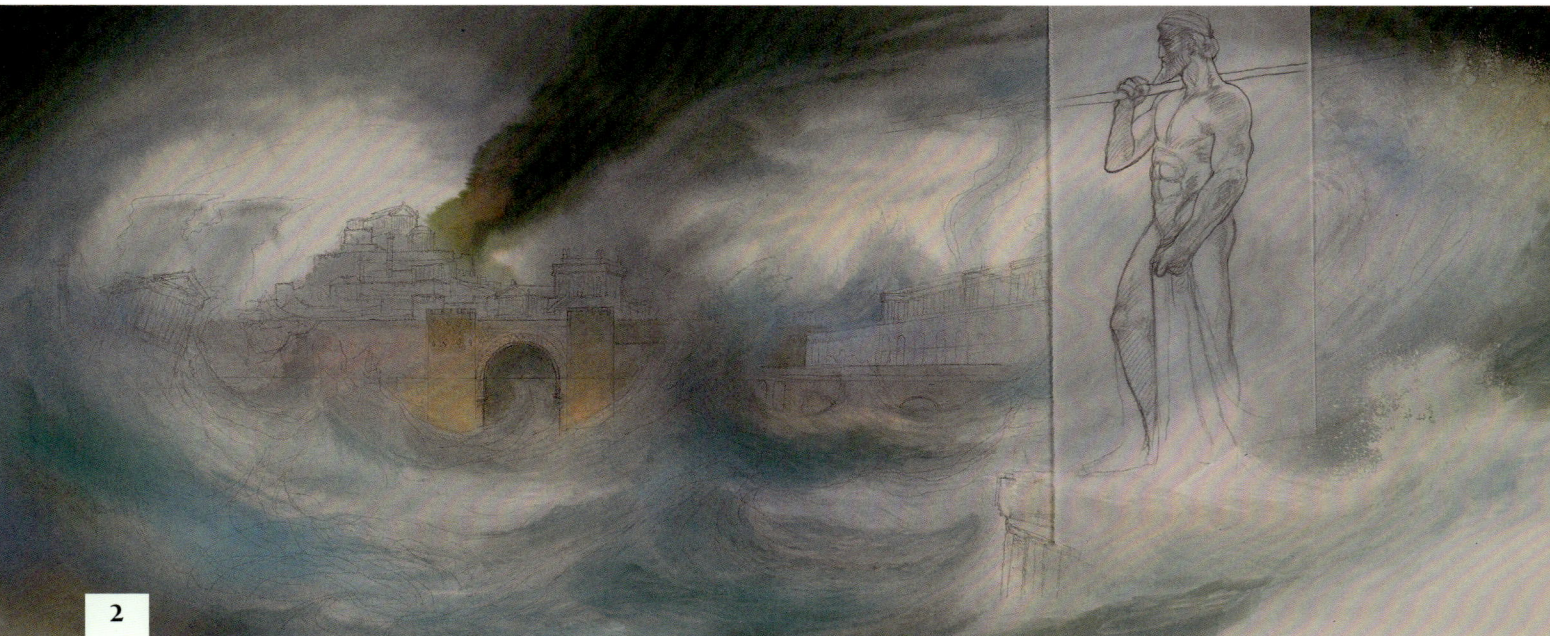

2

Stage 1
Initial colour wash

In cataclysms of this nature, the sky opens and clouds boil, waterspouts dance and waves churn. Using the sketch, I blocked in the sky and a few waves to determine the atmosphere. It may not look like much now, but it contains the guidelines I need to carry on. Time is limited – too much re-dampening of the paper will eventually disturb the colours. Squint at the page from a low angle to areas that are drying too quickly. Use a hair dryer to ensure that no pooling of water occurs, which results in a hard line along the edge of the puddle.

Stage 2
Establishing scale

The city has been sketched in and a horizon line determined. Dampening the whole sheet a second time, I've added the smoke from the fire and started to block out the masses of the water and the waves. Rather than be hindered by thinking of the statue (as he's much darker than the rest, there's no need to mask him off), redrawing him on tracing paper allows him to find the best position, then be folded back out of the way. A vanishing point in the middle of the central arch will draw the eye back to that point as well as fixing the surrounding structures.

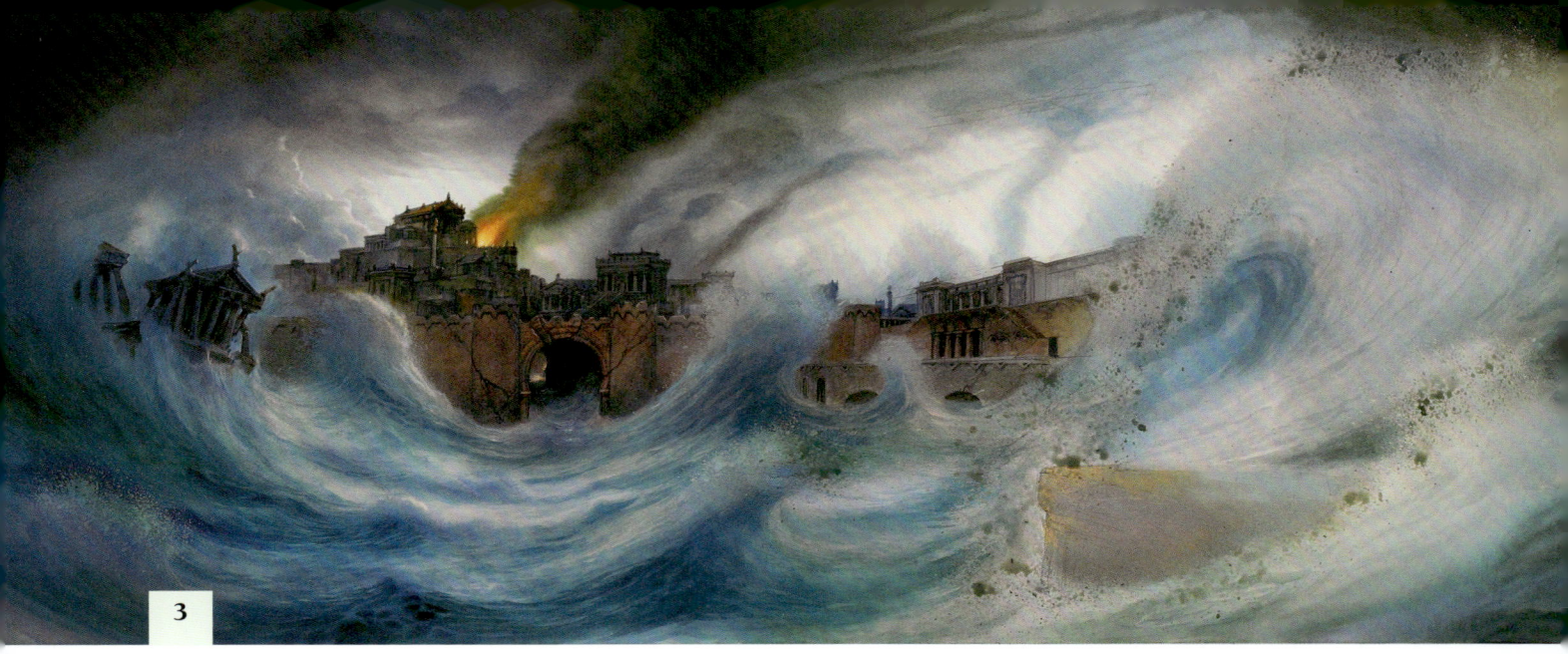

3

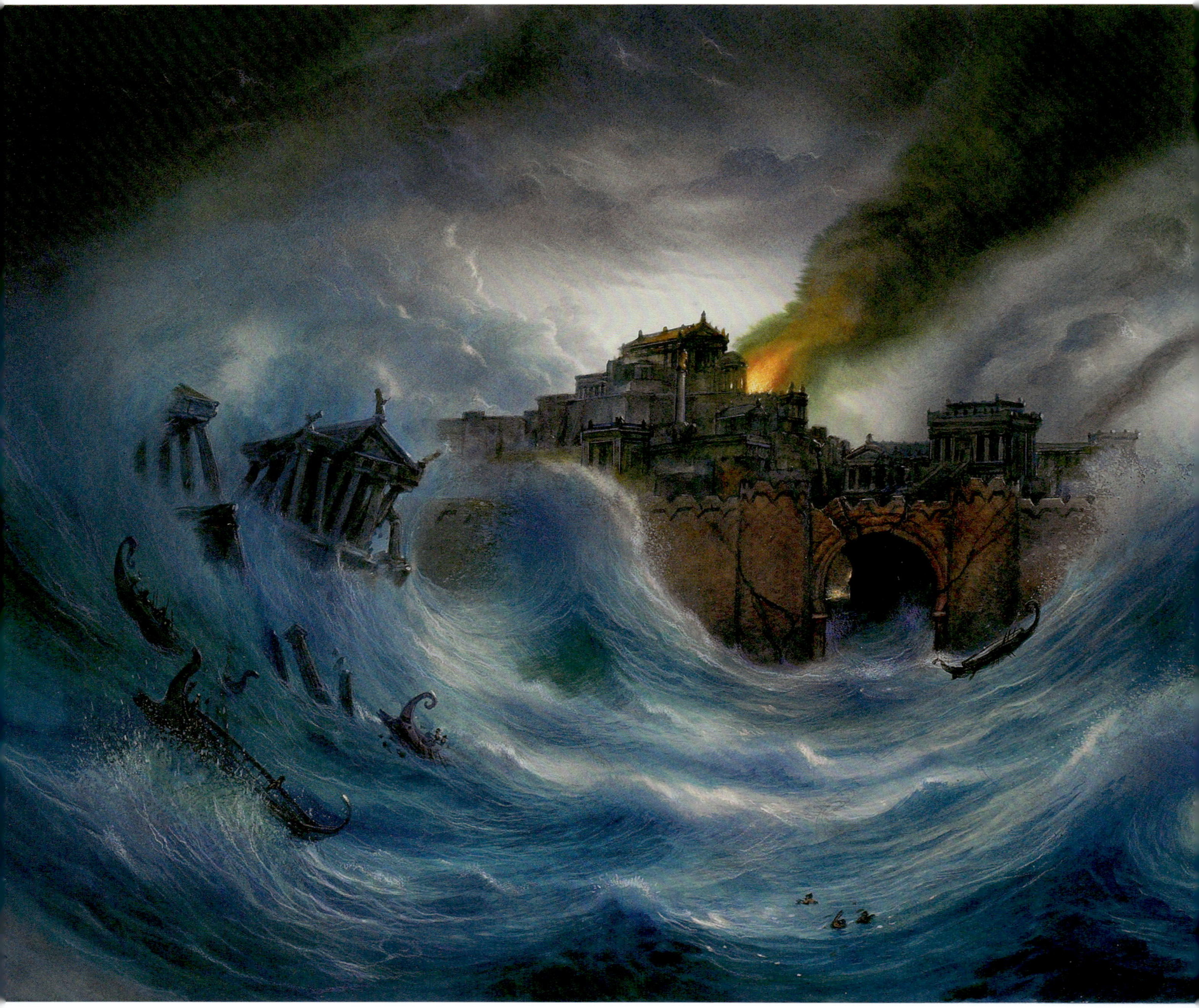

Stage 3
Making waves

That awful looking sticky latex splattered all over the sea is just what it looks like: awful-looking sticky latex, or masking agent. A lot is used for a picture with raging waters and crashing waves – I'm already on my second toothbrush. Mindful of the need to keep a low-contrast wave to the left of the image, there is still room for dark water to add depth.

⬇ Final artwork

I've added Poseidon, built the pedestal under his feet, added fleeing Atlanteans and capsizing galleys, and finished the wave that must support the text. Each wave is designed to bring the eye back around and into the centre of the image – the visual equivalent of an undertow – so there's no escape from the image itself or from the doomed city of Atlantis.

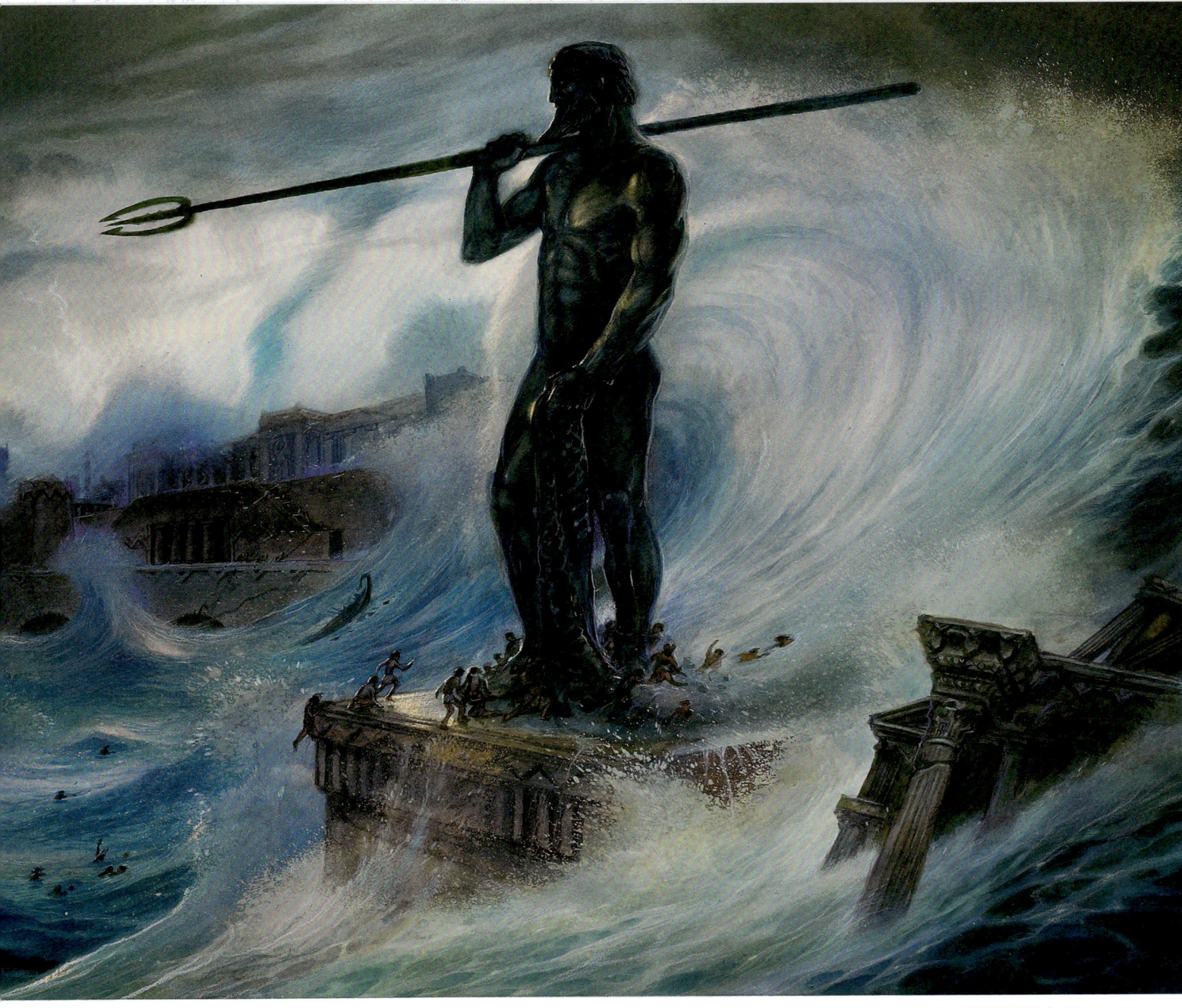

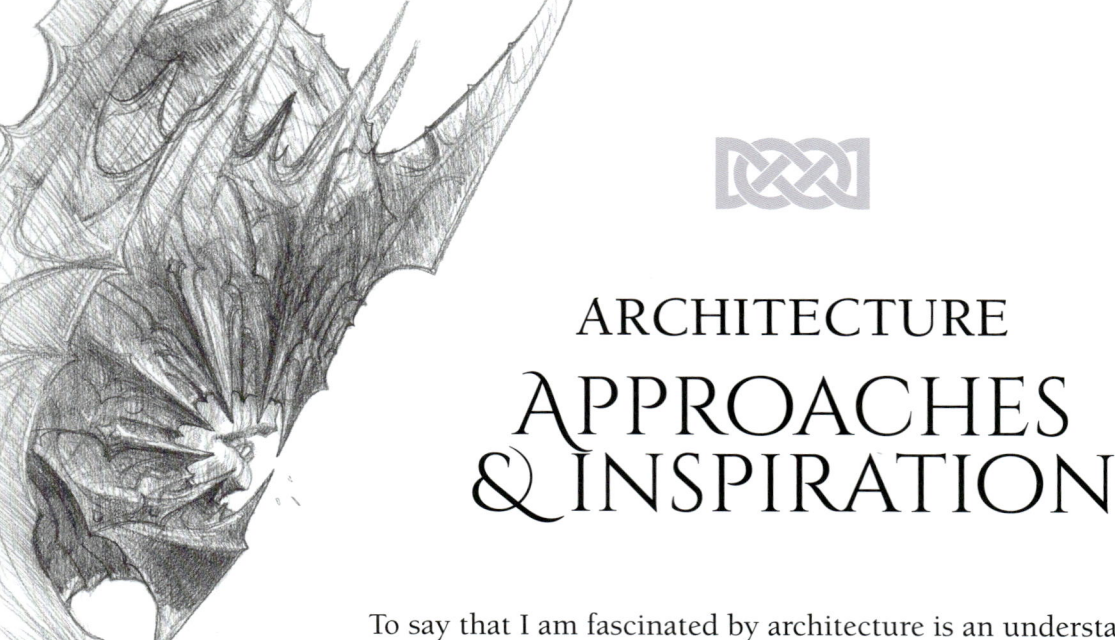

ARCHITECTURE
APPROACHES & INSPIRATION

To say that I am fascinated by architecture is an understatement. The world has a history of seven thousand years of placing one stone or brick atop another, and everywhere I go I spend spare moments snapping photos and making quick sketches.

I am enraptured by the patterns of paving stones, captivated by corbels, bewitched by belfries, I'm charmed by Corinthian, delighted by Doric, beguiled by Gothic, ensorcelled by Art Nouveau. Castles conquer me without siege, monuments arrest me mid-stride. I love all forms of architecture (except modern glass and steel, which is awe-inspiring, but affords little pleasure in rendering it). Architecture, like all human endeavours, is often a summing-up of a culture. This notion came home forcefully when in New Zealand working on the *Lord of the Rings* trilogy, several thousand miles away from any architecture more than a century or two old.

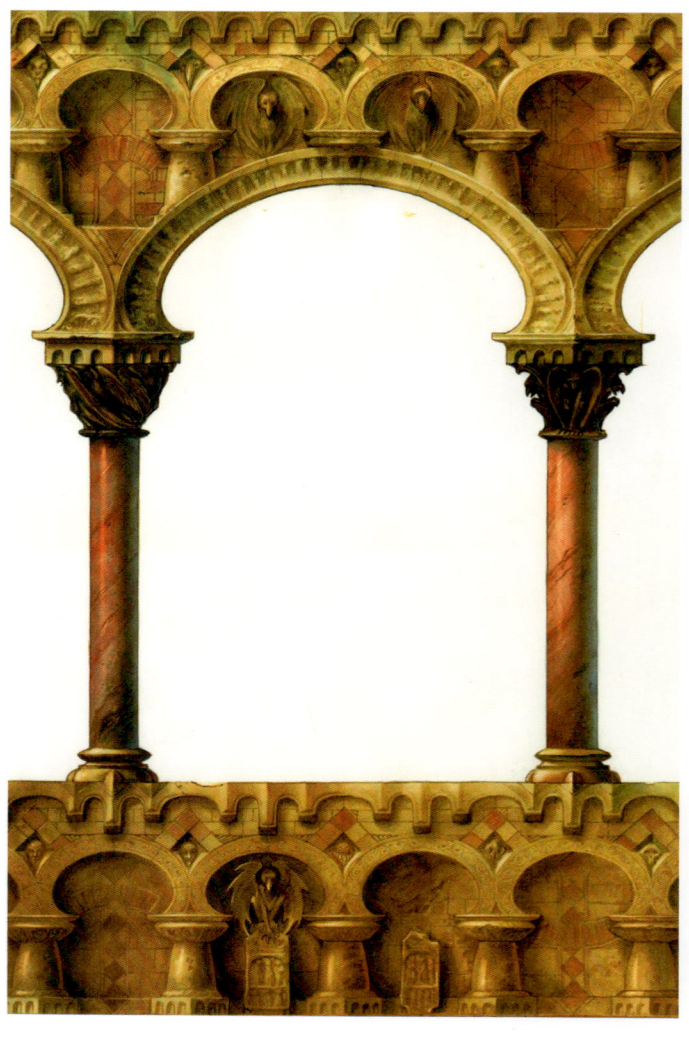

⬦ The Mouth of Sauron
The helmet of the Mouth of Sauron, from Tolkien's *The Return of the King*. The helm echoes in miniature the Towers of the Teeth flanking the Black Gate of Mordor, with their jagged ramparts and crenellations.

➼ Architectural Border
Each foray into an author's universe is a chance to explore a parallel history of art and architecture. Spain's Moorish architecture is one of the most beautiful in the world.

→ Winter of the Raven

I was overjoyed with a commission set in the Pacific Northwest. Drawing something I grew up with would be fun ... It was a nightmare. I have strong feelings about Northwest Coast First People's art. I am deeply touched by it (at 15, I carved a thirty-foot totem out of a fallen telephone pole), but lay no claim to any. I've walked through abandoned Nootka villages, a couple of hours by Ford Zodiac from anywhere. Rotting totems lay askew in the forest, an eerie requiem sung by screaming gulls. And an unwilling son of conquerors in damp hiking boots, rain on my glasses and in my heart. I'll never forget. Decades later and many miles away, the raven was no problem, but there are no photos of Haida poles in Switzerland: no book in a library or shop. I got lucky at the local Museum of Ethnology. I've since acquired several books on totems. Will I need to draw them again? Better safe than sorry ...

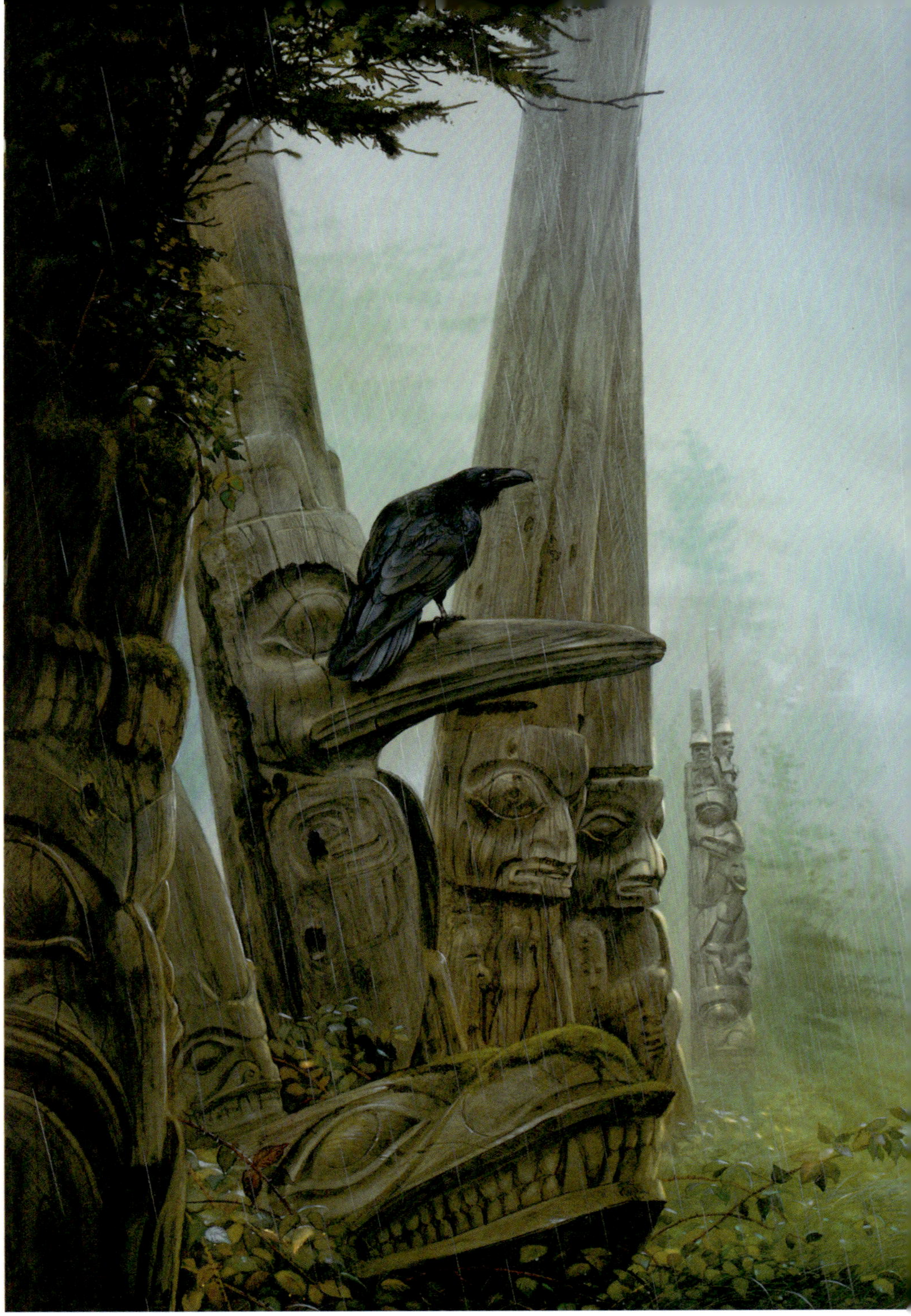

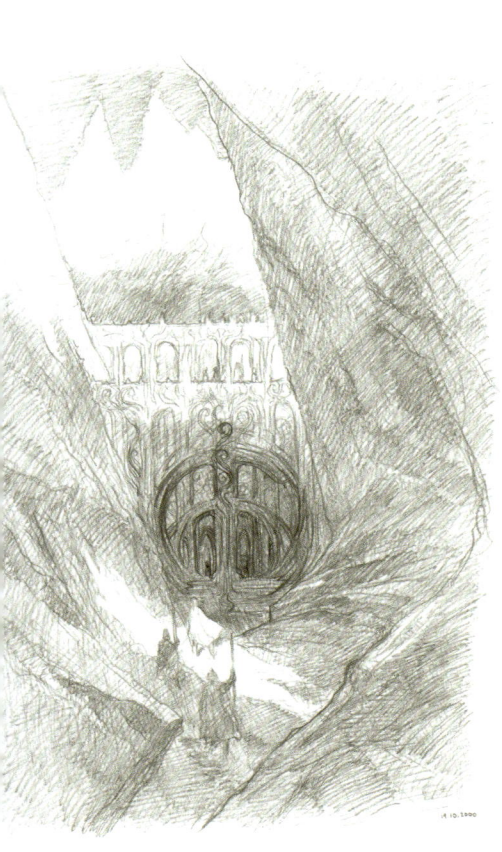

← Gates of Gondolin

First of a series of sketches for the seven gates of Gondolin, from Tolkien's *The Silmarillion*. Art Nouveau always springs to mind where elves are concerned. The supple lines, inspired by nature and plants, transformed into motifs, seem more elven than any other architecture.

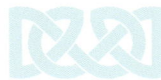

ARCHITECTURE
FANTASY & REALITY

Building fantasy architecture requires no diploma, no engineering skills, no degree. The construction is not done with quarried stone, moulded bricks or adzed timbers. The finished building is not intended to house generations of families, but to provide convincing, if temporary, lodgings for the imagination.

Of course, real architecture convinces. Whether ancient or contemporary, exotic or vernacular, it is real. We can admire or dislike it, but it is indisputably there. Fantasy architecture needs implicit approval without this facility. The idea is to briefly believe in what you are dreaming up, within the context imposed by the architecture itself. It's a process not so far removed from the work of medieval architects, who possessed ideal castles in their minds that could rarely be built. But every version that was constructed is an expression of a culture. The grasp of perspective required for illustrating is pretty basic. It's more a question of identifying that niggling sensation that something is 'not quite right' and possessing the solutions. It is a logical and mathematical process, but far less daunting than it can appear when tackled without method. It's only lines and points, after all.

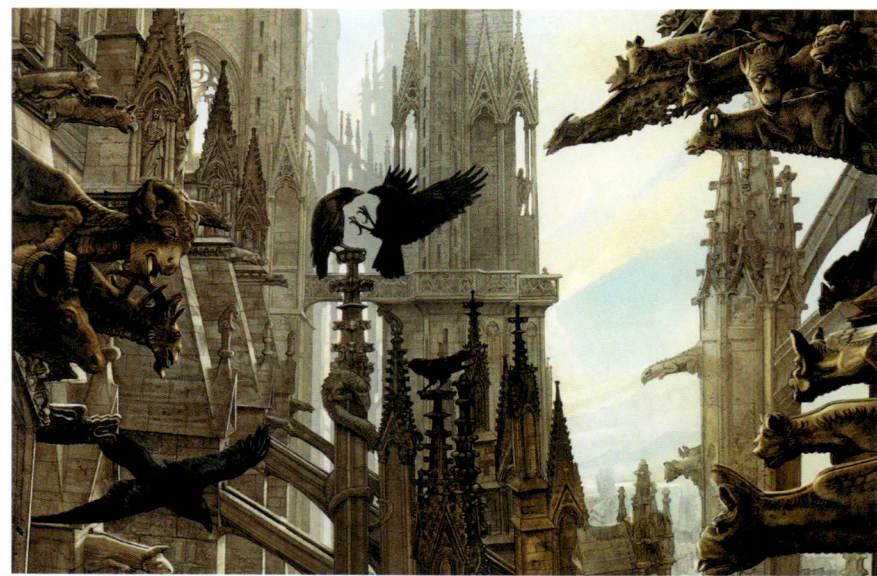

"IT'S A PROCESS NOT SO FAR REMOVED FROM THE WORK OF MEDIEVAL ARCHITECTS"

⬆ *Ravens*
This watercolour is actually a sort of collage. I took hundreds of photos of Strasbourg Cathedral, and stuck them all together. The superimposed rows of pinnacles and buttresses in the image are all actually the same row, seen from different heights.

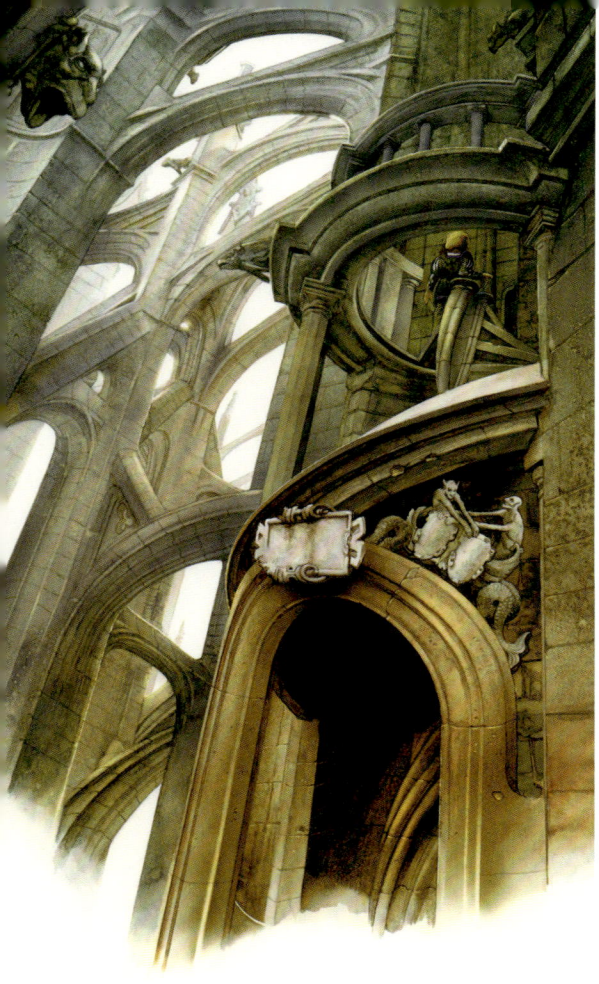

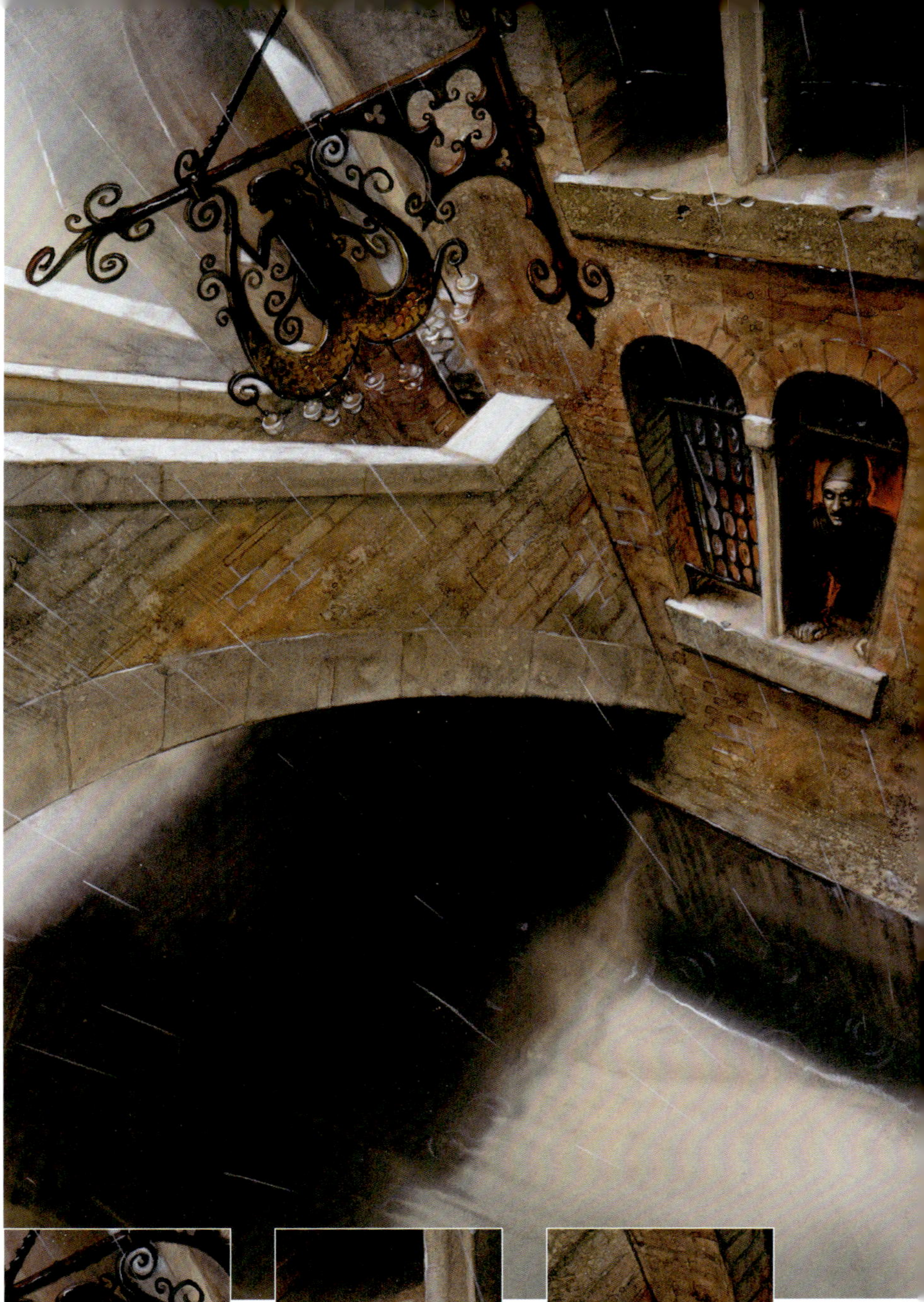

⬆ Stairs

This spiral staircase is a few stories up on the cathedral; I changed nothing. The flying buttresses are from Mont Saint-Michel. Since I worked from photos taken from close up and pinned together, the change of angle results in a bending of perspective. Add to this the twisting stairs and circling forest of buttresses, and the result is a visual updraft spiralling upwards.

➥ The Glassblower's Workshop

The story this painting illustrates is based on a charcoal drawing by Fernand Khnopff. Any period can be defined by architectural style, materials and techniques, to determine a 'look' for your fantasy world. Brick is a marvellous material to depict. Endlessly varied, it also occupies that portion of the spectrum where a hint of colour can make it warm or cold.

The Glassblower's Workshop, from *La Ville Abandonnée*, John Howe © CASTERMAN S.A.

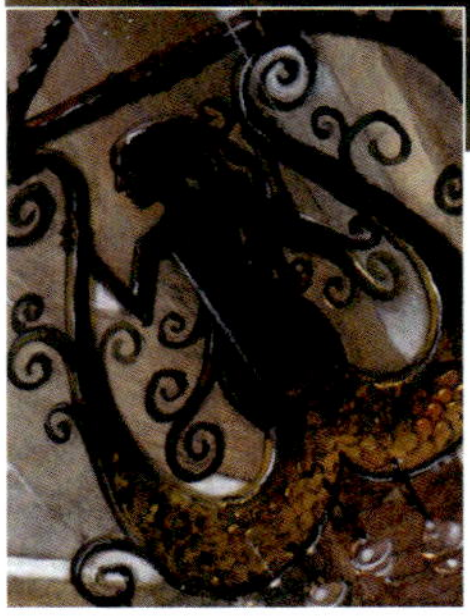

✦ The Melusine, a woman with a serpent's or fish's tail, is a heraldic motif often depicted with a double tail. This one was inspired by medieval models.

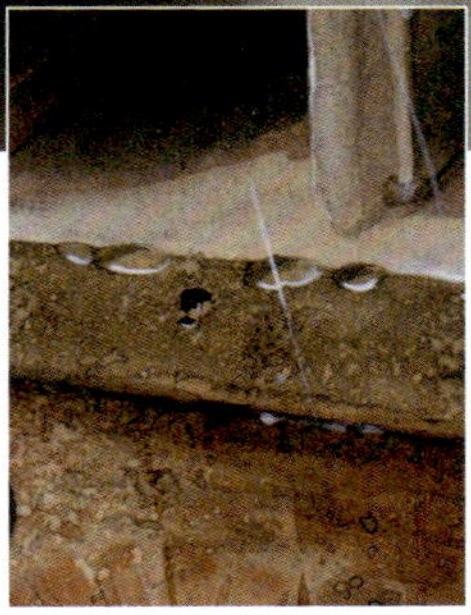

✦ Paying attention to chips and fissures, the wear and general patina bestowed by the elements, can help to make fantasy architecture convincing.

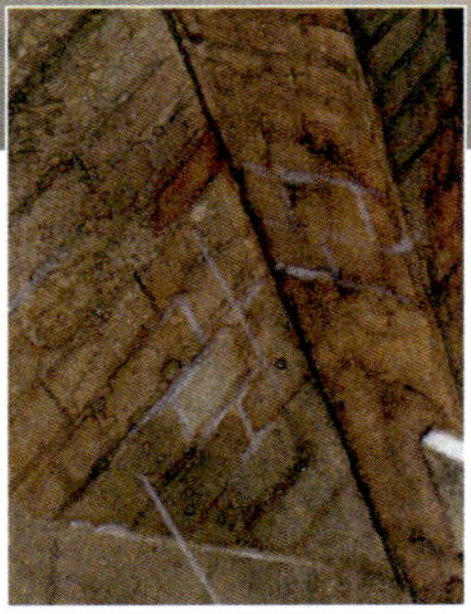

✦ As with dragons' scales, I either draw in each block on a lighter ground, or block in a whole wall and work up the lighter mortar with a coloured pencil.

ARCHITECTURE

THE ARRIVAL OF THE AIRSHIPS

This is the poster for a summer 2007 fantasy-oriented festival in the little town of Saint-Ursanne in the Swiss Jura. It's a well-preserved medieval town on a river, with a beautiful bridge. The image hopefully suggests the arrival of all manner of fantasy elements in the town for the event.

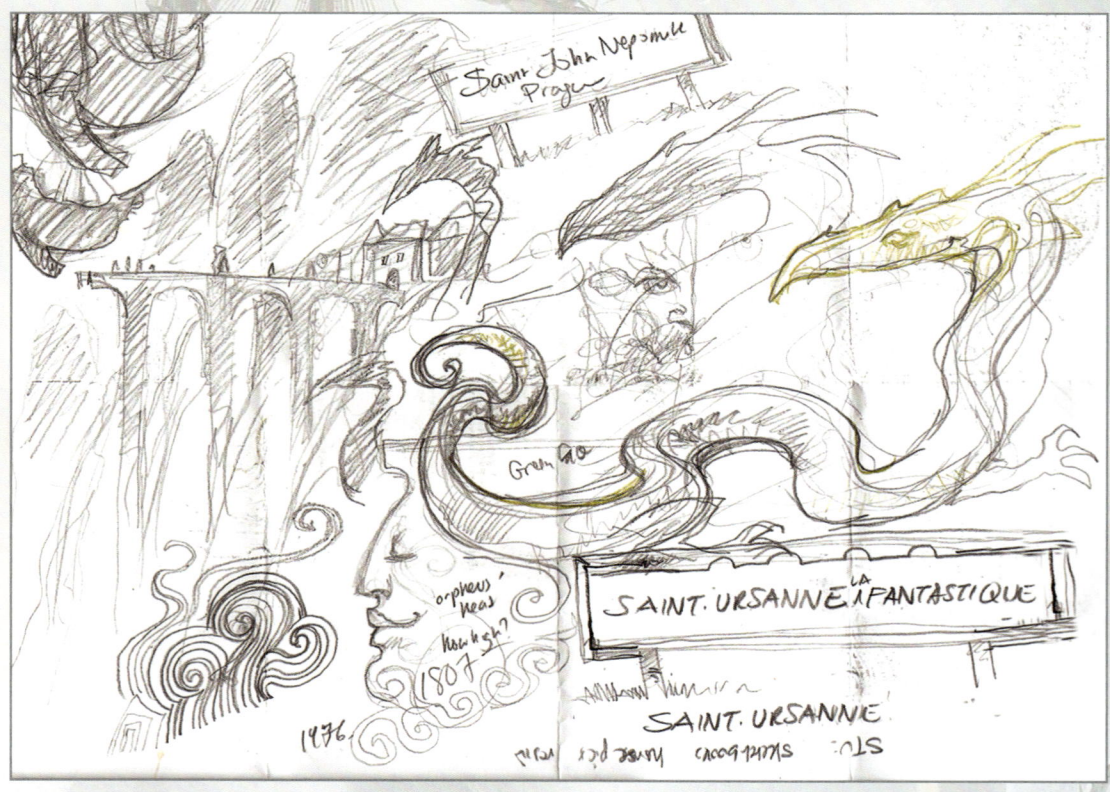

Sketch

The sketch is a scribble on a paper tablecloth, done in a restaurant when the idea popped into my head. Working from a photo – although the bridge is of course not that high and doesn't end in mid-span – it was enough to sketch the houses and bridge right on to the paper itself.

Stage 1
Initial washes

Thinking very hard about the Yellow Mountains in China and Milford Sound in New Zealand, I got the paper (it is big) exceedingly damp and worked in a few suggestions of mountains and waterfalls. I wetted the whole paper three times for three successive washes, which is about all any paper will take before too many colours run into each other.

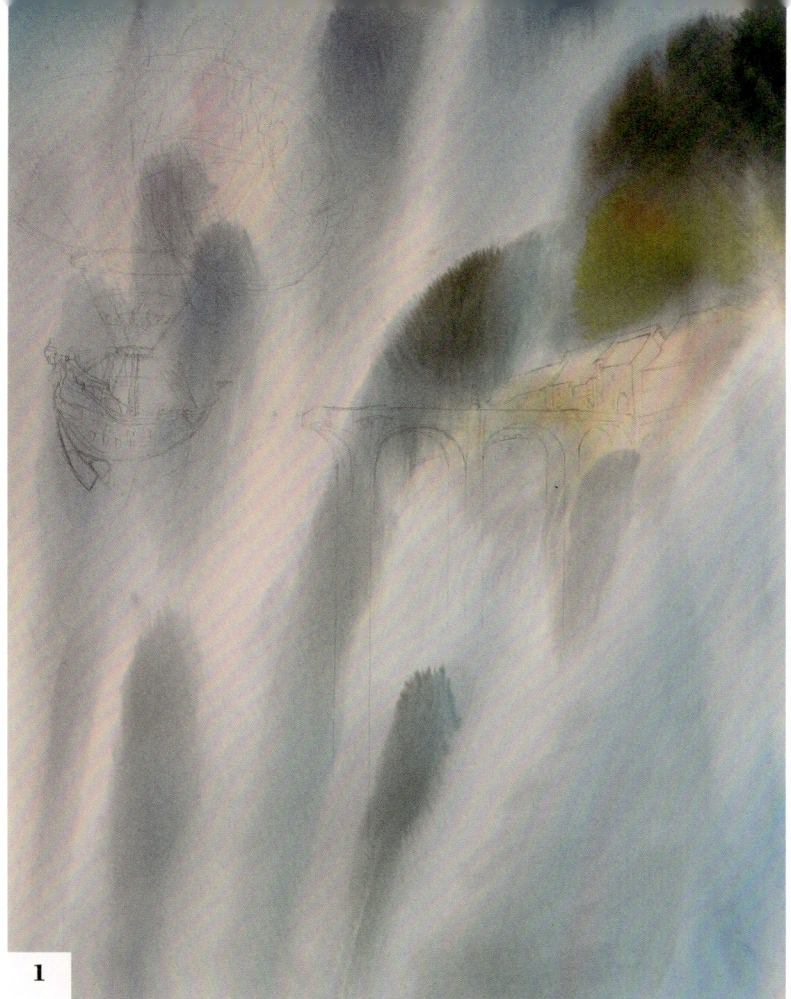

Stage 2
Blocking and defining

I have re-sketched the town more tightly, blocked in the bridge and added some clouds at the top, and have continued working up details on the bridge and the town itself, leaving a spot behind the lower dragon's head. (I moved the dragon later, so eventually painted in the light spot.) I've added a hint of cloud and mist and started to work in the nearer waterfalls. Masking off elements such as the pillars is helpful in keeping them vertical. On a whim I decided to add the enormous stone head in the distance – rather close to the edge of the painting, but a little clone stamping in Photoshop will allow the image to extend past trim edge so hopefully it can stay.

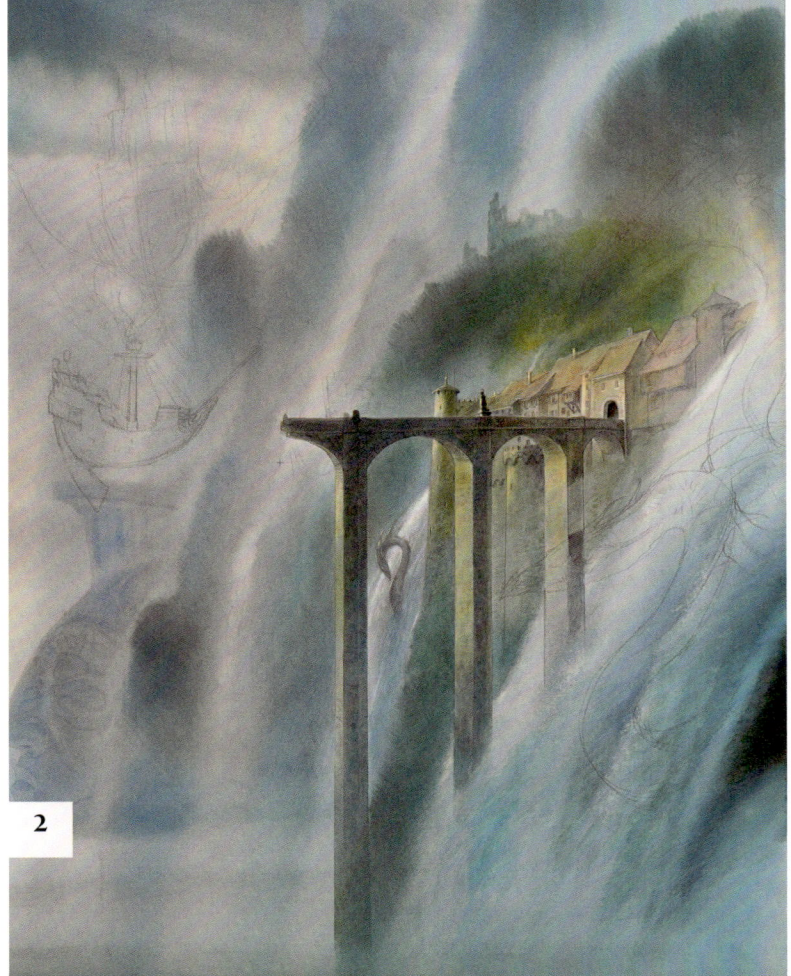

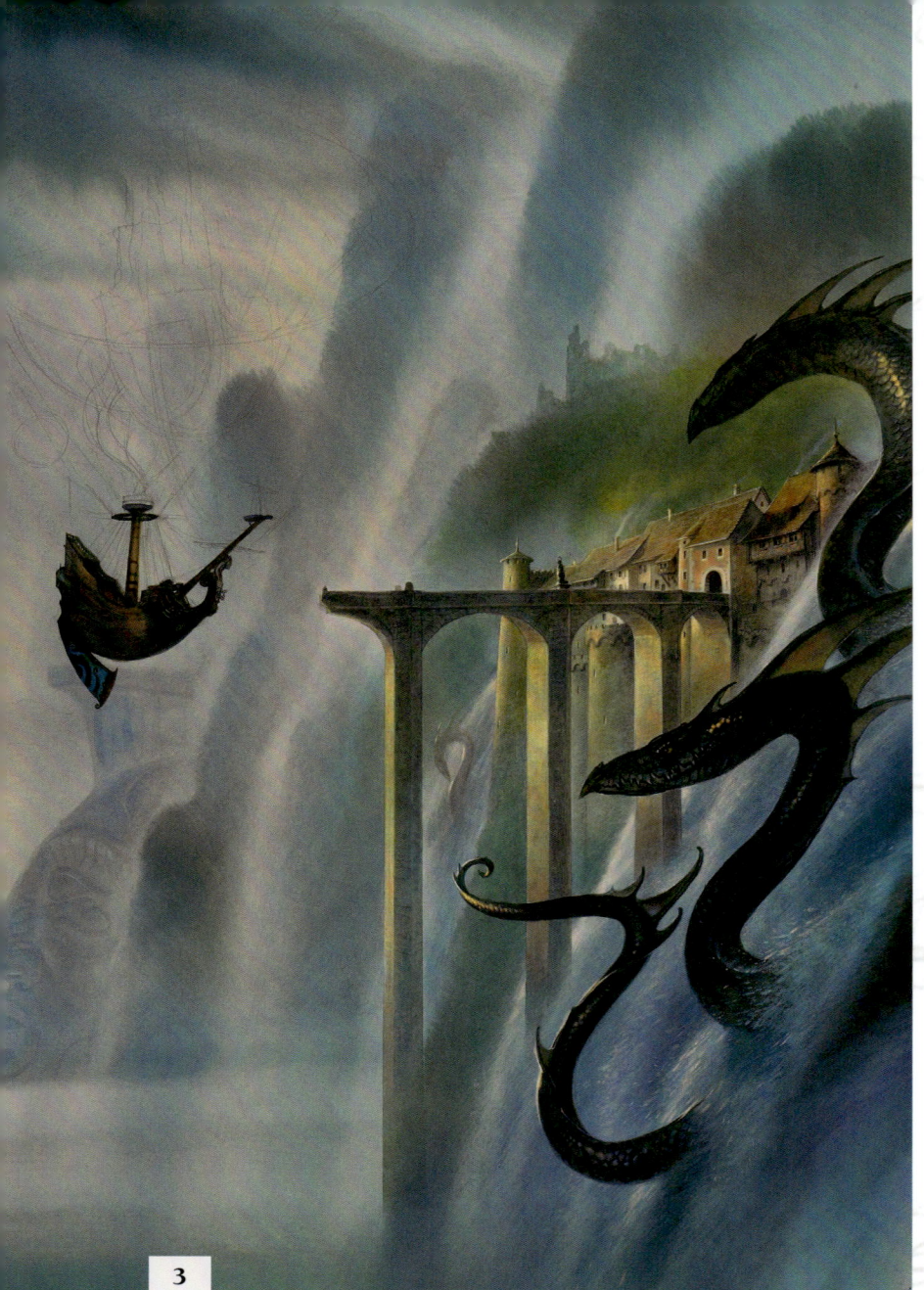

3

Stage 3
Placing the dragons

Options are becoming indelible decisions. The dragons have found their places (the tail of the lower dragon was decided with a rapid, no-going-back stroke of the brush, more akin to calligraphy than drawing, but this is often a way of retaining energy and movement) and the foreground waterfall is now properly contrasted. The airships are finding their positions, more or less following the initial sketch. I have also, in a moment of annoyance, run a wash over the far dragon and his waterfall, and erased a lot of white pencil crayon that I had put in prematurely, trying to find the values for the middle ground. The cascade and creature are now well in the background where they belong.

"THE TAIL OF THE LOWER DRAGON WAS DECIDED WITH A RAPID, NO-GOING-BACK STROKE OF THE BRUSH, MORE AKIN TO CALLIGRAPHY THAN DRAWING"

➨ Final artwork

The two airships – freely inspired by existing ships and images of early balloons – are in place. They might have been a little better moved slightly to the right, but it seemed important to maintain the distance between the ships and the quay. The empty spot in the middle is now occupied by the birds, added on the spur of the moment at the end, but a certain amount of empty space has been left to accommodate all the text that posters require.

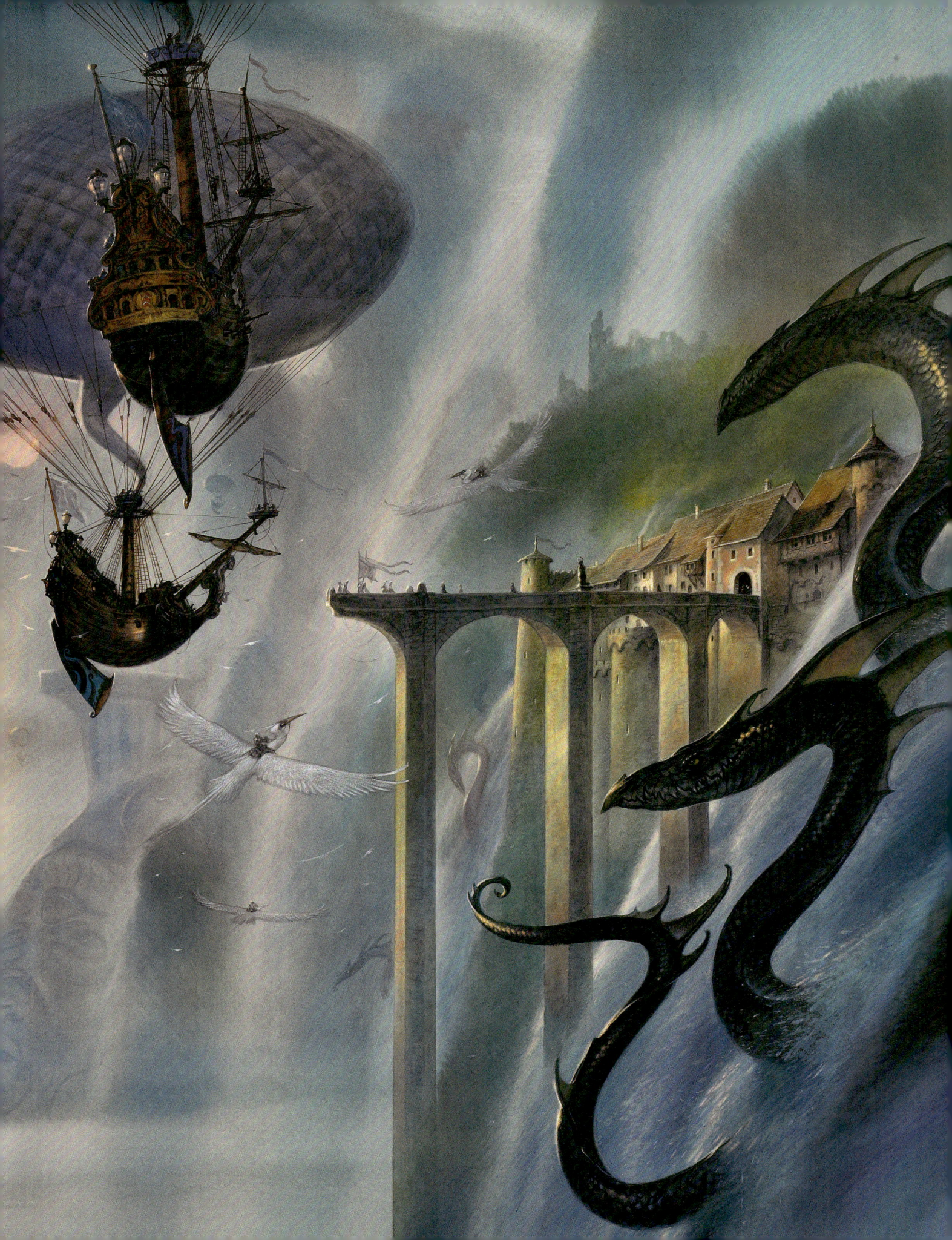

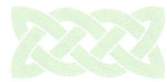

ATMOSPHERES
APPROACHES & INSPIRATION

If I had to settle on one reason for drawing pictures, the key word would be 'atmosphere'. Light and dark are the most powerful themes in history, the most constant in allegory and the grandest graphic opportunity afforded to fantasy illustrators.

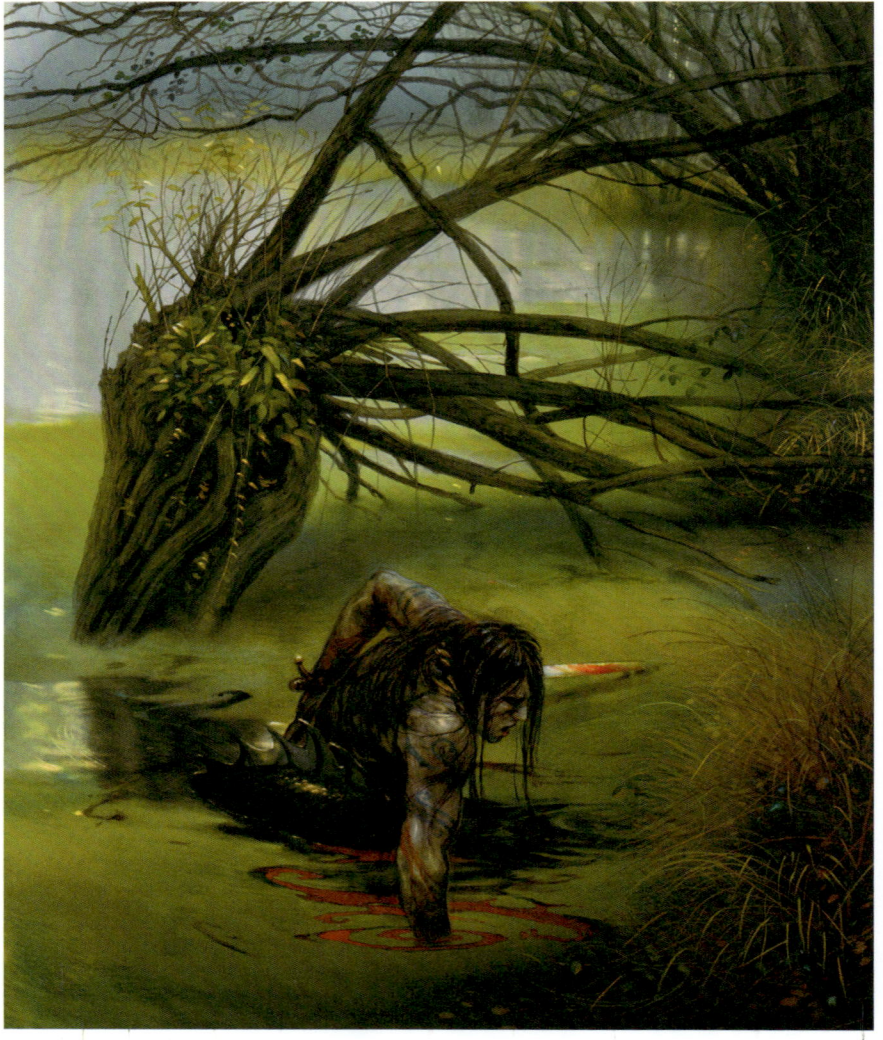

I would prefer to compromise on graphic straitjackets such as perspective and proportion rather than undermine any opportunity to treat every image as an atmospheric whole. Treating atmosphere with the attention it deserves allows you to exploit every possibility an illustration offers. There is also a pragmatic side to this. As the pot of water one uses to rinse brushes grows steadily more opaque, a little of every colour ends up in every other. While it's crucial that water be clean initially, the residue, both on the palette and in the rinse, adds to the coherence of the whole work.

← *Celtic Dragon*
The scene is set amongst the marshes that border the Rhine. I've always loved still water with algae or weeds, and the possibilities offered by juxtaposing the different surfaces.

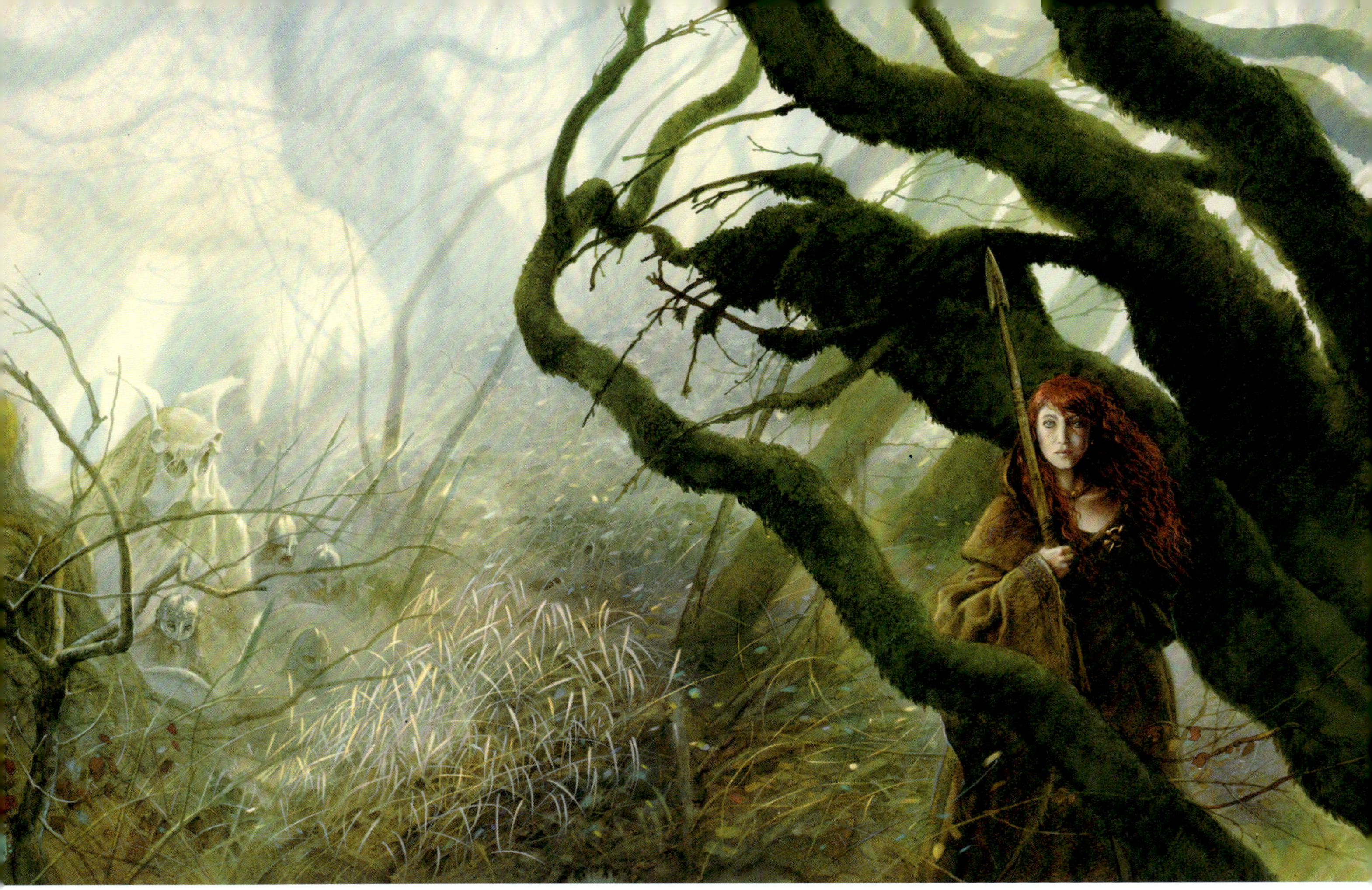

↑ *Mythago Wood*

Occasionally authors open wide worlds into which you fall headlong. Robert Holdstock is one of those writers who has stumbled on a unique world that he alone occupies. The landscape is local, along the shores of Lake Neuchâtel; all I did was add the characters. I'd used the same landscape over a decade before in *Merlin* (*see* Sketching Tutorials), and it's likely that I'll use it again one day.

"TREATING ATMOSPHERE WITH THE ATTENTION IT DESERVES ALLOWS YOU TO EXPLOIT EVERY POSSIBILITY"

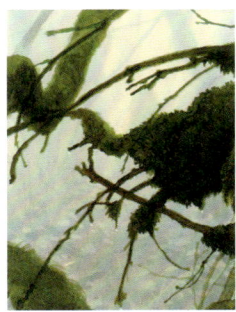

◆ I have a deep drawer of photos of mossy trunks and branches. You cannot do better than nature does, and it's often worth allowing a composition to be guided by the elements you find.

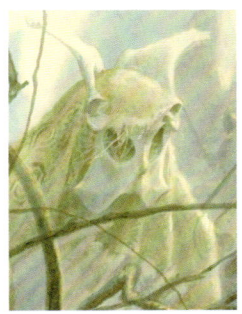

◆ Years ago, a schoolfriend and I built a costume using a deer's pelvis as a mask, with a tunic made of a hessian mattress cover, with Celtic spirals printed by rusty springs. Now and then an excuse arises to get out the photos.

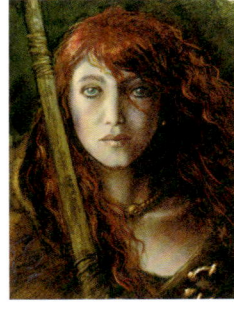

◆ The character Guiwinneth of *Mythago Wood* is a daydream brought to life from a romanticized Celtic past. This portrait is loosely based on an acquaintance, but also on a daydream of my own.

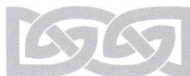

ATMOSPHERES
DARK & LIGHT

The balance of light and dark is a
powerful symbolical tool as well
as a handy pictorial device.

D ark is often mistakenly thought of as black,
but it is usually composed of a variety of
colours. Dark areas can indicate depth,
but black alone will give you only a flat
opaque surface. It is wise to reserve black for surfaces black
in colour, or the darkest corners of your image. The best
darkness is a mix of complementary colours – I'm fond
of Prussian Blue and Sepia, as they can easily become a
warm or cold darkness, depending on how they are dosed.
Shading doesn't consist only of dark and yet darker areas.
It's about the contrast of shade and light, so you always
have to remember to make highlights. For this I use mainly
white (or light-coloured) pencils in my paintings.

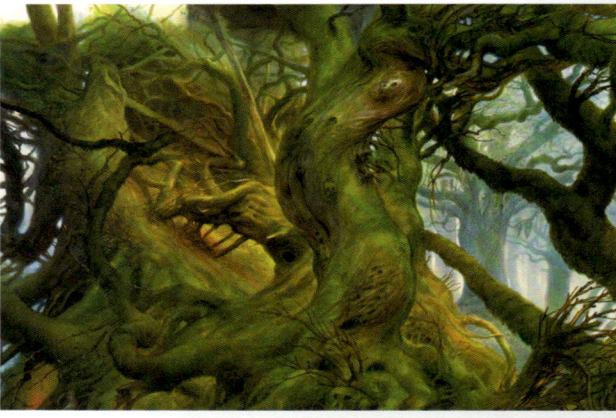

⬆ The Perilous Wood

Forests are studies in contrast, and
often abbreviations of perspective,
where line is replaced by juxtaposition
of value. This image was for a book
cover, with a large white 'hole' on the
right, but I eventually completed it
for its own sake. I often paint in the
whitened glare of sky visible through
trees afterwards, letting the light spill
over the edges to increase the effect.

➥ Rainstorm

I always marvel at medieval stonework
and the intricate Gothic tracery on
cathedrals. Ocean salt often creates
the same kind of tracery in rock, so
this picture is a mingling of Strasbourg
Cathedral and the Pacific Northwest
coast. Raindrops are particles of falling
light or shadow: as a tool available to
render atmospheric perspective, they
rank second only to mist and fog.

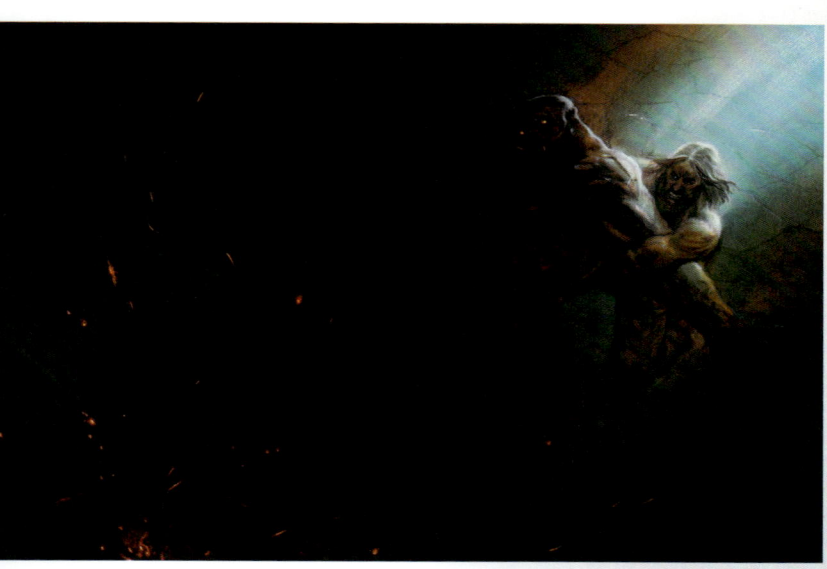

⬅ Beowulf and Grendel
Originally done for a board game, only
a small portion of this image was to
be used, but it is always good policy
to do an illustration that can stand on
its own. I shifted the perspective to
an overhead view – far more dramatic
with the embers of the fire.

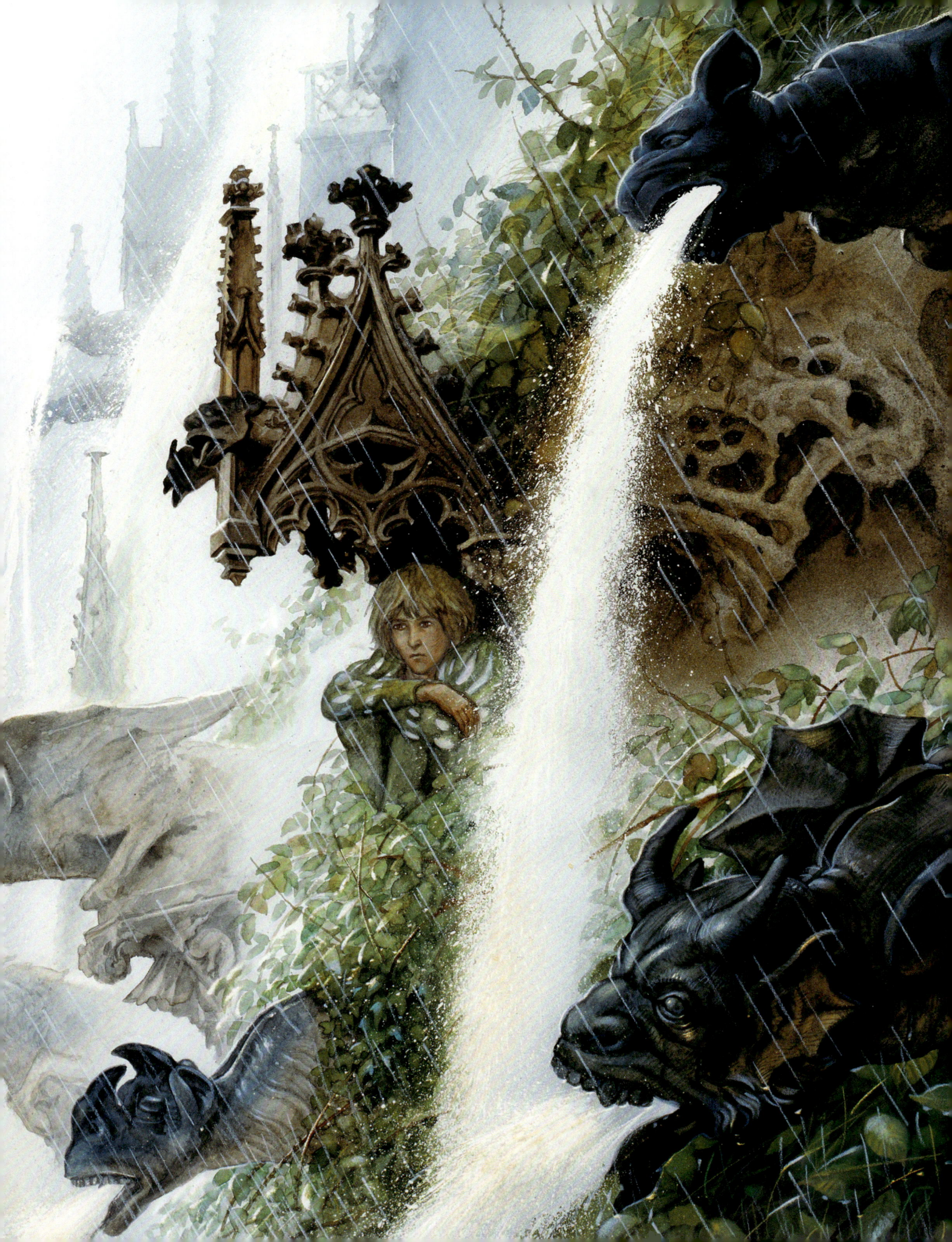

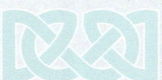

ATMOSPHERES
BHARGEST LAND

Collectable cards are to me a relatively frustrating medium. While they are for the most part brilliantly reproduced, the print size is very small. Nonetheless, a landscape must be treated as if it were to be a poster and not a postage stamp. When landscape includes no humans to provide scale, it is crucial to use a 'lens' close to a standard 50mm, carefully placing the viewer at human height above the terrain.

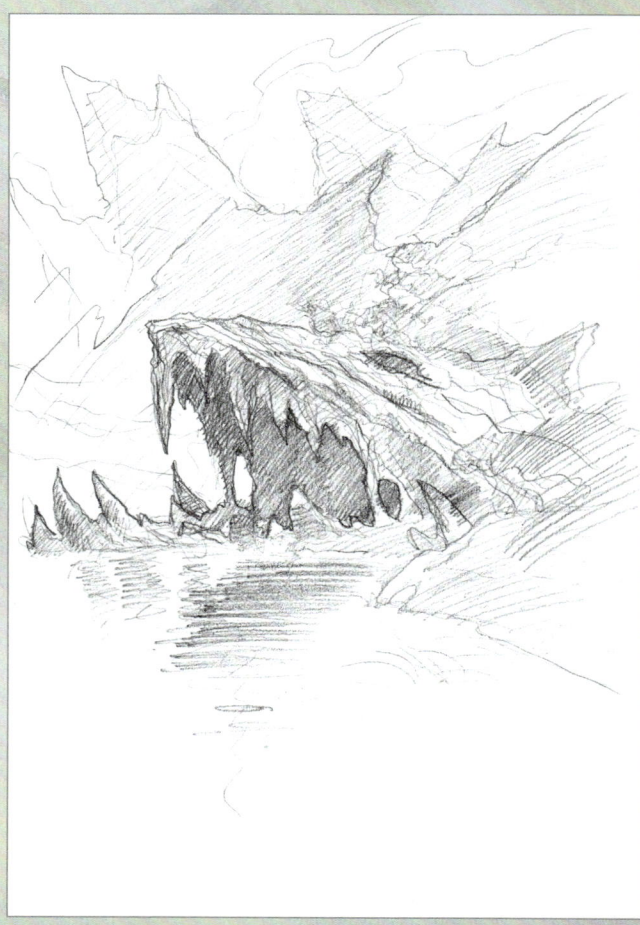

Sketch

A rough sketch, but with all the elements in place, for a card in the series *Magic – The Gathering*. The brief: 'This is one of five lands that represent a huge creature that's been integrated into the terrain – sleeping, petrified, hidden, or otherwise neutralized. In this case it's an enormous, evil, wolf-like, "demon-dog" creature of folklore: a barghest. Show a large, dark cave in a bog that barely resembles the barghest's huge mouth. Behind the cave mouth, a cluster of hills slightly resembles the barghest's crouched body. The general impression should be that the cave only vaguely resembles a huge black wolf with its mouth agape – it shouldn't be too obvious.'

Stage 1
Strike one

The initial wash with a colour scheme blocked in. I was careful to work to the sketch I transferred prior to wetting the paper. But the result wasn't satisfying – the colours weren't as I had imagined. Also, I had stopped short of blocking in the foreground values, which was an error.

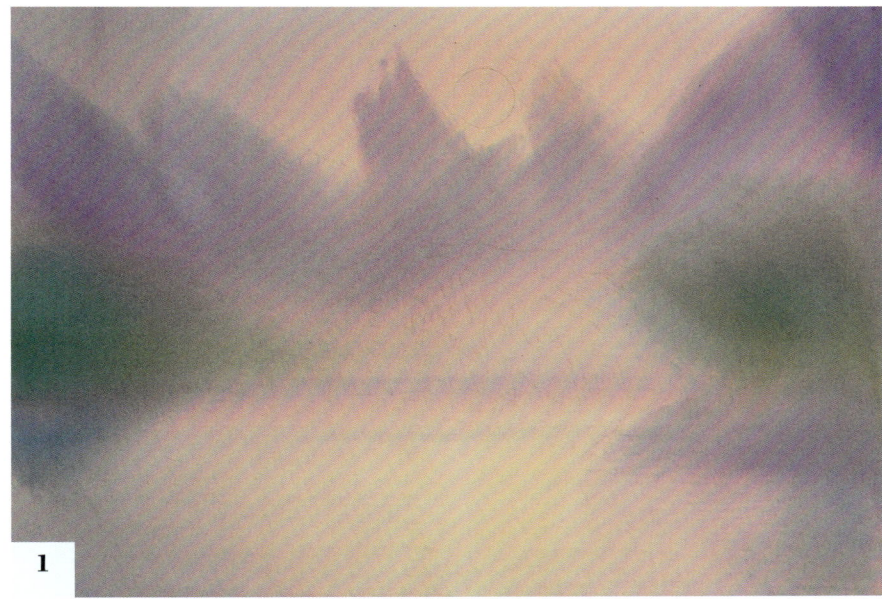

Stage 2
Stage second time luckier

I decided that the first version was far too tame and boring, so I brought out another board, set up my sketchbook so I could see the sketch, and blocked this in on a very damp ground, without any pencil work beforehand. It's a shame it can't be left like this.

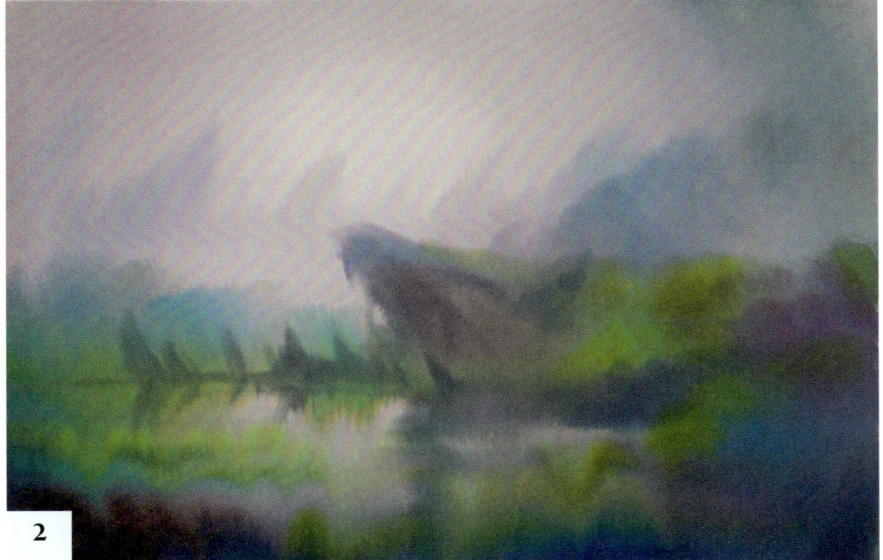

Stage 3
Adding detail

The details are being worked up using drybrush in order to keep lines and zones from forming; a medium-wide oil painting brush is often the solution. Also, putting clear water in the airbrush (with the pressure turned well down) allows portions of the paper to be dampened without forming hard edges when drying, allowing you to work in the middle of that zone for a moment. The tree branches are done in coloured pencil.

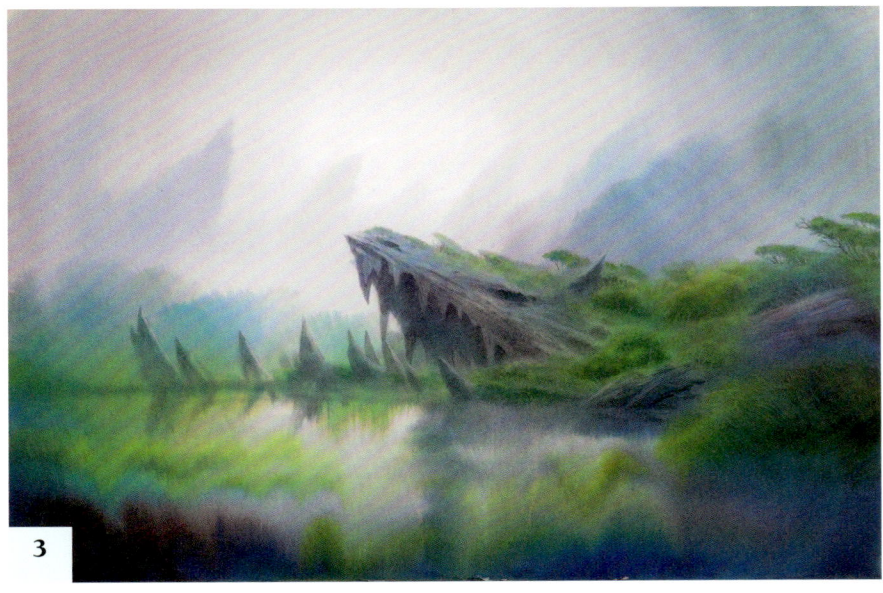

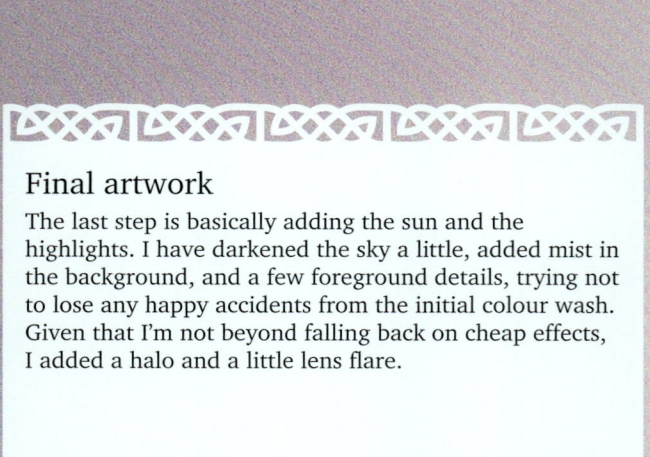

Final artwork

The last step is basically adding the sun and the highlights. I have darkened the sky a little, added mist in the background, and a few foreground details, trying not to lose any happy accidents from the initial colour wash. Given that I'm not beyond falling back on cheap effects, I added a halo and a little lens flare.

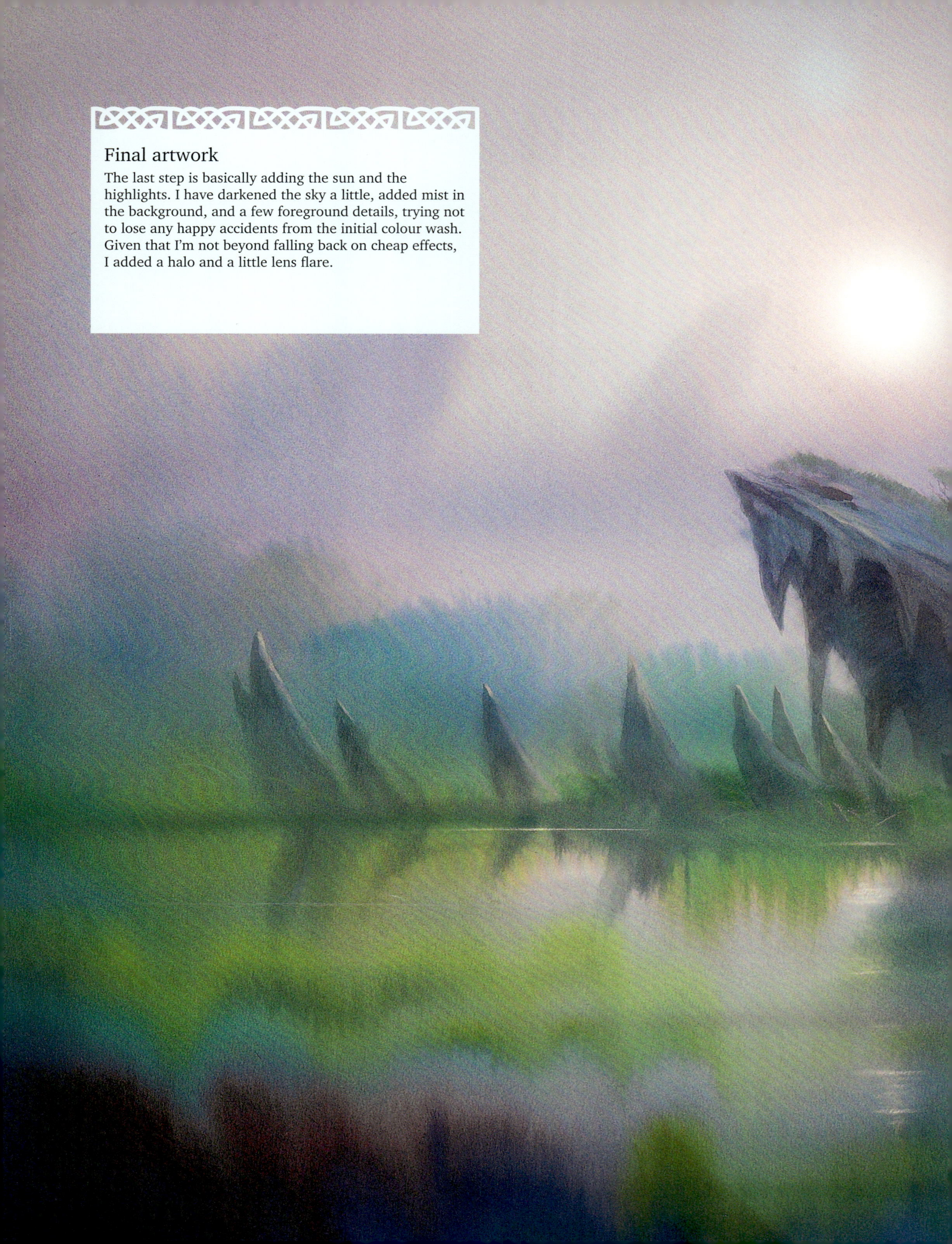

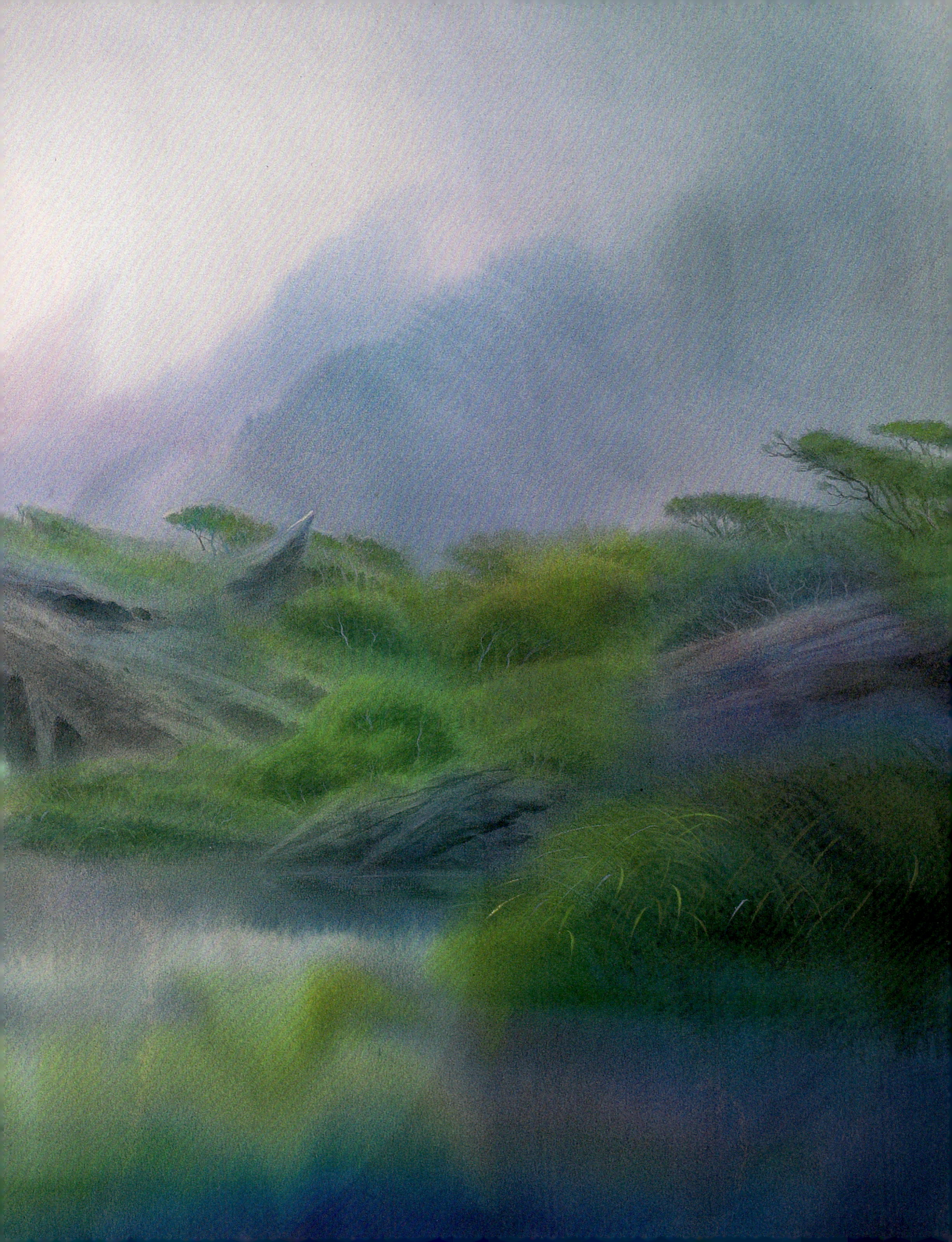

WORDS & PICTURES

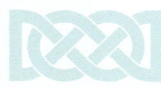

In the years since I wrote the original books, I have of course not paused: projects follow projects, paintings succeed each other on the easel, words fill pages. I am ever more fascinated by the imagery of words and the stories pictures tell. The world is full of layers, of depth and meaning; art in all its forms is there to help us perceive it better. Here is a small selection of those creations, presented as a portfolio of images and thoughts.

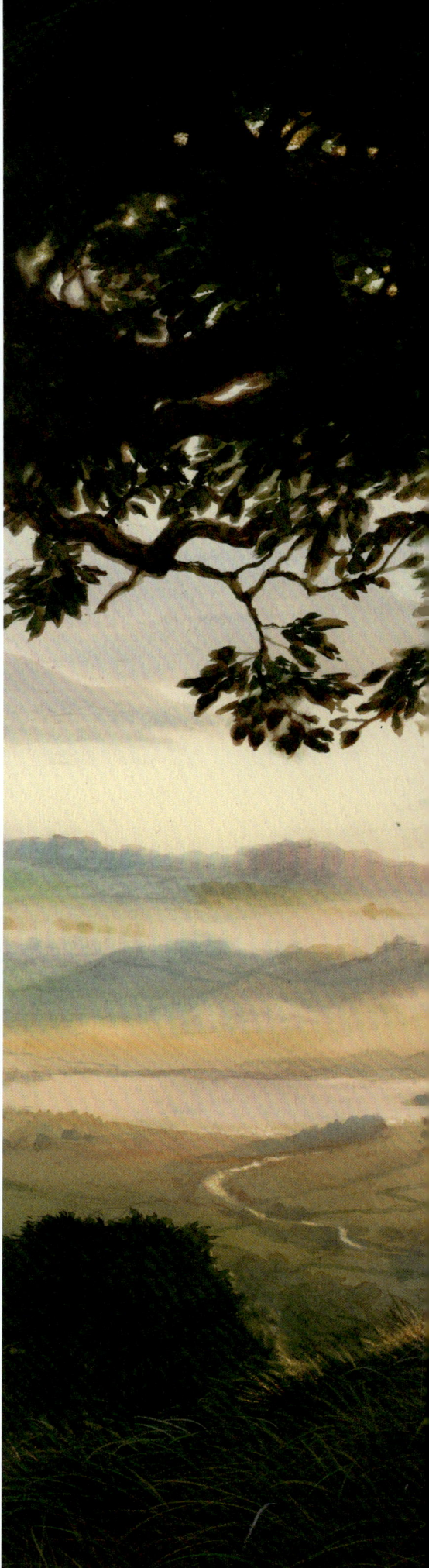

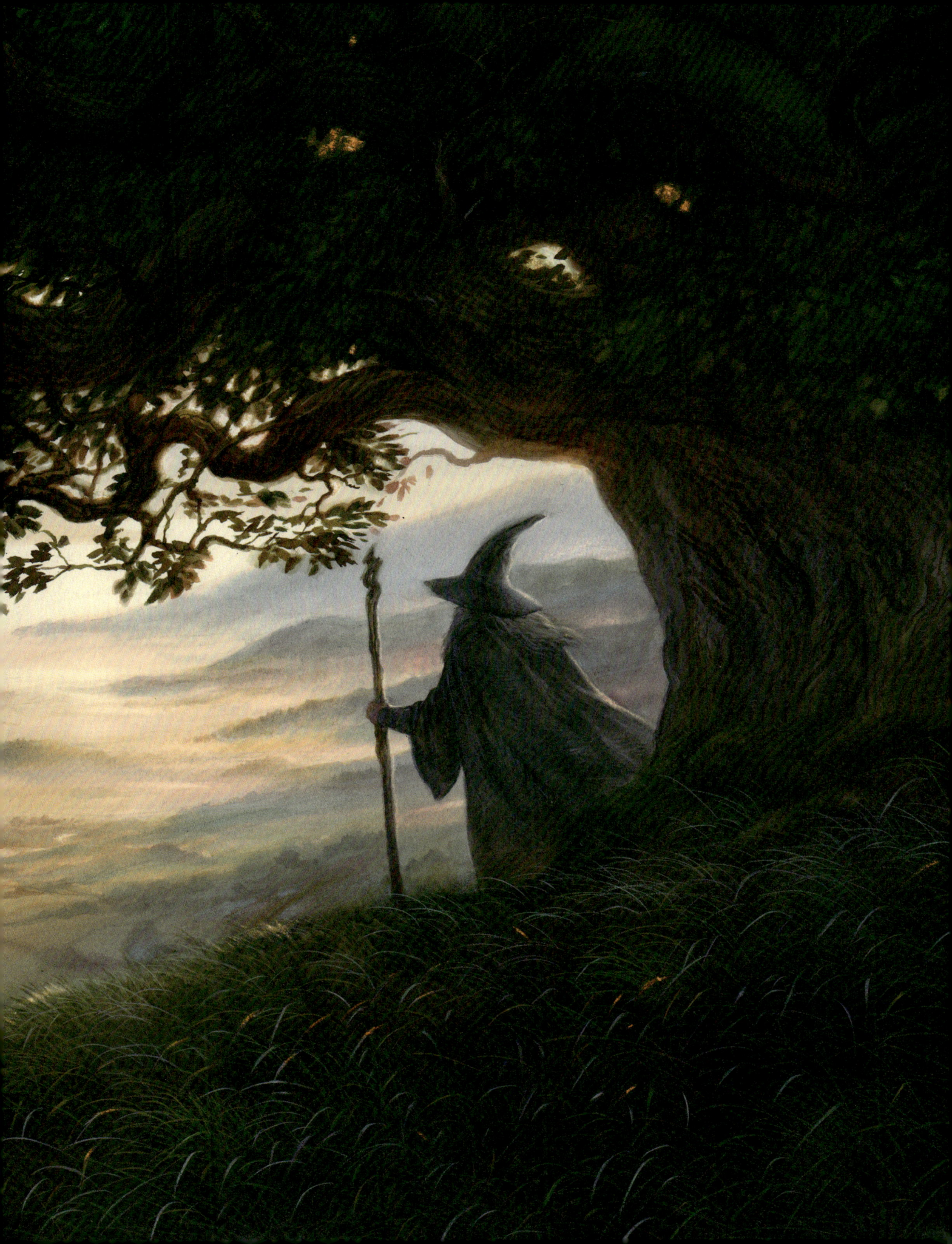

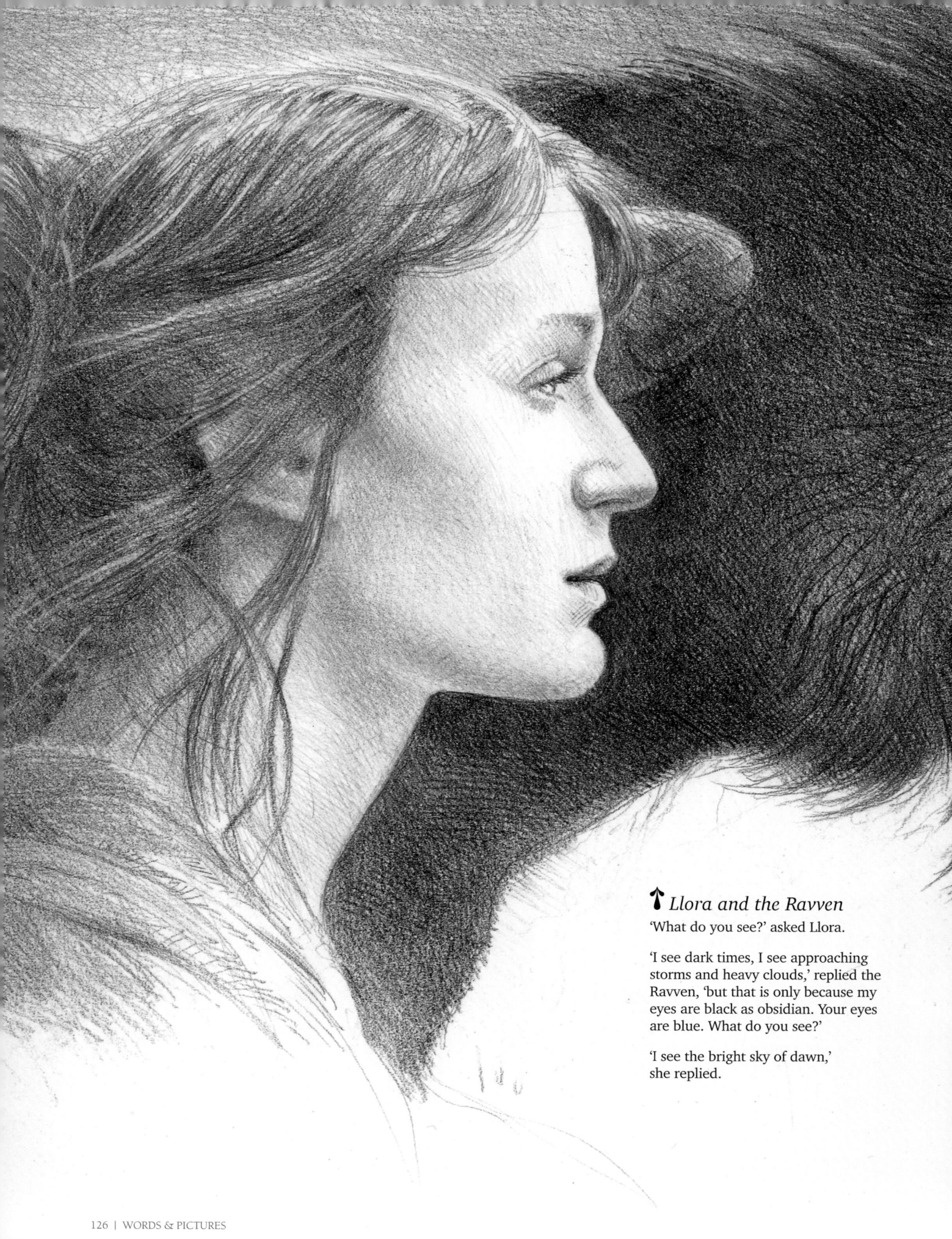

⬆ Llora and the Ravven

'What do you see?' asked Llora.

'I see dark times, I see approaching storms and heavy clouds,' replied the Ravven, 'but that is only because my eyes are black as obsidian. Your eyes are blue. What do you see?'

'I see the bright sky of dawn,' she replied.

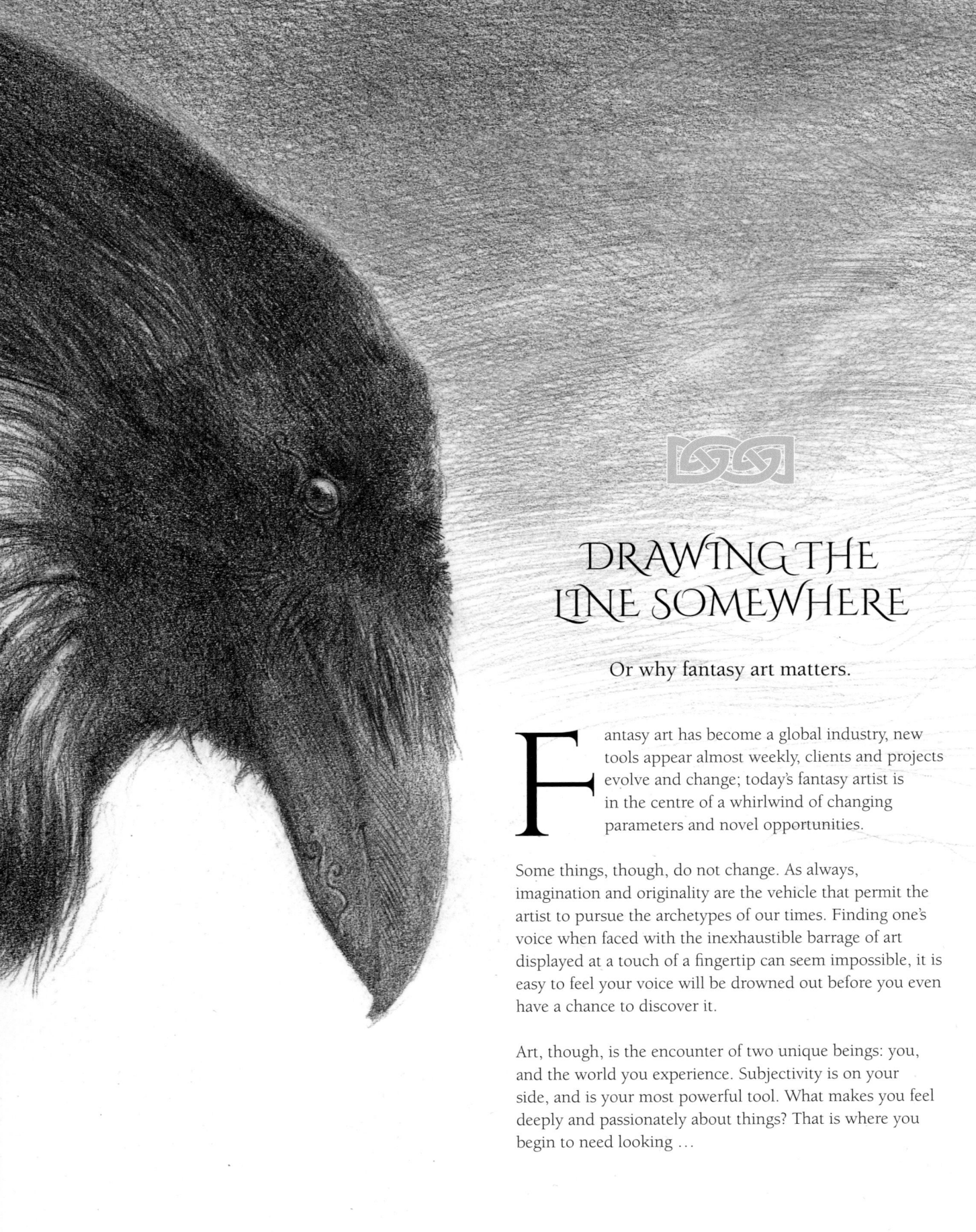

DRAWING THE LINE SOMEWHERE

Or why fantasy art matters.

Fantasy art has become a global industry, new tools appear almost weekly, clients and projects evolve and change; today's fantasy artist is in the centre of a whirlwind of changing parameters and novel opportunities.

Some things, though, do not change. As always, imagination and originality are the vehicle that permit the artist to pursue the archetypes of our times. Finding one's voice when faced with the inexhaustible barrage of art displayed at a touch of a fingertip can seem impossible, it is easy to feel your voice will be drowned out before you even have a chance to discover it.

Art, though, is the encounter of two unique beings: you, and the world you experience. Subjectivity is on your side, and is your most powerful tool. What makes you feel deeply and passionately about things? That is where you begin to need looking …

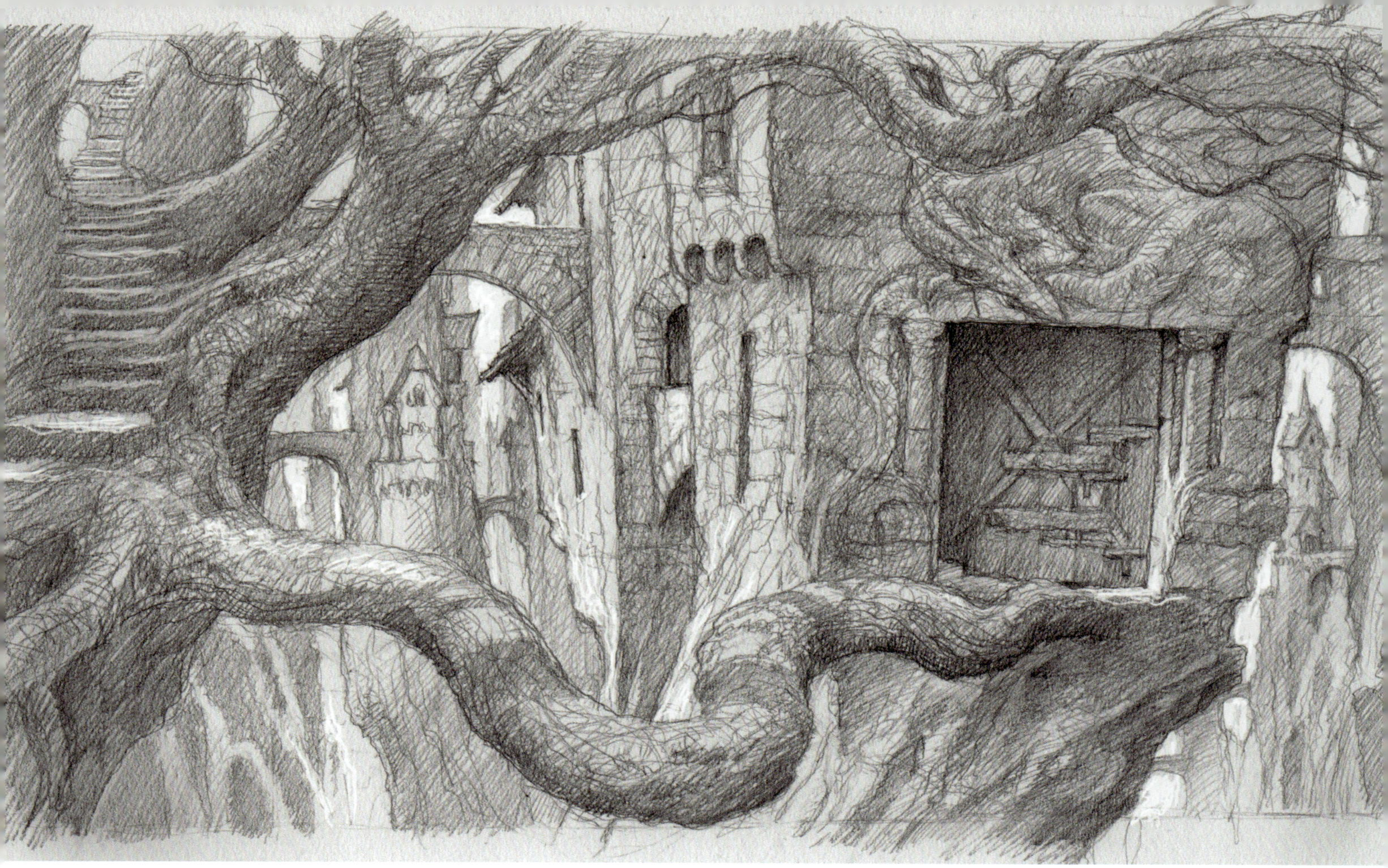

INTO THE WHITE

Entering infinite space.

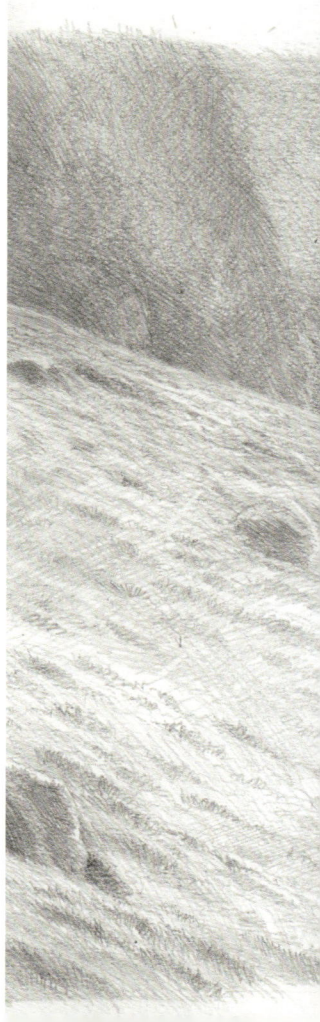

I am often asked about artist's block, about what to do when faced with a seemingly unassailable expanse of white paper and a dearth of ideas and inspiration. I agree, it can be daunting. But it does not exist.

I used to believe that images were in our heads, that talent was defined by the ability to externalize them, to get them out and down on paper. I know now how misguided that was. What we have in our heads is the desire, the experience and tools – the images are out in the world. They are there already, but hidden,

or buried. If we are sharp-eyed and patient, we will uncover them, like archaeologists discovering a buried statue or a wanderer watching the clouds part to reveal a breath-taking landscape. That is how our imagination works. Art is all about capturing that moment.

So relax. Get comfortable. Perhaps your sketchbook is open on your knees, pencils and eraser to hand. Let your mind empty itself of even the idea of trying to draw something.

Then, when you are ready, *imagine a door*. A story will be waiting on the other side …

IMAGINE A DOOR...

But this is not just any door. Maybe it is carved into stone, or leads through a castle wall. Perhaps the lintel is sculpted with fantastical forms. It might be made of aged oak, carved and worn, fitted with intricate iron hinges and several locks. The key is in your pocket.

You open the door and step into the world you will create. The sheet of paper is not a sheet of paper. It is a three-dimensional infinite space into which you reach with your pencil and begin to uncover the world that is there.

That's the thing, of course. It is all there. You simply need to discover it. When I am doing concept work, and must design a city or a civilization, I have a purely pedestrian approach. I start from far off, imagining the landscape and the atmosphere. I might draw a section of the road or path I am on. There might be a milestone or a marker, engraved with a god of the crossroads, some Hekate of a fantasy world. Vista by vista, I draw myself closer, until the city is in front of me. I draw my way through the gates (if there are any) and explore, exactly as one might a city you visit for the first time. I remark on the architecture, note the ages of the buildings, little by little imagine the culture they represent.

When you step through that metaphorical door, you step into worlds you create as you wander in them, leaving drawings and paintings in lieu of footprints.

⬅ *Unexpected Journey*

When you pick up a pencil, you are never sure where it will take you.

⬎ *The Unopened Door*

'You are late,' said Althea.

'The Ravven are far ahead of us. Come, we must hurry!'

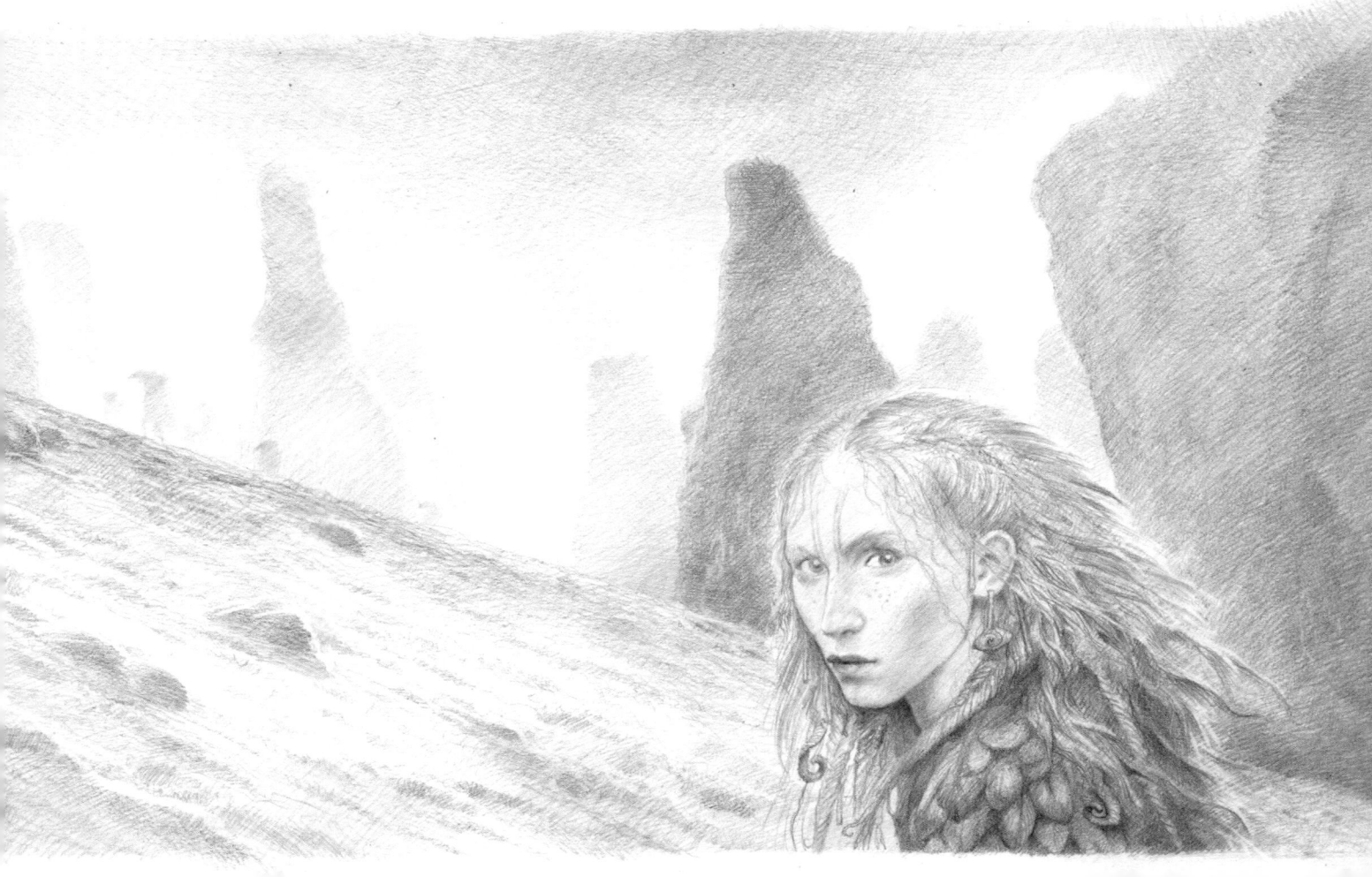

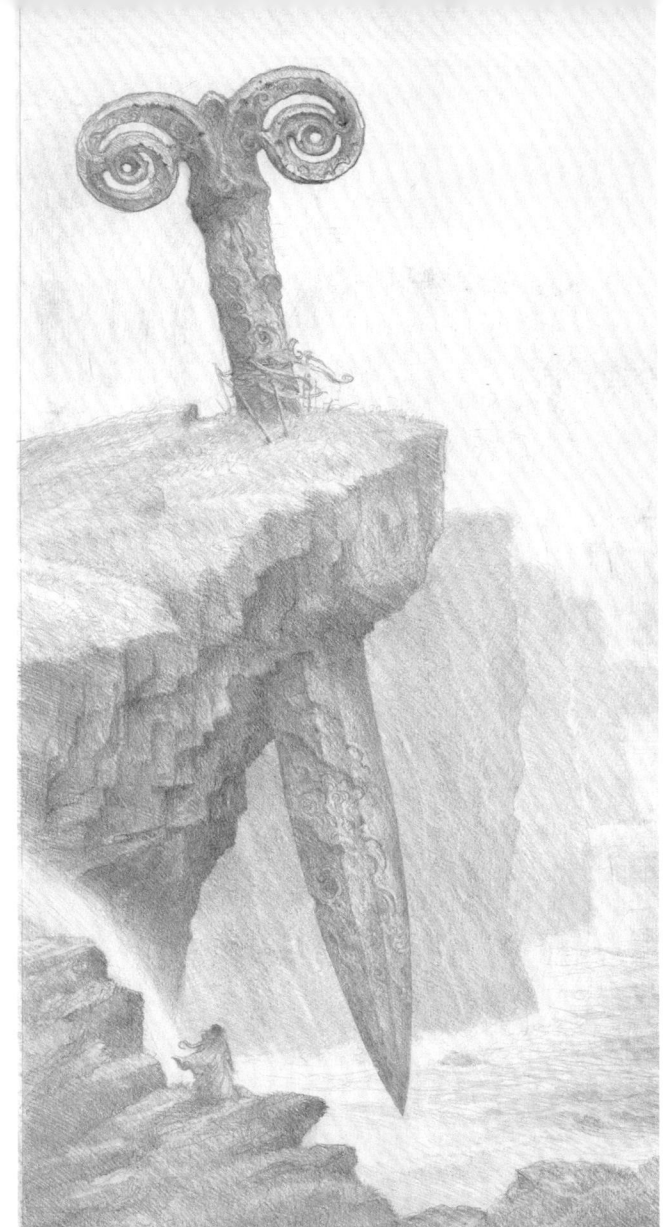

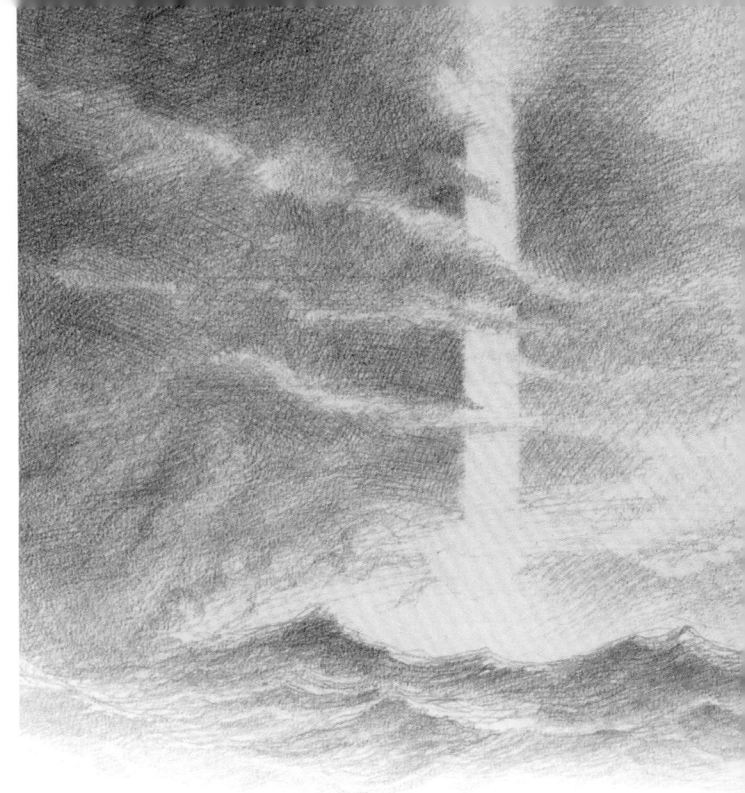

Letting the pencil wander

I almost loathe to give these drawings specific titles, or at least for now. They tell stories, or fragments of stories, which change every time I look at them. Perhaps as I write the stories down, I will be able to add captions with more confidence.

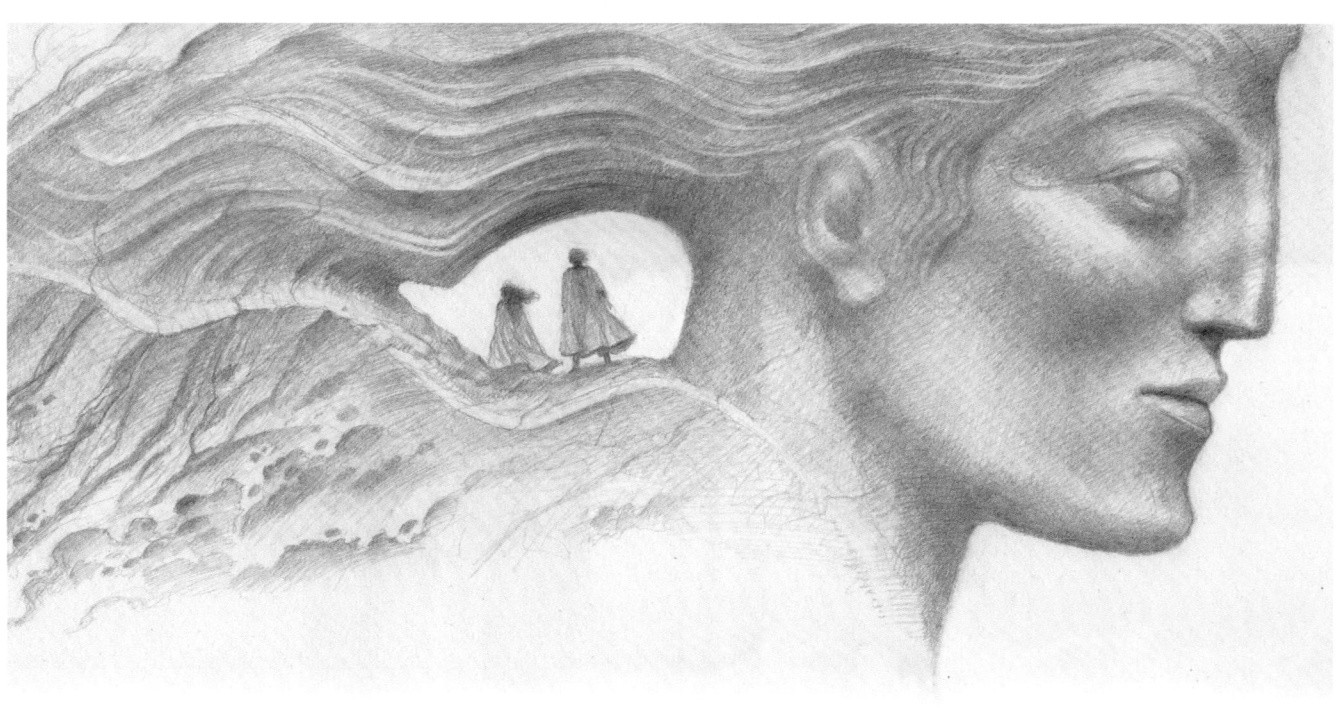

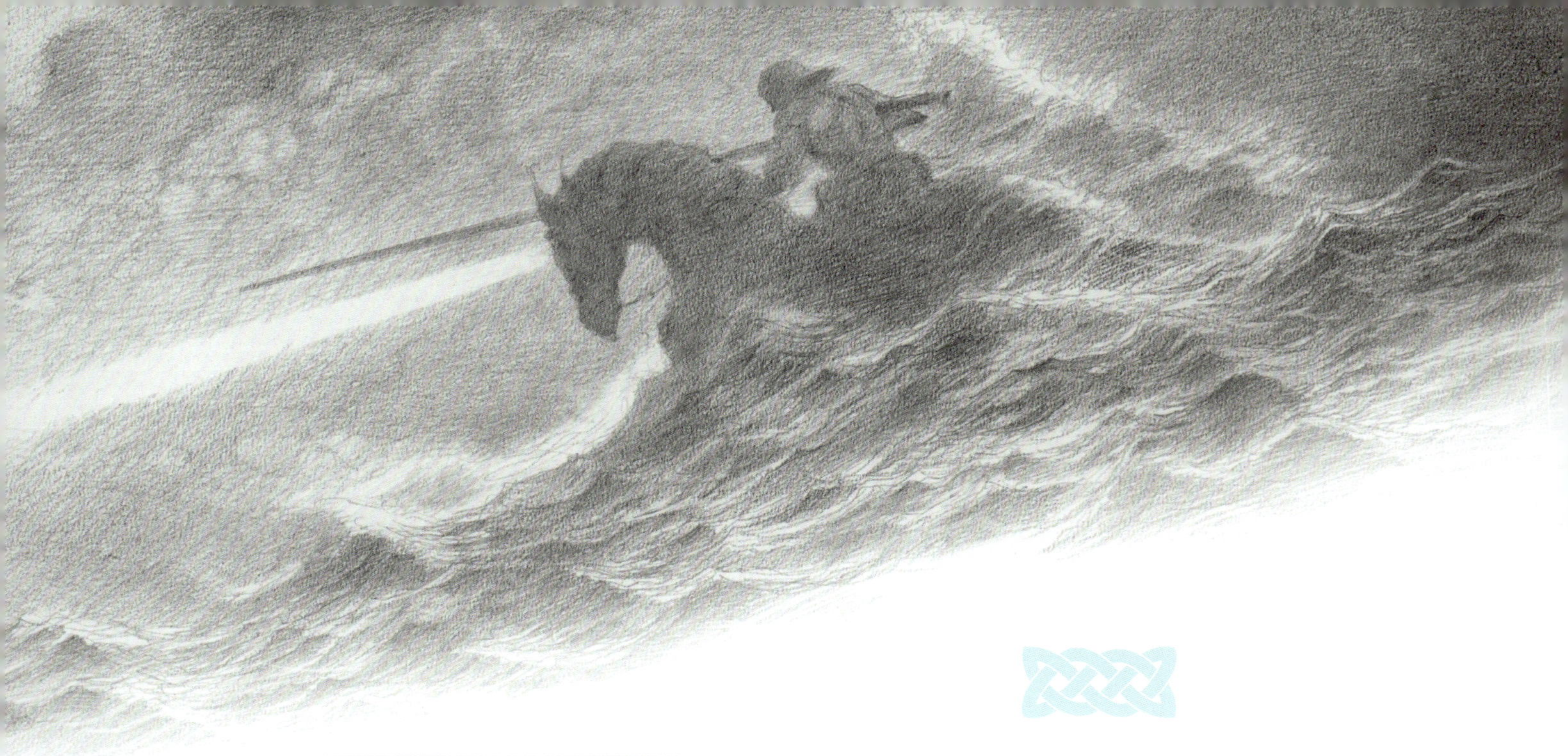

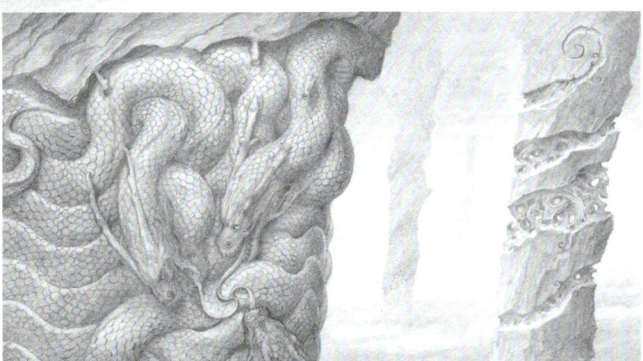

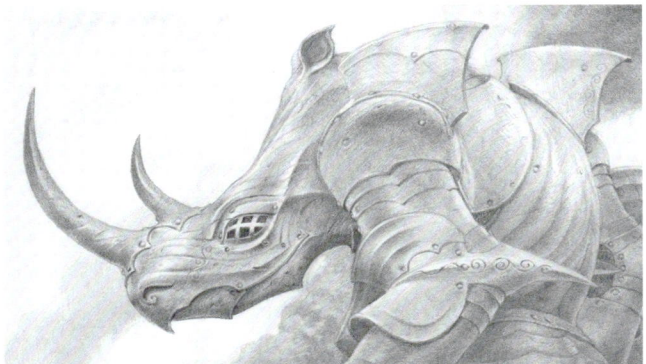

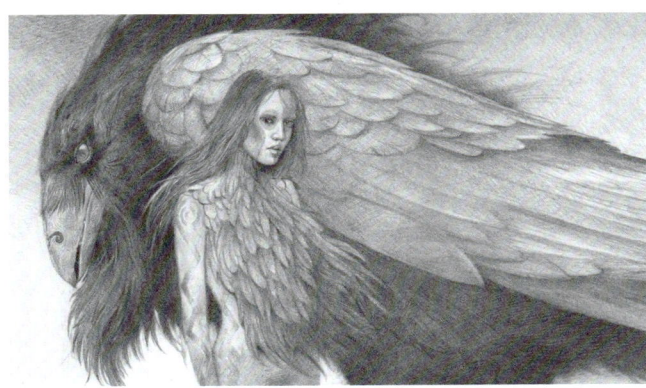

WANDERING BUT NOT LOST

Or letting a drawing decide for itself.

I have often painted skies I liked very much, only to cover them with a foreground element. Nonetheless, the remaining patches of the sky carry a credibility that might not be achieved by simply painting in the visible portions.

All you need, besides a few well-sharpened pencils, is the hint or premise of a theme or an element. It might be an archway. What shape is it? How were the stones quarried? Is the lintel carved? You might be standing in front of the Lion Gate at Mycenae, or at the gates of Minas Tirith, Gormenghast or Castle Dracula, or about to enter a world of your own. The drawing will soon tell you where you are.

Once you have drawn the portal, you can choose: step inside and draw what is beyond, or turn about and draw from where you have come. This approach can be applied to any spare moment you have; the sketches you do are ideas you set aside for later, nothing is lost. You can return and wander at will, encounter the inhabitants, listen to their stories. Before you know it, you will have built a world.

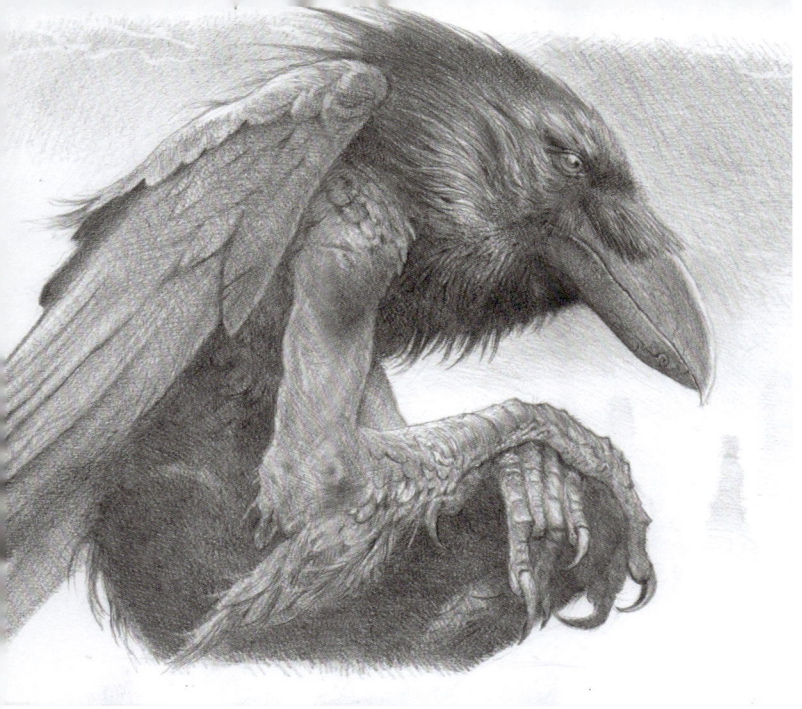

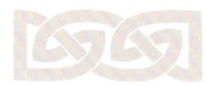

TO THE WORLD'S EDGE

Building worlds of your own.

The best worlds are, of course, the ones that you build on your own. Narration is the key to world-building, but the choice of word or image need not be consistent. Let your sketches tell you stories.

Let your stories take shape and clamour to be put into images. The more thoroughly you ignore the difference between writing and drawing, the quicker your world will take shape. Consistency will impose itself as needed, as the relationships between characters, geography and culture gather weight. Let things happen of their own accord.

Perhaps draw a map, imagine you are a medieval cartographer receiving information of faraway climes piecemeal and filling in the blanks as you go. Above all, have fun! Serious work will begin soon enough if you pursue; the accumulated weight of your world will demand rationalization and consistency.

'What country, friends, is this?'

These pieces were done either as personal works or festival posters. They are not part of the same world, though I confess that a world (or worlds) of sorts is taking shape as their number grows. As I go, I find that each image contains stories that call out to be illustrated, or themes that need to be explored.

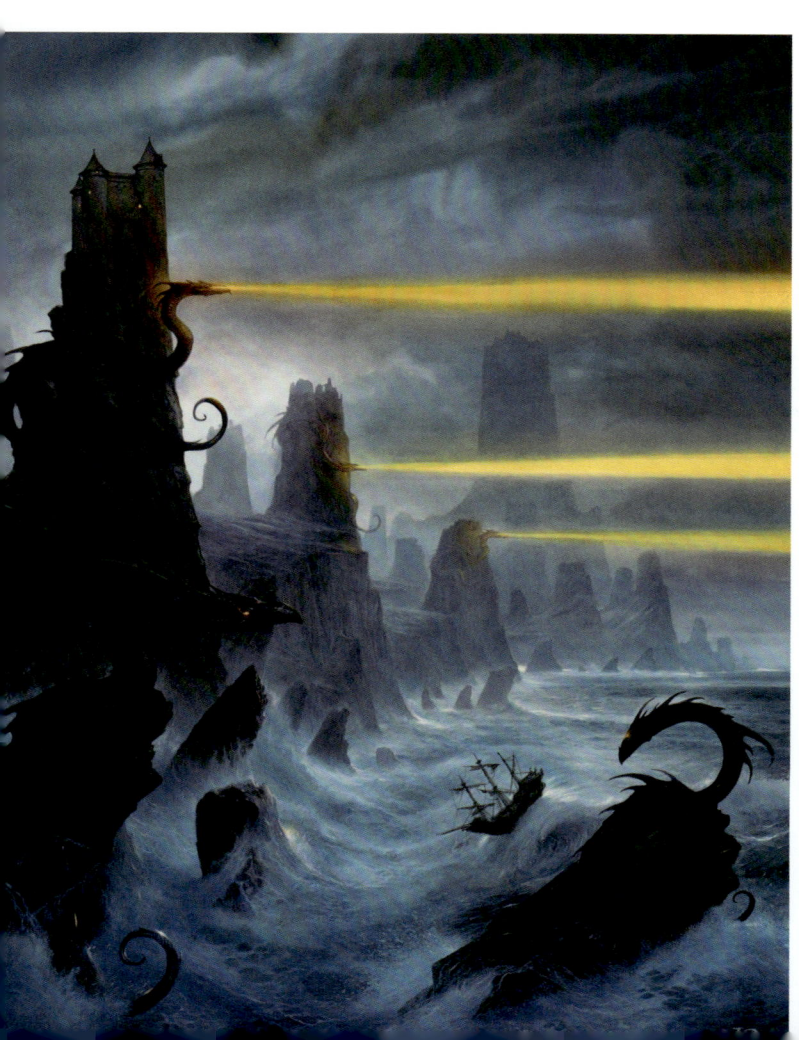

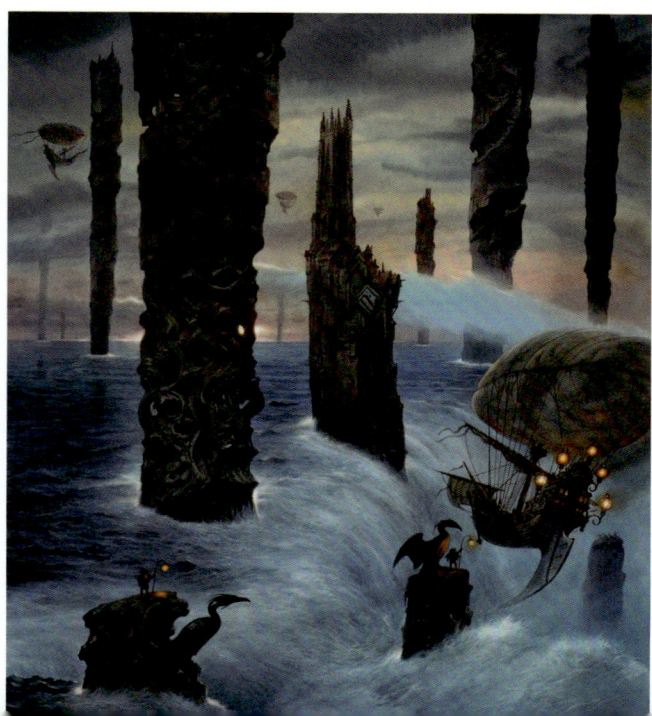

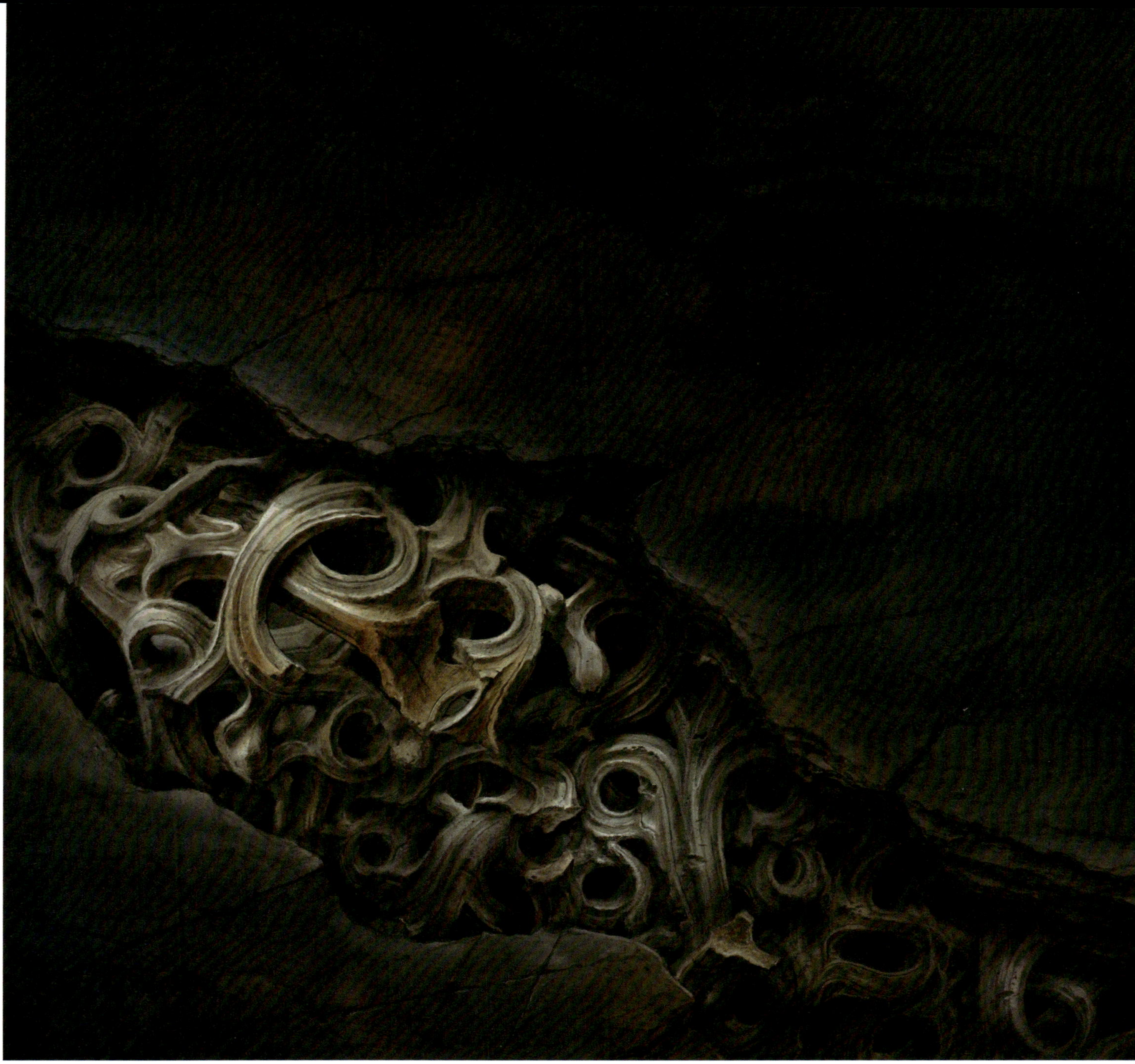

Do try, though, if you can, to leave parts blank, the equivalent of those empty spaces marked 'hic svnt draconis'. They will fill themselves in when inspiration dictates that they should.

There is a passage I love in Shakespeare's *Twelfth Night*, where Viola exclaims, to the sailors who have rescued her from a shipwreck: 'What country, friends, is this?' That is precisely how I feel when an idea or whim takes shape on a page, offering the first glimpse of a new world to explore.

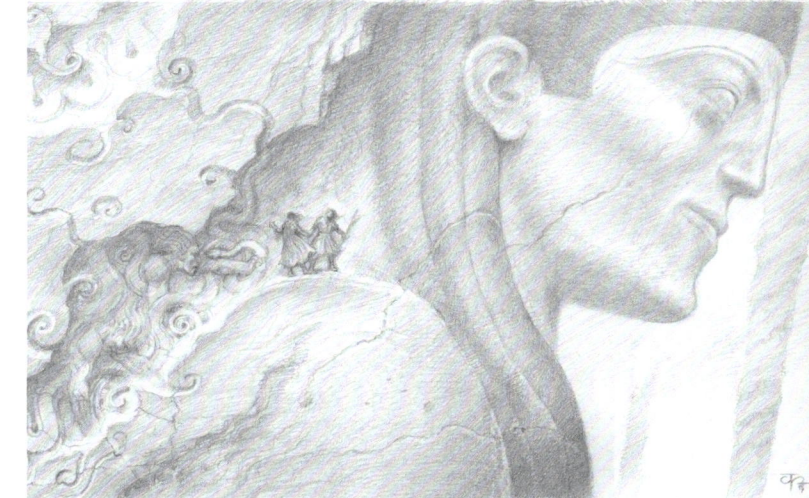

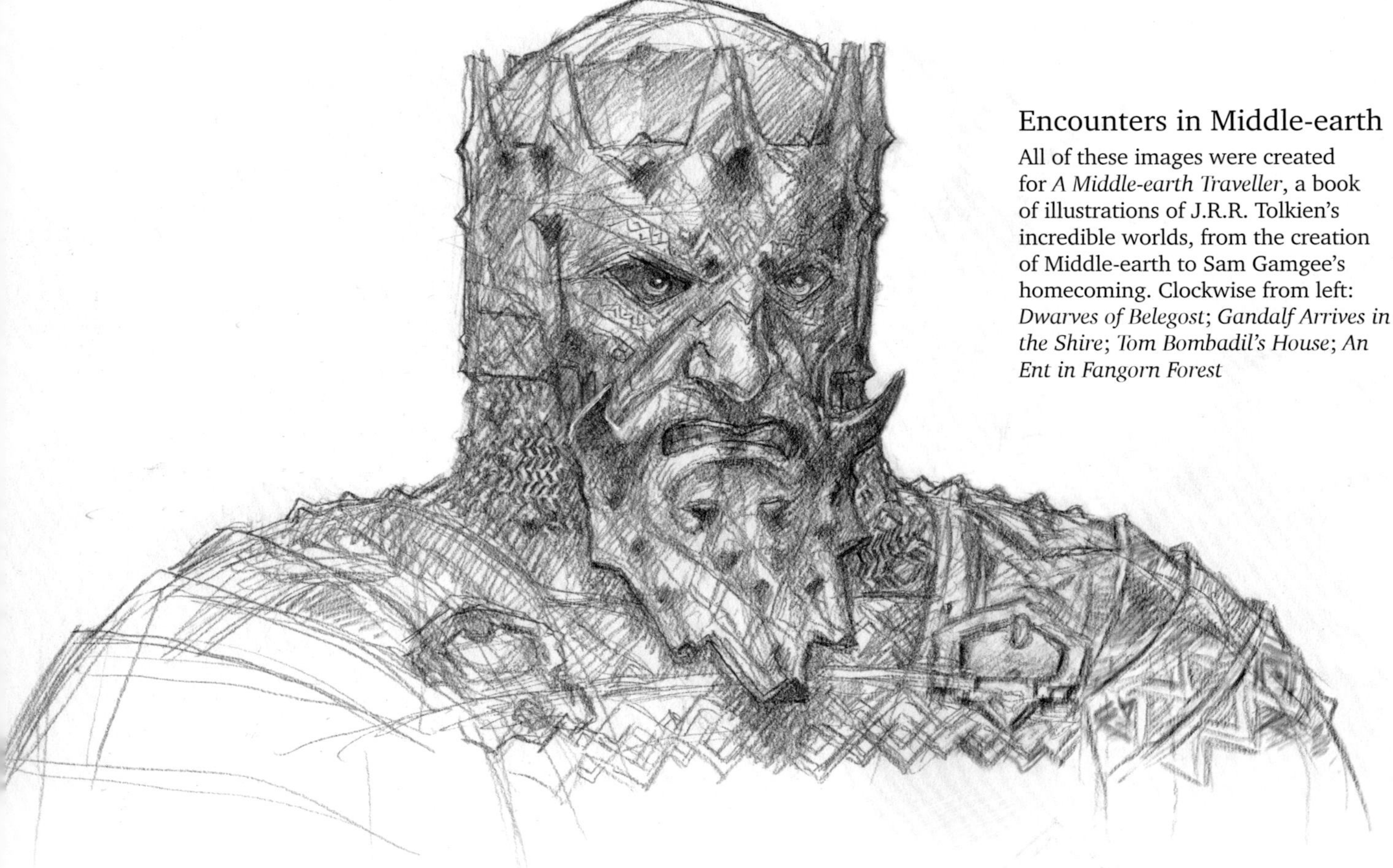

Encounters in Middle-earth

All of these images were created for *A Middle-earth Traveller*, a book of illustrations of J.R.R. Tolkien's incredible worlds, from the creation of Middle-earth to Sam Gamgee's homecoming. Clockwise from left: *Dwarves of Belegost*; *Gandalf Arrives in the Shire*; *Tom Bombadil's House*; *An Ent in Fangorn Forest*

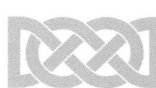

LOST IN WILDERLAND

Travels in Tolkien's Middle-earth.

After four decades wandering in Middle-earth, from the earliest forays in school to the latest concept art, I have, above all, the feeling that I have honestly not seen very much of it. The depth of a fantasy world is the result of the author's work, but also the desire to not consider anything established, to remain open to new ideas and experience in relation to the themes therein.

Not all those who wander in Middle-earth are lost. Some are just artists, seeking a place to set up their easels, or sit down a while with a sketchbook on their knees.

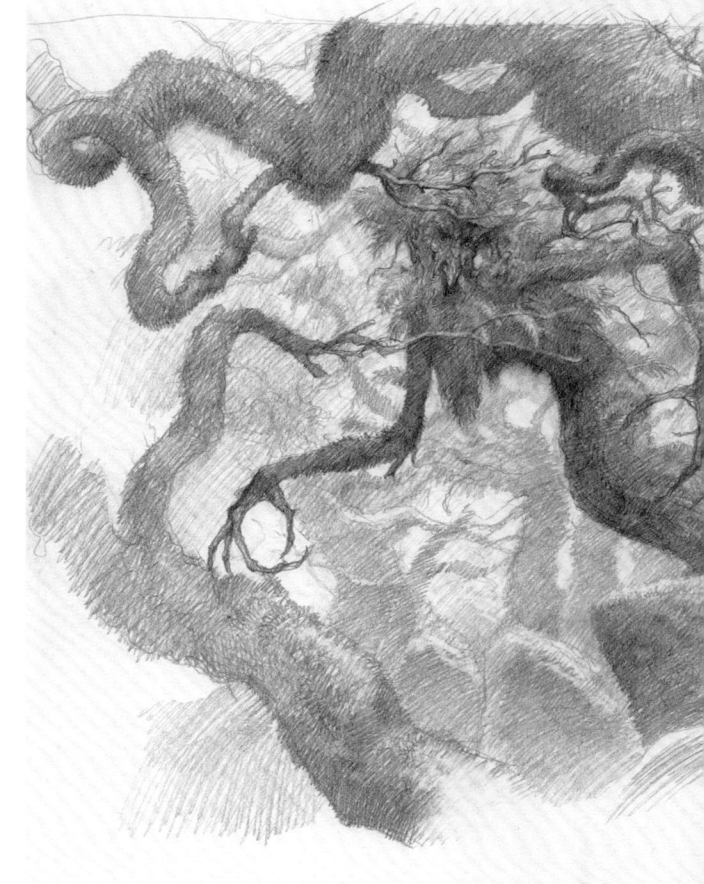

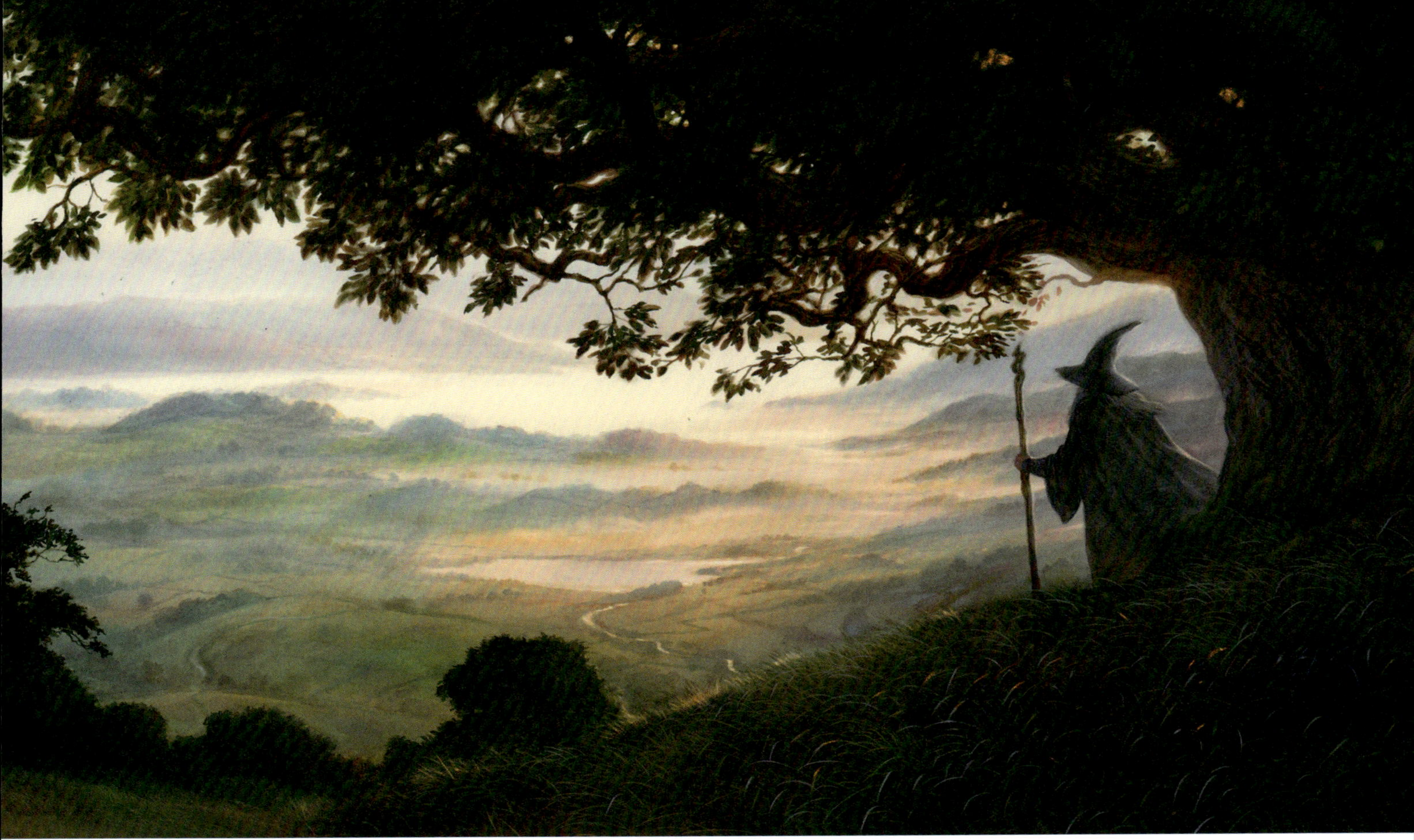

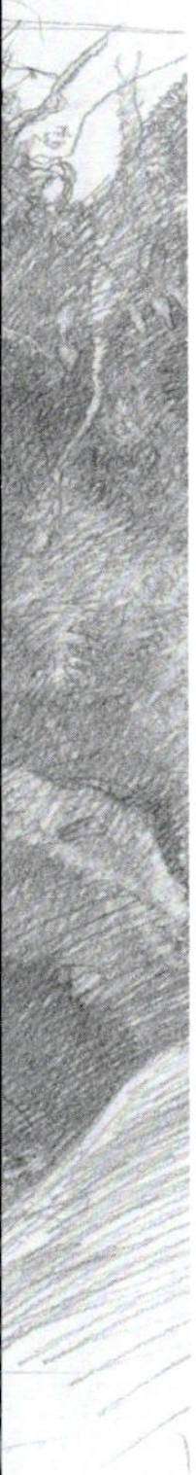

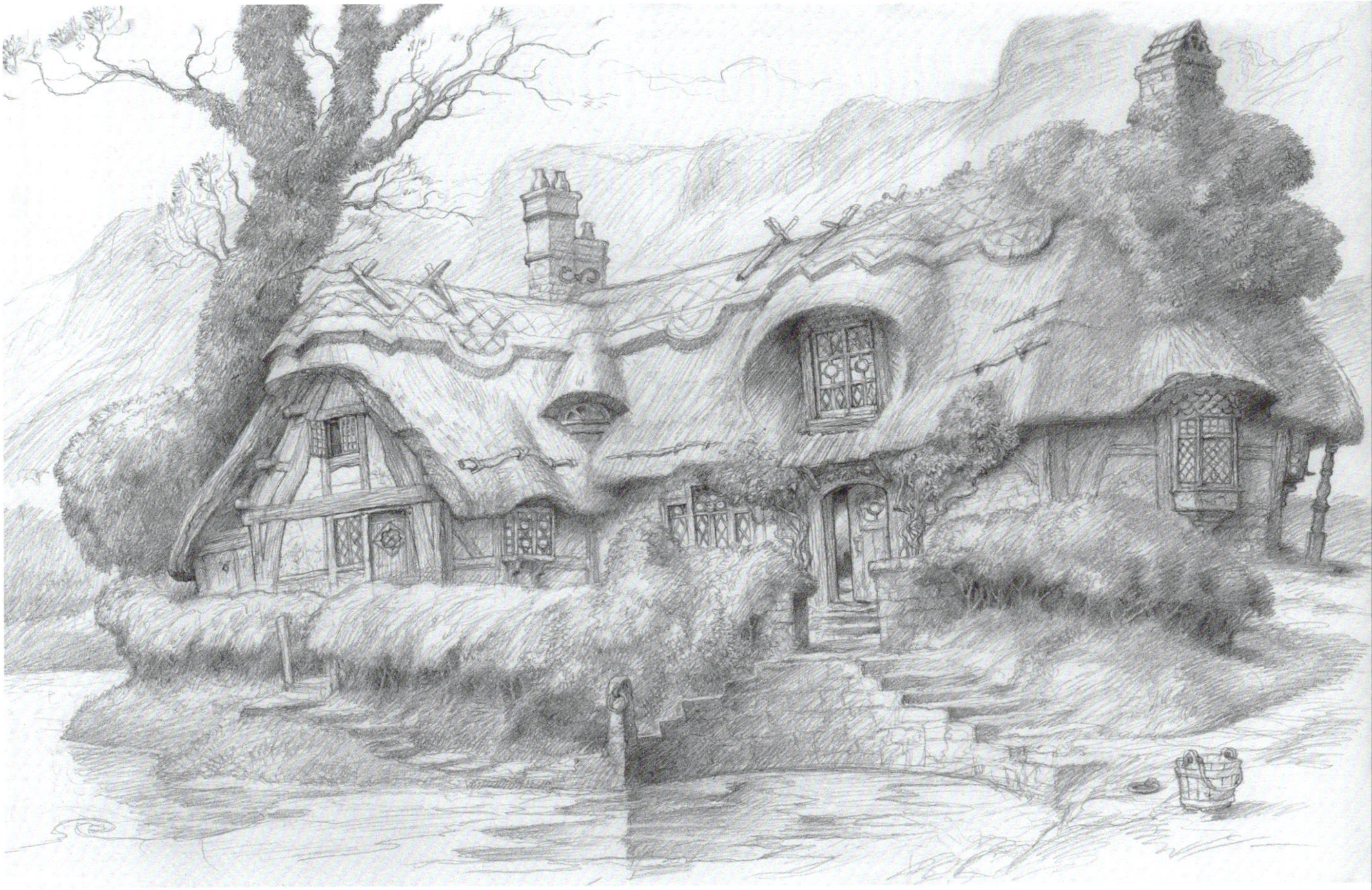

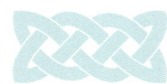

IMAGES WERE MAGIC ONCE

Or how to find the line that's right for you.

Images were magic once, establishing in ochre and madder and soot the sacred, intimate connections to the world. The earliest artists drew the world in the same spirit that the first humans in many mythologies are said to have named the animals: an act of appropriation, preparatory to the act of propitiation. These drawings traced the visible borders of the world and the invisible borders of humanity's spiritual connections therein. The gesture of image-making was equally sacred, some practised in secret, some in ceremony; Neolithic art is only the residue of the act of its making. Eventually the very act of drawing was dissociated from the drawing itself, the sanctity being invested in the image itself, the making no longer a part. Nonetheless, in images both sacred and profane magic exists in the intangible made tangible.

Of course, our relationship to imagery is very different now. The Renaissance saw the heroization of the artist as the initiator and the sole creator of art, no longer simply the conduit of a katabasis of the divine. The image no longer comes from the gods or God, but originates with and travels outward from the artist, whatever the destination. Art is the paradoxical juxtaposition of the intimate and the universal.

All very well, you might say, but what does it mean for me? Where do I, and what I do, fit in? Where do I start?

First, forget yourself and fall back on your experience. Your mind is full of images. The key is to establish a three-way conversation between your experience, the theme, and the drawing. Like any conversation, if one drowns out the others, it is just a monologue. A chance line may prompt a change of direction, both unexpected and refreshing. (The most exciting moments in concept art are when a simple line inadvertently opens up a complete change of direction.) The drawing is the tangible trace of this exchange; once it no longer asks or answers questions, it is time to move on.

There are things you can do to help:

1 Pencil posture: If you have not kept in touch with drawing your whole life, you may be unsatisfied with your efforts when you pick up a pencil again. There is a simple test: compare how you hold your pencil to draw to how you hold it to write. If the same, then you may wish to modify the way you hold the pencil to draw. Try holding it lightly, as far away from the sharpened end as possible.

2 Keep the pencil moving: When it stops, ideas stop flowing; let your pencil do the thinking and drive the drawing. A drawing is non-linear, even though there is a certain logic to any procedure, you are free to draw as you will.

3 Keep it light: Leave your lines to find the right place, do not be in too much of a hurry to pin them down.

4 Start again: A drawing, and even more so a sketch, is incidental. Do not linger on a drawing if you feel it is no longer responding.

5 The eraser is your friend: Never be afraid to rub out something that is not working; you can redraw it. (The hardest is when you have drawn something you are very happy with in just not quite the right place. Let it go, it will be even better next time.)

6 Get to the point: Keep your pencil well-sharpened – a dull pencil lead leaves but approximate lines.

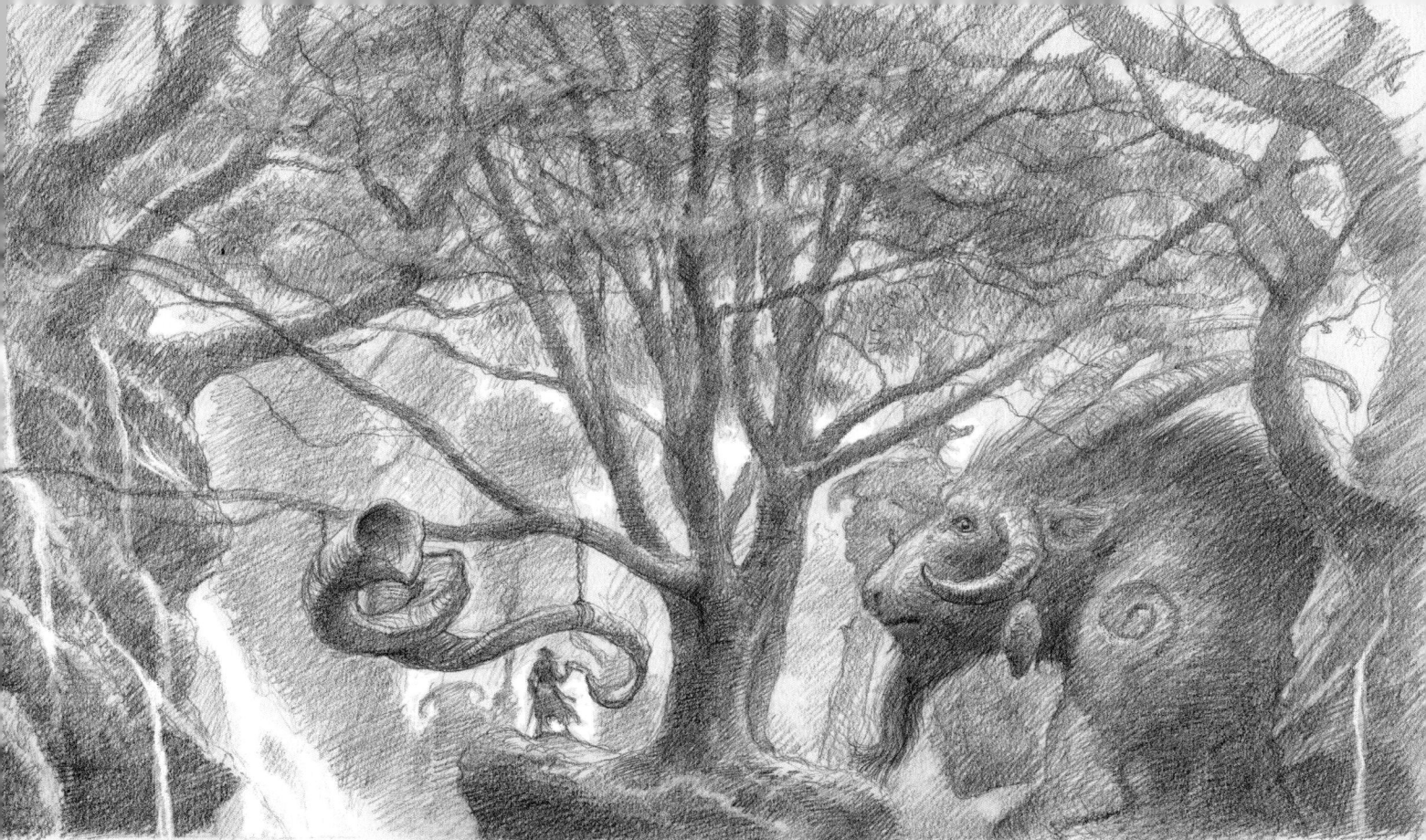

7 Draw what you see, see what you draw: Your drawing may not resemble the image you have in your mind when you begin. The whole process is an ongoing, evolving exchange until you set the pencil down.

8 A line is not a line: There are few lines in nature. They are a handy, legible convention, the quickest way to translate volumes. When drawing a contour, remember that it is not a simple line, but a succession of disappearing and reappearing forms. Represent the volume of an object or body, even if you are summarizing it with a line.

9 Making lines is non-linear: There is no inevitable procedure, only pitfalls to avoid as your confidence and skills build. While it is wise to block in volumes and establish horizon lines initially, these do not need to be on the paper. Jump from one part or the other at will.

10 Have sketchbook, will travel: Sketchbooks are wise investments; they require no chargers or Wi-Fi and will faithfully accompany you in any situation. As big as you can comfortably carry, not spiral-bound and with good paper, rough or smooth, it's up to you.

↑ *The Summoning*

Imagining one world ending at cliffs' edge, and a horn to summon the creatures who live beyond. Images like this are visual reminder that there is always a story to follow.

11 Don't design by default: (I call this the 'insert-large-search-engine-name-here school of design'.) Enlarge your experience, enhance your visual palette. If you are working in fantasy, you should have the enlightened amateur's knowledge of culture, architecture, costume and decoration the world over, through the ages. Be interested. Look things up; do not fall back on familiarity. Every element in a drawing is a chance to augment the credibility of your invention. Neglect nothing. Make informed choices. Be a judge of what constitutes a good reference or not.

12 Just start: Don't think too much. Drawing is an intuitive exercise founded in experience and interests. Turn off your brain. Let the pencil find the images; they are there, you simply haven't uncovered them yet.

SKETCHING TUTORIALS

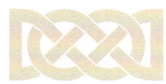

Welcome to the practical section of the book. Sketching is meant as a dialogue, so learning the language and acquiring the vocabulary will allow you to develop your personal style. Remember, a sharp pencil is an extension of a sharp eye; a lightly held pencil the equivalent of agility of imagination. The dialogue is as much about listening as expressing oneself. Learn to listen to what your sketch is telling you as you draw.

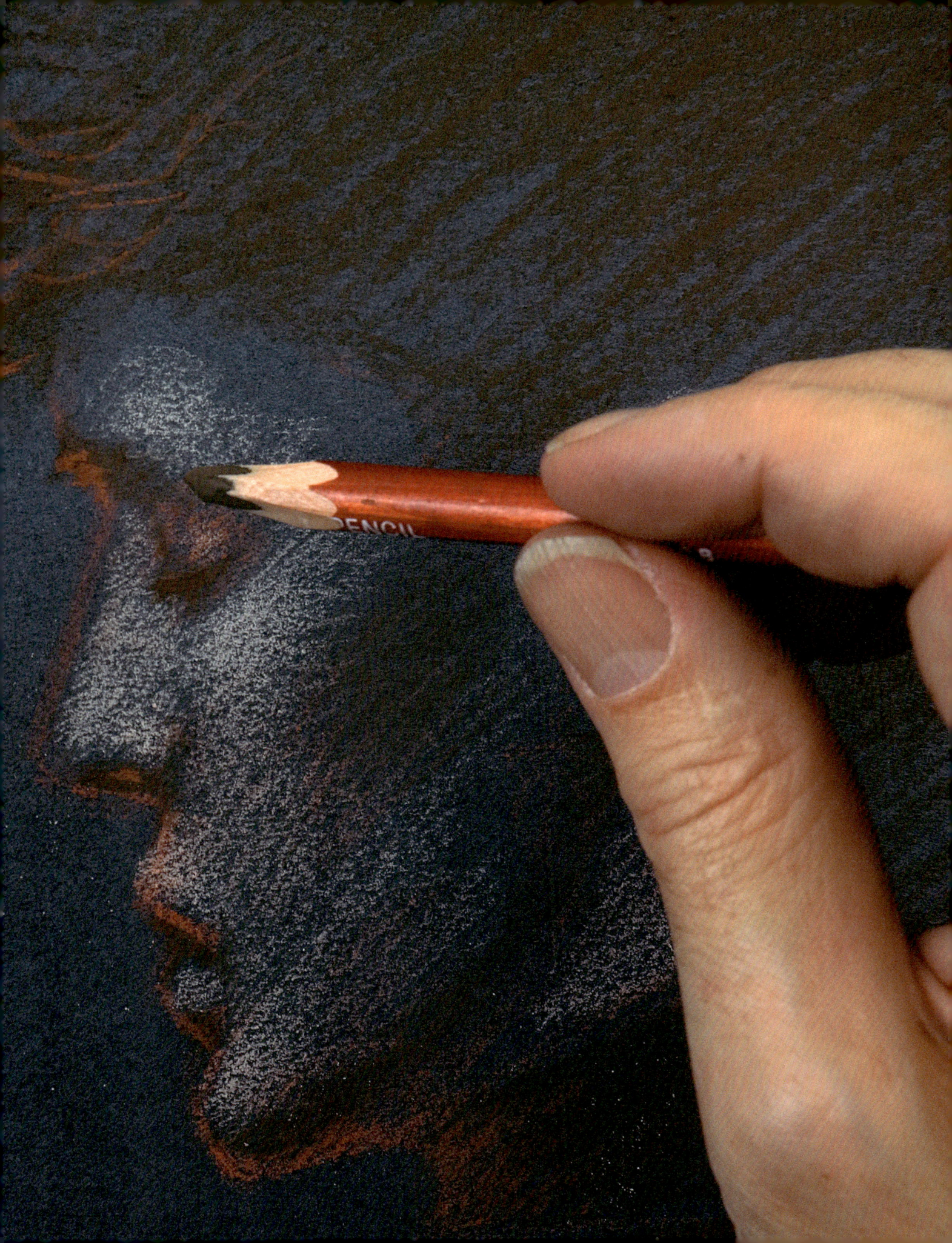

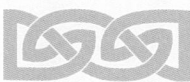

MERLIN

There are as many Merlins as there are texts that mention him. He is the hero, or the figure in the shadows – kingmaker, prophet, bard, druid, keeper of secrets – of countless stories in Welsh literature and Arthurian legend. Drawing Merlin means choosing time and landscape, costume and context, imagining a story that creates the implicit frame of the portrait.

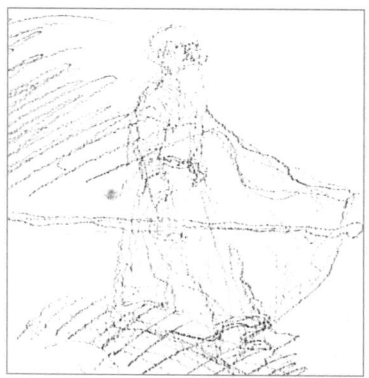

Techniques
✦ Building a basic character composition
✦ Using a thumbnail to establish composition
✦ Simple shading for volume

Ideas and inspiration
This is the kind of pencil study I would do before beginning a painting, to establish the character's basic composition in terms of pose and initial detailing. This is a classic pose – Merlin standing on a cliff top facing out to sea with the wind and rain driving behind him.

Visual references
Since there's no one Merlin, I have one of my own – a retired civil engineer from the Swiss Alps, who graciously allowed me to take a series of portraits. I tracked him down through a photo glimpsed in a magazine and he's been my Merlin ever since.

⬆ Thumbnail sketch
Thumbnails are quick and can rapidly resolve many issues, helping you to decide how you want to place different elements. Tucked away at the lower right of my drawing, the thumbnail will come in handy as the drawing takes shape although it will likely get drawn over in the process.

Costume drama
Cloaks are a wonderful element to play with and do so much besides establish context; they can gracefully depict the wind, its direction and strength and so create atmosphere.

1 Working with a 4B pencil, first lightly sketch in Merlin's torso and head. 'Lightly' is the key word here; normally just the weight of your pencil is enough to leave guiding lines sufficiently clear for you to build upon without getting in the way later.

2 Further define the torso and sketch in Merlin's arm. Now lightly sketch in his legs as a reference point – this helps to anchor standing figures early in the process. Then sketch his robe billowing out in the wind. Place the sloping ground on which he is standing below the robe, then sketch his staff.

3 Add the edge of Merlin's cloak billowing out before him in the wind.

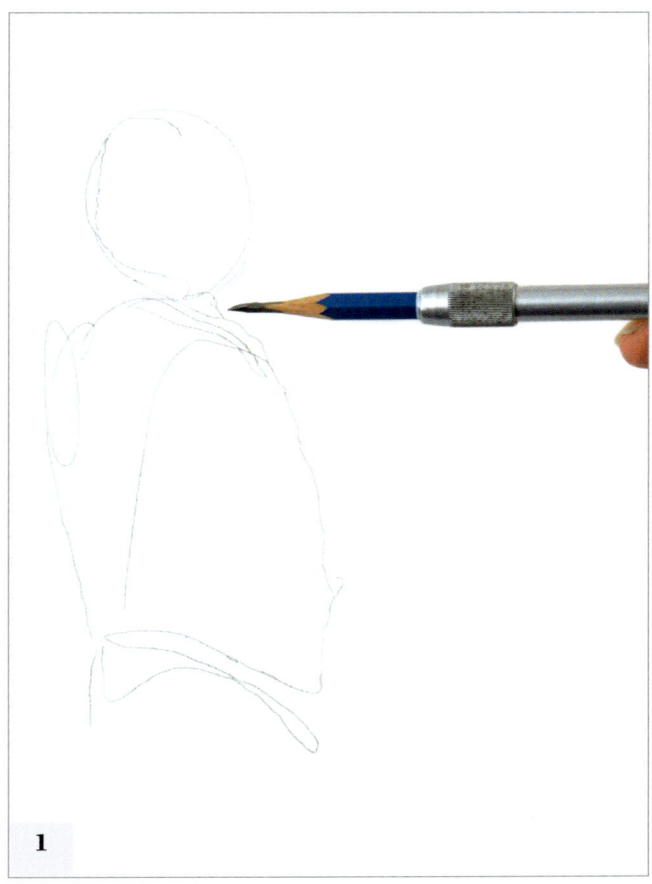

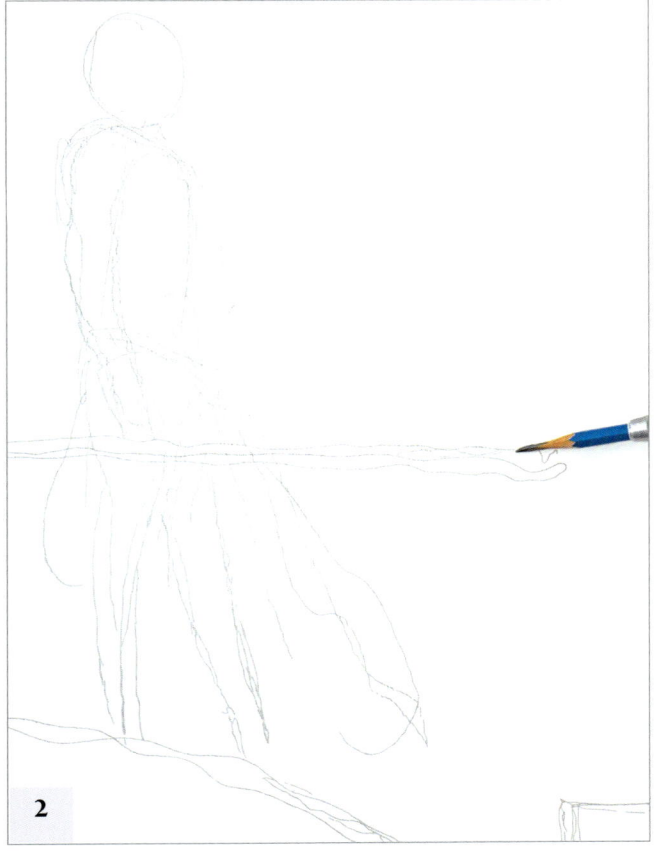

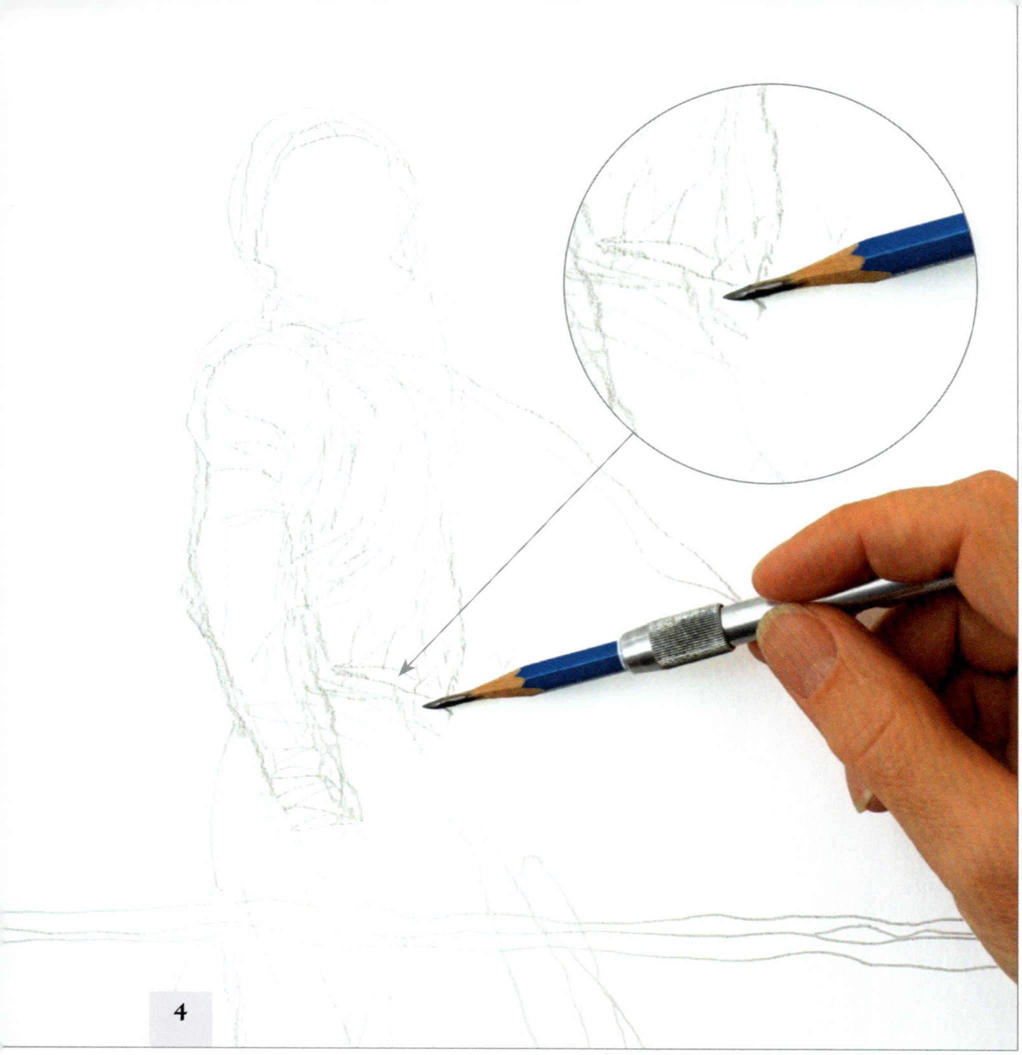

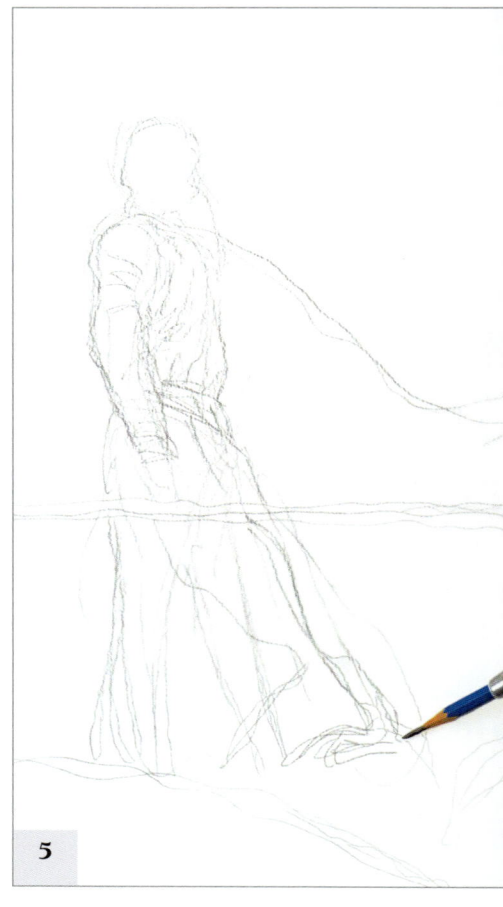

4

5

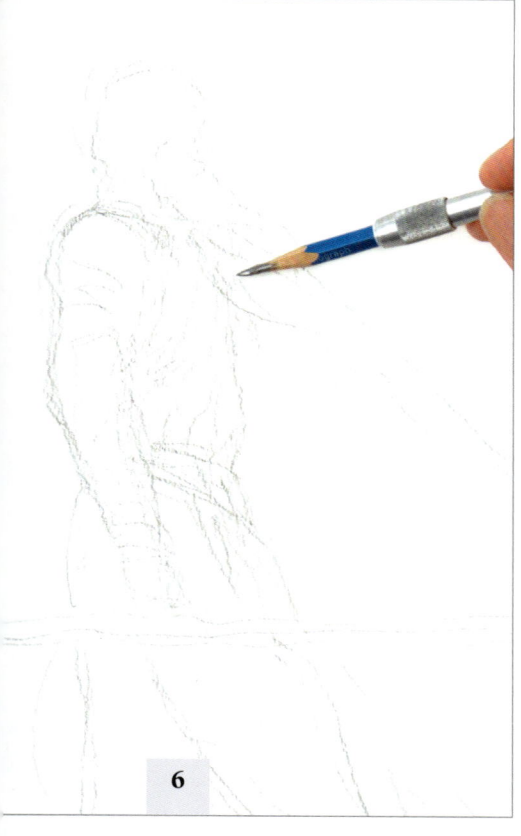

6

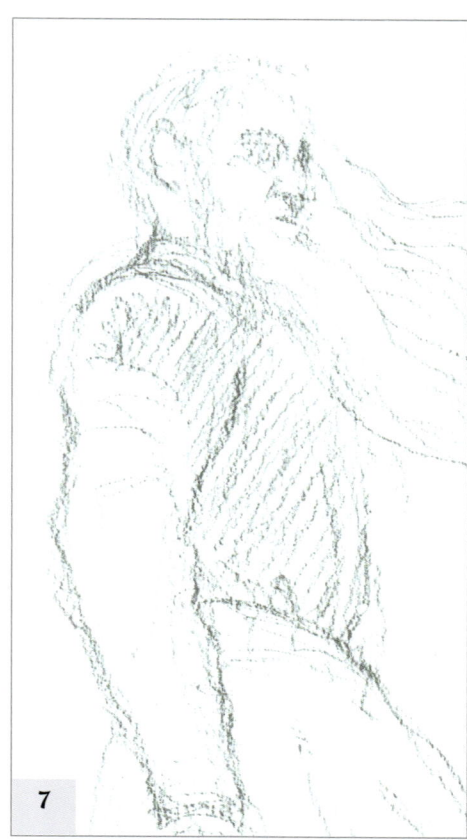

7

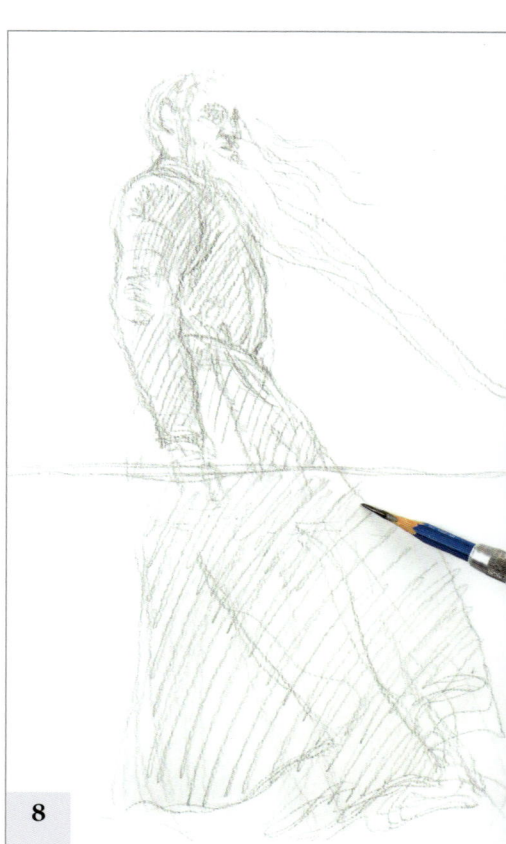

8

4 With everything more or less in place, start building up the first layer of details. Fill in the belt and sketch in contour lines and cloth folds on the torso and shoulder area. Begin to lightly shade down the body.

5 Sketch more lines down the robe to represent folds. Start to define the hem, relating billowing edges to these folds. This working garment has no flowing sleeves or big details.

6 Define the edge of the arm; there is a body under the cloth, so define the shape across the shoulder. (If in doubt, lightly draw in the body – it will be hidden later.) Then start to sketch his beard, taking your lead from the flow of the robe.

7 Sketch in eyebrows, ear and hairline. Add light shading for eye sockets, nose and mouth. Shade the torso with bold directional lines, and further define the arm and shoulder.

8 Reposition the staff and erase the old one. Add further shaping to the front of the torso, then shade down the arm and over the lower robe area.

9 Now draw a firmer edge to the robe and move back to work on the hand that needs to grasp the staff. Here, we'll keep it relatively simple – just the hand with some indication of the fingers grasping the staff.

10 Start to establish the character in the face. Gently erase earlier positional sketch lines and re-establish the basic head shape. Position the eyebrows and eye sockets, and the outline of the nose. Place the hairline and ear adding some shading around the neck and collar. Then add more depth to his flowing hair and beard.

Drawing hands

Observe and sketch hand positions whenever you can to gain familiarity with their structure and movements. A mirror will let you draw both hands. A person willing to pose can be ... handy.

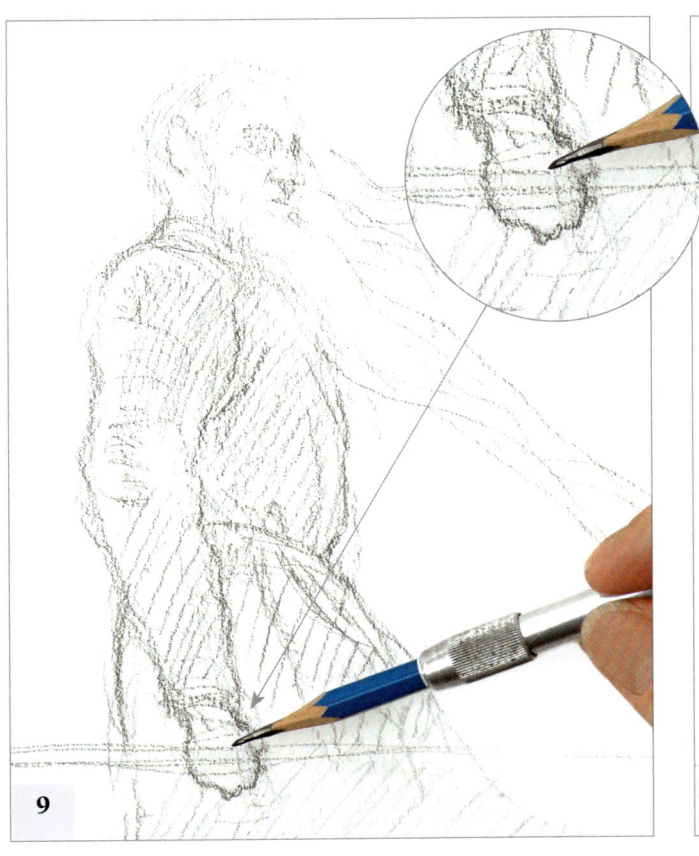

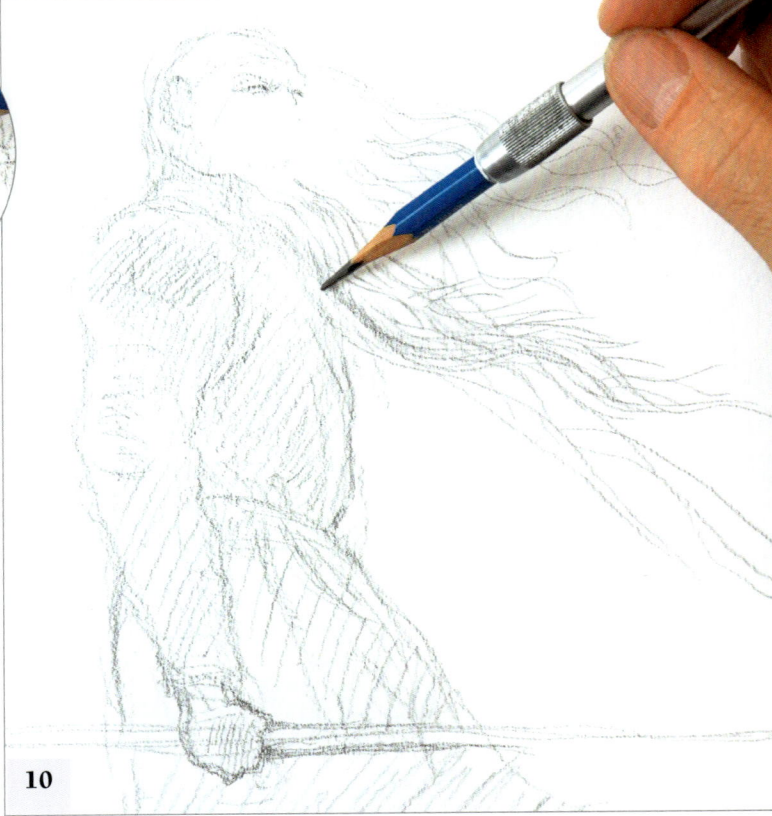

11 Add more depth to the belt and firmly establish the front of the torso. Lightly smudge some of the shading to build the volume. Then sketch in the sword, held in Merlin's unseen hand. Even such a discreet element can add a background story and imply a narrative.

12 To build more volume on the torso, hatch across the top of the shoulder and down the front of the torso, smudging some of the line work to create depth. Suggest where the belt buckle will go, and extend the belt end out in front to show it blowing in the wind.

13 Add further shading on the torso and arm to increase the depth and volume. Keep the shading in one direction, gently curved to denote the shape of the chest, then shade the arm with crooked pencil work to form material folds. Firmly establish the outline of his arm and hand grasping the staff. Sketch a pouch hanging from the belt, with a little detail.

14 Add further detailing at the top of the pouch where it attaches to his belt. Then shade down the inside of the cloak, the hatching following the movement of the cloak.

15 Do further work on the lower half of the figure, sketching in stronger folds in the robe, using an eraser to lift out highlights and deepening the shading between folds. Work down to the base of the cloak and deepen the hemline, shading below it to indicate shadow. Lightly sketch his feet to give a loose indication without detail.

16 Add further shading on the inner cloak to build volume. Now take an eraser and run through the length of the staff to define a clear shape through the shading. If you erase your original line work, draw that in again. Once the staff is clearly established, add decorative elements. The little shape sketched here is to remind me of a bronze ornament I picked up abroad that will work well as a model.

17 Once happy with the staff outline, gently shade it. Keep the line denoting the lower edge strong to indicate shadow. Do not use a ruler – this detracts from the fluidity.

18 Erase the original sketched landline and shade around the base of the figure to denote a grassy slope. Build up texture to show grass blowing forwards in the wind.

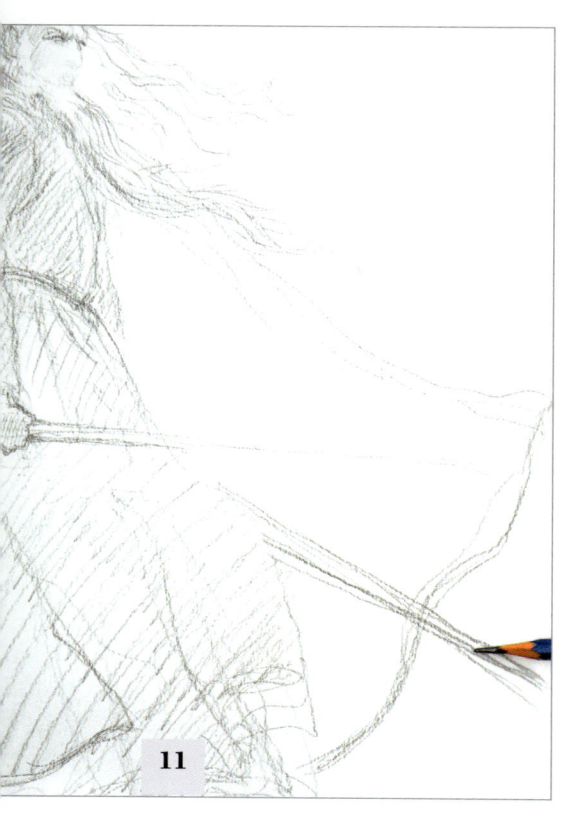

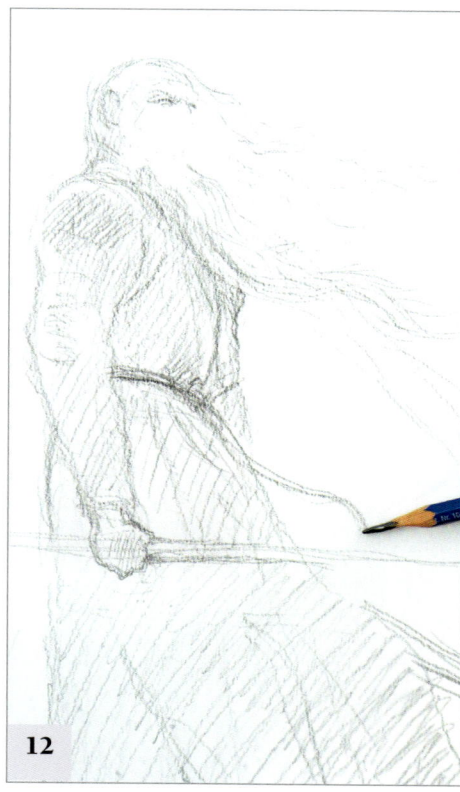

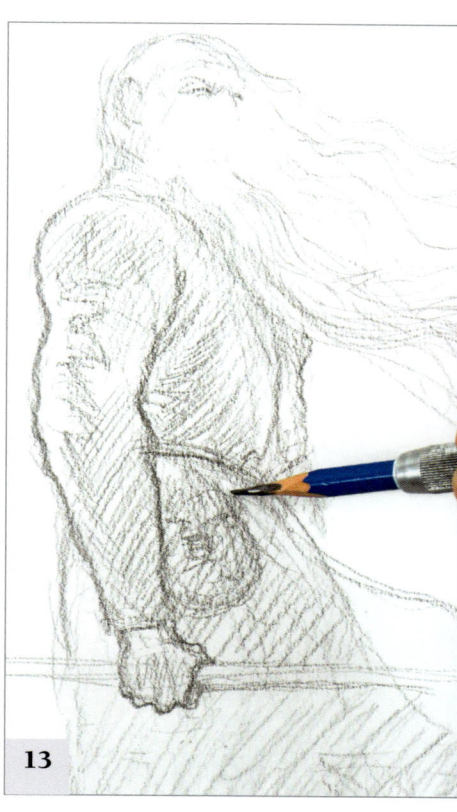

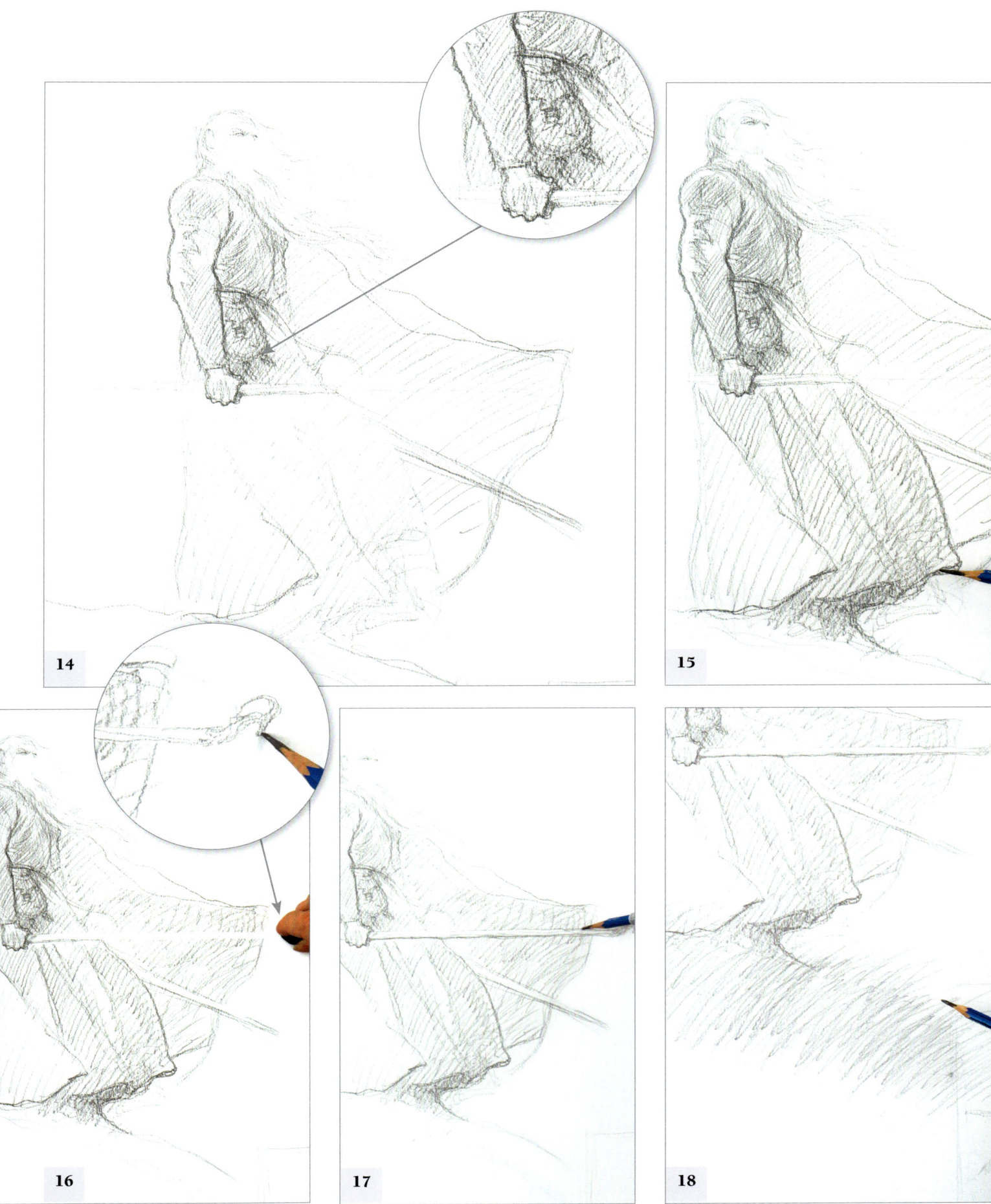

14

15

16

17

18

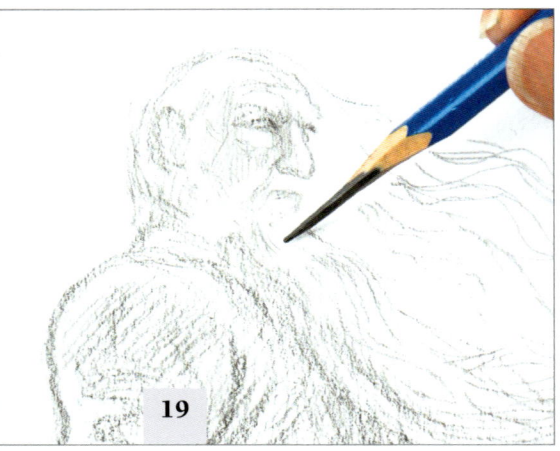

19 Now move back to the face. Change to a finer 3B pencil to capture the detail and first establish the nose, working in a straight line down from between the eyes. Then add the mouth with a line to denote the creases either side. Shade upwards into the cheek and up the side of the nose, leaving a highlight for the top of the nose. Add further shading below the chin for the beard.

20 Add further light shading around the mouth, and a firm line for the lip. Further define the contours of the nose and face, and deepen the shading on the eye sockets. Add the tattoo near the corner of Merlin's right eye.

21 Add further shading to the cheek area, adding depth to the cheekbones. Then move back to the eye sockets and add further definition. Add fine lines over the forehead to define Merlin's windswept hair and the wrinkles beneath.

22 Add the outline of a cliff in the background and sketch in some clouds; this is all to enhance the atmosphere of the piece and requires very little definition. With bold strokes, indicate the driving rain.

23 To indicate the rain driving across Merlin's body, take the eraser and drag strokes through the shading.

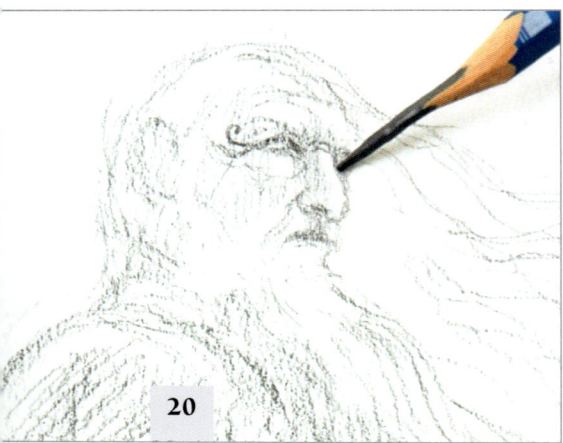

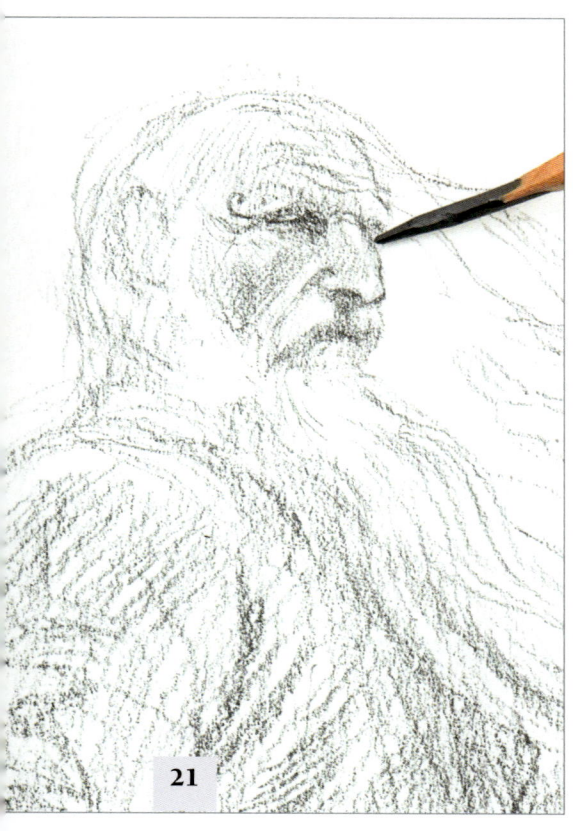

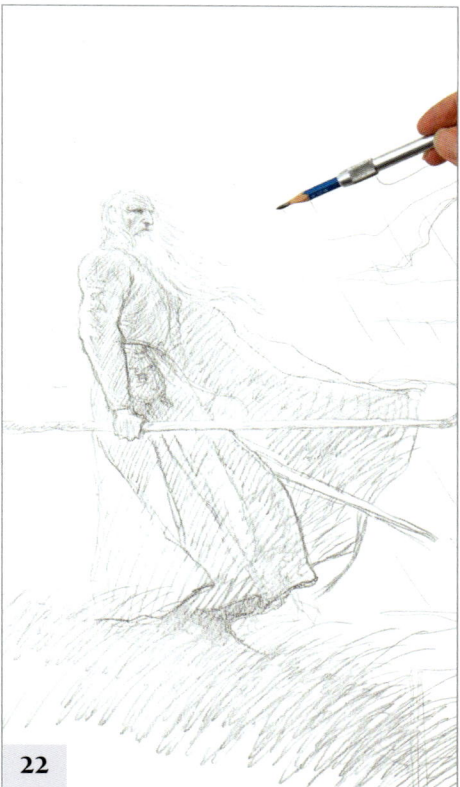

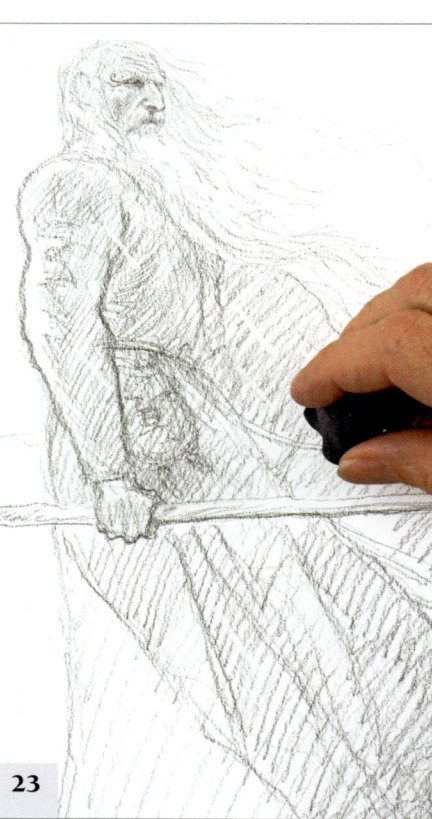

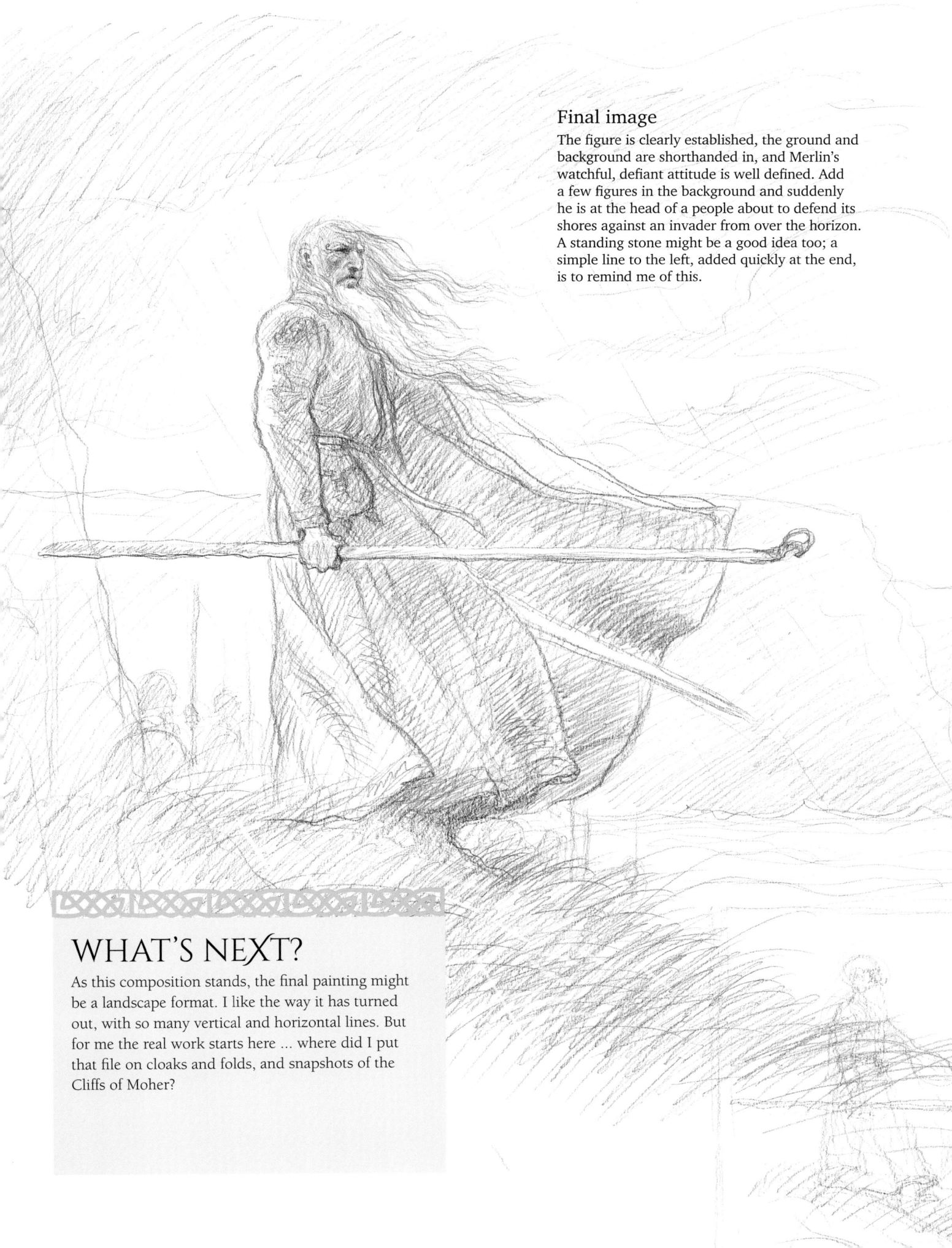

Final image

The figure is clearly established, the ground and background are shorthanded in, and Merlin's watchful, defiant attitude is well defined. Add a few figures in the background and suddenly he is at the head of a people about to defend its shores against an invader from over the horizon. A standing stone might be a good idea too; a simple line to the left, added quickly at the end, is to remind me of this.

WHAT'S NEXT?

As this composition stands, the final painting might be a landscape format. I like the way it has turned out, with so many vertical and horizontal lines. But for me the real work starts here ... where did I put that file on cloaks and folds, and snapshots of the Cliffs of Moher?

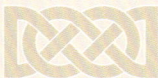

DRAGON

This might best be described as the archetypal dragon (of St George and the dragon fame), with a storybook knight eagerly galloping to the fight. One might imagine he has shattered his lance on a first pass, and now must come in to rather closer (and possibly much warmer) quarters.

Techniques
✦ Design and form through contour
✦ Conveying energy and action

Ideas and inspiration
I wanted to create a drawing with implied narrative. Who is the knight, why is he battling the dragon and what will happen? Graphically, though, the scene must be self-contained, focusing on this moment's action, rather than what has gone before or what will come.

Visual references
There is no pictorial reference for this image; it is more about energy and lines of motion, about focusing all the attention on the imminent point of contact between the two combatants. It is important to keep documentation out of the way at this stage and concentrate on the action. Detail can come later.

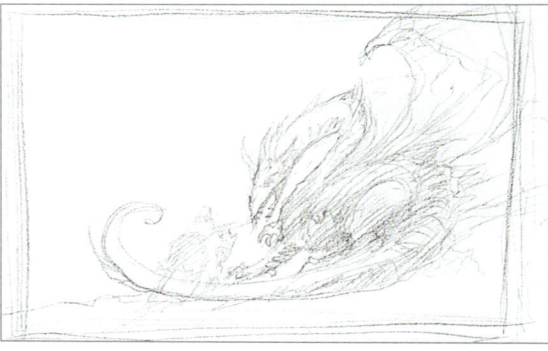

⬥ Thumbnail sketch
A quick sketch was done to plan the scene. This helps me to work out how the piece will work graphically within the page. The dragon's wing and tail 'contain' the image and help the viewer stay in the moment, drawing the eye into the scene. I would work up this drawing as a prelude to a colour painting of the subject.

Position and pace
Freedom of movement is crucial in this kind of sketch: large format, pencil held lightly and as far as possible from the point, with wrists and elbows clear of the paper. Also, maintain a brisk sketching pace until the main elements have found their places.

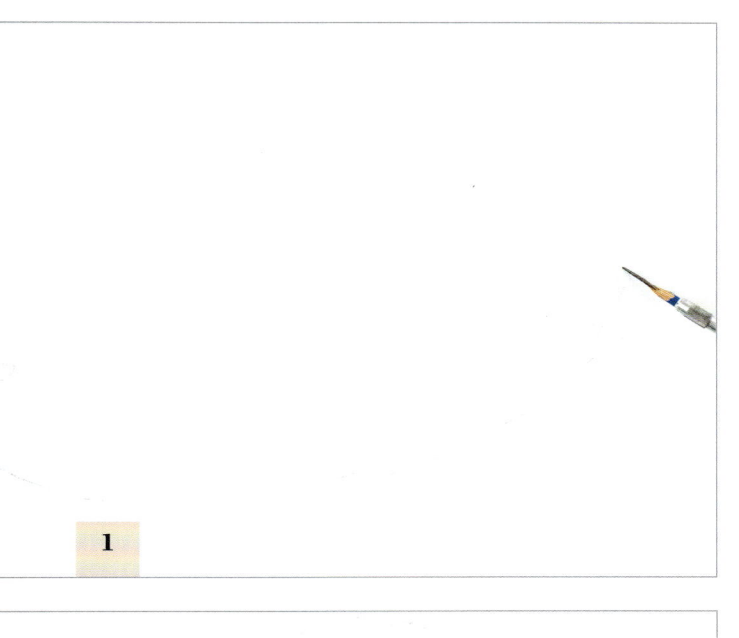

1 Working with a 4B pencil, sketch in the long, curved tail of the dragon. This will provide the initial building block on which the whole image will be developed. It's the most important part, despite what will be added later, so it should have a certain energy.

2 Sketch the long neck of the dragon, forming a full backwards 's' shape where it curves around to become the creature's chest. Also start to sketch in the body. These lines need to work as pure lines since they are all about establishing energy and movement rather than any particular physical detail.

3 Sketch in the foreleg and the haunch of the hind leg. Move on to the head and start to put in some structure here by sketching the dragon's open mouth and the various spikes and spines. Then work back into the neck, feeling out the shape here and adding some initial cross-hatching for volume and texture.

4 From the neck move up to further establish the shape of the wing. Then return to the neck and add some further contour shading. Begin to suggest the dragon's other foreleg with its raised clawed foot. Add the crest around the curve of the neck. Move down to the tail: strengthen its shape and add a crest. Lightly sketch in the ground.

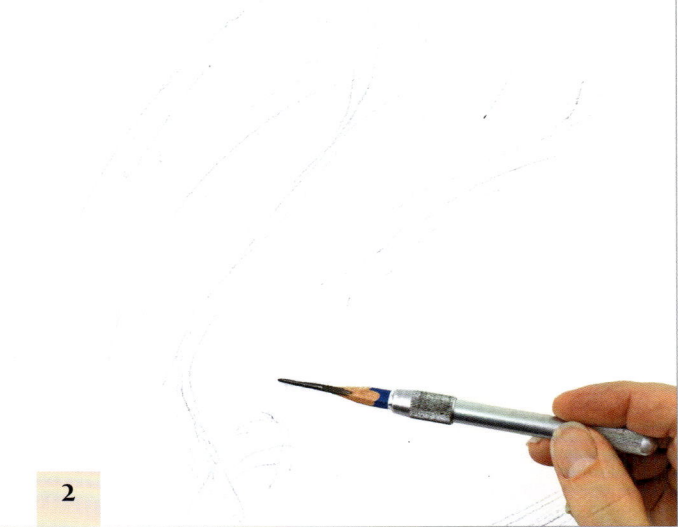

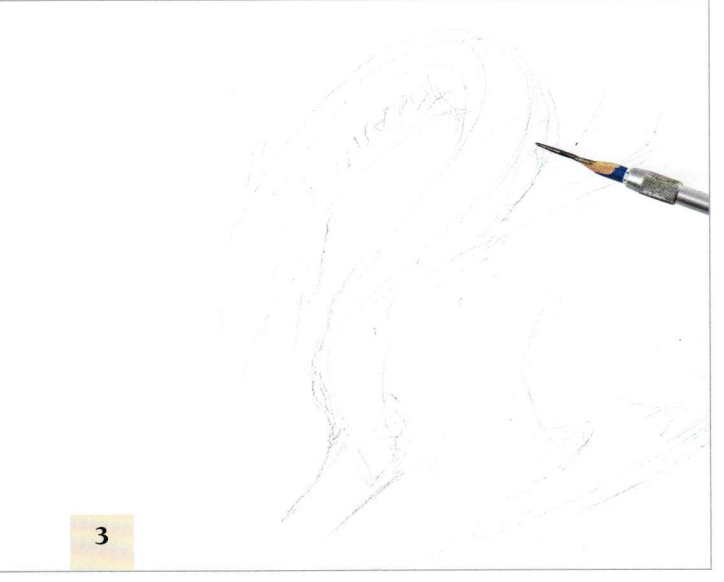

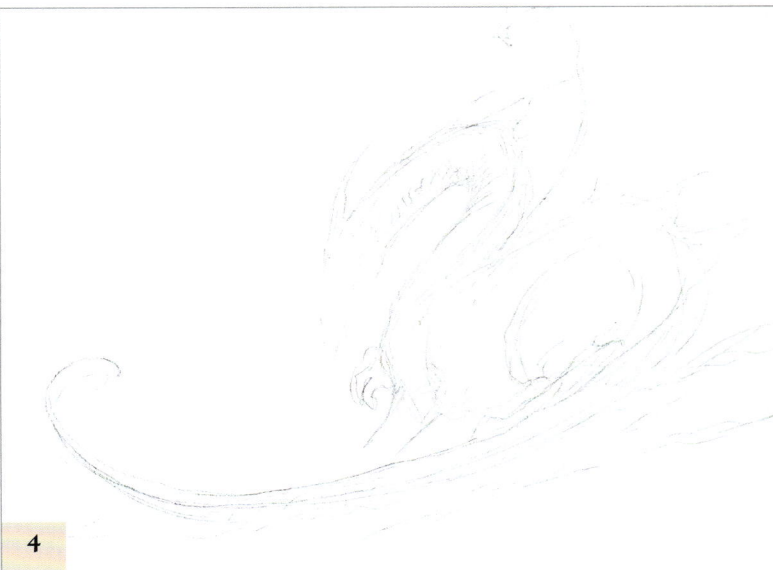

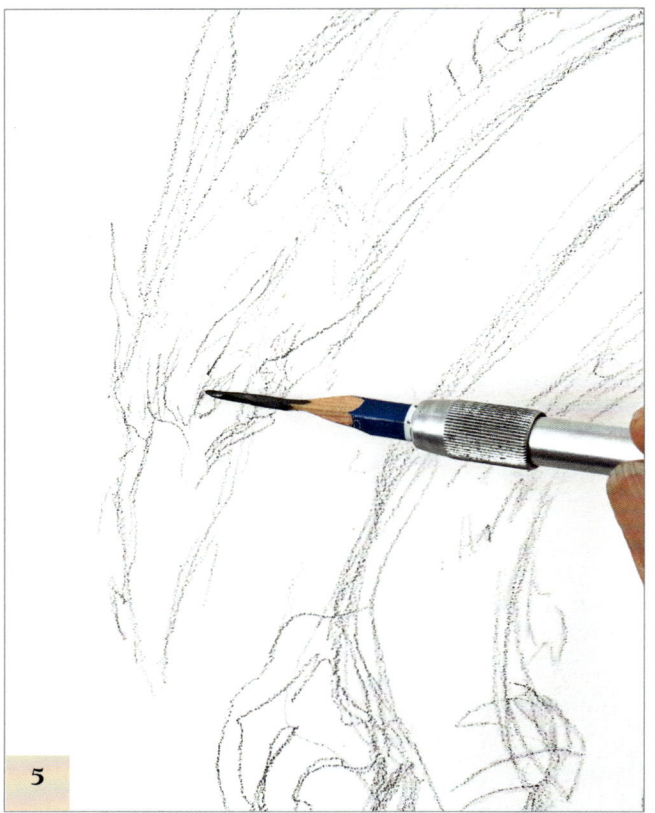

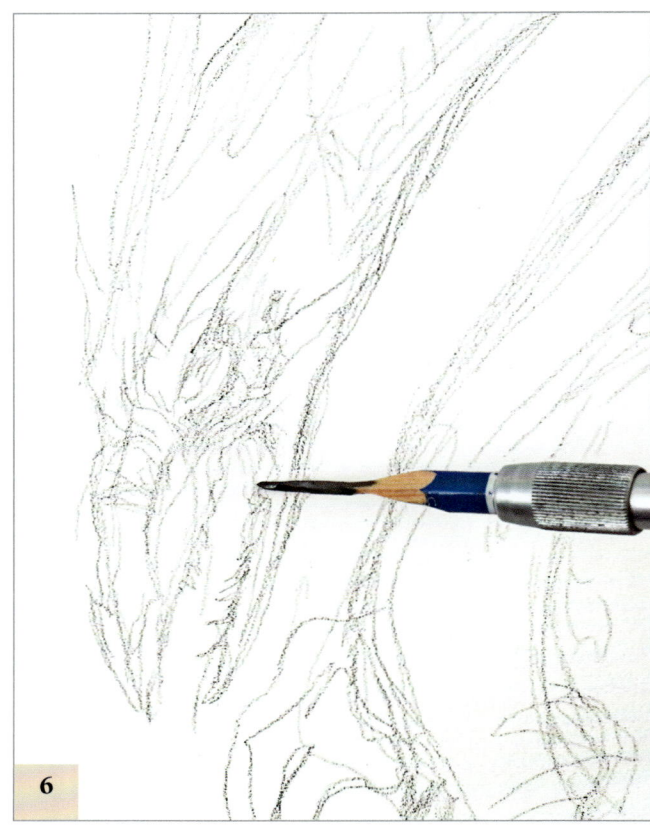

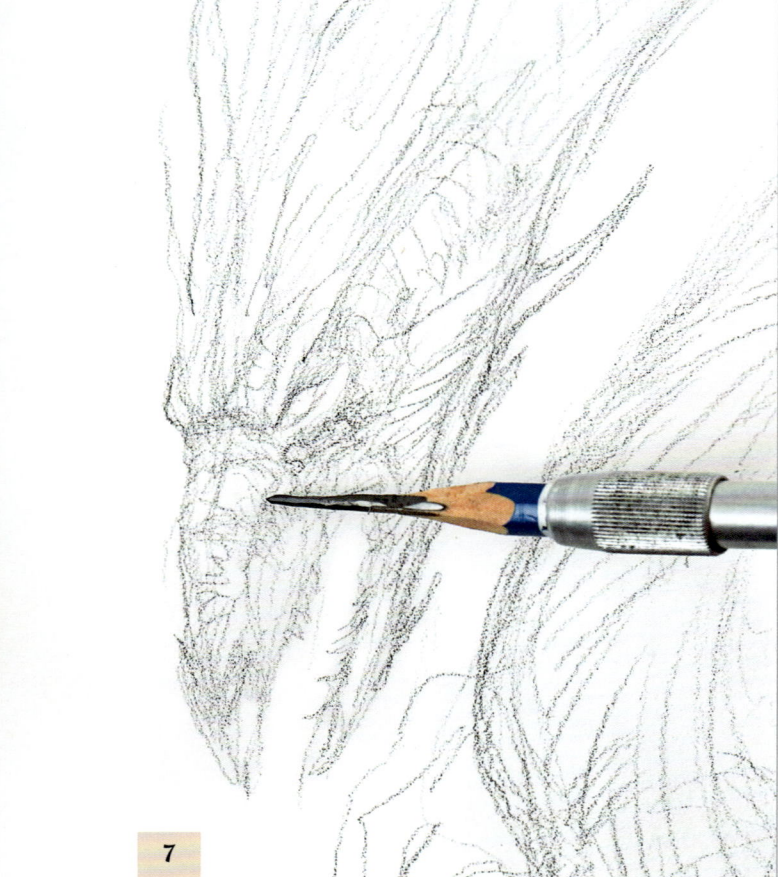

5 Now the basic structure is in place, it is time to return to the dragon's head. Place the eyebrows and the eye sockets, and begin defining the structure around the eyes.

6 Suggest scales and texture with a few lines, working down to add the nostrils. Start to add further detailing to the mouth, filling in the lower jaw and adding jagged teeth.

7 Add some contour shading around the front of the dragon's chest. Move back to the head and develop the crest with stronger lines, including a spike protruding back from the jaw. Add further detailing lines on the muzzle, working up to create a ridge between the eyes. Start to lightly shade the area to create texture and volume.

Keep moving

It is tempting to focus on the detail at this point, but resist the temptation to dwell in one place too long. Continue while there is energy in the sketch – you can build the detail later.

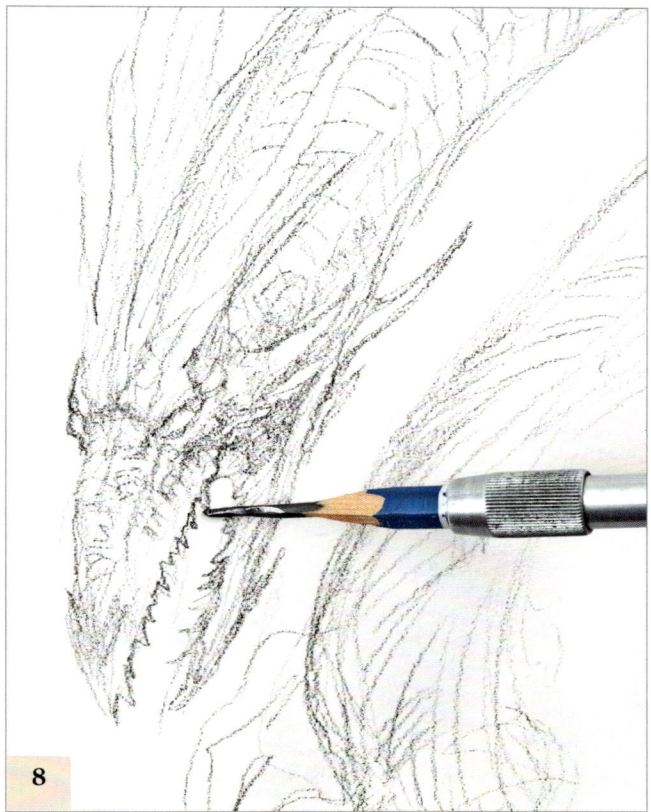

8 Move into the neck and build up the texture and shape by adding further cross-hatching. Establish the eye sockets further and apply further shading over the head to block it in. Work around the teeth with a bold line to create a strong, jagged edge.

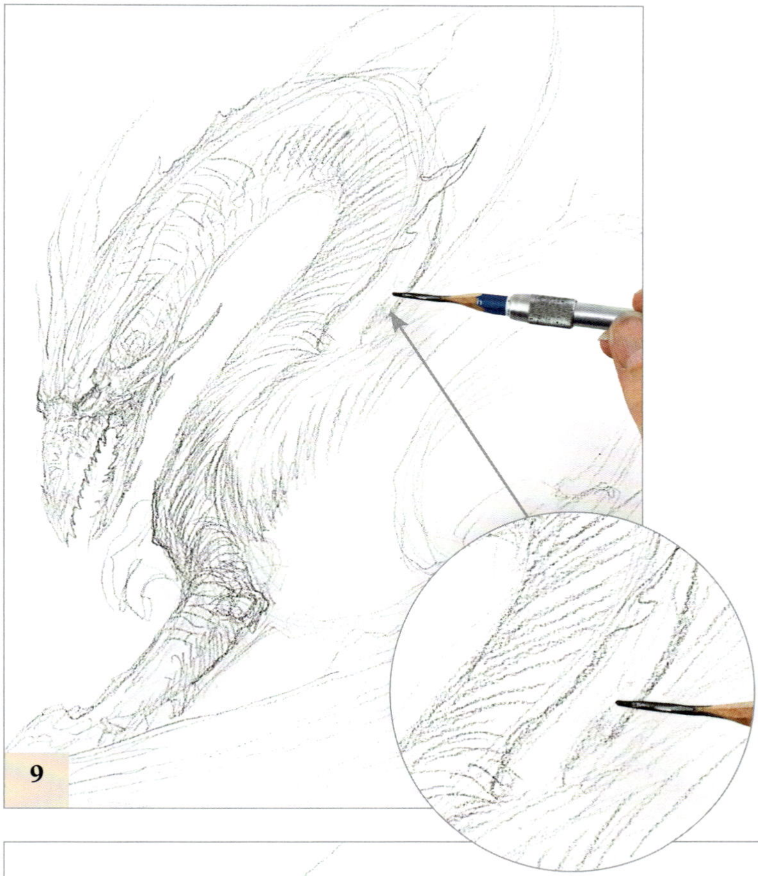

9 Apply further shading on the chest and reinforce the contour line, working down into the foreleg. Start to shade in the foreleg, and sketch in the claw. Continue shading up into the chest and neck. The neck of a dragon, like the body of a snake, is pure muscle. To capture the energy of the living creature do not think of an outline as a simple continuous line, but as a collection of lines appearing and disappearing around the volume they delineate.

10 Move up into the wing area, roughly establishing its shape. The wing is not represented in detail in this drawing but it is an important visual element which helps to contain dramatic effect within the image.

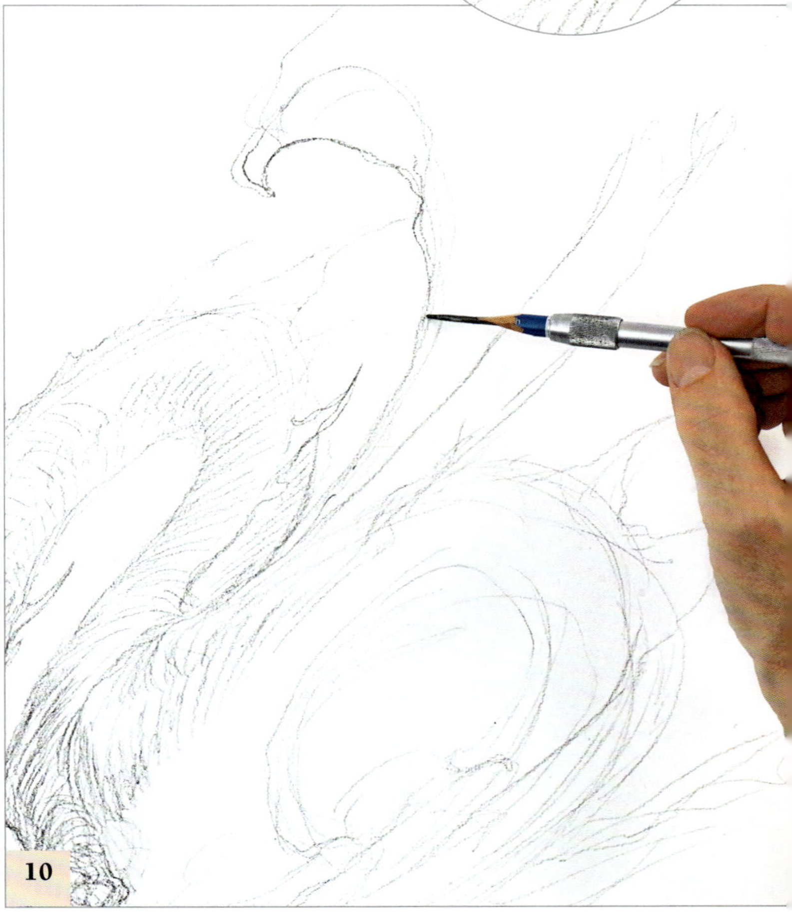

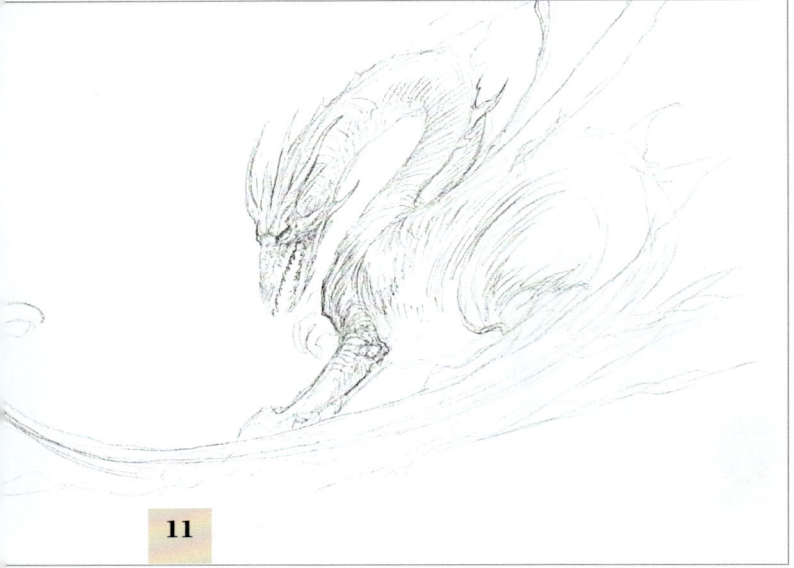

11 Strengthen the outlines on the dragon's neck and head. Lightly shade the haunch to begin establishing the shape.

12 Draw in the hind leg; shade and establish with a firm outline. Delineate the outline of the belly, working from the foreleg back. Firmly outline the foreleg and draw in the claw, and lightly shade. Shade over the chest and under the dragon's belly. Further establish the tail's shape, adding a strong ridge, and shade here too.

13 Draw in the crest on the dragon's back, and move up into the wing area with strong directional hatching.

14 Firmly establish the ground on the right-hand side of the drawing and shade. Continue building up the shape and shading on the tail.

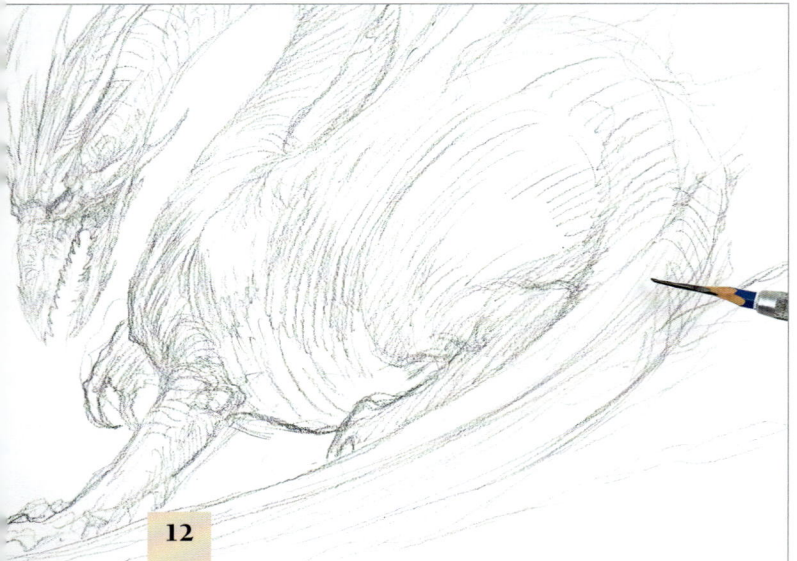

15 Now the knight enters. Start by drawing a loose outline sketch of the horse and rider. Then add the horse's tail and hind leg, and the knight's outstretched arm holding his sword, defining the shield at his right-hand shoulder. Add the saddlebag and sweeping folds of fabric at the knight's back. Define the horse's head then shade in the sketch.

16 Add flames from the dragon's nostrils with thin, wavy lines. Lightly add long, trailing, wispy lines to suggest flames and billowing smoke in the background to the left of the knight as a reminder of what could be created in the further development into colour (*see* What's Next?).

17 Add more contouring and shading to the smoke to add weight and shape. Further define the end of the dragon's tail and add a small crest. Loosely shade the whole of the foreground with strong, directional hatching.

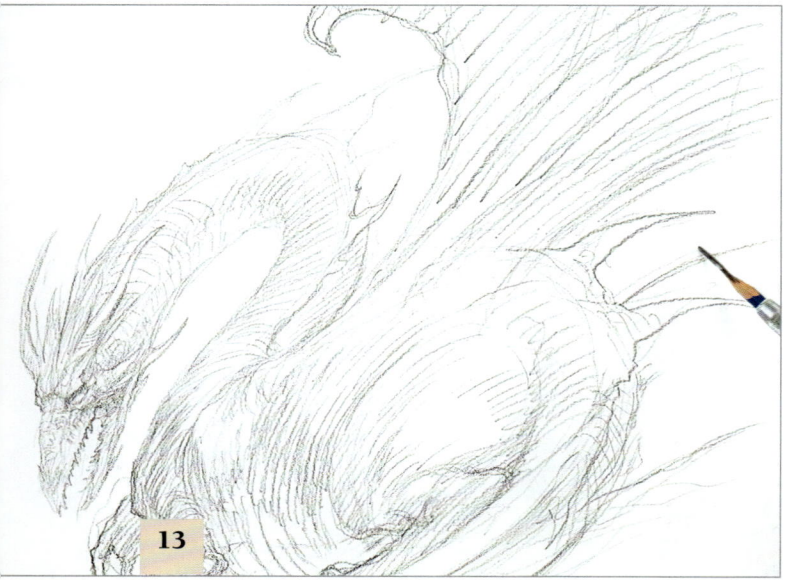

Directional hatching

Directional lines are dependant on which hand you use, so if you are left-handed, these may feel awkward. As long as they don't contradict the movement and volumes, they can be done however best suits you.

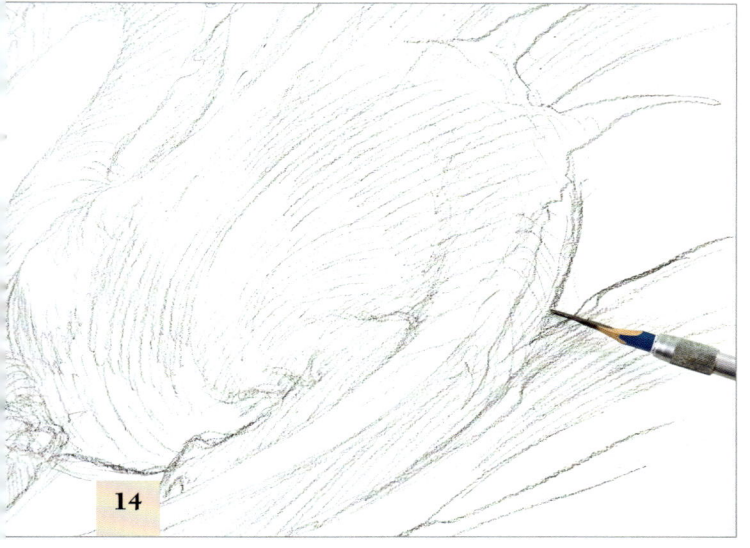

14

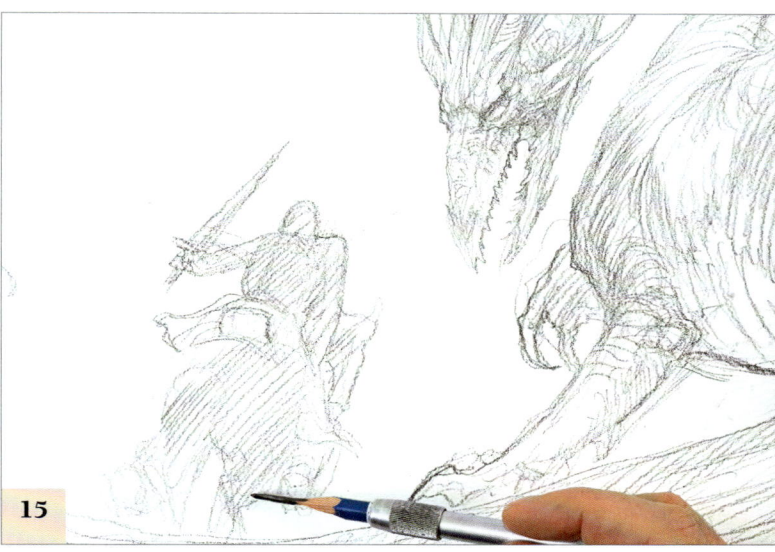

15

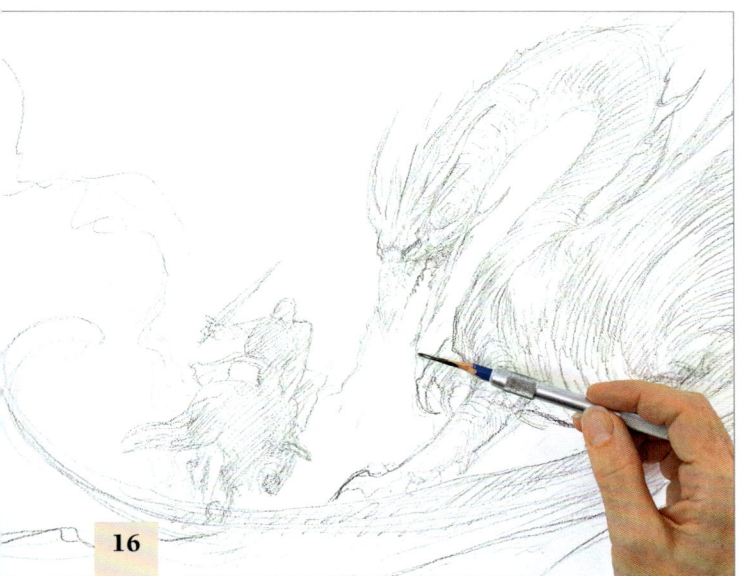

16

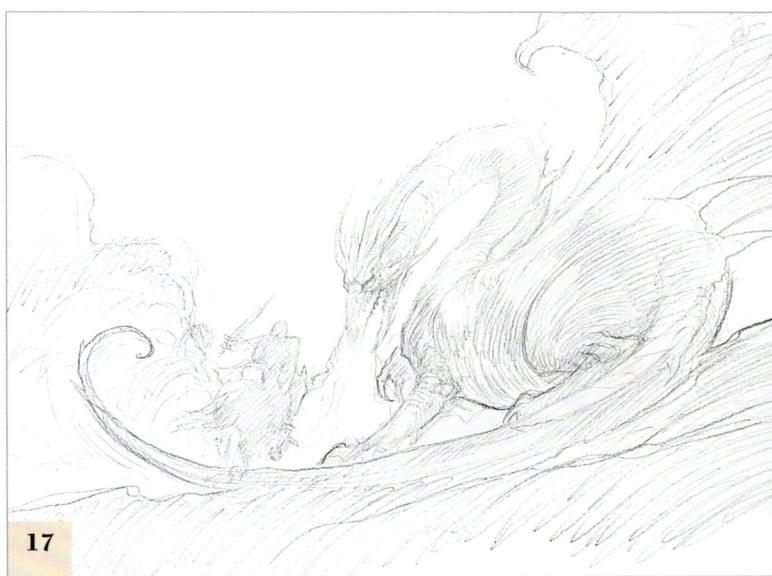

17

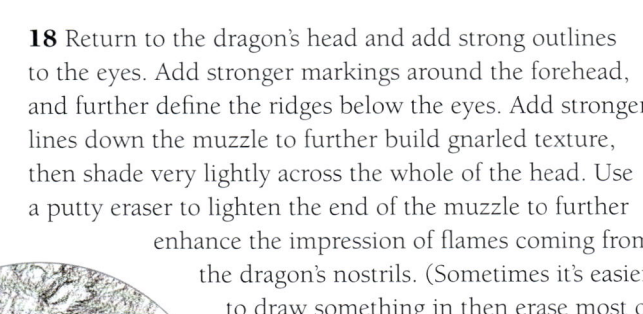

18

18 Return to the dragon's head and add strong outlines to the eyes. Add stronger markings around the forehead, and further define the ridges below the eyes. Add stronger lines down the muzzle to further build gnarled texture, then shade very lightly across the whole of the head. Use a putty eraser to lighten the end of the muzzle to further enhance the impression of flames coming from the dragon's nostrils. (Sometimes it's easier to draw something in then erase most of it than to draw it in faintly.)

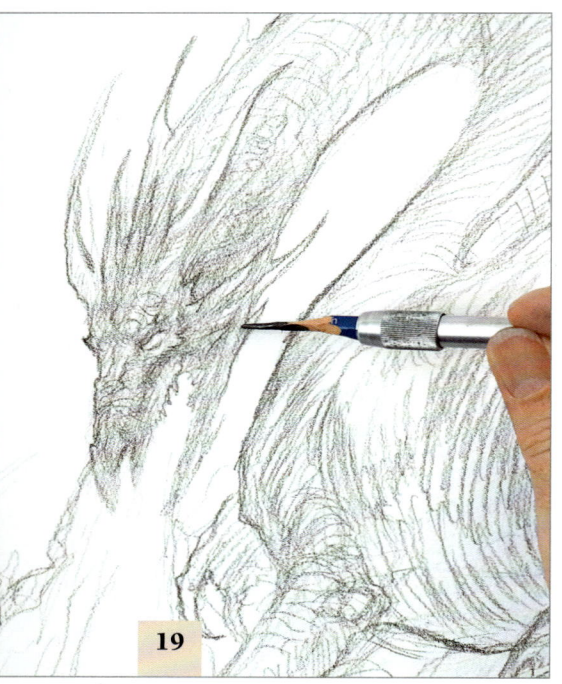

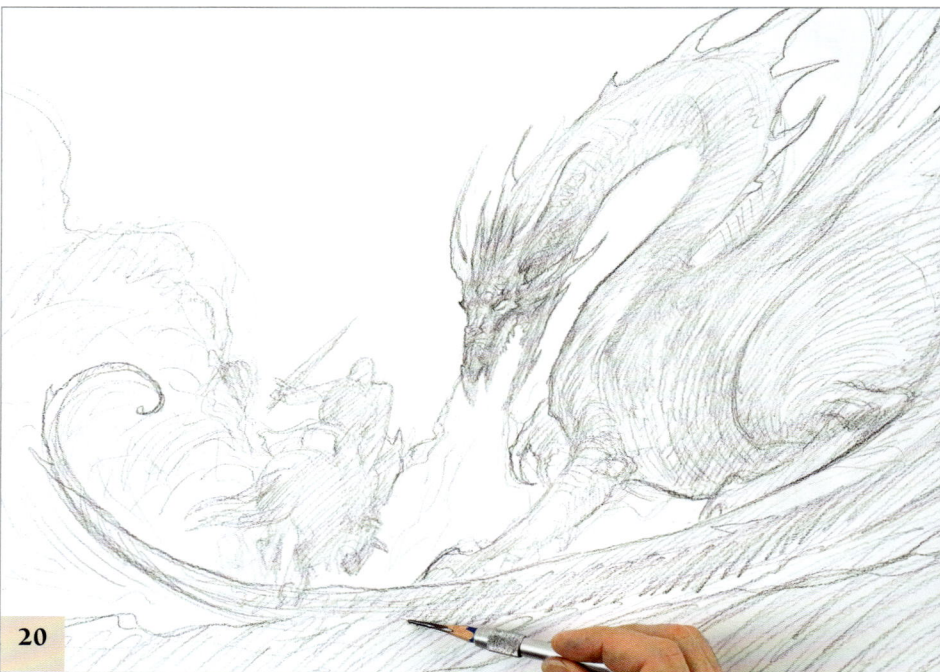

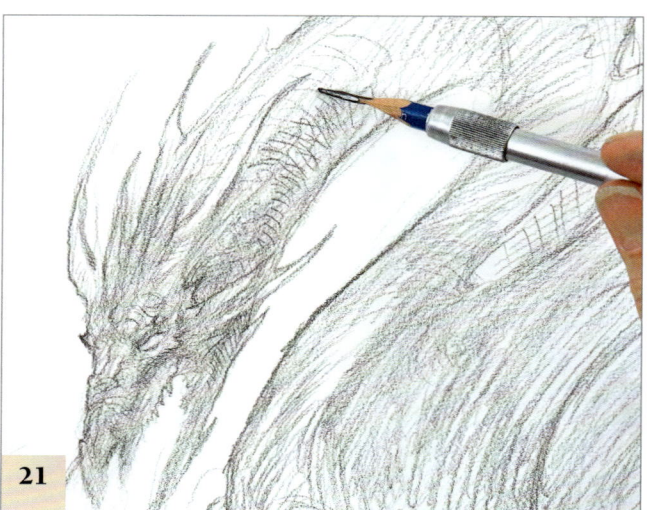

WHAT'S NEXT?

This is a sort of shorthand to establish the energy of the final piece – until then the detail will not be added. The background will then be developed, the knight properly realized, and the dragon rendered in all his reptilian glory. Drawing smoke and flames in pencil is a thankless task, but they come to life in colour. I will be glad that I did not spend too much time on the wing shape here – in the final painting it is likely to be moving and therefore blurred.

19 Add further contour lines across the muzzle, around the eyes and into the neck. Apply stronger outlines still to the crest and spines.

20 Again shade across the belly, this time with cross-hatching to suggest the texture. Work down the tail with strong, short marks to enhance the volume and texture.

21 Return to the dragon's neck to apply some final shading working with strong marks to give the impression of scales.

Final image

I have loosely sketched in a few lines in the far background to give the impression of mountains, a barren and hostile realm where dragons dwell. This is what I'd call a 'useful' sketch. There are awkward spots still to be resolved, and the dragon is missing a wing, but the essential ingredients are there. While the drawing may be short on detail, it has much movement and energy.

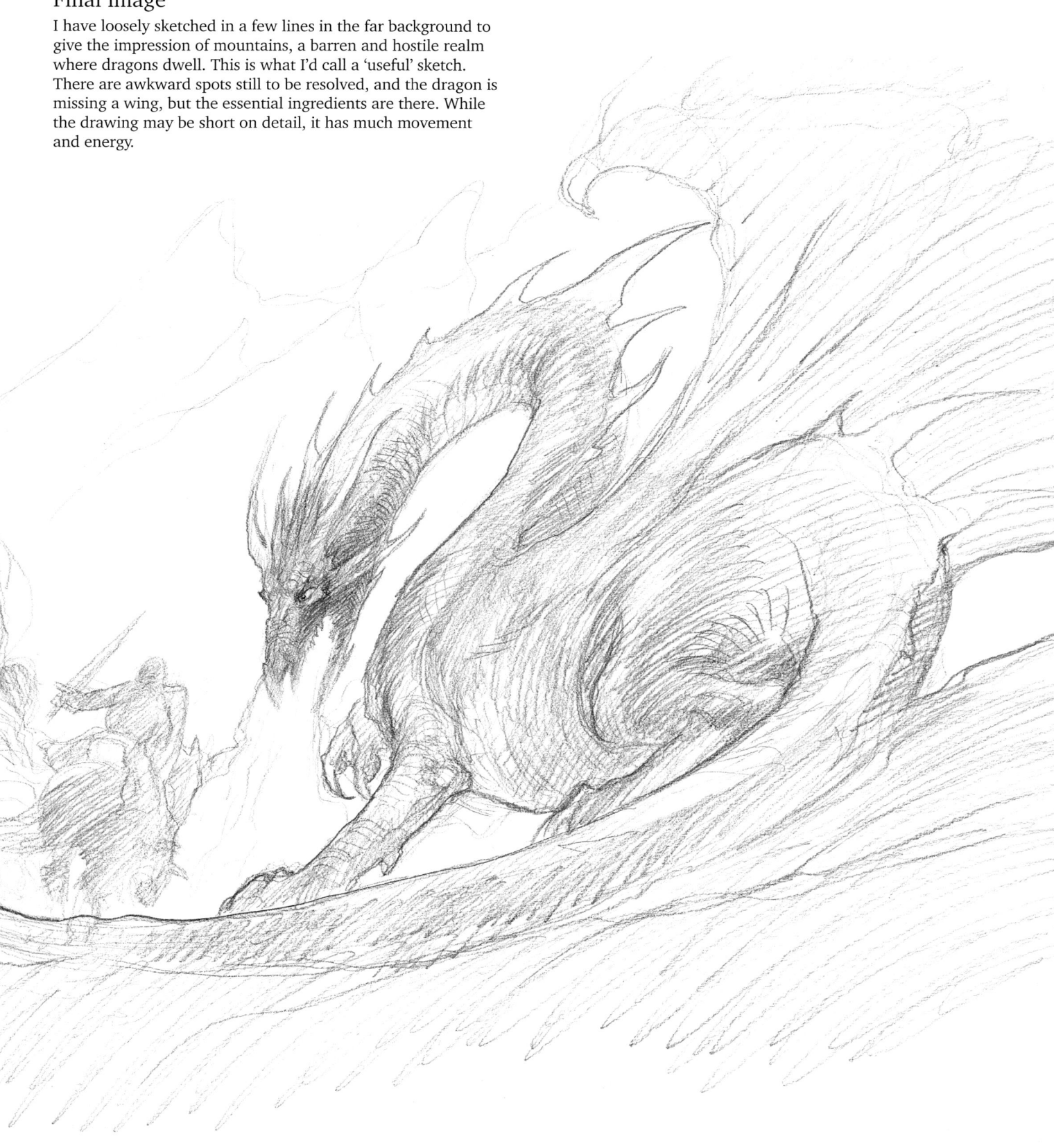

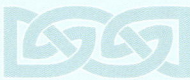

THOR AND THE GIANT

Thor, the Norse god of Thunder, persuades the giant Hymir to take him fishing, lopping the head off the giant's prized ox as bait. He is after not just any fish, but Jörmungandr, the World-Encompassing Serpent who sleeps beneath the Middle Sea, his tail held in his mouth. The serpent takes the bait, and an agitated scene follows.

Techniques
✦ Drawing with energy
✦ Interaction of two characters
✦ Making a scene

Ideas and inspiration
I wanted to depict these larger-than-life characters tossed upon stormy seas in a simple fishing boat, the giant battling to keep control against the towering waves while Thor is engaged in an intense struggle of his own with his catch.

Visual references
I dug out a number of pages cut out of a range of different magazines from my drawer marked 'Body – Male'. From fashion adverts to body building articles, several came in useful as I progressed my ideas. Reference to a good history book helped me to get the fishing boat right.

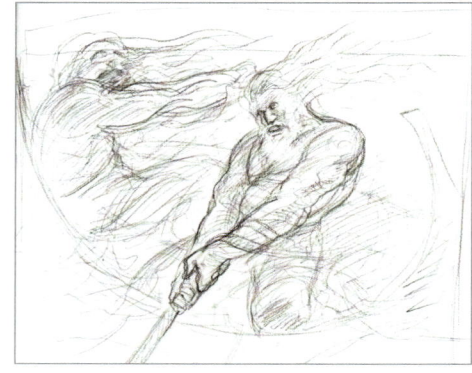

⬆ Thumbnail sketch
This is useful where more than one figure occupies a space. The thumbnail places the characters, and its tonal density gives an indication of the dramatic atmosphere I hope to achieve. But the full drama – driving rain and the boat-tossing waves – has yet to be developed.

Using references
A variety of references is essential for researching the details needed to create a convincing depiction of both the figures and the boat. Getting the detail right helps establish a reality for your imagined worlds.

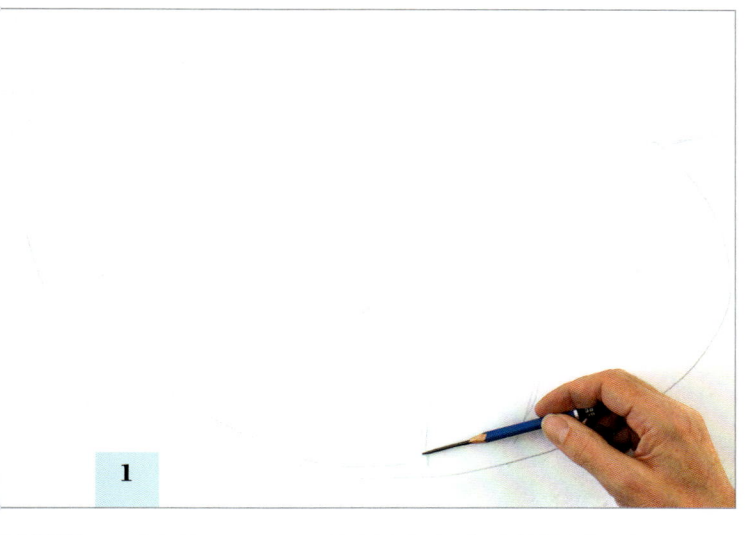

1 Working with a 3B pencil, first establish the main components of the drawing. Sketch in the gunwale of the boat as the initial building block. Then sketch in the body of the giant to the left of the boat – his torso and arm, his head and his leg. Now sketch Thor – his torso outline and his upper legs seen as he kneels in the boat.

2 Now start to work on the giant. Roughly draw in the outline of his head and a few wavy lines for his hair. Establish the outline of his torso and arm down into his hand (which will be grasping the rudder), then start to lightly shade over these areas to build up some volume.

3 Build up the giant's face. First sketch in his eyebrows and nose, and add some light shading across his cheeks and around the mouth area. Then establish his hairline and sketch in his long flowing hair, and start to shade this.

4 Now begin work on the giant's leg. Establish the leg outline then start to lightly shade the areas of shadow here. Define the line of the rudder.

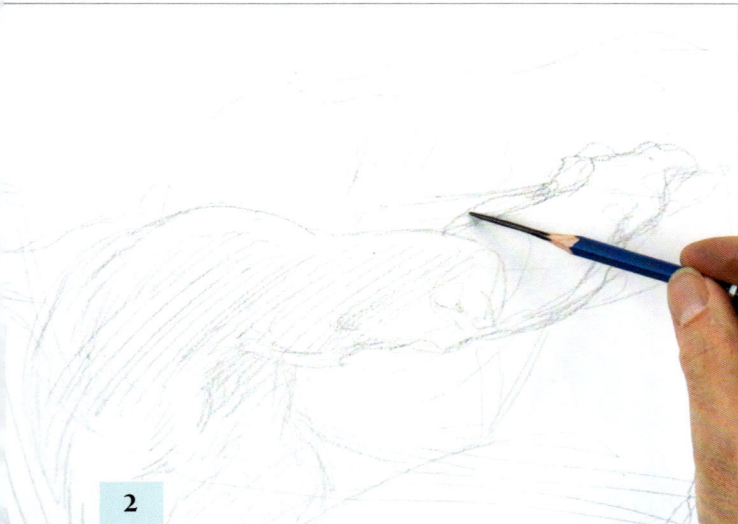

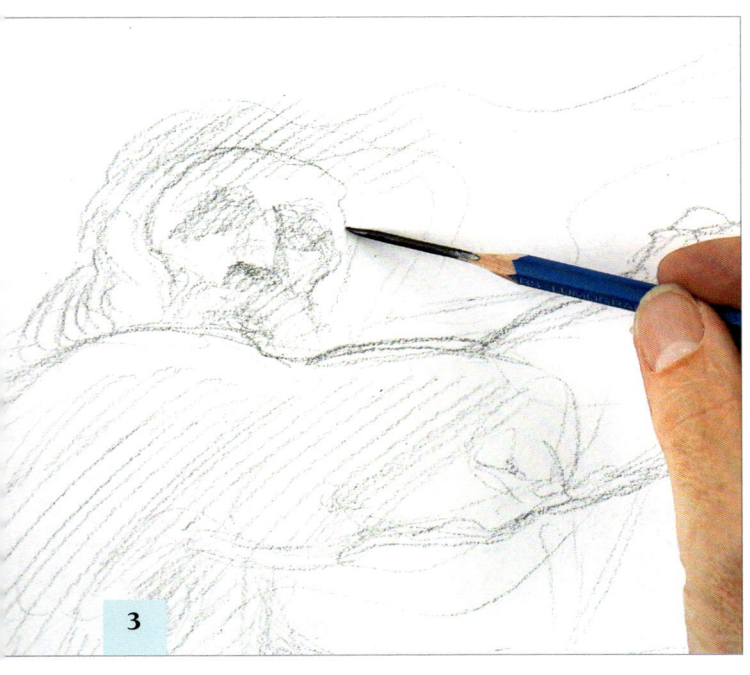

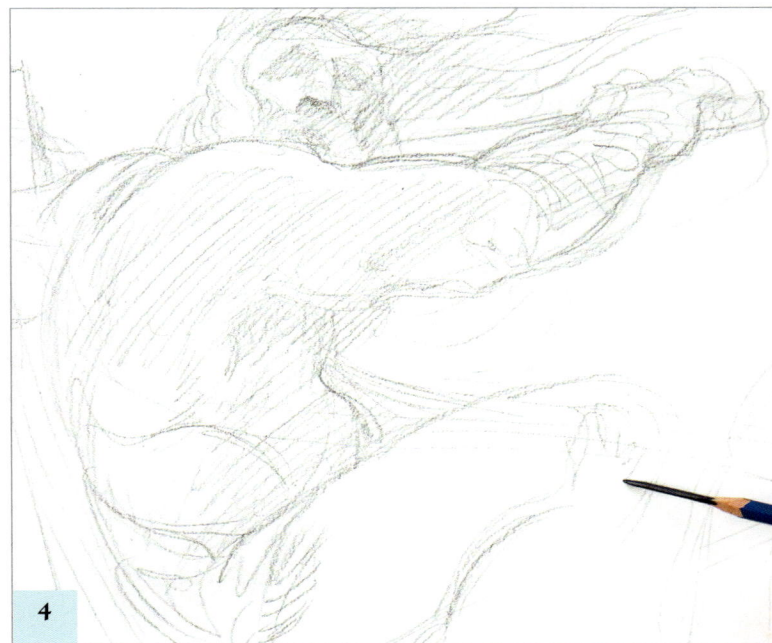

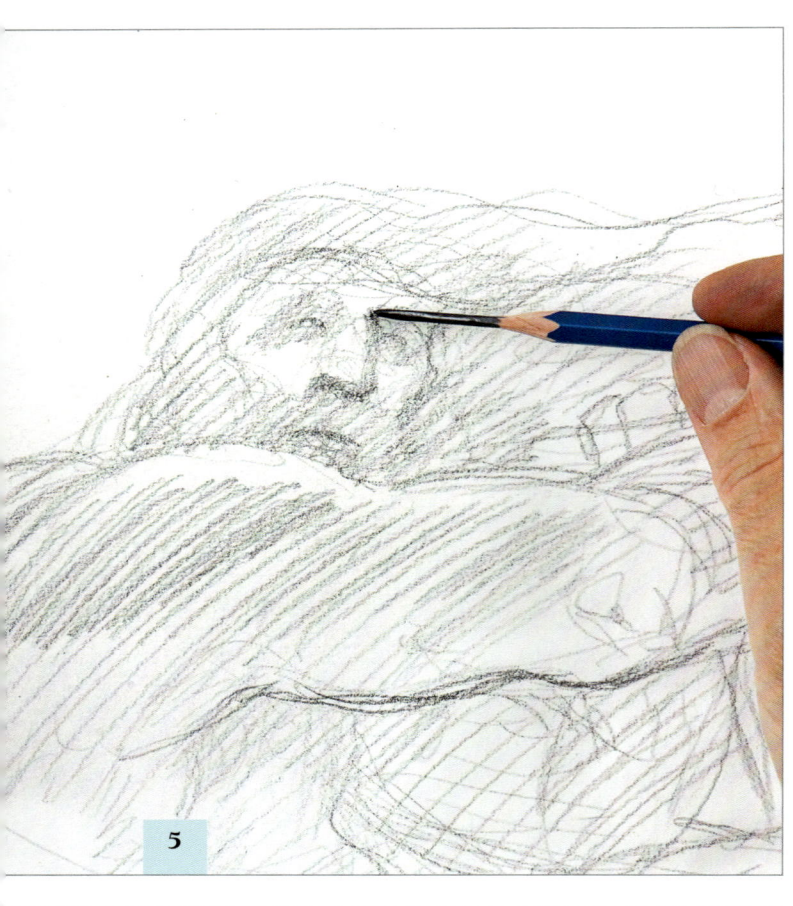

5

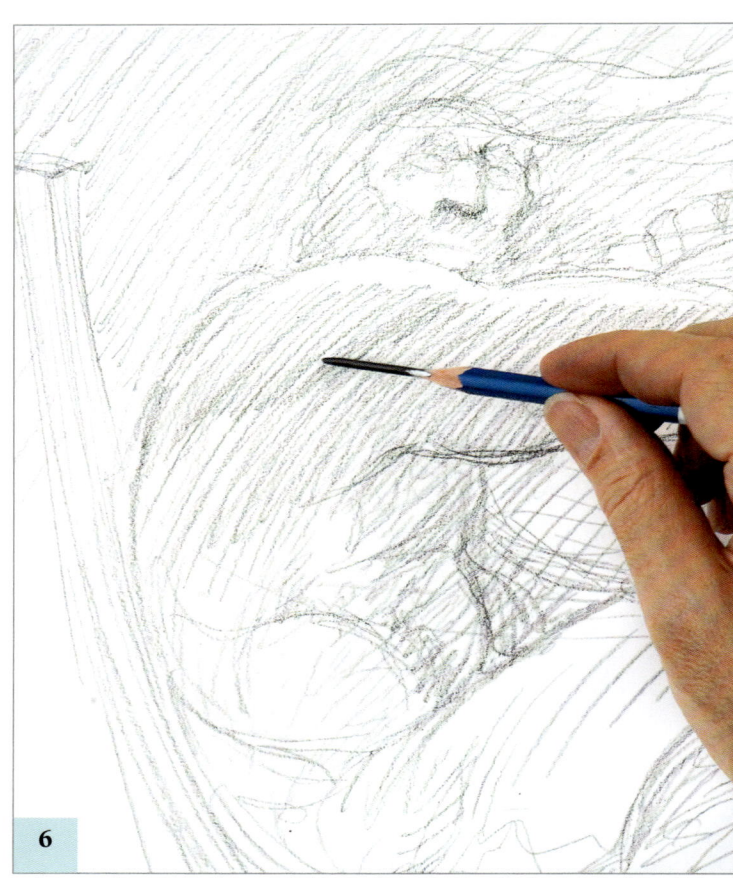

6

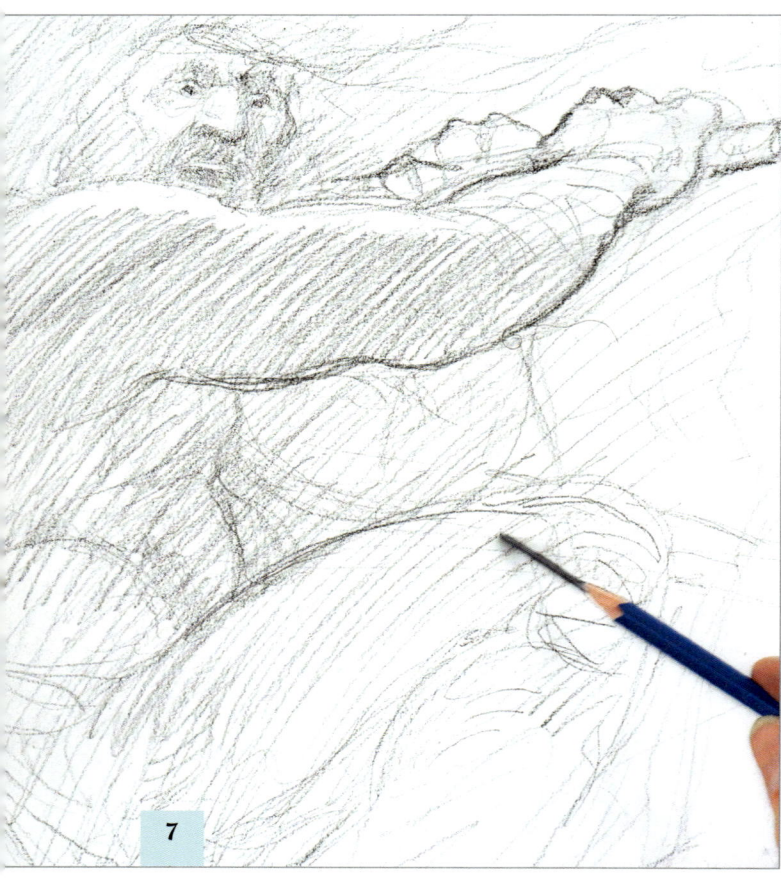

7

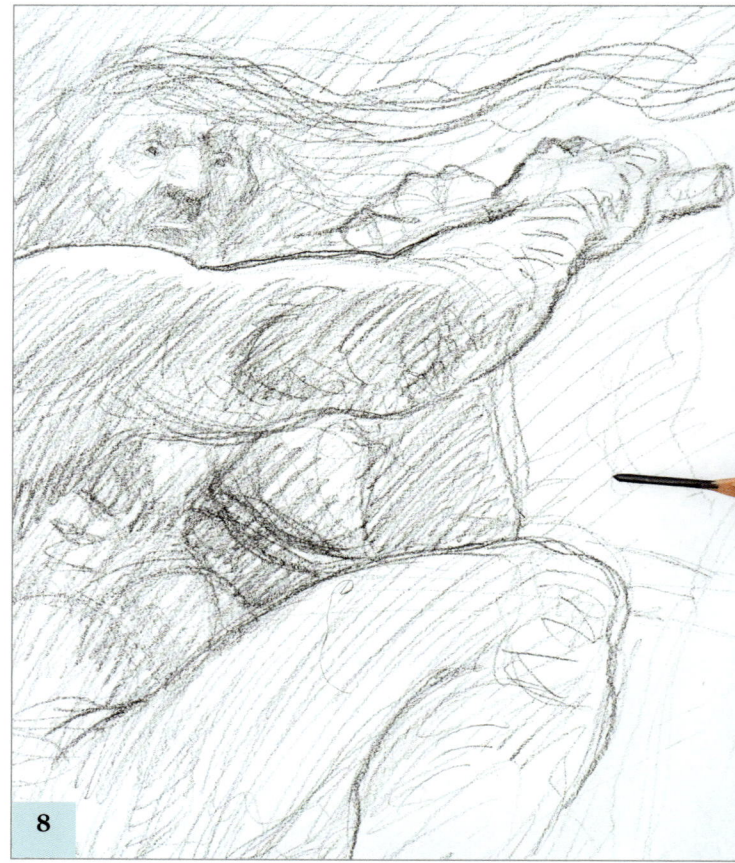

8

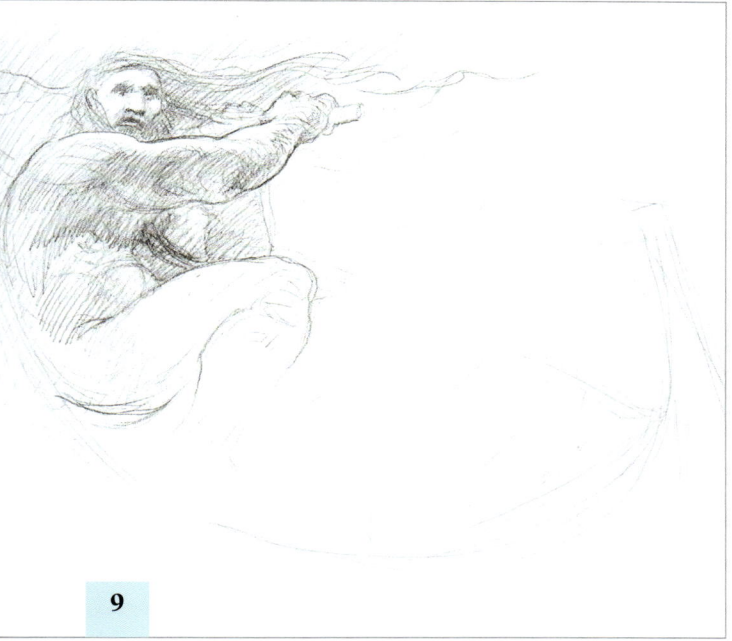

9

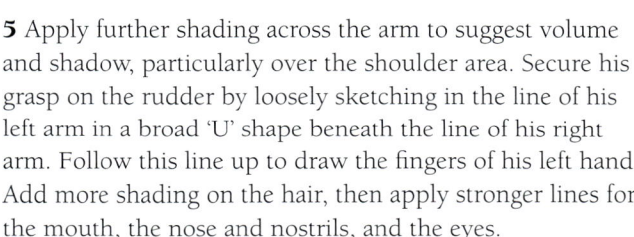

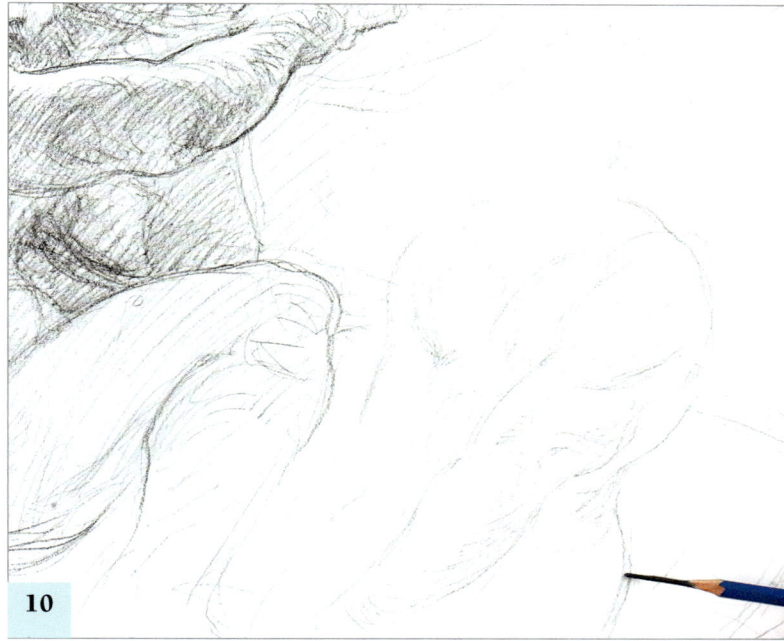

10

5 Apply further shading across the arm to suggest volume and shadow, particularly over the shoulder area. Secure his grasp on the rudder by loosely sketching in the line of his left arm in a broad 'U' shape beneath the line of his right arm. Follow this line up to draw the fingers of his left hand. Add more shading on the hair, then apply stronger lines for the mouth, the nose and nostrils, and the eyes.

6 Firmly establish the stern of the boat and the giant's back braced against it. Shade the background to the left of the giant with broad strokes. Establish the outline of his body with directional shading across it to further build volume.

7 Use a strong pencil line to build the outline of the right arm and hand gripped around the rudder. Firmly establish the left hand alongside. Define the mouth, adding strong shading to suggest a moustache and beard. Add pupils to the eyes, then work out to clearly establish the cheekbones. Continue shading across the body and background.

8 Add to and strengthen the wavy lines that convey the giant's flowing hair. Firmly establish the giant's leg and continue to shade his body, particularly on his torso and arm to build shape and volume. This shading should define the muscles down the right arm and across the body and begin to define the giant's partly hidden left arm. Continue to build up the shading in the background.

9 Begin moving to the right of the giant. Add a shadow down the inside of the boat's stern, and following the line of the free-flowing hair, continue to draw in broken wavy lines to the left and the right to give the impression of the sea's waves. Returning to the giant's face, increase the shadowing around the eye socket to give the impression of raised eyebrows. Use a putty eraser to knock back the facial details and clean up the hair across the forehead. Shade the mouth. Increase the shading in the hair to enhance the thickness.

10 To begin Thor, start establishing the shoulder and right-hand arm, then build up the left-hand arm and torso. Shade lightly, and draw the line of his back and mid-section.

The giant's face

Before moving on from Step 9 to begin Step 10, I redrew the mouth. If you got it right the first time, there is no need to do this. However, I find it tempting to over-define recognizable facial elements, so often erase details and rework them more freely.

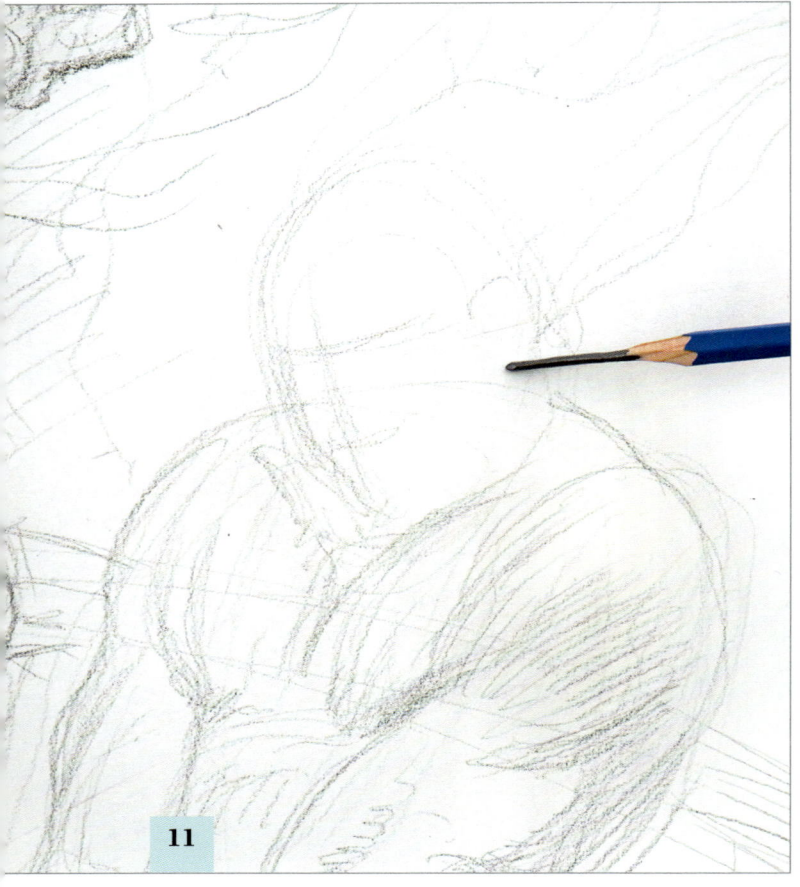

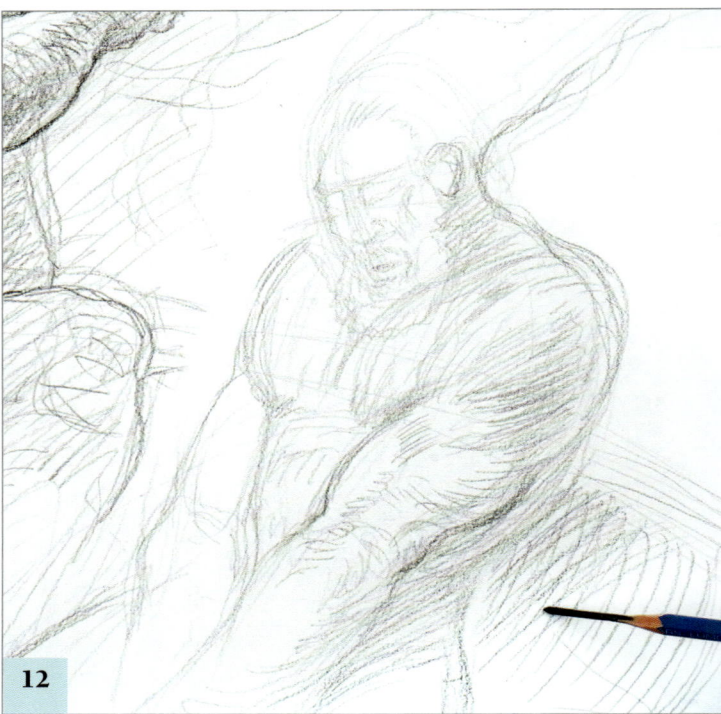

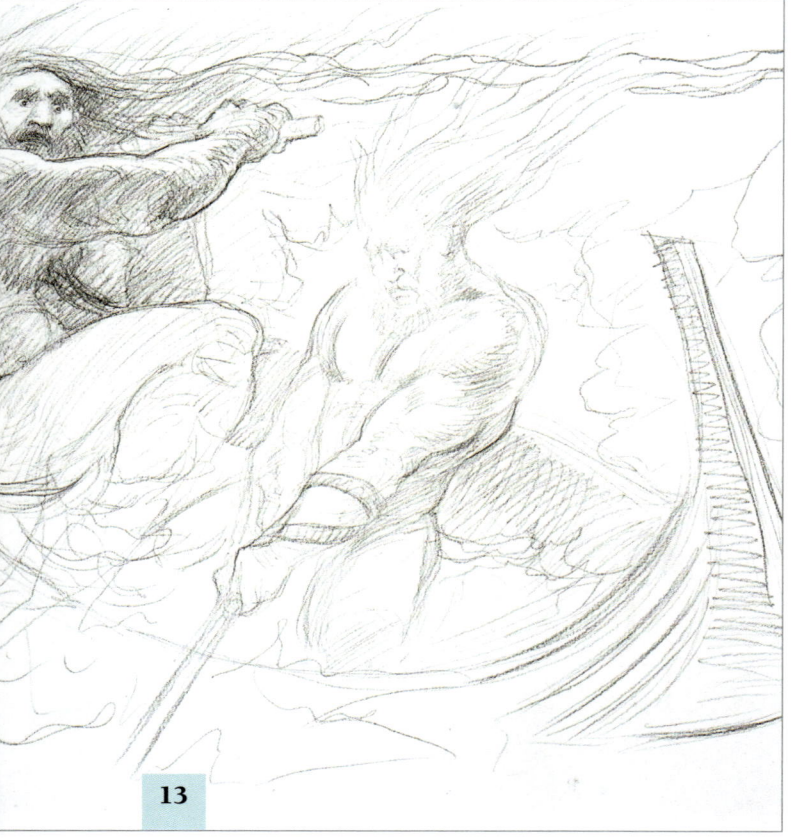

11 Apply further shading on Thor's upper chest to define his straining muscles. Then start work on his head, using guidelines to establish the head angle, and lightly sketch the outline of the skull.

12 Lightly sketch in Thor's eyes, nose, mouth and beard. Establish the left-hand profile of his face then draw a flowing line up from the right-hand shoulder to form his neckline, moving into an outline for his long, flowing hair. Continue shading down Thor's right-hand side. Work into the body of the boat to convey its concave shape.

13 Extend Thor's arms down to define his hands grasped around the fishing line. Draw two straps across his forearm and cross-hatch to shade. Apply light shading across the face. Define the mouth, nose, eyes and right-hand ear, and convey the shape of the cheekbones with contour shading. Work long strokes up from the head for flowing hair and lightly shade. Define the prow of the boat and the planking of the boat's sides and lightly shade. Lightly sketch in a rough sea and lightning flashes behind Thor.

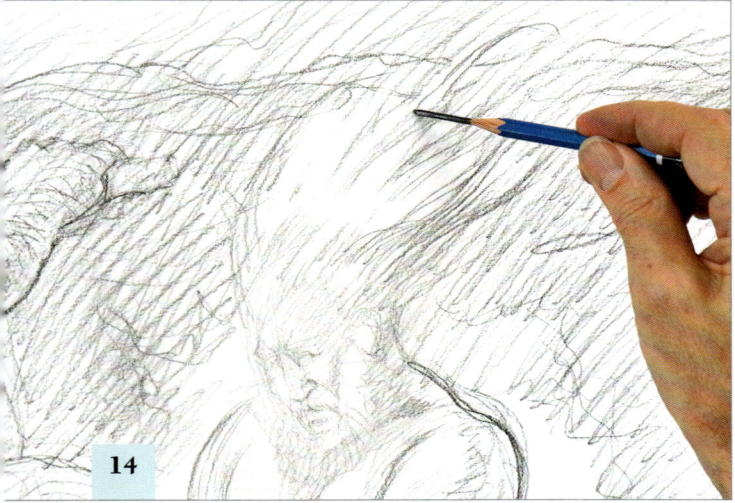

14 Apply bold shading across the sea area, then add more waves to build the dramatic backdrop. Use an eraser to lift Thor's hair from the shading, and re-define his hair strands.

15 Add further definition to the outline of Thor's arms and torso, then move back to work on his face. Further define his beard, mouth and nostrils, and start to apply the creases on either side of his mouth.

16 Add more texture to Thor's moustache and beard, then further define his left-hand profile, shading to convey shadow. Add raised eyebrows to convey exertion, then fill in the pupils. Working up full details in faces that will eventually be painted in colour isn't always necessary of course, but faces with dramatic and well-defined expressions – in this case teeth-gritting determination and fear – are always worth exploring.

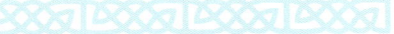

Go for it

On a rough sketch like this, let go and work vigorously. Occasionally, you will find power in unexpected lines and energetic shading. Never be afraid to 'go for it' if you feel you might capture something. You can always erase and draw it again.

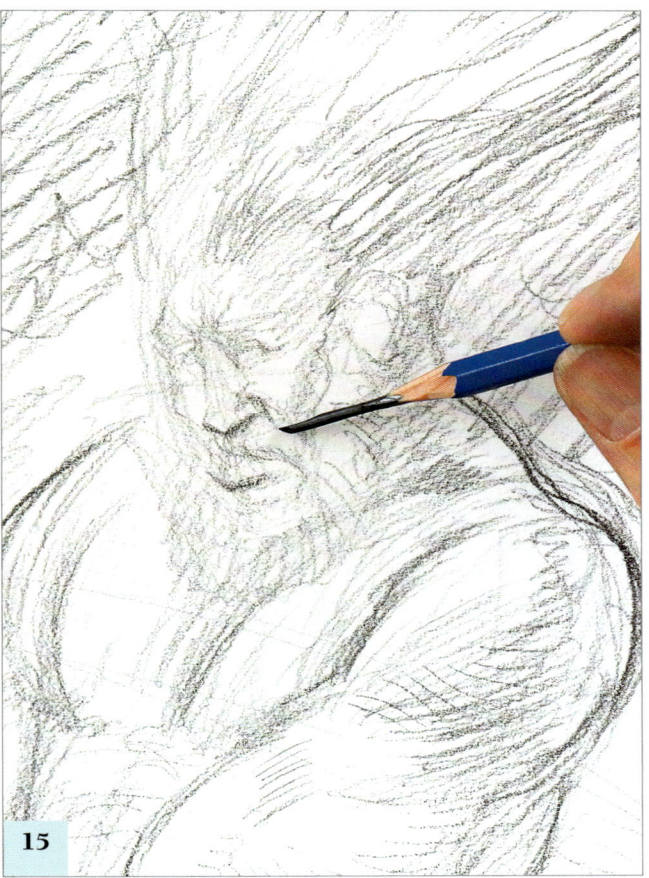

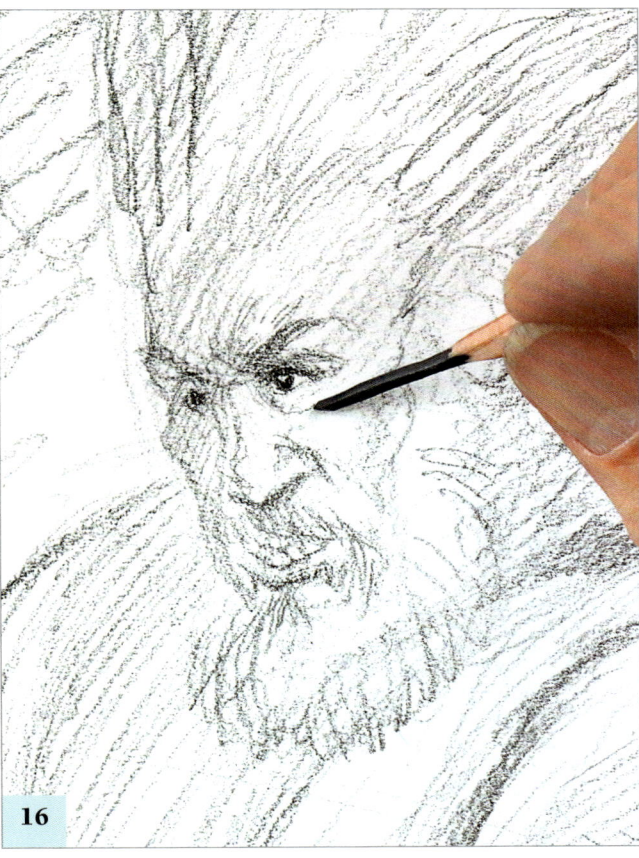

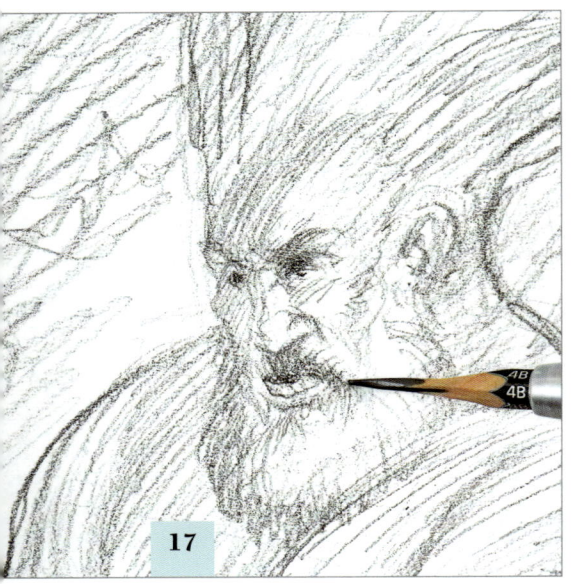

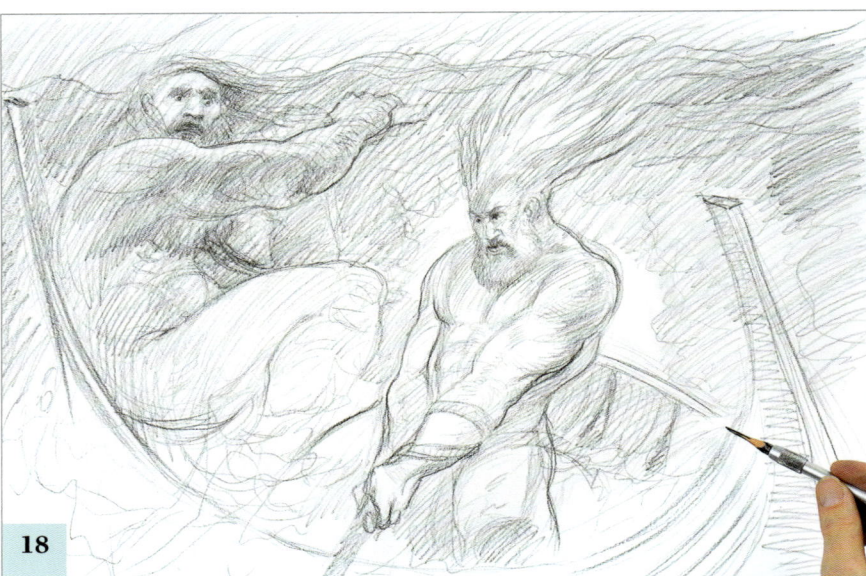

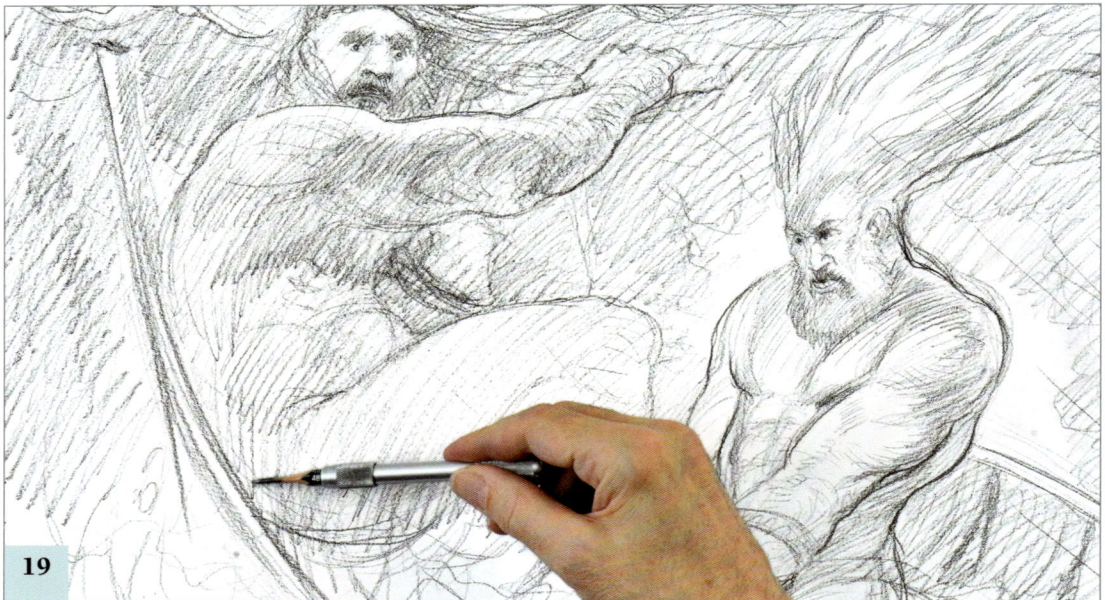

17 Work a line of contour shading down the side of Thor's face to define his cheek. Further develop his moustache and the edge and volume of his beard with strong shading. Shape his ear, and re-define the outline of his arms.

18 Ensure the boat details are as authentic as possible. Define the edges, stern and prow. Add detail inside the boat, shading to define the planks and the ribs.

19 Add sheets of rain across the image in bold directional strokes from left to right. Continue shading the background and add more hair lines to both figures so that they appear to merge with the waves. Build up more bold shading on the giant's body to begin to balance out the sketch.

Look again

Refer often to your source material. Ensuring authenticity of period objects and historical details in a sketch will help to establish credibility for the imagined characters.

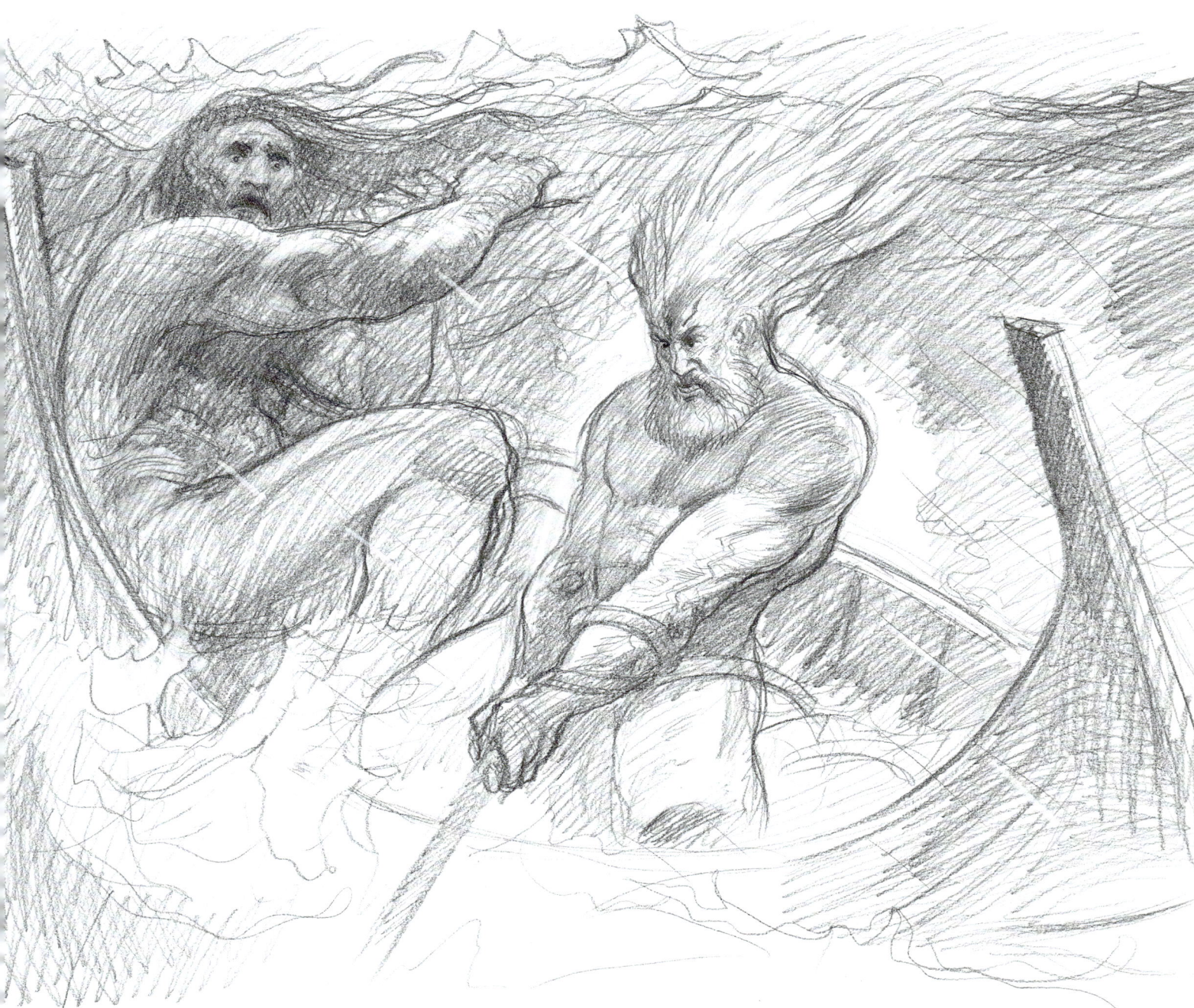

Final image

This drawing succeeds in capturing a fair bit of the energy and tension that I was looking for. Still quite a rough sketch, with little in the way of worked up details, the final image more than adequately defines the dark wall of water behind and Thor lit up by lightning, and makes a very atmospheric piece.

WHAT'S NEXT?

I look forward to developing this into a colour painting. The wall of water and the storm clouds running diagonally across the sky will be fun to paint, and the foam and spray offer many possibilities for contrast. Thor is a little on the big side though, compared to the giant, so I'll reduce him slightly.

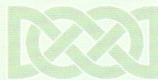

LANCELOT

Lancelot has become, over many retellings of the legend of King Arthur, a complex and intriguingly flawed character. The greatest and most trusted of the king's knights, Lancelot's flight to France with Queen Guenevere precipitates the fall of Camelot and the end of Arthur's kingdom.

Materials
+ Derwent pastel pencils: white, light blue, terracotta, light terracotta, umber, light violet
+ Blue-grey cartridge paper

Tinted paper
Tinted paper is a job half done before you begin; you can work both ways, dark and light, from the mid-tone.

Techniques
+ Introducing pastel pencils
+ Drawing armour
+ Making a scene

Ideas and inspiration
I wanted to show Lancelot on his ship in a pensive mood, perhaps a sorrowful look back to home shores, and contemplating the gathering clouds on the far horizon. Also, I have a confession to make: I have never used coloured pencils on coloured paper, so this is a bit of an experiment.

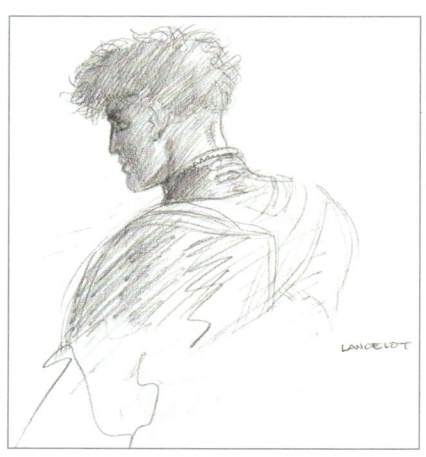

Graphite pencil sketch
This preliminary pencil sketch didn't really capture what I was after, but served to eliminate a few things which would not have functioned in a larger sketch. Concentrating too much on the armour to the detriment of Lancelot's profile was an error. Both need to be treated equally.

Visual references
I have a big collection of armour images – postcards, posters and photographs. Time spent looking at period costume, armour and weaponry is well spent. It can also be a constraint if authenticity overshadows imagination, so leave historically inspired details to one side until you've captured the spirit of your piece. For Lancelot himself, images of male models cut from fashion magazines over the years helped me to capture the desired wistful look.

1 With **terracotta**, establish Lancelot's basic outline. Start with the shape across the shoulders then work up into the jaw line. Place the profile then work up into the hair area, establishing the hairline. Lightly shade across the cheek then work down from the hair to form the smooth curve of the neck. Now you are ready to begin shading.

2 With **white**, shade a clear highlight down the left-hand shoulder, then lightly apply white shading in broad strokes across the shoulder. Start blending this initial shading with **light blue**.

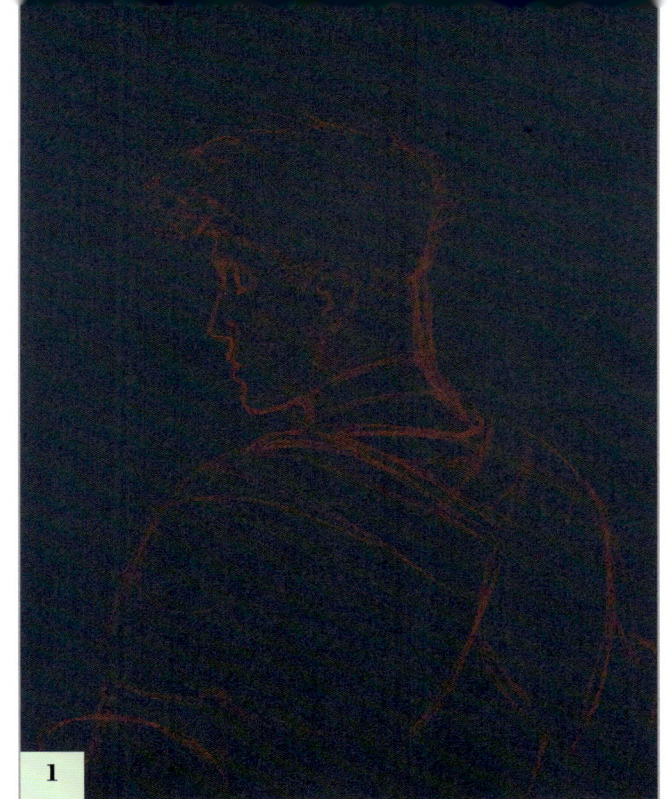

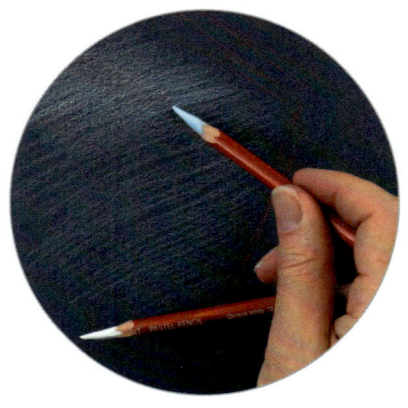

Blending duo
When building up blending with two colours, it helps to hold both pencils in one hand at the same time.

3 Start to slowly build up the colour by blending the two pencils, adding a strong **white** highlight on the top of the shoulder. To emphasize the ridge of the shoulder armour, pull a putty eraser through the shading. As the colours are lightly applied – the weight of the pencil itself is almost enough to leave a line – you will have no trouble 'drawing' a clean line with the eraser. You will need to re-shape the eraser between strokes to keep the line clean and sharp.

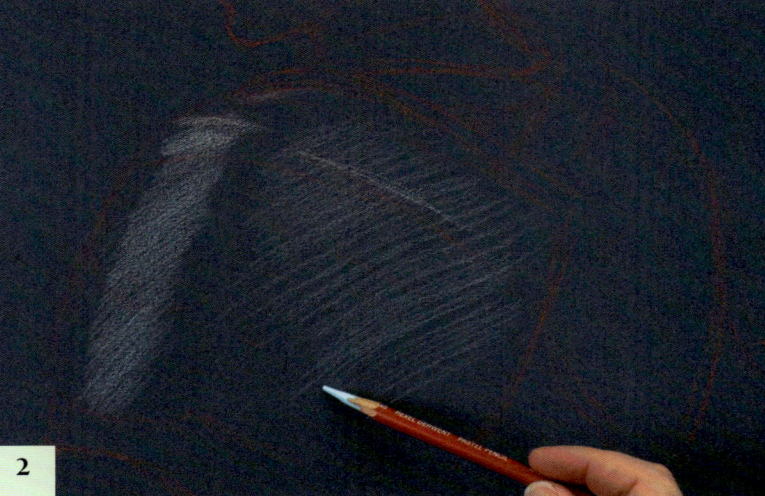

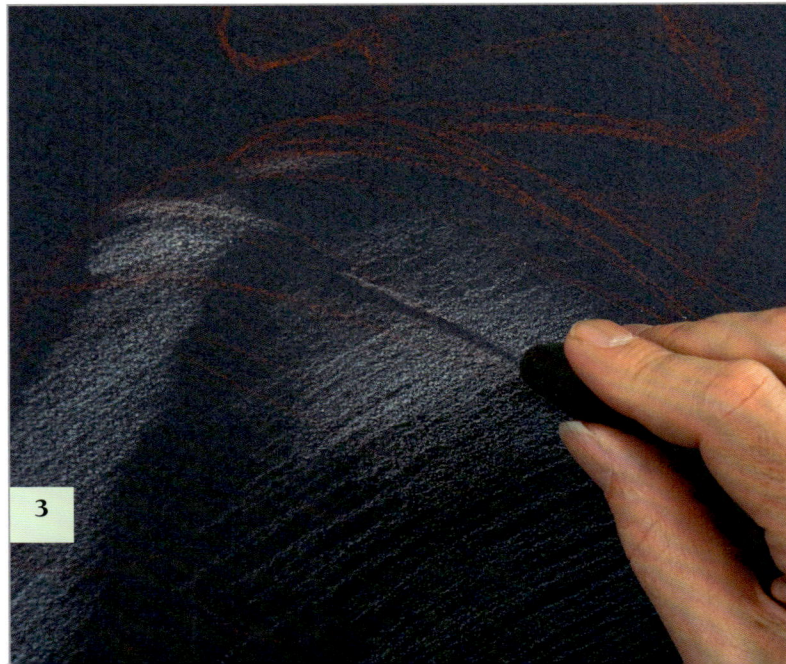

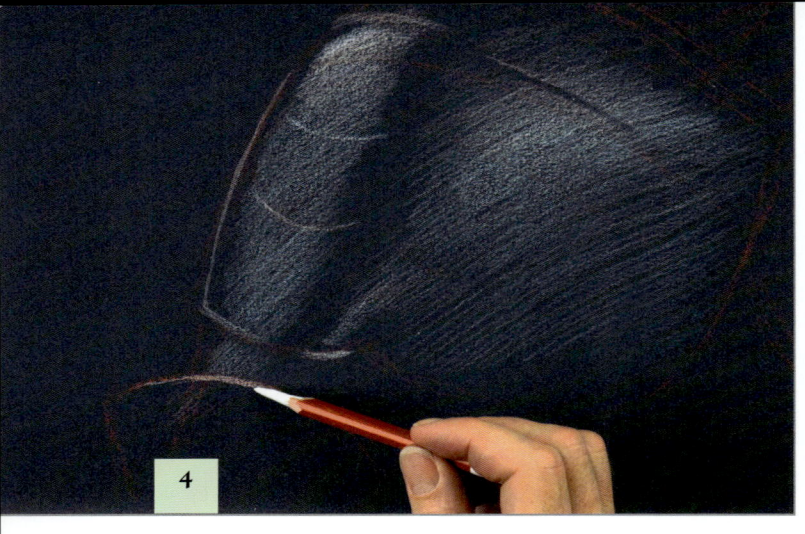

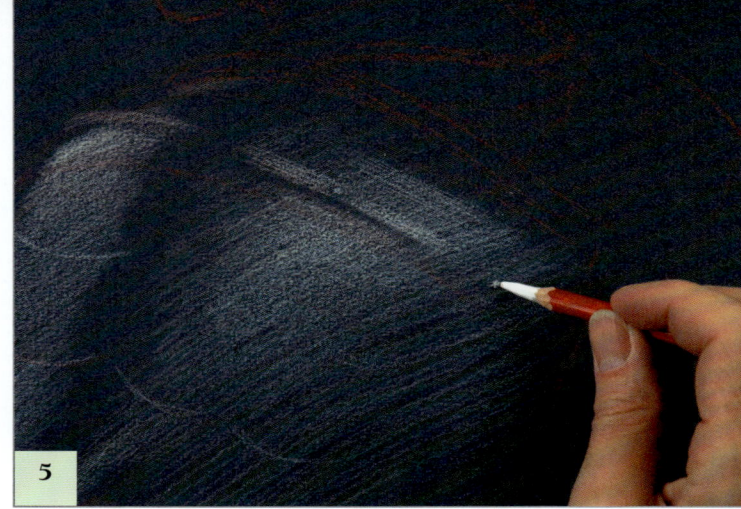

Understand structure

When drawing armour, it helps to know a little of how it is constructed and the purpose of the component parts. Rivets, for example, are decorative but also hold the stop rib in place. This metal bar prevents the point of a weapon sliding into an opening.

4 Continue one directional shading with **light blue** down the back of the shoulder. Increase the depth of shading on the edge of the shoulder with **white** and draw contour lines to denote the armour plating. Add a **white** edge to the **terracotta** outline around the pauldron (shoulder plate) and the couter (elbow guard).

5 Continue with white directional shading down the back. Mark a defined line across the top of the shoulder for the stop rib. Erase small round marks at equal intervals along this line and fill with small **white** dots to create rivets.

6 Continue shading with white down the shoulder, now cross-hatching across the original shading to create highlights. Add white highlights at the neck edge of the pauldron, and start to shade into the v-shape. This is where the back plates of the pauldrons overlap. Switch to **light blue** to fill in at the top of this area, then shade down the right-hand shoulder with rounded directional shading.

7 Now with **umber**, lightly shade the area at the base of the pauldrons. Use the **umber** pencil to go over the **terracotta** outlines on the left-hand pauldron.

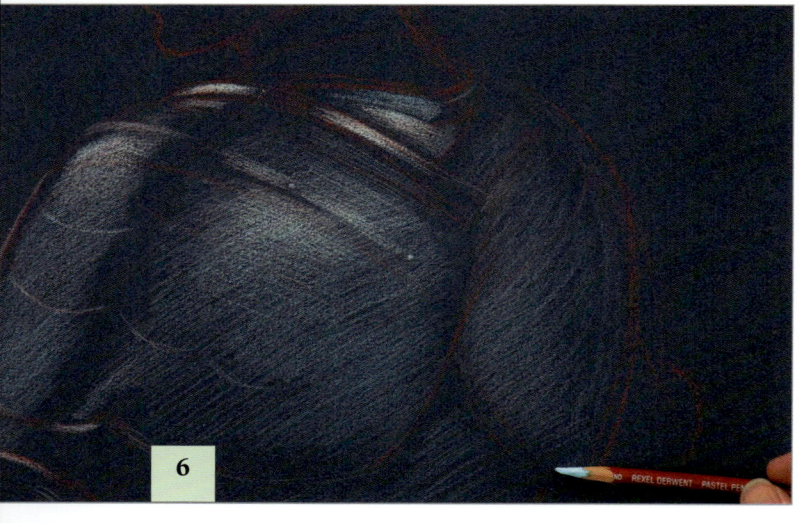

Safe shading

To avoid smudging, work with your hand in the air. Smudging is a technique in its own right, but once introduced there is no going back as the colour is rubbed into the paper's fibre. Instead, light, regular cross-hatching creates an area of solid colour that can be worked with the putty eraser if adjustments are needed later.

8 Switch back to **white**, and shade with rounded contour strokes down the left-hand edge of the pauldron. Add a stronger highlight to the lower edge, then continue to build up shading using the **white**.

9 Continue building up the shading on the back shoulder plate in **white**, using cross-hatching over the original shading. Add further plating details and a strong highlight to match the highlighting along the left-hand edge.

10 With **light violet**, re-define the **terracotta** edge of the right-hand shoulder plate and start to add more shading to this far shoulder. Build up the depth of shading in stroke directions that match the shading previously applied here.

11 To define the right-hand shoulder, use the putty eraser to pull a thick line downwards through the shading to create a clean highlight.

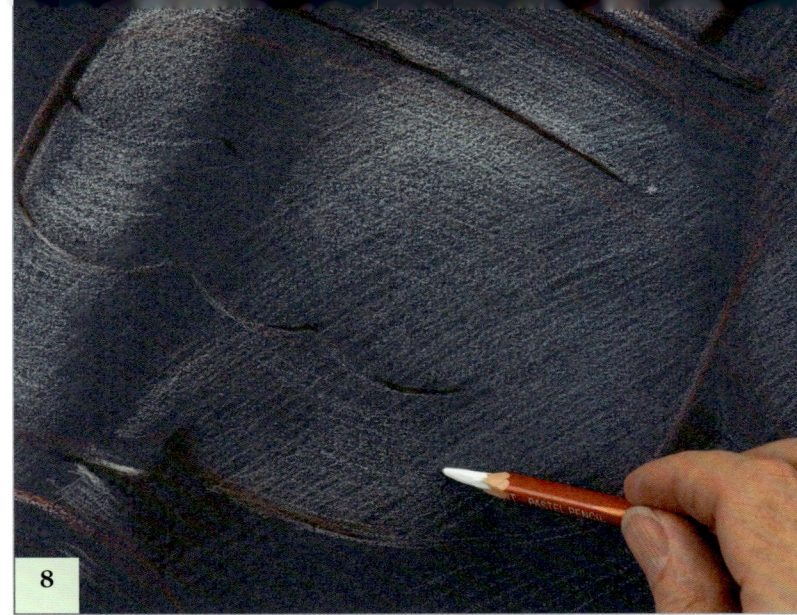

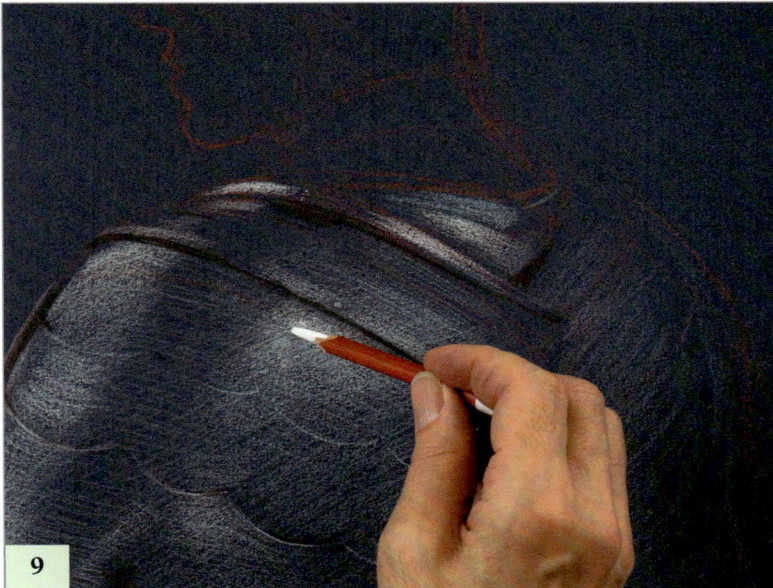

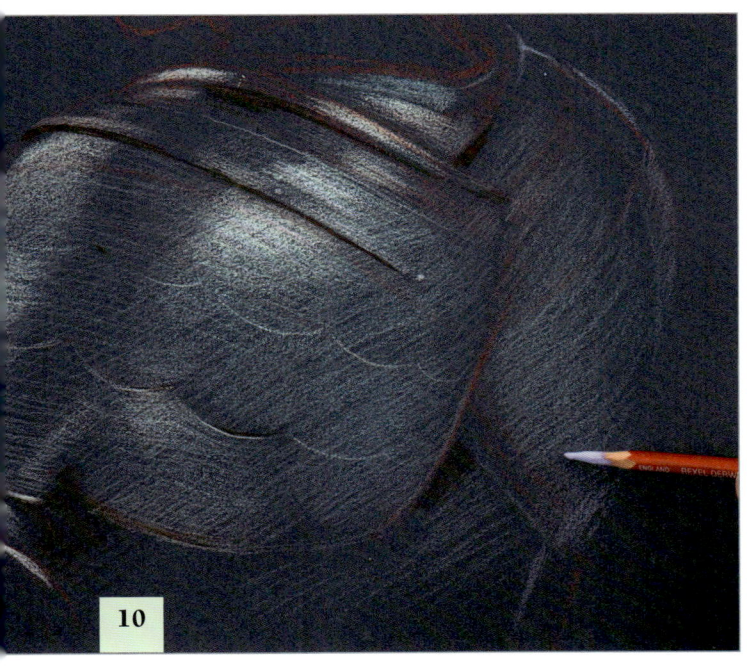

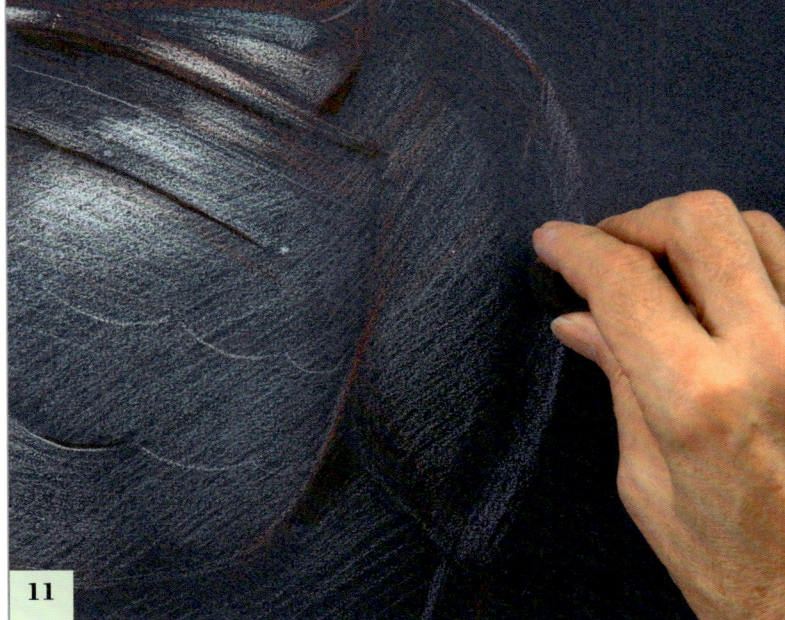

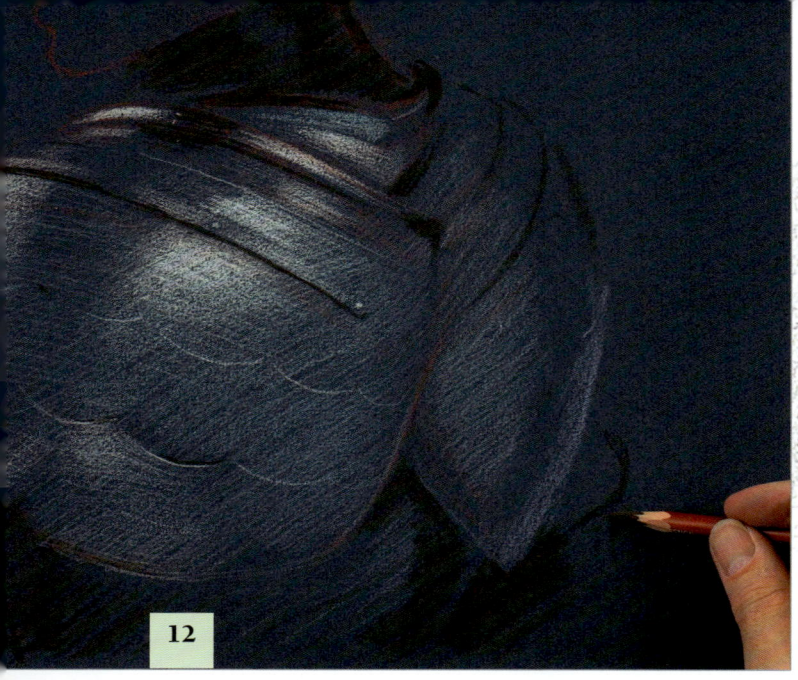

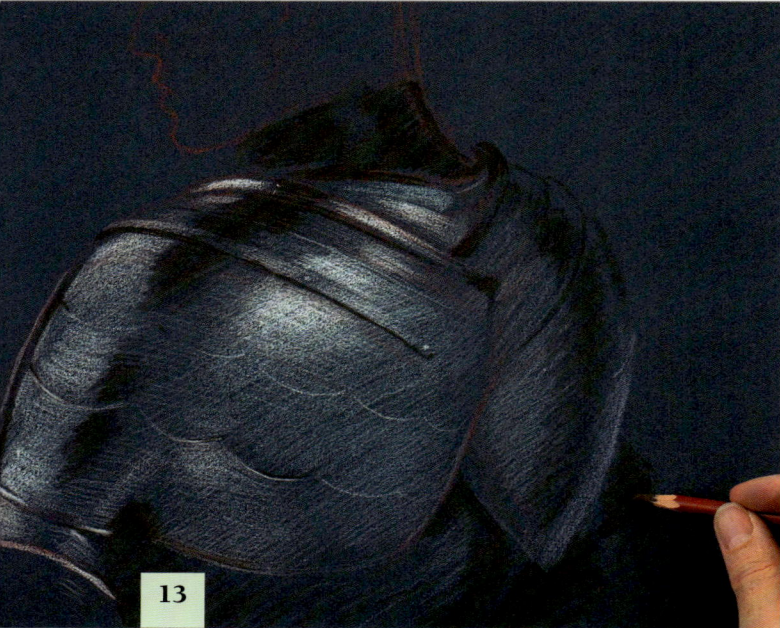

12 Use **umber** to start blocking in the chain mail collar on the neck. Shade in freely then use the putty eraser to lift a clean line down the centre of the neck. Build up further shadow in the centre back where the plates overlap to create deep shadows, then start to shade below the right-hand pauldron to begin to establish the right-hand couture.

13 Continuing with **umber**, add shadow to define the top edge of the couture, and continue with the **umber** to add shading working down through the area erased in Step 11.

14 With **light violet**, apply further shading up the edge of the right-hand shoulder plate, add plating details across the back, and further define the bottom edge of both plates.

15 Time to return to the face. Using **light terracotta**, shade in the nose and cheek. Apply a small amount of **terracotta** to the cheekbone, and continue to shade with the **light terracotta**, gently blending the two colours on contact.

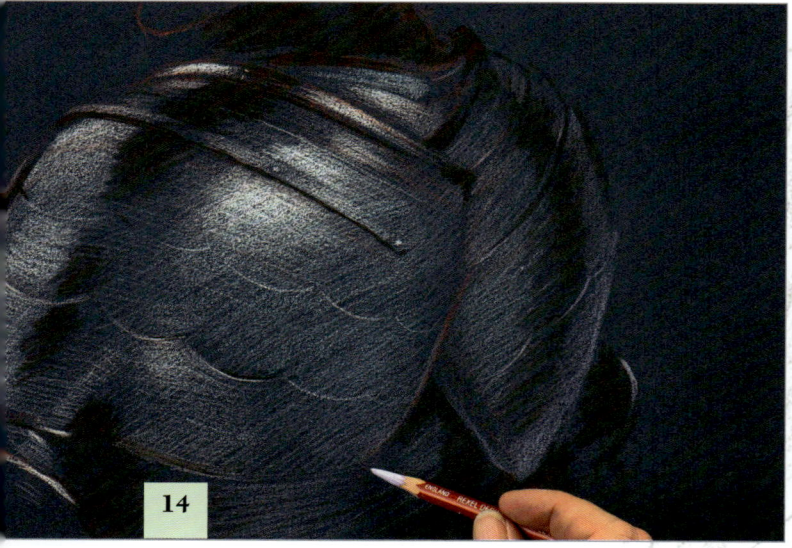

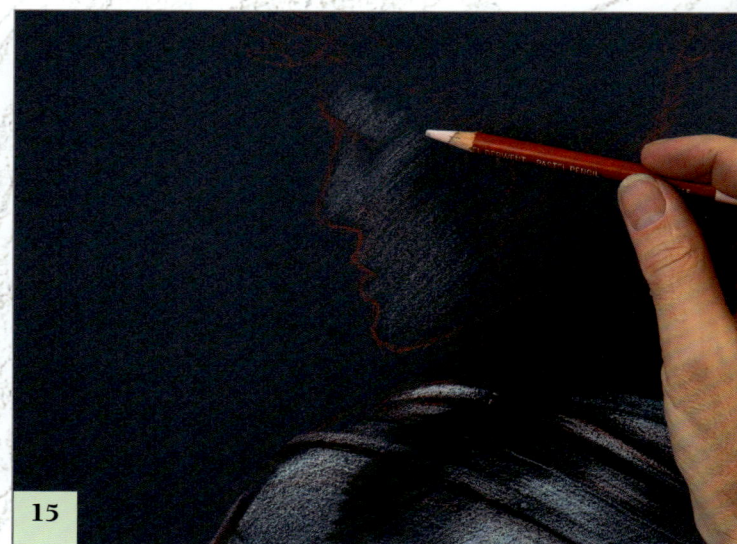

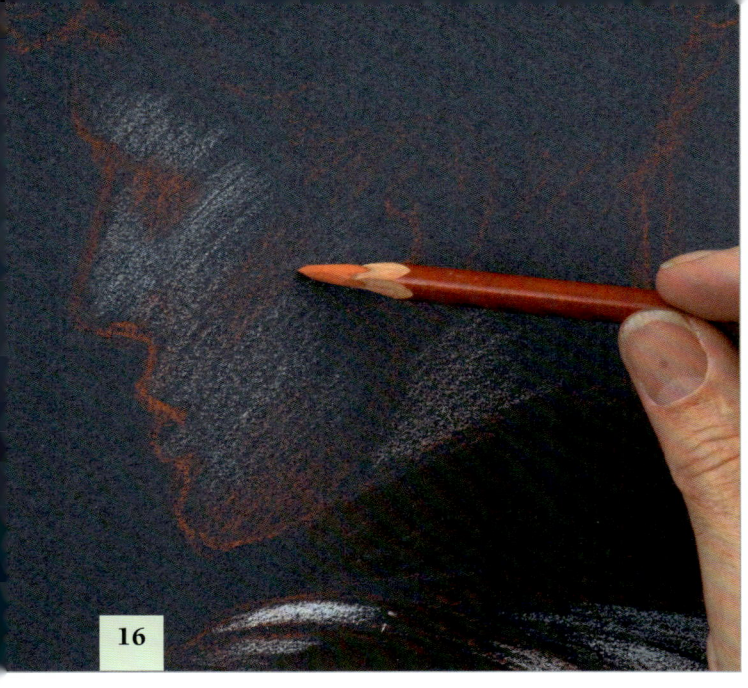

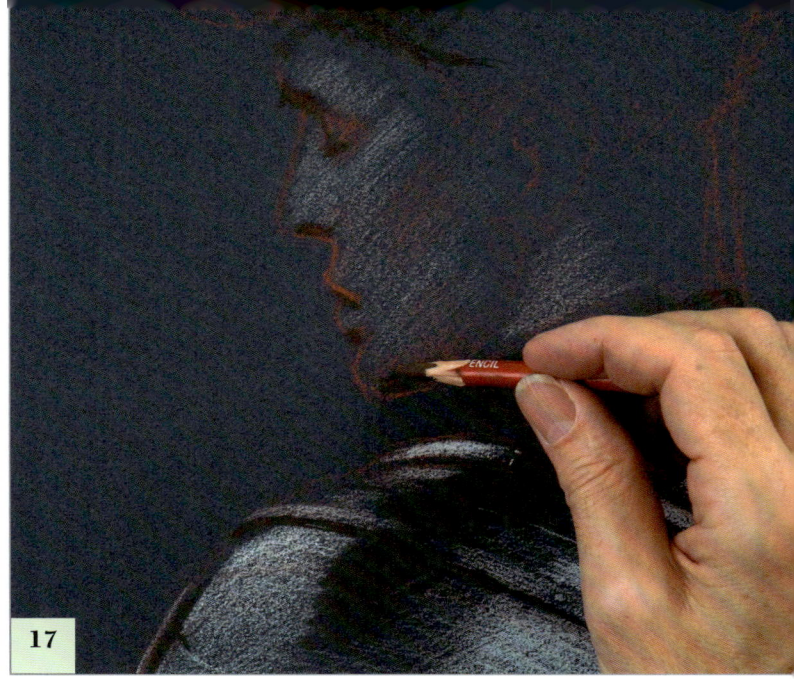

16 Use **light terracotta** to shade down into the upper neck area, then switch back to the **terracotta** to re-define the profile outline and shade below the chin and cheek.

17 With **umber**, shade the hairline just above the eye, then the eyebrow, lower eyelid and nostrils, mouth and chin.

18 Now use the **light terracotta** to build up volume and contouring on the face. Lightly shade around the eyes, creating strong highlights here with cross-hatching. Place a strong highlight across the upper lip and work to blend together the shading across the face. Move to the ear and add some shading here to define its shape.

19 Switch to **umber** for the hair. Add bold directional shading across the whole of this area. Fill in some curly texture as you go, particularly above the forehead.

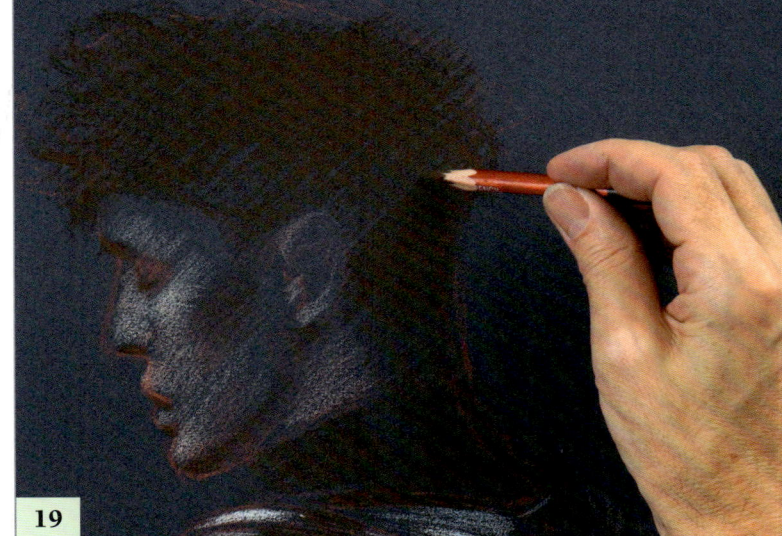

Portraying hairstyles

Many fantasy knights sport hairdos more suited to a businessman clutching a briefcase than a broadsword. Don't fall back on the 'Prince Valiant' haircut. Research relevant period styles to make your fantasy illustrations all the richer.

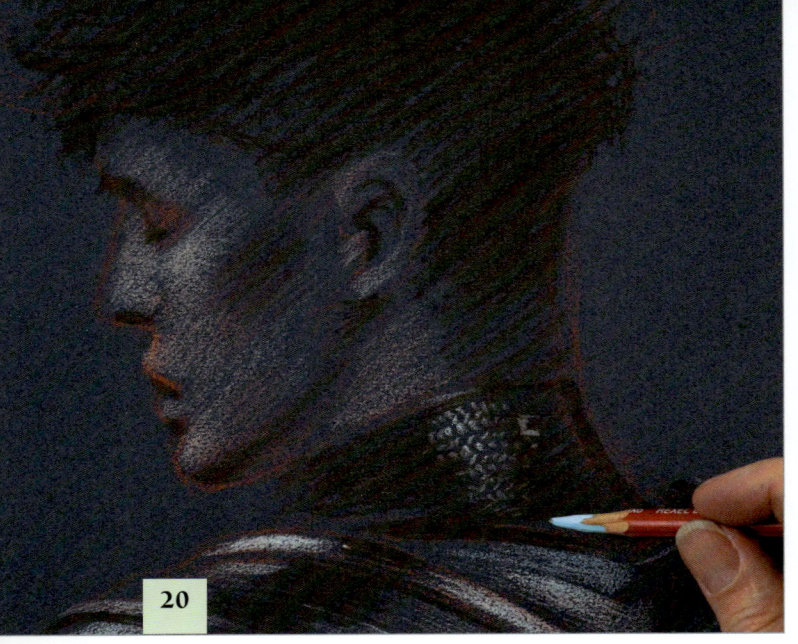

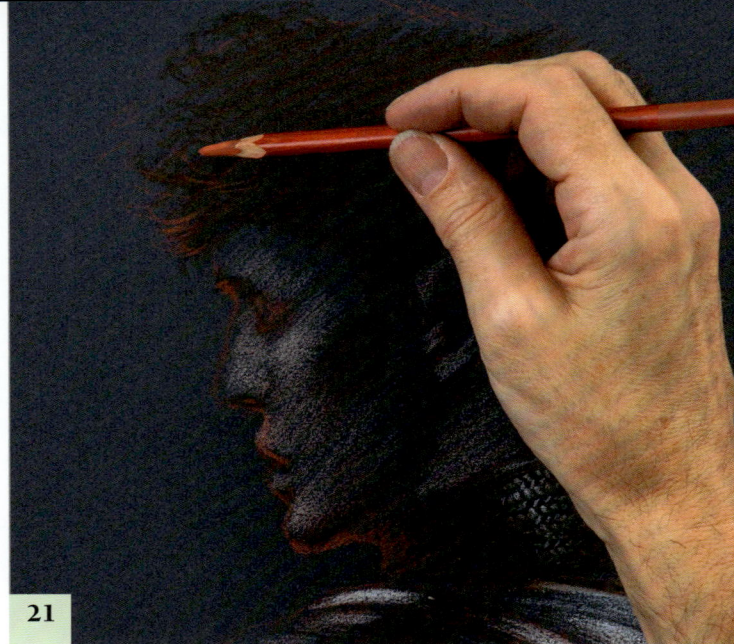

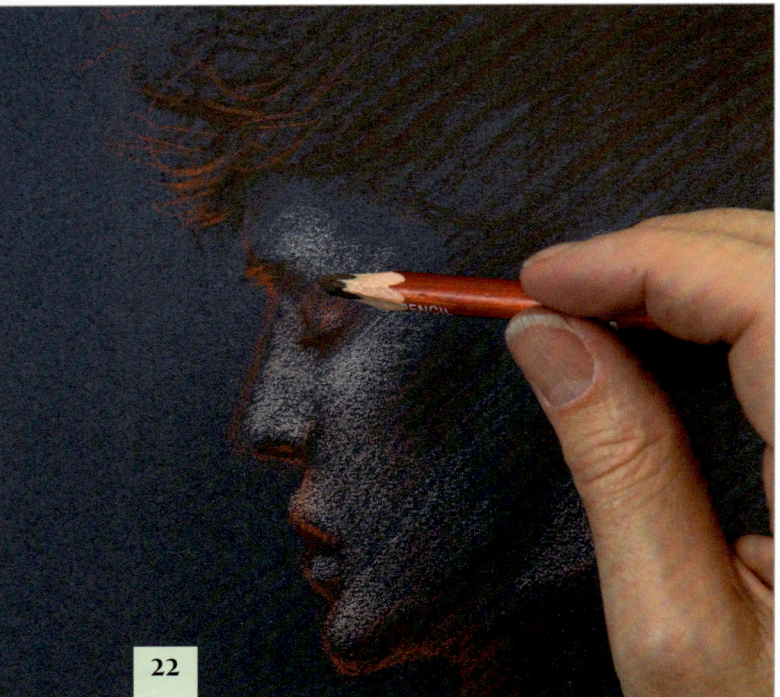

Chain mail

An effective way to render chain mail is to work quite dark for most of the surface, keeping a hint of volume. Then pick out a line of highlights where it best fits with alternating short strokes, slightly curved to suggest rings.

20 To build up detailing on the chain mail collar, alternate **white** and **light blue** in short, curved marks in the space between the shaded areas.

21 With **terracotta**, thicken the outline on the base of the chin and around the nose. Then add textural detailing at the front of the hair.

22 Highlight the eye by applying first **terracotta**, then a spot of **light terracotta**. Then use **umber** to deepen the shadow of the eye socket.

WHAT'S NEXT?

This is one of those in-between pictures. Meant as a sketch, it could easily be fully rendered in coloured pencil or even paints. Watercolour, which I generally use, would not be entirely satisfactory as it would fail to capture the gloomy atmosphere. Oils would be more appropriate for the subject.

Final image

I added a background of stormy seas, the heavy waves a metaphor for Lancelot's inner turmoil. Sketch the waves with light blue, white and light violet. For the sky, shade these colours plus **umber** and lightly smudge with your finger to blend. This will define the atmosphere without detracting from the figure. I also added the gunwale of the boat with a few lines in **umber** and a small **white** highlight.

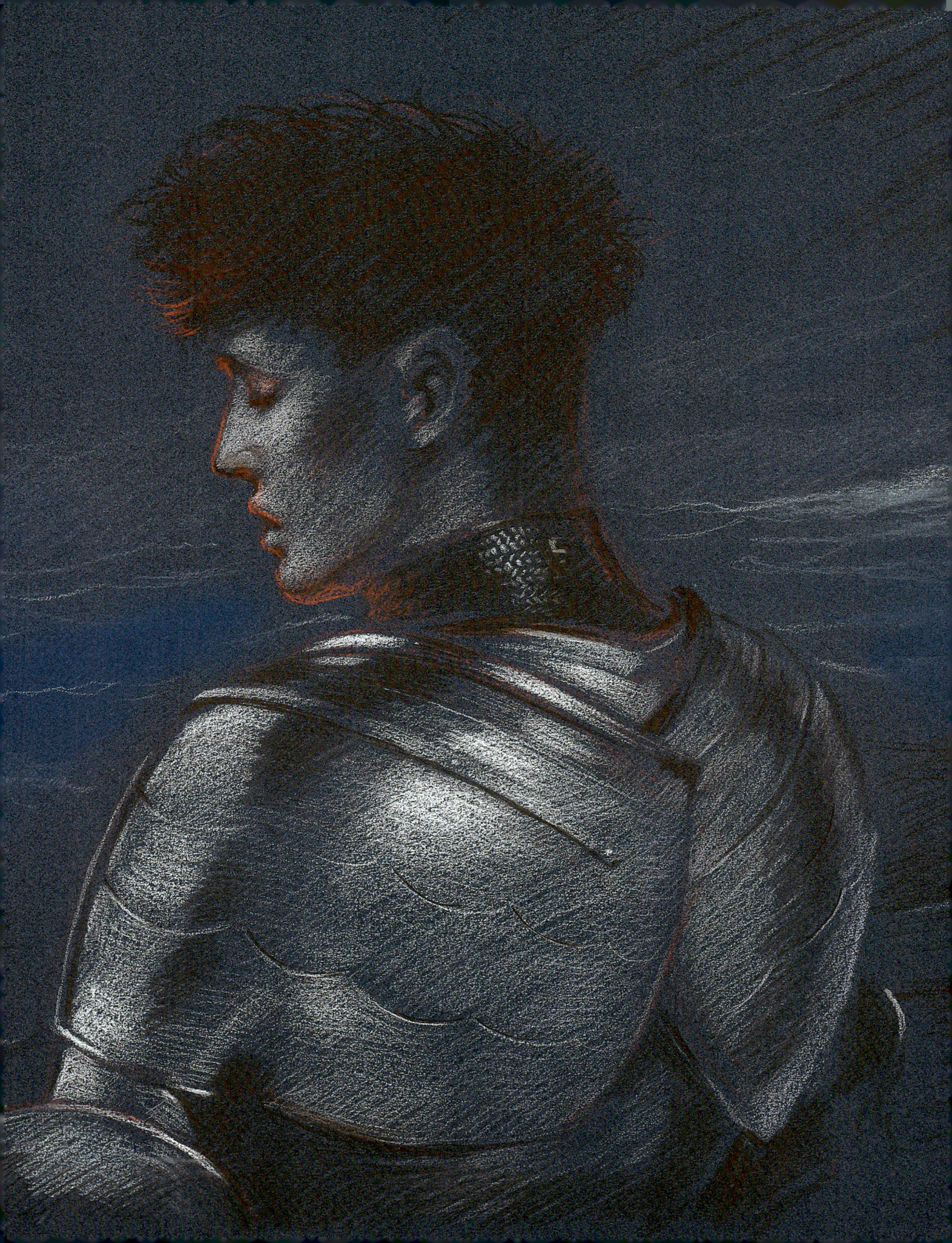

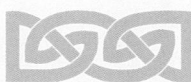

CENTAUR

Centaurs are associated so intimately with classical Greece that it's rare to see interpretations that go farther afield. This mythological creature is half-human and half-animal – the torso of a man joined at his waist to the horse's withers. Consorts of Bacchus, they were often pictured brawling and fighting.

Techniques
✦ Combining anatomy of different species
✦ Creating a centaur culture in a concept sketch
✦ Inventing armour and weapons

Ideas and inspiration
Taking a classical creature from its 'normal' environment is very much what myth-transferral is about. Myths gain in richness and complexity as they travel from culture to culture. I was inspired by the winged hussars of 16th and 17th century Poland who had extraordinary styles of armour and were famous for the huge wings worn on their backs or attached to their horses' saddles.

Visual references
As an enthusiastic admirer of Russian painter Viktor Vasnetsov (1848–1926), I thought, why not a medieval bogatyr centaur? His painting *A Knight at the Crossroads* (1882) was my starting point, but in my drawing, the Russian knight-errant has merged to become one with his steed, a centaur ready to do battle.

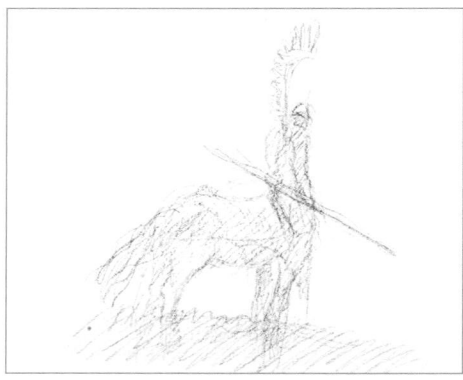

⬆ Thumbnail sketch
Use this preview to avoid common mistakes like starting in the wrong part of the sheet. Nestling in the bottom right-hand corner of my drawing, the thumbnail helps me to position the centaur to fit him all in, from wings to tail.

Armour glossary
✦ **Barding:** a defensive covering for horses
✦ **Coif:** the chain mail hood worn beneath the helmet, covering neck and shoulders
✦ **Helmet:** for the head, this one incorporates an ear guard
✦ **Nasal:** a strip of metal on the front of the helmet to protect the nose
✦ **Disc and splint:** light arm guard defence (here it protects the outside of the upper arm)
✦ **Vambrace:** armour covering the lower arm

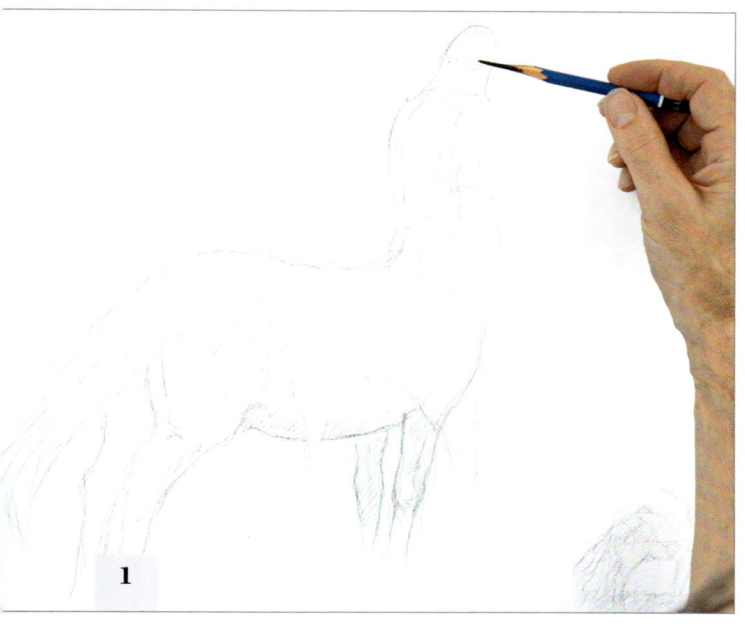

1

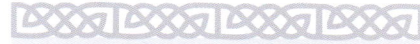

Pace yourself

Don't work on tiny details before positioning them correctly. First, set out the basic figure outline in the right proportions. Once happy with that, you can build on the details, confident of their position.

1 With a 3B pencil, lightly sketch in the basic outline. Place the legs and belly, and lightly shade them in. Then sketch the barding and the tail. Move on to sketch the torso and arm, lightly shaded. Finally add the helmet and the coif.

2 Establish the helmet and the coif falling down over the shoulders, then sketch in the profile of the face.

3 Sketch the shield on the centaur's back and the wing outline reaching up behind him and over his head. Place the helmet's top spike; lightly shade the whole helmet. Start detailing the arm and lightly shade. Sketch in the horns.

4 Add further detailing to define the shape of the helmet and coif, concentrating on shading in the cheek guard area. Define the outline of the head with a bold line. Place the eyes, nose and beard. Define the ear guard and add a short line to indicate the nasal. Add the curved tip of the all-but-hidden horn and shade in the visible horn.

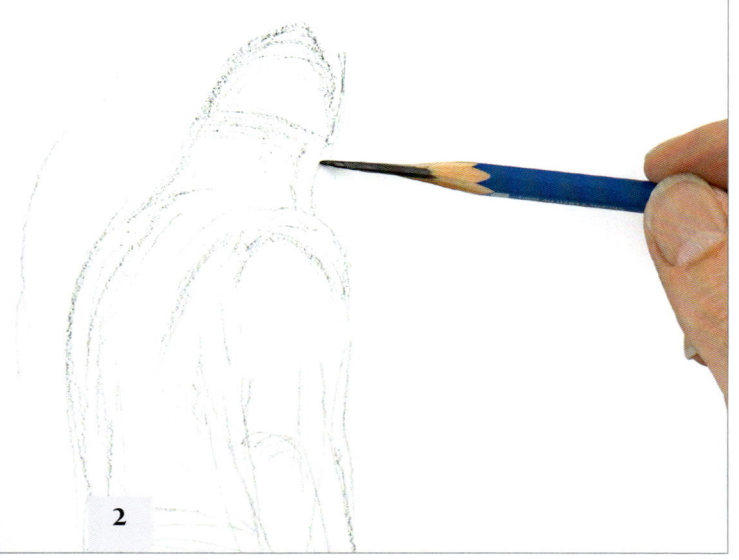

2

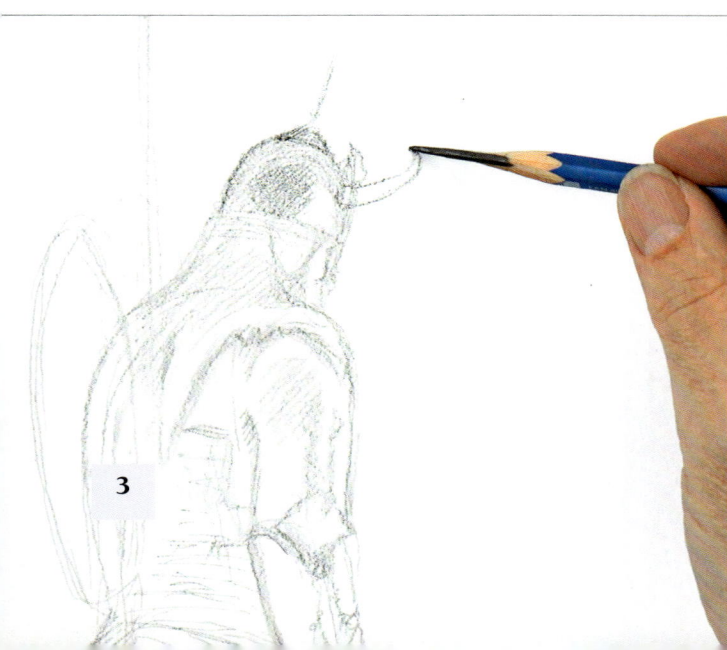

3

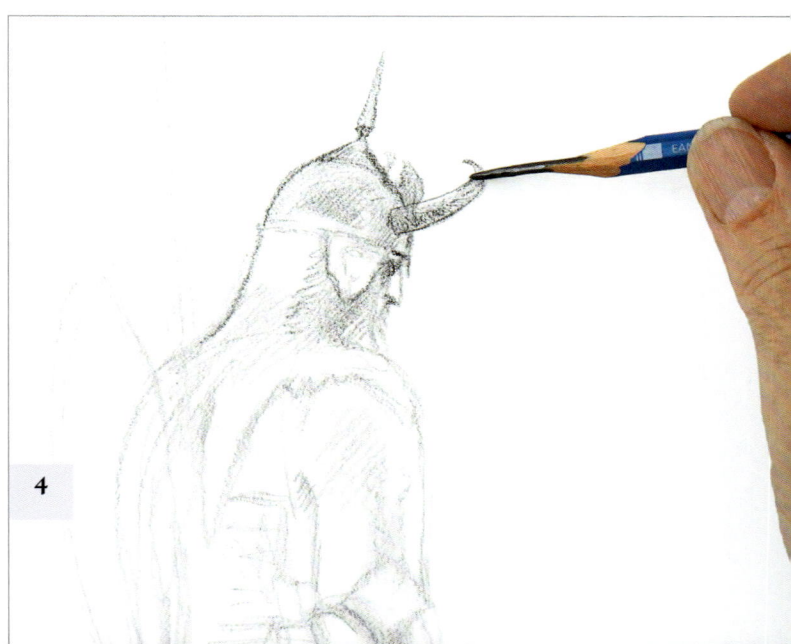

4

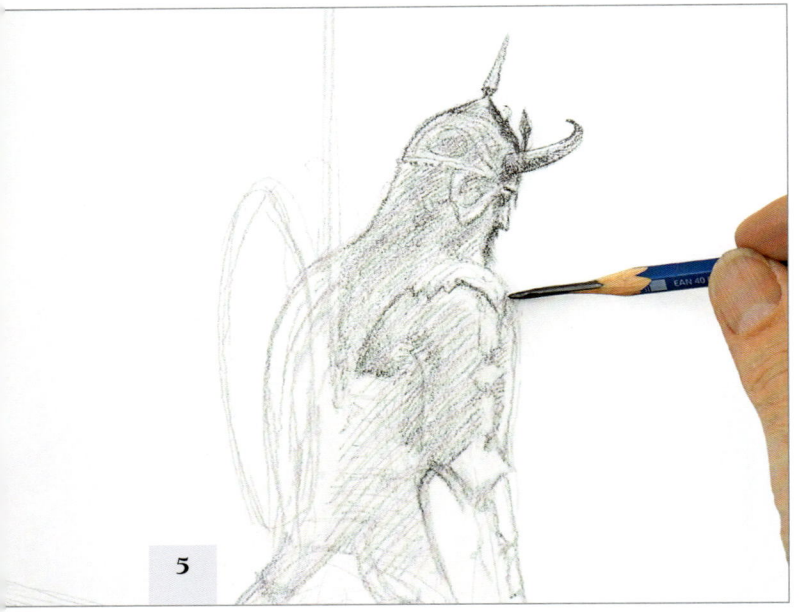

5 Apply further shading down the back of the coif, then more detailing to the ear guard. Shade down the shoulder and arm, adding an outline for the chain mail over the shoulder, and the disc and splint arm guard and vambrace. Lightly shade the lower half of the torso. Lightly sketch the quiver at the base of the torso.

6 Begin to sketch in the lance, then continue working on the right-hand arm adding discs and splints to the vambrace. Build up the shading here as you go.

7 Add further shadow shading to the coif and horn, and outline the ear guard. Now define the strapping across the centaur's back and clearly establish a belt.

8 Add rivets around the centaur's helmet and use a putty eraser to pull out some highlights here. Develop the shading down the back of the neck. Then move back to the arm and add further stronger outlines and shading here.

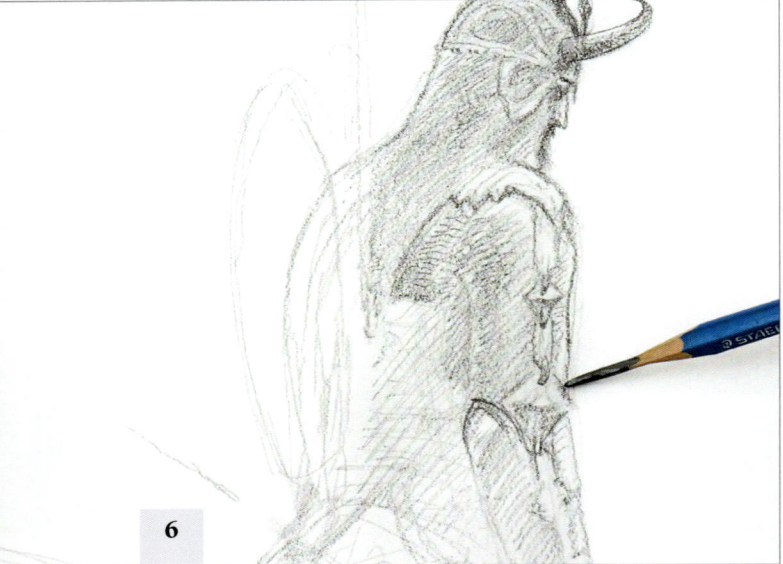

Avoid stereotypes
Research armour and weaponry details to avoid stereotypical, often erroneous movie imagery. For example, the leather wrist guards often seen on fantasy warriors are fine for role play, but are otherwise not convincing.

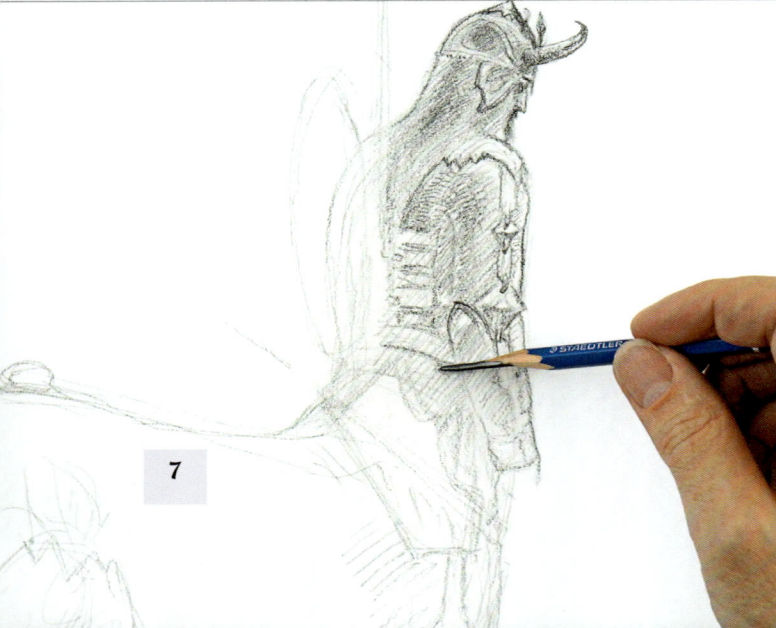

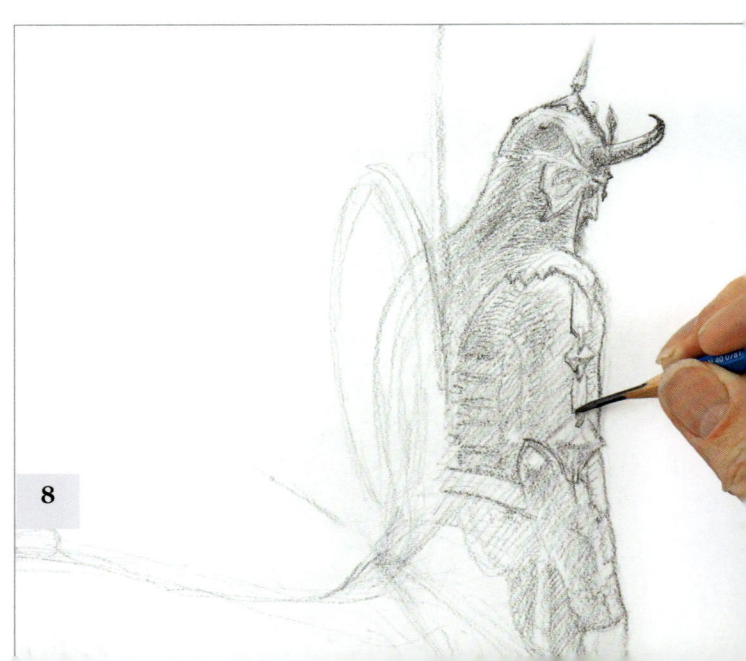

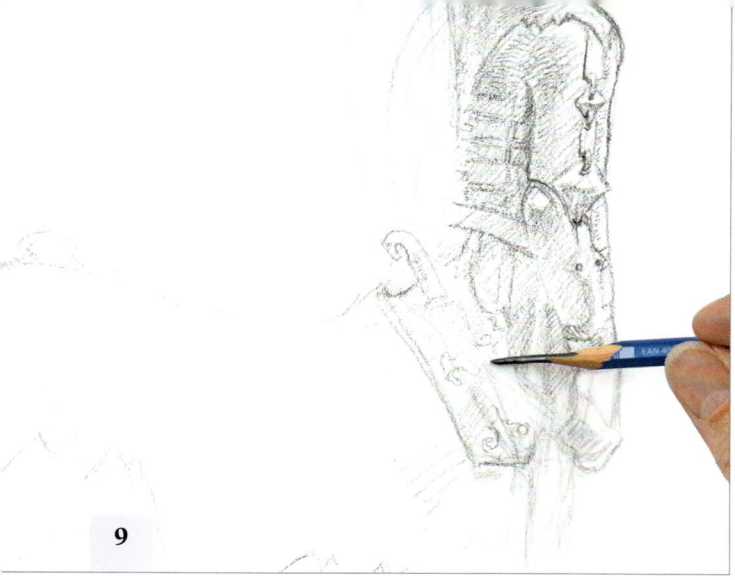

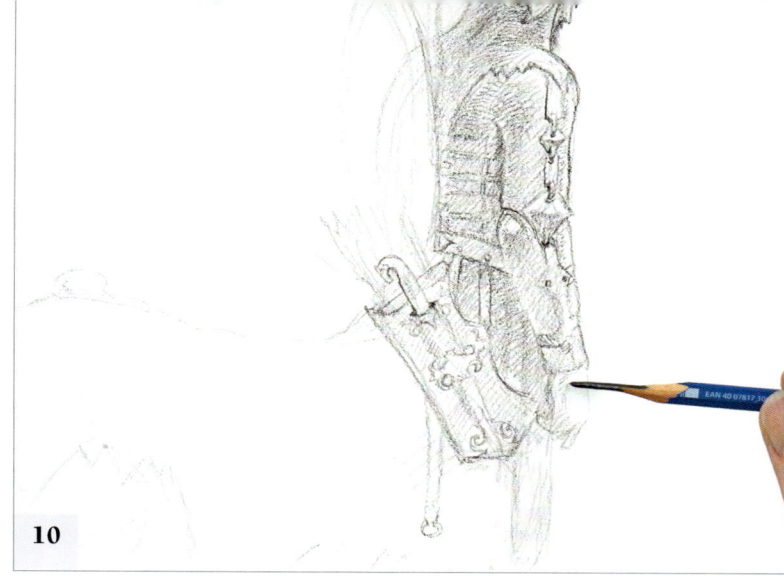

9 Now sketch in the dagger handle and scabbard. Establish the edge of the quiver and shade across it.

10 Sketch in the arrow ends and add detailing on the scabbard. Draw in the quiver suspension straps then re-define the edges of the belt and back straps. Lightly draw the centaur's hand.

11 With a ruler, use the putty eraser to pull a line for the lance through the body area, making sure that this passes within reach of the sketched hand.

12 Use the ruler to create two straight lines in this space to form the lance. Re-establish the hand grasping the lance, then shade down the length of the lance. Draw the spearhead on the end of the lance.

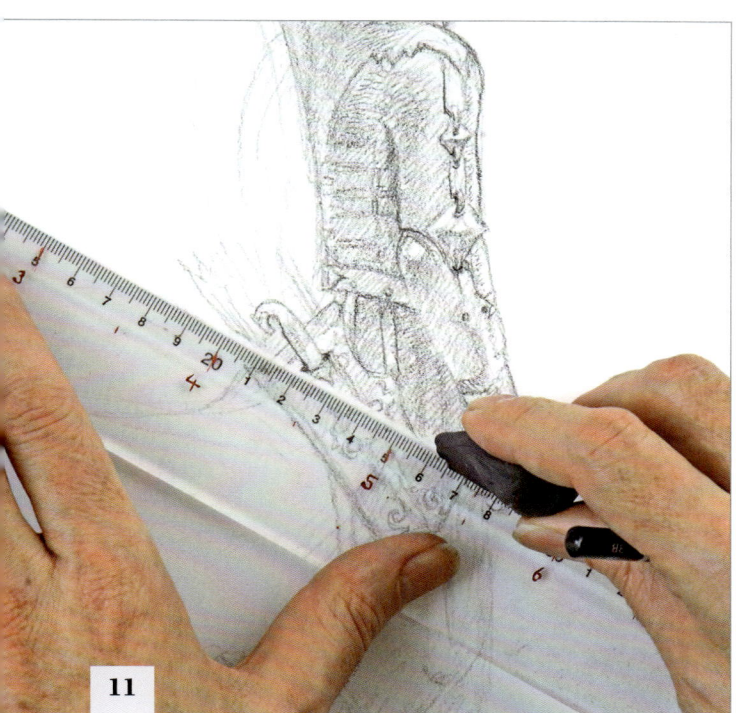

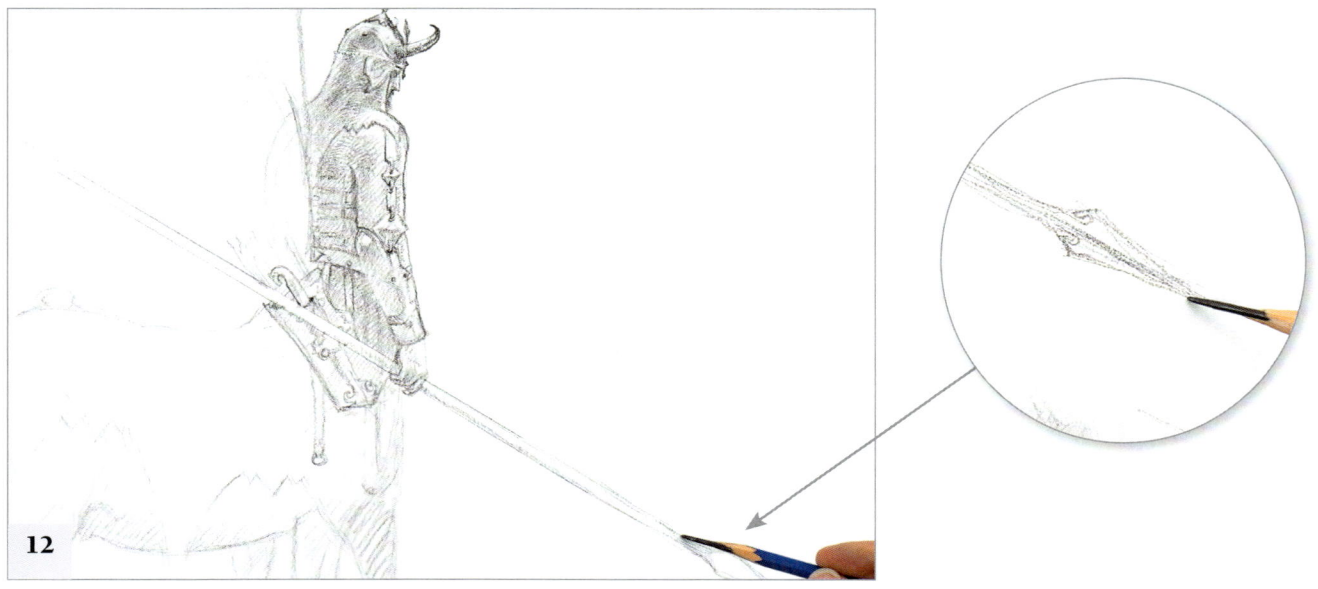

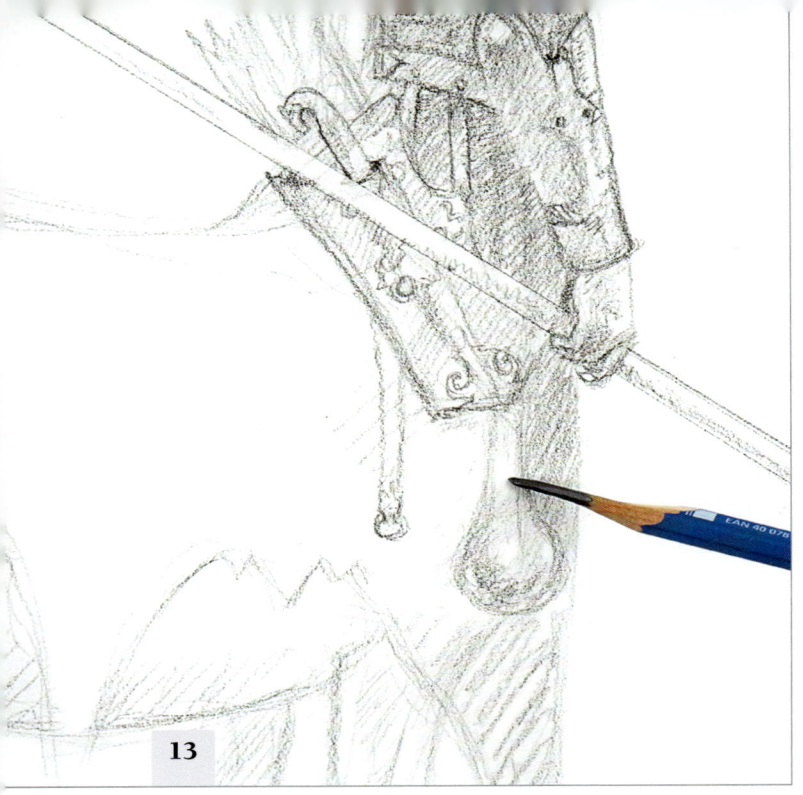

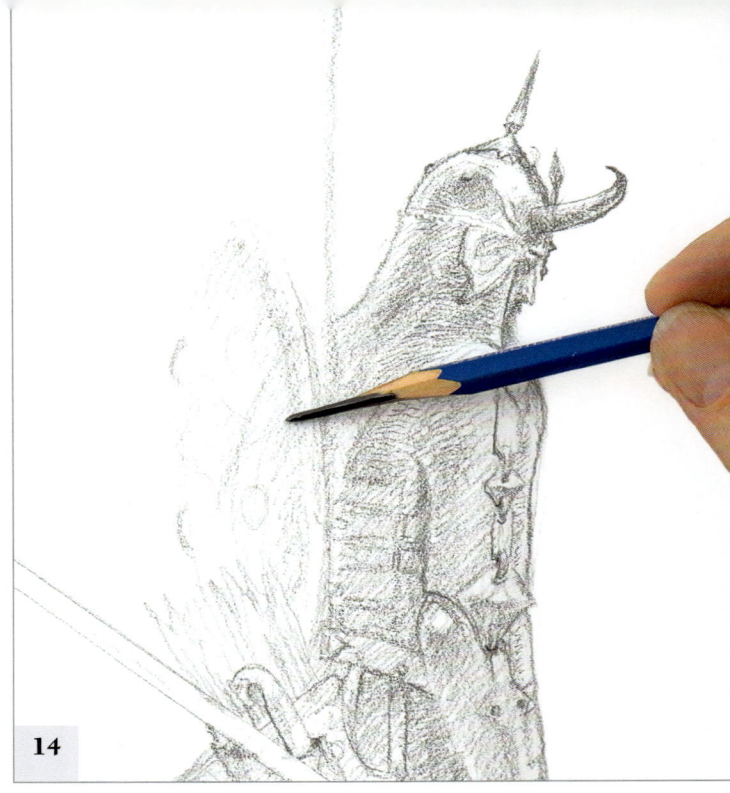

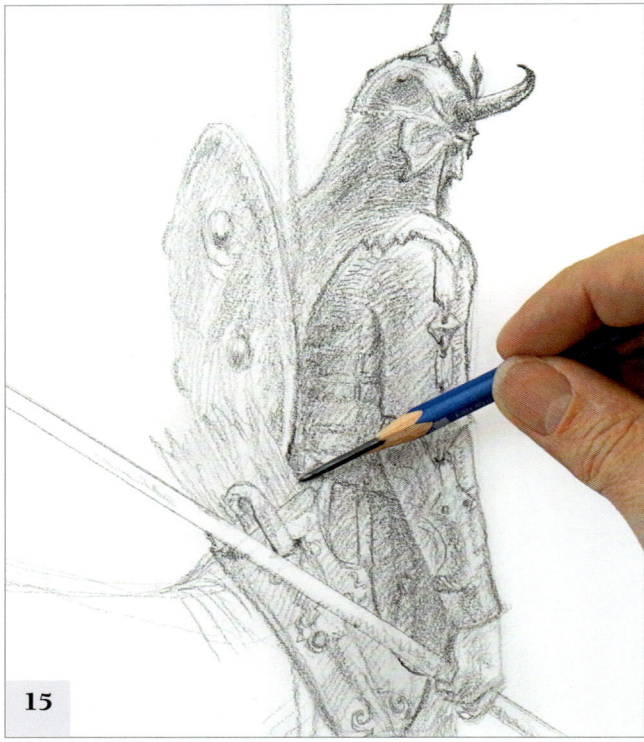

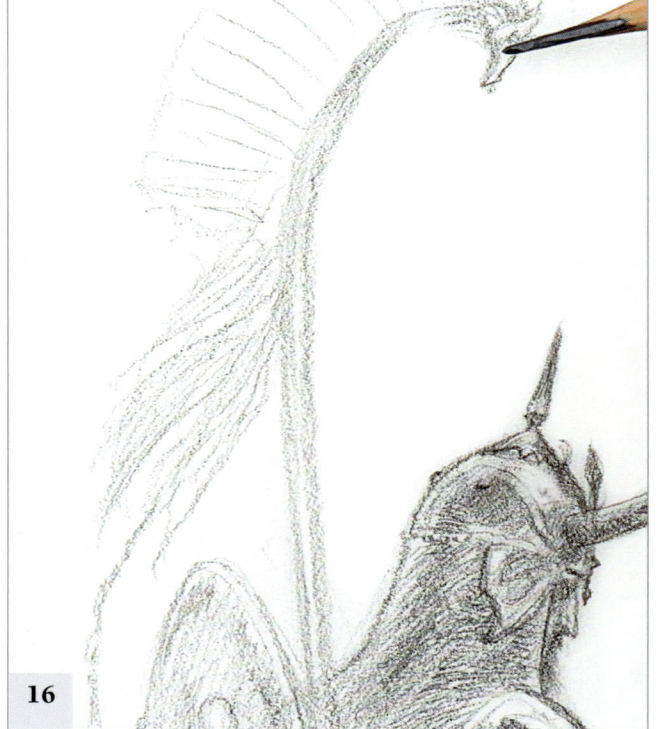

13 Now establish the outline of a mace. Re-establish the edge of the barding and start to shade down the front of it. Add some contour shading to the mace.

14 Add more arrowheads to the quiver then start to work on the shield. Sketch in the four bosses then lightly shade the shield and define its edge.

15 Build the shading here, and darken the shadows below the bosses. Finally add some darker shadows down the back of the torso behind the shield.

16 Clearly define the outline of the wing then start to add the plumes. Move up to the summit of the wing and draw its end detail.

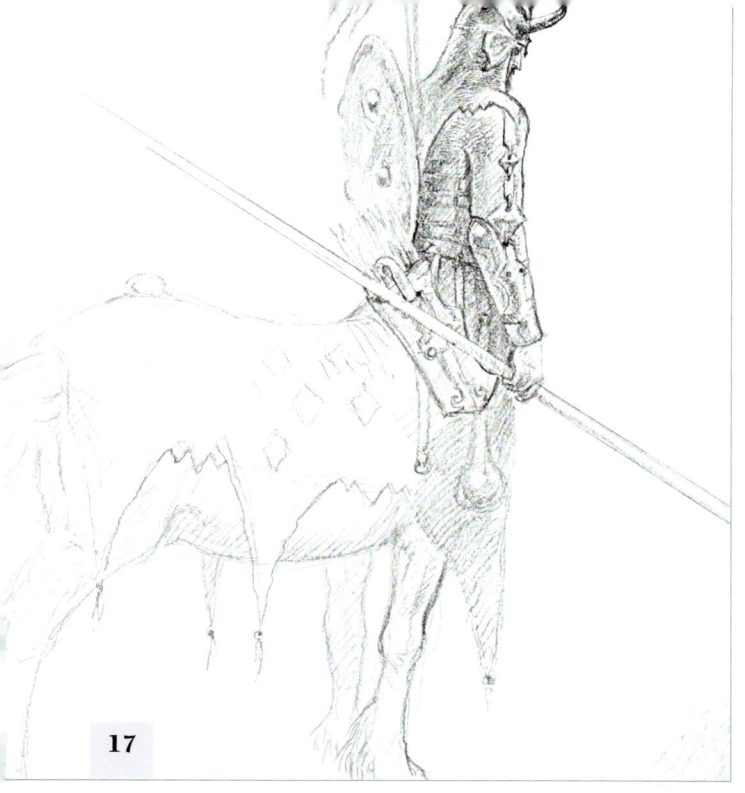

17

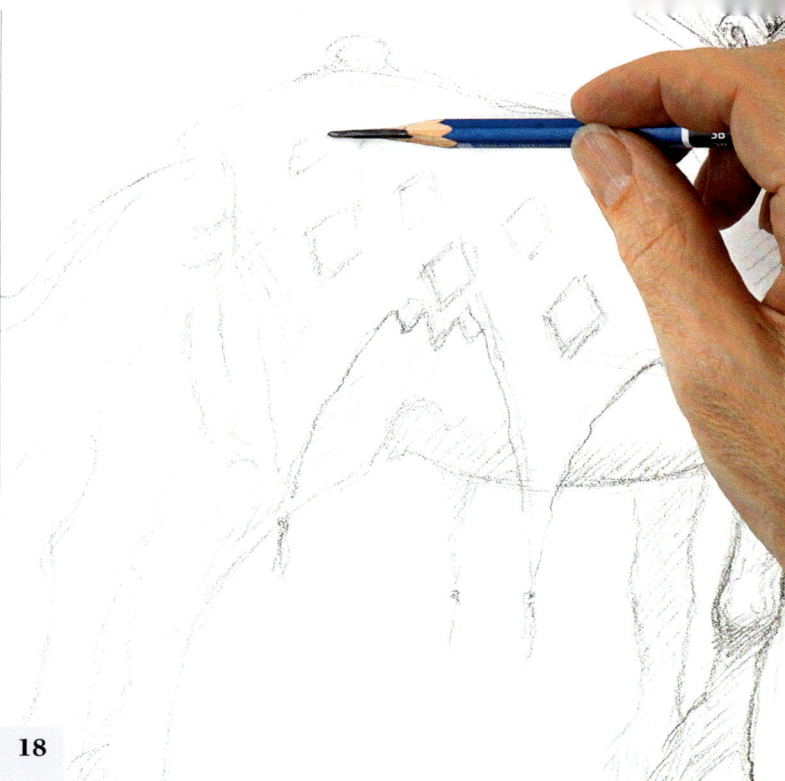

18

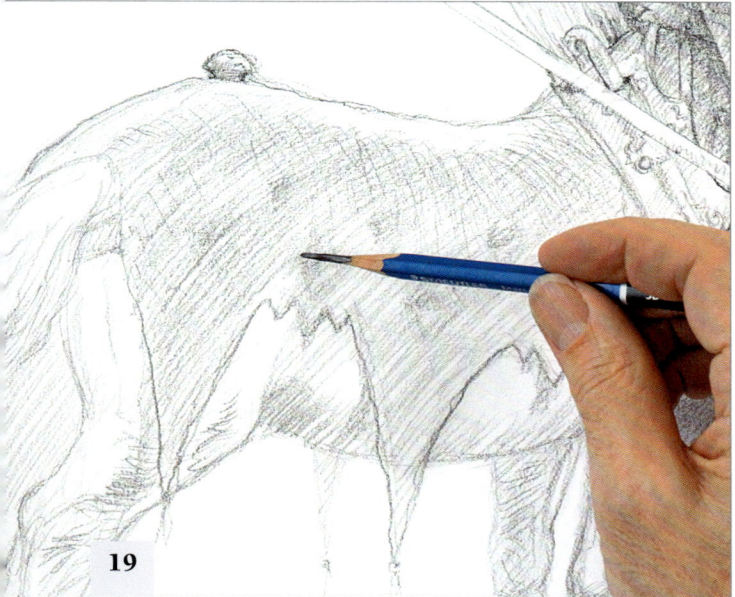

19

17 Apply further shading down the right-hand foreleg and hoof, and further define the edge of the barding adding the tassel detailing.

18 Lightly sketch guidelines across the barding then apply diamond-shaped decorations, using the guidelines to ensure equal spacing. The barding's decorative metal plates echo the shapes of the discs on the arm guard, and are an interesting way to break up an expanse of armour.

19 Outline and darkly shade in the stop to establish its volume. Shade across the barding with clean, directional hatching to give a unified tone. Shade the body working down to the hooves, defining the line of the hind legs, and filling in the shading on the left-hand foreleg. Fill out the tail with wavy lines to create depth. Add dark shadows on the diamond-shaped plates of the barding, then cross-hatch here to build the shape and volume.

20 Further define the edge of the barding, then erase highlights. Add a hill shape in the background, with a lightly shaded shadow on the ground beneath the centaur.

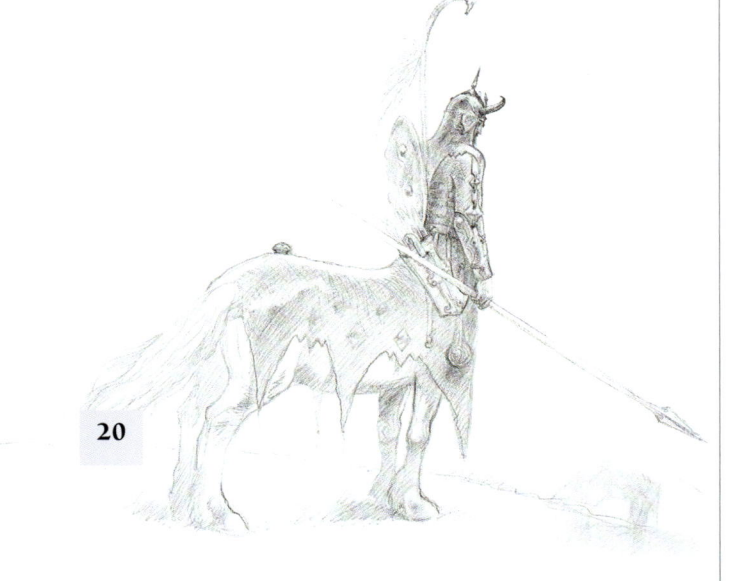

20

Artistic tip

The barding's decorative metal plates are an interesting way to break up the huge expanse of armour.

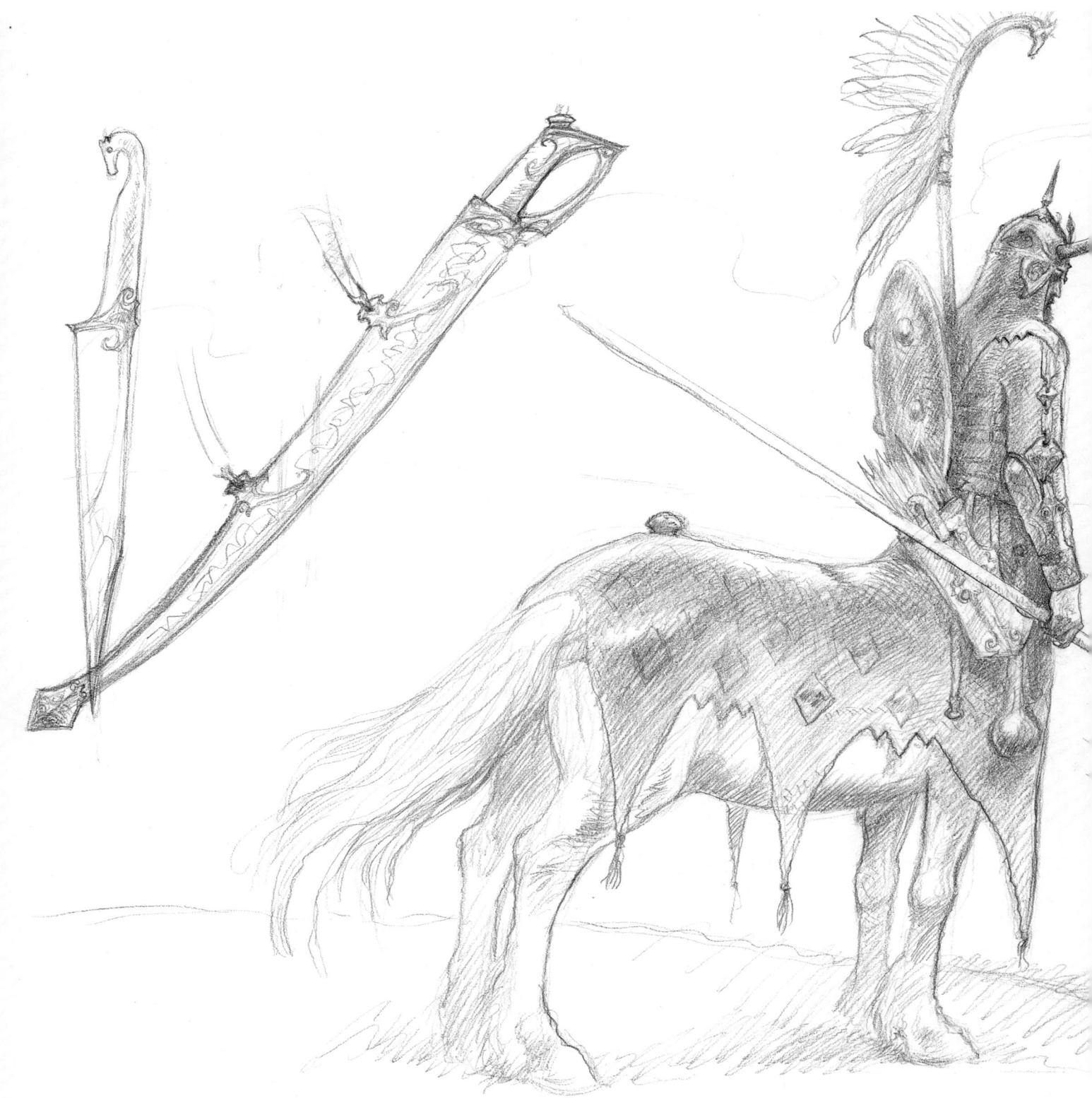

Final image

Rather than develop the background landscape, I used the
final image to focus on the detail of the weapons and armour
with larger drawn details, filling the edges of the piece.

Adding detail

More than a nodding acquaintance with actual period weaponry can give authenticity to your fantasy work.

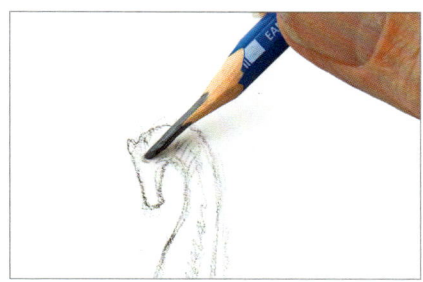

◆ A horse head motif seems fitting for the dagger hilt.

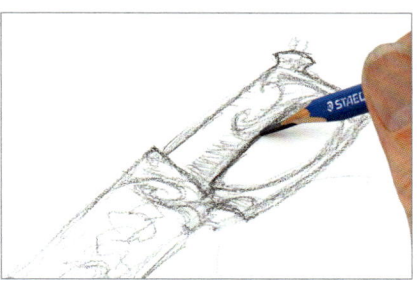

◆ The sword isn't visible in the drawing, but I'm tempted to design the hilt anyway.

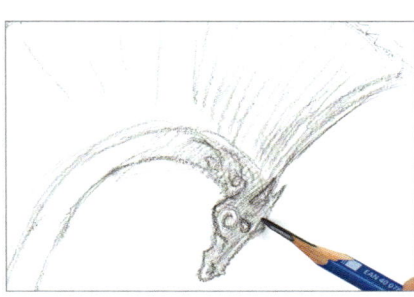

◆ I am totally dissatisfied with the wing end – it's far too overstated. I will need to find a different solution.

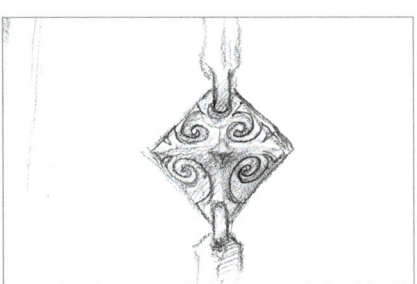

◆ I have a file on discs from a variety of medieval sources, and add one to the arm guard. They seem to be quite rare.

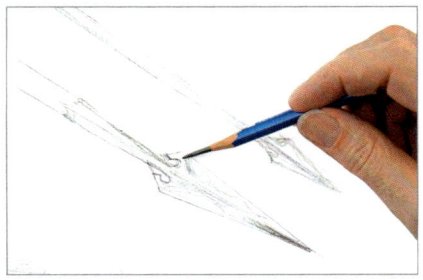

◆ I am trying to find a novel design for the spearhead, something a little more complex than the original.

WHAT'S NEXT?

This 'concept' sketch offers detail to develop later. As you define the physical practicalities of fantasy creatures, you ask more questions than you answer. Pursuing these as sketches can be very enriching.

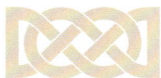

ARWEN

Arwen is a dark-haired elven beauty and daughter of the Lord Elrond of Rivendell. Caught between two worlds, she is one of Tolkien's more tragic feminine characters. Her love for Aragorn, a mortal man, forever sunders her from her people and from her immortality.

Techniques
+ Characters in situation
+ Implying a back story without action

Ideas and inspiration
Critics often dismiss Tolkien's female characters as inconsequential, which is a grand shame. They simply require more attentive reading. The object of this sketch is to try to capture Arwen's beauty and to hint at her sense of loss.

Visual references
I gathered all the pictures of female actors and models, collected from magazines over the years, to provide me with inspiration for my work. However, my Arwen has a look all of her own.

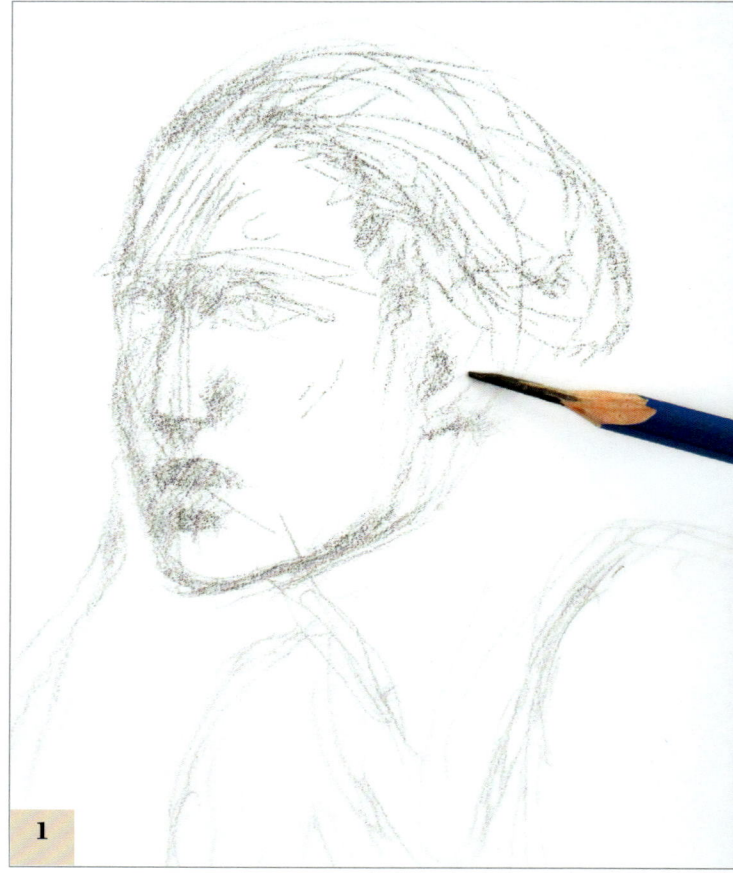

1

1 With a 3B pencil, sketch the shoulders and neck. Lightly sketch in her head, profile and jaw. Work in her eyebrows then nose and mouth, so that her cheeks and chin begin to take shape. Work on the outline of her hair, starting to lightly shade this, and begin to suggest the shape of the ear.

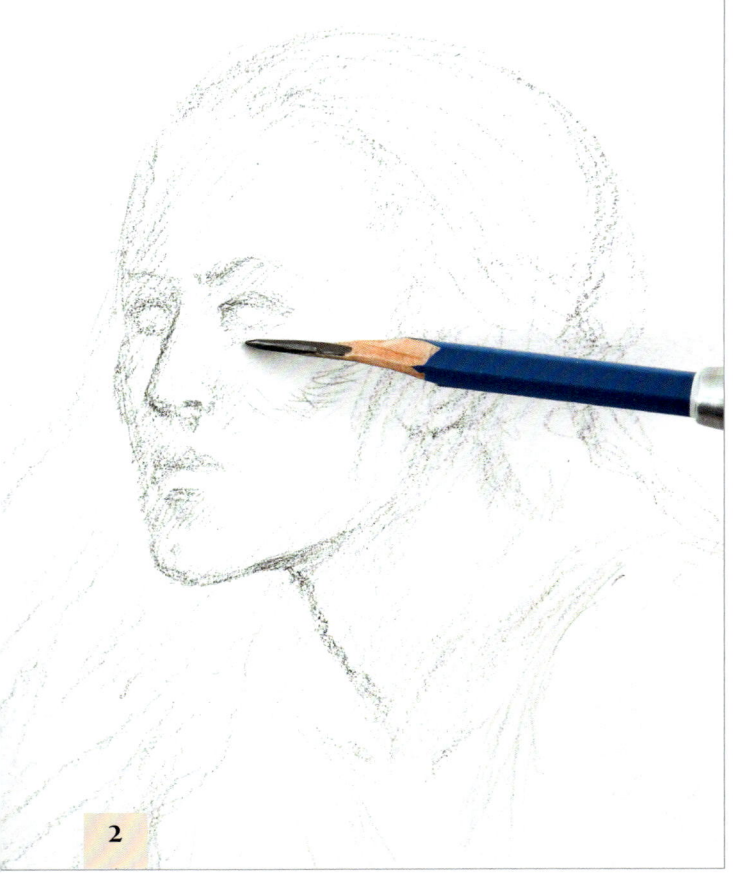

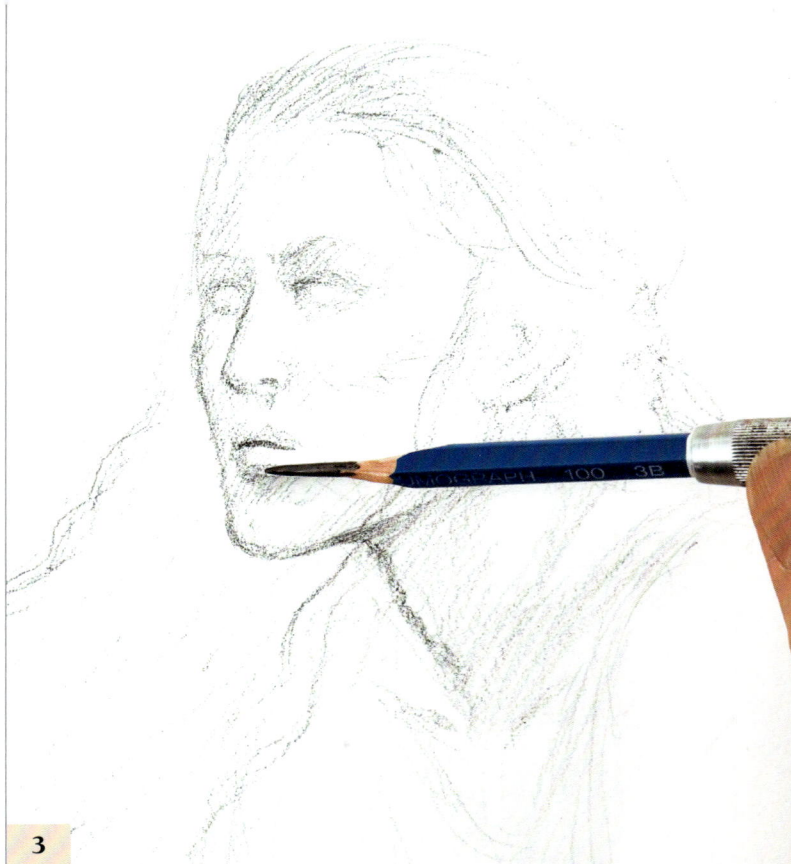

2 Continue shading the hair and neck, establishing a shadow under the chin. Position the ear, then sketch in more hair flowing across Arwen's shoulders. Clearly define the jaw line and chin, then the mouth and nose. Shade around the mouth, then establish the rest of the profile. Firmly position the eyes and eyebrows.

3 Shade down the left-hand side of the face and continue to develop the hairline around the forehead, shading in the hair itself. Firmly establish the outline of the hair flowing over the left-hand shoulder, then return to the mouth to add firm definition.

4 Shape the lips with shading and re-define the profile and neck outline. Start to shade boldly in front of the neck and lightly on the chin to establish shape here.

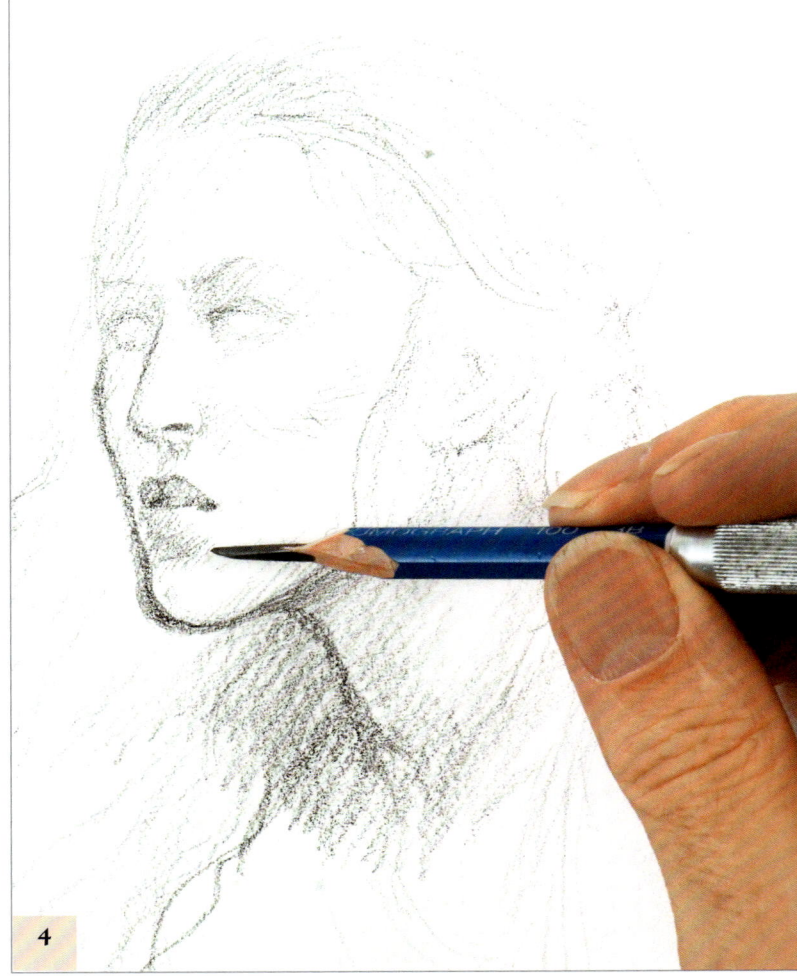

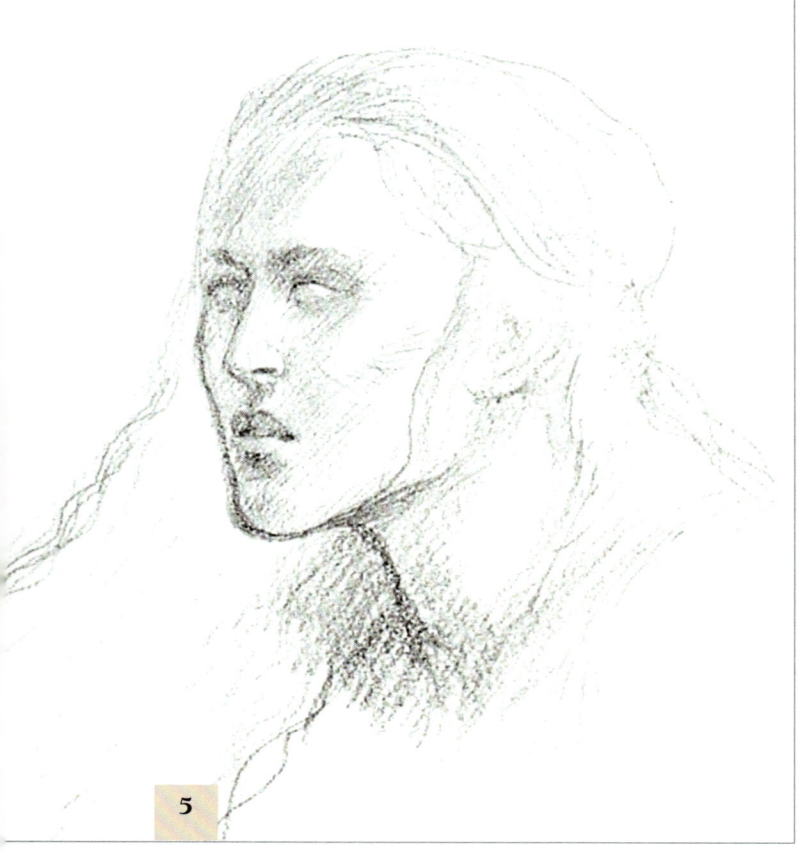

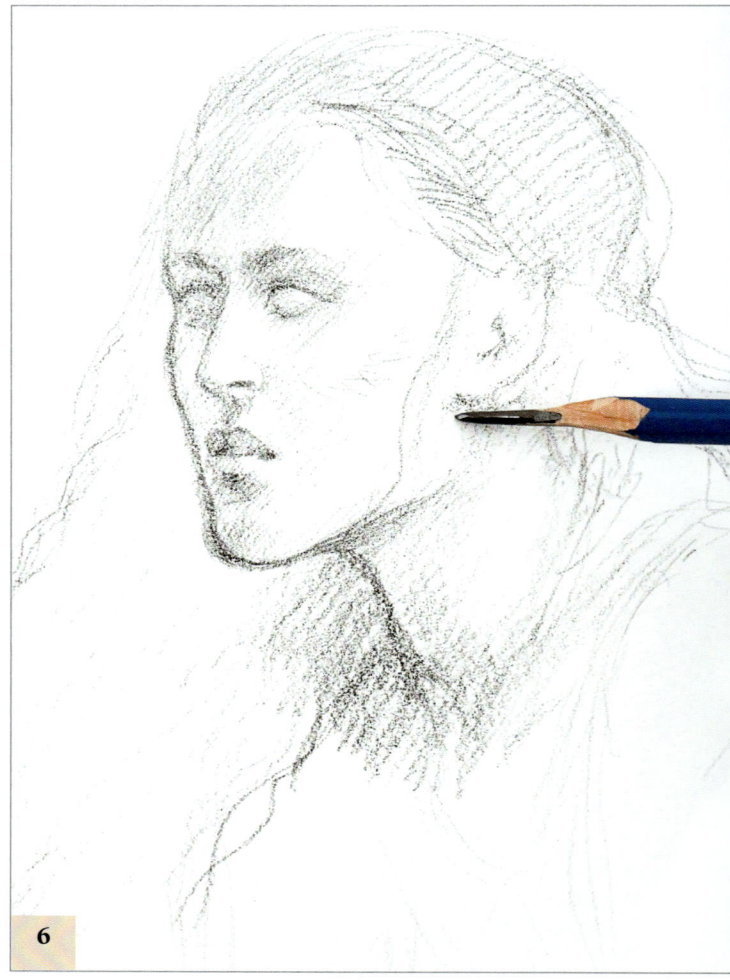

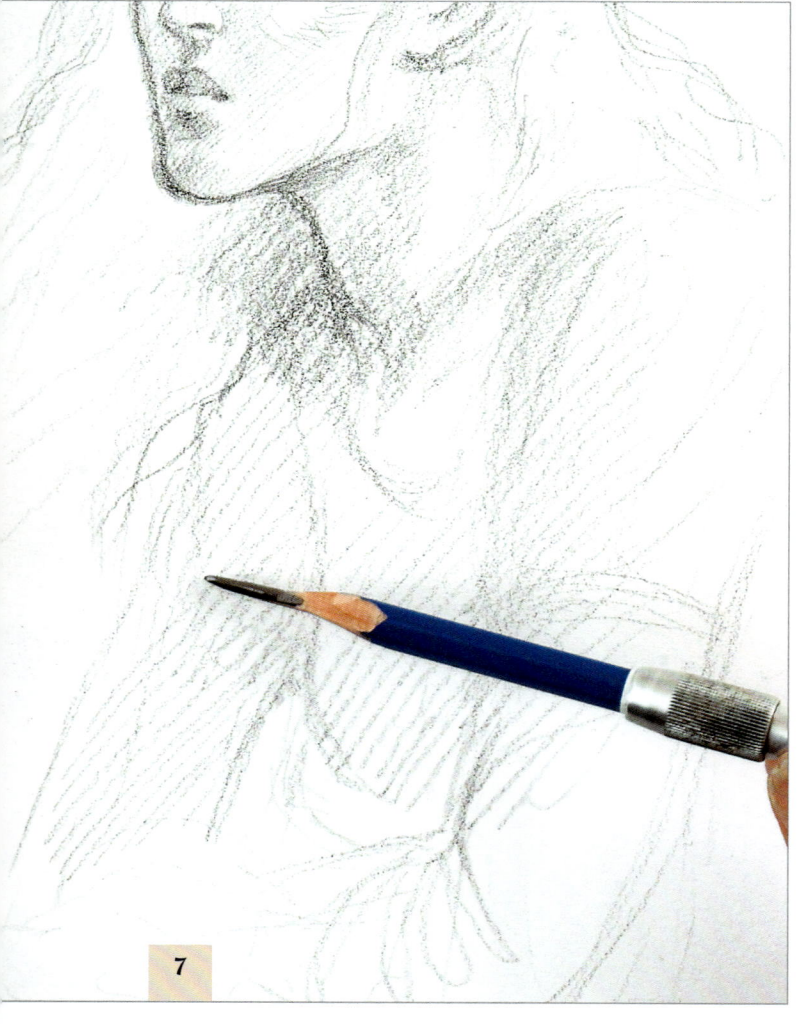

5 Continue to develop the facial features. Block in the mouth then define the upper eyelids, shading above them. Shade around the face to build the contours, particularly on the cheekbones and forehead.

6 Working on the hair, build the shape of the hairline and the back of the head – lightly shade. Then start to cross-hatch on this to quickly develop volume and texture. Define the ear with a clear outline.

7 Now work on the body. Increase the shading around the base of the neck, then sketch the right-hand shoulder and down into the arm, and suggest the curve of the elbow that will be resting on a balcony. Sketch the neckline of Arwen's dress and her bust line, and lightly shade through. Then start to sketch the left-hand arm and lightly shade.

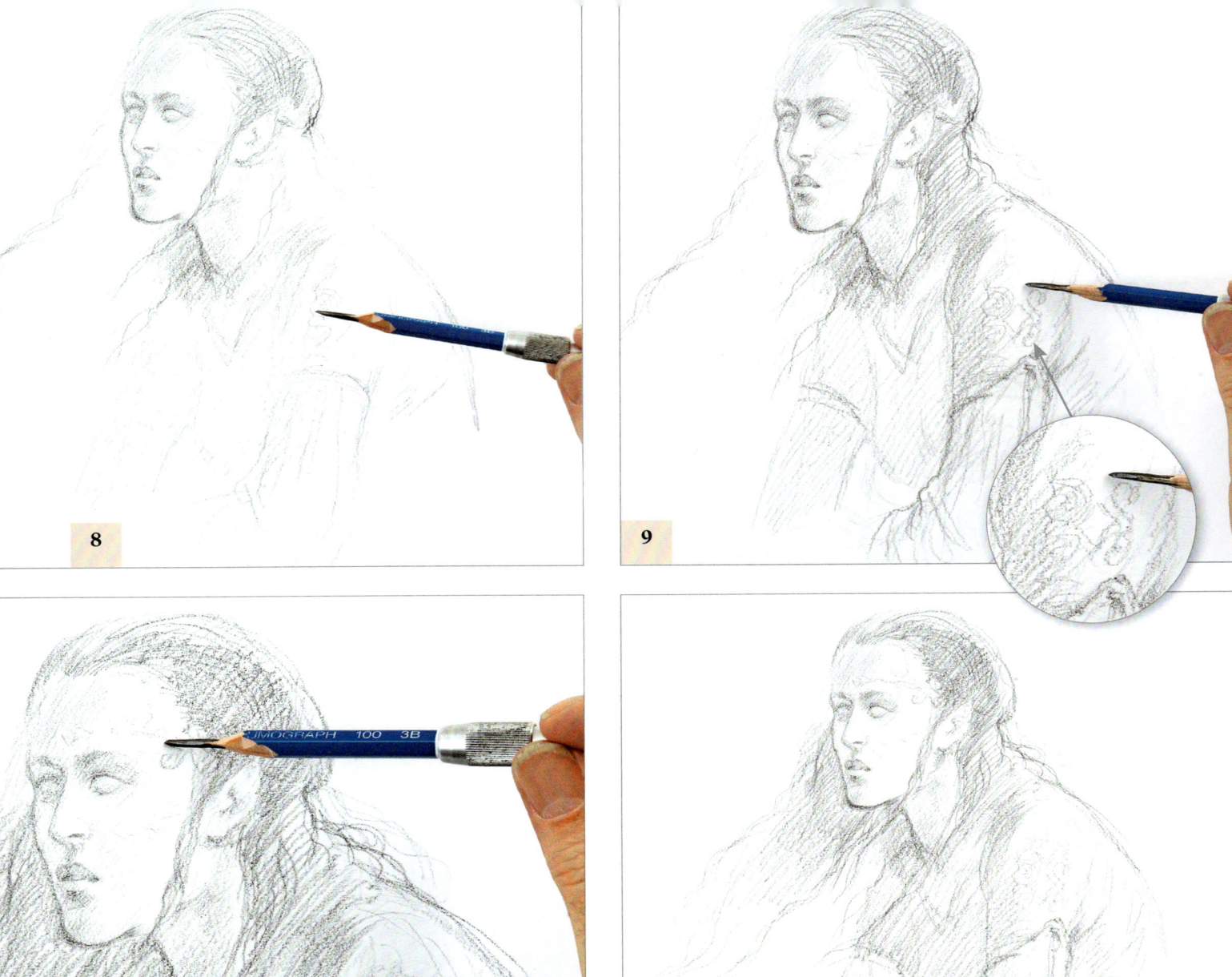

8 Add more detail to the ear and the hair falling in front of it; then work again into the hair building the volume and texture. Follow through the line of the wisps of hair at the back of the neck to define the curve of the back. Establish the v-shape neckline, then add further shading over the shoulder and contouring to the sleeve.

9 Working from the nape of the neck, develop the hair with strong directional shading. Shade down the sleeve to build shape and fabric texture. Draw the upside down v-shape of the upper sleeve and the drape of the fabric over the lower arm. Add light pattern detailing to the upper sleeve.

10 Build the hair hanging down on the left-hand side. Firmly shade the volume over the left-hand shoulder then extend the strands right down, using directional shading. Now build the hair volume and texture on the head with cross-hatching, and sketch the circlet across the forehead.

11 Add further shading below her ear. Define the outline of the whole torso and shade this with directional hatching.

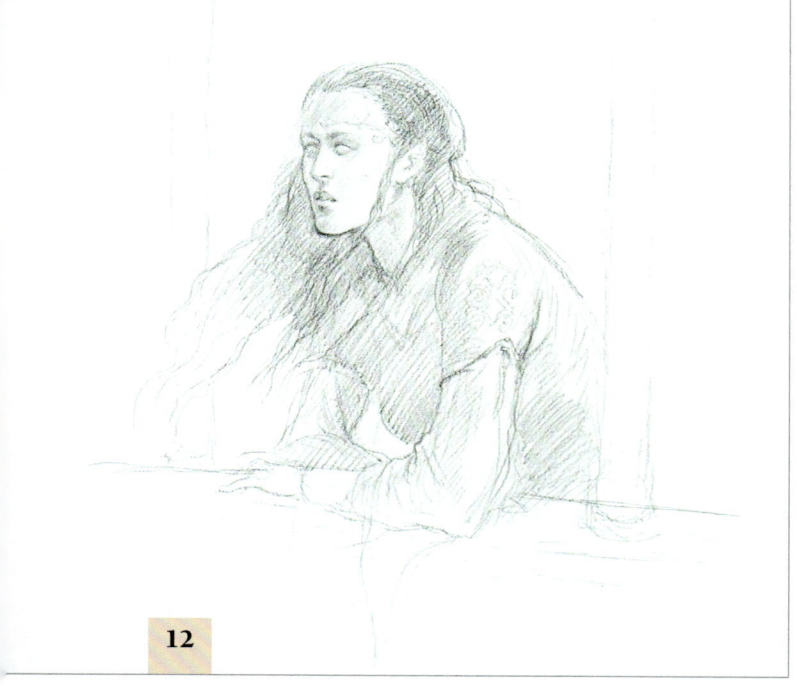

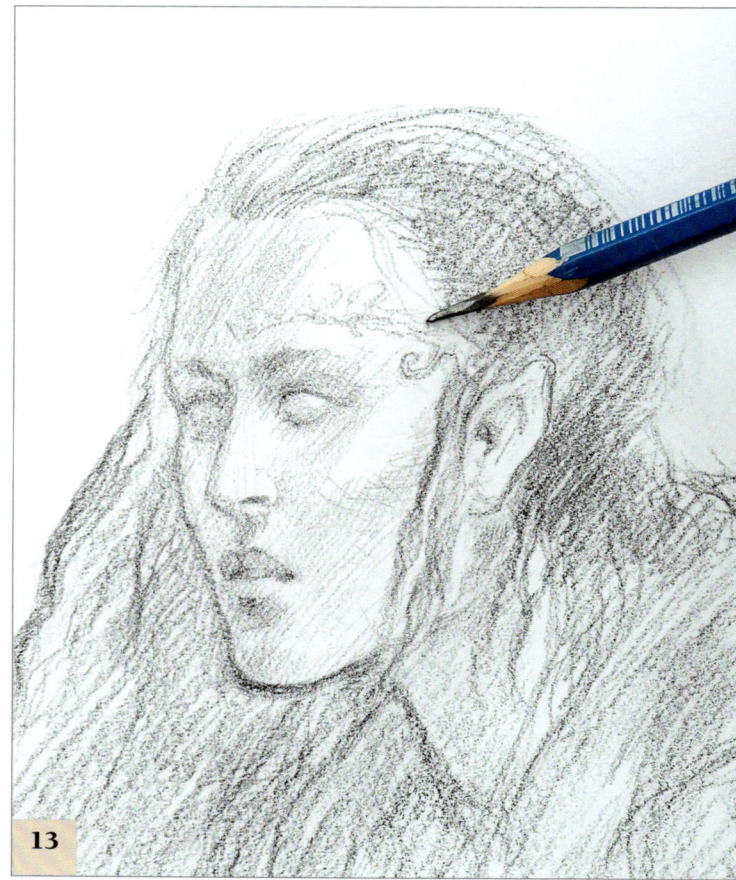

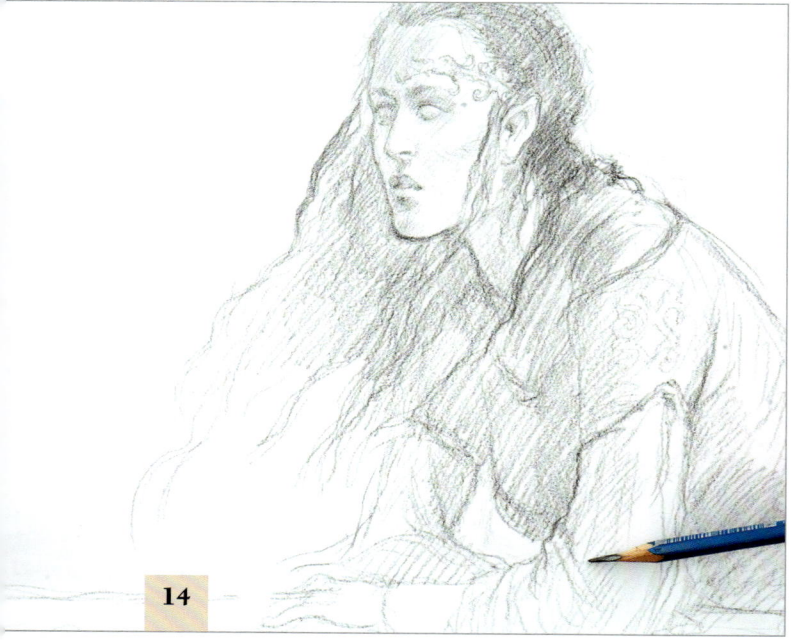

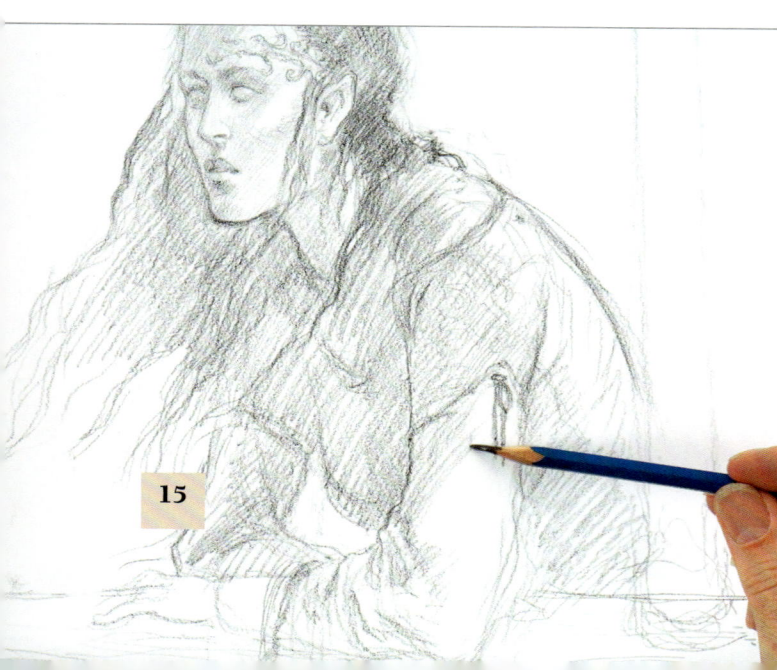

12 Add balcony columns either side of Arwen. Continue contouring her arms and develop the right arm through to the wrist and hand as she rests on the balustrade.

13 Switch to the 4B pencil to continue developing Arwen's hair. Further define the outer edge and add strands curving around her back. Deepen the shading around the hairline. Erase shading around the ear and re-establish an elven ear protruding here. Add detailing on her forehead.

14 Deepen the shading over the right shoulder and down into the body. Shade the sleeves' fabric folds at the elbow.

15 Further establish the curve of her back as Arwen leans over the balcony, then add deeper shading to the chest and left-hand arm. Working from the upside-down v-shape of the upper hem on the sleeve of the right-hand arm, add a ribbon detail, then start to lightly shade the shadow here.

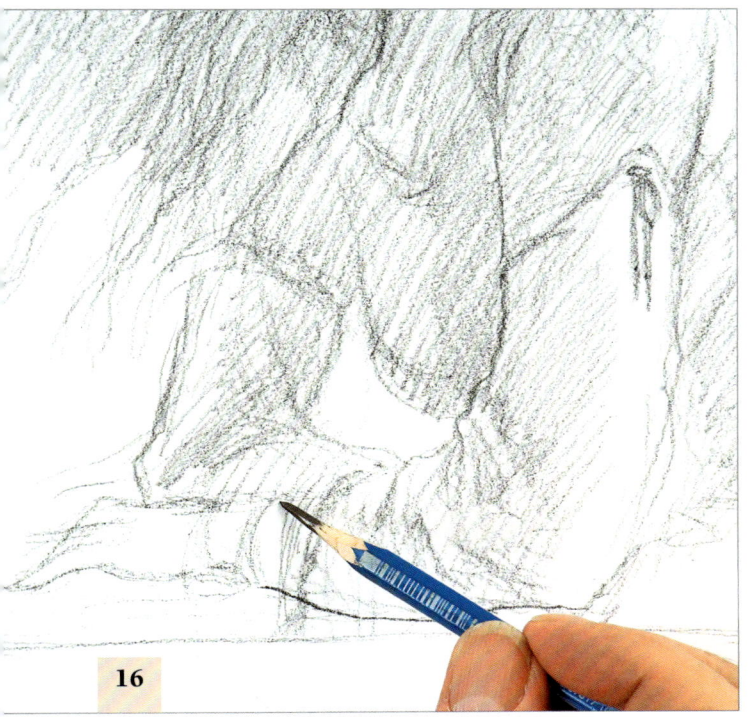

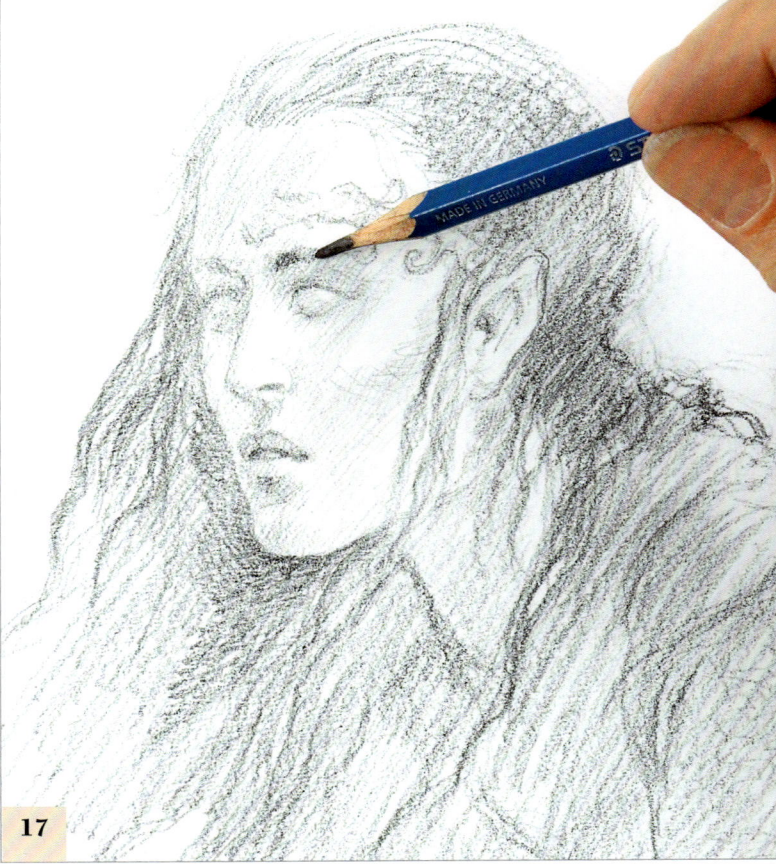

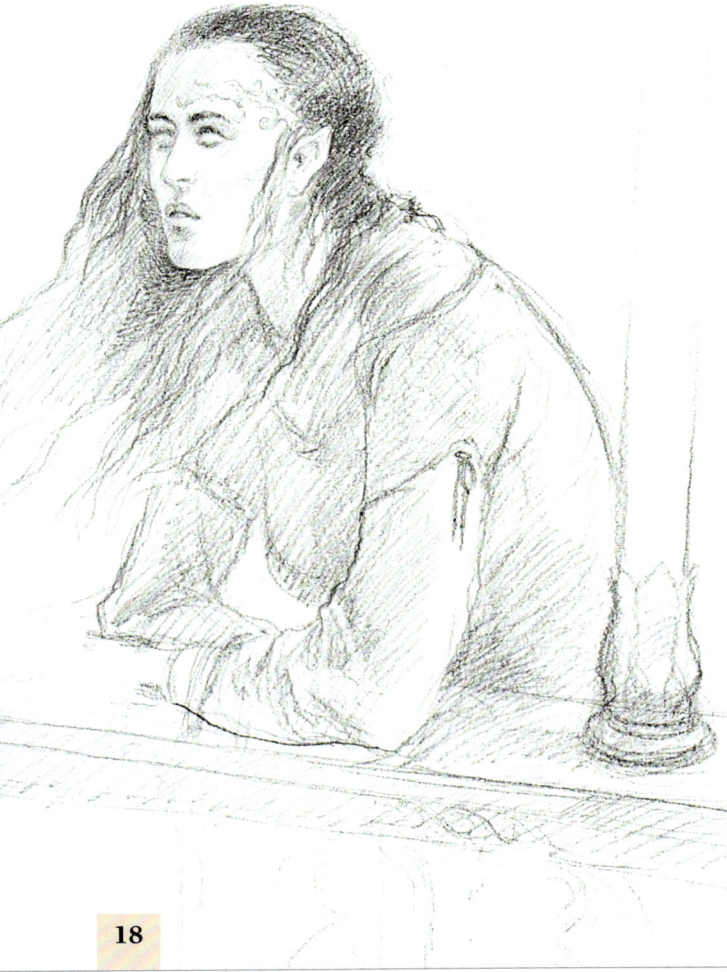

16 To finish the arms, add more contour shading on the forearms to denote fabric folds. Firmly establish the outline of the hand as it rests on the balustrade. (I said 'firmly establish ...' then promptly erased the hand as it didn't seem to work the way I wanted. It reappears in Step 21.)

17 Continue shading Arwen's hair to add depth between her chin and the left-hand shoulder using a 4B pencil to strongly define strands within the hair flowing there. Returning to the 3B and Arwen's face, add further detailing on her mouth and increase the shadow below her nose, then build up the eyebrows.

18 Deepen the outline of the eyes and the shading of the hair, particularly on the crown of the head. Start to build the setting by adding detail to the column and the balcony.

Background

It's easy to forget the environment when caught up in getting the character right. At the very least block out the background you have in mind. You can choose whether to develop it later.

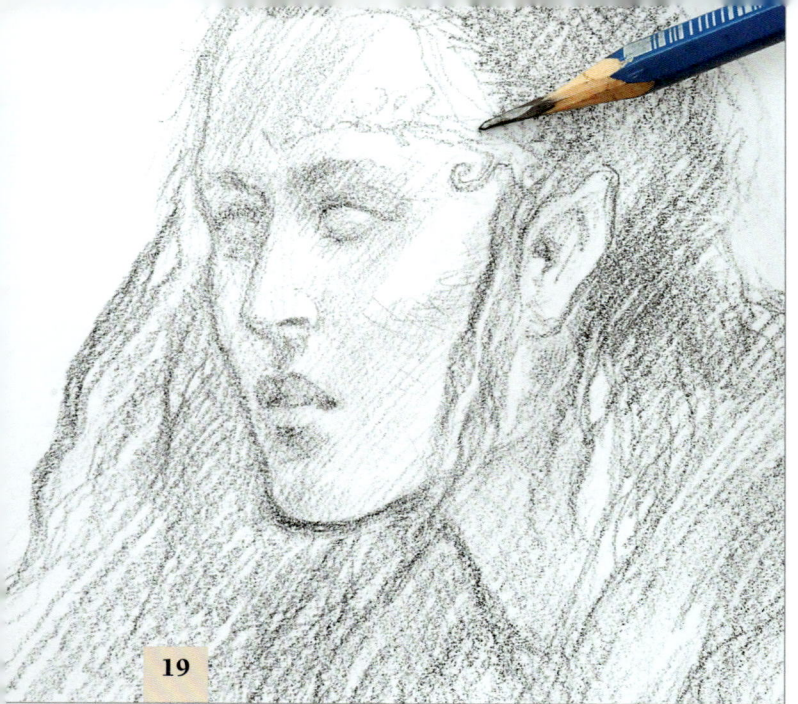

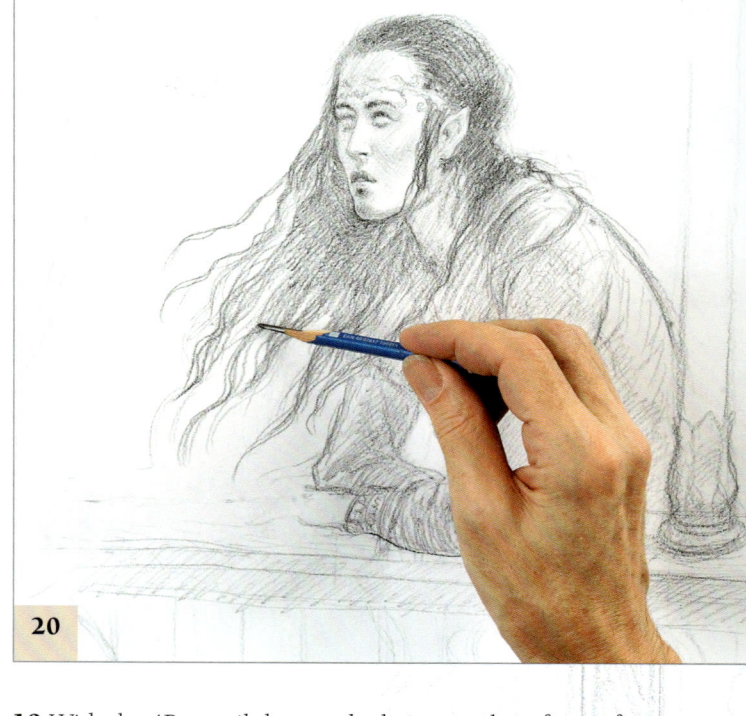

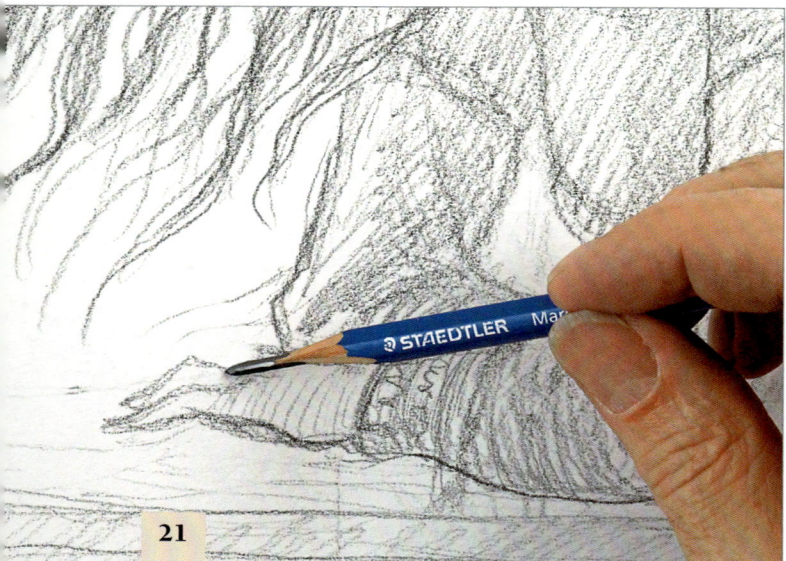

19 With the 4B pencil deepen the hair strands in front of and behind the ear, then deeply shade the chin. Switching back to the 3B, deepen the shading on the lips and nostrils then return to the forehead to build the circlet detail and further define the hairline.

20 Continue adding light shading around the facial contours and further extend the hair strands falling over the chest. Add further directional shading across her chest and define the edges of the forearms and sleeves. Continue to develop the flowing hair.

21 Outline the shape of the hand and define the fingers. Shade beneath the hand and all the way along the length of the forearm.

22 Build the backdrop. I have provided some pointers for this in the caption to the final image, but return here to complete the character's face. Re-define her eyelids then add the pupils. Refine the shading around her eyes and the shape of her mouth. As you can see opposite, at the very last minute I redrew the curve of her back, making it slightly straighter.

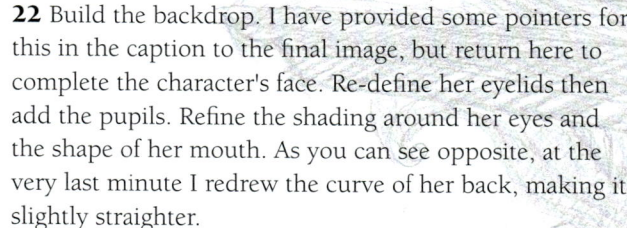

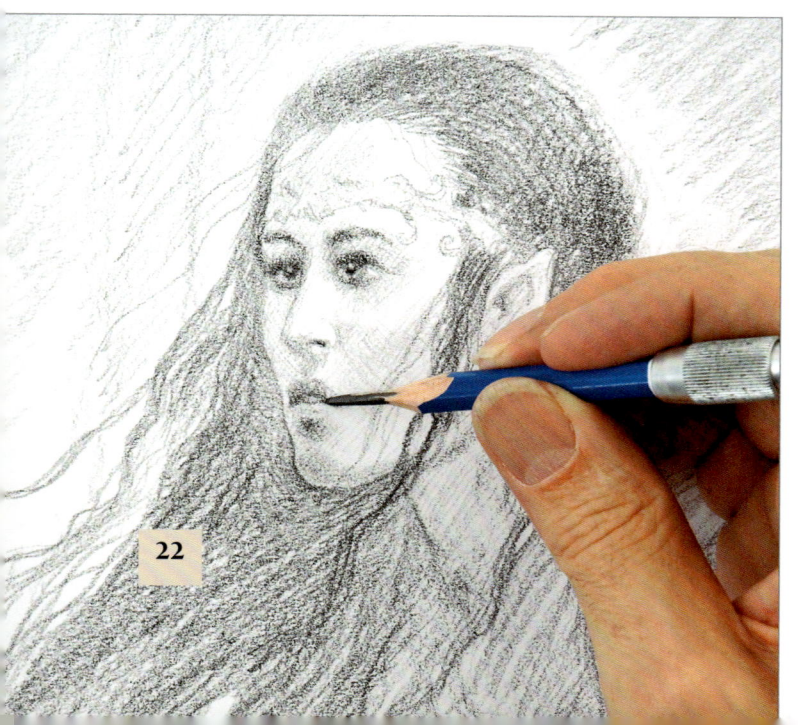

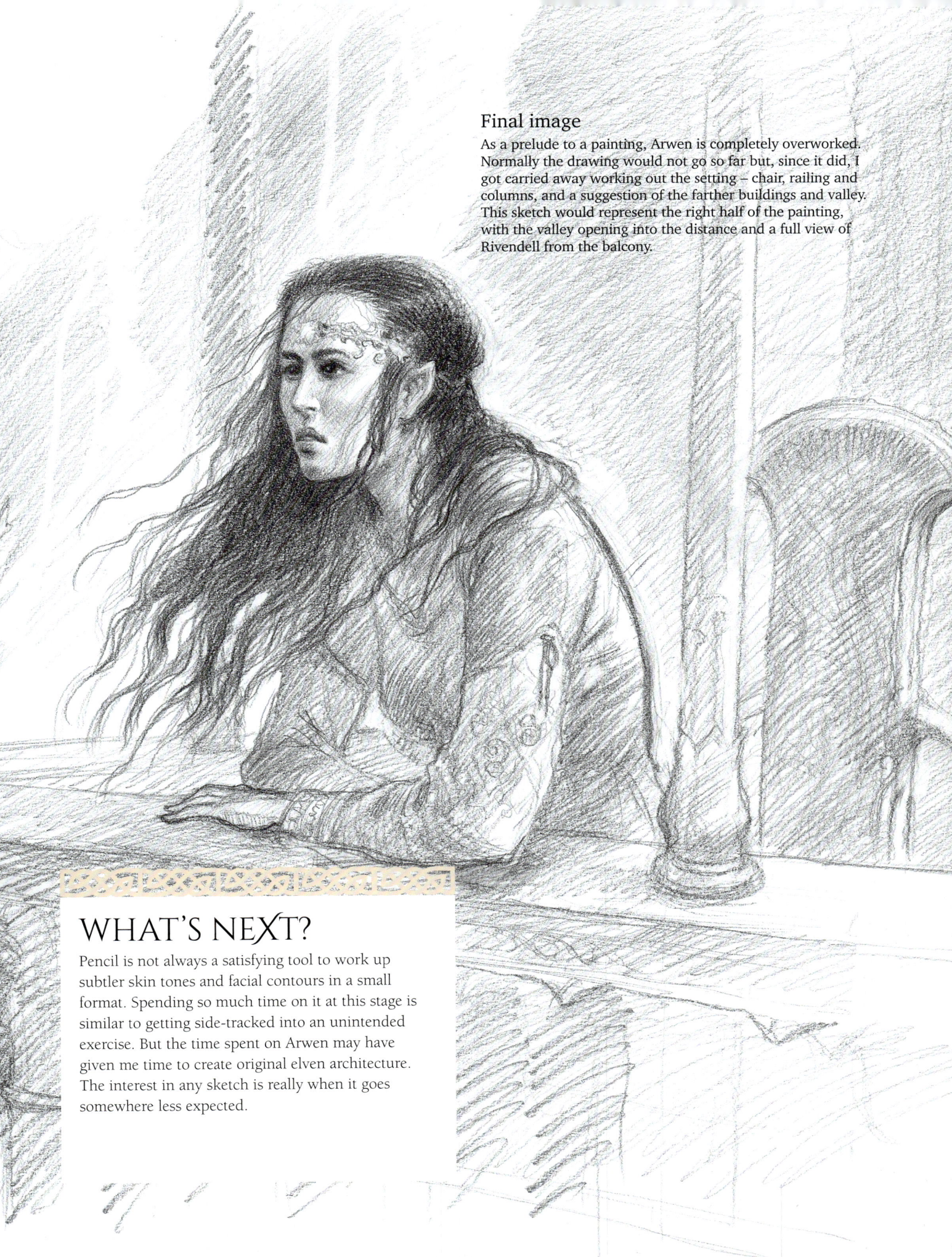

Final image

As a prelude to a painting, Arwen is completely overworked. Normally the drawing would not go so far but, since it did, I got carried away working out the setting – chair, railing and columns, and a suggestion of the farther buildings and valley. This sketch would represent the right half of the painting, with the valley opening into the distance and a full view of Rivendell from the balcony.

WHAT'S NEXT?

Pencil is not always a satisfying tool to work up subtler skin tones and facial contours in a small format. Spending so much time on it at this stage is similar to getting side-tracked into an unintended exercise. But the time spent on Arwen may have given me time to create original elven architecture. The interest in any sketch is really when it goes somewhere less expected.

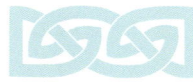

BALROG

Because the balrog in the Mines of Moria is never fully described by J.R.R. Tolkien, one can be quite free to do one's own interpretation. My balrog is fearfully strong and menacing, shrouded in fire, darkness and shadow, clutching his long sword. It should not surprise that this fierce and fiery demon is said to rival the dragon in its capacity for destruction.

Techniques
✦ Shading and smudging
✦ Drawing by erasing

Ideas and inspiration
There is huge debate amongst Tolkien fans as to whether the balrog has wings or not. Here, I've decided not to decide with merely a suggestion of them. The balrog is a creature of smoke and flame, both rather unsatisfying elements to render in black and white. It is, however, an excuse to indulge in a lot of smudging.

Visual references
One is one's best model – or at least the most readily available – so I stand in for creatures from Gollum to balrogs. A photo of my arm slightly bent with muscles flexed has enough detail to serve as a guide.

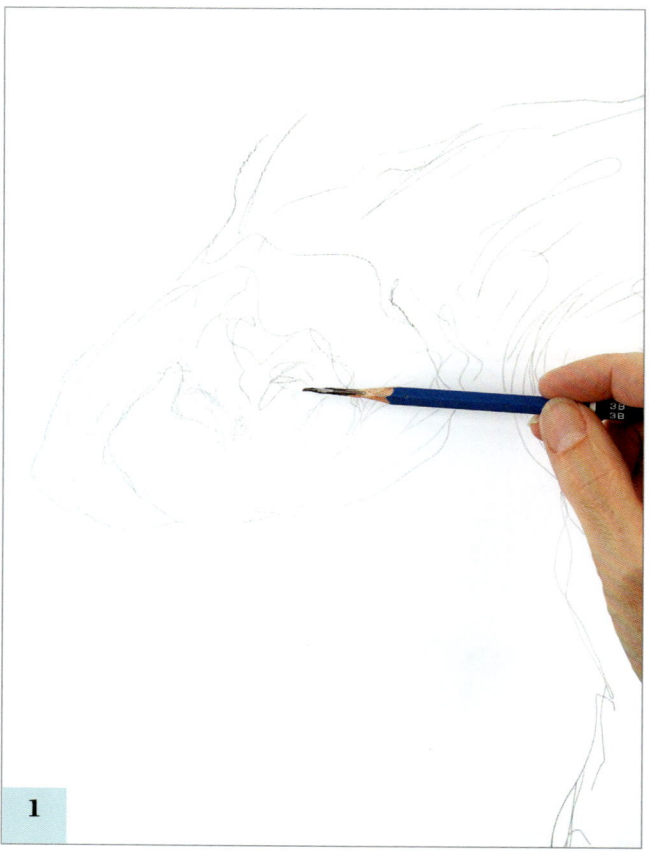

1

1 Taking a 4B pencil, lightly draw the outline of the body and the arm. Then work on the basic head shape by drawing the jaw line, the horns and the eyes.

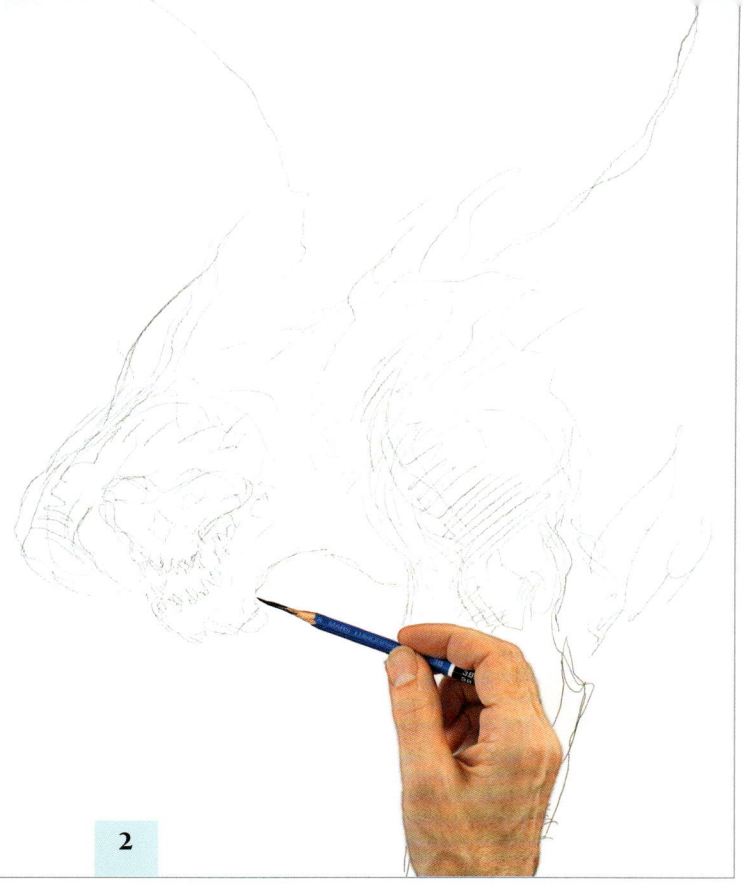

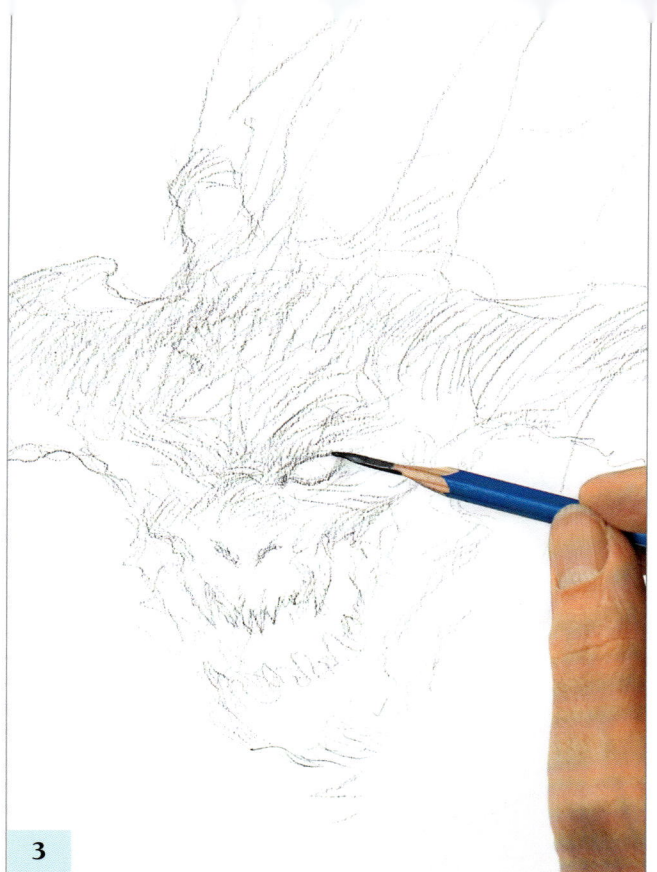

2 Continue to sketch the shape of the arm and the base of the wings where they attach to the shoulders. Add some initial shading, then build the mouth by lightly sketching in some teeth.

3 Add a second pair of horns then shade across the head into these. Build the face by placing the nose and further establishing the mouth and jaw. Start to establish the eyes. Keep your lines light so that changes can still be made.

4 Extend the lower horns right out from either side of the head with firm outlines and shade along their full length.

5 Start to work the balrog's full body shape. Build the arm with stronger contour lines and shading to denote the shape and muscle. Work right down to the hand.

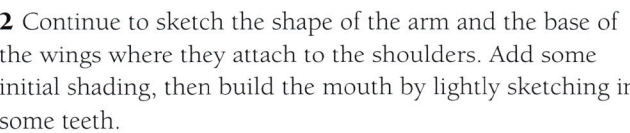

Natural references

A visit to a natural history museum will provide excellent reference for horns, skulls and other details. Remember to take your sketchpad.

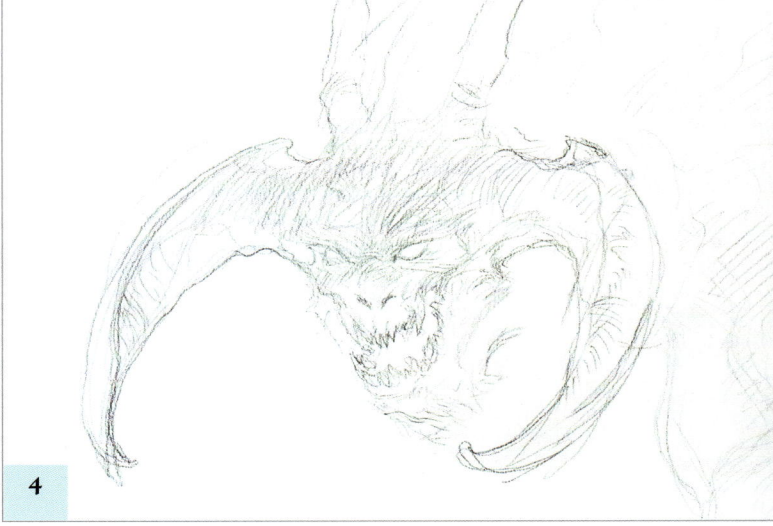

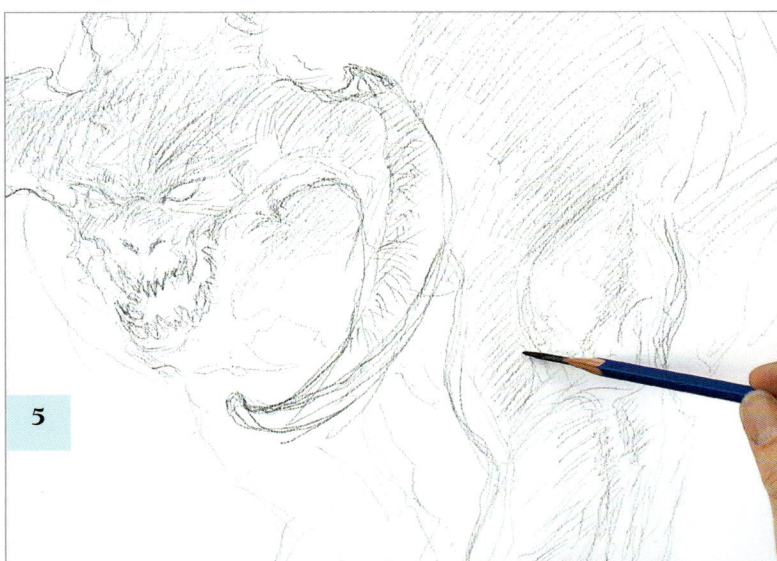

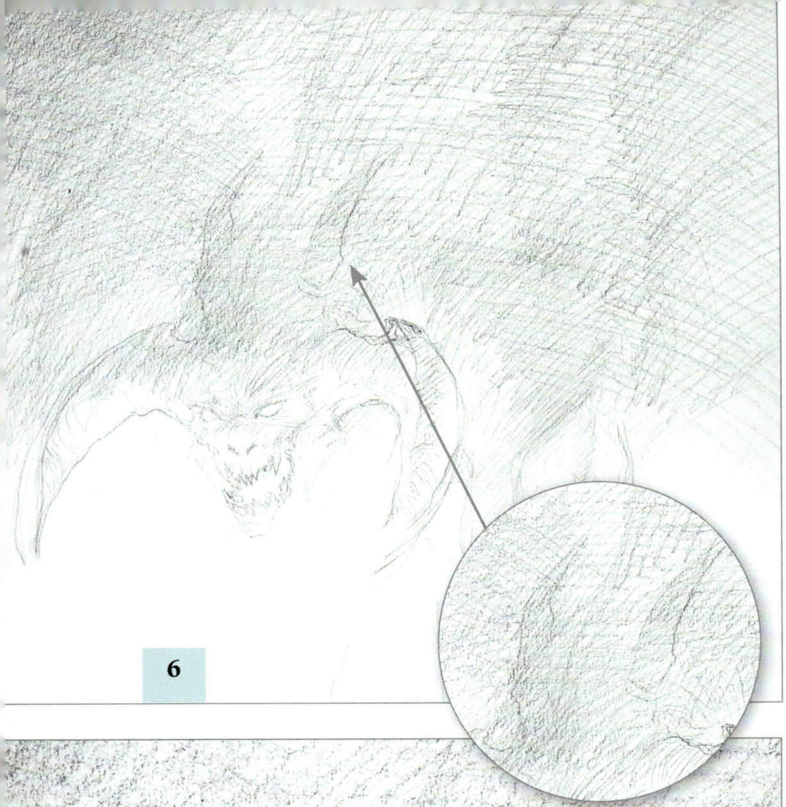

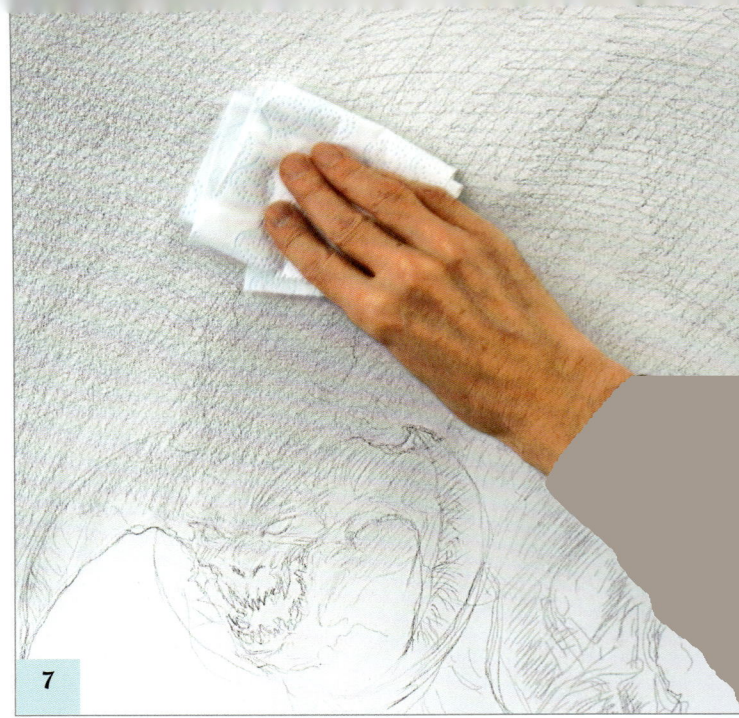

6 Lightly sketch the wings. Shade the neck and upper horns. Start to shade the background with sweeping strokes, cross-hatching to increase density, lightly covering the balrog too. Create strong shading to the left of the beast. If your pencil is neither too short nor the lead too hard, and sculpted into a long point, its weight will leave a line when held at the very end. Building up cross-hatching in this way can be very effective, as all the lines are of a similar density.

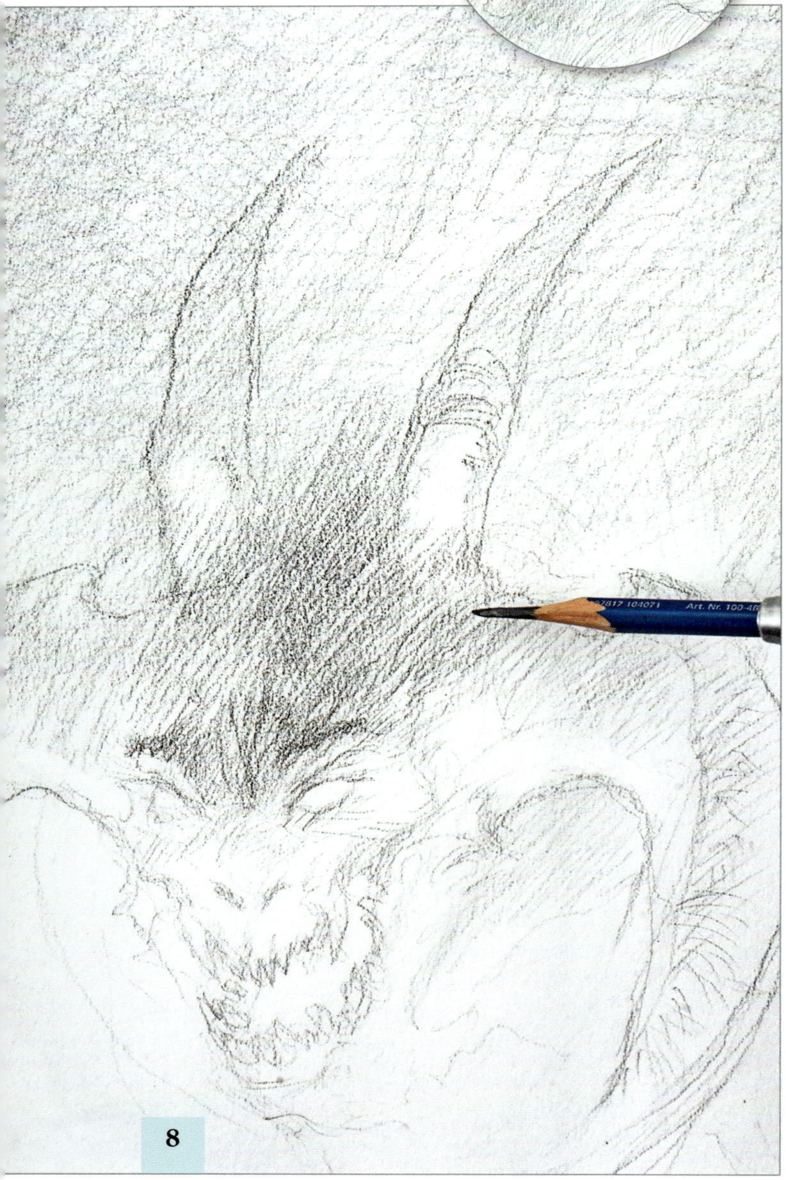

7 Using facial tissues, rub over the whole of the cross-hatched background to smudge the shading, but avoid smudging the face or anywhere else where the detail has still to be built up.

8 Re-define the balrog's horns, working back into the smudged area. Add further shading to the forehead, and start to establish the cranial structure with creases rising from the nose. Further establish the eyes and eyebrows, then develop the horns using the putty eraser to lift highlights and applying darker shading for form.

Smudging technique

I don't generally use smudging, but it can have specific applications where it's useful, as here. It can be messy but is a good way to darken an area quickly.

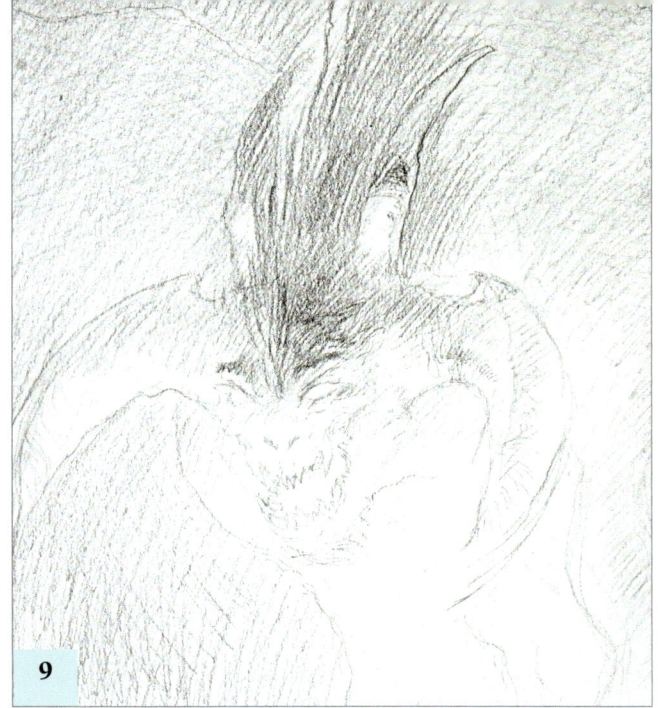

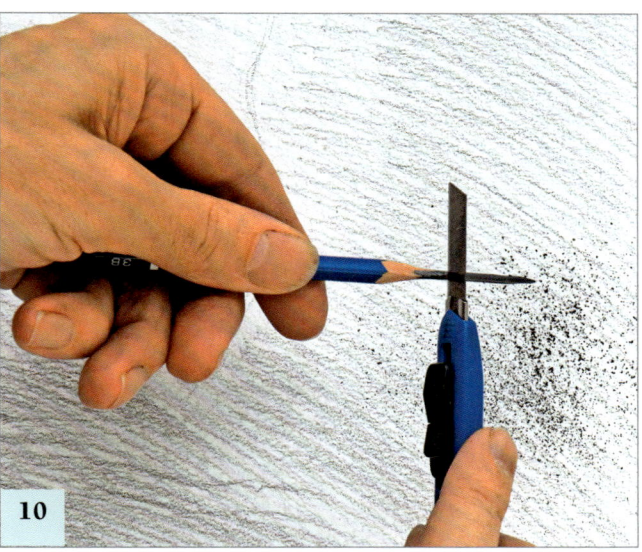

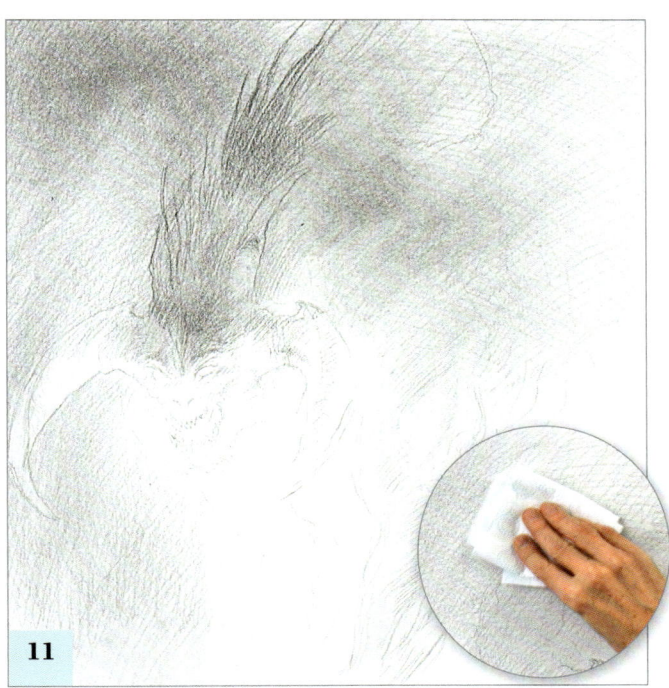

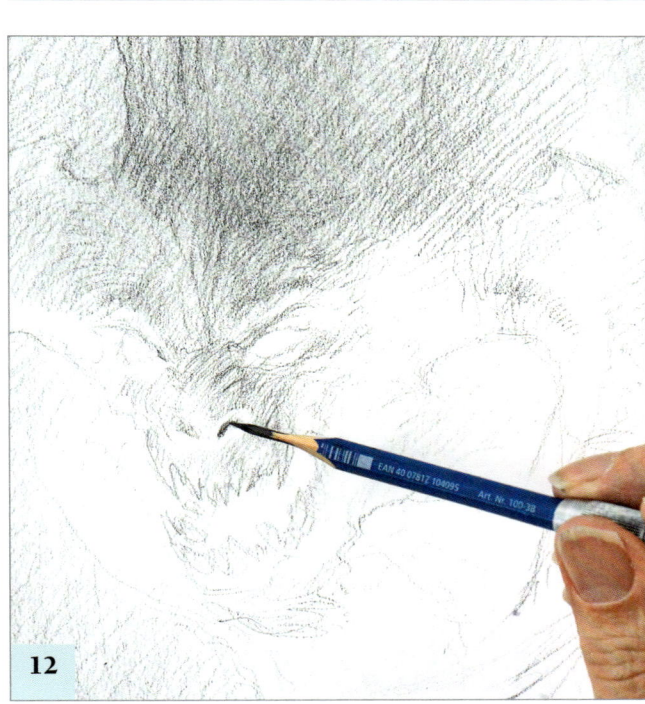

9 Apply darker tones below the upper horns where they attach to the head creating a gnarly texture with squiggles. Draw the mane between them with bold directional strokes. Shade to establish the balrog's cheekbones then move to the background and shade below the lower horns.

10 Continue shading around the base of the horns and lift highlights with a putty eraser to build the shape. Develop the shading around the beast, using the craft knife to shave graphite powder onto the left-hand side. Use facial tissues to smudge the graphite and blend the shading.

11 Use the same smudging technique down the left-hand side of the image, and in the wing area to deepen the smoky effect. Re-establish the mane through the smoky background with bold strokes, then re-define the outline of the upper horns.

12 Lightly shade the neck then return to the face, switching to a 3B pencil which will allow a little finer lines. Shade down the nose and place the nostrils. Then shade below the nose and around the cheekbones. Use heavy marks to denote the ridges on the nose.

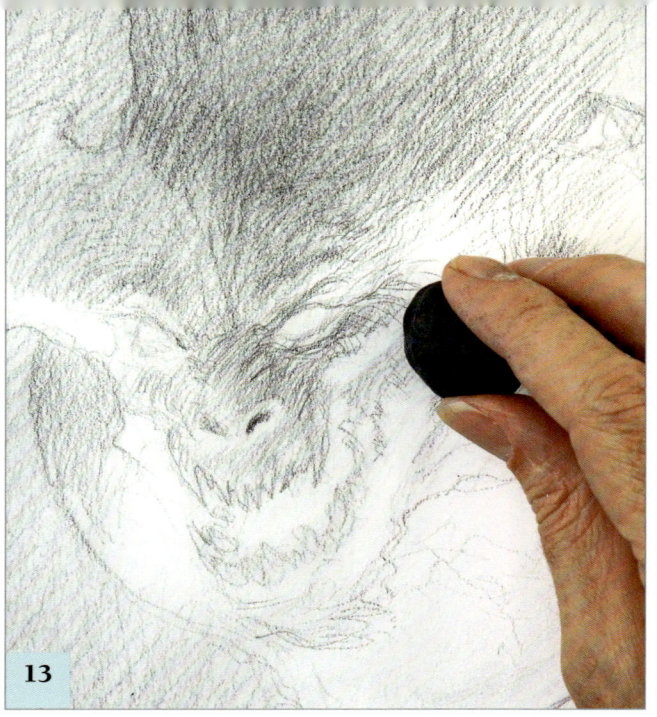

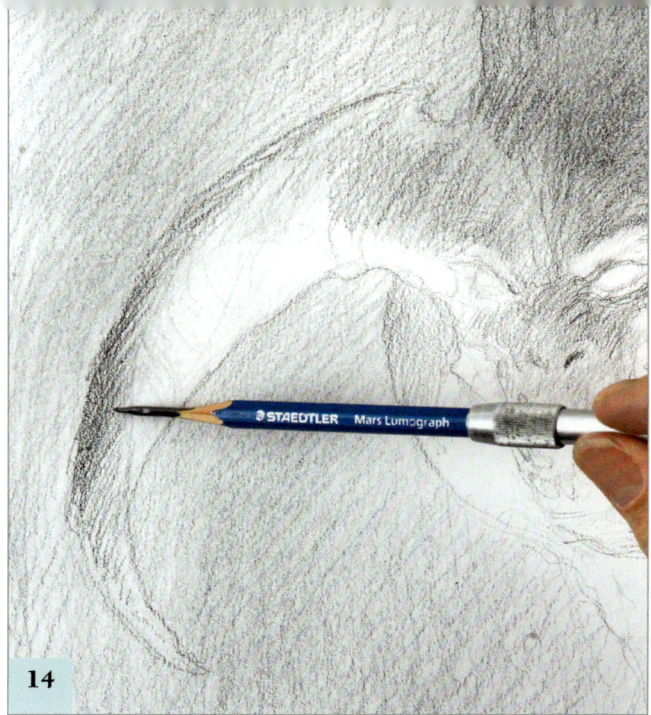

13 Cross-hatch around the eyes to create form and wrinkles. Continue shading the neck and define the outline of the just-visible left-hand shoulder. With the putty eraser lift a highlight from the right-hand cheek.

14 Continue building the shading around the forehead. Develop the left-hand lower horn by re-defining its outline and establishing its ridge with heavy shading. At this stage the rest of the horn is left white; detailing can come later.

15 Deepen the shading above the left-hand eye then work across the top of the head to protrude the cranial structure. Deepen the shading up into the mane.

16 Now work on the right-hand lower horn. As the main part of this will be in shadow, shade down from the horn ridge. Use cross-hatching to denote the ridged texture here.

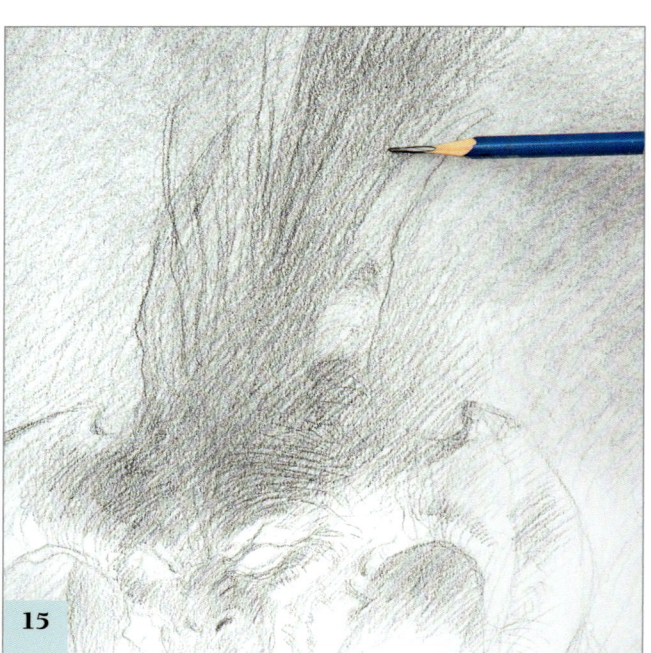

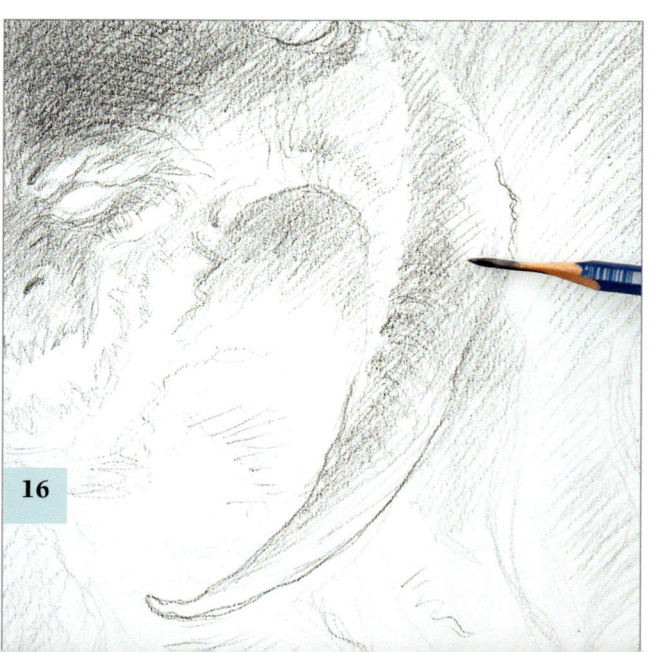

Letting it rest

Curiously, graphite benefits from being allowed a little time to 'settle', so moving around from one spot in a picture to another can be more effective than trying to build up a large dark area in one go.

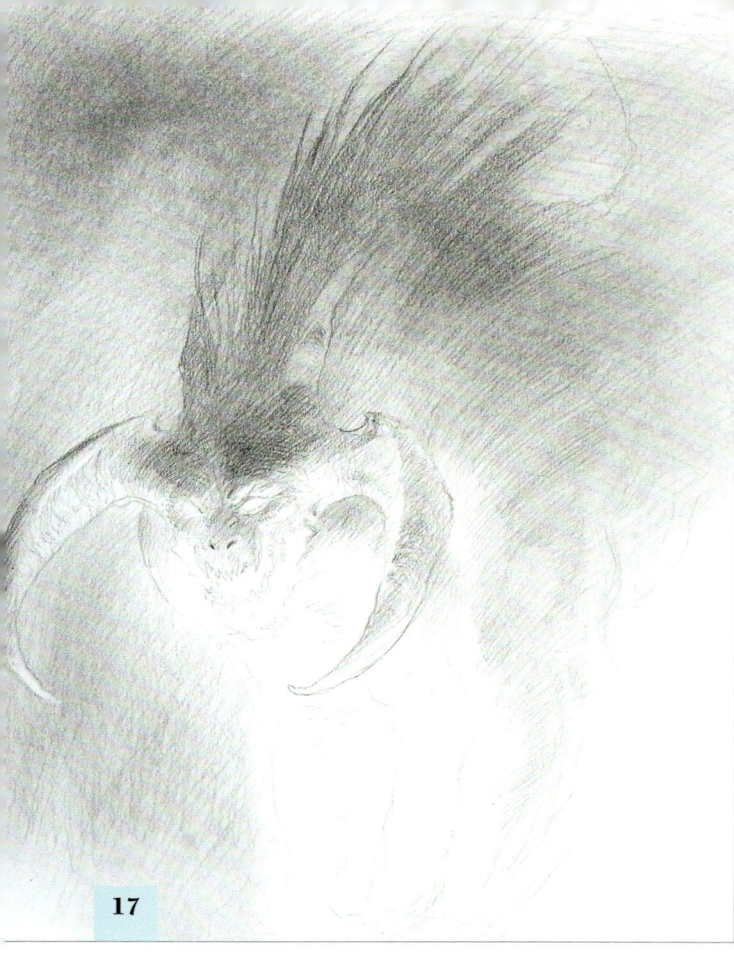

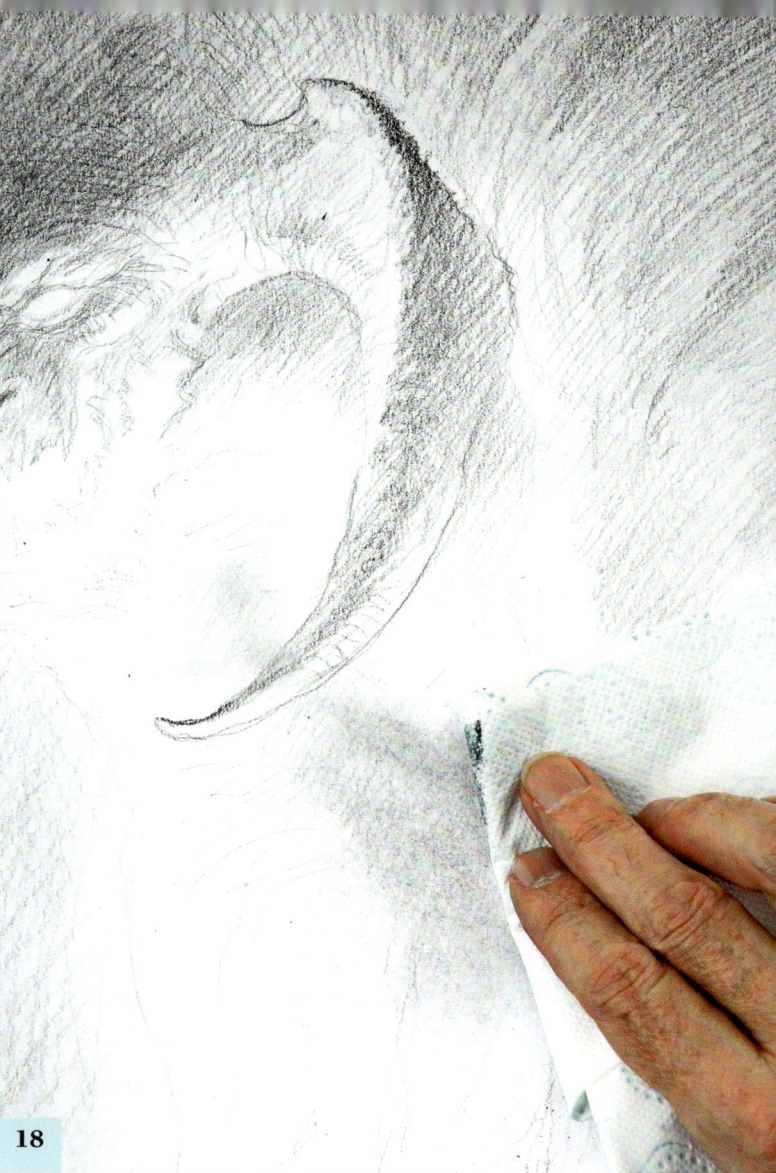

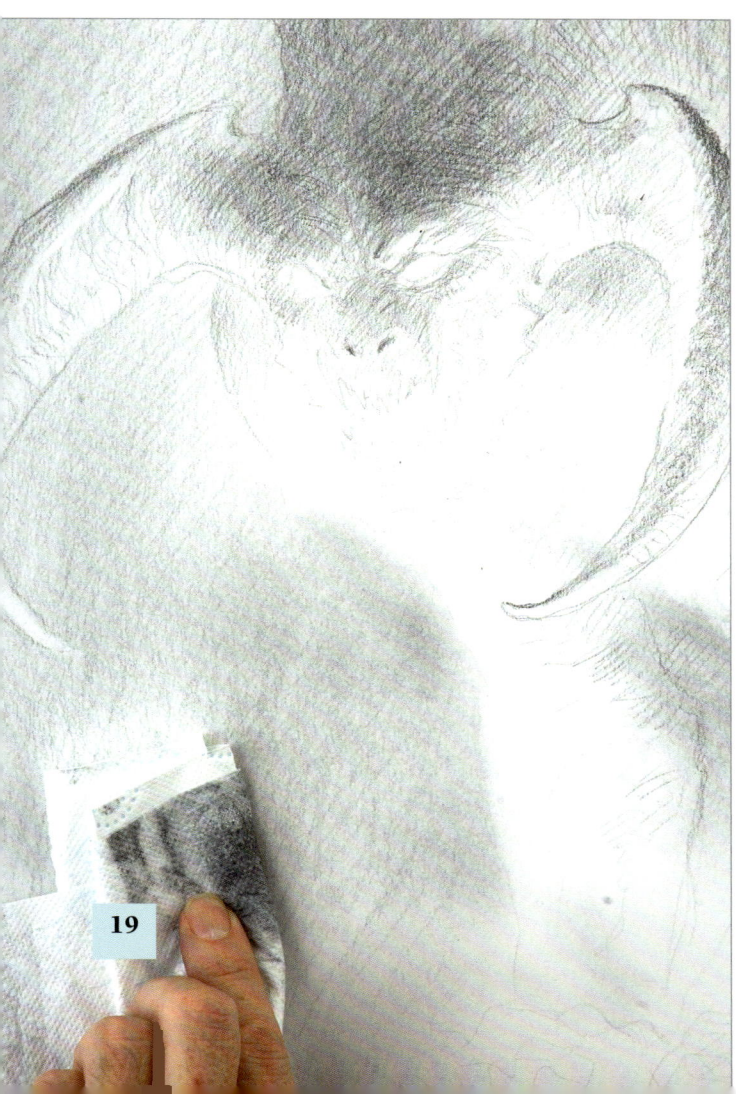

17 Further define the two front arms of the balrog, and lightly position the claws. Lightly shade this area. Firmly establish the join of the lower horns to the head.

18 Begin to define the balrog's strong neck, working down into the right-hand shoulder with contour shading. Now smudge with the facial tissues to define where the top of the arms join the chest. Some detail will be lost, but you can easily work it back up again.

19 Shade the area below the lower left horn and smudge as before. Use a putty eraser to lift the highlight on the left arm.

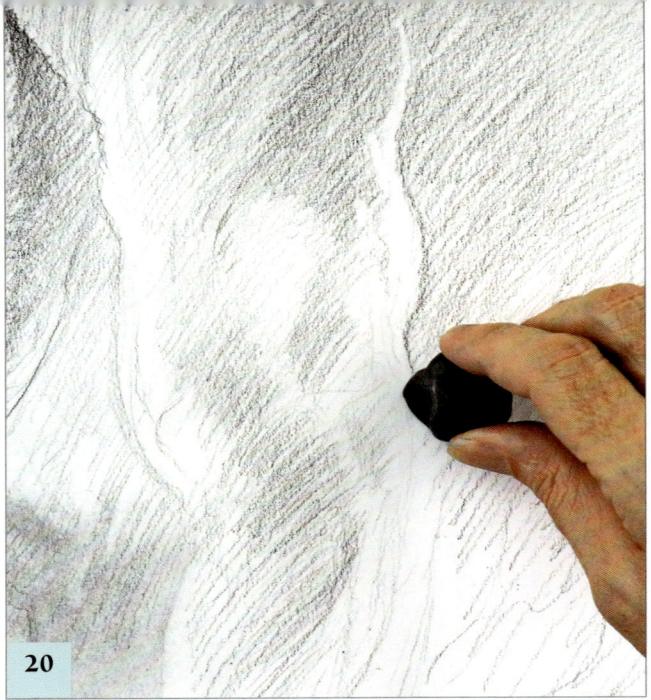

20

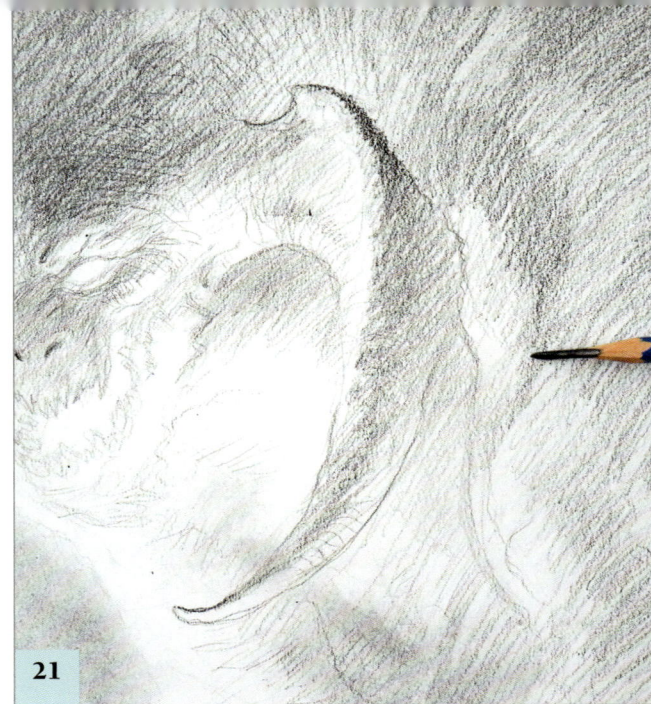

21

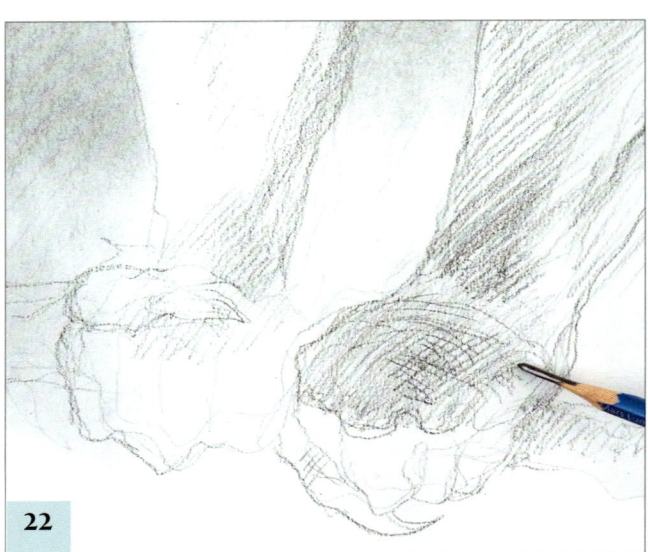

22

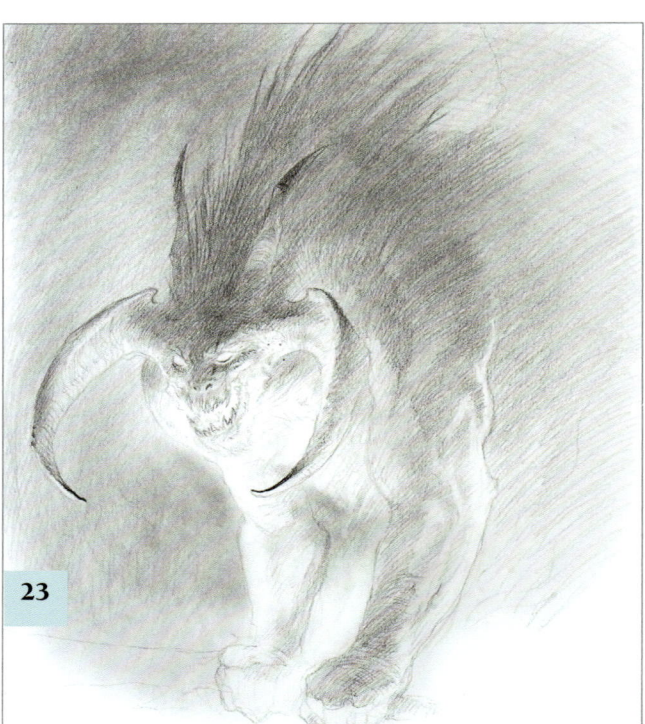

23

20 Move to the right-hand arm. Outline with a firm line and build the contour shading, strongly denoting the muscles using your reference photo. Then use the putty eraser to pick out highlights and shape from the shading.

21 Strongly increase the shading above the shoulder with bold directional strokes.

22 Increase the shading on both arms. Sketch in the claws clutching what will be a sword. Block in both hands with bold shading, using an eraser to lift highlights at the wrists.

23 Further establish the edges of the lower and upper horns, adding dark shaded details to each tip. Define the teeth and add further texturing to the face. Add a highlight below each eye by drawing in a lower eyelid. Finalize the shading around the body and background, smudging and lifting highlights to enhance volume and shape.

WHAT'S NEXT?

This kind of sketch is akin to painting in graphite. A little more work would turn it into a fully finished black-and-white rendering. Then the decision is made whether to retain the incidental nature of the sketch, or create a piece of finished art that stands on its own.

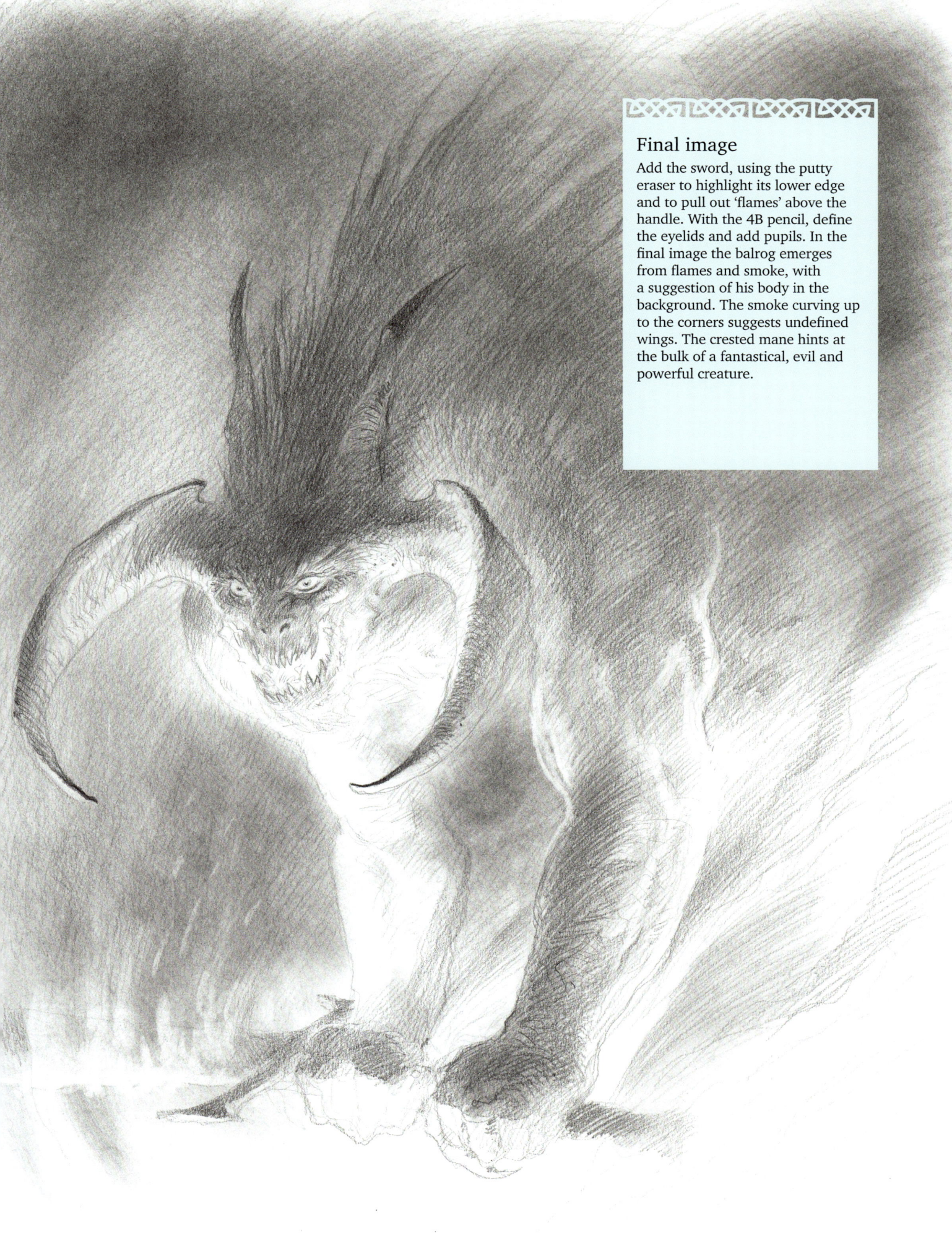

Final image

Add the sword, using the putty eraser to highlight its lower edge and to pull out 'flames' above the handle. With the 4B pencil, define the eyelids and add pupils. In the final image the balrog emerges from flames and smoke, with a suggestion of his body in the background. The smoke curving up to the corners suggests undefined wings. The crested mane hints at the bulk of a fantastical, evil and powerful creature.

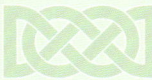

MERMAID

Mermaids are so much a part of our common cultural heritage
that not only do we have a solid idea of what they look like,
but they lend themselves to being re-invented with ease.
Half-fish and half-woman, the word mermaid comes from
'mere' – the Old English word for sea – and 'maid'.

Materials
✦ Derwent pastel pencils: terracotta, pale green,
  pale blue, cadmium yellow, pale yellow, olive,
  white, pale flesh, dark flesh, pale violet, pale
  orange, umber, dark green
✦ Grey-brown cartridge paper

Techniques
✦ Basic human form and features
✦ Building coloured flesh tones
✦ Smudging with pastel pencils

Ideas and inspiration
I wanted to draw a classical mermaid as if she had
suddenly appeared in front of an underwater diver,
like a hallucination out of the sea's depths.

Visual references
I used a number of pages cut from photo and fashion
magazines marked 'Body – Female' as reference. For
the fish-tail, we won't see enough to require back-up.

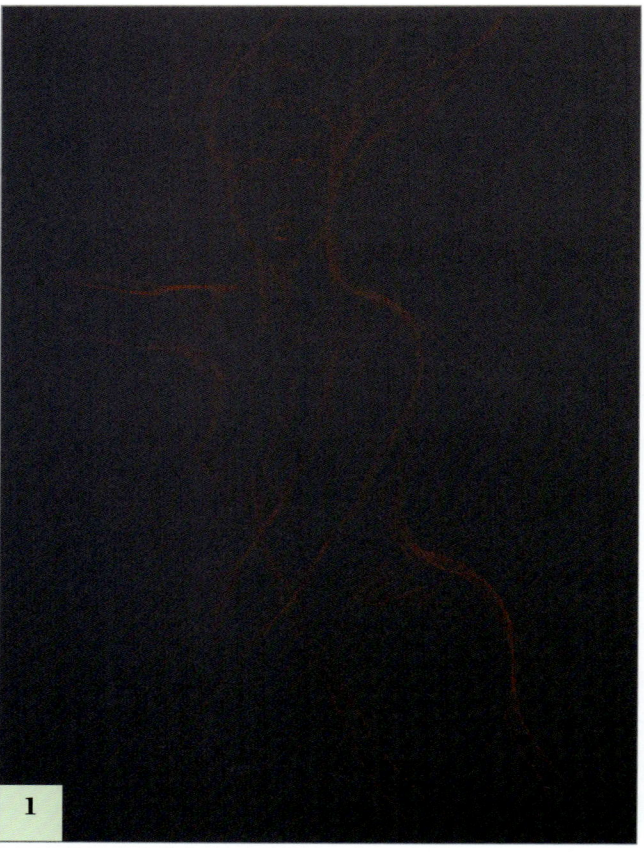

1 With **terracotta**, sketch the head and flowing hair, the
neck and the shoulder line. Work down into the arms and
add the curve of the back, extending down into the tail.
This is the basic outline of the mermaid.

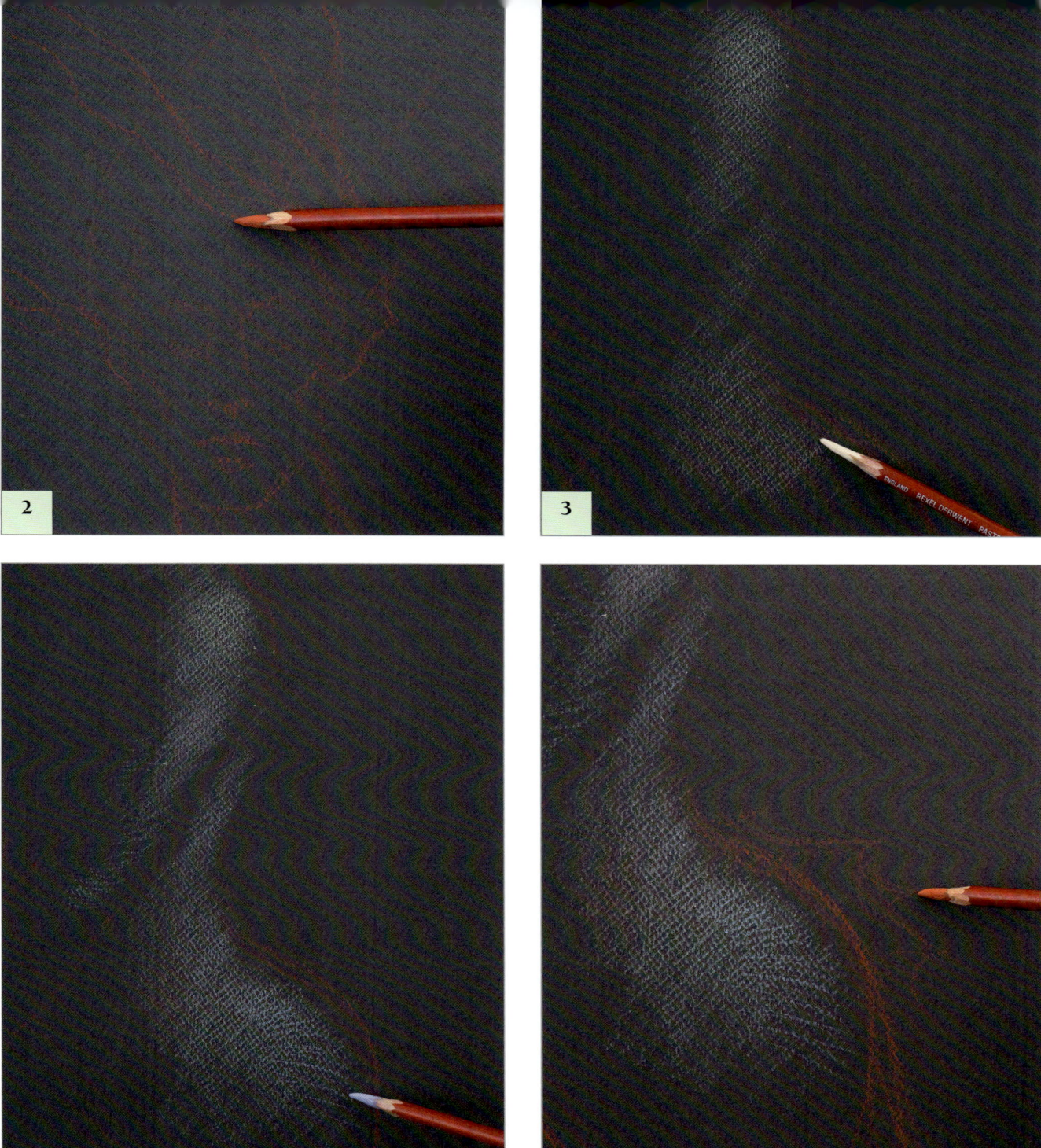

2 Firmly establish the outline of the face then sketch in the mouth, nostrils, eyes and eyebrows. Work out to create fin-edged ears, then start to add shape to the flowing hair.

3 With the **pale green** pencil start lightly shading down the neck and right-hand shoulder. Switch to **pale flesh** to work down the shoulder and arm, and into the hips and tail.

4 With **pale green** continue to shade this area, and extend down the right-hand arm. Switch to **pale violet** to add further light shading to the arm, then cross-hatch down the shoulder and hips to build volume and texture.

5 With **terracotta**, firmly establish the curve of the tail and sketch in the dorsal fin.

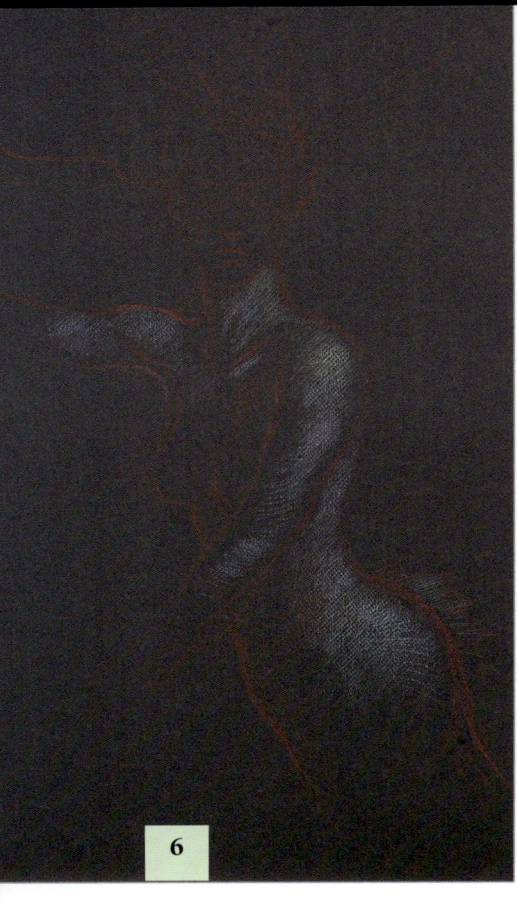

6

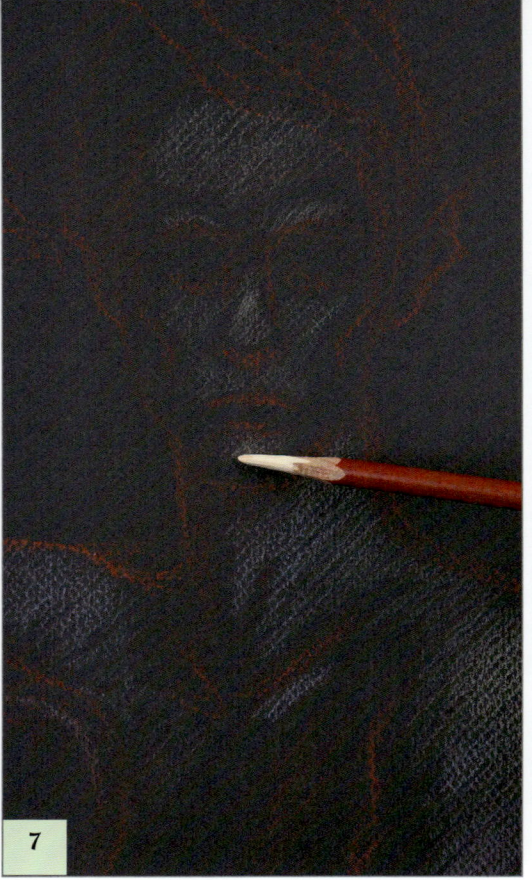

7

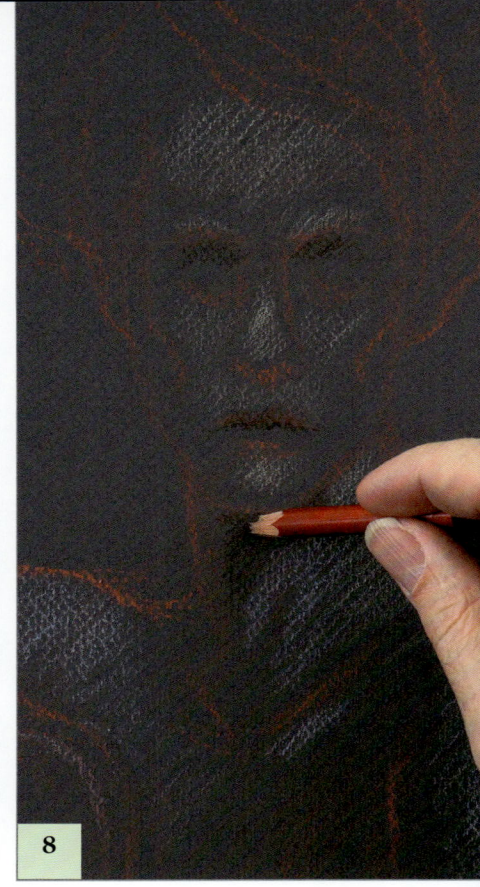

8

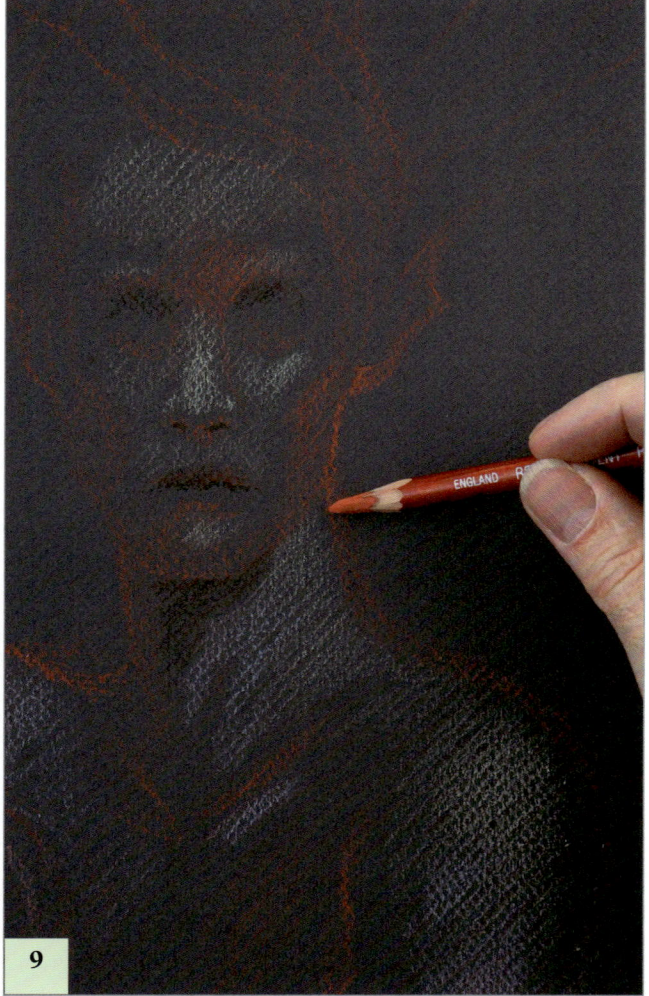

9

6 Continue establishing the outline around the chest and into the arms as far as the hand, which is only suggested at this point (and a good thing too as it ends up getting erased and redrawn). Add shading to the neck and collarbone with **pale violet**, and work out into the left-hand arm. Shade down the right-hand arm, curving your strokes to enhance contours. Using **pale green** lightly shade in the dorsal fin.

7 With **pale flesh**, start shading the mermaid's face over the forehead, eyebrows and nose, then down across the cheeks and onto the chin.

8 With **umber**, shade around the eye sockets, across the mouth then across the base of the chin and into the neck.

9 With the **pale green** lightly shade the nose, then with **terracotta** shade the bridge of the nose, the jaw line and the cheekbone, working down to re-define the neck.

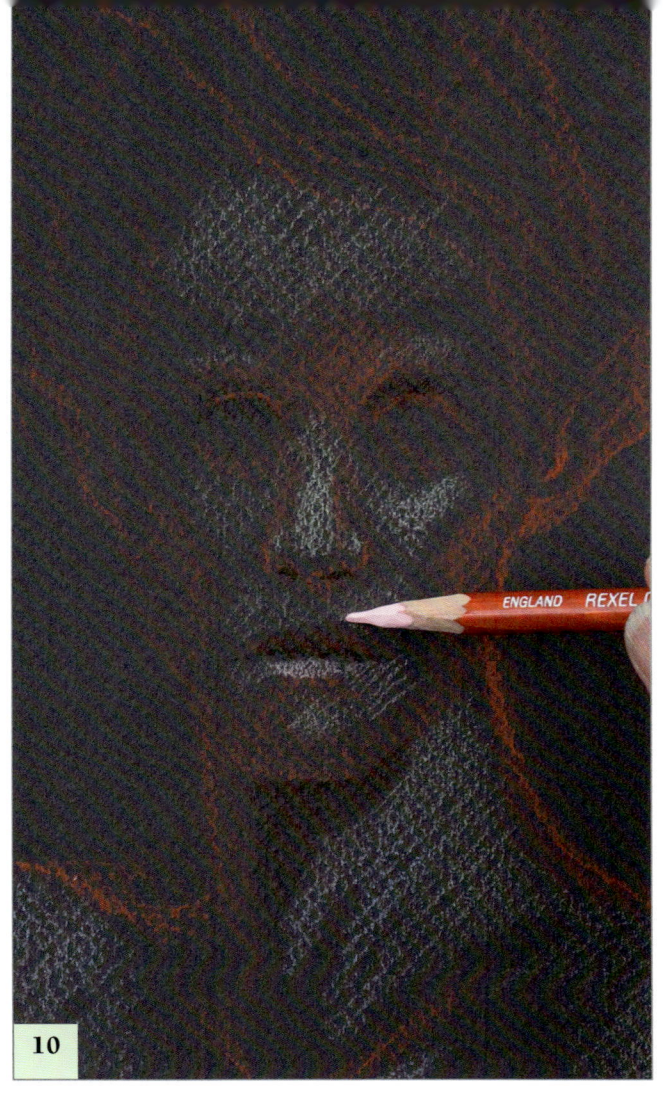

10 Continue to define the edge of the nose with **terracotta**, then use **pale flesh** to shade the lower lip.

11 With **dark green** shade above the upper lip and lightly up the lower half of the right-hand side of the face to define the facial contour. With **umber** darken the left-hand side of the face; apply a strong outline then work light shading here. Lightly shade the mouth. Shade into the chest area to create a v-shape around the collarbone and work light directional pencil strokes from the left-hand shoulder and across the chest.

12 Continue with the **umber** and shade in the eye sockets and across the bridge of the nose. Use **dark flesh** to place a highlight on the chin, the lower lip and around the nostrils; then **umber** to start defining the hair. With **cadmium yellow** establish the upward sweep of the hair and lightly shade across the forehead. Continue down the nose and add a highlight to the right-hand cheek and the right-hand side of the upper lip.

13 With **pale violet** gently blend across the forehead and add highlights above each eyelid. Switch to **olive** and shade down the right-hand side of the face.

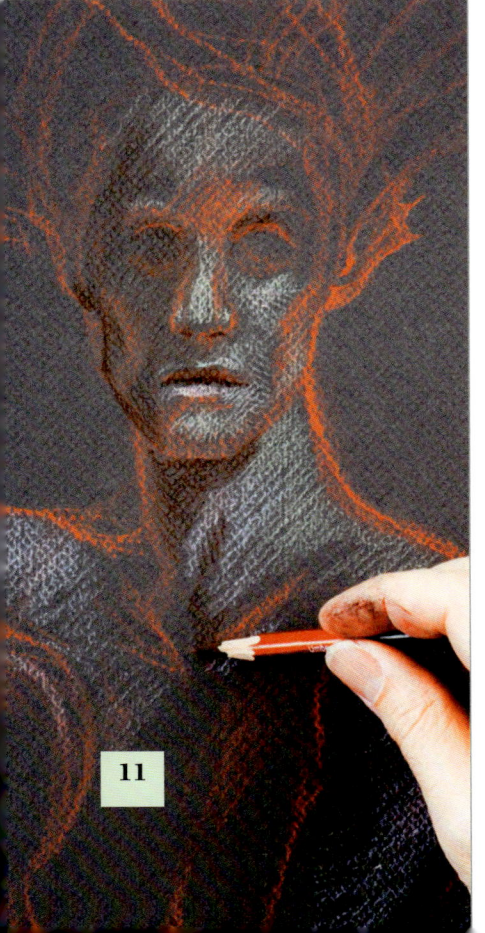

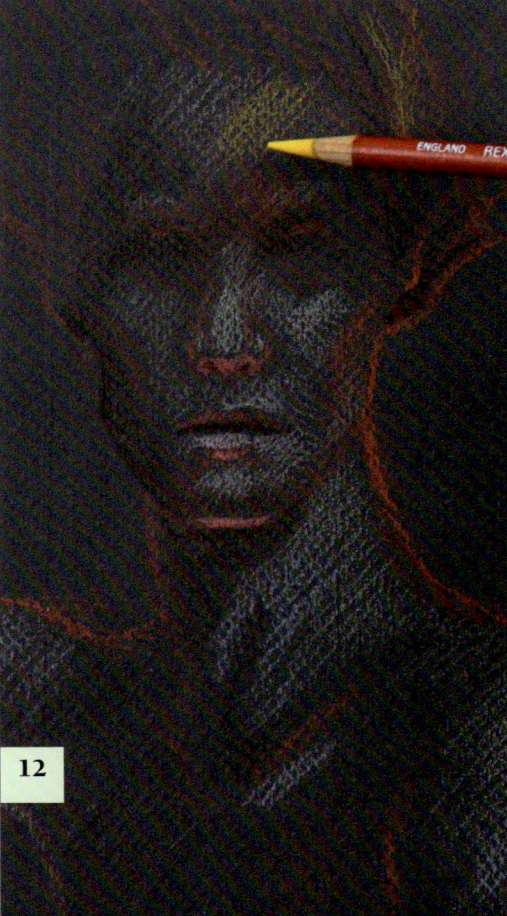

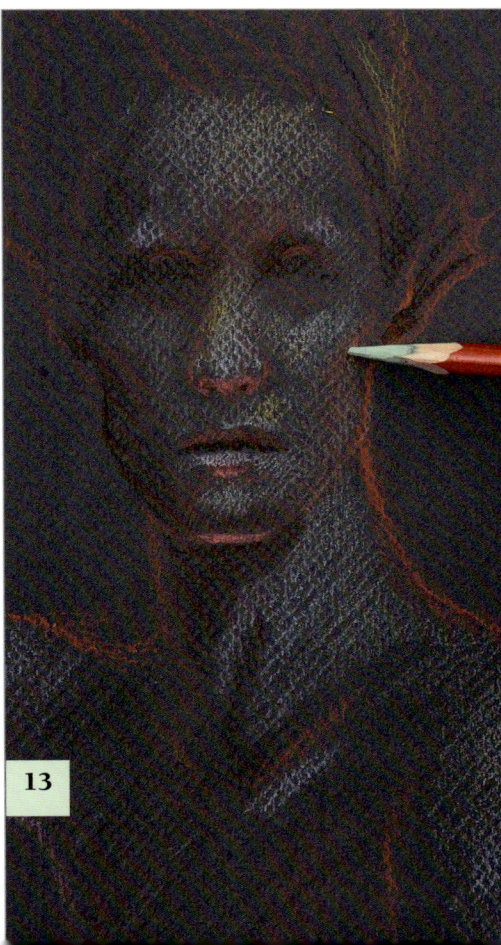

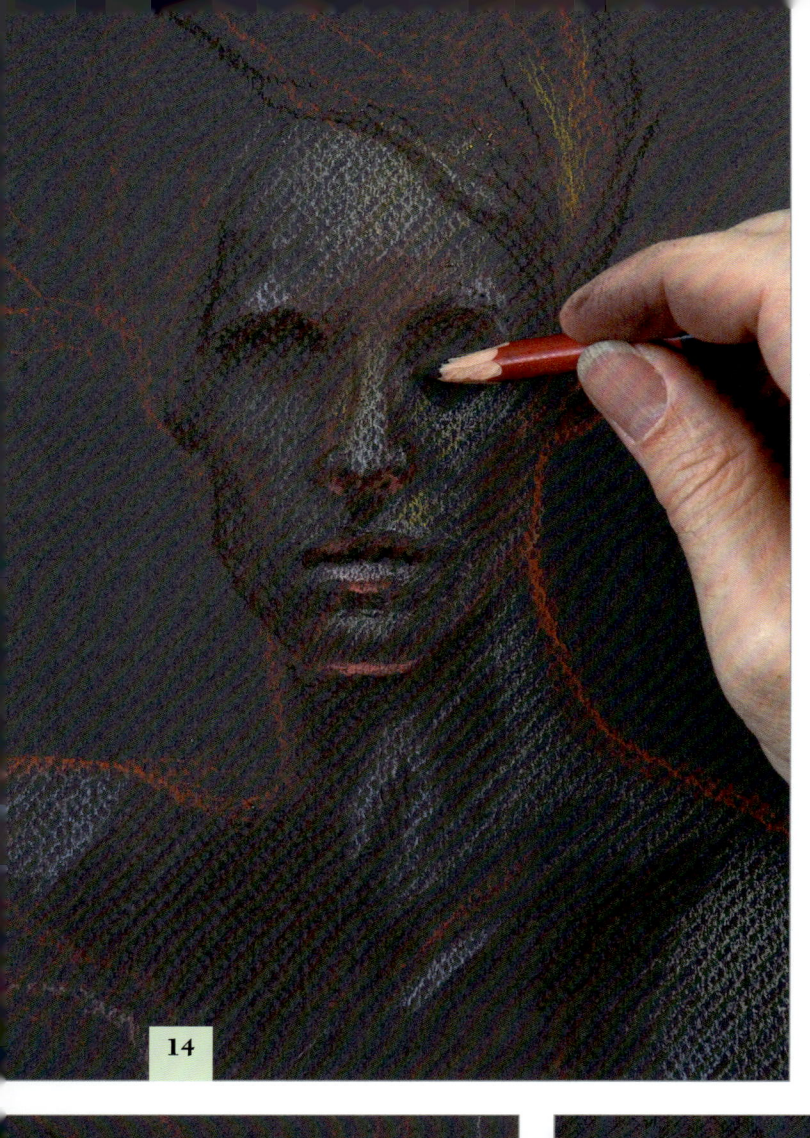

14 With **umber** deepen the shadow on the left-hand side of the face, establishing the hairline here. Continue to outline other key details: the eye sockets, nose, mouth and chin, and around the eyes. Add further shading to the chest.

15 With **pale flesh** continue highlighting the forehead, ear (working into the hair), upper lip and right-hand side of the face; then fill in the eyes.

16 Continue using **pale flesh** to build up the shading on the face and add a star shape in the centre of the mermaid's forehead on the bridge of the nose. Back with the **umber**, develop the contouring under the left-hand eye and down the cheeks, then shade up into the hair with bold strokes. Also boldly fill in some shading in the background.

17 Continuing with **umber**, add further shading to the forehead and deepen the shadowing on the right-hand side of the face. Clearly define the lower eyelids with bold lowlights here. Fill in the eyes.

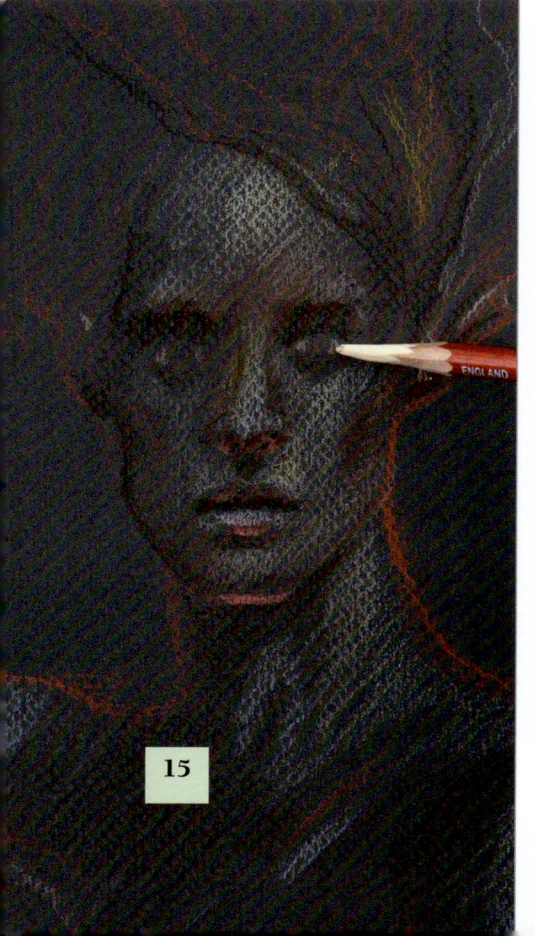

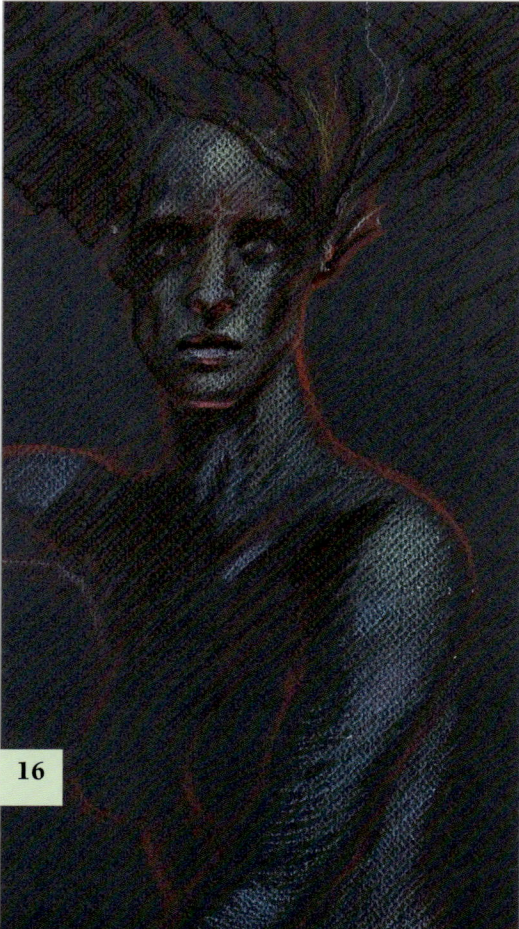

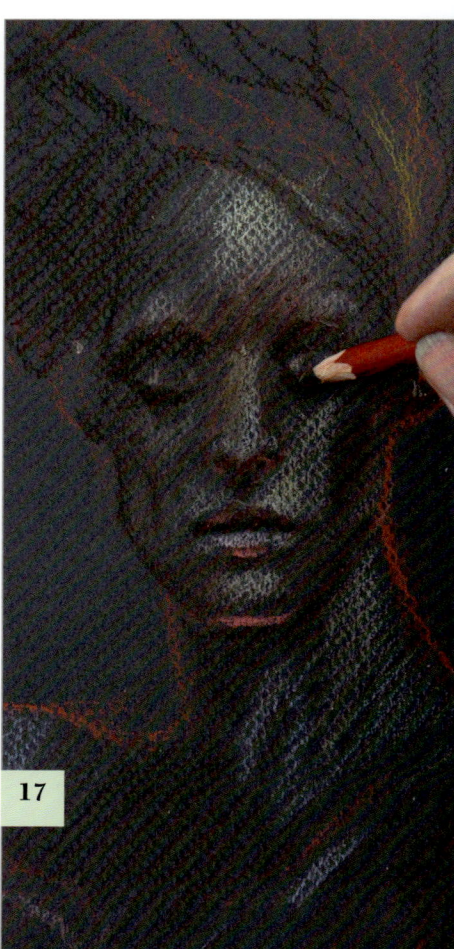

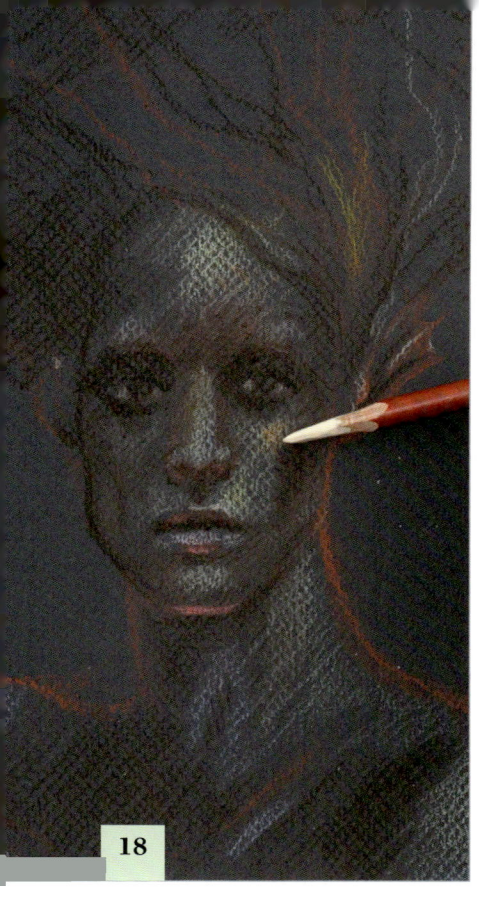

18

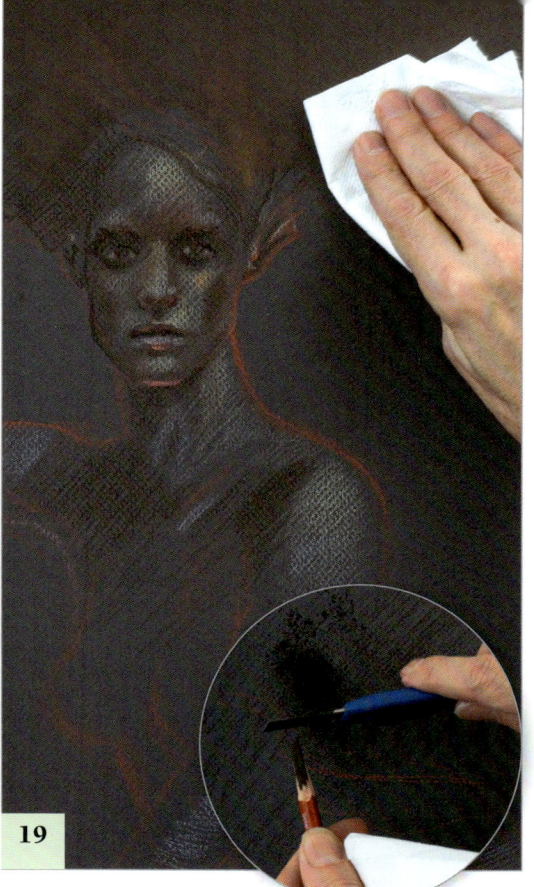

19

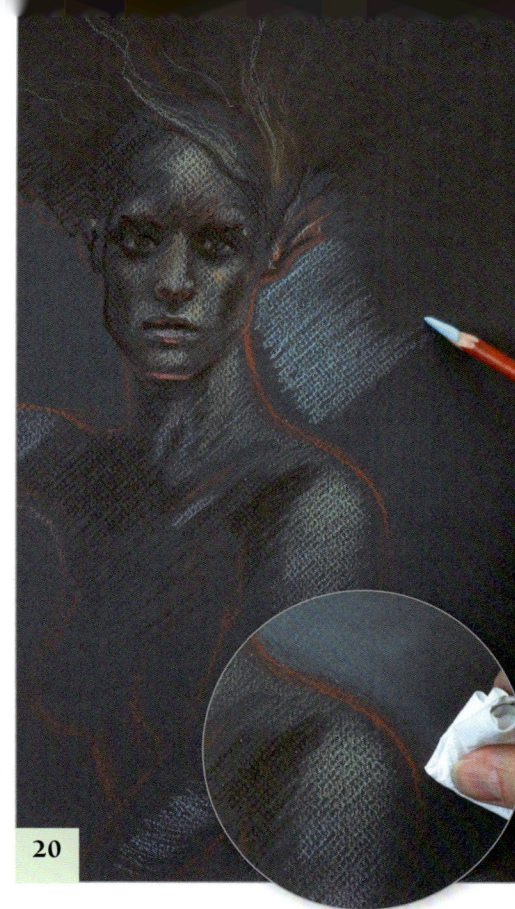

20

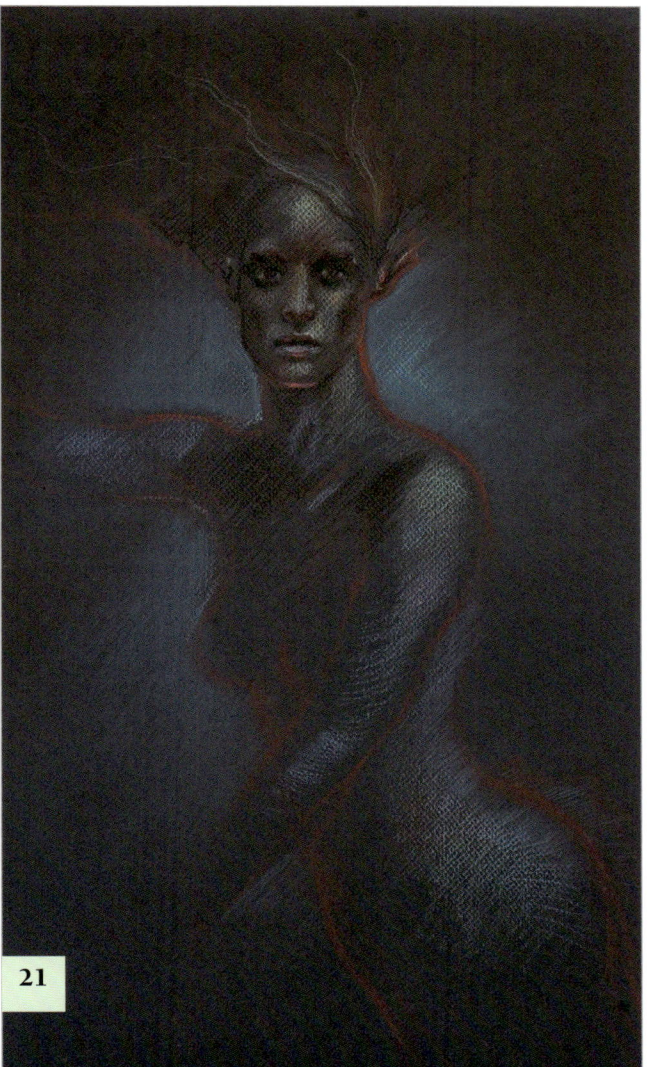

21

18 Apply a touch of **pale orange** to the forehead and right-hand cheek to create a strong highlight; then use **pale flesh** to further lift highlights on the lips, nose and cheeks.

19 To darken the hair and background we are going to smudge. Use the craft knife to scrape **umber** shavings onto the background and hair. Use facial tissues to smudge and blend the colour.

20 With **pale green** add some further shading to the cheek and forehead, and work strands up into the hair area. Then with **pale blue** boldly shade the background to the right of the neck. Again, smudge.

21 Continue shading the background on the left-hand side of the mermaid with the **pale blue**, gently smudging the colour as you go.

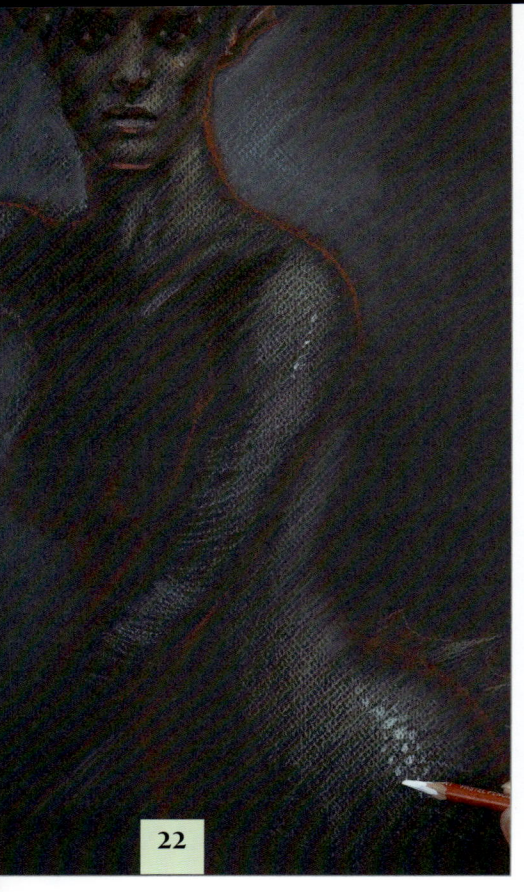

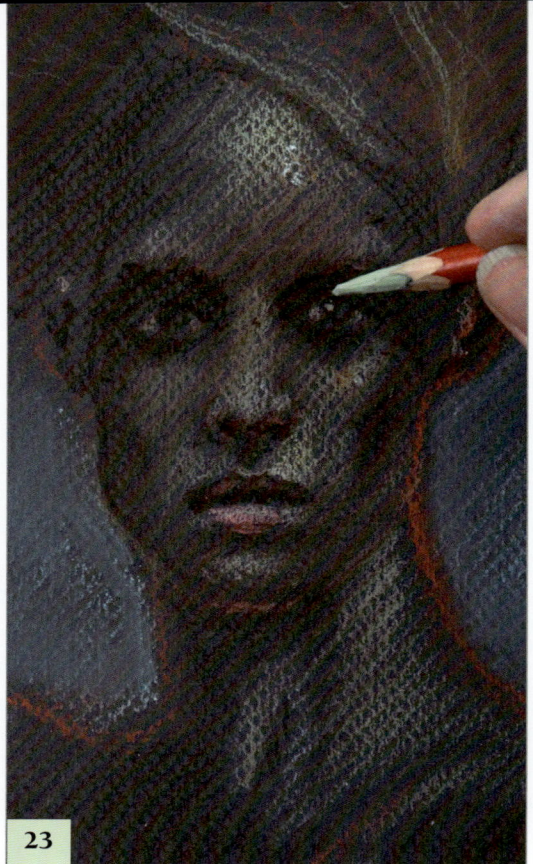

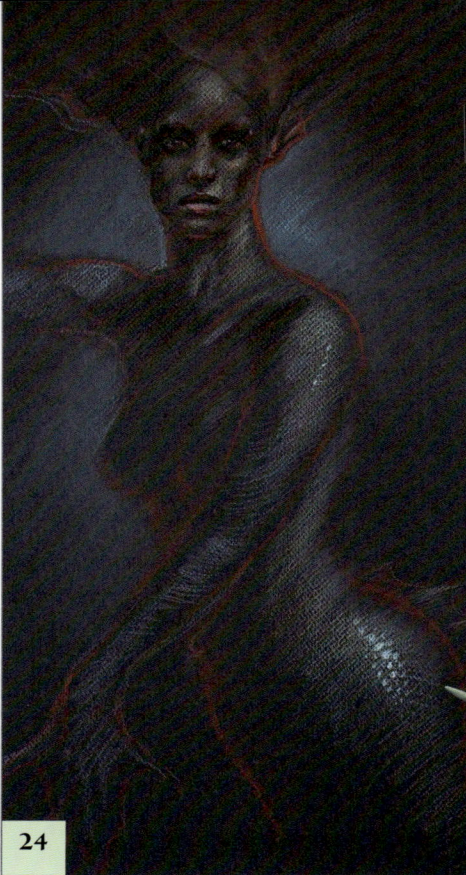

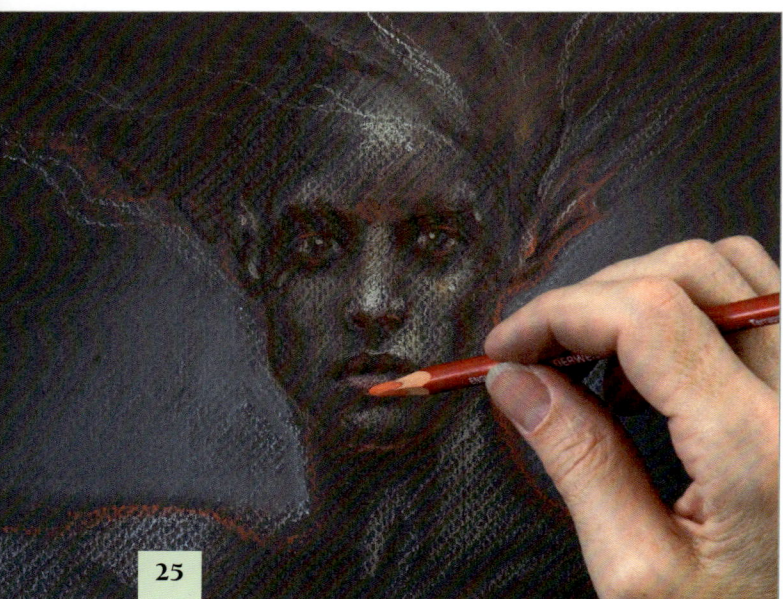

22 With **olive**, add further shading on the side of the neck, working down into the collarbone. Move back to the face to shade on the chin, cheeks and forehead. Then shade highlights onto the dorsal fin. Now with **white**, place highlights down the top of the arm, then mark a small section of scales on the tail.

23 With **umber**, add further depth around the eye sockets and lips. Then use **olive** to add highlights in the eyes.

24 With **pale yellow**, add more strands into the hair then smudge again. Switch to **olive** and apply light shading to follow the contours of the chest then down around the right-hand arm; continue working down the arm with **pale blue** and add a fin by the wrist. With **terracotta**, sketch in a hand, then use **pale violet** to lightly shade. With **olive**, cross-hatch over the hips and down the tail.

25 With **pale yellow** and **olive** add further small highlights to the face and stranding in the hair. With **terracotta** further define the eyelids, the bridge of the nose, the chin and the outline of the torso deeply shading into the left-hand shoulder (*see* Final Image). With **umber** finish the deeper facial shadows and contouring.

WHAT'S NEXT?

This is the kind of image that feels like a preliminary study, not of any one figure, but of a genre. It would be fun to work on a series of sketches. I did not achieve as 'alien' a face as I wished, so it would be worth revisiting in another format to redesign.

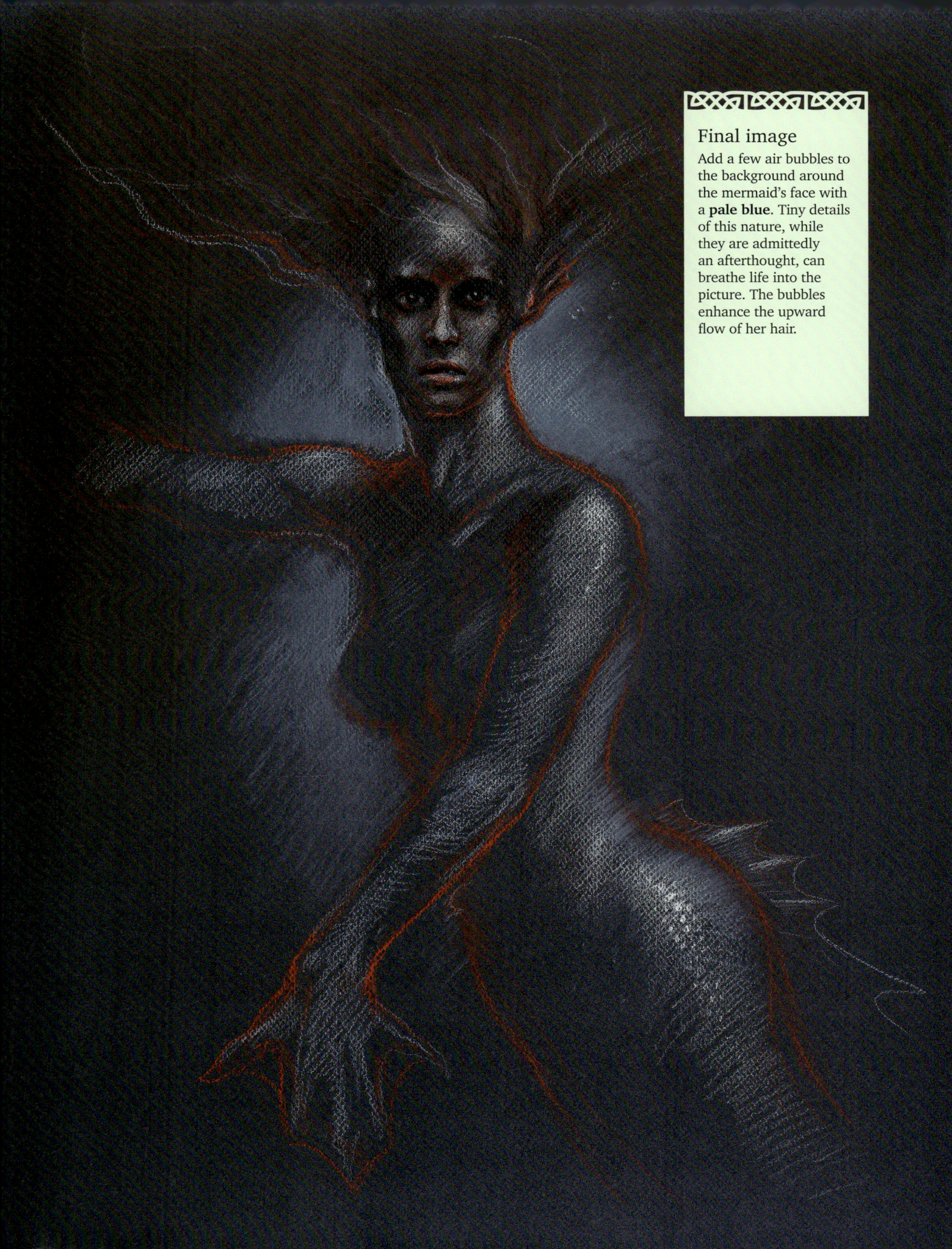

Final image

Add a few air bubbles to the background around the mermaid's face with a **pale blue**. Tiny details of this nature, while they are admittedly an afterthought, can breathe life into the picture. The bubbles enhance the upward flow of her hair.

THE BUSINESS OF FANTASY

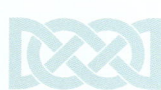

I am still asked what I really do for a living and even when I reply that painting fantasy is a profession, I am then occasionally asked why I don't use my talent to deal with real issues. I can only say that I've never been more serious in my life. This chapter looks at fantasy art in the real world, in books, films and other settings, and offers a basic introduction to getting your work out there and published.

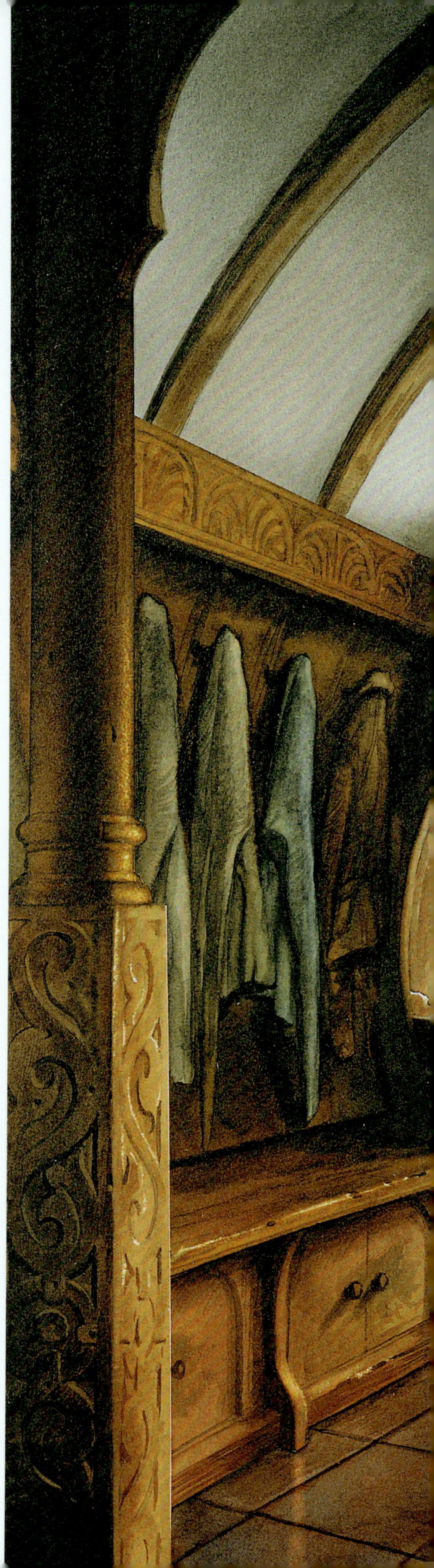

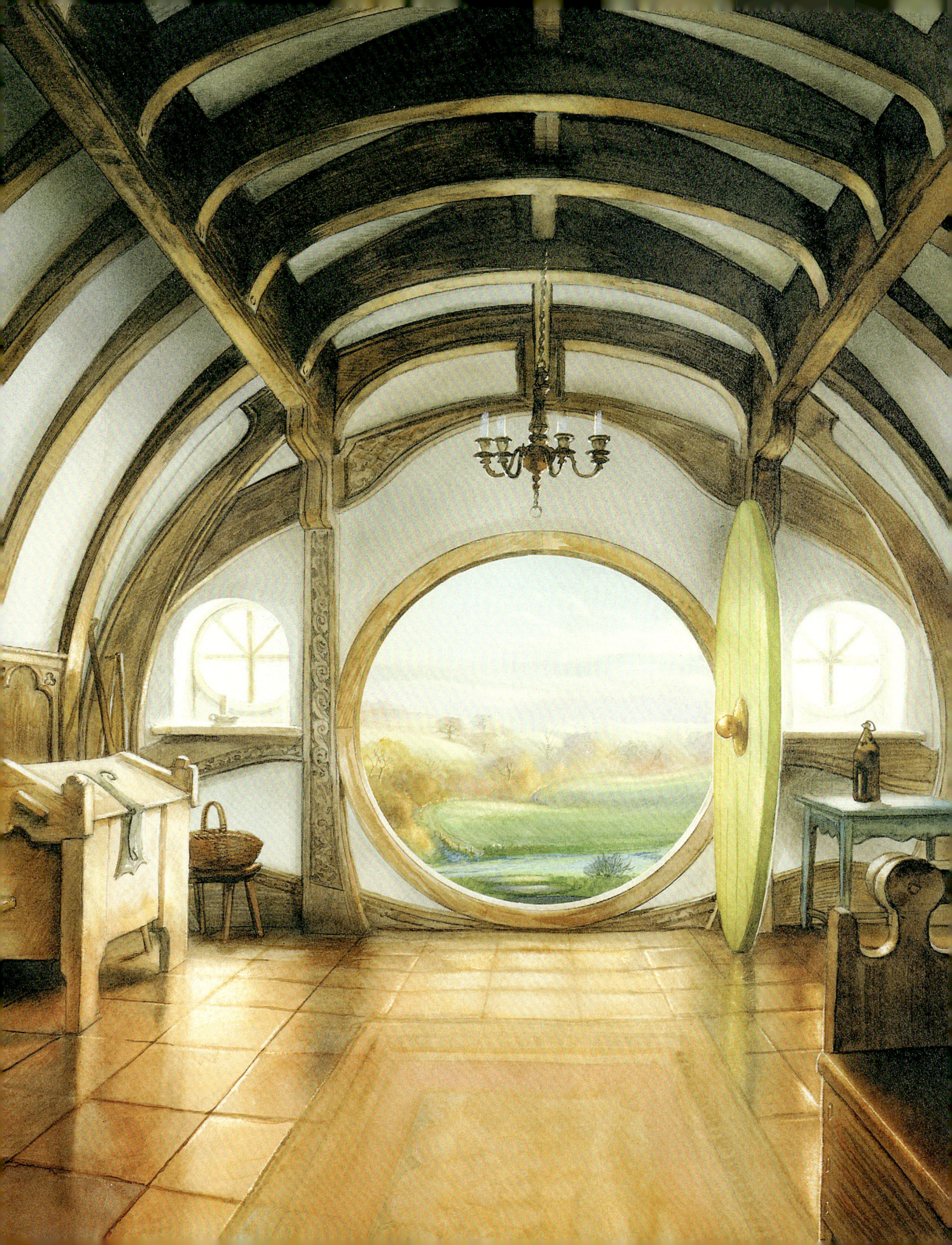

THE BIG BAD WORLD

Working freelance is no easy undertaking. Any
independent will regale you with stories of being cheated,
of broken relationships, both business and personal,
unpaid bills and mysteriously invisible creditors.

Being a freelancer combines sensitivity, business sense, an open
attitude and a hard-sell approach: a contradiction in terms.
Would-be artists starting out generally evolve amidst a public
consisting of admiring family and friends. Stepping into an
art education is both humbling and exhilarating – you're suddenly in a
world of peers, most of whom are likely as good or better than you.

But there is a 'magic' moment, though it is hard to know when it has
arrived, when you can start expecting to be paid for what you do. It is
difficult to determine fees. (It does not stop there: it took me decades to
separate the human relationship with a client from the money side of it.
It can be fraught, believing you're jeopardizing a working relationship
over money, because – like it or not – not just money is involved. I am
miserable when all I get in return is a cheque with no note saying the
work is appreciated. It's like dumping the job in a well.) Also, no matter
your rates, publishers have budgets. You can't always get what you want.
Much of the job is determining a decent return based on print runs,
possible sales, cession of rights, exposure, and so on; calculating a fee
can be difficult. Generally, the less you relish doing the job, the more
you ask. (A parenthesis on 'exposure': when evoked, it is simply a way
of being told that the client expects the job for free. I can't imagine them
trying that with a restaurant or a car mechanic. One word: say no.)

Fantasy art may not always pay the bills on time, but you are doing
something unique, that only you can do. It's worth considering that; if it
cannot occupy the major role in your life, find another spot for it. Don't
lock it away and try to forget. If you feel the need to make pictures, then
it is not a whim – it's a part of your balance as a human being.

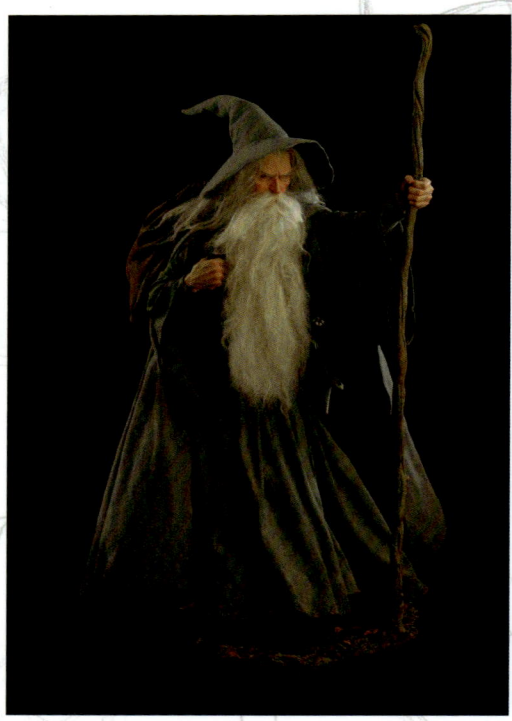

⬆ *Gandalf the Grey*

The original painting of Gandalf was stolen,
along with others, from an exhibition years ago.
It has not been recovered, and I decline any
requests to repaint it. Instead, I commissioned
Oscar Nilsson, a remarkable Swedish sculptor
and model maker, to create a Gandalf based
on that image. (One day, I'll very likely paint
another Gandalf based on Oscar's sculpture.)

Working practice

When you do an original piece of art for a publisher, for an agreed fee, the original artwork remains yours. (Film work and advertising is often work-for-hire, and the original will likely belong to the employer – the contract will specify the conditions.) The publisher is buying the right to use the image for a specific use, such as a book cover. There may not be a contract if you are working for a flat fee (not royalties), but still get something in writing. There is no 'standard' contract you are obliged to accept. It is an offer to be amended and discussed. Once signed, however, stick by the terms, even if you capitulated due to timidity or inexperience. You need not make the same mistake a second time.

There is a fairly strict protocol to delivering work. Once the sketch has been approved, the artwork is based on that sketch. The editor should not ask you to change details that were in the sketch. (For example, if the girl fighting the dragon has long windswept hair and you have clearly indicated that in your sketch, they should not send back the finished artwork and request a braid.) Depending on changes, a second sketch may be requested, but you should have a clear road ahead when it comes to the original. On the other hand, don't make spontaneous changes without notifying the editor: stick to what you have sketched.

If a piece of artwork is refused, you should still be paid, but do not expect the full fee. You are free to sell your picture rights to someone else, so it is rarely lost. If a commission is refused after the sketch stage, one third of the fee is normal compensation. I have had projects die after a few sketches and heard surprise at the temerity of asking to be paid for them. If you have no contract, file that information away. It's a small world – one day the client may be in touch for another job, when you can say: 'Speaking of sketches, remember ...?' and tell them to get lost unless they own up. Generally, though, editors like illustrators and want to do well for their work, so this does not happen so often. Those who rip you off have no intention of working with you again – you are better rid of them. Every profession has sad stories of creator/client malcontent, usually the result of questions left unasked or unanswered and a lack of clarity at crucial junctures. If you do not understand a contract or an arrangement, if you are even just vaguely unhappy or concerned, ask.

Time management
Delivering late puts you in a poor position, so be on time (pot calling kettle black here). Generally, editors allow a margin of time, but don't count on it. The deadline may be just that.

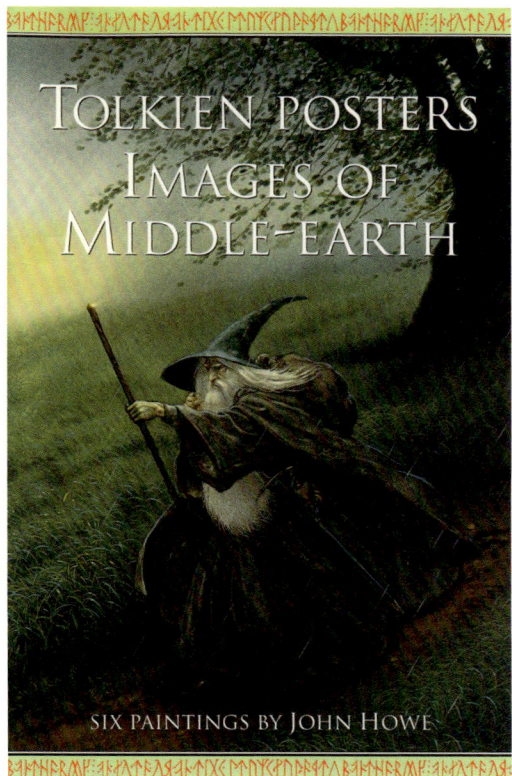
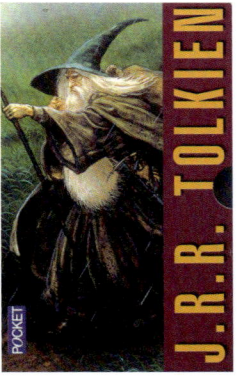
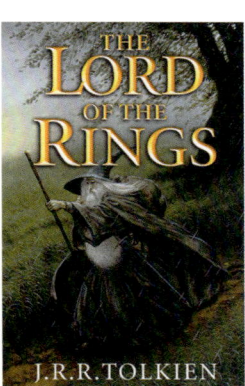
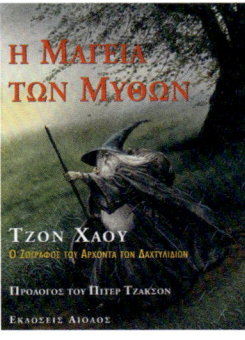
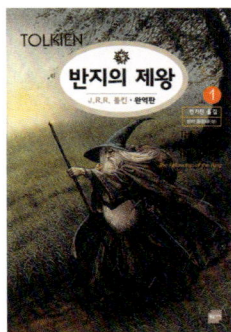

⬆ *Gandalf the Grey* in print

Perhaps my most ubiquitous image, *Gandalf the Grey* has appeared in many places (he is always in a hurry), often without either my or the publisher's permission, and has been repeatedly pirated on the most unlikely articles worldwide.

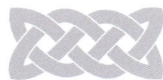

BOOK COVER ILLUSTRATION

You can't judge a book by its cover, or so it's said – but prospective buyers do. Each cover is meant to state loudly, '*Pick me up. I am far more interesting than the other books. BUY ME!*' A striking image can draw the eye from across a room.

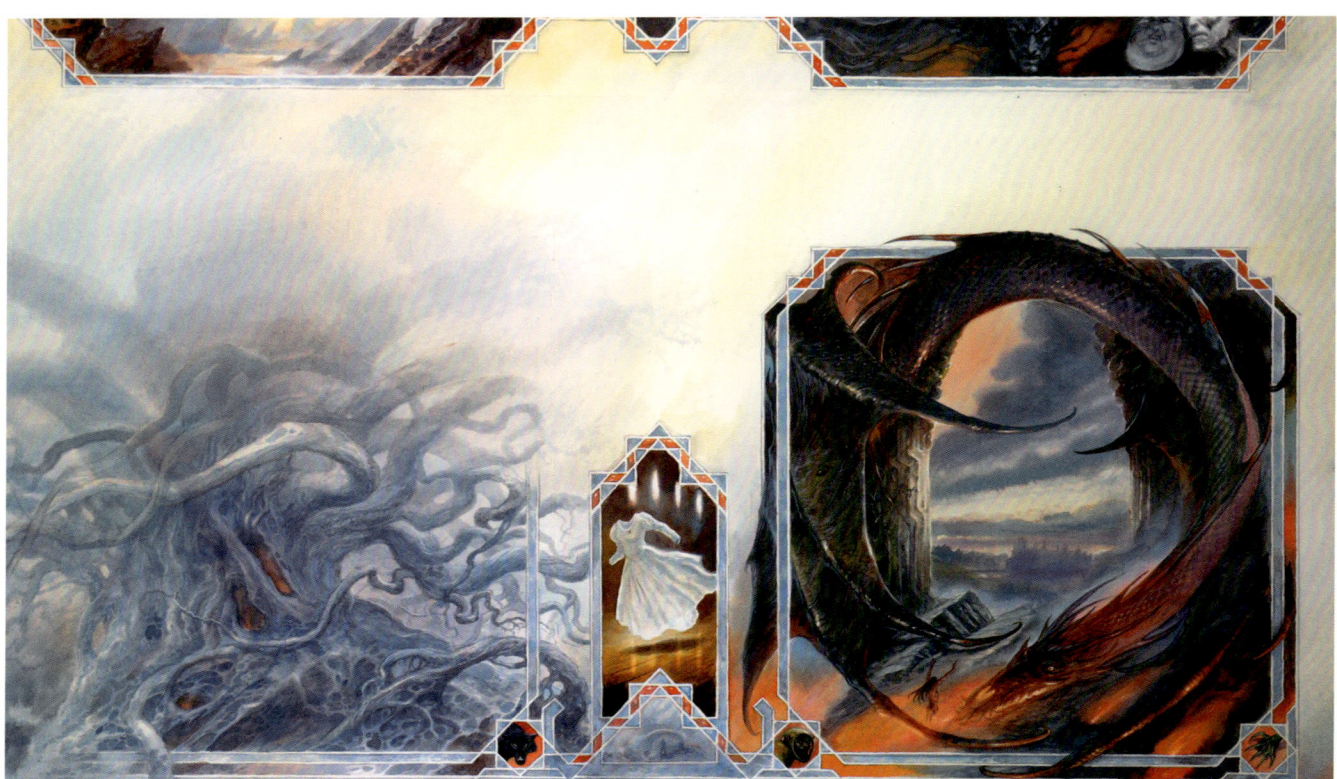

A manuscript may be cumbersome to read, but if you are commissioned for a cover, it is important to know details such as hair colour and length, straight or curved sword, black dragon or red. But a collection of details does not make a cover – a read-through of the book, unhindered by note taking, gives an idea of the story's tone and atmosphere. Some cover commissions come as a brief – a short description of pertinent images, designed to let you know what the editor would like, perhaps with comments from the author and often accompanied by a cover layout, complete with title copy and dimensions.

⬧ *The Dragon-Charmer*

I've always called this image my fake Alan Lee cover. Alan had done the artwork for the first book in the series, Jan Siegel's *Prospero's Children*, but had no time to do the second. The publishers asked if I could step in. I declined. They asked again. I demurred. They persisted and I gave in. I used Alan's layout, and thoroughly enjoyed trying to find a continuity of style and technique.

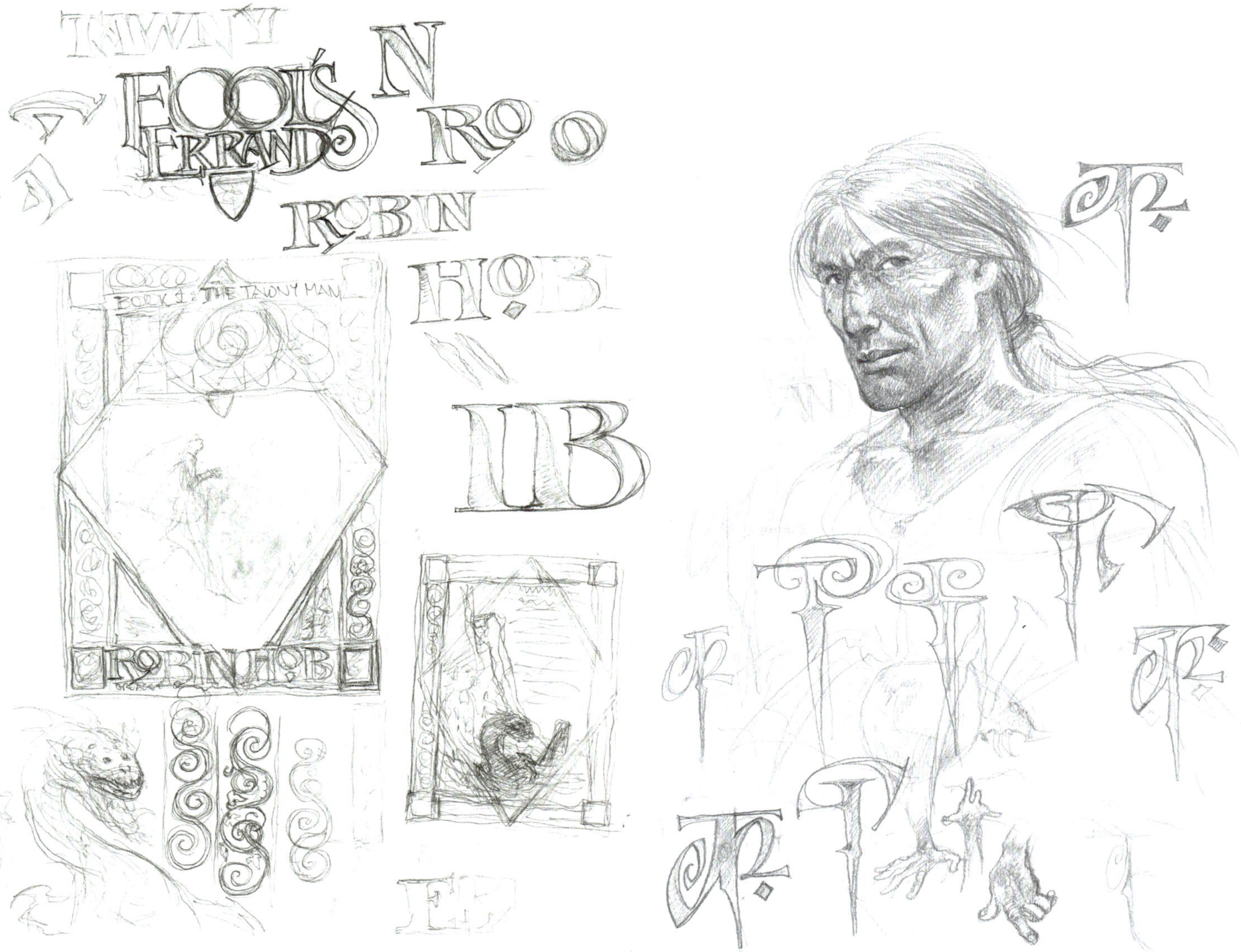

Hobb scribbles

I very much enjoy fiddling with signs and symbols. In Robin Hobb's trilogy *The Tawny Man*, abandoned stone obelisks called 'skill pillars' allow brave individuals to be teleported from stone to stone. The enticing theme resulted in doodling to find an appropriate set of symbols. I would happily have designed all the skill pillars in the land. (I also found an attractive new signature on the way – you never know where a skill pillar will lead you.) The three Robin Hobb series I've worked on have decorative panels around the cover artwork. These remain the same throughout, new images being dropped in for each novel.

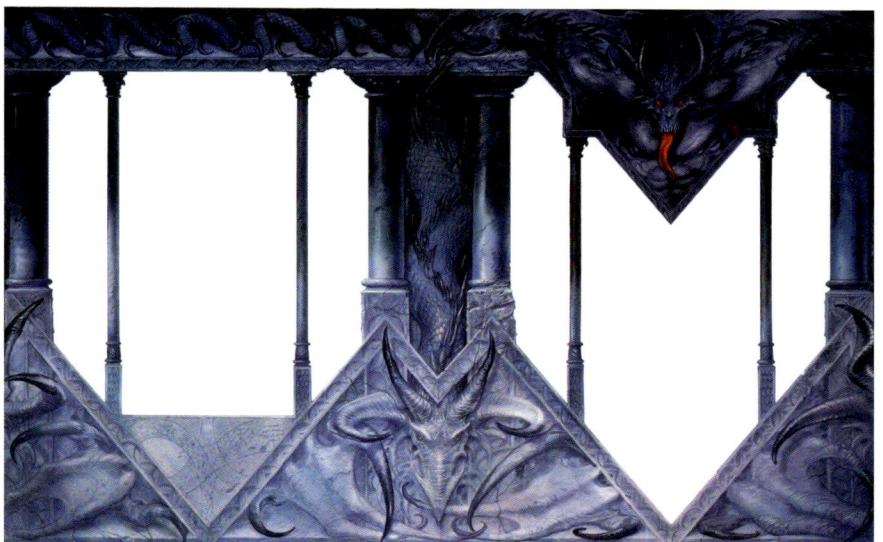

The Tears of Artamon

I enjoy doing decorative borders, especially reproducing stonework and aged masonry. I have a deep drawer full of images of crumbling stone walls. Each trip finds me lagging behind snapping façades and plinths in every style.

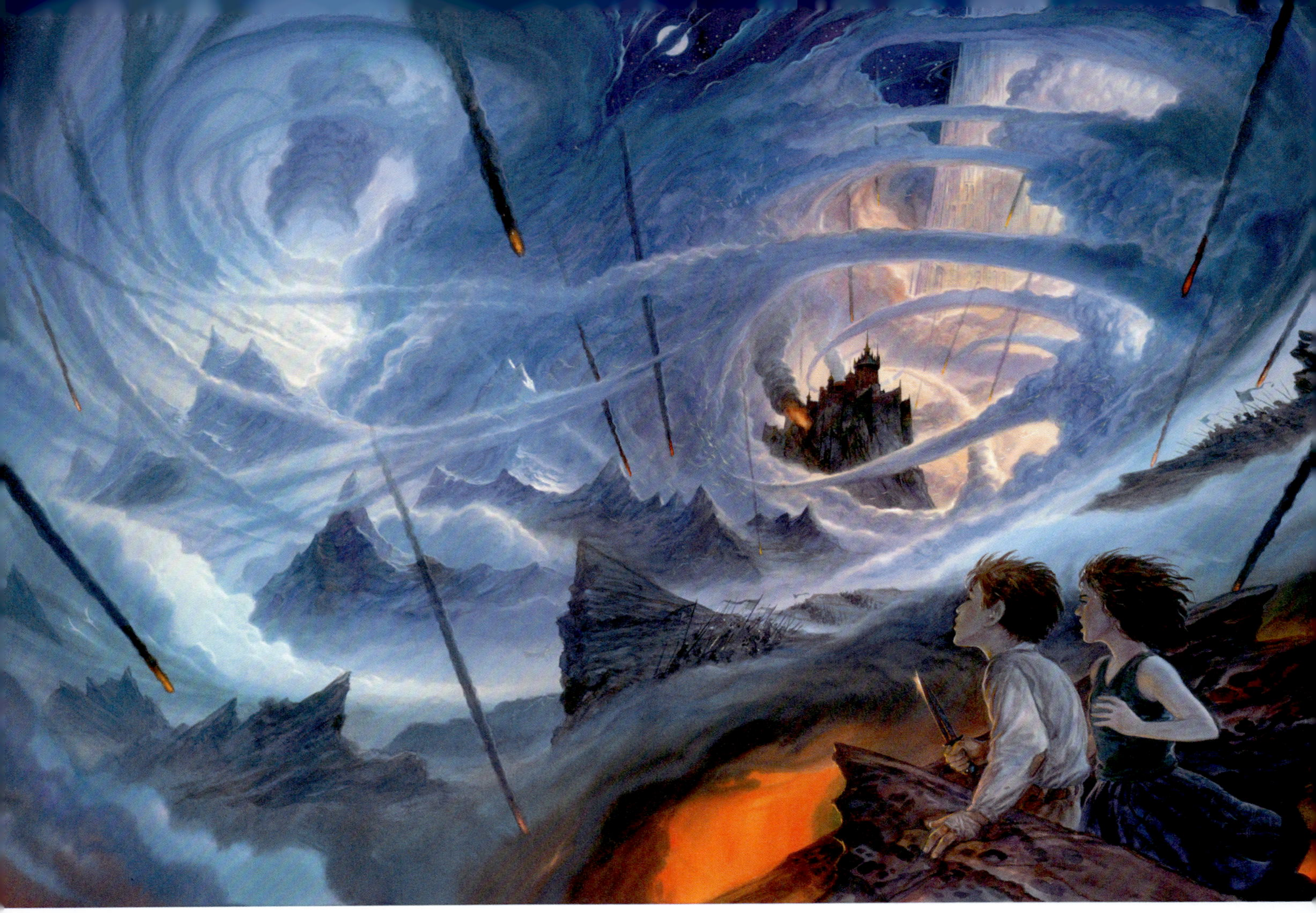

Sometimes a cover brief can live up to its name – the shortest I ever had was: 'Subject: Elves. Treatment: Fantasy.' Another said: 'John Howe as artist. Tree border to bleed into the front cover from the left side, covering the spine and back cover. Front cover image, a grassland background impaled by a cavalry sword. Details to come from author.' Ideally, though, your image should intrigue, not give the story away.

I prefer when the images literally leap straight out of the text. Many authors are visual writers, so the images come easily; others are less so, and it can be a struggle to find an image in a text. You may go straight to the author for information, but only with the editor's prior approval.

Your image should leave room for layout contingencies (however constricting this might seem) but should not be a concentration of detail on an otherwise vague, empty ground; it should function on its own without the copy, not ruined by the intrusion of texts. It is also advisable to finish your image completely, as a painting that can stand on its own, regardless of what will appear on the cover. Every image deserves that care, and you may be able to resell the rights in the future. I advise generally doing vignettes and borders separately, but it's up to you.

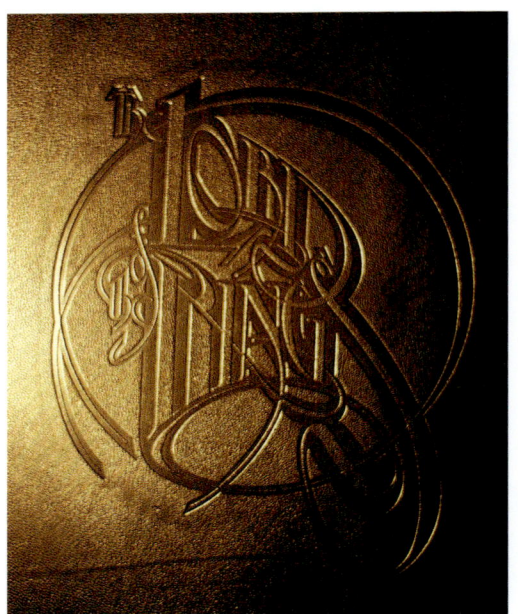

↑ *Lord of the Rings* logo
My love of lettering dates from school, where I designed banners for school events, and later painted signs to pay for art school.

⬅ *The Amber Spyglass*

This illustration was done for the cover of Philip Pullman's novel. It was turned down. So I did it again. That was turned down, too. This was one of the few times I have had a cover refused, and certainly the only time twice.

➡ *Yvain's Madness*

Spurned by the woman he loves, the knight Yvain goes mad with grief and retreats into the forest. Though the focus of the picture, he is isolated and remote: the oppressive canopy of the tree clinging to the precipice and the fathomless fog express his state of mind.

⬇ *Saffron Fool*

This is more an elaborate doodle than an actual illustration. It began with a spiral and ended up with a bit of a story attached.

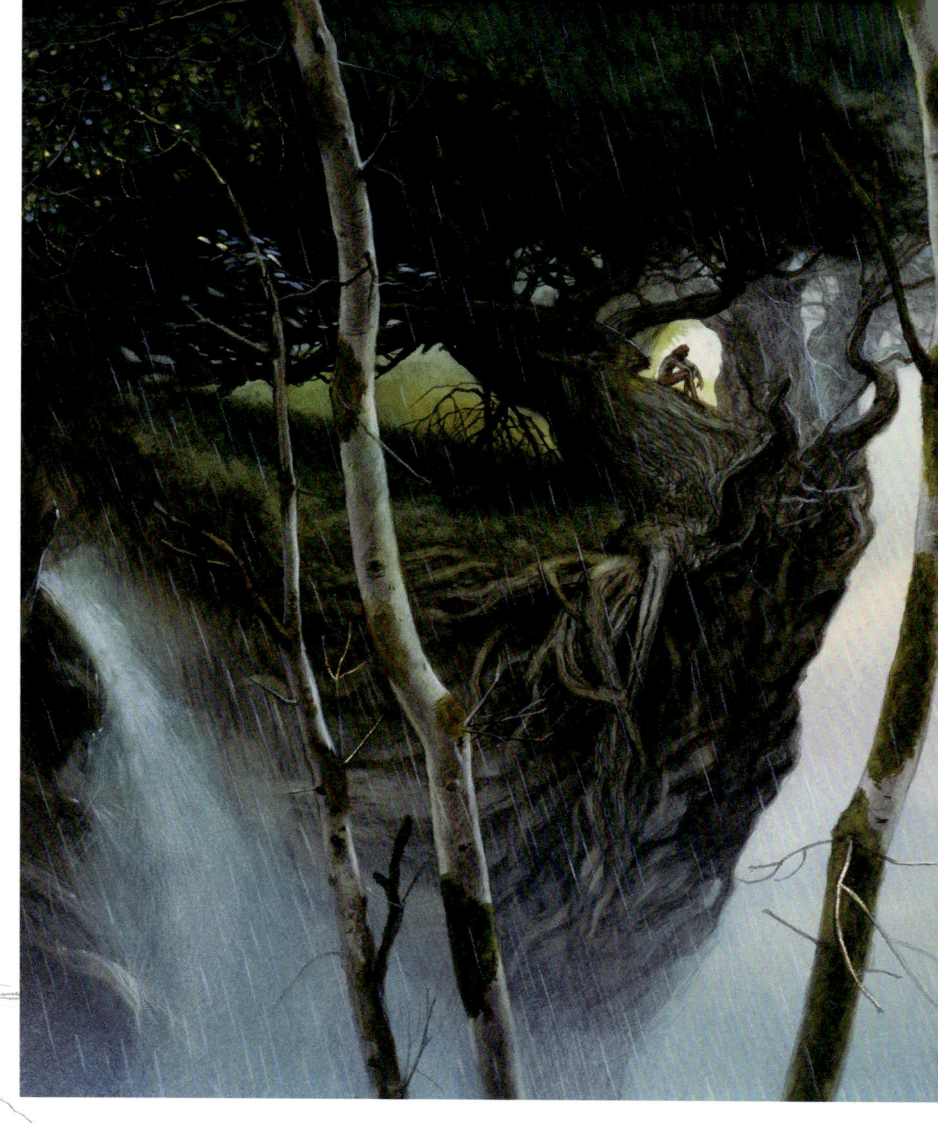

Illustrated books

Illustrating the interior of a book is a rather different undertaking from the cover. The narrative is the primary guide, and the images should possess a narrative logic of their own. Moreover, with children's books, it is mandatory that the image and the text to which it refers be on the same double spread. Children's books are a vocation in themselves. For novels, try to space the illustrations as evenly as you can throughout the book.

Graphic novels

These are another member of the extended family of illustrated books, perhaps the border region between the kingdoms of illustration and comics. Less image-intensive than comics, they nonetheless impose the same strict discipline. Many artists are able to navigate with happiness between the two.

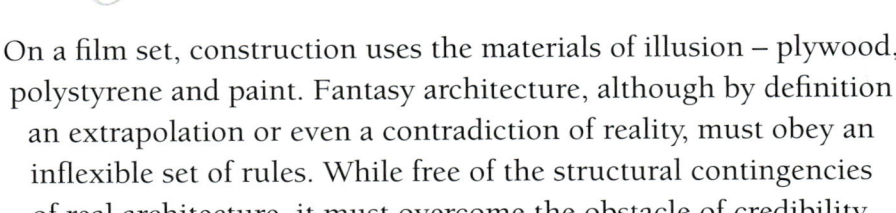

THE BIG SCREEN: SET DESIGN

On a film set, construction uses the materials of illusion – plywood, polystyrene and paint. Fantasy architecture, although by definition an extrapolation or even a contradiction of reality, must obey an inflexible set of rules. While free of the structural contingencies of real architecture, it must overcome the obstacle of credibility.

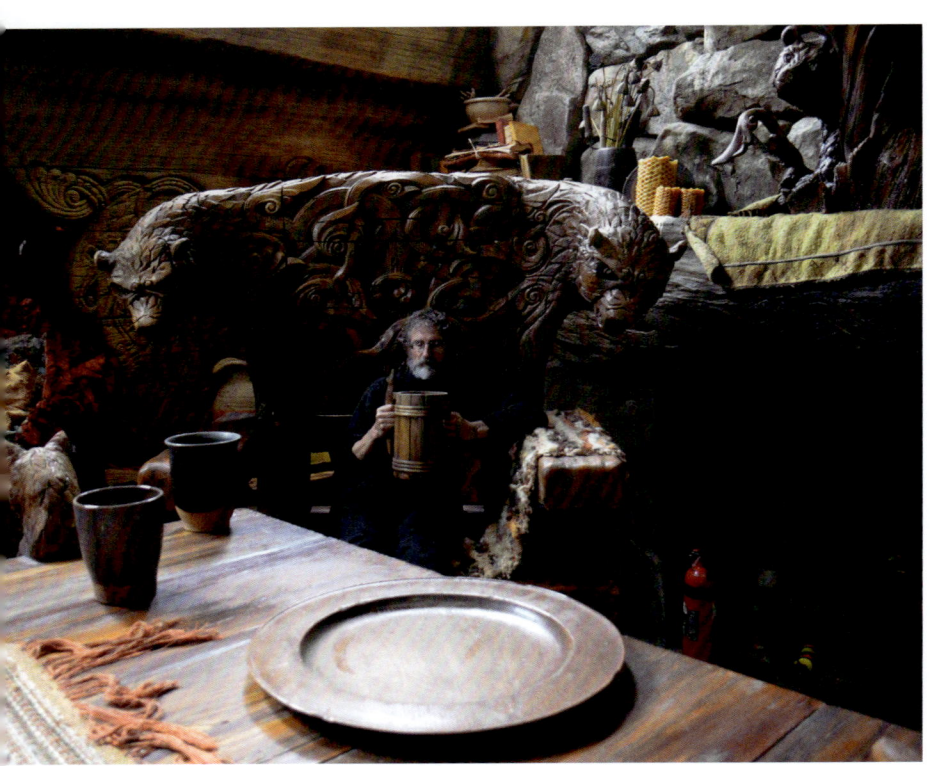

⬆ Sitting in Beorn's chair

'I'll never finish this,' I'm thinking … The outsized set of Beorn the Shape-shifter's house in *The Hobbit* trilogy was a delightful place to wander in. We are so accustomed as adults to having everything built to our scale – any disproportion of familiar objects is enchanting *and* disconcerting. Every element of the set was designed to underline Beorn's nature. Every element of design in a film is an opportunity to enhance the credibility of the whole.

A leap of faith is required for a fantasy world to appear real on the screen – any element that hinders this transition will compromise the willing suspension of disbelief. The best compliment I can imagine for it is that it is not noticed – it is participating so fully in the storytelling that it draws no attention to itself. The homeliness of Bag End, for example, plays a crucial role in 'selling' *The Fellowship of the Ring* (and by extension, the remainder of the trilogy) to the audience.

A set is the embodiment of a culture portrayed, one that is often impossible to describe in great detail, depending on the script. Like costume, a set underlines a (probably fictional) culture and helps to provide a convincing atmosphere. Much is added digitally in post-production, but the set gives the actors an environment to work in. (Actors typically do not see sets until shoot day; it is gratifying to hear exclamations of surprise and delight when they first see it.) Fantasy film environments have no reality beyond the internal logic of the film, but still must strive for acceptance at face value. Our experience of film prior to computer technology told us landscapes had to be real; creating the illusion of a wide landscape was near impossible. Now, as the sky (and

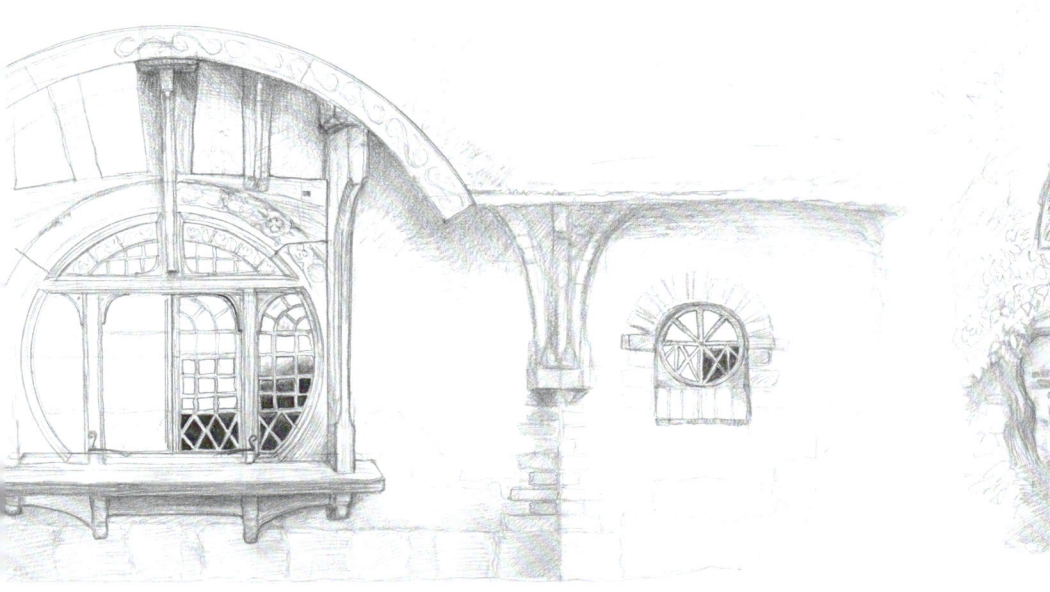

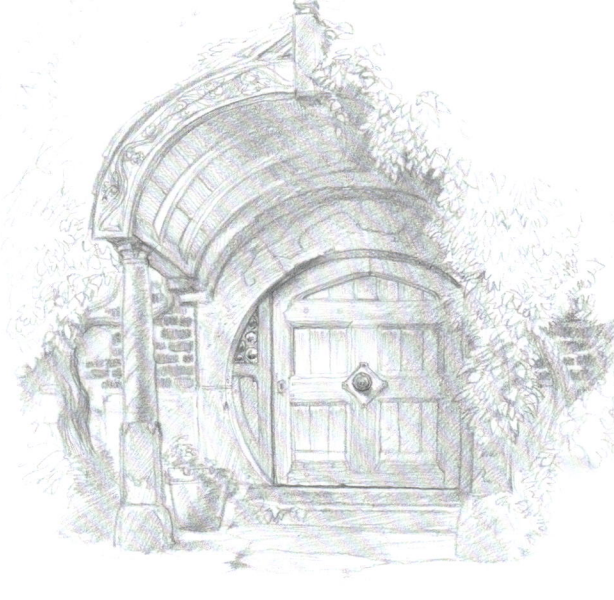

Bag End

Bilbo's home is the grandest in Hobbiton, but like many old houses, all is not perfectly symmetrical. I'm quite proud of the little sliding shutter over the window on the left, and the fact that one corner shows the remnants of arches.

Bilbo's Back Door

Beside the world-famous round green front door, Bag End of course has a back door. (I also designed a secret door, but it was of course never built, and wouldn't have been visible anyway.) The designs for the hobbit houses were endless variations on simple shapes. Thinking in terms of the materials used and staying true to certain motifs and design elements will usually lead in the right direction.

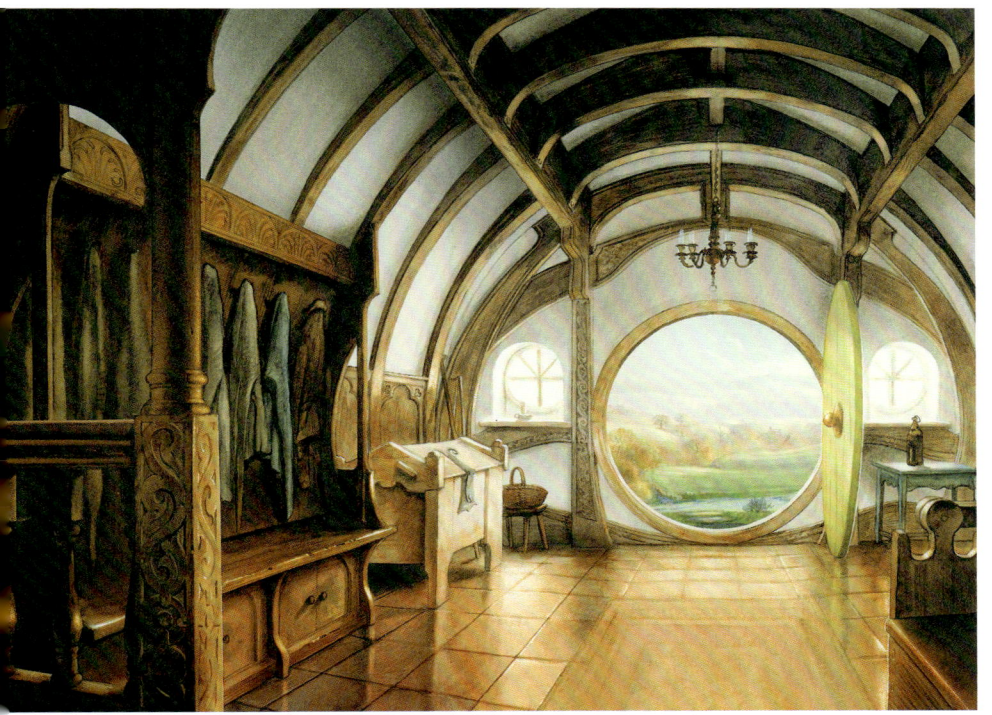

Barad-dûr

I had already designed the Dark Tower and the Fell Beasts earlier on, so this illustration was an opportunity to revisit the Nazgul against a wider background. The river of fire running parallel to the road to Mount Doom is borrowed from one of J.R.R. Tolkien's own depictions of Barad-dûr. The plain of Mordor is twisted rock in swells and waves, as if a rough sea had suddenly turned to stone.

Hobbit Dwelling

This image was commissioned for the cover of a map of Bilbo's adventures. It draws on several influences: the description by Tolkien, of course, but also a love of Norwegian stave churches and Scandinavian Jugenstil. Several years later, Peter Jackson said: 'I know what the hall looks like, but how about the rest of the place? Can you just do an about-face and draw the other rooms?'

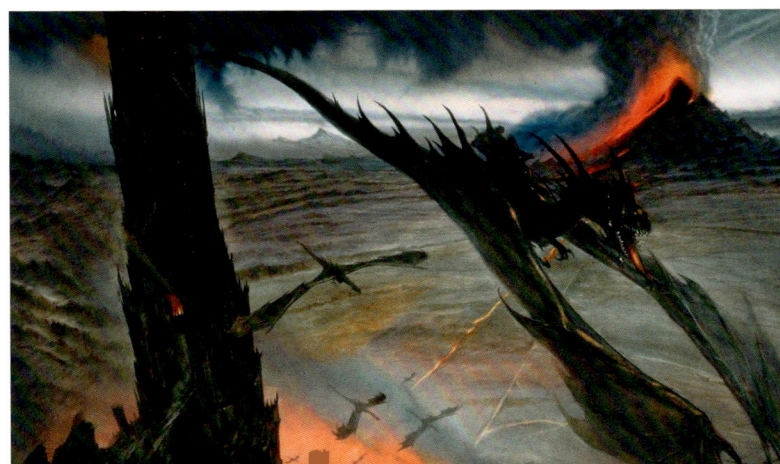

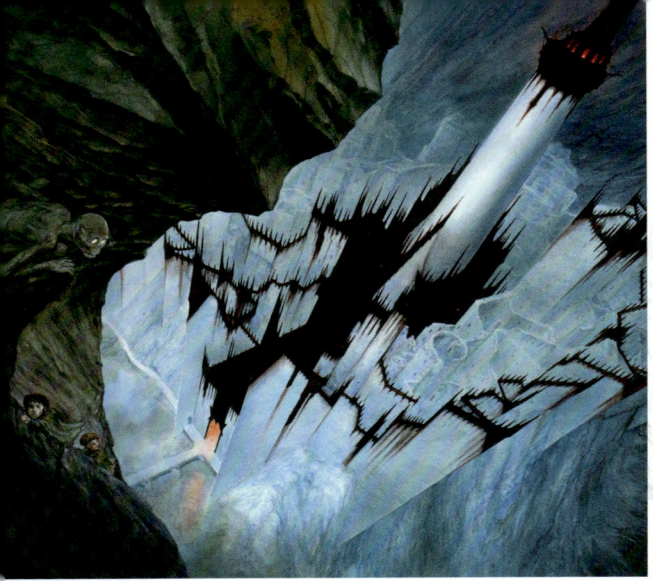

⬆ *The Endless Stair*

In the films, the Endless Stair was placed directly opposite the causeway leading out of Minas Morgul: the idea was that the hobbits and Sméagol would be dangerously exposed when the army issued forth. The overhanging rock creates a visual whirlpool of vertigo dragging at the desperately clambering hobbits.

⬇ *The Foundations of Barad-dûr*

The full drawing (this is a detail) was several yards across, and took hours to draw. This enforced delay is valuable: the mind is always just an element or two ahead of the pursuing pencil, and the design has time to grow and change throughout. It's a process rather like discovering a landscape through heavy mist, as the wind pushes it aside.

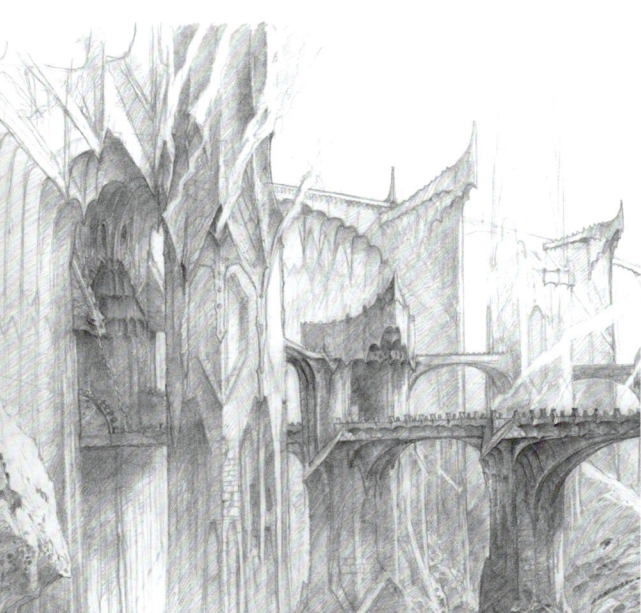

beyond) is the limit, the threshold of credibility is not so lightly passed without stumbling; the audience's expectations have matured with the technology. Fantasy elements are often nestled in real environments, or a real environment is pieced around them. The harmony of this relationship is crucial, to be carefully managed ahead of post-production compositing. In interiors, the 'real' may be present in materials used and views glimpsed beyond windows, but only when actual locations are chosen does the real world come to the fore. The choice of location is based on the atmosphere created by the concept art, but the two rarely match exactly. Other factors – accessibility, rights of way, budget – generally carry far more weight, and original concepts are adapted to fit.

A nodding acquaintance with history is a plus for the concept designer, especially with fantasy, which often has deep roots in myth and legend. The larger your vocabulary, the more intricate and convincing your work can be. Knowledge of techniques is also useful – techniques as much as culture define the 'look' of any fantasy world. Credibility is the goal. The largest outdoor set built for *The Hobbit* trilogy, the city of Dale, was big enough to wander around as you would in a real town. Many people told Alan and I that Dale reminded them of somewhere they had visited abroad, but no two named the same place. Beorn's house was entirely inspired by Cyclopean stonework, stave churches, Haida longhouses and Norse carving. The carvers creating the set were intimately familiar with Maori culture and carving. The result is a mix of all those things, at a size that dwarfed humans. We are clearly in another world.

Rather than an inconvenience, the adaptations made to blend original concept with location are the best and final exchange between fiction and reality. Concept work can become, rather than a pure flight of fancy, an apprenticeship in a foreign culture. The acquired knowledge (fictitious, but coherent) lets the designer adapt the idealized structure to the contingencies of the terrain, accepting the intrusion of reality. This is the best way to avoid the 'designer's dream' look, the deadliest trap. The abrupt slope, inconvenient incline, sudden bend in the river: these are the jumping-off points from concept artist to real architect in a non-existent world. If you are going to make make-believe, then believing yourself, even briefly, even as a sort of game, has no serious side effects, just special ones. This is also true for the other visual departments. Nothing dates faster than bad design. History, however, never looks fake. While this doesn't at all mean that historical reference should be a cut-and-paste image bank, it can be a never-ending source of inspiration.

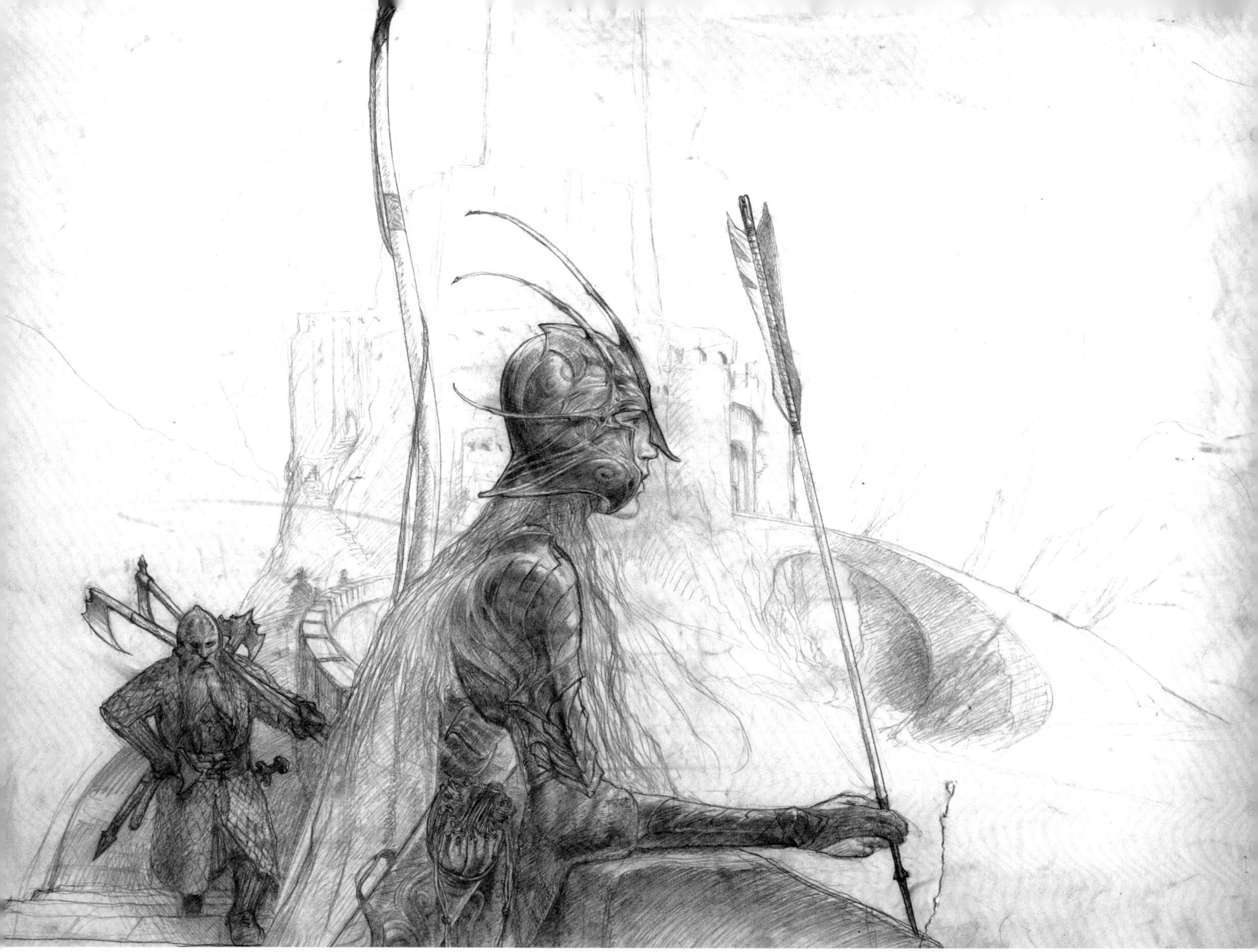

↑ *Legolas and Gimli at Helm's Deep*

A doodle that started with Legolas' helmet, this quickly expanded into a full view of the Deeping Wall with Legolas and Gimli awaiting the arrival of the enemy. (Luckily I started more or less in the middle of the paper.) I ended up designing elven armour, the shooting glove, quiver, arrows and bow along the way. This is the kind of pencil-in-hand musing I prefer, when the sketch is begun with no precise idea in mind and simply grows of its own accord.

↪ *The Breaking of Narsil*

This scene was originally sketched out as a possible fresco in Rivendell, but is rather too focused on the action and not sufficiently on the decorative elements. One of the ambitions for the movie was to create a proper armour for Sauron, who was to appear in the prologue.

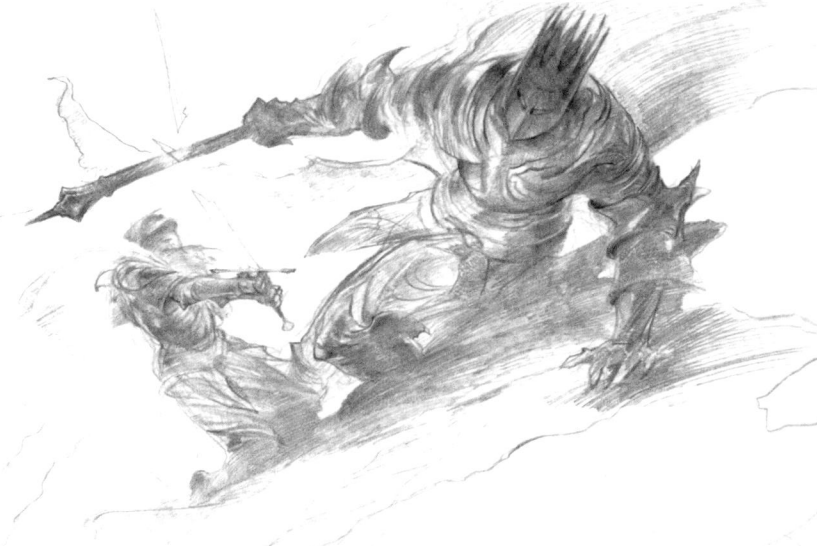

PUTTING YOUR WORK UP FRONT

Presenting your work is secondary in importance only to the work itself. Remember that first impressions aren't entitled to replays, so it's worth doing it well.

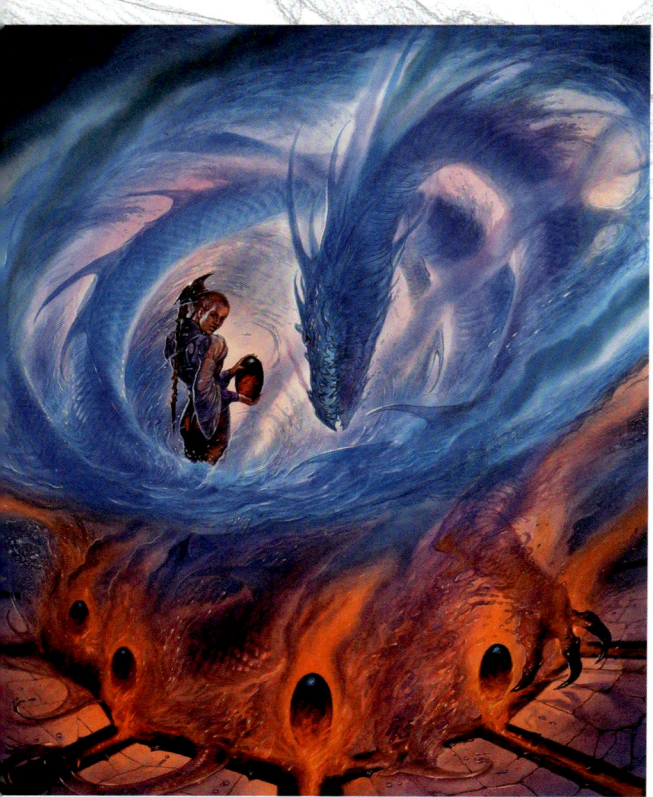

⬧ *Mistress of the Pearl*

A water spirit dragon imprisoned in a cage of smoke and flame was one of the more novel requests I've had for a book cover. I enjoyed rendering the dragon coruscating and dissolving in his airborne whirling tempest. But the paper was too tensely stretched on the board and split across the middle when I was cutting it free. I would now take both pieces to the scan shop and put them back together in Photoshop.

You may be shy – many illustrators are – otherwise you might have chosen a different profession, but don't let that hinder you. Your first encounters may leave you in a bit of a lather, but they do get much easier. Broadly speaking, presentations can take two forms: a wide palette showing your capabilities, or focus on what you think represents you more deeply and clearly. The former will show that you have a variety of skills, which may land you with a variety of commissions. If you're at ease with changing styles and techniques, this is not a bad way to go. The latter will reduce your potential array of clients, but eventually gets you work that suits you more intimately.

The big appointment

✦ Whatever you do, make your portfolio painless to shuffle through; art directors see a lot of work, so make it easy for them.

✦ Never apologize for your work while showing it – remain relaxed and make comments only if you see a spark of interest in a piece, otherwise let them do the looking.

✦ Don't over- or under-present your work. Run-of-the-mill student work beautifully mounted is as bad as professional work spilling from a tattered portfolio. You are dealing with professionals – they have seen it all before, but are ever hoping to discover new talent.

✦ Keep your presentation simple and smart; it can be in a stylish press-book or a portfolio. Work of varying sizes can be mounted on simple sheets of sturdy paper (not mat boards) to unify the presentation. Plastic sleeves will protect it and present a homogeneous format.

✦ Have something you can leave with the person you see: this can be a card with link or QR code, a printout with your details and a few illustrations. Take their card. Offer to send follow-up samples.

✦ Do not leave originals with anyone you have only just met. You can send them a low-resolution file or a printout.

Afterwards

✦ Don't be discouraged by a polite refusal or a 'come back next year': all this means is that they don't need your skills that month or for that particular publishing schedule.

✦ If you got along well, send samples of new work in a month, saying what a pleasure it was to meet them.

✦ Don't hover over your inbox waiting for news; it's not constructive. Yes, you desire a response, but you should be knocking on many doors, not fretting about one or two.

✦ Don't worry about editors stealing your work: anyone in their right mind prefers a happy illustrator to a disgruntled person they can only rip off once (unless you have a poor memory). This said, work is still pirated or reproduced without permission – unless you have assigned rights to a third party, all rights are yours. Non-commercial use is acceptable (I am thinking of kids printing out your work to have it signed at conventions) but any commercial use should be the object of an agreement.

Online challenges

New technology brings incredible advantages *and* challenges to the freelance artist. I have lost count of the times I have had t-shirts, posters or mugs with my artwork on them removed from online shops. Here, you can measure the distance that separates the law from its application. If your work is pirated abroad, there is little chance of obtaining satisfaction. Closer to home, the chance of reaching an agreement is good. (My work is popular with Russian death metal bands, for example; you learn to live with it.) Online platforms do their best to attract sellers to their marketplace, but make it arduous to have illegal knock-offs taken down. Filling out often elusive forms can be time-consuming and complicated. Be patient – decide which violations are worth the trouble to pursue.

Why is an agent useful?

It is simple: selling yourself and your work is hard – a job in itself. Either you go where the work is or your work goes there for you. The first is not always possible, but an agent will ensure that the latter happens. Good agents keep in touch with clients, update portfolios regularly and of course provide a guarantee of sorts that you are a safe bet. Agents aren't afraid of using the 'M' word – money – and usually their commission is compensated for by the fact that they won't accept your being underpaid. But if you don't want the job, you can refuse. Given the profusion of platforms, you certainly can get your work out there yourself. You can self-publish: prints, posters, cards, etc. You can sell prints at conventions, or use platforms such as Kickstarter to publish your work. (This can be successful, but demands a grand investment in time and energy.)

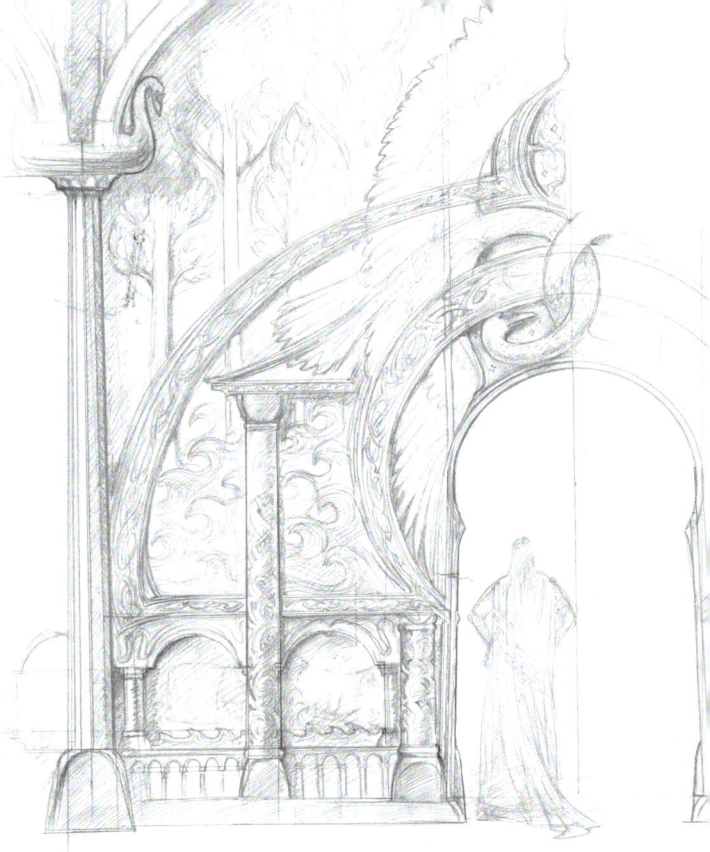

⬆ *Elrond's House*

Of the numerous designs I did for elven architecture, this is one that I prefer. Scandinavian and Slavic Art Nouveau were the principal guides, using a number of themes conceivably dear to elves: ships, swans, waves and trees.

Same again?

Inexperienced illustrators often approach publishers who have just published a book that appeals to them. These could be the last publishers to approach – if they've just done that book, they often have no plans to do a similar one for years. (If it's part of a series or they are a specialist publisher, this may be different.)

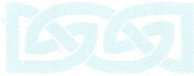

THE FUTURE ...

While it's a cliché to ponder upon tomorrow at the end
of a long book of thoughts, if you've gotten this far
I'm sure I will be forgiven and you will read on.

Career plans and agendas are an illusory exercise, given the nature of the illustrator's profession. It is a full global undertaking, while remaining very personal. I seldom know what I will be working on in three months' time; to have a year's work planned in advance is a rarity.

I have become aware of the increasing weight of managing one's own little empire of copyrights and originals. It can be time-consuming; the temptation is to spend more time doing that, than actually working. Even more tempting is being invited to talk about what I do – it is easy to end up not doing anything, just talking about it. I decided to keep my drawing to myself and not take on assistants or manage any pencils other than my own. I enjoy contact with people whose lives are made up of words. Pursuing the visualization of a world growing in a writer's mind is exciting and rewarding. They are generally strong-minded – if they don't like your interpretation they will say so.

Years ago, I penned the chapter 'Why I Don't Do Sketches' in the first book of my collected work (*Myth & Magic*, HarperCollins, 2001). Since then, I've filled nearly a 100 sketchbooks – about 4,000 drawings. While this reveals a remarkable inconsistency of view, I'd prefer to present it as a shift of certainties from the practical to the philosophical.

I am far less determined now to apply particular methods and techniques, and ever more unshakably convinced that means should not be confused with ends. Increasingly, I want to leave irreversible decisions as late as I can, to keep the dialogue with a painting going as long as possible. It seems clear to me that the pursuit of the pictures in one's head can never be reduced to a recipe and I am ever more wary of my own opinions. I will gladly offer guidance and advice, but never mail-order methodology. That's why this book is, or at least I hope it is, an artful fraud. Disguised as a how-to-draw book, it's actually something from which,

in the doing, I have learned as much as you. Trying to put into words thoughts I have only ever put into images has convinced me of many things about which I had never reached any valid conclusions. Hopefully the answers this book provides will not interfere with your work, and the questions it poses (which considerably outnumber the answers) will allow you to draw conclusions of your own and in turn ask the right questions about what you do.

Finding your own voice is a quest. It will lead you both inward to meet the artist inside, and outward to experience the world. In the world is where the images are, but to find them, you need to cultivate interests, build skills and learn to trust your imagination. It truly is a never-ending journey.

How many words is a picture worth? A few anyway. Thank you for reading them.

25.10.2000

➼ *The Abandoned City*

The pastel by Fernand Khnopff, who produced exquisite paintings of Bruges, has always struck me, with the empty pedestal and sea lapping at the cobbles. I sent a postcard of it to Parisian author Claude Clément, asking if she would write a story for it. We went to Bruges, where I sketched and took photos. The book was published by Éditions Casterman. This is my rendering of Khnopff's painting, almost unchanged. Anchoring fantasy in real places lets you strip away centuries of urbanism and discover the spirit of a place. *The Abandoned City*, from *La Ville Abandonnée*, John Howe © CASTERMAN S.A.

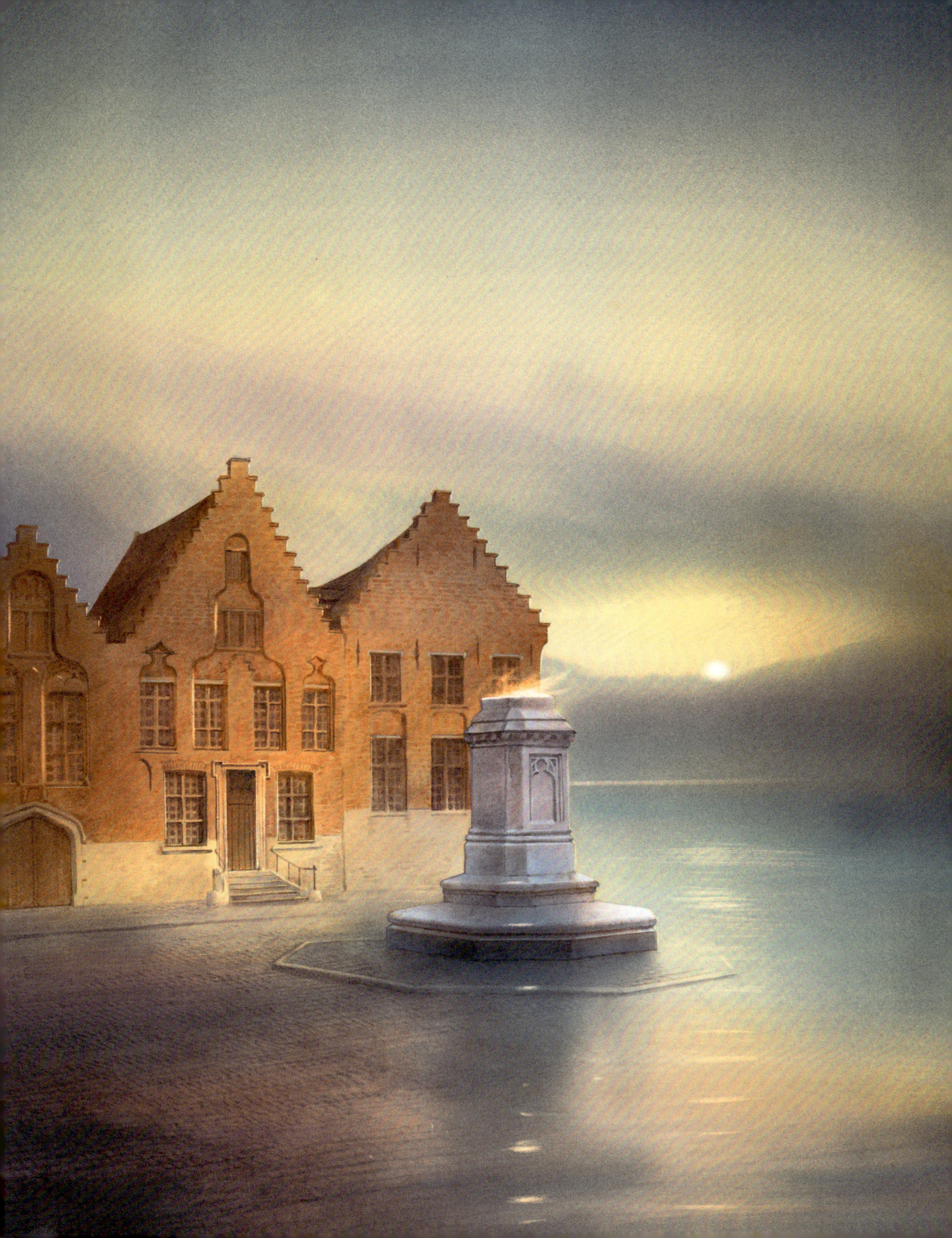

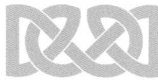

AFTERWORD
BY ALAN LEE

There is an eternal fascination with the idea of the artist revealing the secrets of the studio; as though by studying its layout, the arrangement of paints on palette, or the way that those pencils are sharpened we can grasp the methodology and absorb some of the inspiration.

I've looked at many of these 'How To …' books over the years – usually while leaning against a shelf in a bookstore – mentally checking off their tips and wrinkles against my own, and filing away any new ones for future use. Sometimes the pleasure is akin to that of a well-produced recipe book – despite all those beautiful photographs of the ingredients and dishes, the luscious descriptions of tastes and smells, I know I'll never get around to cooking anything more complicated than pasta. I'll avidly read descriptions of the process of Fresco painting, memorizing luscious words like 'arriccio' and 'intonaco', reckoning up the amount of fresh plaster I could cover in a day, even when I know that I'll be doing nothing but fiddly little watercolour illustrations for the next year.

Occasionally though, I'll stumble across something that offers more than daydreams and wishful thinking; John is a dreamer too, but he is also very practical, well-organized and – crucially – articulate, and is able to drip feed those vital insights into his artistic processes without either confusing or boring the pants off his readers. Brilliant! At last I'll have a book about an artist I admire which engages the mind, stimulates those parts of me that get excited by pictures of paintbrushes, and which, most importantly, inspires me to further experiments and efforts. And all that for the price of an afterword!

A few years ago, John and I contributed to a book called *Fantasy Art of the New Millennium* (since 'Millennium' won't be a buzz word again for a while the publishers changed the title to *Fantasy Art*). We were together at one end of the technological spectrum, with our burnt sticks and pigment, with those who work entirely on computers at the other. We were both quite happy to be part of the rearguard in this forward march; amazing work is being done by illustrators working in digital media at the moment, but there is always the slightly uncomfortable feeling that you are exploring a playground designed by people who are much smarter than you. This love of traditional methods is also tied in with a mutual fascination for earlier times and ancient stories.

What I really like about working in these older techniques – along with the satisfying smells and smudgy fingers – is the sense of being in a dialogue with your materials. At times the dialogue is awkward – or even abusive – but there is always the sense of responding to, or being inspired by, how the paint is behaving on the paper. It is this quality of immediacy, fluidity and lightness of touch that appeals to me, and John's work is a perfect example of how a liveliness of mind, acuteness of vision and an urge to look at things from every possible angle can be reflected in the translucent, shimmering surface of a watercolour.

"THIS LOVE OF TRADITIONAL METHODS IS ALSO TIED IN WITH A MUTUAL FASCINATION FOR EARLIER TIMES AND ANCIENT STORIES"

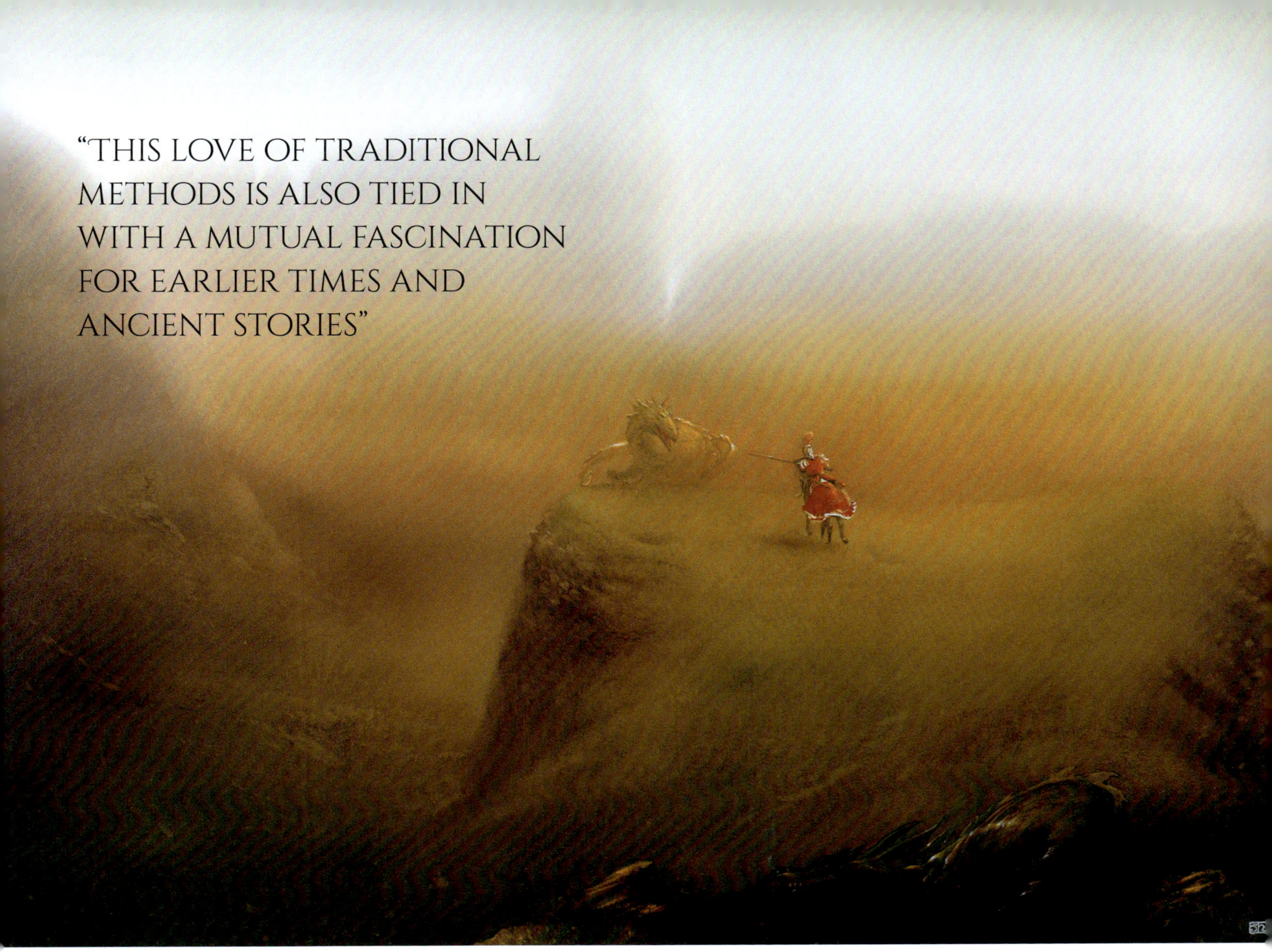

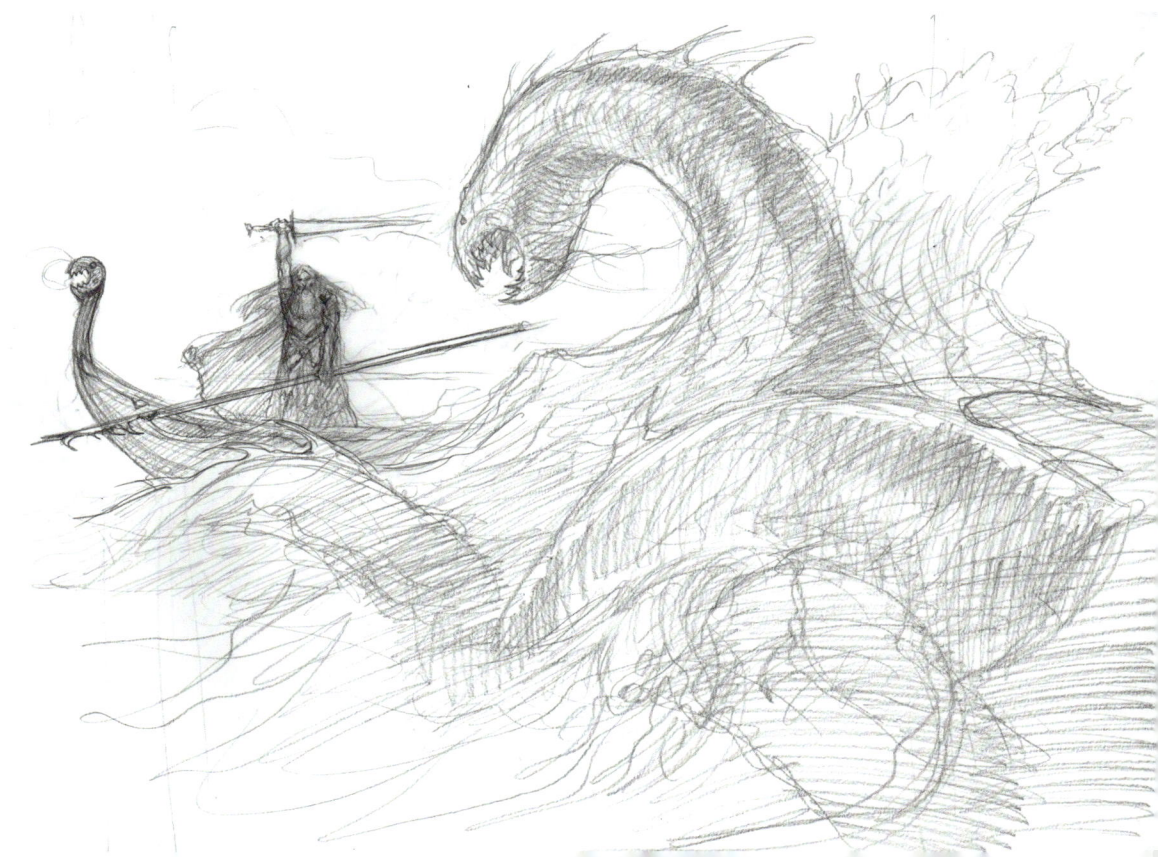

⬩ The Last Dragon

This is a tragicomic postscript for the age of chivalry. What does a knight do when there are no more dragons? The world needs Sir Pellinores, as much as it needs the quests they cannot fulfil.

➡ The Grey King

A scene of the confrontation between the Grey King and a sea monster, from George R.R. Martin's epic series *A Song of Ice and Fire*.

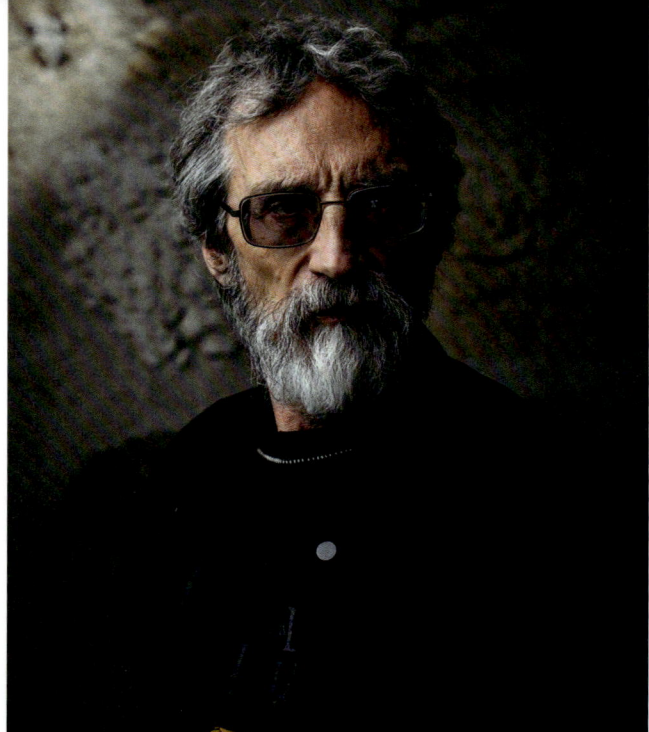

Photo © Lucas Vuitel

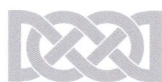

ABOUT THE AUTHOR

John Howe was born in Vancouver in 1957 and grew up in British Columbia. He can't remember ever not drawing and John's talents and passion for the arts became evident at a young age; he then went to France to study at the École des Arts Décoratifs de Strasbourg. A gifted painter, illustrator and writer of children's books, John has been highly acclaimed for his work on J.R.R. Tolkien's books and associated merchandise over the last three decades. In recent years, John and fellow Tolkien illustrator Alan Lee have mesmerized audiences across the globe with their award-winning work as Conceptual Designers for Peter Jackson's *Lord of the Rings* and *Hobbit* film trilogies. John's work can frequently be seen in exhibitions the world over, from London to Shanghai and from Paris to Tokyo. He has given regular master classes in Switzerland, France, Italy and Spain for many years and teaches at a local art school.

John's imaginative power is truly an inspiration. He is passionate about the need to construct fantasy on a foundation of authenticity, creating credible, if often magical, worlds that are plausible and familiar in some way. His knowledge of the medieval period is outstanding, and as a former practitioner of living history, he extends his experience and knowledge of weapons, armour and fighting styles through re-enactment. This energy spills into his work – a distinct fusion of Celtic, medieval, Gothic and Art Nouveau inspirations. And inextricably woven into John's fabric of detail is his love of mythology and heroic tales. Combining serious craftsmanship and technical skill, vitality of communication and depth of dimensionality – John's art is as experimental as it is visual. John lives in Switzerland with wife Fataneh (also an artist).

To view John's portfolio visit www.john-howe.com

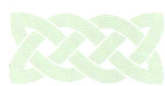

ACKNOWLEDGMENTS

Thanks to all those who contributed to this book in ways big, small, straightforward or mysterious. Thanks to my mother, who couldn't quite draw that cow, thanks to all my art teachers for persisting in the belief art could be taught. Thanks to the team at David and Charles for affording me the opportunity to try words instead of pictures. Thanks to Terry for the words before and Alan for the words after. For the words between special thanks to Imola Unger, Beverley Jollands and Ian Kearey for helping me arrange the words in the cluttered attic that is my mind. Thanks to my wife for her sharp eyes, perfect visual memory and impeccable taste; and to our son who chose music but still thinks art is a respectable occupation. And finally, thanks to Jenny Fox-Proverbs for making the assembling of the two books into one a painless and exciting process.

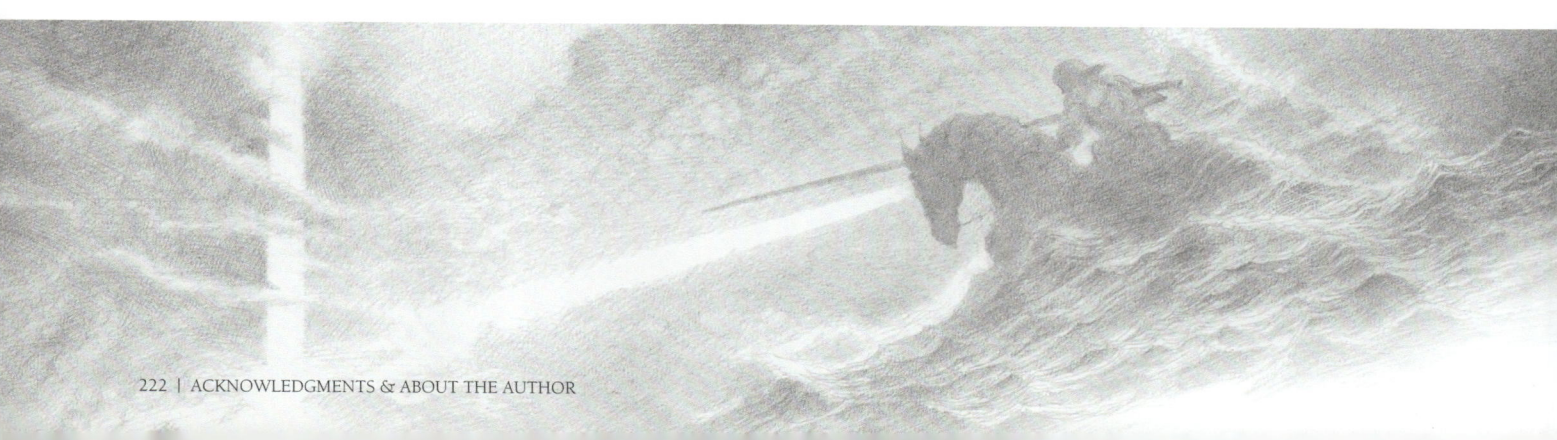

INDEX

A DAVID AND CHARLES BOOK
© David and Charles, Ltd 2021

David and Charles is an imprint of David and Charles, Ltd
Suite A, Tourism House, Pynes Hill, Exeter, EX2 5WS

Text and Illustrations © John Howe 2021

First published in the UK and USA in 2021
Some of the content in this book was originally published in Fantasy
Art Workshop (2007) and Fantasy Drawing Workshop (2009)

John Howe has asserted his right to be identified as author of this
work in accordance with the Copyright, Designs and Patents Act,
1988.

A catalogue record for this book is available from the British Library.

ISBN-13: 9781446308929 paperback
ISBN-13: 9781446381120 EPUB

This book has been printed on paper
from approved suppliers and made from
pulp from sustainable sources.

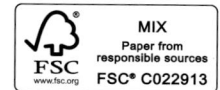

Printed in the UK by Pureprint for:
David and Charles, Ltd
Suite A, Tourism House, Pynes Hill, Exeter, EX2 5WS

10 9 8 7 6 5 4 3 2 1

Publishing Director: Ame Verso
Managing Editor: Jeni Chown
Project Editor: Jenny Fox-Proverbs
Designers: Blanche Williams and Lucy Waldron
Pre-press Designer: Ali Stark
Production Manager: Beverley Richardson

David and Charles publishes high-quality books on a wide range of
subjects. For more information visit www.davidandcharles.com.

Layout of the digital edition of this book may vary depending on
reader hardware and display settings.

CREDITS